Campus and Classroom

Making Schooling Multicultural

Second Edition

Carl A. Grant
University of Wisconsin–Madison

Mary Louise Gomez
University of Wisconsin–Madison

Merrill
Prentice Hall

Upper Saddle River, New Jersey
Columbus, Ohio

Library of Congress Cataloging-in-Publication Data

Campus and classroom : making schooling multicultural / [edited by] Carl A. Grant,
Mary Louise Gomez.–2nd ed.
 p. cm
 Rev. ed. of: Making schooling multicultural. c1996.
 Includes bibliographical references and index.
 ISBN 0-13-948878-2 (alk. paper)
 1. Multicultural education–United States. I. Grant, Carl A. II. Gomez, Mary Louise.
 III. Making schooling multicultural.

LC1099.3 .M34 2001
370.117'0973–dc21

00-030985

Vice President and Publisher: Jeffery W. Johnston
Editor: Debra A. Stollenwerk
Editorial Assistant: Penny S. Burleson
Production Editor: Mary Harlan
Design Coordinator: Diane C. Lorenzo
Cover Design: Rod Harris
Cover Art: Kenneth Henson
Text Design and Illustrations: WordCrafters Editorial Services
Production Coordination: Ann Mohan, WordCrafters
Production Manager: Pamela D. Bennett
Director of Marketing: Kevin Flanagan
Marketing Manager: Amy June
Marketing Services Manager: Krista Groshong

This book was set in ITC Garamond by The Clarinda Company. It was printed and bound by R. R. Donnelley &
Sons Company. The cover was printed by Phoenix Color Corp.

Previous edition entitled *Making Schooling Multicultural: Campus and Classroom.*

10 9 8 7 6 5 4 3 2 1
ISBN: 0-13-948878-2

*This book is dedicated to the possibilities
of all children, including our own—
Alicia and Carl Grant and Lily Gomez Sasse.*

Preface

This second edition of *Campus and Classroom: Making Schooling Multicultural* was written, in part, because our efforts in the first edition were so well received. However, we learned from readers' responses to the first edition. Prospective and practicing teachers requested more examples of linkages between theory and practice in each field. So, we asked the contributors to the initial volume to revise their work with these requests in mind. Furthermore, we asked the authors to enhance their original work by confronting current dilemmas in their fields, providing readers with multiple perspectives on these problems and considering various ways teachers might respond. An excellent example of the ways in which the authors met the challenges we raised is evident in the work of Ann DeVaney in her chapter on reading film and television in the classroom (Chapter 18). Professor DeVaney offers new ways for teachers and students to think about and interrupt the often stereotypic images all of us receive daily in various media. Professor DeVaney concentrates on reading the representations of one group, African Americans; however, the tools she offers for understanding the presentation of images of African Americans can be applied to conceptions constructed of other peoples as well.

We also prepared this second edition because readers asked us to address a particular dilemma—how to think about teaching reading in ways that engage all children's interests and needs. We believe that Patricia Enciso, of The Ohio State University, has provided all of us with new ways to think about the theories we bring to teaching reading and the materials and methods with which we translate those ideas into action.

✤ About the Text

As we work with elementary, middle school, and university students and our university and school colleagues, there is one important theoretical and practical question we are asked time and again. Which approach or definition of multicultural education should we (i.e., universities and K–12 schools) use to prepare our students for life in the 21st century?

Education that is multicultural and social reconstructionist, with its focus on all aspects of education—curriculum, instructional pedagogy, staff, personal awareness, advocacy—has become the choice for educators who are developing a vision and constructing or reforming their programs for today's schools. *Campus and Classroom: Making Schooling Multicultural* was written from this perspective.

The book contains four parts. Part 1 comprises two chapters—the first offers readers a theoretical orientation to the volume and a summary of the individual chapters, and the second contains a historical overview of multiculturalism in the United States. Chapters in Part 2 focus on general issues of pedagogy—how to create teaching and learning environments that are multicultural and social reconstructionist.

Part 3 engages readers in considering how individual academic disciplines such as mathematics, science, and art can be taught in ways that invite all students to learn. The chapter authors explain how to infuse into each academic discipline the theory and practices of education that are both multicultural and social reconstructionist. The authors provide examples of teachers' struggles to transform their teaching for equity and social justice.

Part 4 helps prospective teachers and teacher educators on campuses and in elementary and middle school classrooms make the teacher education experience one that embraces multicultural and social reconstructionist goals and practices. Throughout the volume, the authors describe and discuss the personal tensions that proponents of multicultural teaching often experience.

There is no simple answer or recipe for infusing education that is multicultural and social reconstructionist into elementary and middle school education, teacher education programs, and/or class assignments. We know this from personal experience and our extensive reviews of the education literature. We do believe, however, that *Campus and Classroom: Making Schooling Multicultural* charts an excellent course for preparing teacher educators and their students, as well as classroom teachers and their students, for educating the diversity of people they will encounter.

✤ Acknowledgments

Campus and Classroom: Making Schooling Multicultural resulted from the efforts of many colleagues, students, and friends. We are indebted to them for their patience and understanding as we toiled to express our vision of how multicultural and social reconstructionist education can become a reality. We especially thank the chapter authors who embraced the opportunity to discuss their academic disciplines from this point of view. We learned a great deal from them.

We also thank Merrill/Prentice Hall and its staff members—particularly our editor, Debbie Stollenwerk—for their support and patience. Debbie was always encouraging and full of good humor. We also extend our appreciation to Amy Hutler, Kathy Galloway, Jennifer Austin, and Jennifer Stone for their skillful support in helping us bring this project to completion.

We thank our students, whose questions and quests for learning pushed us to take on this project. We also thank the reviewers of this book for their insightful analyses during the review process: Novella Carter, Illinois State University; Dianne L. Common, University of Regina, Saskatchewan; Brenda Hill, University of Oklahoma; and Mary Roosevelt, University of California, Irvine.

Finally, we have to thank each other, because we each broadened our understanding of collegiality and friendship through our work on this project.

Carl A. Grant

Mary Louise Gomez

Discover the Companion Website Accompanying This Book

The Prentice Hall Companion Website: A Virtual Learning Environment

Technology is a constantly growing and changing aspect of our field that is creating a need for content and resources. To address this emerging need, Prentice Hall has developed an online learning environment for students and professors alike—Companion Websites—to support our textbooks.

In creating a Companion Website, our goal is to build on and enhance what the textbook already offers. For this reason, the content for each user-friendly website is organized by topic and provides the professor and student with a variety of meaningful resources. Common features of a Companion Website include:

For the Professor—

Every Companion Website integrates **Syllabus Manager**™, an online syllabus creation and management utility.

- **Syllabus Manager**™ provides you, the instructor, with an easy, step-by-step process to create and revise syllabi, with direct links into Companion Website and other online content without having to learn HTML.
- Students may logon to your syllabus during any study session. All they need to know is the web address for the Companion Website and the password you've assigned to your syllabus.
- After you have created a syllabus using **Syllabus Manager**™, students may enter the syllabus for their course section from any point in the Companion Website.
- Clicking on a date, the student is shown the list of activities for the assignment. The activities for each assignment are linked directly to actual content, saving time for students.
- Adding assignments consists of clicking on the desired due date, then filling in the details of the assignment—name of the assignment, instructions, and whether or not it is a one-time or repeating assignment.
- In addition, links to other activities can be created easily. If the activity is online, a URL can be entered in the space provided, and it will be linked automatically in the final syllabus.
- Your completed syllabus is hosted on our servers, allowing convenient updates from any computer on the Internet. Changes you make to your syllabus are immediately available to your students at their next logon.

For the Student—

- **Topic Overviews**—outline key concepts in topic areas
- **Electronic Bluebook**—send homework or essays directly to your instructor's email with this paperless form

- **Message Board**—serves as a virtual bulletin board to post—or respond to—questions or comments to/from a national audience
- **Chat**—real-time chat with anyone who is using the text anywhere in the country—ideal for discussion and study groups, class projects, etc.
- **Web Destinations**—links to www sites that relate to each topic area
- **Professional Organizations**—links to organizations that relate to topic areas
- **Additional Resources**—access to topic-specific content that enhances material found in the text

To take advantage of these and other resources, please visit the *Campus and Classroom: Making Schooling Multicultural,* Second Edition, Companion Website at

www.prenhall.com/grant

Contents

Chapter 6 Reconstructing Bilingual Education from a Multicultural Perspective   93

Chapter 7 Multicultural Concerns and Classroom Management   109

✤ Part 3
The Subject Matters   135

Chapter 8 Telling and Critiquing Stories of Our Teaching—
for Literacy   137

Chapter 9 Reading Within Multicultural Education: Beyond "Silent"
and "Silenced"   155

Chapter 10 Mathematizing and the Democracy: The Need for an Education That Is Multicultural and Social Reconstructionist   175

Chapter 11 Learning Science as a Transformative Experience   189

Chapter 12 Teaching Social Studies for Decision-Making and Citizen Action   205

Chapter 16 Integrating Diversity and Multiculturalism in Health Education 281

Chapter 17 Multiculturalism and Educational Theatre 295

Chapter 18 Reading Film and Television in the Classroom: African American Representations in Popular Culture 313

Contributing Authors

Veronica M. Acosta-Deprez

Veronica Acosta-Deprez is currently an Assistant Professor at the Department of Health Science at California State University, Long Beach. Her professional interests are in the fields of international health, multicultural health education, curriculum development and evaluation, and human sexuality and HIV/AIDS education. She has published several articles related to multicultural approaches in health education in various settings such as the school and community. Her research involves examining how multiculturalism is integrated into health educators' work and the health education profession itself. Actively involved in professional organizations, she is Chair of the Multicultural Involvement Committee of the American Association for Health Education, Chair of the Minority Affairs Committee, and Director of the Council for International and Cross-Cultural School Health in the American School Health Association.

James A. Banks

James A. Banks is Professor of Education and Director of the Center for Multicultural Education at the University of Washington, Seattle. He has been President of the National Council for the Social Studies and has held fellowships from the National Academy of Education, the Kellogg Foundation, and the Rockefeller Foundation. Known internationally for his work in social studies and multicultural education, he was named a Distinguished Scholar/Researcher on Minority Education by the American Educational Research Association (AERA). In 1994, he received the AERA Research Review Award. He received an honorary Doctorate of Humane Letters (L.H.D.) from the Bank Street College of Education in 1993. Professor Banks has published over 100 articles in such journals as *Educational Researcher, Phi Delta Kappan, Social Education,* and *Educational Leadership.* His books include *Teaching Strategies for Ethnic Studies, Teaching Strategies for the Social Studies, An Introduction to Multicultural Education,* and (with Cherry A. McGee Banks) *Multicultural Education: Issues and Perspectives.* He is the editor (with Cherry A. McGee Banks) of the *Handbook of Research on Multicultural Education* (Macmillan, 1995).

Marilynne Boyle-Baise

Marilynne Boyle-Baise is an Associate Professor at Indiana University. Her special areas of interest are multicultural education and social studies, and she is active in defining multicultural social studies education. Professor Boyle-Baise has centered her research in helping inservice teachers implement multicultural education. She is the founder of a teacher-oriented advocacy group for multicultural education.

Jepkorir Rose Chepyator-Thomson

Jepkorir Rose Chepyator-Thomson is an Associate Professor at the University of Georgia. She received her B.A., M.A., M.S., and Ph.D. degrees from the University of Wisconsin–Madison. Her research interests center on issues of race, class, and gender in curriculum and teaching; women and sport in Kenya; and child development and children's games in Keiyo society in Kenya. Her most recent work has been published in *Interchange, Social Development Issues,* and in the *Journal of Teaching in Physical Education.*

Ann DeVaney

Ann DeVaney is Professor Emerita in the Department of Curriculum and Instruction, University of Wisconsin–Madison, where she led a graduate program in Educational Communications and Technology. Her scholarship appropriates literary models to analyze representation of women and people of color in educational and popular media and software. Her latest publication is an edited volume, *Watching Channel One: The Convergence of Students, Technology and Private Business.*

Mary Catherine Ellwein

Mary Catherine Ellwein was an Associate Professor of Educational Studies at the Curry School of Education at the University of Virginia until her death in 1994. Her work in assessment merges interests in qualitative research methodology, measurement, and teachers' ways of knowing their students. Her dissertation, *Standards of Competence: A Multi-Site Case Study of School Reform,* won the outstanding dissertation award from the American Educational Research Association in 1987.

Patricia E. Enciso

Patricia E. Enciso is an Assistant Professor in the College of Education at The Ohio State University. Her research on children's and teachers' interpretations of the imaginative and sociocultural aspects of children's reading has been published in *Language Arts, Reading and Writing Quarterly,* and the *English Journal* and has been supported, in part, by a Spencer Postdoctoral Fellowship and an NCTE Grant-in-Aid. This research informs her work with preservice and practicing teachers who are interested in extending the purposes and pedagogies of culturally relevant reading education.

Kerry Freedman

Kerry Freedman is a faculty member in the Department of Curriculum and Instruction at the University of Minnesota. Her research focuses on questions concerning art and the sociology of education, particularly in the areas of the teaching and learning of aesthetic knowledge, technological influences on visual culture, and the relationship of culture to curriculum. Professor Freedman has published in art education and curriculum books and journals, including *Studies in Art Education, Art Education,* and the *Journal of Curriculum Studies.* She is co-author of a book titled *Postmodern Art Education.*

Mary Lou Fuller

Mary Lou Fuller earned her doctorate in Multicultural Education from the University of New Mexico. Her research, professional presentation, consultation, and teaching include both classroom management and multicultural education. Dr. Fuller has been a classroom teacher and a school psychologist and is currently a Professor in the Center for Teaching and Learning at the University of North Dakota.

Geneva Gay

Geneva Gay is Professor of Education and Associate with the Center of Multicultural Education at the University of Washington–Seattle. She is the recipient of the 1990 Distinguished Scholar Award, presented by the Committee on the Role and Status of Minorities in Educational Research and Development of the American Educational Research Association, as well as the 1994 Multicultural Educator Award, the first to be presented by the National Association of Multicultural Education. She is known nationally and internationally for her scholarship in multicultural education, particularly as it relates to curriculum design, staff development, classroom instruction, and culture and learning. Her writings include more than 90 articles and book chapters, the co-editorship of *Expressively Black: The Cultural Basis of Ethnic Identity* (Praeger, 1987), and author of *At the Essence of Learning: Multicultural Education* (Kappa Delta Pi, 1994).

Maureen Gillette

Maureen Gillette is Assistant Dean in the College of Education at William Paterson University in New Jersey. Professor Gillette serves as a consultant and researcher in multicultural teacher education.

Mary Louise Gomez

Mary Louise Gomez is an Associate Professor at the University of Wisconsin–Madison, where she codirected Teach for Diversity, a master's degree program (offering certification to teach in grades 1-6) grounded in concerns for social justice and equity in schooling. She currently codirects a research and professional development project, Teachers Helping Teachers: Language and Literacy for Young Children. This is a collaborative effort between university faculty and primary teachers aimed at increasing the achievement of young, struggling readers living in poverty, many of whom are children of color. Professor Gomez's research focuses on how teachers' perspectives challenge, enhance, and limit literacy teaching. Her published work includes articles in *Language Arts, Teaching and Teacher Education*, the *Journal of Education for Teaching*, and *Teaching Education*, as well as numerous book chapters. She also is the co-editor of *Complexities of Reform in Teacher Education* (Teachers College Press, 1996).

Carl A. Grant

Carl A. Grant is Hoefs-Bascom Professor of Teacher Education in the Department of Curriculum and Instruction at the University of Wisconsin–Madison. In 1997, he received the School of Education Distinguished Achievement Award. He has written or edited 18 books or monographs in multicultural education and/or teacher education. These include *Multicultural Research: A Reflective Engagement with Race, Class, Gender and Sexual Orientation,* 1999; *After the School Bell Rings* (2nd ed.) (with Christine E. Sleeter), 1993; 1995; *Making Choices for Multicultural Education* (with Christine E. Sleeter), 1994; and *Dictionary of Multicultural Education* (with Gloria Ladson-Billing), 1997. He has also written more than 100 articles, chapters in books, and reviews. Several of his writings and programs that he directed have received awards. Professor Grant is a former classroom teacher and administrator and has been a Fulbright Scholar in England, researching and studying multicultural education. In 1993 he became President of the National Association for Multicultural Education (NAME), and in 1996 he became Editor of *Review of Educational Research* (RER).

Beth Graue

Beth Graue is a Professor in the Department of Curriculum and Instruction at the University of Wisconsin–Madison. Her work addresses issues in early childhood education, assessment, and qualitative research methods. She is the author of *Ready for What? Constructing Meanings of Readiness for Kindergarten.*

Toni Griego-Jones

Toni Griego-Jones is Professor and Chair of the Department of Curriculum and Development at the University of Arizona. Her research interests include minority parent involvement in educational reform and teachers' knowledge of the educational needs of language minority students.

Julia Eklund Koza

Julia Eklund Koza is an Associate Professor in the Department of Curriculum and Instruction and the School of Music at the University of Wisconsin–Madison. She also is a faculty affiliate in the Women's Studies Program. Her research focuses on diversity issues in music, education, and music education. Professor Koza's recent scholarship has appeared in the *Musical Quarterly,* the *Journal of Research in Music Education, Educational Foundations,* the *Music Educators Journal,* the *Review of Education/Pedagogy/Cultural Studies,* and *The Quarterly.*

Jean Lythcott

Jean Lythcott is retired from the faculty in Science Education at Teachers College, Columbia University.

Mark Riherd

Mark Riherd is the Program Director for the Creative Arts Team (CAT), the professional educational theatre company in residence at New York University. By combining original theatre productions and participatory drama workshops, CAT motivates youth to examine pertinent social issues and curricular themes. He is also an instructor in the Program in Educational Theatre at NYU, where he teaches courses in both Drama-in-Education and Theatre-in-Education. Additionally, he conducts staff development workshops nationally and internationally in Critical Thinking Through Drama.

Christine E. Sleeter

Christine E. Sleeter is Professor of Teacher Education at the California State University–Monterey Bay. Formerly she was a high school learning disabilities teacher in Seattle. She earned her Ph.D. from the University of Wisconsin–Madison in 1981 and taught at Ripon College and the University of Wisconsin–Parkside before assuming her current position.

On the basis of her active record of publication, she recently was awarded the University of Wisconsin–Parkside annual award for Excellence in Research and Creative Activity and the Research Award of the National Association for Multicultural Education. She has published articles about multicultural education in numerous journals. Her most recent books include *Empowerment through Multicultural Education, Keepers of the American Dream*, and *Making Choices for Multicultural Education* (with Carl Grant). She also edits a series of books for SUNY Press titled *The Social Context of Education.*

Peter N. Stearns

Peter N. Stearns is Dean of the College of Humanities and Social Sciences at Carnegie Mellon University, where he regularly teaches a world history course for first-year students. His book *Meaning over Memory: Recasting the Teaching of Culture and History* (University of North Carolina Press, 1993), deals with a variety of issues in humanities education. His most recent monograph is *American Cool: Developing a Twentieth-Century Emotional Style* (1994). Peter Stearns also is active in a number of curricular projects, including the College Board's Pacesetter World History project, and is a member of the National Board of Teaching Standards, History and Social Studies unit.

James Stewart

James Stewart is a Professor in the science education area of the Department of Curriculum and Instruction at the University of Wisconsin–Madison.

Nancy Swortzell

Nancy Swortzell serves as director of the Program in Educational Theatre at New York University where she also teaches courses in acting, directing, and theatre-in-education practices. In 1973 she designed and led the NYU Study Abroad Program to introduce American students to the educational theatre scene in England. The Study Abroad Program continues each year with a distinguished faculty that has included leaders in the field such as John Hodgson, Gavin Bolton, and Cecily O'Neill. She holds a D.F.A. in directing from the Yale Drama School and has directed many NYU productions for young audiences, including *Gulliver's Travels, The Little Humpback Horse,* and *The Hobbit.*

William F. Tate

William F. Tate is an Associate Professor in the Department of Curriculum and Instruction at the University of Wisconsin–Madison. His articles "School Mathematics and African American Students: Thinking Seriously about Opportunity-to-Learn Standards" in *Educational Administration Quarterly* and "Toward a Critical Race Theory of Education" in *Teachers College Record* (with Gloria Ladson-Billings) reflect his interest in the political dimensions of African American education.

An Introduction to Multicultural Teaching

❖ ❖ ❖

The journey of a thousand miles begins with a single step.

Lao-Tse

The acceptance of women as authority figures or as role models is an important step in female education. . . . It is this process of identification, respect, and then self-respect that promotes growth.

Judy Chicago
Through the Flower; My Struggle as a Woman Artist, 1975

You see things as they are; and you ask "Why?". But I dream things that never were and I ask "Why not?".

George Bernard Shaw

I touch the future. I teach.

Christa McAuliffe

Even if I knew that tomorrow the world would go to pieces, I would still plant my apple tree.

Martin Luther

1 Journeying Toward Multicultural and Social Reconstructionist Teaching and Teacher Education

Carl A. Grant and Mary Louise Gomez
University of Wisconsin-Madison

In Barry Lopez's fable *Crow and Weasel* (1990), two young men travel farther north than any of their people have ever gone. During their journey, which is spiritual and self-reflective as well as physically challenging, they encounter varied experiences. At one point, they come upon Mouse, a weary fellow traveler who is resting by the roadside, and exchange the following remarks.

> "We come in peace," said Weasel.
> "Good" said Mouse. "I'm a peaceful man."
> "We are traveling north through these woods," said Crow.
> "I am going to the west. I am on a vision quest."
> "We are trying to go farther north than our people have ever gone before," offered Weasel, getting down from his mare. "Already we have come farther than anyone, but we are still going on."
> "I am traveling a long way myself," said Mouse. "Among my people, west is the direction we fear most, so that is the direction we travel when we go on a vision quest."
> "We have that custom among our people as well," said Crow, who had also dismounted. "Only with us, we do not travel far."
> "We travel very far," said Mouse. "We travel to some high place and fast and wait for a dream that will give our lives a good direction."
> "We have that same custom," said Weasel.
> The three of them remained silent for a while.
> "It's very difficult to lead a good life," said Crow finally. "What you have set out to do," he said, turning to Mouse, "is hard. But our older people tell us that without a dream you do not know what to do with your life. So it is a good thing, I think, what you do, what your people believe."
> "Yes. To be a good hunter," said Mouse, "is to be a good family man, to be truthful instead of clever with people, to live in a community where there is much wisdom— that is what all of us want."
> "Ah," said Crow. "But it takes your life to learn to do these things."
> "Hah!" said Mouse, and they all laughed.
> They camped the night together. (pp. 19–21)

Like Crow and Weasel, we are travelers. Our journey, like theirs, is both self-reflective and corporeal. We, too, are seekers after dreams. Today, when teachers must negotiate the terrain of teaching in increasingly complex contexts, it seems timely to invite you to come with us—and our friends and colleagues who have contributed to this book—in pursuit of dreams.

We ask you to join us in seeking how to teach and learn across the disciplinary areas in ways that are equitable and just for all people. While our pathways are not always smooth or easy, we are propelled by social, economic, and moral imperatives. In this chapter, we outline the concerns that motivate our work and clarify what a multicultural social reconstructionist perspective on teaching and teacher education entails.

In part, our work is fueled by a sense of urgency concerning the social and economic distress in which many U.S. children live. As Haveman and Wolfe have recently written: "The debate over educational reform—school choice, magnet schools, busing— starts from a common judgment that neither schools nor families are serving children well" (1994, p. 3).

Haveman and Wolfe document a bleak picture of many U.S. children's family lives:

- One-quarter of children in the United States are born to unwed mothers.
- Fewer than 75 percent of children live with two parents.
- Parental child care time has been reduced from 30 hours of contact per week in 1965 to 17 hours per week in the late 1980s.
- Thirty percent of children experience divorce, up from 19 percent 30 years ago.
- Twenty percent of children live in poverty—up from 15 percent in 1973—and 40 percent of children of color live in poverty. (p. 3)

Children's lives are challenged not only by the decreasing support offered them at home, but often at school as well. Recently, countless educational reports have reminded us that as more children of color, low-income children, students with other than English language backgrounds, and students with special learning needs come to U.S. schools, rates of dropping out, violence, and truancy increase, and achievement (as measured by grades and standardized test scores) falls. We and our colleagues do not consider students' disillusionment with schooling and their academic failures to be entirely their fault or that of their families. Rather, we see universities and schools—along with other representatives of U.S. economic and social institutions—acting with families and children to reproduce these unjust conditions.

Haveman and Wolfe (1994) argue that children's life success is determined by three primary factors: a social or government investment in their lives, a parental investment, and the choices each child makes over time. While at first glance, and without explication, this model can appear somewhat linear and deterministic (as Haveman and Wolfe also posit), it highlights for us the significant role that social institutions—like schools—play in children's lives, and the importance of good schools and teachers.

We developed this book with the schooling of all U.S. children in mind, because we recognize the crucial role that good teachers play in everyone's life success. We are especially concerned, however, with providing children who are the most socially and economically distressed with the knowledge, skills, and dispositions to make choices for their future—choices that provide them with a safe haven for their bodies and spirits. Because we as teachers are so critical to children's opportunities, we ask you to consider why we require personal and professional self-reflection and teacher Education That Is Multicultural and Social Reconstructionist.

Statistics concerning who teachers are and who children are in our schools may not surprise or concern you at first glance. However, in the next paragraphs, we make the case that differences in the race, social class, language background, and sexual orientation of U.S. teachers should concern us all—not because people who are different from one another should be apart, but because the differences among us often lead to unjust, inequitable treatment of those we see as "Others."[1] Who are teachers and what are their perspectives on people who are not like them?

Gomez (1994) has written that there are great differences in the races, socioeconomic groups, and language backgrounds of U.S. teachers and students. These, along with differences in sexual orientation of teachers and students, often lead to diminished expectations and different educational experiences for children who are unlike their teachers—children who are already more likely to live with one parent in poverty. Gomez writes:

> In 1990, for example, when the kindergarten through grade 12 population of the nation was 40 percent children of color, nearly 90 percent of teachers were White (National Center for Education Statistics, 1992). The race of those teaching and those taught will continue to differ in the future as numbers of school-age children of color increase and numbers of teachers of color decrease in the U.S.A. (Hodgkinson, 1991). There are also increasing social class differences between students and their teachers. In 1989, for example, 15 percent of White children, 44 percent of African American children and 36 percent of Latino children lived in poverty and these numbers continue to rise (Children's Defense Fund, 1991, p. 24). Nearly half of all children living in poverty in the U.S.A. live in central cities (Children's Defense Fund, 1991, p. 2). In contrast, most U.S. teachers come from lower middle-class and middle-class homes and have grown up in rural and suburban areas of the nation (Zimpher, 1989). There are also increasing gaps in language background between U.S. teachers and students. There were 2 million limited English proficiency students enrolled in grades K–12 in the U.S.A. in 1990; this is a 36 percent increase from 1986 (Olsen, 1992), yet most U.S. teachers continue to be monolingual in English (Zimpher). (1989, p. 320)

On the surface, these differences only say that, as teachers, we differ from our students. Unfortunately, these differences lead to negative perspectives or biased beliefs and classroom actions toward some children. In analyses of several large-scale studies concerning teachers' attitudes toward "Others," their willingness to live near and be part of communities with "Others," to teach "Others," and to expect that "Others" can learn, Gomez found the following:

> Those new teachers working in inner cities, small towns, and rural areas were more likely to cite influences outside of school as challenging students' ability to learn than were their counterparts teaching in suburbia. Teachers working with students of color and students from low-income families were also more likely to point to outside-of-school influences as detrimental to students' learning and achievement. Taken together, these responses from novice teachers indicate that early in their careers, many teachers locate problems of learning and achievement not as outcomes of teachers' beliefs about and behaviors towards children in school, but as consequences of children's outside-of-school lives—beyond the purview of teachers, schools and schooling. (p. 321)

We believe that classroom and campus experiences in teacher education that support or maintain such beliefs about children must be changed, or the already bleak future of many of our nation's children becomes unimaginable. Changes in teacher education experiences offered to new teachers become imperative as four factors assure us that, for some time in the future, we will continue to educate prospective teachers resembling those in our current cohort to teach increasingly diverse populations of children.

These are (a) the predictions of demographers regarding the characteristics of and numbers of different incoming student populations (see Hodgkinson, 1985, 1991, for discussion of contemporary population trends); (b) the continuing availability of higher-status, higher-paying positions in professions outside of teaching for people of color; (c) current efforts to "professionalize" teaching (e.g., the National Board of Professional Teaching Standards, various state department mandates for selection, credentialing and licensure) that often result in rejecting or sifting out people unlike those already credentialed; and (d) the pervasive racism, sexism, and homophobia that mark life in the United States (Gomez, 1994).

Clearly, it is difficult to make changes in teachers' beliefs and attitudes toward "Others"—even when teachers are highly motivated to do so. As Paley (1989) vividly portrays in *White Teacher,* it is nearly impossible to make such changes alone. In her book, Paley examines how she thought and acted when she first taught African American children in her kindergarten classroom at the University of Chicago Laboratory School. She ruefully acknowledges how she alternately practiced first a color-blind and then a color-centric focus in her teaching as she struggled toward teaching that invites all children's learning. It was only through discussion with African American and White colleagues in her campus school, through talking with children in her classroom and their families, and through reading and self-reflection that Paley could initiate changes in her theories and practices.

Paley tells us that her story, "like anyone's story, is a morality tale" (p. xv). We believe the tales told in the following chapters are also morality tales; that is, teaching and teacher Education That Is Multicultural and Social Reconstructionist are aimed deliberately at changing the ways that teachers and schools as institutions work.

✥ A Multicultural and Social Reconstructionist Framework for Teaching

Several interpretations can be assigned to multicultural education. These interpretations are usually related to how issues of race, class, gender, disability, and sexual orientation are dealt with in school policies and practices. Banks (1994), for example, posits four approaches to integrating cultural content into curriculum. These approaches to multicultural curriculum reform are

1. The contribution approach, in which content presented about ethnic and cultural groups is linked, for the most part, to holidays and celebrations;
2. The additive approach, in which the cultural and ethnic concepts, content, and themes included in the curriculum do not modify the basic goals structure of the classroom activity and characteristics;
3. The transformation approach, in which the structure of the curriculum is changed to provide students the opportunity to examine concepts, problems, events, and issues from the perspectives of different ethnic and cultural groups;
4. The social action approach, in which students investigate social issues and problems and take civic action to further learn about concepts and events that they have studied.

Sleeter and Grant (1999) assigned five interpretations or approaches to multicultural education. These include curriculum reform, and they address race, class, gender, disability and sexual orientation in societal goals, school goals, instruction, and other classroom- and school-wide concerns. These approaches are the following:

- Teaching the Exceptional and Culturally Different
- Human Relations
- Single-Group Studies
- Multicultural Education
- Education That Is Multicultural and Social Reconstructionist

Teaching the Exceptional and Culturally Different

This approach fits students into the existing social structure and culture. By building bridges between the students' backgrounds and the schools, teachers teach a dominant traditional academic curriculum. Instruction builds on students' learning styles and is adapted to their existing skills. This approach accommodates students who are exceptional or culturally different through the use of teaching strategies or culturally relevant materials that otherwise might be used in a "pull-out" program for students with "special needs." While this approach may help students remain in their regular classroom and enable them to participate in its ongoing daily life, the problem of cultural discontinuity remains that of the individual student.

Human Relations

This approach to multicultural education attempts to assimilate individual students into the dominant discourse and practices of the classroom. The focus is on fostering positive affective relationships among students of diverse backgrounds and personal characteristics in the school so that each student has a strong self-concept and can work in harmony with the group. The Human Relations approach undergirds a curriculum that includes lessons about stereotyping and individual differences. It encourages instruction that includes collaborative and cooperative learning among students.

Teacher education grounded in a Human Relations approach prepares teachers to honor the diverse backgrounds of the students whom they will teach and to promote good will among all students. Actual conflicts between individuals and groups can be glossed over in support of an "I'm okay, you're okay" ideology.

Single-Group Studies

This approach promotes social structural equality for and the immediate recognition of an identified group. Commonly implemented in the form of ethnic studies and labor studies, this approach assumes that because of past curriculum biases, knowledge about particular oppressed groups should be taught separately from conventional classroom knowledge in either separate units or separate courses.

The Single-Group Studies approach seeks to raise consciousness levels about an identified group by teaching both its members and others about the history, culture, and contributions of the group, as well as how that group has been oppressed by or has worked with the dominant group in society.

Multicultural Education

This approach to education promotes social equality and cultural pluralism. Curriculum is organized around the contributions and perspectives of different cultural groups. It pays close attention to gender equity. For example, teachers drawing on a multicultural approach learn how gender-biased socialization and oppression are located in their own teaching practices; they learn to alter these as well as to become aware of how males and females from different ethnic backgrounds are socialized.

Teachers build on students' learning styles, adapt instruction to the existing skills of students in the class, and involve students in thinking through and analyzing the life situations of different people. This approach encourages both the maintenance of students' native languages and multilingual acquisition for all students. Further, proponents of multicultural education advocate the staffing of schools with a diverse population.

Education That Is Multicultural and Social Reconstructionist

We believe this approach is the responsible interpretation to use as the theoretical framework for *Making Schooling Multicultural: Campus and Classroom,* because it extends the previous approaches and supports education for everyone. It promotes social and structural equality and cultural pluralism. It provides a climate in which students can work toward structural equality, accept lifestyles different from their own, and understand the importance of equal opportunity for all people. The curriculum is organized around social issues involving race, class, gender, disability, and sexual orientation. It also involves the history and lives of many United States peoples and uses the lives of students in the classroom as the starting point for analyzing oppression, teaching critical thinking skills, and developing social action and empowerment skills.

From this viewpoint, instruction involves students' active and democratic decision making. It builds on students' learning styles, adapts to students' skills, and encourages student cooperation and collaboration. Education That Is Multicultural and Social Reconstructionist affirms the active involvement of parents, families, and other community members in children's learning and the evaluation of their progress in school and outside of school.

We advocate this approach for several reasons. It provides teachers with an ideology of what "ought to be." It is a set of beliefs that advocates changes in the prevailing social structure and order—changes that promote cultural pluralism and structural equality. Education That Is Multicultural and Social Reconstructionist provides teachers with the theory and (guide to) practice to help them shape their educational philosophies and develop teaching strategies for successfully teaching all students.

This approach contributes to an awareness and understanding of the changing student demographics in many classrooms across the nation. It validates and supports the need for second-language instruction and the importance to non-English language students of maintaining their native language as well as learning a new one. It prepares teachers to make both their formal and informal curriculum developmentally appropriate and culturally authentic. It shows teachers how to integrate multicultural education into different academic disciplines, it creates an awareness of how student evaluation and assessment are interpretive and contextual, and it includes parent participation.

Education That Is Multicultural and Social Reconstructionist prepares teachers to understand that successful and student-appropriate classroom discipline and management are based on a teacher's knowledge of self, a teacher's knowledge of students and their homes and communities, and a teacher's willingness to involve parents as partners in their children's learning.

Finally, this approach helps teachers prepare students to examine and conceive of ways to challenge the problems and issues that impede self-empowerment. It prepares students to take charge of their lives, work collectively with others, and speak out to bring about social change.

❖ Making Schooling Multicultural in Every Discipline

In the chapters that follow, our colleagues offer their perspectives on achieving a multicultural, social reconstructionist approach to teaching and learning in their disciplines. In chapter 2, Peter Stearns reminds us that multiculturalism has a long history in U.S. educational traditions. He traces how U.S. schools, like their counterparts in other parts of the world, have been designed for the assimilation and acculturation of citizens aimed at "a single ultimate Americanness." Stearns also shows how recent political and demographic shifts in our nation and in the world—as well as changes in how thinkers in various disciplines are reconstructing their fields—have created a more welcoming climate for multiculturalism. Yet he cautions that much of what people apparently sympathetic to multiculturalizing schools say can also be read as new cloaks for homogenizing school curricula.

In chapter 3, Geneva Gay discusses curriculum development, instruction, and assessment with a chapter focusing on definitions and components of curriculum. She draws attention to how the formal and informal curricula of schools operate simultaneously in classrooms, and how teachers pursuing multicultural practices must be aware of and work toward altering both of these. She points out that multicultural curriculum reform is most effective when it is target-specific, developmentally appropriate, and culturally authentic.

Carla Cooper Shaw's work on instructional pluralism in chapter 4 complements Gay's chapter on curriculum through discussion of how students' varied approaches to learning are outcomes of their individual characteristics and of their membership in cultural groups. Shaw lays out the debate on the merit of recognizing and teaching to accommodate varied student learning styles. She helps readers understand how building on what students bring to the classroom as their preferred ways of learning and their "cultural habits of thought" can enhance learning.

In chapter 5, Mary Catherine Ellwein and M. Elizabeth Graue present a strong case for rejecting positivistic and fragmented ways of knowing how and what students are learning. They argue for the recognition that assessment of students' learning is an interpretive act, and they call for exploration of evaluative tools that consider individual, social, and contextual dimensions of learners and learning.

Ellwein and Graue begin with a description and critique of the development of testing in the United States. They point out that most teachers have not received education or formal training in assessment; and that teachers who do receive such training find that it often fails to meet their specific classroom needs. Ellwein and Graue offer realistic vignettes that contrast traditional and technical means of understanding children's learning with new efforts to comprehend how and what children are learning in collaboration with their families.

In chapter 6, Toni Griego-Jones explains that what is now known as the United States has always been a multilingual, multicultured land, from the time it was dominated by diverse American Indian cultures, speaking hundreds of American Indian languages. In the chapter "Reconstructing Bilingual Education from a Multicultural Perspective," Griego-Jones traces how people in the United States from various language groups have attempted to maintain their cultural identities through schooling in their native tongues.

Griego-Jones points out that bilingual education is conducted in this country in varied ways. Bilingual education programs differ with regard to the amount of time and effort expended on the maintenance of a student's native language versus that devoted to the learning of additional languages. She envisions a future in which all children in the United States learn another language and appreciate the heritage and traditions of other peoples. As she puts it, bilingual education could then be an enhancement to all children's lives rather than a remedy for some.

In chapter 7, on classroom management, Mary Lou Fuller explores various models of teachers managing classrooms and argues that teachers must understand students' behavior as an outcome of both their personal motivation and as a consequence of their cultural group membership. To illustrate her discussion, Fuller depicts a prospective teacher struggling both to understand the behavior of students from varied ethnic groups and also to teach them effectively. Readers see the complex dimensions of managing a classroom of students with diverse backgrounds through one novice teacher's experiences.

Mary Louise Gomez's chapter on teaching for literacy—chapter 8—launches a series of chapters in which authors discuss how students can understand and construct knowledge in various disciplinary fields via a multicultural, social reconstructionist approach. Through stories of her own teaching experiences and those of prospective teachers with whom she has worked, Gomez shows how reading, writing, and other communication skills can be taught in culturally relevant and inviting ways. She demonstrates critical reflection through a form of narrative inquiry that asks participants to tell stories about their own teaching and to critique their own actions as well as those of others in supportive communities of peers.

In chapter 9, Patricia Enciso considers both how children learn how to read words and link these to ideas, and how the words that are most powerful are those that have meaning in children's lives. She encourages teachers to draw on the varied, powerful words and images in children's lives to support their learning to read and to share what they know and have read with one another. Enciso highlights for us that as teachers we often are encouraged to judge and categorize our students' learning. She urges us to quell our own and others' impulses to judge and label readers' skills. Rather, she shows how readers of various skills and backgrounds can work together to construct meanings from texts as they learn to increase their reading skills.

In chapter 10, focusing on teaching mathematics from a multicultural and social reconstructionist perspective, William F. Tate IV argues that the values of the mathematizer or the person doing mathematics play a large role in how a situation is quantified and understood. Concomitantly, he argues that the ways mathematics has been framed as an activity—one that fosters the economic, social, and cultural advancement of a society and that is best suited for an elite group practicing a deductive system of logic—have played a large role in how mathematics is presented in schools and how it has served as a gateway to higher education and high status jobs. Tate argues for teaching mathematics from a centric perspective, one that locates students within the context of their own cultural references so they can create their own mathematical knowledge and critique that made by others.

In chapter 11, "Learning Science as a Transformative Experience," Jean Lythcott and James Stewart take their readers on an exploration of science materials as they show us how elementary and middle school children can learn about solids, liquids, and gases. The authors embark on a lively discussion about what it means for teachers and children to construct—within a diverse classroom community—conceptual understandings about the world. Lythcott and Stewart point out, however, that multicultural and social reconstructionist science education is about more than conceptual and intellectual understandings; it is also about enabling learners to transform themselves and their world as they come to know and understand it.

James Banks, in chapter 12, "Teaching Social Studies for Decision Making," describes four major periods in the development of social studies education in the United States. He lays out the goals of social studies education in a pluralistic and democratic society that result in a decision-making/social-action model of curriculum. Further, he demonstrates how the model comes to life in a junior high school social studies classroom. Banks shows how, in a social studies curriculum focused on decision making, students can learn the following: to identify the sources of their values, to determine how their values are compatible or conflictive with one another, to identify and choose among alternative values, and to justify their values and the actions based on them in light of societal values such as social justice, equity, and dignity for all people.

In chapter 13, "The Social Reconstruction of Art Education: Teaching Visual Culture," Kerry Freedman challenges the purposes that Western art teaching has served. Rather than instill the aesthetic values of an elite few into all, Freedman argues for art education that presents all visual cultures as socially constructed, meaningful, and changing. Rather than focus on the individual as a "self-expressive maker of art" who is therapeutically treated via art production, Freedman argues that art can be at the center of a curriculum on culture. Understanding the dimensions of visual culture, including artifacts, ceremonies, and costumes, she maintains, is fundamental to understanding human existence. She suggests that teachers of art can provide the foundation for students to produce and critique art and explodes seven common myths that reflect current debates about multiculturalism in education.

In chapter 14, which focuses on a social reconstructionist approach to music education, Julia Eklund Koza first describes how music educators in the United States have been developing a multicultural agenda since the late 1960s. Next, she suggests how changes in schooling at large, in the music education paradigm, and in the curriculum and instruction of music education can facilitate a multicultural social reconstructionist agenda. She grounds her arguments in four principles she views as "departures" from "business as usual" in music teaching and learning: (a) music is a worthwhile and basic matter for inclusion in the elementary and middle school curriculum, (b) any teacher is capable of creating an environment in which children can learn music, (c) classroom teachers as well as music specialists are responsible for helping students learn music, and (d) the compartmentalization of music as a "special" subject area is artificial and marginalizing. Koza argues for developing music education that is diverse, inclusive, and respectful of all people.

In chapter 15, Jepkorir Rose Chepyator-Thomson creates a new vision for physical education that embraces the interests and activities of many peoples. She places contemporary physical education curricula and instruction in a historical context, arguing that, from its inception in U.S. schools, physical education has been Euro-centered. Chepyator-Thomson outlines four paradigms that have dominated physical education practices in this country to date: a physical fitness model, developmentally based physical education, movement education, and humanistic physical education.

She follows this discussion with a multicultural and social reconstructionist perspective on physical education that, in addition to inviting students' participation in the games and sports of diverse peoples, fosters analyses of how sports have developed—who has been encouraged and who has benefited from playing them—and helps students find ways to be fit and powerful in active play.

Veronica Acosta-Deprez argues in chapter 16 that health education can be effective only when teachers take into account the cultural beliefs and values that students hold regarding what constitutes health and how one maintains it. She explores seven principles of planning and teaching a health curriculum. These principles involve teachers' acquisition of knowledge regarding the health practices of varied peoples and transforming the role of health educator from information provider to partner in problem solving with students, their families, and community members. Acosta-Deprez emphasizes the importance of looking first to students' interests and needs in planning and teaching for health.

In chapter 17, "Multiculturalism and Educational Theater," Mark Riherd and Nancy Swortzell describe two movements in educational theater, *drama-in-education* and *theater-in-education*. Both are predicated on the belief that people's behavior and the social institutions that we create can be changed. Riherd and Swortzell show how educational theater teams around the world have responded to oppression through the making of theater experiences for and with audiences of young people. They offer principles on which educational theater aimed at social change is predicated and give a detailed example of a theater experience grounded on these postulates.

In chapter 18, "Television and Film in the Classroom: The Presence and Absence of People of Color," Ann DeVaney focuses attention on how the available images surrounding us help us to construct portraits of ourselves and of the possibilities that lie before us. In particular, DeVaney shows how the representations of people of color on television and in films create and sustain images that are narrow, stereotypical, and oppressive. She offers readers a structural method for critically reading media images and gives examples from familiar contemporary television programs and films to illustrate how teacher-viewers can employ this method themselves and with their students.

In chapter 19, "Field Experiences: Planting Seeds and Pulling Weeds," Marilynne Boyle-Baise and Christine Sleeter draw attention to the knowledge and experience—the perspective or "web of beliefs"—that everyone brings to teacher education. The authors show how teachers' perspectives serve as filters or interpretive lenses through which they view students and families and their role as educators.

Boyle-Baise and Sleeter note that field experiences generally serve as transitions in which prospective teachers move from roles as students to classroom leadership that often imitates their cooperating teacher role models. But they argue that field experiences can also be opportunities for reflection and rethinking of one's perspectives. The authors describe how prospective teachers can take responsibility for examining and altering their perspectives on people different from themselves through field experiences.

In chapter 20, Maureen Gillette closes the text with "It's Got to Be in the Plan: Reflective Teaching and Multicultural Education in the Student Teaching Semester." Gillette focuses on what is generally the capstone of teacher preparation—the student teaching semester—and contrasts the work of two student teachers whose goals are to become multicultural and social reconstructionist teachers. Gillette explores how two sets of cooperating teachers and student teachers work together with a supervisor colleague to examine the encouragements and constraints of implementing a multicultural and social reconstructionist pedagogy across the curriculum.

✢   Finally

As you read, we hope that you, like Crow and Weasel, will continue to be self-reflective in your preparation for teaching and in your classroom practices. We hope that, like their journey, yours has offered you new ways of thinking and acting. As Weasel says to Crow after they have finished their trip, "Our journey, seeing different ways of life, has made me wonder about many things."

He adds the following:

One day perhaps my son will return and the people will listen to what they have to say. And then their children. It will go on like that, and that way our people will look into the heart of wisdom.

Crow pondered his friend's words. His eyes followed an Appaloosa mare on the hill below them. "The wonder and the strangeness," he said, "the terror of the world will never be over." He turned and regarded Weasel. "Imagine our daughters," he said. "Traveling." (pp. 78–79).

We imagine you traveling as well.

Notes

1. Grumet (1988) uses the phrase *Other people's children* to heighten our sense of responsibility for teaching all children as we would teach our own. Delpit (1988) uses the same phrase to challenge teachers to acknowledge how their participation in the "culture of power" constrains their understanding and teaching of diverse children.
2. Tabachnick, Zeichner, Densmore, & Hudak (1983) point out that the notion of perspective has its theoretical roots in the work of Mead (1938) and his concept of the "act." Contemporary uses of the term *perspective* to discuss teachers' beliefs about their work and the classroom actions that give meaning to these beliefs date to the Becker, Geer, Hughes, & Strauss study of medical students' socialization (1961). Becker et al. define *perspective* as "a coordinated set of ideas or actions a person uses in dealing with some problemetic situation; a person's ordinary way of thinking about an act or situation." (p. 34)

References

Banks, J. A. (1994). *An introduction to multicultural education.* Boston: Allyn and Bacon.

Becker, H., Geer, B., Hughes, E., Strauss, A. (1961). *Boys in white.* Chicago: University of Chicago Press.

Delpit, L. (1988). The silenced dialogue: Power and pedagogy in educating other people's children. *Harvard Educational Review, 58,* 280–289.

Gomez, M. L. (1994). Teacher education reform and prospective teachers' perspectives on teaching "other peoples'" children. *Teaching and Teacher Education, 10*(3), 319-334.

Grumet, M. R. (1988). *Bitter milk: Women and teaching.* Amherst, MA: University of Massachusetts Press.

Haveman, R., and Wolfe, B. (1994, Winter). America's children: Status, prospects, policy. *The Follette Policy Report, 6*(1), 3-5.

Hodgkinson, H. L. (1985). *All one system: Demographics of education—kindergarten through graduate school.* Washington, DC: Institute for Educational Leadership.

Hodgkinson, H. L. (1991, April 10). Remarks made on a video teleconference. *Who's missing from the classroom? The need for minority teachers.* Washington, DC: American Association of Colleges for Teacher Education and the ERIC Clearinghouse on Teacher Education.

Lopez, B. (1990). *Crow and Weasel.* New York: HarperCollins Perennial.

Mead, G. H. (1938). *The philosophy of the act.* Chicago: University of Chicago Press.

Paley, V. (1989). *White teacher.* Cambridge, MA: Harvard University Press.

Sleeter, C. E., & Grant, C. A. (1999). *Making choices for multicultural education: Five approaches to race, class, and gender* (3d ed.). Upper Saddle River, NJ: Merrill/Prentice Hall.

Tabachnick, B. R., Zeichner, K. M., Densmore, K., & Hudak, G. (1983). *The development of a teacher.* Paper presented at the annual meeting of the American Educational Research Association, Montreal.

2

Multiculturalism and the American Educational Tradition

Peter N. Stearns
Carnegie Mellon University

The current goals of multicultural education bear a positive relationship to many features of the American educational tradition as it has developed for more than 150 years. The decentralized quality of American education, though modified in recent decades by increased planning at state levels, contributes to a certain amount of cultural flexibility. Nothing in the American tradition compares to the classic centralist model of French schooling, which deliberately set out to crush regional distinctiveness as the public system confirmed its hold in the late 19th century. No American education official has ever rivaled the boasts of the French minister in the 1880s who would look at his watch and claim to know what was happening in every classroom across the nation—and no serious official ever wanted this degree of homogenization (Stearns, 1997).

The American system has long been committed to an ethic of social mobility, which has also opened educational access to people of many different backgrounds; here, too, the national tradition has been more flexible than that of many other nations where more deeply rooted social hierarchies tempered mobility messages. In seeking to use education to reflect the validity of differing norms (for example, in religion) and to help people of varied cultural backgrounds achieve their goals, the American schooling tradition may prove congenial to the new appeals for more explicit attention to diverse identities. The nation's educational history provides positive background for some aspects of multiculturalism (Cremin, 1970, 1980, 1988).

This is not the whole story, however. American education has also long been seen by the bulk of its leadership as a source and enforcer of vital values, essential to creating a degree of national consensus amid a varied population. Schooling, in other words, has from its inception worked to change habits on the part of groups regarded as foreign or inferior. Education formed a key center of efforts to convert traditional workers into modern, efficient producers imbued with appropriate middle-class zeal and to mold new arrivals into "good Americans." The tradition of using education to shape children and youths according to a powerful if not always fully defined set of values is at least as profoundly rooted as the tradition of tolerance and flexibility. Here, multiculturalism as currently conceived must do battle with established habits, and its advocates must be aware of the powerful momentum toward insistence on conformity.

American educational traditions, in sum, embody deep-seated tensions that must be understood and sorted out if a realistic multicultural approach is to emerge. The traditions, not surprisingly, mirror and help explain current debate about multicultural issues, with both partisans and opponents pointing to different features of our educational past. Partisans of multiculturalism, for example, correctly emphasize the long-standing association of schooling and curricula with democracy and religious tolerance, because Americans have taken pride in the openness of their educational system and its ability to group students of varied backgrounds. Opponents, however, also correctly point to the long-standing link between schooling and the shaping of citizen consensus of definitions of Americanness and how the United States fits into the cultural panoply of the larger world (Himmelfarb, 1987; Ravitch & Schlesinger, 1990). To these opponents, multiculturalism is a dangerous, divisive innovation. Their arguments can be understood only if current political disputes are seen in the perspective of more durable features of our educational past.

Nothing more clearly reflects the double-edged quality of American education, confronting varied cultural strains within society at large, than the hallowed image of the melting pot, taught to generations of school children through the first three quarters of the 20th century. On the one hand, the melting pot image was welcoming. It not only recognized but also celebrated the unprecedented racial and ethnic diversity of the United States after 1900. Folded into the image was pride in the American tradition of religious freedom and separation of church and state, which had infused public education (after initial decades of sectarian domination) by the middle of the 19th century. Schools imposed no single denomination. Despite disproportionate Protestant influence, they came to include many Catholic and Jewish students, and by the middle of the 20th century (despite common insistence on some Christian symbolism) the schools made this ecumenicalism a positive virtue. Religion aside, the melting pot imagery treated the variety of peoples of the nation (particularly, of course, the ethnic immigrants) as a source of strength. A distinctive national character resulted from the combination of diverse peoples and their own special qualities.

Yet the pot was supposed to fuse its mixed ingredients, which is where the consensus strand re-entered strongly. The melting pot ideal was carefully couched to emphasize a single ultimate Americanness, an evolutionary product to be sure, enhanced by the (often unspecified) qualities contributed by immigrant cultures. Ongoing diversity was not the point. To be sure, the melting pot was compatible with after-school excursions into specific religious programs or the occasional folk festival, seen as compatible with "real" Americanness, but on essentials a single set of values predominated: There was one proper set of fundamental political beliefs (by the 1920s socialism and then communism need not apply); there was one valid set of economic values, with emphasis on hard work, productivity, and commitment to a capitalist order. The verb "Americanize," coined at about the same time that the melting pot idea began to enter classroom currency, expressed this authoritative aspect of the educational culture explicitly. The melting pot was viable because its components had been Americanized, and the very school system that held up the melting pot symbol played a vigorous and self-conscious role in the Americanization process. As current proponents of multiculturalism recognize, the traditional celebration of diversity was predicated on a firm understanding that, in the habits that counted, diversity would quickly yield to a single American standard.

The lessons of the melting pot apply to the implications of American educational history more generally. There are traditions to cherish, curricular themes that can be embellished in providing a framework for multiculturalism. Yet many educational emphases are also hostile to significant diversity; exacerbating the tension, a certain amount of myth-making may mask the strong homogenizing impulse.

❖ The Burdens of Schooling's History

The framework for American public education began before diversity issues loomed large—though, in fact, as revisionist educational historians have emphasized, they were present in some forms from the outset. Katz (1968, 1987) and others have noted how the schools that began to spread in the northern states from the 1830s complacently built curricula on middle-class and disproportionately urban values, held to be valid standards for a growing working class, new immigrants, and the rural majority. Local school board control modified the impositions somewhat, particularly for agricultural districts. Sincere beliefs in the openness of the American system concealed the impositions to some extent. The fact remained that educational authorities pushed not only a single set of basic skills but also a single set of republican virtues, highlighted by embellished stories of national heroes such as George Washington. Students either were sufficiently similar to accept this common fund or should be made similar by accepting it.

The distinctiveness of the American political system, at this educational incubation point, reduced explicit awareness of the homogenizing impulse. The early establishment of political democracy (for White males) and, in most northern states, of extensive public school systems and attendance requirements obviously linked mass education to political empowerment and to social mobility. By the 1830s many Americans were being taught that, whatever their backgrounds, education provided them a means of participating in intelligent citizenship and gaining opportunities for advancement. The American educational system did not have the elitist bias of most of the systems being established (usually more gradually) in Europe in the 19th century. The state did not set up special kinds of secondary schools, like the German *Gymnasiums,* that would be open only to a tested, select few. As a university system emerged, it was relatively heterogeneous, again avoiding the rigid tracking that described European systems. A related sign of openness was the relatively early American commitment to substantial co-education, despite debates and misgivings that extended from 1850 into the early 20th century (Tyack & Hansot, 1990). Women were not systematically shunted into separate school tracks, and while their curricula emphasized certain subjects appropriate for domestic life—like the ubiquitous home economics of the 1900s—they also shared many substantive classes with their male counterparts.

The rise of the American high school, as a unique institution designed for relatively broad access, at precisely the time that other industrial countries (including Japan by the 1880s) were firming up a highly tracked and discriminatory secondary educational system, symbolized and furthered the unusual equation of American education with wide access to students of diverse backgrounds (Perlmann, 1988). Small wonder that educational leaders had little sense that they were imposing cultural standards, in contrast to their more frankly authoritarian counterparts in 19th century Europe.

There were serious qualifications to the love affair between educational tradition and American democracy, however, well before 1900. Until the 20th century a minority of high school students were working class; economic differentiation posed a formidable barrier to opportunity. University access, though not constrained by a single, state-run hierarchy, was even more limited. On another front, the domination of most public school systems by Protestants repelled many immigrants, who fled to the growing parochial school network. Nineteenth-century Americans tolerated a certain amount of diversity in education—including local pockets of foreign-language schools, like the German systems in rural Wisconsin—but their tolerance mainly involved parallel institutions, not widely acknowledged diversity under a single school roof.

The public school system, as it spread in the northern states, had a reasonably well-defined, if somewhat implicit, value system. It was open-ended in welcoming students from reasonably diverse backgrounds, but it expected to homogenize them in crucial ways. Members of the working class, rural and urban, were taught middle-class standards of punctuality, avoidance of political excess, and cleanliness and hygiene. Dress codes carried the message, as did lessons in civics. Immigrants, like the Irish who flooded in from the 1840s onward, were to learn similar habits—which, along with religious differences, helps explain considerable interest in alternative school systems and a tendency to pull students out of schooling at a relatively early age. Diversity in background was fine in principle and to an impressive degree in fact; diversity in outcomes or in educational process was not sought. Rather, schools operated as institutions of social control, where socially dubious segments of the population could be taught appropriate standards. From this process, in turn, talented students could rise in an education-linked mobility pattern that depended on the combination of openness and assimilation to middle-class values (Vinovskis, 1995).

It was also true that separate private schools, classical high schools and elite colleges offered a distinct educational tradition for many upper middle-class Americans, emphasizing Latin and Greek and European high culture as superior products of a superior education tradition. The Western cultural tradition could attract others—many educated former slaves were steeped in the tradition—but it tended to separate elite styles from the more diverse patterns of the general American population. By 1900 certain cultural figures, like Shakespeare, were being removed from popular stages and treated as hallowed museum pieces, to be reverenced by those truly educated (Levine, 1988).

The tensions embodied in the American educational tradition boiled over after 1900, when for a time widespread access no longer seemed compatible with instilling a single set of values. At the lowest educational levels in the north, to be sure, older traditions largely prevailed. Students were mixed in the primary schools (except where residential segregation constrained the process—and 20th century suburban flight played a growing role in constraining real classroom diversity) and taught a growing array of lessons about political propriety, diligence at work, and personal grooming. The growing cultural diversity of the overall student population, however, as a result of new waves of immigration plus growing (if limited) incorporation of African American students during the Great Migration from the South threatened to overwhelm the system as defined by the dominant White, Protestant middle class, particularly at the high school level. The opportunity for opening to a wider cultural array within individual classrooms was not seriously considered, except for women's education, which steadily advanced. Rather, new forms of institutional separation were introduced to keep distinct cultural groupings apart, except for those talented and adaptable individuals who might break through.

Separation took two forms. In Southern states, which were just establishing full public school systems and attendance requirements after 1900, segregation kept Whites and Blacks apart. African American education had advanced considerably during Reconstruction, through efforts by freedpeople themselves (Wiener, 1978). It was not systematically focused on a distinctive African American culture. Nor of course was pervasive school segregation designed explicitly to avoid multiculturalism. The result of separation, however, limited any need to confront diversity issues in the South. Separate educational systems also affected many American Indians, as the reservation system spread, despite impressive earlier literacy gains by some tribes (Spring, 1994).

Northern cities had experimented with racially segregated schools, at least de facto. The onslaught of immigrants from southern and eastern Europe, held to be inferior to Yankee and old-immigrant stock, led to slightly more subtle efforts to keep various groups apart. Batteries of aptitude tests were developed as the basis of tracking into different high school programs (Chapman, 1988). Academically talented students aimed in one direction, while various technical sequences received the students who tested less well. It was assumed that groups like Italian Americans, Slavs, Hispanics, and, soon, the growing flood of African American migrants from the South would largely test into the non-academic tracks, and like many prophecies this one proved self-fulfilling. The new testing mania assumed, of course, that one set of standards accurately identified student quality. Diversity was shunned, recognized only through the existence of separate programs with largely separate career results. Not coincidentally, this same early 20th-century transition saw the reduction of the autonomy of local school boards within major cities, as more standardized controls and curricula were spread through the big urban systems.

Test-based tracking, despite the racist thinking that underlay it, was based as much on the impulse to homogenize as on that to exclude. Students who could demonstrate their talent could be admitted to the top standardized programs. Those programs would lead them to the most prestigious urban high schools and soon, despite more outright discrimination, to the "best" universities. Many children of Jewish immigrants thus made it into places like Boston Latin or Philadelphia's Central High School. A significant number of talented African Americans and others also made it in the terms of the system— like Margaret Lawrence, the first African American woman psychiatrist, whose academic success took her from the South to the classical Wadleigh High School in New York and ultimately to Cornell (Labaree, 1988; Lightfoot, 1988). The point was not only that the cards were stacked against most minority aspirants, but also that they were expected to internalize the standard cultural baggage of the White Protestant majority. Their talent for assimilation, not their diversity, was rewarded; their ethnic or racial background was officially ignored, not highlighted. As Nathan Glazer recently put it, referring to the period when Jewish and Italian American students dominated New York City's public schools, students were told that the European American forefathers of the American republic were their forefathers, not that they had a distinct or valued identity or history (Glazer, 1991). The message that being American was a single experience, launched in the primary grades, was maintained in the tracked system that confronted the reality of increased diversity in the early decades of this century.

With time, of course, the effect of early 20th century school reforms was modified. Students from a wider variety of backgrounds managed to pass into the academic mainstream. Cessation of massive immigration between 1923 and the 1960s eased fears of diversity somewhat and permitted the development of such comforting notions as the melting pot (modified, of course, by growing residential separations). In the 1950s and 1960s, the Civil Rights movement, zeroing in on educational targets, produced legislation that further limited school segregation and other forms of separation.

It is important to recognize that the educational reforms of the early 20th century, though undeniably racist in assumption, were dealing with important educational issues. Defining and maintaining academic standards in a mass educational environment can prompt concern even aside from racism. When high schools became normal and not exceptional experiences, by 1910 or 1920, they had to consider more bureaucratic methods of sorting students. Balancing local and systemwide curricular responsibilities in growing urban school systems involved complex issues after 1900, as is the case today. Furthermore, outside the South the solutions adopted did not totally block out any cultural grouping, while as we have seen the historical treatment of immigrants produced some curricular support for at least limited recognition of the value of diversity. American education retained some fruitful tension between the implications of its openness and the use of schooling for standardized acculturation.

It remains true that the American educational tradition, from its founding to its first clear multicultural crisis around 1900, opted largely for a single cultural standard, to which minority groups were expected to bow. The standard did not embrace all beliefs; religious diversity, most obviously, was still tolerated and to some degree honored. Yet growing emphasis on political conformity (amid the "Red scare" of the 1920s), increasingly detailed rules about sex and hygiene (amid germ theories and residual Victorianism), and pervasive assumptions about proper economic discipline drove the single standard home. Agreement on the key values to be conveyed, and institutional mechanisms to keep students apart who were seen as too diverse, kept potential multicultural issues largely at bay for decades.

Only in the aftermath of Civil Rights legislation and amid sweeping changes in student demography resulting from differential racial birthrates and the massive renewal of immigration—this time from Latin America and Asia, with heritages still more distinctive than those brought by the immigrants of the turn of the century—have the educational tradition and the reforms introduced to support it been challenged anew. The contemporary debate about multiculturalism looms, historically, as the second great challenge to dominant educational assumptions created in the 19th century and asserted victoriously against initial challenge between 1900 and 1920.

✥ Americanization Through Curriculum

The same tensions that produced institutional changes in response to growing diversity in the population, without totally closing access to varied groups (save in the South), inevitably shaped characteristic curricula. Pervasive curriculum themes drove home the standard messages authorities wanted students to learn; all subject areas reflected a concern for emphasizing a single basic standard, a unitary truth. Gradual movements toward greater curricular standardization worked in the same direction from one school to the next. This occurred in citywide school districts, as part of college preparation with the formation of College Board guidelines early in the 20th century, and more recently with the powerful trend toward statewide curricular mandates (Valentine, 1987). At the same time openness to diversity was not entirely cast aside, as programs in literature and some aspects of history showed some sensitivity to varied interests and contexts.

Courses in science reflected dominant cultural beliefs in a single set of valid methods and findings, and as science was increasingly worked into the curriculum, by the later 19th century, this helped set the general tone for education. Religious explanations for natural phenomena were entertained concurrently for a time, but faded in the face of scientific claims, particularly after the dramatic Scopes trial of the 1920s. Scientific truth was singular, and science remains the most difficult area to adapt to multicultural goals because of assumptions that proper research methods produce replicable findings whatever the cultural factors involved.

Through most of the 20th century, programs in music and literature were particularly revealing of the avoidance of diversity issues. Literature taught great works in the European and American tradition, as defined by scholarly arbiters of taste. Art and music appreciation involved exposure to great works in the same traditions. Civilized taste, in other words, focused on appreciation for a single set of works: Shakespeare—as his work was removed from boisterous popular appreciation and sterilized in classrooms by the later 19th century (Levine, 1988)—leading 19th-century novelists, and a few more recent figures. Music was Bach and Beethoven, art the wonders of Greece and Rome and the Italian Renaissance. Literary and artistic productions from other parts of the world, by other groups within European and American society, or in forms other than standard genres, need not apply (Bloom, 1987).

Reading programs enforced another kind of value—setting—even before students were old enough to receive the great canon. Reading materials featured standard (or idealized-standard) middle-class settings, logical to most of the authors involved and essential (seemingly) in creating agreed-upon cultural values. People lived in individual houses with chimneys; they were usually blonde; they were clean and family size was small. Readers began to form these images with materials presented in the first grade, and they were rarely subjected to additional nuance as their student careers continued.

The consistent strand in the humanities curriculum, beginning with pablum reading and moving on to high school literature courses, was the belief in a clear and singular cultural standard. Students should be taught, through early reading, that there was one civilized way to live—the houses and the smiling mothers—and they should progressively learn that there was also one civilized definition of humanistic culture. A result, for many students—not only recently, but in the early 20th century as well—was a massive disparity between life as lived, culture as experienced in popular media, and what was learned about proper standards. To an extent, this was precisely the intention of the curriculum planners, for reading and art materials were designed to help children, culturally inferior by dint of age, and groups judged culturally inferior because of their racial or ethnic origins, gain access to the knowledge required by propriety and good taste. Diversity was not specifically shunned; it was simply not seriously considered. Underlying assumptions even had a certain optimistic quality, since it was believed that movement toward more civilized standards was possible; the inferior were not forever condemned.

One final facet of humanities curricula reflected national concern with standard-setting. Foreign languages received short shrift as subjects to be introduced early or seriously. Language concern centered on teaching "standard" English and displacing immigrant languages and dialects. This focus, and the desire to instill familiarity with American literature staples as part of building a national cultural consciousness, permitted, and perhaps caused, a striking national neglect of foreign language teaching. Treatments in history or, as became increasingly common after the 1930s, social studies programs, in some respects simply replicated the assumptions of the arts and literature courses. Social studies advocates long emphasized an even more explicit assimilationist message than more traditional advocates of standard classical or American history courses (Armento, 1986). New work in civics, while diluting the historical diet, was designed to show how American institutions worked and what proper American citizenship entailed, on a definite assimilationist model.

There were, additionally, some specific twists in this general social studies-history-social sciences area that warrant particular attention. They reveal deeply held assumptions about what the United States was and how it fit into the world, assumptions that not only ignored much diversity but in some ways explicitly combatted it.

As in literature courses, topic selection leaned heavily on elite or elite-led developments. The evolution of constitutional structure, major wars, major presidencies, and reform movements such as Progressivism headed the list in American history, with occasional excursions into cultural topics such as transcendentalism or pragmatism. By the 20th century some attention to immigration leavened the mix, but there was no consistent attention to popular behaviors; for a considerable time even slavery was largely passed over. America was shaped primarily by the thoughts and actions of formal leaders, like the framers of the Constitution or presidents like Lincoln. The values and institutions they shaped in turn formed the centerpiece requirements of civics. Here was the historical and social studies equivalent to the Great Books diet of high school literature.

Beyond this, certain theoretical assumptions, rarely trotted out for explicit debate, enhanced the monochromatic portrait of the past. American history was given a central place in the social studies curriculum, with remaining attention (if any) devoted largely to West European societies (particularly Britain), seen as progenitors of American values. To the allocation of attention was added an implicit belief in American exceptionalism: The United States, as it formed from the 17th through the 19th centuries, proved to be a unique society, which could be understood in terms of American context alone (brief bows to West European antecedents notwithstanding) and which could be credited with an array of distinctive and mainly beneficent achievements. Religious freedom, political democracy wedded with unusual political stability (the Civil War aside), belief in individual initiative, unusual equality of opportunity joined with exceptional upward mobility—these were some of the themes that followed from the American exceptionalist framework. At times, international claims might be added: Americans acted unselfishly in their diplomacy, compared with the grasping European imperialists; Americans did not start wars, though of course they won them (Lipset, 1995).

American exceptionalism encouraged students, and many of their teachers, to ignore patterns in the rest of the world as irrelevant to their own lives and lamentably inferior. It encouraged them to claim more distinctiveness in their society, concerning social mobility rates, for example, than real comparison would have warranted (Kaelble, 1986). It encouraged them to overcome any lingering sense of cultural inferiority to Western Europe by pointing to the nation's political superiority, business dynamism, and freedom from greedy international entanglements. It encouraged neglect of some of the complexities of American history itself (Gifford, 1988; Stearns, 1993).

Reliance on rags-to-riches mobility themes might explain a lack of explicit treatment of lower-class groups, which after all would ultimately rise to become part of the great, homogeneous national middle class. American political stability brought rather unconsidered praise for the two-party system and distaste for political ideology. The same history might be interpreted in terms of an unwillingness to confront difficult political issues and a tendency to force dissent into nonpolitical behaviors such as violent protest and crime. Even when troublesome issues were confronted, they were often given an optimistic, American-superiority twist. Thus textbooks paid more attention to the end of slavery than to the experience itself or to subsequent racism. Even today, comments on problems such as low voter turnout in the United States offer explanations such as a distinctive American commitment to freedom that makes voting seem less essential, arguing that European countries where voting levels are higher have shakier rights; since many American nonvoters are also racial minorities who can hardly celebrate a secure tradition of freedom, the explanation may seem somewhat forced.

In sum: The curricular assumptions in the major fields of study, focused on conveying a fairly uniform set of values and standards and an inordinately simple definition of the national past, shaped in the late 19th century with the waning of classicism, have persisted in most respects to the present day. The emphases may be judged entirely justifiable. Nevertheless, the most obvious result of a long and durable curricular pattern, bent on instilling standard definitions of cultural and personal and political goals, offers a massive challenge to serious multicultural education. As most of the essays in this volume suggest, no subject area can be easily converted from present practice to genuine multiculturalism. Undoing current routines is vital, because these routines are built on curricular goals that either ignored diversity or consciously combatted it (Ravitch & Vinovskis, 1995).

❖ Recent Change and Illusion

To be sure, the curricular tradition has not been immune to change, even apart from recent developments such as the California curriculum reform. Political currents set in motion by the Civil Rights and feminist movements have produced modifications. The science tradition remains largely immune, given beliefs in its ability to generate demonstrable and unitary truths. Literature courses, on the other hand, added works by African American authors, and more basic readers included more stories and illustrations based on inner cities and the experiences of racial and ethnic minorities. Social studies courses, correspondingly, generated new lessons on the African American experience. History texts introduced at least supplemental sections on women and other groups. More and more high schools shifted from Western civilization to world history courses, including items such as the great African kingdoms of Ghana, Mali, and Songhay.

Changes of this sort during the past two decades point in some promising directions. They have not, however, as yet overcome the homogenization tradition. At best they have modified, at worst merely cosmeticized. The content of many world history courses turns out to be Western civilization barely altered. The average high school world history text is two-thirds Western. Additions to American history are often inserts that do not seriously alter the standard political and cultural emphases. Even women's studies, though widely discussed, have not recast the basic emphases in most mainstream texts. Crucial issues, such as the complex pattern of discrimination and moral praise in the 19th century, are ignored. Certain other trends, indeed, move in contrary directions: While attention to minority groupings has gone up, so have standardized, statewide testing programs, which tend to highlight familiar factual fare along with presumably "basic" skills (Resnick, 1980).

Even apparently sympathetic educators reflect a distressing, if unsurprising, ability to adopt multicultural labels while maintaining a homogenization thrust—and this aside from the vociferous outright opponents of multiculturalism. Thus Ravitch (1990), long a perceptive commentator on social studies curricula and more recently a sometime critic of multiculturalism in favor of the need for a national consensus, offers a revealing aside. Noting specifically that the old melting pot idea, suggesting erasure of group differences, has yielded to the idea of variety as a national strength, she proclaims: "Cultural pluralism is a national resource rather than a problem to be solved."

She quickly adds: "The unique feature of the United States is that its common culture has been formed by the interaction of its subsidiary cultures" (Ravitch, 1990, p. 339). The words are new, the understanding and curricular implications less clearly so. A common culture remains front and center, overshadowing subsidiary elements; how this differs from the melting pot is not apparent. Further, the hallowed belief in American uniqueness is triumphantly reasserted, with no felt need to demonstrate through comparative analysis. A curriculum derived from this kind of thinking would surely allow a bit more space for the idea that various groups in American society brought distinctive and valid cultural contributions, and this would be an adjustment for the better. It would not, however, serve as the basis for a real multicultural examination of the presentation of American history or of the larger world context into which American history should fit. Again, the potency of the assimilationist tradition, bent on instilling a mainstream, assertively distinctive American standard, stands out. Reform statements easily turn into mere tinkering formulas when confronted with the tradition's force.

Against this force, built into a host of curricular routines cherished by many able teachers—the comforting litany of major presidencies, the awesome power of Shakespeare, the message of a distinctive American commitment to social mobility—serious reformulation faces many obstacles. Many educational authorities, sincerely attracted to some multicultural goals, will find conversion impossibly traumatic; many, of course, will persuasively argue that big chunks of the tradition remain objectively valid.

The power of conservative opposition to curriculum reform was dramatically demonstrated in 1994, when new standards for history teaching in U.S. and world history were issued by a government-sponsored task force. The *Standards* were not revolutionary, but they did give unusual attention to the political reactions of African Americans, Native Americans and women, and they pressed for world history over purely Western civilization history. Conservative commentators howled against these changes, arguing for the necessity of paying more attention to White men and to the Western tradition and to the importance of consensus education in American democracy; at one point, amid a rightwing Republican political surge, the U.S. Senate voted 98 to 1 to condemn the *Standards*. In fact, history teaching continued to evolve—the forces for change were strong as well. But the battle had not been fully redefined (National Center for History in the Schools, 1994).

✛   The Force for Multiculturalism

There is, however, another recent historical ingredient to insert. The context for American education obviously continues to change, raising challenges for the assimilationist tradition that are arguably greater than at any time in the more distant past. This is an obvious statement at one level: Why else would multiculturalism be so vigorously on the agenda? Yet a brief historical assessment is useful, in pointing to the several strands that combine to suggest change, rather than the one or two most commonly emphasized.

Student demographics have shifted dramatically and will continue to shift. Differential birth rates and the most impressive tide of immigration in our history—and from largely non-European parts of the world—produce a more diverse student body than ever.

The effects of desegregation and other Civil Rights measures put this huge change in student body composition into a distinctive political context as well. More self-conscious feminism adds another political ingredient working in the same direction. These developments do not automatically assure a fundamental reevaluation of assimilationist curricula. Many opponents of multiculturalism emphasize the need for a single canon, in literature and history, precisely because of new degrees of student diversity. They, too, reflect change: The canon they point to is far more rigid than is traditional in American curricula, particularly in literature. Nevertheless, the case for multiculturalism commonly begins with the new student body, sometimes adding human relations criteria related to goals of tolerance and personal adjustment. Too often, indeed, the case ends with these factors, and many convinced multiculturalists surely believe that student diversity and adjustment needs amply justify the reevaluation of assimilationist traditions in the K–12 curricula.

Two other important changes, however, add to the force of the argument and give additional direction to the multiculturalist thrust. The first, related admittedly to the new student body, involves the changing position of the United States in the world. Europe remains a vital reference point for American culture and diplomatic and economic activity, but it has long lost its monopoly on attention and effect. Latin America has been of vital concern for more than 150 years, and the Middle East, other parts of Asia, and Africa now figure in strongly (McNeill, 1988). The international context for life in the United States has become truly global, even apart from its new immigration patterns, and this impels curricular development sensitive to issues of cultural diversity even vaster than represented within the nation itself.

Finally, key disciplines from which curricula are logically drawn have shifted dramatically during the past 25 years, for the most part in directions relevant to multiculturalism. The study of literature at the scholarly level no longer simply involves a standard summary of great works. It opens these works to new kinds of assessment, in terms of wider cultural context, implicit assumptions about such issues as gender roles, and audience interaction. The same scholarship also turns to other works—novels by less prominent authors—as attention moves to understanding culture, not insisting on a single aesthetic standard (Kennedy, 1991). Historical scholarship has shifted at least as fundamentally, particularly through the growing dominance of research in social history (Gardner & Adams, 1983). Social historians argue that societies and social change must be grasped in terms of the interactions of various groups: elites with ordinary folk; women with men; regional, racial and ethnic groups with more centralizing forces. The past is not simply constructed by the doings and ideas of great men. Social values cannot be understood simply through the ideas of the most creative thinkers; indeed, their ideas are shaped, revised, supplemented, sometimes rejected outright by various cultural groups in the wider society. Political structures involve not only formal constitutions, but also power relationships at work in the family, even in leisure pursuits; they also involve recurrent protest and violence. The past expands, and the nature of change has been fundamentally reconceived.

Major shifts in scholarship, particularly in social studies and humanities fields, provide vital support and some guidance for multicultural educational change, in combination with the other conditioning factors. Too often, pressure for multicultural reform seems purely political, and sometimes the political interests deriving from a changing student body do indeed have a life of their own. Thus Nathan Glazer, largely supporting the multicultural implications of the recent New York report on diversity, primarily emphasizes political impulses (Glazer, 1991). Yet the new scholarship must be recognized in allowing educational reform to combine multiculturalism with a better understanding of how cultures operate and how societies function. Deciding what groups to serve through multiculturalism is not the only reorientation required; reconceiving key disciplines, in light of some extraordinarily fruitful innovations, figures in as well.

Three strands of change, then, mutually interrelated, serve as the basis for reassessing longstanding assumptions and routines in American education. Student needs and related political interests do not stand alone. Broader international developments and a real recasting of scholarship in the humanities and social sciences provide powerful support for many multicultural arguments and further basis for directing these arguments into practical curricula. Multiculturalism in this context means finding ways to address varied groups in the student population, but also raising levels of global understanding and building teaching programs, even in the early grades, in explicit relationship to exciting changes in scholarship. Arguments on behalf of multiculturalism broaden correspondingly.

✛ Conclusion

American education has an impressive history. Despite varied problems, the achievements of American education, including the ability to reflect a genuine commitment to beliefs in considerable democracy of opportunity, are substantial by any comparative standard. On balance, however, its historical role has emphasized provision of chances for people from diverse backgrounds to learn some common "American" values, largely middle class, and to use their education to advance in the larger society on these terms. Even for the nonmobile, it has helped teach a common fund of beliefs about what the nation stands for and about the values that define appropriate political, economic, and in some respects even personal behavior.

The educational system indeed contributes greatly to one of the striking features of the American historical record: the ability, despite unprecedented ethnic and racial diversity, to avoid permanent political groupings and conflicts based on race and ethnicity alone. Curricular traditions have been shaped to fill these functions, though not without some ambivalence. They have been open enough to allow new claimants some space: Thus African Americans have long had a few representatives in American history textbooks, like Booker T. Washington, carefully selected to highlight individuals who largely accepted the American system and achieved success within it.

Similarly, choices of American literary works have been flexible enough to give at least token voice to groups seeking greater recognition and identity. Nevertheless, the insistence on a distinctive and definable national value system, mastery of which was held to be part of appropriate assimilation into the national society, clearly predominated, particularly in the history and civics courses that most directly purported to teach what the American system was all about.

The emphases and tensions of the American educational tradition raise a host of fascinating historical and policy questions. How fully did the focus on assimilation dampen group identities and complicate the process of functioning in the United States? How essential was the assimilationist approach, and the curricula that translated it, in maintaining political stability and in encouraging some individuals to achieve "American" success more rapidly than they could have done without school guidance?

Will a shift toward real multiculturalism destroy schooling's role in maintaining American unity and political capacity, as some critics seriously claim?

The American educational tradition helps explain the persistence of these kinds of questions in the current policy context. The successes and the limitations of the tradition play directly into current debate. Opponents of multiculturalism, most obviously, while arguably incorrect in their goals, accurately reflect important ingredients of our educational past; this helps explain their fervor and their strength. They exaggerate certain elements—claiming, for example, a more uniform canon in literature than ever really prevailed in the past, while downplaying prior diversities; however, they are correct in pointing to the assimilationist bent of the educational tradition.

Correspondingly, teachers who work in a more multicultural environment must be aware not only that many powerful educational authorities disagree with them—that's obvious enough—but also that elements of their own curricular experiences as students need to be rethought. This enhances the task of taking hard looks at the principles that should guide the presentation of American and more general history or at selections and interpretations of literature. Multiculturalism does not attack all the basic principles of American education, but it certainly challenges some deep-seated impulses. It builds, however, on a number of far-reaching changes not only in the schools but in underlying scholarship that must themselves be appreciated to mount effective alternatives. A grasp of the factors history thrusts into current debates helps improve an understanding of the choices to be made and the disputes to be faced. The same history does not make the choices simple or the results secure.

References

Armento, B. (1986). Research on teaching social studies. In M. C. Wittrock (Ed.), *Handbook of research on teaching* (pp. 131–173). New York: Macmillan.

Bloom, A. (1987). *The closing of the American mind: How higher education has failed democracy and impoverished the souls of today's students.* New York: Simon & Schuster.

Chapman, P. D. (1988). *Schools as sorters: Lewis M. Terman, applied psychology, and the intelligence testing movement, 1890–1930.* New York: New York University Press.

Cremin, L. A. (1970). *American education: The colonial experience, 1607–1783.* New York: Harper and Row.

Cremin, L. A. (1980). *American education: The national experience, 1783–1876.* New York: Harper and Row.

Cremin, L. A. (1988). *American education: The metropolitan experience, 1876–1980.* New York: Harper and Row.

Gardner, J. B., & Adams, G. R. (Eds.). (1983). *Ordinary people and everyday life: Perspectives on the new social history.* Nashville, TN: American Association for State and Local History.

Gifford, B. (Ed.) (1988). *What shall we teach: History in the schools.* New York: Macmillan.

Glazer, N. (1991, September 2). In defense of multiculturalism. *New Republic, 205,* 15–22.

Himmelfarb, G. (1987). *The new history and the old: Critical essays and reappraisals.* Cambridge, MA: Belknap Press.

Kaelble, H. (1986). *Social mobility in the nineteenth and twentieth centuries.* New York: St. Martin.

Katz, M. B. (1968). *The irony of early school reform: Educational innovation in mid-nineteenth century Massachusetts.* Cambridge, MA: Harvard University Press.

Katz, M. B. (1987). *Reconstructing American education.* Cambridge, MA: Harvard University Press.

Kennedy, A. (1991). Memory and values: Disengaging cultural legacies. *Liberal Education, 77*(3), 34–39.

Labaree, D. F. (1988). *The making of an American high school: The credentials market and the Central High School of Philadelphia, 1938–1939.* New Haven, CT: Yale University Press.

Levine, L. (1988). *High brow, low brow: The emergence of cultural hierarchy in America.* Cambridge, MA: Harvard University Press.

Lightfoot, S. L. (1988). *Balm in Gilead: Journey of a healer.* Reading, MA: Addison-Wesley.

Lipset, S. M. (1995). *American exceptionalism: A double-edged sword.* New York: Norton.

McNeill, W. (1988). Pursuit of power: Criteria of global relevance. In B. Gifford (Ed.), *What shall we teach: History in the schools* (pp. 129-137). New York: Macmillan.

National Center for History in the Schools (1994). *National standards for U.S. history* and *National standards for world history.* Los Angeles, CA: National Center for History in the Schools.

Perlmann, J. (1988). *Ethnic differences: Schooling and social structure among the Irish, Italians, Jews and Blacks in an American city, 1880-1935.* Cambridge: Cambridge University Press.

Ravitch, D. (1990, Summer). Multiculturalism: E pluribus plures. *American Scholars, 59,* 339-347.

Ravitch, D., & Schlesinger, A., Jr. (1990, October). Statement of the committee of scholars in defense of history. *Perspectives, 26,* (15).

Ravitch, D. & Vinovskis, M. (Eds.). (1995). *Learning from the past. What history teaches us about school reform.* Balitmore, MD: Johns Hopkins.

Resnick, D. P. (1980). Educational policy and the applied historian: Testing, competency and standards. *Journal of Social History, 14,* 539-559.

Spring, J. (1994). *Deculturalization and the struggle for equality: A brief history of the education of dominated cultures in the United States.* New York: McGraw-Hill.

Stearns, P. N. (1993). *Meaning over memory: Recasting the teaching of culture and history.* Chapel Hill, NC: University of North Carolina Press.

Stearns, P. N. (1997). *Schools and students in industrial society: Japan and the West.* Boston: Bedford Books.

Tyack, D., & Hansot, E. (1990). *Learning together: A history of coeducation in American schools.* New Haven, CT: Yale University Press.

Valentine, J. A. (1987). *The college board and the school curriculum: A history of the college board's influence on the substance and standards of American education, 1900-1980.* New York: College Entrance Examination Board.

Vinovskis, M. (1995). *Education, society and economic opportunity: A historical perspective on persistent issues.* New Haven, CT: Yale University Press.

Wiener, J. M. (1978). *Social origins of the new South: Alabama, 1860-1885.* Baton Rouge, LA: Louisiana State University Press.

Curriculum, Instruction, and Assessment

❖ ❖ ❖

Teach the young people how to think, not what to think.

Sidney Sugarman

Those of us who stand outside the circle of this society's definition of acceptable women; those of us who have been forged in the crucibles of difference; those of us who are poor, who are lesbians, who are black, who are older, know that *survival is not an academic skill.* It is learning how to stand alone unpopular and sometimes reviled, and how to make common cause with those others identified as outside the structures, in order to define and seek a world in which we can all flourish. It is learning how to take our differences and make them strengths. *For the master's tools will never dismantle the master's house.*

Audre Lorde

Had she paints, or clay, or knew the discipline of dance, or strings; had she anything to engage her tremendous curiosity and her gift for metaphor, she might have exchanged the restlessness and preoccupation with whim for any activity that provided her with all she yearned for. And like any artist with no art form, she became dangerous.

Toni Morrison

I learned to make my mind large, as the universe is large, so that there is room for paradoxes.

Maxine Hong Kingston
The Woman Warrior
(New York: Vintage, 1977), p. 35

3

A Multicultural School Curriculum

Geneva Gay
University of Washington

Curriculum can be confusing and intimidating. This is due in part to inadequate understanding of its basic features, of how it is defined, and of its various shapes and forms. However, curriculum plays a fundamental role in the design and implementation of educational processes at all levels of schooling. It is the anchor of instruction and evaluation, and the embodiment of educational ideals, goals, purposes, visions, and missions.

Effective multicultural education reform requires that the various types of school curricula be dealt with directly and forthrightly. Some ideas for reform are developed in greater detail in this chapter. Specific issues discussed are curriculum definitions, different types of curricula, some guidelines for multiculturalizing the curriculum, and strategies for reforming two types of curricula to incorporate cultural pluralism.

✢ Curriculum Definition

Curriculum is usually defined in five ways: as a product, content, program, intended learning outcomes, and the experiences of learners (Beane, Toepfer, Conrad, & Alessi, 1986; Cushner, McClelland, & Safford, 1992; Zais, 1976). Curriculum as *product* translates into documents, such as subjects offered, course syllabi, lists of objectives and content to be mastered, and titles of textbooks. Curriculum as *content* means the specific information or data to be taught in a course or subject. The teacher of an introductory literature course might describe the curriculum as poetry, prose, drama, and the essay, short story and novel.

When thought of as a *program,* curriculum usually refers to the courses of study offered or the subjects taught by educational institutions. For example, a magnet school specializing in the fine arts might have a curriculum each for dance, music, and theater. Or a middle school curriculum might be described as math, science, social studies, English, physical education, and exploratory units.

Curriculum as *intended learning outcomes* deals with the specific knowledge, skills, attitudes and behaviors students are supposed to learn. They, too, are typically identified in some kind of written documents. Some examples are school or district level student learning objectives (SLOs), lists of state minimum competencies, individualized educational plans (IEPs) for students in special education, and scope and sequence charts.

Curriculum as *experiences of learners* reports what actually happens to students, whereas the other concepts only indicate what should happen. It includes planned and unplanned experiences, because students learn from the formal instructional encounters sanctioned by the school as well as from the structural arrangements and social environments in which materials are presented and teaching-learning interactions occur (Cushner, McClelland, & Safford, 1992; Zais, 1976). Students can experience a curriculum of cultural hegemony, racial prejudice, and social class bias without these being deliberately taught. They can be transmitted by allowing rules, regulations, and materials used in instruction to stem from Eurocentric, middle-class cultural frames of reference.

Another curriculum concept is a *plan* or *blueprint* for instruction. Taba (1962) calls it "a plan for learning" (p. 11); Glatthorn (1987) says it is "the plans for guiding learning in schools . . ." (p. 3); and Saylor, Alexander, and Lewis (1981) describe it as a "plan for providing sets of learning opportunities for persons to be educated" (p. 8). The definition Armstrong (1989) offers is consistent with these views, but is more precise and encompassing. He sees curriculum as "a master plan for selecting content and organizing learning experiences for the purpose of changing and developing learners' behaviors and insights" (p. 4). The emerging notions of Afrocentricity, whole language instruction, and transitional bilingual education programs are examples of master plans for instruction.

In this chapter, the concept of curriculum as a plan for guiding instruction is used. Some attention is given to the processes involved in making decisions about the components of this plan, and how these can and should be modified to be more inclusive of ethnic, cultural, and social pluralism.

✛ Curriculum Components

Scholars agree that curriculum as a plan for instruction should include five common elements, regardless of its magnitude or level of operation. These elements are what is to be taught, why, how, with what, and how its effectiveness will be determined. They are called goals and objectives, rationale, content, activities, and evaluation, respectively. Together they constitute the "anatomy of the curriculum" (Zais, 1976). The interrelationship of these components is shown in Figure 3.1. Frequently, resources, timelines, and tables of specification are added to these.

Curriculum components and the designs they produce may be simple or elaborate, depending on whether the intent is to create a plan of instruction for a single lesson, a unit of study, a course, a series of courses, or an entire program for a given school or district. The components of the curriculum, and their configuration, offer different challenges and possibilities for multicultural education reform.

Knowing some of the key traits of each of the constituent parts of a curriculum is necessary to make them more multicultural. A *rationale* is a general statement of why curriculum designers believe certain knowledge and skills should be taught in particular ways. It embodies values and assumptions about "the role of the individual in society, the societal role of education, the nature and purposes of society and human beings, the relation of the future to the present, the question of what knowledge is most useful, and the purpose for which it should be useful" (Posner & Rudnitsky, 1986, p. 42).

The rationale is one of the most difficult parts of the curriculum to devise, and it is often ignored or merely implied. Yet, it is a critical one, because it establishes the parameters for all the other components. The rationale justifies the learnings students are to acquire and the teaching methods and procedures; it guides and directs decisions about goals, objectives, contents, activities, evaluation, and resources; it sets the emphasis and tone for the teaching and learning processes; and it is a benchmark for determining internal consistency about the other components (Posner & Rudnitsky, 1986).

Goals and objectives are expected learning outcomes, expressed as knowledge, attitudes, values, and skills. An example of a goal statement might be to "understand and

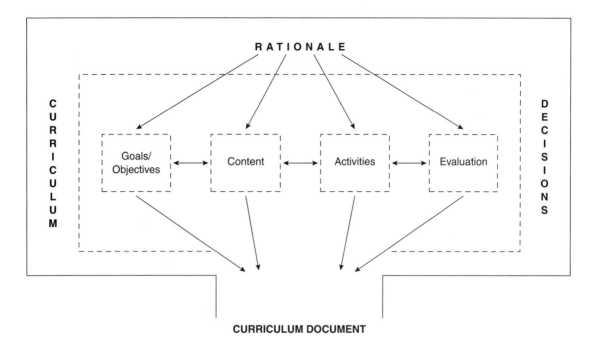

FIGURE 3.1   Curriculum Development Process.
This diagram shows that a rationale establishes the parameters and directions for all other curriculum components, and all of the other components influence and reflect each other.

appreciate the contributions of different ethnic and cultural groups to the culture of the United States." Related objectives would specify the groups and areas of contribution, such as "Compare the gifts of Asian and African Americans to medicine in the United States," or "Name the foods common in the U.S. diet that were introduced by American Indians, Hispanics, and Africans."

The *content* component of the curriculum is the database or information source for teaching the goals and objectives. It includes knowledge (facts, observations, explanations, principles, definitions, relationships), skills (numerical calculations, map-making, persuasive debating, original research), processes (thinking, analyzing, deciding, communicating), and values (beliefs about right/wrong, good/bad, just/unjust, beautiful/ugly). Curriculum content may be in the form of books, reports, films, videotapes, recordings, newspapers, magazines, personal observations, real and vicarious experiences, and interviews.

Learning activities identify what students will do with the content as they practice the skills embedded in the goals and objectives. These may include analyzing films, taking field trips, conducting surveys, doing library research, writing critical essays, engaging in peer coaching, simulating experiences, or participating in role plays. To a large extent, the nature of the activity is shaped by the kind of content to be taught. To illustrate, students might be asked to look at films in the "Eyes on the Prize" or "Profiles in Courage" series to compile information about different women and people of color who have made significant contributions to science, technology, politics, music, art, and literature. Other activities might have students interviewing people from different race, socioeconomic, age, and gender groups to see how they feel about the significance of ethnic contributions to U.S. development. A third activity might involve students in finding out how ethnic contributions, nationally and internationally, affect their lives from day to day.

The *evaluation* component of the curriculum deals with performance assessment. It identifies the methods, techniques, and procedures that will be used to determine how well students have achieved the intended learning outcomes, or objectives. These may include pencil-and-paper tests, analysis of individual and group projects, portfolios, behavioral observations, inventories, student journals, and oral and written reports (Beane, Toepfer, Conrad, & Alessi, 1986). Thus a point-counterpoint team debate on how and why *X* groups have made more significant contributions to the development of the United States than *Y* groups can be as effective in assessing learning as giving a pencil-and-paper test on ethnic gifts or having students write reports on individual contributors.

✥ Types of Curricula

School curricula are often identified as *formal* or *informal*. The formal curriculum is expressly stated in school documents such as textbooks, guides, scope and sequence charts, policy mandates, and other legally sanctioned plans for instruction, and officially taught in the classroom. It is intentional because it is composed of learning experiences that the school system plans deliberately (Glatthorn, 1987). Glatthorn refers to this form as the *written curriculum*.

Manifestations of Formal Curricula

He refines the category further to include three other manifestations: the recommended, supported, and tested curricula. The *recommended* curriculum comes from requirements of federal and state policy makers, and proposals of individual scholars, professional associations, and reform commissions. Examples of this type are Public Law 94-142, which requires IEPs and "least restrictive environments" in educating students with disabilities; the America 2000 strategy and National Education Goals adopted by President Bush and the state governors in April 1991 (U.S. Department of Education); the Paideia Proposal offered by Adler (1982); and the recommendations of the American Association for the Advancement of Science (1989) in *Science for All Americans.*

The *supported* curriculum is reflected in and shaped by the resources allocated to its development and implementation, including funds, time, personnel, facilities, and materials. Two of the best illustrations of this type of curriculum are the textbooks adopted for use in the classroom and the subjects and skills that are given priority in the hiring and assignment of teachers. The *tested* curriculum is the learning assessed by district and state competency tests and norm-referenced standardized tests, such as the Iowa Test of Basic Skills (ITBS), the California Achievement Test (CAT), and the various National Assessment of Educational Progress (NAEP) tests.

Several terms exist for the *informal* curriculum. Among these are the hidden, subtle, covert, invisible, lived, and experiential curriculum (Beane, Toepfer, Conrad, & Alessi, 1986; Glatthorn, 1987; Goodlad, 1979; Snyder, 1971; Zais, 1976). Because many of its intents and content are coded in and conveyed through a network of school symbols, it can also be called the *symbolic curriculum*. While the formal curriculum is official and focuses on what is taught overtly and directly, the symbolic one is more covert and indirect. It has de facto legitimacy and is grounded in customary practices, rituals, routines, and codes of behavior.

Some of the major benchmarks of the symbolic curriculum are the assignment of students to different instructional programs; attitudes and values attached to various subjects and skills; school systems of rewards and punishments, sanctions, and incentives; and the celebrations and ceremonies routinely practiced in elementary, middle, and high schools. In traditional schools, the symbolic curriculum transmits values that emphasize individualism, competition, conquest, control, division of labor, and fragmentation (Giroux & Penna, 1981). Although these are consistent with the capitalistic cultural ethos of mainstream U.S. society, they are contradictory to the values of many groups of color, females, and children of poverty. They also are incompatible with the goals and visions of multicultural education that emphasize common destiny, interdependence, and reciprocity among diverse groups.

Significance of the Symbolic Curriculum

The hidden, informal, or symbolic curriculum is especially evident in the type of schoolwork students from different social and economic backgrounds receive and how this accesss operates as tacit preparation for adult roles as laborers, managers, leaders, and policy makers in the world of work. Curriculum offerings, teaching practices, and instructional materials are not necessarily the same across socioeconomic and ethnic groups of students and the schools they attend. Middle-class, European American students tend to be treated more favorably in all aspects of curriculum and instruction than lower socioeconomic group students and children of color. These discrepancies cause inequities in access to knowledge capital, personal competence, power and authority relationships, and leadership skills acquired in school that are subsequently reproduced in society (Anyon, 1981).

The customary ways of "doing schooling," the social, emotional, and valuative contexts and procedural rules that surround the formal curriculum, transmit certain powerful and pervasive messages to students about which attitudes, values, behaviors, and personas are likely to be rewarded. Jackson (1990) summarizes some of the most significant messages in *Life in Classrooms*. Among them are learning how to (1) exist in crowds but operate in social solitude; (2) function in what are basically and persistently evaluative settings; (3) understand the clear distinctions between powerless students and powerful teachers; (4) be patient and passive; (5) recognize that violations of institutional expectations are more consequential than academic attainment; (6) develop work ethics and habits of conformity, compliance, obedience, and docility; and (7) that access to the system of praise, encouragement, recognition, and reward is differentiated by socioeconomic, racial, ethnic, and gender group identity.

The symbolic curriculum and its messages have different forms and are transmitted through various media. These include the structures, relationships, etiquette, expectations, and ambience that exist in schools; the institutional rules and regulations that govern the social behaviors of students and teachers; the organizational mechanisms used to manage students within the educational program; the social values taught by example; the types of knowledge and learning experiences accessible to different groups of students; the procedures used to make the school acceptable to the larger society; and the system of symbols and rituals instituted to embody the image and essence of the school.

Students must learn to master both the formal and the symbolic curricula to succeed in school. This requires at least two systems of skills, because those that contribute to intellectual achievement may not necessarily facilitate successful social adaptation to institutional norms. Furthermore, what is taught through the symbolic and formal curricula is often dichotomous, with the lessons learned from the former frequently being much more powerful, lasting, and transferable to life beyond school than those of the latter (Anyon, 1981; Beane, Toepfer, Conrad, & Alessi, 1986; Giroux & Penna, 1981). In addition, both types of curricula must be actively engaged in teaching all students knowledge of and respect for cultural diversity, skills for living in a pluralistic world, and commitment to constructing a more morally just and egalitarian society. All aspects of all kinds of curricula have tremendous ramifications for orchestrating multicultural curriculum reform relative to priorities, content, techniques, and focus. However, specific strategies need to be tailored differently for formal and symbolic curricula.

✥ Guiding Principles for Curriculum Reform

Efforts to multiculturalize the curriculum should be contextually specific, developmentally appropriate, and culturally authentic. *Contextualizing* curriculum reform involves awareness that certain techniques are better for some subjects, units of instruction, grade levels, student populations, and school environments than others. For example, because education in the elementary school tends to concentrate on reading and math skills development and evoke the "Learning activities" component of the plan, multicultural education reform in formal elementary curriculum should be similarly focused. In the arena of symbolic curriculum, elementary schools typically do a lot with school and classroom decorations. These are fertile avenues for incorporating cultural pluralism. By comparison, high school teaching emphasizes mastery of subject matter, thereby giving priority to the "content" component of the planning process. Evidence of their symbolic curricula appears as various types of celebrations, recognition assemblies, and social dances.

The predominant middle school focus is less definitive, even though ideally it includes a combination of subject matter and skills, thus highlighting both the content and activities components of official plans for instruction. The symbolic representations of the hidden curriculum are more similar to those of high school, as can be seen in school songs, insignia, rituals, clubs, and activity programs. Multicultural education curriculum reform in middle and high schools also should parallel these emphases. This approach may not be ideal, but it is a realistic starting point. Educators are more amenable to change when some of it can be accomplished within their existing points of reference than when totally new frameworks, information, and operational styles must be accommodated simultaneously.

Achieving *developmentally appropriate* reform simply means matching techniques and efforts to the competency levels of the reformers and the intended consumers of the reform, or the curriculum designers, teachers, and students. The details of specific strategies will differ according to the levels of expertise about and ideological commitment to multiculturalism among those who are creating the reform.

Banks (1989), Gay (1983), and Sleeter and Grant (1988) suggest that approaches to dealing with cultural pluralism in instructional programs increase in complexity as those providing the leadership become more informed and sophisticated. This progression has tended to move (1) from studying single ethnic groups to multiple ethnic groups to multiple cultural groups; (2) from supplementary multicultural information, lessons, and units added to existing curricula to integrating multiculturalism into all dimensions of curriculum and instruction; and (3) from teaching the contributions of diverse groups to transforming all aspects of schooling to reflect cultural pluralism and developing skills for the ultimate reconstruction of American society.

This developmental character of multicultural education reform recognizes that individuals just beginning the task are not capable of accomplishing the same changes as those who have been working in the field for a long time. While studies of contributions and profiles of separate ethnic groups may be appropriate for novices, they are not so for experts. It would be more developmentally reasonable to expect educators experienced in multiculturalism to design strategies for infusion across the entire spectrum of schooling, curriculum transformation, and social reconstruction. Yet, both novices and experts should be held accountable for the highest quality of multicultural curriculum reform within their respective developmental levels.

Another important dimension of developmental appropriateness is the readiness level of the students and the climate of the school for which the curriculum is designed. The essentials of multicultural education must be translated into instructional delivery systems suitable for students and schools in different psychosocial states based on such factors as age, attitudes, previous experiences, existing knowledge levels, and the diversity mixes among school and classroom populations. Dealing with racism is a fundamental component of multicultural education. Although combatting racism is a complex and volatile issue, it is nonetheless imperative that skills for this purpose be taught to all students, beginning in kindergarten. The challenge for curriculum designers is how to do this in meaningful and appropriate ways for students in early elementary, intermediate, middle, and high school grades; for students of color and European American students; for students in single- and multiracial school settings; for students in social studies and language arts as well as math and science; for school environments experiencing racial tensions and those that are harmonious.

Cultural authenticity in curriculum reform requires that the information included in instructional plans about diverse ethnic, racial, social, and gender groups is accurate and significant, and covers a wide range of experiences and perspectives. This means curriculum designers must bring to their task a clear understanding of the elements of different groups' heritages, lifestyles, sociopolitical experiences, and cultures that factor most directly into defining the various components of the curriculum.

Of particular relevance are cultural values and contributions, communication styles, learning styles, interrelational patterns, levels of ethnic identity development and affiliation, and how ethnic attitudes and cultural values are encoded in and transmitted through expressive human behaviors. Knowledge of these components of culture helps curriculum designers avoid common pitfalls in dealing with diversity in schools, such as focusing on a few individuals who have achieved exceptional feats or fame, exotic rituals and ceremonies, and historical experiences to the exclusion of contemporary issues. It is also necessary to incorporate appropriate elements of cultural pluralism into all parts of formal plans for instruction (that is, goals, objectives, rationale, content, learning activities, and evaluation) and into the climates and contexts that constitute the school culture, or symbolic curriculum.

❖ Strategies for Multiculturalizing the Curriculum

Examining the implications of every element of formal and symbolic school curricula for multicultural reform is beyond the scope of this chapter. Suffice it to say that all are susceptible, and should be affected by reform. The focus here is on those parts of the curricula that make up much of what goes on routinely and habitually in schools and classrooms, and are most fundamental in shaping the quality of learning experiences provided to students. Because they require different techniques, multiculturalizing the formal and symbolic curricula are discussed separately.

The Formal Curriculum

Various proposals have been offered for revising the official school curriculum to include ethnically, culturally, and socially pluralistic content, experiences, and perspectives. These have ranged from adding facts to existing frameworks, to introducing new courses, to replacing entire programs of study. What has been lacking in these recommendations are operational explanations for how to mesh these proposals with other curriculum mandates. For example, how does one systematically integrate ethnic contributions into the teaching of basic skills, higher-order thinking skills, and standard subjects like algebra, science, geography, family living, and industrial arts?

Curriculum designers, teachers, administrative leaders, and anyone else in the school who influences learning can accomplish this by answering four key questions within the parameters of different subjects and skills routinely taught in elementary and secondary schools. These are:

1. What do you want students to learn about ethnic and cultural pluralism?
2. Why are these learnings particularly desirable for diverse students, the various subjects and skills taught, and a culturally pluralistic society?
3. How will these learnings be facilitated and accomplished within culturally pluralistic contexts?
4. How will culturally pluralistic frameworks, techniques, and procedures be used to determine if or when the desired learnings have been accomplished?

These questions respectively address the goals/objectives, rationale, content and activities, and evaluation components of plans for instruction.

Some hypothetical situations may help illustrate how answering these questions can help educators successfully multiculturalize the formal school curriculum. Three examples are presented here:

Middle School Curriculum Reform   Suppose that middle school math teachers want their students to "apply computational skills in understanding ethnic and gender disparities in employment." This is their *goal* statement. Related objectives might include learning how to read ethnic employment statistics, working cooperatively to complete learning tasks, and becoming aware of different types of ethnic and gender discrimination in local businesses and industries. The teachers then explain that this is desirable because (1) mathematical skills are learned more thoroughly when they are connected to meaningful life experiences of students; (2) students live in a society inundated with devastating examples and effects of inequities in educational and economic opportunities by race, gender, socioeconomic, and ethnic group; and (3) learning how to apply math skills in analyzing social problems increases students' social consciousness, equips them with tools to make better decisions about social issues, and cultivates a sensitivity to the need for social change. These are parts of their *rationale.*

The teachers decide the desired learnings will be facilitated by teaching students how to use state and federal labor charts on ethnic and gender employment statistics, how to conduct surveys of local businesses to determine patterns of employment by race and gender, and how to calculate percentages, ratios, and comparison distribution charts of the types of jobs performed by different ethnic and gender groups in various businesses. These suggestions constitute the *content* and *activities* portions of their curriculum.

The students' understanding and mastery will be assessed by the accuracy with which they are able to plot their numerical calculations of employment distributions on a variety of charts and graphs, and extrapolate and explain the different ethnic, racial, and gender employment trends embedded in them. Thus, translating information from one form to another and interpreting it accurately replace the traditional pencil-and-paper tests used so often for *evaluation.*

Language Arts Curriculum Reform   The eighth-grade language arts teachers use a somewhat different approach to answering the key questions. In revising the literature segment, they decide to leave intact the general objective of having students "learn how social and political points of view are expressed through different literary forms and techniques." Previously, they had used various political essays and debates as the *content* for this objective, and students spent most of their *learning activities* examining their structural elements. The teachers had justified these emphases on the basis that students needed to know the technical components of various literary genres.

They decide to create culturally pluralistic *contexts* in which the objectives are taught and learned. They modify the content to reflect their hypothesis that literary forms and techniques of social and political commentary vary by ethnic, gender, and cultural groups, and by time of occurrence. The emphasis on examining different examples of commentary shifts from structure and form to substance, aesthetics, and effect. A variety of examples by ethnic and cultural groups are used to demonstrate these differences in techniques. The selections include the "sermon" for African Americans, the "debate" for European Americans, the "song" for Hispanics, "body adornment" for the youth counterculture, "protest" politics for American Indians, and "literary criticism" for women. Learning outcomes are evaluated by having students explain how the literary techniques they learned about in their case studies analyses are translated into other expressive forms, such as poetry, paintings, symbolic dress, and dramatic performance.

K–1 Curriculum Reform   The K–1 teachers choose "learning activities" and "classroom climate" for their reform efforts. They decide to culturally diversify all the experiences provided to help their students master the basic, routine skills or reading, writing, arithmetic, and social and physical development. They want to create a classroom environment that radiates pride in cultural diversity. Their list of specific reform strategies includes the following:

- Design and use multiethnic alphabets in which each letter stands for different groups, their cultures, and contributions. For example, "A" is for Asian and African Americans.
- Consistently use culturally diverse items, images, and artifacts in classroom decorations.
- Use ethnic games and folk dances to practice gross motor coordination, for recreation, and for physical education skills development.
- Always use culturally diverse books of myths, facts, fiction, and folklore to teach basic reading skills.
- Practice spelling skills with words from different ethnic and cultural traditions.
- Have culturally diverse individuals regularly facilitate story time, through personal or mediated appearances.
- Change the focus of routine seasonal activites (such as pilgrims and turkeys for Thanksgiving, jack-o-lanterns for Halloween, and snowflake cutouts for winter) to reflect ethnically diverse experiences, practices, and celebrations.
- Institute a cross-ethnic "Adopt a Grandparent Program" in which students from one ethnic group choose grandparents from a different group.
- Create a "media center" with time allotted regularly to present students with positive visual images of culturally diverse individuals and experiences.
- Have students practice writing skills using ethnically and culturally diverse issues and themes.
- Institute a ritual of celebration of diversity in which students conduct a monthly "ceremony of praise" for specific features of cultural diversity, such as remembering historical people, giving thanks for how diversity enriches their daily lives, and recognizing how their peers are honoring diversity.

These three scenarios give a quick glimpse of a single segment of an entire revised curriculum. They represent how different concentrations for change can be translated into specific curriculum components. They also demonstrate the points made earlier that (1) each of the standard five components of the formal curriculum is amenable to multicultural reform but that it is not always necessary to change all of them to be effective, and (2) changes made in the curriculum should be appropriate for the human, grade, and subject or skill contexts for which they are intended.

The Symbolic Curriculum

As is true with the formal curriculum, efforts to change the informal or symbolic curriculum to reflect more sensitivity to cultural diversity need to be target-specific. This can best be achieved by identifying its different components, and then designing change strategies specific to them.

Because the messages of the informal curriculum are embodied in and transmitted through symbols and rituals, the curriculum can be multiculturalized by revising, expanding, and even replacing them. Demonstrating how to do this for all school symbols is a mammoth task, which far exceeds the boundaries of this chapter. Therefore, only four types are developed here to illustrate the process. These are the arrangement of physical space, work habits and rituals, recognitions and awards, and institutional affiliation. Other dimensions of the symbolic curriculum which should be included in the total range of reform are rules regulating the movement of students throughout the school; protocols that surround teaching-learning interactions regarding permission to participate, paying attention, and appropriate performance and presentation style; interactions among students during instruction and on learning tasks; and how behavior is sanctioned and rewarded.

Rules, rituals, and ceremonies are the primary conduits of the symbolic curriculum. They are to it what goals, objectives, content, and activities are to the formal curriculum. Invariably, the values and beliefs taught through these symbols are those of the Eurocentric, middle-class society. Among them are such prized American values as individuality, competition, rationality, linearity, objectivity, productivity, control, and conquest.

The arrangement of traditional school environments discourages familiarity, collaboration, group effort, and personal enjoyment in learning. The austerity of the color schemes and the relative lack of decorations in classrooms (especially in middle and secondary schools) create antiseptic environments that appear cold and uncaring. They imply formality and social distance in interpersonal interactions, attaching a certain somberness, even severity, to the learning process. Some students from culturally different groups, such as Hispanics, African Americans, American Indians, and Appalachians, find these environments distractive to learning. They prefer warmer settings that are more friendly, informal, social, communal, interactive, and animated. To accommodate these preferences, schools and classrooms can do the following:

- Change color schemes to warmer and brighter pastel colors, instead of the conventional institutional gray, beige, or green.
- Replace the standard 6-by-6-block seating arrangement with circles and small clusters of chairs.
- Close the "existential distance" between students and teachers by having teachers become more like friends and partners with students, rather than distant, authoritative directors of learning.
- Use cooperative learning as the standard structure of instruction instead of the current model of large-group, direct teaching, and competitive individualistic learning.
- Make the physical space of the school and classroom a reflection of and testimony to the value that accepts cultural diversity as a regular and prized feature of everyday life by always having visual images of diversity on display.
- Make the classroom into a participatory laboratory of learning in which students are habitually engaged in active inquiry, discovery, and application of learning instead of the current model of passive absorption of facts.

Homework and the conditions under which it is assigned are symbolic approximations of the American capitalistic work ethic—individual effort and the survival of the fittest. Homework tends to reinforce achievement distinctions between students. Those who are already doing well are more likely to do homework than those who are not. Also, many students do not have the resources to successfully complete their homework at home. Unquestionably, practice is necessary for learning for most students. But it does not necessarily have to be relegated to "homework." This component of the symbolic curriculum can be reformed by changing school schedules and mind-sets to allow time and assistance during the school day for students to work together in study teams and do their "practice work." This revision has the added benefit of promoting cooperative learning and making time, space, materials, supervision, and expertise readily available to students who need them.

Awards and recognition ceremonies in school serve similar purposes for students as those in society do for adults. The implicit objective of choosing homecoming courts, conducting honor society initiations, granting varsity letters for athletic accomplishments, and giving perfect attendance and citizenship awards is to publicly praise and celebrate individuals who personify the institution's values and norms in exceptional ways. These rituals create folk heroes and heroines who serve as models for other students to emulate. They can be multiculturalized in two major ways.

First, the criteria used to select candidates for consideration in existing areas of recognition should be broadened to be more culturally pluralistic. For example, committees judging beauty kings and queens can include traits specific to different ethnic groups. Thus, an African American female selected to be a beauty queen would have classic African American features instead of looking like a Black imitation of European American images. Other modifications in these standards might include not considering any slate of candidates for special recognition unless it is racially and ethnically diverse, and applying affirmative action standards to the selection of members to organizations such as the student government and extracurricular activities.

A second way awards rituals can be multiculturalized is by creating new categories for recognition and celebration that symbolize the school's commitment to cultural pluralism. A new citizenship award might be granted to a student who models desirable ways to respect cultural diversity, such as being a leader in eliminating racial and gender biases in the school. Achievement awards could be given on the basis of exceptional mastery of significant learnings related to understanding, appreciating, and promoting cultural pluralism. These could be cultivated and acknowledged through "odyssey of the mind," academic olympiad, and scholarship bowl competitions that test students' knowledge of different ethnic groups' cultures, histories, and heritages. Service awards could be designed for students who do something noteworthy in communities and groups that are culturally different from theirs. And, in general, greater emphasis should be placed on *group achievements,* because this format is the preference of some ethnic groups in the United States.

The efforts of schools to develop institutional allegiance among students is analogous to what the larger society does to evoke feelings of corporate affinity and national loyalty. Many of these are embodied as school songs, mottos, mascots, and insignia. They parallel, in purpose and function, the national anthem, the flag, the red, white and blue colors, and the Pledge of Allegiance. The problem with these is that they may conjure up images and emotions that are either irrelevant or undesirable to some students from different ethnic, racial, social, and national origin backgrounds. Two cases in point are the reactions of some African Americans to schools whose spirit song is *Dixie,* and the responses of some American Indians to schools that use "Braves," "Indians," and "Chiefs" as mascots.

These symbols of institutional allegiance and affiliation should be revised to avoid stirring up negative historical experiences, eliminate stereotypical racial images, and include more culturally diverse perspective and experiences. In many instances, this will mean abandoning old symbols and creating new ones which embody new value commitments to pluralism. These should include inspirational mottos, emblems, jackets and T-shirts, songs and pledges. The school's commitment to cultural pluralism as transmitted through its symbolic images will be unmistakable, and students from many diverse cultural backgrounds will wear them equally proudly because their perspectives are an integral part of the symbols.

The rituals and symbols adopted by the Carson Montessori Elementary School in Cincinnati, Ohio, to daily praise the worth of each student and demonstrate the need for students to work together illustrate how school symbols can be used to teach powerful lessons about diversity. For the 1991–92 academic year, the school adopted "RESPECT" as its guiding motto, with the added slogan, "Together We Can Make It Happen." Each letter in the motto was expanded to represent an element of respect: **R**esponsibility; **E**nvironment; **S**elf-discipline; **P**ride; **E**ffort; **C**onfidence; and **T**ruth. A song was composed, assemblies were conducted, bulletin board displays in the halls and classrooms were created, and formal lessons were taught regularly on what each letter of RESPECT represents, as well as the entire concept. Students of all ages took leadership roles in conducting these activities by planning the programs, writing and reading pertinent essays, and sharing personal experiences before the student body. Students also learned a pledge written by the principal.

I Am a Special Human Being

❖ I am a special human being
❖ There is no one like me.
❖ I have unique ideas that make me proud of me.
❖ No one can challenge my originality only
❖ Because it signifies who I am supposed to be.
❖ Others may have questions about what makes me exceptional,
❖ The only answer that I may give is that the Creator only
❖ Made one of me.
❖ And since the mold is broken I must feed
❖ My mind to become the best that I can be!

The students at Carson sing their RESPECT song and recite their school pledge with the same regularity in classes and assemblies that they sing the national anthem and recite the Pledge of Allegiance. They also wear T-shirts, display pennants, and use folders and book covers emblazoned with their motto and pledge. A strong feeling of institutional identity, pride, and communal bonding radiates throughout this school, which is racially and culturally diverse. Even the youngest students recite their motto and pledge with vigor and conviction. This school is successfully creating visible symbols that represent its value commitment to diversity. It is institutionalizing a set of rituals for students to regularly practice this value at the same time they are learning about cultural pluralism and their academic subjects. Thus, the formal and symbolic curricula are complementary extensions of each other. This is a model well worth emulating as a way to teach multicultural education through informal or symbolic curricula.

❖ Conclusion

Most advocates of multicultural education agree that its successful implementation in schools requires systemic and intentional change. Within the context of curriculum, or plans for instruction, this means recognizing that there are two major types of curricula operating in schools simultaneously. The formal curriculum is the officially stated plan of what students are expected to learn in various subjects or skill areas, and the tools and techniques that will be used to facilitate this learning. The symbolic curriculum is less explicit and conscious. It exists in the environment, the ecology, and the ethos of the climates we create for learning. It comprises the values that underlie the codes of behavior, social etiquette, and work ethics that students are expected to practice as they go about the process of living and learning in schools. These lessons are embodied in and transmitted through sets of rules, rituals, symbols, ceremonies, celebrations, and sanctions. Both the formal and symbolic curricula must be revised to be more culturally pluralistic, because both now tend to disproportionately reflect the experiences, perspectives, cultures, and contributions of mainstream, Eurocentric middle class.

Efforts toward multicultural curriculum reform are more effective when they are target-specific, contextualized, developmentally appropriate, and culturally authentic. These guidelines require that curriculum designers identify the specific dimension of learning or curriculum component to be revised and ensure that the intended reform is in sync with the subject being taught, the principles of multiculturalism, and the developmental levels of students and teachers. The guidelines also require that the information included about culturally different groups is accurate, significant, and representative of a wide range of perspectives and experiences within and among them.

The ultimate challenge and purpose of multicultural curriculum reform is to demonstrate how mastery of subject matter, academic skills, and cultural pluralism can be natural complements of each other, and all can be accomplished simultaneously without doing injustice to any. This must be the goal of curriculum design if it is to play a central role in preparing students to be fully functioning and socially responsible citizens in a society and world that are increasingly ethnically, socially, racially, and culturally pluralistic.

References

Adler, M. J. (1982). *The Paideia proposal: An educational manifesto.* New York: Macmillan.

American Association for the Advancement of Science. (1989). *Science for all Americans.* Washington, DC: Author.

Anyon, J. (1981). Social class and the hidden curriculum at work. In H. A. Giroux, A. N. Penna, & W. F. Pinar (Eds.), *Curriculum & instruction: Alternatives in education* (pp. 317–341). Berkeley, CA: McCutchan.

Armstrong, D. C. (1989). *Developing and documenting the curriculum.* Boston: Allyn and Bacon.

Banks, J. A. (1989). Integrating the curriculum with ethnic content: Approaches and guidelines. In J. A. Banks & C. A. McGee Banks (Eds.), *Multicultural education: Issues and perspectives* (pp. 189–207). Boston: Allyn and Bacon.

Beane, J. A., Toepfer, C. F., Jr., Conrad, F., & Alessi, S. J., Jr. (1986). *Curriculum planning and development.* Boston: Allyn and Bacon.

Cushner, K., McClelland, A., & Safford, P. (1992). *Human diversity in education: An integrative approach.* New York: McGraw-Hill.

Gay, G. (1983). Multiethnic education: Historical developments and future prospects. *Phi Delta Kappan, 64,* 560-563.

Giroux, H. A., & Penna, A. N. (1981). Social education in the classroom: The dynamics of the hidden curriculum. In H. A. Giroux, A. N. Penna & W. F. Pinar (Eds.), *Curriculum & instruction: Alternatives in education* (pp. 209-230). Berkeley, CA: McCutchan.

Glatthorn, A. A. (1987). *Curriculum leadership.* Glenview, IL: Scott, Foresman.

Goodlad, J. I. (1979). *Curriculum inquiry: The study of curriculum practice.* New York: McGraw-Hill.

Jackson, P. W. (1990). *Life in classrooms* (Reissued). New York: Teachers College, Columbia University.

Posner, G. J., & Rudnitsky, A. N. (1986). *Curriculum design: A guide to curriculum development for teachers.* New York: Longman.

Saylor, J. G., Alexander, W. M., & Lewis, A. J. (1981). *Curriculum planning* (4th ed.). New York: Holt, Rinehart and Winston.

Sleeter, C. E., & Grant, C. A. (1999). *Making choices for multicultural education: Five approaches to race, class, and gender.* (3d ed.). Upper Saddle River, NJ: Merrill/Prentice Hall.

Snyder, B. R. (1971). *The hidden curriculum.* New York: Alfred A. Knopf.

Taba, H. (1962). *Curriculum development: Theory and practice.* New York: Harcourt Brace and World.

U.S. Department of Education. (1991). *America 2000: An education strategy.* Washington, DC: Author.

Zais, R. S. (1976). *Curriculum principles and foundations.* New York: Thomas Y. Crowell.

4 Instructional Pluralism: A Means to Realizing the Dream of Multicultural, Social Reconstructionist Education

Carla Cooper Shaw
Northern Illinois University

An air of anticipation pervades the school auditorium as parents, brothers and sisters, teachers, and administrators await the parting of the stage's curtain. The audience soon will witness fifth graders dramatizing original plays and reading stories they have written about American Indians. Members of the audience will be invited onstage to join a fireside tale-telling session. Student scholars will point to charts while they deliver minilectures on shifts in American Indian populations and solutions to environmental crises from an American Indian perspective. When the curtain has fallen and both students and teacher have taken their bows, audience members will exit through the lobby, where they will see American Indian-style artwork on display.

This evening's entertainment is the culmination of an interdisciplinary unit focusing on a variety of American Indian cultures, as well as on the collective American Indian experience. The whole language approach begins with the teacher reading aloud children's literature about American Indians. Students then read silently and out loud, individually and in groups. They have written original folktales, as well as stories from the points of view of American Indian characters envisioned with the help of guided imagery.

Students brainstorm conflicts that might arise between American Indians from various tribes. Using what they have learned about their systems of governance, students role-play tribal councils as they resolve these conflicts.

In cooperative groups, students construct concept maps for the cultures of several American Indian tribes. Later, the class works together to merge the maps into one large web representing aspects of culture shared by these tribes. Eventually, students use this web to compare American Indian cultures with their own and to European American culture.

Students locate the territories of various American Indian tribes on the map and research the plant and animal life, topography, and climate of these regions. They take field trips to the countryside, where they practice the observational skills in which American Indians from traditional cultures excel.

Drawing on the literature they have read, students explore views of nature common to various tribes, developing concept maps or other visual representations of the American Indians' relationship with nature. They discuss how today's environment might be different if European settlers had never come to the New World and how American Indians might solve current environmental problems.

Students write and solve mathematics word problems relevant to American Indian day-to-day life, as well as problems using demographic figures related to the population of American Indians now and in the past. They devise bar graphs and pie charts, which the teacher uses to reinforce fractions. Students draw conclusions about changes in American Indian populations over time, hypothesize reasons for shifts, and make projections.

Interspersed throughout the unit are art experiences in which students use natural materials that American Indians from traditional cultures use today.

This unit exemplifies what Sleeter and Grant (1993) call Multicultural Education. It promotes equal opportunity to learn for all students, cultural pluralism, and respect for those who differ from the mainstream, and it has the potential to become Education that is Multicultural and Social Reconstuctionist. Further, this unit takes a transformational approach to the integration of ethnic content into the curriculum. When implemented with similar units focusing on a variety of cultural groups, it enables students "to view concepts, issues, events, and themes from the perspectives of diverse cultural groups" (Banks & Banks, 1993) and to channel their insights into social action. This unit is praiseworthy not only for its emphasis on cultural pluralism, but also for its incorporation of *instructional* pluralism. That is, the unit displays a sensitivity to diverse learning styles and translates this sensitivity into diverse and meaningful learning experiences.

Learning style refers to the characteristics students bring to situations that influence how they learn. There are several possible dimensions to learning style. For example, students may have perceptual preferences. Auditory learners learn best when they hear instructional material, visual learners prefer material to be presented in a visual format, and tactile-kinesthetic learners learn most effectively with hands-on experiences.

Another dimension of learning style is conceptual level. Students with high conceptual levels need a minimum amount of structure in their learning experiences, while students with low conceptual levels require highly structured activities. Another dimension concerns social preferences—whether students learn best by working individually, in pairs, in small groups, or as a whole class.

No matter which dimensions the educator emphasizes, there are four central aspects of style. First, everyone has a learning style. Second, while one's learning style is amenable to change, it is relatively consistent over time. Third, no particular learning style is innately superior to another; rather, certain styles may be more or less effective in given situations. Finally, style is pervasive in that it reveals itself not only in the formal environment of school, but also in the wider context of life, from social situations to job tasks. As such, learning style serves the astute observer as a window to the personality of the individual.

Hilliard (1989) defines style as the following:

> Consistency in the behavior of a person or a group that tends to be habitual—the manifestation of a predisposition to approach things in a characteristic way. (p. 67)

While Hilliard's definition captures the essence of other conceptions of individual learning styles, it also attributes style to groups. Much as individuals have preferred ways of knowing, so do cultures. Individual learning style is to the personality of a person as cultural learning style is to the personality of a culture.

Hilliard identifies key aspects of style as it relates to culture. Culture, as opposed to nature, is an invention of humankind, and thus, cultural styles are learned, not innate.

They can also be unlearned—or at least changed. Consequently, people can learn to use more than one style, or "code switch." Hilliard says "style tends to be rooted at a deep structural level and so may be manifest in a highly generalized way" (p. 67). How, then, do these roots develop, and what are their behavioral outgrowths?

The roots of learning style may lie in how children are raised and how their families function. Cohen (1969) makes a compelling case for the origin of two opposite "conceptual styles," relational and analytic, that emerge from deeply ingrained socialization practices. Cohen argues that relational learners come from shared-function families in which *family* is defined to include relatives, friends, and neighbors. Group functions are shared among all members, and status roles change easily, with no one person being in power for an extended length of time. The following passage from a short story by Hunter (1973), *You Rap, I'll Reap,* illustrates a shared-function group. The narrator is Gloria, an African American teen-ager, speaking of life in her housing project.

> Take last week when old Mrs. Dawkins across the hall was late getting her check.
> I borrowed ten dollars toward her rent from Mrs. Stevens, the lady I work for after
> school. Mrs. Dawkins got the rest from Lola, the new girl my age down the hall who
> has a baby, and from Po Boy, the numbers writer, and Madame James, the card reader, and
> Pork Chop, who runs the newsstand on the corner. Then her check finally came,
> so on Sunday she cooked a big dinner, ham and fried chicken and yams and cornbread
> and greens, and invited everybody in the building who'd helped her make her rent. . . .
>
> Course, Mrs. Dawkins couldn't pay us back right away, not after buying all that
> food. We didn't ask her to. How could we, when she'd been so nice to us? We don't
> exactly keep books on each other in the projects, but it all works out somehow. Mrs.
> Dawkins, now, she does favors for everybody. At the party she offered to keep Lola's baby
> anytime she couldn't pay a sitter. And she lets *me* stay over her place anytime I want.
>
> I stayed with Mrs. Dawkins two whole months one time. My Aunt Lou and her
> daughters had come up from down South and had no place to go. I didn't mind giving
> them my room. . . . Over Mrs. Dawkins' I can do anything I want, study and read in
> peace and quiet or stay up all night and watch TV. (pp. 89–90)

The shared-function group in this passage operates as an extended family. Members consist of family, neighbors, and friends, who share their money and time freely with one another. Child care is no one person's exclusive responsibility, just as no one is the boss all the time. Whatever happens to one person influences everyone. "One for all and all for one" defines the pragmatic approach to life of the shared-function group and its relational members.

For relational learners at the extreme end of the continuum, learning is an intensely affective, social experience. They learn material with a human and social theme more easily, and their writing is peppered with personal references ("you," "we") to their audiences. Relational learners tend to be field dependent; they focus on the whole picture, rather than on individual parts, and the context of learning is important to them. In many instances, the affective and social preferences of relational learners help them survive in the real world, where cooperation and sensitivity to context are important. However, the relational style is at odds with the style of most schools, which tends to be analytic.[1]

Analytic learners, in contrast to relational learners, often come from families in which group functions are specialized, formally defined, and assigned to status roles.

These roles, along with relationships within the family, seldom change and are often hierarchically organized. That is, authority figures remain constant over time. The formally organized group is exemplified by the prototypical, 1950s nuclear family of *Leave It to Beaver* in which Ward brings home the bacon, June cooks it, Wally tells Beaver how to eat it, and Beaver sticks it in his ear. Analytic learners tend to come from White, middle-class homes. Males, in particular, from this background are often analytic learners.

For analytic students at the far end of the continuum, learning is neither particularly affective nor social. They do not require emotional or social themes in the material they learn, and their writing often is impersonal, with the writer being referred to in the third person. Analytic learners tend to be field independent; they are able to focus on parts of the whole picture, and context is not especially important for them. They are confident about control over their environments, as they are about their intellectual problem-solving abilities. This confidence translates into an ambitious approach to learning. Alex Keaton of television's *Family Ties* caricatures the extreme analytic learner when he says, "I'm going to read these books and find out what my feelings are. And memorize them." However dissonant the analytic style may be with regard to many demands of life outside school, where cooperation and consideration of context are required, the analytic style is consonant with the style of most schools, which emphasizes individual competition.[2]

Another origin of cultural learning style may lie in the adaptation of cultures to their environments. For example, many African Americans appear to be acutely sensitive to spoken language—in terms of intonation, rhythm, inflection, connotations of words, and verbal variation. They also appear to be sensitive to nonverbal cues, or body language (Pewewardy & Huber, 1990; Shade, 1982). Such sensitivity may have developed in part out of a need to detect both overt and subtle cues—to survive—in a hostile, racist world.

Correspondingly, American Indians in traditional societies display well-honed spatial abilities and are especially observant and perceptive of the natural world (Diessner & Walker, 1986; Marashio, 1982). It is likely that such skills grew out of the need to navigate and survive in nature.

✥ The Debate

Whatever its origins, cultural learning style, like individual learning style, predisposes people to respond in characteristic ways to certain learning situations. Learning style, then, is resonant with implications for instruction. One goal of multicultural education is to improve the achievement of all students. An obvious and logical means to fulfilling this goal would appear to be matching cultural learning styles with teaching styles. For example, because American Indians tend to excel in the spatial domain, Diessner and Walker (1986) suggest that visual formats might be used to teach material to American Indian students. In addition, many Mexican American children tend to be less competitively oriented and more cooperatively disposed than their European American counterparts (Kagan & Madsen, 1971). It would seem logical, then, to employ cooperative learning as a dominant instructional method for them.

Advocates of matching learning style with instructional style say empirical evidence supports their argument. They believe that learning style is resistant to change, and when instruction accommodates learning style, students score significantly higher on measures of attitudes and achievement than when instruction proceeds as "business as usual" (e.g., Dunn, Beaudry, & Klavas, 1989).

Critics oppose matching students' learning styles and teachers' instructional styles. They find scant evidence to support matching, which they say might even be detrimental in some cases. Further, they believe learning styles are malleable, not static. Critics of matching argue that children can "code switch"; that they are able to adapt to the demands of a variety of learning tasks and out-of-school situations.

Questions of feasibility also arise when matching is considered. The task of deciding which dimensions to emphasize can prove overwhelming. For example, given the dimensions discussed previously, should the teacher concentrate on perceptual preferences, on conceptual level, or on social preferences—or perhaps some combination?[3]

Even after one has identified the dimensions to emphasize, practical and ethical considerations arise. When exposed to *cultural* learning styles, well meaning, prospective and experienced teachers alike often respond with exasperation: "Must I plan a different activity for each ethnic group in my class? What about the girls?" The planning of such instruction clearly demands more time than most teachers have. Newcomers to cultural learning styles continue their complaint: "And doesn't all this differentiation smack of stereotyping?"

Some educators would answer "yes," that familiarity with cultural learning styles cannot substitute for in-depth knowledge of students as individuals. These educators highlight several factors related to learners' backgrounds which may influence the extent to which an individual exhibits the learning style associated with his or her culture. Among these factors are: degree of identification with one's culture, socioeconomic status, child-rearing practices, ethnic subculture, length of residence in the U.S., and degree of assimilation into the dominant culture (Irvine & York, 1995).

Other educators dispute the existence of cultural learning styles altogether. They contend that consistent style does not hold within families, much less whole cultures. For these critics, learning style is strictly an individual matter, and variation is the rule (e.g., Dunn, Beaudry, & Klavas, 1989).

✢   The Solution

If matching is not advisable, how are multiculturally minded teachers to use their knowledge about learning styles? And what if they do not hold with the notion of cultural learning styles? They can use their sensitivity to diverse learning styles, whether individual or cultural, to make instruction more varied. The multiculturally minded teacher, as Hilliard (1989) puts it, can make instruction "better for all," for the "traditional approaches have tended to be rigid and uncreative. They are far from exhausting the wonderful possibilities of teaching and learning" (p. 68). This is a statement with which numerous educational reformers have concurred.

The solution to the problem of rigid, uncreative teaching does not lie in strict matching. Rather, it lies in building on learning styles, as advocated by four of the five approaches to multicultural education described by Sleeter and Grant (1993), and in drawing on cultural "habits of thought":

> *Every* culture brings habits of thought . . . which have built into them vehicles that promote learning and inquiry. Accordingly, children of *any* culture can and should

have curriculum and instructional practices that draw from that culture. (Jones & Fennimore, 1990, p. 16)

Building and drawing involve using ones' awareness of diverse learning styles to suggest diverse learning experiences. They involve instructional pluralism, or variability. Highly effective teachers know that more than one instructional path can lead to achievement of the same objective. In other words, there is more than one way to skin a cat—as the rest of this chapter shall make clear.

Instructional pluralism consists of a variety of possible learning experiences, which grow out of the interplay between cultural learning styles and goals of Education That Is Multicultural and Social Reconstructionist.

The goals listed below represent a synthesis of the goals enumerated by Sleeter and Grant (1993) for Multicultural Education and Education That Is Multicutural and Social Reconstructionist. Listed under Goals 3 and 4 are prerequisite classroom goals.

1. Promote equal opportunity to learn; improve achievement of all students, especially those from victimized groups.
2. Promote cultural pluralism.
3. Promote respect for those who differ.
   a. Help students develop positive attitudes toward people who differ from them; encourage the reduction of prejudice.
   b. Develop perspective-taking skills.
   c. Aid the development of empathy.
4. Prepare citizens to work actively toward social structural equality.
   a. Develop attitudes and skills necessary for personal and group empowerment.
   b. Facilitate the growth of a propensity for social action.
   c. Develop critical thinking skills.

Following are discussions of instruction based on the interaction of learning style characteristics and goals of Education That Is Multicutural and Social Reconstructionist. The discussions illustrate how teachers can plan instruction with their educational goals as well as students' learning styles in mind. The following examples include general approaches, such as interdisciplinary teaching; broad methods, such as cooperative learning; specific methods, such as guided imagery; and particular strategies, such as using the concrete as a vehicle to the abstract.

Cooperative Learning

Recommended by Sleeter and Grant (1993) as a key instructional practice of Education That Is Multicultural and Reconstructionist, cooperative learning is in tune with the affective orientation and social, cooperative preferences of students from shared-function families. Such applicability is especially apparent among American Indian students. As members both of extended families and of a culture that values harmony with self, others, and nature, American Indian children are already advanced in the social skills of getting along with others, taking turns, and sharing—and so are predisposed to benefit from cooperative learning (Soldier, 1989).

Of 68 studies reviewed by Slavin (1990), 49 showed positive effects in terms of academic achievement for the groups involved in cooperative learning. In five studies investigating cooperative learning's effectiveness, Black students and students with learning and physical disabilities outperformed both their control counterparts and White, high-achieving, and nondisabled treatment students. The studies were conducted at elementary and middle school levels.

Cooperative learning also has been shown to improve ethnic relations. Students in Grades 2–8 in schools with non-White populations ranging from 13 percent to 61 percent (who were involved in cooperative learning for 10–12 weeks) gained more in interracial friendships than did control students. As one of these studies found, gains persisted into the following year when treatment students indicated that about 38 percent of their friendship choices were from outside their race compared with 10 percent for the control students.

In another study, more cross-racial interaction during free time was observed among students in cooperative classes than among those in individualized classes. Other researchers found that cooperative learning with teams composed of White, Black, and Hispanic students resulted in fewer teacher reports of interethnic conflict.[4]

The potential uses of cooperative learning are many. Kagan (1989–90) outlines 14 structures, each with its own academic and social functions. Among the most promising for multicultural education are activities called Jigsaw, Team Word Webbing, Three-Step Interview, and Numbered Heads Together.

After being assigned a topic for Jigsaw, students in "home" groups number off and then convene with students having the same numbers. In numbered groups, students learn about an aspect of the topic. Once back in their home groups, students teach their expert knowledge to their team members. For example, in science, when studying fish, numbered groups might study the characteristics of various classes of fish and collect examples of these. In social studies, numbered groups might study different aspects of a particular country, such as demographics, religion, natural resources, and commerce. As an interdisciplinary variation on this activity, the teacher might direct numbered groups to investigate a particular culture's approaches to science and mathematics and contributions to art and music.

This activity would attain interdisciplinary status by segueing into Team Word Webbing. In this activity, students create concept maps showing different aspects of a topic and their relationships to one another. In the previous example, numbered groups would devise concepts maps for science, math, art, and music, and then home groups would attempt to connect the four maps into one large concept map representing the culture as a whole.

Team Word Webbing might operate on a less grand scale as well with topics as concrete as "animals" or as abstract as "prejudice." In numbered groups, students might develop individual concept maps and then synthesize them into one in their home groups, or they might all work together from the outset. Teachers might use Team Word Webbing at the beginning of a unit to ascertain what students already know about a topic, then build on it. They also might use the webbing to conclude a unit by reinforcing students' knowledge of a topic's components and how they fit together. More on concept mapping as an instructional response will follow.

Three-Step Interview provides a structure for sharing personal information related to stimulus material, such as hypotheses and responses to stories, poems, and provocative newspaper articles. Within groups, students interview each other in pairs and then share with the group information gleaned from the interviews. The teacher might enhance the potential for instructional pluralism by encouraging students with different learning styles to interview each other.

The Numbered Heads Together framework provides a cooperative structure for recitation, which usually is driven by competition among students. After learning material, either in groups or as a whole class, students number off within teams. The teacher asks a question and instructs teams to put their heads together to come up with an answer. The teacher then calls a number and students with that number may raise their hands. A student is chosen and if the response is incorrect, the teacher calls on a student from another group whose hand was raised.

In addition to surrounding the often dull practice of drill with a gamelike, motivating atmosphere, Numbered Heads Together provides for competition within a context of cooperation. To the extent that both competition and cooperation are necessary for success in school and life, this combination of learning styles should benefit both relational/field dependent and analytic/field independent learners.

Using the Concrete as a Vehicle to the Abstract

Using the concrete as a vehicle to the abstract in the classroom helps relational learners, who tend to think concretely. The teacher first finds something with which students are familiar, then links this to new, potentially difficult, abstract material, referring back to the familiar when necessary. Teachers can use the concrete ("your family") as an example of an abstract concept ("interdependence"). Or a concrete analogy may be used to explain abstract material, as in General Schwarzkopf's comparing the Gulf War military strategy to strategy used in football. Similarly, the teacher of science or health might explain the body's use of nutrients by referring to an automobile's use of fuel.

In the film *Stand and Deliver,* Jamie Escalante uses the concrete as a vehicle to the abstract to dramatic effect. Explaining the concept of negative numbers, he exhorts Angel, who, like most of his classmates, is Latino and lives near the ocean, to think of the space left on the beach from scooping out sand as analogous to negative numbers. By filling in the space, the beach becomes level again, which is like zero. Escalante further explains that zero is a concept first conceived by their ancestors, the Mayans.

The rest of the lesson is noteworthy for Escalante's rapid fire variability. After his interaction with Angel, he leads the class in a spirited chanting of "A negative times a negative equals a positive." Satisfied that they have memorized the rule, he abruptly asks, "Why?" In the space of a few minutes, Escalante takes his students from a concrete analogy to an abstract notion to concrete memorization and back to the abstract.

Relevance

Relevance involves relating material to be learned to something from students' lives, something in which they are interested. Literature is replete with opportunities for injecting relevance. For example, as an introduction to *Romeo and Juliet,* the teacher of students living in neighborhoods where gangs are prevalent might ask students to relate the gang life in their area to that between the Montagues and Capulets. With such an emphasis on relevance to their lives, students would be more motivated to tackle *Romeo and Juliet.*

As a preamble to reading *The Secret Garden,* the teacher might ask students if they have their own special places where they can escape to be alone and daydream. "What is it like?" "If you could have any kind of special place, what would it be?" The teacher then might entice students to read by informing them that the book they are preparing to read is about a girl and her special place.

Sometimes tapping the relevance of a subject involves grasping the "teachable moment." For example, as soon as a tornado warning has been lifted, the teacher might take advantage of students' curiosity by teaching about tornadoes then and there, or at least taking time to discuss their observations and feelings. In science class, the teacher might seize the burning out of a fluorescent tube as an opportunity to teach about electricity.

There are numerous instructional opportunities for making math and science relevant to students' lives and cultures. For instance, *Applied Mathematics* (Center for Occupational Research and Development, 1988), a series of workbooks and videotapes used in rural Illinois, presents students with problems from the farmer's world. In St. Paul, Minnesota, Henke (1992), a math teacher of multicultural classes, reinforces math skills by drawing on students' cultural heritages. For example, after reading about Benjamin Banneker, an African American who was one of two surveyors of Washington, D.C., in the late 1700s, students use their protractors to draw property lots according to specifications. In another instance, students learn of the original purposes of the Great Wall of China and how it was constructed; then they compute the area of a cross section of the wall.

In science, students at Wound School in South Dakota learn that American Indians used ingredients now found in more than 200 modern medicines and that the origin of the science of ecology lies in American Indian cultures. After studying Black astronauts, students at Malcolm X Academy in Chicago delve into African American ancestry by discussing the means by which slave ships were powered and the physiological effects of lying chained in the bottom of slave ships for extended periods of time (Ross-Flanigan, 1992).

Of particular relevance to multicultural education is the use of statistics regarding the changing population and poverty demographics of the United States. Students might solve problems using figures from *Statistical Abstracts* related to the current and projected ethnic and socioeconomic composition of the country, as well as constructing bar graphs and pie charts and writing their own word problems (Shaw, 1993).

When teachers are aware of the interests and concerns of the students' families and communities, they can build on this knowledge to create culturally relevant instruction. For example, one teacher, who was aware of her Latino students' high level of interest in building and construction, implemented an instructional unit in which students engaged in a wide variety of learning activities, all related to building and construction. Students, parents, and the community responded enthusiastically, and students were more motivated to learn crucial literacy skills than they had been with more traditional, less culturally centered approaches (Saulter 1994).

Simulations

Simulations often incorporate perspective-taking and empathy exercises, cooperative learning, and using the concrete as a vehicle to the abstract, and they draw on virtually all cultural learning style characteristics. Simulations take complex situations and systems from the real world, such as cross-cultural communications and urban planning, in which students make realistic, well-informed decisions, often in collaboration with others. As such, the simulation epitomizes the hand-on learning experience with all its motivational appeal. Simulations may take the form of role playing or board games or a combination; they also may be computerized.

Simulations often, but not always, involve group decision making. In one particularly innovative simulation, *Sound Foundations,* students with learning disabilities develop math skills as they act as managers of rock bands over the course of the year. There are daily quizzes, and each band must achieve 10 "milestones," including Formation, Equipment Purchase, Recording Contract, and Concert Publicity. Of the students involved in the first year of *Sound Foundations,* 92 percent of the group passed the New York Regents Competency Exam, compared with 20 percent of a similarly composed group the previous year with traditional instruction (Gerver & Sgroi, 1983).

Many commercially packaged simulations are on the market, but with a little imagination, a creative teacher can customize simulation experiences to the curriculum. For example, students learning computer programming might simulate the functioning of a computer as they role play parts of the computer. As the Central Processing Unit follows on foot each line of a program written on butcher paper and placed on the floor, he or she does the following: directs Output to write the appropriate output on the chalkboard, indicates to the User when it is time for input, instructs Memory to write values for variables on index cards and place them in the correct memory boxes. In addition to reinforcing programming skills, this simulation draws on tactile-kinesthetic learning styles.

In studying the nature and effects of prejudice, students might engage in a short version of the well-known simulation, *Brown Eyes–Blue Eyes,* in which students are divided into two groups according to eye color or some other physical characteristic. The first day, one group is discriminated against by being ignored, subjected to inferior treatment, and having its privileges arbitrarily suspended. The next day, the roles are reversed. During the ensuing debriefing session, which is of crucial importance given the intensely emotional nature of the simulation, students discuss the injustice of discrimination, how they felt as both victims and victimizers, and steps they might take in their own lives and in society to minimize discrimination.

Literature provides ample opportunity for students to identify with the lives of characters through simulation experiences. For example, after reading *Island of the Blue Dolphins,* a novel in which children live on an island, students from the Texas School for the Deaf took a field trip to an area lake. Working in cooperative groups, students explored the area and used survival skills they had read about to locate a site for a shelter, collect samples of materials to use in building the shelter, and devise means for getting water and food. Students presented their plans to the teachers in charge, who evaluated them according to criteria that teachers and students had agreed upon beforehand.

Guided Imagery

As a teaching tool, guided imagery derives from theories relating the role of the subconscious to learning and creative thinking. By tapping visual and right hemispheric dimensions of thinking, guided imagery exercises help students focus in imaginative ways on upcoming tasks. Following is an example of such an exercise.

In a soothing voice, a teacher tells the students to get comfortable, close their eyes, become aware of the rhythm of their breathing, and relax their bodies from their toes to their facial muscles. She then invites students to visualize themselves waking up to a morning 20 years in the future. She asks them to imagine how they will look and how they will feel as they read the headlines on their Compu-view news screen. She tells them they are members of a special presidential task force that will decide who will travel on the Space Ship Save to a space station, gleaming silver and silent in the far reaches of space, to form a new society. She asks students to envision the society they will create and the kinds of people they will select to be the pioneers. The teacher instructs students to gradually and slowly return to this time and this place, but to remember their thoughts and their feelings on that day in the future.

On mentally returning to the classroom, students envision a future society, creating travelers on the Space Ship Save and pioneers of the new world and justifying their decisions in light of the ideal, multicultural societies they imagine. It is likely that these students will engage in more lively discussions and come up with more original and elaborate ideas than students who are asked simply to describe future societies.

There are two types of guided imagery of interest to the classroom teacher, cognitive and affective. Two examples of guided cognitive imagery follow.

- The teacher of reading and social studies takes his students on mental journeys into the past or the future and to distant places. He includes many sensory details to help students remember factual information and obtain a feel for the times and places in which reading selections and periods of history are set.
- As an introduction to the circulatory system, the teacher "shrinks" students to microscopic proportions. Students travel in a tiny submarine through veins and arteries and in and out of the heart, as the teacher describes what the travelers see, hear, and feel.

In contrast to cognitive imagery, which focuses on fairly specific aspects of academic performance, guided affective imagery seeks to influence more general attitudes and behaviors.

- Galyean (1983) describes a study in which students, who ranked in the lowest 25th percentile in reading ability and were involved in gang activities, meditated for 5 minutes at the beginning of each Spanish class for 4 months. They visualized themselves being bathed in warm light on top of a beautiful mountain and saw themselves doing everything well. Results indicated a substantial decrease in disruptive behavior and an increase in Spanish language skills.
- Before reading *The Secret Garden,* students might take mental journeys to their secret places, visualizing their hideaways in elaborate detail and summoning their feelings while there. In addition to using this guided imagery to relate *The Secret Garden* to students' own imaginative experience, the teacher might take students on return trips to their secret places when they seem to be under stress, much as the Spanish class students found respite by visualizing themselves on mountaintops.

Perspective-Taking/Empathy Exercises

Perspective-taking and empathy exercises help develop in students a crucial trait of the multicultural sensibility—flexibility of perspective. Children low in prejudice show sensitivity and openness to other points of view and are able to think critically. Research suggests that activities and materials with a strong affective component that invite children to enter vicariously into the lives of people of different ethnic groups help develop this flexibility of perspective (Byrnes, 1988). Once students begin to feel empathy, they are well on their way toward respecting diverse points of view, thereby becoming less prejudiced and self-centered in their organization of experience.

Literature, especially multicultural children's literature, films, and creative writing, all provide potent possibilities for emotional identification with characters of diverse cultural groups. Potential for the growth of empathy and flexibility of perspective is embedded in several instructional responses, such as simulations and guided imagery. Cooperative learning, by its very nature, depends on the contributions of members who are heterogeneously grouped. More particularly, cooperative learning structures that promote sharing of personal responses, such as the Three-Step Interview, are especially conducive to the growth of respect for other points of view. Using the Jigsaw structure, the teacher might instruct students in the home groups to assume different perspectives on a particular issue or event, such as American Indians' fishing rights in Wisconsin. In their numbered groups, students flesh out their positions for presentation in their home groups, where they attempt to reconcile their diverse points of view.

Similarly, debates might serve as opportunities for perspective taking. Not only should students develop their positions on issues, they should also argue positions that diverge from their own. Debates can take place in virtually all subject areas—from such issues as capital punishment and affirmative action in social studies to genetic engineering and national health plans in science.

If students are to attain true flexibility of perspective—which is a habit of mind, rather than an occasional performance of mental acrobatics—perspective and empathy exercises should be woven throughout the curriculum. In social studies, the teacher might routinely ask students to consider the points of view of various players in history. For example, in studying the Westward Expansion (or the Invasion from the East), students might write journals from the perspectives not only of male settlers and White cowboys, but also of Black cowboys, women both in towns and on farms and ranches, male, female, and juvenile American Indians and Mexicans.

Perspective-taking exercises need not always be used in reference to cultural groups or individual people. In math, the teacher might encourage students to assume different physical points of view by asking, "How would a sphere look if you were inside it?" In science, in lieu of the guided imagery exercise described previously, the teacher simply might ask students to imagine how blood vessels would look from the points of view of passengers in a tiny submarine traveling through the circulatory system. Or the teacher might instruct students to take the roles of electrons, protons, and neutrons and describe and act out the activity inside an atom. In addition to reinforcing the skill of perspective-taking, these brief exercises in math and science draw on tactile-kinesthetic learning styles.

Concept Mapping

Everyone has schemata, or internal representations of knowledge. One way students and teachers can externalize schemata is through concept maps, which are visual, nonlinear depictions of the aspects of a topic and their relationships to one another.

Teachers can use completed concept maps to visually present complex, interrelated, and potentially difficult material. When used in this way, concept maps enhance student understanding. However, the true value of schemata as teaching tools in the classroom lies in students actively constructing them and in building on what they already know.

The uses of concept maps are limited only by the imagination of the teacher and students. To introduce students to concept mapping, the teacher might select a current event or other topic familiar to students and model the process. Students are asked to brainstorm aspects of the topic and then decide on the most important ones. On the chalkboard, the teacher visually arranges these aspects, encouraging students to discuss, debate, and justify their placement of important aspects and the means of showing relationships among them.

Once familiar with the process, students are ready to construct their own concept maps. Following are several suggestions.

- As homework, students might construct concept maps to show understanding of reading assignments.
- Before teacher presentations and other relatively passive activities aimed at the acquisition of information, the teacher might provide students with skeletal maps as advance organizers, with only the most general and inclusive aspects filled in. As the teacher presentation progresses, students add more specific features.
- To analyze current events, students might construct concept maps showing cause-and-effect relationships. These connections might extend beyond the past and present into predictions about future, related events. Using concept mapping in this way enables students to arrive at an understanding of the global consequences of seemingly localized events, such as the lingering effect of South African apartheid on world business. Students might use the understanding gleaned from these maps to deliberate solutions to the problems posed by current events and to communicate their insights to people in power.
- As discussed previously for cooperative learning, students might use the structure of Team Word Webbing to construct group concept maps.
- Instead of constructing maps on paper, students might develop *physical* concept maps. After writing aspects of a topic on cards to which magnetic tape has been attached, students might construct concept maps by arranging and rearranging the cards on a magnetized surface, such as a chalkboard or a filing cabinet. Using another variation, students themselves, with the appropriate labels attached, might represent aspects of a topic by physically arranging themselves in relationship to one another, using yarn to show the connections.

Many of the cognitive benefits accruing to students from concept mapping depend on particular classroom applications. However, there are two pervasive advantages. One is the transformation of unwieldy masses of information into connected sets of knowledge. The other advantage is the "aha!" perception of relationships, which might not be as apparent in less visual representations. Students with relational learning styles may be especially inclined to grasp such relationships through the use of concept maps.

Other cognitive advantages in using concept mapping include the following:

- Drawing on visual and nonlinear styles of learning and encouraging their development.
- Building on tactile-kinesthetic preferences in the case of physical concept maps.

- Building on the facility of field dependent learners at perceiving whole entities and constructing meaning within contexts.
- Facilitating the organization of knowledge, which leads to improved retention, accessibility, and retrievability of information for problem solving.
- Prompting students to analyze their organization of knowledge and thus to think about their own thinking. By thinking metacognitively, students become more capable critical thinkers in all subject areas.

The multicultural teacher, too, stands to benefit from concept mapping. It is probable that students from diverse cultural and socioeconomic groups possess qualitatively different internal schemata (Reynolds, Taylor, Steffensen, Shirley, & Anderson, 1982). By encouraging students to externalize these representations before instruction, the teacher can accumulate a wealth of information about her students' backgrounds. This information can be especially useful if the teacher's culture differs from that of her students. Thoughtful interpretation of these data can provide the teacher with direction in planning instruction.

In a similar vein, the teacher can use these early concept maps to gain insight into students' initial conceptions of material to be covered. When detecting faulty connections, the teacher can parlay his or her insights into diagnostic tools. However, the teacher should exercise caution in labeling such connections as erroneous, for they may reflect cultural practices and world views different from his or hers. Hence, students may draw on their internal stores of information to make inferences that don't match the teacher's, but are still "correct" in terms of their own cultural backgrounds (Smith, 1982).

Interdisciplinary Teaching

Interdisciplinary learning and teaching represent the full flowering of instructional pluralism, especially for relational learners. The term *relational* implies an ability to readily perceive connections between and among dissimilar bodies of knowledge. But this is not necessarily the case. Relational learners could more aptly be called "holistic" learners, for they tend to focus on global characteristics rather than parts, and they have self-centered orientations to topics. On tests of sorting ability, relational learners usually are able to come up with only one means of classifying items (Cohen, 1969). Without instructional intervention, their initial perceptions are likely to become lasting and resistant to transfer to other areas.

Interdisciplinary teaching is a viable approach to improving the chances for transfer from one academic task to another, from subject to subject, and from school to outside life. In constructing many connections among subjects, students are more likely to touch upon topics of relevance to them. Indeed, when engaged in interdisciplinary or thematic learning, students capitalize on their brains' natural tendency to seek and make connections (Caine & Caine, 1994).

Possibilities for interdisciplinary learning are contained in several of the instructional responses suggested in this chapter. Concept mapping and certain cooperative learning structures, such as the Jigsaw and Team Word Webbing activities, can help students make connections between and among disciplines. Further, using concrete analogies to make abstract concepts more easily understood facilitates the perception of relationships between dissimilar subject areas.

A teacher or team of teachers might incorporate these instructional responses into full-blown interdisciplinary units. Examples of such incorporation include the following:

- Four subject areas converge to provide students with a multifaceted understanding of stars. In social studies, students learn of various cultures' beliefs about the heavenly bodies, while they read related myths and legends and write their own in language arts. In science, students construct sun dials, study the life of a star, and discuss how this life cycle might be represented in myths they have read and written. Finally, students learn the mathematics of rudimentary astronomy (adapted from Baker, Cross, Mills, & Rogers, 1991).
- Students master the scientific method through the combination of science and language arts. They read detective fiction, write endings to incomplete mysteries, compose original stories, play board games such as *Clue* and *221B Baker Street* and computerized games such as those in the *Carmen Sandiego* series, and participate in detective simulations. In tandem with these activities, students conduct scientific experiments designed to highlight the scientific method. Throughout the unit, students are encouraged to note similarities in the thinking of detectives and scientists.

The first unit focuses primarily on the relationships among the content of different subjects, while the second focuses on process. Ideally, interdisciplinary units emphasize both, as in the unit described at the beginning of this chapter. This unit, centering on individual American Indian cultures and American Indian culture as a whole, represents the intersection of two areas—*content* of social studies and *processes* of social studies, reading and writing, science, math, and art—with the skill of perspective-taking woven throughout. A collection of this and similar units focusing on a variety of cultural groups might attain the status of Education That Is Multicultural and Social Reconstructionist by encouraging students to apply their new understandings to functioning in multicultural communities.

❖ The Place of Instructional Pluralism in Elementary and Middle School Programs

If, during the discussion of instructional responses, readers have heard some new ideas, thought about the corollaries of some responses (e.g., individualized instruction for cooperative learning, outlines for concept maps), and best of all, generated ideas of their own—then they have gotten the chapter's message, and they possess a frame of mind crucial to the multicultural teacher.

This chapter's message is instructional pluralism—or sensitivity to multiple learning styles and consequent variability of instruction. The teacher's personal style of delivery should be varied and animated, but instructional pluralism also must encompass classroom activities and the entire curriculum.

The willingness to embrace variability entails a certain frame of mind—which is heuristic, rather than prescriptive, in nature—on the part of teachers. Multicultural teachers are creative people who consider the interaction of their students' learning styles and needs, their teaching styles, the demands of the subject matter, and the goals of Education That Is Multicultural and Social Reconstructionist when planning instruction. They also are cognizant of their own learning styles and use their awareness to avoid one-dimensional instruction and favoritism toward students of the same style.

Multicultural teachers do not feel compelled to ignore differences to avoid stereotyping; they see not only unity in diversity, but also diversity in unity.

Multicultural teachers think schematically—with one idea generating another, which generates yet another. They also think in a more linear, logical fashion in organizing instruction so as to achieve tangible outcomes. They possess expertise in instructional implementation, which includes selecting and planning both traditional and alternative learning experiences, dealing with logistics, stepping in and out of various teaching roles, evaluating student learning, and effecting good classroom management.

Implementation of instruction pluralism in its entirety should post no problems in elementary, self-contained classrooms and in middle schools with interdisciplinary teams of teachers. When flexibility is not possible, teachers of diverse subjects need to confer with one another, for they can still point out connections or help their students discover them.

Instructional pluralism is feasible in the nation's classrooms. It does not require massive restructuring of the current system. Rather, it requires a willingness to embrace variability, together with a frame of mind that is creative and logical, by turns.

Proponents of special education for the gifted believe that talented youth should receive instruction that is different from the regular fare. It should be more varied, and it should require higher levels of thinking and more active student involvement. No doubt these educators are right, but all students, gifted or not, need varied instruction. A change in the definition and practice of "regular" instruction is imperative if all learners are to succeed.

By setting instructional pluralism into motion, we not only come closer to "exhausting the wonderful possibilities of teaching and learning" (Hilliard, 1989) but we also build and draw on various learning styles and provide *all* students with an equal opportunity to learn. In educating our students to be adept in diverse ways of knowing, we prepare them to code switch—to function multiculturally, as situations require, in a pluralistic society they will help to construct. Cultural pluralism demands instructional pluralism.

Notes

1. For discussions of relational style, see Anderson (1988); Cohen (1969); Cooper (1980).
2. For discussions of analytic style, see Anderson (1988); Cohen (1969); Cooper (1980).
3. For critiques of matching learning styles and teaching styles, see Davidman (1981); Doyle and Rutherford (1984); Hilliard (1989); Hyman and Rosoff (1984).
4. For research on the effects of cooperative learning at improving ethnic relations, see Johnson and Johnson (1981); Slavin (1977); Slavin (1979); and Weigel, Wiser, and Cook (1975).

References

Anderson, J. A. (1988). Cognitive styles and multicultural populations. *Journal of Teacher Education, 39*(1), 2–9.

Baker, J., Cross, J., Mills, O. F., & Rogers, M. (1991). *An interdisciplinary study of the stars.* Presentation conducted for CISE 533, Northern Illinois University, DeKalb, IL.

Banks, J. A., & Banks, C. A. M. (1993). *Multicultural education: Issues and perspectives* (2nd ed.). Boston: Allyn and Bacon.

Byrnes, D. A. (1988). Children and prejudice. *Social Education, 52,* 267–271.

Caine, R. N., & Caine, G. (1994). *Making connections: Teaching and the human brain* (2nd ed.). New York: Addison-Wesley.

Center for Occupational Research and Development. (1988). *Applied mathematics, Unit 15: Using formulas to solve problems.* Waco, TX: Author.

Cohen, R. A. (1969). Conceptual styles, culture conflict, and nonverbal tests of intelligence. *American Anthropologist, 71,* 828-856.

Cooper, G. C. (1980). Everyone does not think alike. *English Journal, 69*(4), 45-50.

Davidman, L. (1981). Learning style: The myth, the panacea, the wisdom. *Phi Delta Kappan, 62,* 641-645.

Diessner, R., & Walker, J. L. (1986). A cognitive view of the Yakima Indian student. *Journal of American Indian Education, 25*(2), 39-43.

Doyle, W., & Rutherford, B. (1984). Classroom research on matching learning and teaching styles. *Theory Into Practice, 23,* 20-25.

Dunn, R., Beaudry, J. S., & Klavas, A. (1989). Survey of research on learning styles. *Educational Leadership, 46*(6), 50-58.

Galyean, B. (1983). Guided imagery in the classroom. *Educational Leadership, 40*(6), 54-58.

Gerver, R., & Sgroi, R. (1983). Sound foundations: Math motivation through rock 'n' roll. *Curriculum Review, 22,* 65-68.

Henke, M. E. (1992). *We all count.* Paper presented at the annual meeting of the National Association of Multicultural Education, Orlando.

Hilliard, A. S. III (1989). Teachers and cultural styles in a pluralistic society. *NEA Today, 7*(6), 65-69.

Hunter, K. (1973). *Guests in the promised land.* New York: Charles Scribner's Sons.

Irvine, J. J. & York, D. E. (1995). Learning styles and culturally diverse students. In J. A. Banks & C. A. M. Banks (Eds.), *Handbook of research on multicultural education* (pp. 484-497). New York: Macmillan.

Johnson, D. W., & Johnson, R. T. (1981). Effects of cooperative and individualistic learning experiences on interethnic interaction. *Journal of Educational Psychology, 73,* 444-449.

Jones, B. F., & Fennimore, T. F. (1990). *Restructuring to promote learning in America's schools. The new definition of learning: The first step for school reform.* Guidebook. Alexandria, VA: Public Broadcasting System; Elmhurst, IL: North Central Regional Educational Laboratory.

Kagan, S. (1989-90). The structural approach to cooperative learning. *Educational Leadership, 47* (4), 12-15.

Kagan, S., & Madsen, M. C. (1971). Cooperation and competition of Mexican, Mexican American, and Anglo American children of two ages under four instruction sets. *Developmental Psychology, 5,* 32-39.

Marashio, P. (1982). Enlighten my mind . . .: Examining the learning process through Native Americans' ways. *Journal of American Indian Education, 21*(2), 2-10.

Perney, V. H. (1976). Effects of race and sex on field dependence-independence in children. *Perceptual and Motor Skills, 42,* 975-980.

Pewewardy, C., & Huber, T. (1990). *Maximizing learning for all students: A review of literature on learning modalities, cognitive styles and approaches to meeting the needs of diverse learners.* Paper presented at the annual meeting of the Association of Teacher Educators, Las Vegas.

Ramirez, M. III, & Prince-Williams, D. R. (1976). Achievement motivation in children of three ethnic groups in the United States. *Journal of Cross-Cultural Psychology, 7,* 49-60.

Reynolds, R. E., Taylor, M. A., Steffensen, M. S., Shirley, L. I., & Anderson, R. C. (1982). Cultural schemata and reading comprehension. *Reading Research Quarterly, 17,* 353-366.

Ross-Flanigan, N. (1992, March 15). Educators mix science, cultural themes. *Chicago Tribune,* sec. 5, p. 3.

Saulter, R. C. (1994). Funds of knowledge: A look at Luis Moll's research into hidden family resources. *City Schools, 1*(1), 10-21.

Shade, B. J. (1982). Afro-American cognitive style: A variable in school success? *Review of Educational Research, 52,* 219-244.

Shaw, C. C. (1993). Taking multicultural math seriously. *Social Studies and the Young Learner, 6*(1), 31-32.

Slavin, R. E. (1977). *Student team learning techniques: Narrowing the achievement gap between the races* (Report No. 228). Baltimore: Johns Hopkins University, Center for Social Organization of Schools.

Slavin, R. E. (1979). Effects of biracial learning teams on cross-racial friendships. *Journal of Educational Psychology, 71,* 381-387.

Slavin, R. E. (1990). *Cooperative learning: Theory, research, and practice.* Englewood Cliffs, NJ: Prentice Hall.

Sleeter, C. E., & Grant, C. A. (1993). *Making choices for multicultural education: Five approaches to race, class, and gender* (2nd ed.). Englewood Cliffs, NJ: Merrill/Prentice Hall.

Smith, M. R. (1982). Science for the Native oriented classroom. *Journal of American Indian Education, 21*(3), 13-17.

Soldier, L. L. (1989). Cooperative learning and the Native American student. *Phi Delta Kappan, 71,* 161-163.

Weigel, R. H., Wiser, P. L., & Cook, S. W. (1975). Impact of cooperative learning experiences on cross-ethnic relations and attitudes. *Journal of Social Issues, 31*(1), 219-245.

Young, V. H. (1974). A Black American socialization pattern. *American Ethnologist, 1,* 405-413.

Assessment as a Way of Knowing Children

5

Mary Catherine Ellwein
University of Virginia

M. Elizabeth Graue
University of Wisconsin-Madison

You will have 15 minutes to complete this portion of the test. Use a No. 2 pencil to answer each question by filling in the bubble next to your choice. Keep your eyes on the page and stay in your seat. Raise your hand if you have a question. Do not get up. When you come to the word *stop,* put your pencil down, close your test booklet, and cover your answer sheet.

Sound familiar? You probably have been asked to follow such directions, and you may someday be asked to give them to your students. But for what purpose? And with what consequences? Experience tells us that tests are used to measure what students know about a particular subject. By figuring the number of correct answers, we determine what and how well a student has achieved. This information is then used to assign a grade, flunk a student, or refer someone for special help. We believe this practice is simplistic and too shallow to meet the challenges of diversity and change. This chapter is designed to encourage you to question the assumptions behind conventional teach-learn-test models and ask new and harder questions about how we know students.

Unlike the stereotypical view, the act of teaching is more than merely delivering information to generic students. To be most effective, teachers must also gather data about their students so they know what and how to teach. Traditionally, this has been one purpose of testing. In this chapter, we propose a more inclusive approach to information gathering. We suggest a move beyond the use of static measures (e. g., tests) to an integrated and dynamic activity that can be thought of as a way to know children. Conceiving of assessment as a learning activity can help teachers make the necessary instructional changes that facilitate learning and transformation in all students. Assessment becomes an integral part of classroom life, inseparable from day-to-day teaching and learning.

A multicultural and social reconstructionist approach to assessment attempts to redefine the historical, social and cultural contexts in which children are defined in schools. Traditional psychometric perspectives take assessment as a rational and scientific process based on identifiable characteristics. But new visions of assessment perceive assessment as a social and political act that is essentially interpretive. At its core is motivation to engage all participants in the act of knowing children so that teaching serves all learners.

This chapter is about making the transition from a technological and fragmented way of knowing students to one that is interpretive and contextual. Before making that shift, however, it is important to understand the circumstances that make the transition necessary in the first place. First, we explore the historical and social contexts that led to the traditional place of testing in schools and teacher education.

✢ Historical View of Testing in the United States

The reasons given for testing, the forms it has taken, and the consequences attached to tests have changed over time as the political winds that shape schools have shifted. Since the turn of the century, three historical themes have structured testing practice and focus in the schools: efficiency, equity, and excellence (Linn, 1986). We explore these three themes briefly to highlight how public attention to schools shapes the testing enterprise.

Efficiency

A population explosion in the early 20th century and enactment of child labor laws prompted a crisis for public schools: More children were enrolling earlier and staying longer (Linn, 1986; Wiggins, 1989). Educators sought efficient ways to meet the needs of an increasingly diverse student population. The tracking system developed, with students placed in college preparation, general, or vocational tracks on the basis of test results (Oakes, 1985). Motivated to group students of like ability, educators viewed tests as a more "fair" and scientific way to manage this sorting process than relying on privileges of birth (i.e., favoring children from families of higher social status). The psychology of individual differences took root and the resulting testing technology enabled schools to group students with like abilities through the use of intelligence tests (Resnick, 1989).

Equity

In response to calls in the 1960s for more equitable distribution of educational resources and experiences, the federal government provided millions of dollars on special programs and materials for the "disadvantaged" (Haney & Madaus, 1989). Among these programs were Head Start, Follow Through, Title I, and special education placements such as those for learning disabilities. Testing was used for two purposes. The first was to determine who was eligible for these programs; poor performance on a test was typically a ticket into programs with more resources than might be found in the regular classroom. Second, tests were used to measure effectiveness of the programs— continued funding was contingent on proof that children who had participated in an education program had gained ground educationally.

The purpose of testing was still to help sort children by ability as defined by the test, but the focus shifted to ensuring that those with less got more when they came to school. This focus inadvertently advantaged schools: Identifying more children as having special needs meant more money for school programs. When a close look was taken at exactly who ended up in these special programs, a disturbing profile emerged: Children of color and of the working class were much more likely to be placed in remedial and special education programs. Allegations of bias spread, and critics charged that instead of determining ability, the tests were measuring how much access children had to the mainstream White culture, with its particular language, behaviors, and skills. Tests were seen as confirming the racist orientations that formed the foundations of inequality in the first place (Williams, Mosby, & Hinson, 1976).

In addition, educators began to question the process of identifying, labeling, and placing children in settings away from their agemates (Heller, Holtzman, & Messick, 1982). The identification process was found to be highly variable, and despite promises, many students did not receive the kind of quality education they would have in their regular program. Experts began to argue that unless a special placement had some proven benefit for students, children should remain in the regular classroom program. The use of standardized tests to determine the ability of minority students in particular became less popular, with court challenges reinforcing the doubt (Linn, 1986). Eventually, most in the measurement community agreed that testing minority children was problematic and any claims for benefits of placement in special programs must be weighed against the potential damage of labels that stigmatize and placements that do not provide appropriate challenge (Shepard, 1989).

Excellence

In the 1980s a spate of reports on education led to calls for more testing. Beginning with *A Nation at Risk* (National Commission on Excellence in Education, 1983), these reports asserted that the quality of American schools had deteriorated; the evidence given was lower test performance than our international neighbors. Focusing on the economic effect of being perceived as second best, authors of these reports called for reform. Likening schools to businesses, focus was turned on the quality of the "product," and measurement of these educational outcomes became of great concern.

Tests became levers for educational reform, with scores used as evidence that the schools were doing their job. Districts and states developed promotional gates tests to check whether students had learned the material and accumulated the skills taught at a particular grade level (Ellwein & Glass, 1989). Kindergartners were tested to determine if they were ready for school (Gnezda & Bolig, 1988), and high school students in many states were tested to see if they were ready to graduate. In Texas, teachers were tested for basic literacy skills (Shepard & Kreitzer, 1987). The focus of this testing was the effectiveness of the educational system; a measure of whether the public was getting its money's worth.

✢ The Social Context of Testing and Its Influence on Classroom Life

It is interesting to examine the effects that these two most recent testing eras have had on instructional materials and practices to gain a sense of how we have arrived at our current testing activities. In this section we will compare the focus of the equity and excellence periods, the motivations that drove actions during these times, and how instruction related to testing.

Equity

With a focus on pulling children out of the regular classroom for special instructional programs, educators depended on tests to identify and sort. The guiding idea was that students with special needs would be more effectively taught in homogeneous groups.

The testing industry grew by leaps and bounds as tests were developed to guide and justify placement decisions.

One problem with this approach was that the tests reflected values that unduly narrowed the view on what things were worth learning. Children were compared on these limited dimensions and difference, as portrayed in skills and achievement, was often interpreted as deficit. Trusting the authority of test scores and their own ideas of the "average" student, classroom teachers steered children into these special programs. As we noted earlier, most participants turned out to be children of color or from working class homes, and many practices intended to "compensate" only kept children at a disadvantage by providing watered-down instruction premised on low expectations.

Concerns about normative and potentially biased comparisons fed the interest in criterion-referenced testing, which focused on descriptions of students' performance relative to some task and not other students. Teachers were trained to develop behavioral objectives for all classroom tasks in measurable forms (Baker & Stites, 1991). As a result, teachers' work came to resemble that of a technician running a machine according to clearly specified directions. Concerns about bias receded into the background because many believed that the learning process, as defined by the criterion-referenced tests, was more explicit, concrete, and fair.

Excellence

The reform movement's focus on testing as a prod for progress had pervasive effects on daily practice in many classrooms. Because test results had high stakes, instruction was shaped to avoid the consequences attached to poor performance. Wanting students to do well, teachers focused on the content of the local test, interpreting test content as what should be taught. Because they were not prominent test components, science, writing, social studies, solving complex problems, computer education, and long-term, creative projects were increasingly excluded from the curriculum (Rottenberg & Smith, 1990).

Not only was the content of the curriculum narrowed by the testing movement, but the form of teaching changed as well (Shepard, 1991a). Looking toward an upcoming test, teachers frequently made their teaching more test-like. Constructivist, manipulative-based approaches were abandoned for fill-in-the-blank, find-the-right-answer worksheets that mimicked the test. Schools developed programs to teach "test wiseness" and began to purchase workbooks that practiced certain test formats (Smith, 1991).

The drill mode of instruction was differentially applied to students: Excellence was only expected of some. Low-achieving students were presented with low-level drill activities so that they would get the basics, while high-achieving students, because they were seen as able to perform on the test, were provided with more complex and interesting activities (Darling-Hammond, 1991; Garcia & Pearson, 1991). Darling-Hammond made this chilling conclusion about the misuse of basic skills tests on students in the lower track classes: "In short, they are denied the opportunity to develop the capacities they will need in the future, in large part because our tests are so firmly pointed at educational goals of the past" (p. 222).

In the flurry of attention to test performance, there was, in fact, an increase in scores. But did that rise really indicate better achievement? Were students learning more? Not necessarily. Teaching to the test, lax test security, blatant cheating, and testing only those students likely to score high (e.g., excluding special education or bilingual students) have all been suggested as competing explanations for increased test scores (Koretz, 1988; Linn, Graue, & Sanders, 1990). Charges of fraud directed at both testing companies and schools flew fast and furiously. Faith in the tests as a tool of reform and a measure of student learning diminished until new promises for improved testing technology and practices were made.

✠   Testing and Teachers

Clearly, testing that developed during both the equity and excellence periods has had a significant effect on curriculum, instruction, and students' schooling experiences. In the following section, we investigate the extent to which testing principles influence teacher preparation and eventual practice.

Teacher Preparation

Given its influence, one might reasonably expect that prospective teachers have been educated about testing theory and technology. Historically, that has not been the case, and even today, less than 50 percent of accredited programs require a course in tests and measurement (Schafer & Lissitz, 1987). Few state departments of education, the agencies responsible for certifying teachers, require teachers to take a measurement course or demonstrate competence in measurement-related concepts (O'Sullivan & Chalnick, 1991). Moreover, teacher educators report little to no pressure from public schools to provide such training (Lissitz, Schafer, & Wright, 1986).

Few teachers have taken a course in tests and measurement at either the undergraduate or graduate levels (Gullickson & Ellwein, 1985; Wise, Lukin, & Roos, 1991). A traditional tests and measurement course usually discusses the technical aspects of paper-and-pencil test construction such as writing objectives and items, scoring, and statistical analysis. Other typical units would address the standards by which tests and measures are judged (e.g., reliability and validity); the selection and use of standardized tests; and the evaluation of students and programs. Although social, legal and ethical implications of testing might be addressed, the technical aspects usually take precedence in an introductory course.

While these and other topics are part of the measurement knowledge base, they do not address all that practicing teachers deem important or relevant to their own practice. Teachers say they want to know more about assessing students with non-test methods. With few exceptions, however, textbooks provide minimal information or help in that regard and measurement professors do little to fill the void (Gullickson, 1986; Stiggins & Bridgeford, 1985).

As a result, a small number of teachers begin their careers with some knowledge about testing, but most enter their classrooms without a repertoire for assessing their students. With few ideas as to why, when, and how to assess their students, practicing teachers draw on their own experiences as students, they look to their colleagues, they experiment, and they use tests provided by textbook publishers (Wise, Lukin, & Roos, 1991; Stiggins & Bridgeford, 1985). Practicing teachers do not ask for courses or inservice training in tests and measurement; surveys indicate that teachers do not see them as pertinent or effective ways of dealing with their assessment concerns (Gullickson, 1984; Stiggins & Bridgeford, 1985).

Teacher Practice

The prominent role of testing in schools and its relative absence in teacher education set the stage for a range of problematic situations for teachers. On the one hand, more teachers have been asked to implement or help develop tests imposed by policymakers. On the other hand, teachers have been left to their own devices to figure out how to assess their students. In the following paragraphs, we describe these two circumstances and show how they characterize the traditional and asymmetric relationship between measurement and teaching in the schools.

Traditionally, the lives of teachers and testing specialists rarely intersect. Testing specialists are usually hired to coordinate the selection and administration of standardized tests and, increasingly, they develop tests to satisfy policymakers' mandates. Teachers are often involved, but usually in ways that are prescribed or highly structured. For example, teachers are expected to administer standardized tests according to a central schedule and specific procedures. Although testing specialists can be a resource for teachers during this time, they generally are responsible for ensuring that tests are administered properly. Throughout the standardized testing process, teachers have little choice in the testing process. They collect information over which they have little control and which they have little opportunity or reason to use.

In other instances, extracurricular effort may be required of some teachers. In some settings, teachers have been told that if students did not meet minimum standards on a new set of tests, they would be flunked (Ellwein & Glass, 1989). Under the direction of testing specialists, committees of teachers produced objectives, items, and the minimum score to pass each test. Ironically, teachers produced a test that was intended to limit their own professional decision making. When finished with their task, these teachers returned to their classrooms with more technical knowledge, but knowledge that had no obvious links to their own classroom assessment practices and needs.

Stories like this attest to the fact that the production of reform-oriented tests depends, in part, on the labor of teachers. Some work willingly and enthusiastically while others may act out of a sense of obligation or a fear of leaving the work to others. Whatever their reasons, teachers have contributed time and effort to the development of tests mandated by policymakers and structured by testing experts.

In sharp contrast, few policymakers or testing experts have invested in teachers' classroom assessment practices and needs. These practices affect the day-to-day lives of both students and teachers, and the cumulative effects of these practices may be a greater influence on students' experiences than intermittent testing events. Indeed, some claim that teachers spend 20 percent to 30 percent of their classroom time assessing students (Stiggins, 1988). Nevertheless, relatively few people have asked teachers how they assess and why. Fewer have taken the time to observe and document teachers' practices. And even fewer have asked teachers what they want or need and what can be done to help.

In the last 10 years, however, classroom assessment has gained more attention. Following is a brief discussion of available research on teachers' assessment practices.

Regardless of grade level, most teachers use non-test methods including oral questioning, class discussion, student papers, and performance assessment (Gullickson, 1985; Stiggins & Bridgeford, 1985). Although some studies have shown that elementary teachers use a more diverse set of assessment strategies than teachers in upper grades (Gullickson, 1985), both lower and upper grade teachers say that they rely more on tests to (1) diagnose student weaknesses, (2) group students for instruction, (3) grade, (4) report to parents, and (5) evaluate instruction (Stiggins & Bridgeford, 1985). More primary grade teachers use published tests, many of which accompany textbooks, while upper elementary and middle-school teachers usually construct their own tests. The only time tests are not favored is when primary grade teachers use spontaneous performance assessments to diagnose students.

To summarize, teachers seldom receive training and assistance in the mechanics of classroom assessment. When they do take traditional courses in tests and measurement, teachers find that the content is largely irrelevant to their needs. They consequently enter their classrooms with either no knowledge or highly specialized knowledge that eventually is displaced by trial-and-error and convenience. Instead of emerging from a wide array of methods and conditions, information about students is filtered through standardized and other published tests as well as teachers' own prepared measures. Instead of providing teachers with relevant assistance to expand and improve their practices, policymakers and administrators simply make more demands on them, such as asking them to assist in the development or implementation of external tests.

✛   A Testing Critique

There is an unsettling irony about how external tests and classroom assessments have been valued and used. Tremendous resources are directed to standardized testing activities that are decontextualized from or inappropriate for students' learning experiences. In contrast, few resources are provided to improve practices that have a direct and regular effect on individual students and their schooling.

Because of their scientific organization and techniques, external tests appear to be a meaningful and coherent system to track student learning. Classroom assessments, however, are seen as disorganized and haphazard measurements of student skill, taken at convenient intervals during the school year. Little faith is put in classroom assessment and teachers' capacities to know their students. We suggest that more weight should be given to classroom assessment. If done effectively, it has the potential to be more congruent with the learning goals and instructional practices of the classroom.

Teachers need to be able to think about and practice in ways that facilitate better learning and teaching. Externally imposed tests have not necessarily helped in this regard and have often been shown to counter efforts to work for diversity and change. We suggest that their form and function should not serve as a template for instructional and learning activity in the classroom. One way to understand why is to look at testing situated in an instructional context. In the next section, we describe a common activity— discussion of student progress in a parent-teacher conference—that is unduly limited by an over-reliance on a testing model.

Reading comprehension: 2.6

Nichole Gardner sits outside Mrs. Hamilton's classroom paging through the most recent public relations brochure for the Adams School District. One of the key points is the recent rise in achievement test scores—a goal that school officials tout proudly. As she checks her watch, the door opens. Nichole takes a deep breath, wondering why these conferences make her so nervous.

"Ms. Gardner?" Mrs. Hamilton says with a smile as she stands at the table at the front of the room. "I'm so glad you could come in. Would you like to have a seat?" The room is bright, with colorful bulletin boards and materials everywhere. Ms. Gardner sits down at a table that has neat stacks of folders at one end and a space clear in the middle and books at the other. Settling in the third-grade size chairs, the teacher and parent engage in a little small talk. As they chat, Mrs. Hamilton pulls a thin folder out of the pile at her left and places it on the table.

"I'd like to show you some of the information we have about where Damien is right now. What I thought we would do is to look over the results of the testing we did earlier in the fall that tell us how he is doing relative to lots of other third graders. Damien has had some good growth so far. My main concern is that he seems to struggle in reading. He is in the reading group that has been working on many of the entry-level third-grade skills in the past few weeks. You can see his skill level from his test scores—you'd expect a child in the beginning of third grade to have a grade level score of about 3.0—Grade 3, no months. [She pulls out the test printout and points to the reading section.] Damien falls below grade level in his reading skills: reading vocabulary: 2.5; reading comprehension: 2.6. He is still working at a skill level a little below what we'd like to see for a third grader. His difficulty in reading carries over into the other academic areas because they depend so much on using those reading skills. His math scores are closer in areas that don't require working with words: arithmetic computation: 3.0; arithmetic concepts: 2.9; arithmetic applications: 2.8."

Mrs. Hamilton continues to describe the test results, comparing Damien's achievements with that "average" third grader. His mother tries to make sense of what her son can and cannot do from the test results and begins to wonder what she could do at home to help.

"So overall, the test shows he's working at or a little below grade level in reading, math, and language arts. That can help us understand how he does in the classroom, I think. Damien is a good worker—he gets right in on any activity, but struggles a little because he has to work so hard. Here's his report card . . ." [She pulls out the single sheet that details the academic subject areas and work habits.] "Language arts—mechanics: B−; writing: B−; speaking: B." Damien's mother listens as the grades are read off and tries to imagine her son sitting at his desk for the length of the school day. He has so much energy at home that the image is hard to pull together. She wishes that she could see more of his work—most of it seems to disappear into that black hole between home and school.

"You know, I have thought about having him tested for learning disabilities, to try to get a handle on why he struggles so. But his difficulty seems to be at about the same level across all subjects so he wouldn't qualify. I have a few goals for him that I think you could reinforce at home. Overall, I'd like to get him to the point where he is more comfortable reading. To do that I think we have to have him reading more. If we set a goal for him to read one book a week. . . ."

Ms. Gardner thinks, "It's funny—Damien does read quite a bit at home. He grabs the newspaper every morning and can give minute details about his favorite sports teams. He reads to his little sister—those easy baby books, but he really enjoys that."

"So if you don't have any questions," Mrs. Hamilton says, "I'll ask you to sign his progress report and let you get on your way. You've probably had a long day, haven't you?"

What does Ms. Gardner know now that she didn't know before? She came to the conference hoping to understand her son's school life a little better. Her interaction with Mrs. Hamilton was pleasant and prompted Ms. Gardner to think of ways that she could help Damien at home. But several opportunities were missed in this meeting. Mrs. Hamilton's comments were strongly shaped by the measurement information she used to think about Damien.

She relied heavily on standardized test scores and report card grades to describe Damien and his progress. But the test scores reflected only how Damien performed on a set of tasks taken by a representative group of third graders. They told nothing about his school tasks or how he performed them. There is little sense of the curriculum, and a limited view of Damien as a student. Unfortunately, the discussion focuses on deficit— where Damien falls behind in various subject areas. A competent and enthusiastic child is portrayed as behind in his skills. The rich knowledge that his mother possesses is not solicited and neither is she helped to understand the information that the teacher has about Damien.

Overall, the picture is cloudy and fragmented and gives little prescription for action. Using this kind of information obscures Mrs. Hamilton's vision of possibility for Damien—it seems that all she can see are problems. Damien becomes a composite of discrete skills that need to be improved. For Ms. Gardner, there appears to be a discrepancy between Damien at home and Damien at school. Wanting to help him succeed, she wishes she knew more about what happens in the classroom. The information given is so far removed from what he does in school, however, that she is left with more questions than answers. What could be done to improve the situation? Are these the things that we want to see happen in a multicultural and social reconstructionist setting?

Our reply, as you may suspect, is no. We hold a quite different vision for assessment in schools. Before moving on to new models, we summarize nine elements that have drawn criticism from a growing number of educators across disciplines and academic philosophies. Table 5.1 outlines the elements of our testing critique and summarizes our vision for assessment.

Intent, Focus, and Comparisons

The traditional intent of most large-scale and classroom testing in schools has been to form conclusions about individual students' aptitude and achievement. The information generated from tests reveals a static, almost fossilized glimpse of what students did at the time they were tested. Coupled with a tendency to focus on weaknesses, those who interpret tests have been inclined to draw conclusions about students' limitations rather than their potential. Because tests are like a snapshot of a group of individuals at any given time, interpreters have tended to make normative comparisons among students.

Type of Task

Traditional standardized tests are not "authentic" measures of educational achievement, largely because of the fragmented and decontextualized nature of the tasks (McLean, 1990). Whole activities such as reading are broken down into constituent skills that are presumed to "add up" to good reading comprehension. In addition, many of the questions designed to tap this array of skills have been divorced from contexts that are meaningful to students.

TABLE 5.1   Features of assessment and testing perspectives

Features	Assessment	Testing
intent	generating questions about the learning process	forming conclusions
focus	student strengths and instructional limitations	student weaknesses and program evaluation
type of comparisons	within individuals	across individuals and groups
type of task	holistic and contextualized	fragmented and decontextualized
relationship to instruction	formative and recursive	summative and episodic
role of professional judgment	discretionary	constrained
students' roles	participatory	passive and reactive
parents' roles	collaborative	recipient
role of values	explicit and monitored	tacit and assumed consensus

Tests look this way largely because of the implicit theories that testing specialists hold to be true about learning (Shepard, 1991b). Many testing specialists believe that learning involves the "sequential mastery of constituent skills" (p. 9), which should be explicitly tested at each learning step. Although these beliefs have strongly influenced the nature of testing tasks, they have been shown to be mostly obsolete by research in cognitive psychology and the various subject matters.

Despite their capacity to limit curriculum and drive instruction, externally imposed tests cannot be a regular and meaningful part of the teaching-learning process. Tests are administered infrequently and months-long delays in receiving test results subvert attempts to use them to adapt instruction to meet learners' needs. Even if results were communicated more quickly, they are not sensitive or concrete enough to guide day-to-day learning activities. Although discrepancies in test scores can indicate where students are having problems in general, the scores themselves are too intangible to help teachers or students do what they need to do.

Traditional standardized tests have structured the roles of teachers, students, and parents in particularly disturbing ways. Teachers' professional judgment has been both informed and constrained by traditional tests. As we have discussed, pressure to make a good showing on standardized tests has prompted many teachers to adapt content and form to more closely match a multiple-choice format.

Students also find their roles constrained by traditional testing. Their cooperation is vital, but they have no power to shape their own testing experiences. Moreover, parents are not usually given a part in the testing system; their role has been defined as that of consumers and recipients of testing information.

A final point warrants elaboration. In traditional testing circles, values are not readily discussed. Much of the work invested in test development and use has been premised on the belief that the instruments reflect commonly held values that students should know and teachers should teach. Some people go so far as to say that the tests themselves are value-free.

Asserting that testing is a neutral technique for gathering information implies that methods can somehow be disentangled from human agency and values. This in itself is a value statement that provokes considerable disagreement. Rather than claiming that tests are value-free, we suggest that tests have been based on implicit values about power and privilege as well as the nature of knowledge, learning, and instruction.

When educators and others in power fail to question such values or beliefs, they accept the dominant view of students, teachers, schools, and society. As a result, they unwittingly limit the options of others in nondominant groups such as people of color and those who are poor, female, or disabled. These practices can be seen as hegemonic, and attempts to counter them will not be well received because those in power steadfastly believe that their practices are both reasonable and just (Erickson, 1987).

Multicultural and social reconstructionist education, by definition, supports efforts aimed at identifying and reversing hegemonic practices. Erickson (1987) suggests how this can and should be accomplished:

> Particular individuals can scrutinize the options enjoined by the conventional wisdom of practice. They can decide which aspects of that conventional wisdom to adopt and which to reject, creating learning environments that not only do not stigmatize minority students, but stimulate them to achieve. (p. 353)

To this point, we have focused on acquainting you with conventional testing practice and its critique. Rather than blindly accepting or rashly rejecting all forms of testing, we hope you can use this as a guide for following Erickson's advice to act critically and consciously. The guide is, of course, incomplete without a list of alternatives to conventional practice. The rest of this chapter is devoted to a discussion of multicultural and social reconstructionist assessment. We explain how its dimensions form a basis for practicing in ways that enable rather than limit children and their families. Specifically, we recommend actions that can provide meaningful alternatives to conventional testing practice—alternatives that stimulate learning for children, families, and teachers.

✤ Creating a Vision for Classroom Assessment

Knowledge about subject matter and pedagogy is necessary to facilitate learning, but teachers must also know their students. What do students know? What can they do? What are their interests? How do they learn best? Answers to these questions will change across subject matter, time, contexts, and of course, individuals; therefore teachers need to pose them often and regularly to be responsive to students' individual and collective needs.

This sort of responsiveness depends on your ability to integrate your role as a learner with your developing identity as a teacher. Assessment becomes a vehicle for your own education as well as that of your students. Before elaborating on this point, however, we return briefly to the nine features of assessment and testing to describe how assessment should be distinct from traditional testing practices.

Relationship to Instruction

The purpose of assessment is twofold: (1) to generate questions or hypotheses about the learning process, and (2) to gather evidence to address these questions. Instead of relying on intermittent tests to form conclusions about what individual students know, you will be watching students regularly in response to your own questions about where they are and where they need to go next. The evidence you gather will document the learning process and shape it as you adapt your instruction. It will also serve as a springboard for generating new questions.

Assessment is based on knowledge and assumptions about the learning process that are quite different from those that have driven traditional testing practices (Shepard, 1991b). Learning is not a process of absorption as much as it is one of construction. Any learner actively constructs knowledge in part by applying current knowledge and understandings (Resnick, 1989). This knowledge is situational and subject to change; that is, we do not learn rules and principles in isolation from the contexts in which they are used. The contexts themselves define what can and should be learned.

Because learning depends in part on prior knowledge and skills, assessments need to focus on students' strengths. By asking what children can do, teachers are in a better position to modify their instruction or arrange opportunities that allow children to cultivate their talents or use them to develop new ones.

Weaknesses will inevitably be noted, but they are best used to generate more questions about the student and the contexts in which they work. Such questions should not be geared only to asking why the student is "not achieving." They should first be treated as clues to our own lack of understanding. Indeed, "when children of a different culture do not seem to make sense, it is probably our fault for not knowing how to recognize it" (McDermott & Goldman, 1983).

Whereas traditional practices compare individuals at a given point in time, assessment should be used to document changes over time of individual students within their contexts. Group assessments are also appropriate when you want to understand how a group has changed over time or how group members work together toward a goal. In this way, while any one piece of assessment information is temporary, they can be strung together to provide a picture of an individual that is more comprehensive than a set of abstract scores collected each spring.

Assessments should be taken frequently and regularly enough to guide instruction as well as document learning. Consequently, teachers need a repertoire of methods at their disposal. Some methods allow them to capitalize on spontaneous or naturally occurring events in the classroom. Others may be the result of planned activities designed for a particular purpose. Whether the method or situation is natural or contrived, good assessment tasks include whole activities or some reasonable components that are meaningful to students.

Professional Judgment

Professional judgment is a critical aspect of assessment. Teachers need to exercise a variety of ways to know their students. Tacit or "gut" knowledge can be developed and used in conjunction with more formal ways of knowing (e.g., observing, testing). But freedom to draw on a range of resources includes serious responsibilities. For example, if you need to decide which two students will work with a remedial reading teacher, you cannot rely only on your gut instincts as to who is in most need or who will benefit most. A teacher must be able to gather corroborating evidence and to interpret it wisely; that is, to consider the conditions under which it was gathered as well as the implications for acting on it. Because so much depends on professional judgment, teachers must have strong connections with their peers who facilitate mindful discussion, examination, and questioning of practice.

The Role of Students

Like teachers, students have the opportunity to play much more active roles in classroom assessment. Children at all grade levels can and should be encouraged to generate and collect information about their learning activities. Independent and collective participation in assessment activities enables children to understand their efforts and experiences in a way that is not possible with traditional testing practices.

With changes in the roles of both teachers and students, their relationships can evolve and mature. Traditionally, the unequal distribution of power between students and teachers has often led to adversarial relationships, especially in testing situations (Johnston, 1987). Teachers and students can work together in ways that recast the role of the teacher as an advocate for the students rather than a keeper of the right answers. By shifting the focus to the individual in context, it will not be necessary or desirable to divorce individual students from their natural interactions with their peers and their teachers.

The Role of Parents

Parents, like students, can become active partners in classroom assessment. Teachers and students can generate concrete information that provides complex but accessible and meaningful pictures for parents. With this information, parents will be better able to understand how their children's activity in school compares with what they see at home. Parents' knowledge of their children can and should be welcomed by teachers. By learning about a family or students' reading habits and interests, for example, the teacher will be in a better position to assess the extent to which classroom learning opportunities are either building on or undermining students' strengths.

The Role of Values

Values cannot be ignored in assessment; teachers must identify and monitor the ways their values influence what and how they assess. For every choice to assess a particular concept or action, teachers choose to ignore something else. Teachers should consciously reflect on the values that frame their actions and interpretations so they can begin to understand the filters they use to make judgments about students. Reflection on your own values is coupled with the values of students, parents, schools, and community. By actively reflecting on these contextual forces, participants in schooling can better identify those that dominate, structure and limit learning opportunities.

By regarding assessment as a learning opportunity, we can shift from a reliance on tests and technology to a conscious and deliberate activity that includes all forms of information and understanding. Assessment must occur at multiple levels; that is, teachers must learn about students individually and collectively as well as the contexts in which they teach and students learn. We evaluate students and their responses to our teaching; we also assess our own responsiveness to students. It is this reflexivity, when practiced with sensitivity and informed judgment, that stimulates learning and transformation in students and teachers alike.

✢ Enacting a Vision for Assessment

Let us peek into Claire Morrow's third-grade classroom to see how she integrates assessment into the "readers' workshop." We chose this example to show how assessment is conducted in the service of learning; note how Ms. Morrow adopts the role of a learner as well as a teacher as she asks questions and generates information about Marcus in the context of his reading *Top Secret.*

Me first today?!

The first few bars from George Winston's *Autumn* gently remind Ms. Morrow's third-graders to retrieve their book tubs and find a niche for private reading time. Rachel, Towanda, Juan, Marcus and Chi Li—Wednesday's children—flock behind the bookshelves in the conference corner as Ms. Morrow makes her way toward them. Towanda and Chi Li claim the spot under the table today, leaving the others room to spread out along the table. While children shuffle through their books and reading journals, Ms. Morrow settles into the empty seat next to Marcus.

"Me first today?!" His plaintive tone is a thin mask for his pride and eagerness. "I'm almost done—chapter nine!"

"Good for you! Just let me remind the others of what they need to do. Towanda and Chi Li, Juan and Rachel, remember to write your weekly letter sometime today—either during private or buddy reading time. I like how you have been describing your books and what happens in them—lots of colorful words—so keep up the good work! Remember to think and write about your reactions to the book, too."

Perched on the edge of his seat, Marcus squirms and sighs expectantly, barely containing his impatience to start his conference. Ms. Morrow invites him to bring her up to date on his current book while she retrieves a conference form out of his reading folder. She listens intently to his description, noting on the conference form "Emphasizes characters, plot, & his own reaction to book." As Marcus finishes, Ms. Morrow follows up with, "Did the main character change during the story?" Marcus thinks for a moment before nodding. "How?" And for the next four or five minutes their conference continues until Marcus asks, "Let me read you this one part—it's my favorite so far." While he searches for page and paragraph, Ms. Morrow jots down snippets from their conference on the form:

Date	Book	Comprehension & Strategies
11/30	*Top Secret*	• he asked for Chris's recommendation • said I couldn't remember much about book—he said, "Read the back cover!" • previewed book together • ENTHUSIASTIC!
12/6	*Top Secret* Chapter 9	• excited to tell me about book • emphasizes character/plot/own reaction • knew how character had changed • couldn't tell how change affected plot • wanted to read aloud favorite part

"Marcus, because parent conferences are next week, I'd like to do one more running record. OK?"

Eyes glued to the page, he nods eagerly as she pulls out a grid form composed of 100 empty cells (10 rows by 10 columns). For every word Marcus calls correctly, Ms. Morrow checks one cell. In the first sentence, he says "pond" for "pound" and she quickly pencils in "pound/pond" in the corresponding cell, making similar notes with other miscalls. Some go by unnoticed by Marcus, while he corrects others after reading to the end of the sentence. Once he's read 100 words, she stops marking but continues to listen intently until he comes to a natural stopping point. Beaming, Marcus looks up from the page and Ms. Morrow nods, "I can tell that you really like that part of the story! You read with lots of expression—way more than you did with *Chocolate Fever!*"

"Yeah, that book was too BORRRRRING! And HARD!"

"You know what else, Marcus?"

"Huh?"

"You were a strategic reader! I noticed how you used a new strategy to figure out words you didn't know."

"Yeah?"

"Um hmmm, instead of rereading the entire sentence once you got to an unknown word, you read to the end of the sentence before going back."

"Oh yeah! That helps me figure out what the word might be. Yihua—you know, my 5th grade buddy—did that yesterday."

Before bringing the 12-minute conference to a close, Ms. Morrow asks about the setting, mood, and style of the passage, something they did not discuss at the onset.

"What will you read once you've finished *Top Secret?*"

"Is there anything more by the author?"

"I think so . . . why don't you check on it during library time today? Get back to me if you have any problems, OK?"

"OK. I'm ready to read some more—do you want me to get Towanda?"

"Sure. Thanks, Marcus."

Marcus slips under the table to summon Towanda, ready to snag her place under the table. While Towanda approaches, Ms. Morrow adds a few more notes to Marcus' conference form under the column for comprehension/strategies.

She completes three more conferences before the timer's buzzer splits the silence of the hour-long sustained, silent reading time. Some of Wednesday's children remain at the center to finish their letters or conferences while the individual readers take out their reading logs and record their book titles and comments before snaring a partner for buddy reading time. Before starting her conference with Chi Li, Ms. Morrow pauses and speaks over the low roar, "Remember to continue your interviews with each other—conferences are next week!"

Clearly, assessment was an integral part of instruction and learning during Ms. Morrow's readers' workshop. Ms. Morrow put her careful listening and observational skills to use by recording what Marcus said and did. In the excerpt, we can see how she attended to his interests and strengths as well as her own responses and actions. Ms. Morrow situated her comments about his comprehension and skills in the context of the book Marcus was reading. Marcus was free to influence the conference and she capitalized on his request to read to her by taking a "running record" of his fluency. The conference notes and running record form will be stored in his folder, giving both Marcus and Ms. Morrow access to a growing database of his reading activities over the school year. Taken together, they could construct a dynamic picture of his reading development linked to real world tasks. Finally, students' daily reading logs, their weekly letters, and their quarterly buddy interviews all served as concrete evidence for students' activities as well as how they make sense of them.

Before we discuss the whats and the hows of assessment, we draw your attention to a fundamental theme illustrated in this vignette: Teachers' assessment activities must complement their instructional philosophies and practices. Although we have discussed constructivist assumptions about learning, we have not explicitly addressed pedagogy and subject matter. Because many of the chapters in the book are devoted to this set of topics, we shall briefly outline a pedagogical orientation that is congruent with the specific assessment principles discussed in this chapter and with the general tenets of education that is multicultural and social reconstructionist.

In keeping with constructivist learning principles, a learner-centered orientation requires teachers to see themselves as facilitators instead of experts who deliver knowledge. Their role is to encourage the active construction of knowledge by arranging appropriate learning opportunities that build on students' current knowledge and strengths. Teachers provide assistance and support to help students reach higher ground. Such strategies, including "reciprocal teaching," are congruent with learner-centered orientations in that teachers and students alike have a shared responsibility for thinking and acting (Brown & Palincsar, 1989). This type of teaching requires a classroom organization that provides multiple opportunities to gather information. Assessment occurs in many contexts, in a variety of formats and with multiple components. In addition, arranging these opportunities requires knowledge of how students communicate their understandings. Communication is primarily a cultural activity; therefore, knowledge of student interaction patterns is vital to understanding learning.

Assessment Dimensions

As we noted earlier, testing practices have focused on the "project" of learning, such as the number of correct answers on a mathematics test. Although appropriate in some instances, the focus on achievement is too narrow and often leads to inappropriate conclusions about what students cannot or will not be able to do. Responsive assessments, in contrast, must seek multidimensional and grounded interpretations of students' performance and knowledge. To that end, we suggest that assessment be directed to three general and interrelated dimensions: individual, social, and contextual.

Individual Assessment   Constructivist learning principles suggest that any assessment includes attention to three related qualities. First, attention should be paid to the actual learning process. By assessing the strategies students use in tasks or activities, and the meanings they have for their actions, teachers are better able to appreciate students' perspectives as well as adapt instruction to bring about desired ends. Second, teachers need to consider what students know about their own learning (Glaser, Lesgold, & Lajoie, 1987). This kind of knowledge includes (1) knowing when or what one knows or does not know, (2) predicting the correctness or outcomes of actions, (3) planning ahead and allotting time effectively, and (4) checking and monitoring the results of actions.

Finally, you will want to understand how students' interests and backgrounds shape their attitudes toward school subjects and activities. Their interests, attitudes, motivations, and experiences are more than cognitive; they are emotional, social, cultural, historical, and political. By looking at schooling (e.g., goals, expectations, doubts, fears, resistance) through your students' eyes, you will be in a better position to adapt your expectations and actions to facilitate learning.

Social Assessment   Traditionally, tests have been designed to measure individual student knowledge. But assessment should not rely only on static evidence generated in isolation. It should incorporate interactions among students as well as between teacher and student. This type of information is more authentic in that it is closer to the rhythm of classroom activity. If cooperative learning is a curricular goal, one set of important dimensions includes the assessment of group processes such as planning and group problem solving (McLean, 1990).

A second factor of social assessment is the extent to which students benefit from assistance. Rather than focusing only on what a student can do alone, teachers should assess what the student can do with help from the teacher or a peer. Based on a concept known as the "zone of proximal development," dynamic assessment is premised on the idea that if we look carefully at what students can do with assistance, we can create a glimpse of their developmental future (Vygotsky, 1978). Assessment of assisted performance provides students with a vision of learning potential and the opportunity to gain motivation, momentum, and direction for learning.

Contextual Assessment   Finally, responsive assessment must take into account the resources available to learners, such as the materials used, the specific activities, and the people involved. In other words, you will want to examine the conditions of the learning context. For example, in addition to knowing the strategies they use and the meanings they hold for a task, you will want to understand the demands imposed by the materials (e.g., the topic and difficulty level of the text). The materials and the activities are not the only contextual dimensions to assess. What you say and do, as well as how, will affect what a student does or what you see. Performance is task dependent, and to understand fully how a student learns, you have to understand the activity in which students are engaged.

Assessment Strategies

Classroom assessment, as we have described it, depends on a teacher's ability to use a variety of strategies. The choice of strategies will be influenced by factors that include (1) the subject matter, (2) the levels and dimensions of assessment, (3) who is generating the information, and (4) whether the situation is contrived or naturally occurring.

To think about these ideas, it will help to liken the roles of teachers to that of field anthropologists. As part of their efforts to know and understand a culture, anthropologists rely on three basic strategies: observations, interviews, and the collection of artifacts. In the same way, teachers must watch, listen, and gather evidence to learn about their students and their cultures, both those they bring with them and that which is created in the classroom.

Observation   Perhaps the most accessible but undervalued strategy, observation allows the teacher to look at both the learning process and product. For example, the preceding vignette illustrated how Ms. Morrow used informal observation skills while Marcus read aloud. Her keen perceptions helped her recognize that Marcus was using a new strategy for figuring out unknown words. By noting its appearance and use, Ms. Morrow could see if Marcus's comprehension was enhanced or inhibited by the strategy. She also used a more formal observation—the running record. By systematically recording the number and types of miscalls in a reading passage that was meaningful to Marcus, Ms. Morrow was able to document his oral fluency. The miscalls could be analyzed to determine whether Marcus needed specific help.

In both instances, Ms. Morrow was looking at her student's performance embedded in a regularly occurring instructional activity—the reading conference. Contrived activities allow teachers to observe other types of performance, also. For example, a first-grade teacher may want to assess students' knowledge of basic math combinations. Instead of handing out a math worksheet filled with addition facts to all children at the same time, the teacher can assess individual children at pivotal points in the learning. During math time, individual children meet with the teacher to play the "hand game" for a particular number. For example, together they count out seven small objects held by the teacher. Transferring some to a closed hand and revealing the rest of the set, the student is asked to give the appropriate combination. When three objects are shown, the student would respond, "Three plus four is seven." The teacher works through all the combinations of seven several times until satisfied that the student can quickly and correctly identify them. This provides rich information on student problem solving and knowledge of quantity.

Observations during group activities enable teachers to watch how students interact and work together. They can look for patterns in participation, explanation giving, interpretations, and resolutions as well as noting the roles students do or do not play in providing support or creating conflict (Brown & Palincsar, 1989).

Observations need not be as in depth as implied by the preceding examples. Teachers may "take a pulse" or snapshot of classroom activity to document such things as students' engagement with tasks, their use of materials, and with whom students choose to work. For example, by keeping a running log of students' language activities (planning, drafting, revising, editing, publishing, reading, conferencing, or choosing a book), teachers can determine what areas students might be avoiding or overemphasizing.

As illustrated in the vignette, teachers keep track of their observations by writing notes. Some teachers prefer to keep separate files for each child and subject. Others prefer to develop forms that help them organize their information, and still others may be comfortable with less structure. One simple way of keeping track is to maintain a log or journal. Teachers can observe and record spontaneous, anecdotal events throughout the day along with more formal or systematic activities. Naturally, the level of detail will vary with the available time and situation, but a regular journal will be a rich source of information on student learning. As computers become a common part of classrooms, word-processed journal entries will allow teachers to sort and print out information to share with students, their parents, and future teachers. They might even choose to videotape students engaged in their activities, to provide a more permanent record.

Interviews   Another everyday activity that serves well as an assessment strategy is the interview—a special case of a conversation between two or more people. Like observations, interviews may be spontaneous or planned and can be used at both the individual and group levels. Although teacher-student interviews are common, students can learn how to interview one another. Whatever the format, interviews enable the participants to learn more about the other's perspective.

Clearly, interviews are natural ways to elicit information from students and parents about student interests, attitudes, values, and experiences, but they can also be used to assess their strategies, knowledge, and interests. Conversations that prompt students to explain their procedures or rationales for their actions help the teacher understand how they approach a task and what misunderstandings—whether those of the student or teacher—might be limiting success. Students' explanations may also help the teacher see that different interpretations of an activity are possible and valuable in and of themselves—that there may be more than one "correct" route or process.

Interviews can be used to monitor students' problem-solving and strategic understandings (Glaser, Lesgold, & Lajoie, 1987). Several generic questions may be posed during or after an activity that can shed light on students' understanding of the tasks and their actions:

1. How would you do this?
2. Why would you do this?
3. What does it tell you?
4. What do you think the problem is?
5. What do you plan to do next?

As we noted earlier, such direct questions may be culturally inappropriate for some children; lack of participation should not be taken to mean the students do not understand the task. A teacher must be creative and sensitive in devising alternate ways to assess these understandings. The key is asking the right question or arranging the right opportunity for children to share their knowledge. Integrating these into activities and modeling them so that students can take on the task may be one such way. Keeping track of interview information may be done by recording directly onto an interview form or in the above-mentioned journal. Taping interviews provides information on fluency and interaction style that is not readily available in other formats.

Artifacts   Simply put, artifacts are samples of student work. Portfolios of students' work are increasingly being used to chronicle their development in areas such as math or language. In the following paragraphs, we describe what artifacts might be included in a portfolio as well as how teachers and students might use it.

Like that of an artist, a student's portfolio is an expanding file that holds materials representing the depth and breadth of his or her growing expertise. One type of artifact to include in the portfolio is the work that students naturally produce as a result of their regular learning activities. For example, pieces of student writing at planning, drafting, revising, editing, and publishing stages would permit a look at how students (1) develop and express their ideas, (2) use relevant skills in context (e.g., punctuation), and (3) understand the purposes of the different stages. Such artifacts, if produced in activities that authentically represent the real world task, give contextual and specific insight into what students know and can do.

Any systematic record of what students have done in the classroom constitutes a second type of artifact. For example, the reading logs that students kept in Ms. Morrow's classroom would be logical and meaningful documents to include in their portfolios, because they display the number and types of books that each person read over time. Such logs can be easily maintained for any subject beginning in first grade. By incorporating them into the daily learning routines, students begin to assume ownership of their activities and they create a lasting record that reminds them and others of their accomplishments.

A third type of artifact serves both assessment and learning: the reflective journal (Cambourne & Turbill, 1990). By setting aside 10–15 minutes a day, teachers can provide students with the opportunity to think about what they have done and learned in a particular subject area. Whether their reflections are incorporated into the journal or into a written literacy event, or recorded on tape, they should be shown how and encouraged to consider what they accomplished, understood, and struggled with as they engaged in a learning activity.

Making Sense of Assessment Information

The array of information in the form of written notes, logs, student performance, reflective journals, work samples, and interviews does not lend itself to simple analysis. Teachers cannot distill the information into a "percent correct" or grade level equivalent. Such information is brimming with the intricacies of the learning process and the analysis must honor and preserve that complexity.

The teacher-as-anthropologist metaphor can be extended from the collected information to how teachers make sense of it (Cambourne & Turbill, 1990). First, teachers need to inspect and read their "data" to note recurring categories and patterns. In some instances, they might develop checklists that reflect goals and values about the learning process—but checklists can be misused when assessment information is decontextualized from the learning activity. Rather than spend time developing summary tools, we suggest teachers consider the evidence as pieces they can use to build a mosaic about students' learning. By inspecting the pieces and making connections among them, they can begin to understand how students are faring in their classroom, individually and collectively.

This process requires individual as well as collective deliberation. Critical reflection and meaning-making depend on the teacher's ability to share ideas and concerns with students, their families, and other colleagues. By asking supportive colleagues to play the role of devil's advocate, for example, teachers can uncover potential blind spots and elicit alternative hypotheses for the things they have observed. By discussing their insights and questions, both teacher and students can reach a more conscious understanding of what is and is not occurring in the classroom.

This vision for classroom assessment has limitations, which we will discuss shortly. Before doing so, however, we show how this vision can inform and reshape the parent-teacher conference illustrated earlier. Rather than discuss how this conference is different, we will leave it to you to pick up the important aspects of communication in which Damien is an expert about his own learning. As you imagine the scene, extend it into a three-way conference following this interaction in which Damien, his mother, and his teacher share information and build a vision for schooling.

"It lets you look back and see how you've improved."

Pulling the thick manilla folder out of the drawer, Damien beams as he hands it to his mom. "You won't believe all the stuff in there. It's really cool." They sit at a table outside Mrs. Hamilton's classroom and Damien pulls out his checklist of topics to cover with his mom. At the same time, Ms. Gardner takes a list from her purse that Damien's teacher sent home as a way to help parents see some of the important things in their children's portfolios. On the list is the following:

Notice

Type of writing appearing in the collection

Changes in writing over time

Use of writing in different contexts (language arts, math, science)

Ask questions about what your child has learned and how that shows up in the collection

"So what's in here?" Damien's mother asks as she reaches for the bulging folder. "Is this the reason I don't get to see your work coming home? You really aren't dumping it on the way home so I won't see it?"

"I told you Mama, we keep it at school so we can see all the stuff we do during the year. It lets us look back and see how we've improved. It helps us feel proud of what we're doing."

He opens the folder and pages from back to front. "Like, I look to see how much better my handwriting is now. At the beginning of the year I did an auto—biography—you know, I wrote about me. Now I know how to do paragraphs and words—it's not nearly as bad. See, I didn't even know where to put periods!" He is speaking rapidly now, pointing to one of the papers in the front of the folder.

"There's all kinds of stuff in here," Damien continues. "I have both my rough drafts and my dummy copies. Dummy copies are where you go through and check your rough draft and make sure that everything is what you want. It's before the final thing. We also have these pink slips—they tell why we want to put things in our portfolio. Why we like what we did. I'm interested in writing about cats. So that's what I'm working on a lot." Damien is pointing to various pages in the folder as he talks.

"You did all of this yourself?" his mother asks.

"When I need help with my writing other kids will help me," Damien says. "I put my name on the board and then I can ask them questions. We have these groups in class—we read and we get help one day a week all together. And we have our spelling cards—words we got wrong. Not just the ones we got wrong but the ones we got right too. See how many more I get right now?"

Ms. Gardner smiles and shakes her head, "You have been working hard. I'm really proud of you." She has never seen Damien so excited about school—and it seems to be showing in his work. And he knows so much about what he is learning—he can look at his progress just by going through the things he has done in the past few months.

"So tell me," she asks, "you could see how you know where to put periods in your work. What else have you learned?"

"This picture of me and my science project. Having this in here helps me look back and remember what I did. It was a lot of work but I learned a lot about cats—you know, what they eat, where they live, what they need. I can draw way better than at the beginning of the year. See?"

The door opens and Sylvie and her dad leave the classroom talking. Noticing Damien and his mother, Sylvie pretends to speak into a microphone, "Up next, Damien Gardner!" Gathering up his materials, Damien pokes his mom, "C'mon—now you get to hear about me from somebody else."

✤ Limitations of Assessment

These suggested assessment practices have limitations and cautions that should be discussed. Change of this type does not occur within a vacuum, and to be effective, it will be necessary to rethink other conventional forms of schooling and instructional practice. Four issues must be dealt with to make these ideas viable: beliefs, knowledge, time, and power.

Matching Instructional and Assessment Beliefs

Teachers' instructional practices are rooted in their beliefs about how children learn and how it is best to teach them (Clark, 1988). Assessment practices are no less connected to these beliefs, and researchers are beginning to look at how that relationship plays out in practice. Examining the implementation of portfolio assessment in one district, Lamme & Hysmith (1991) found a relationship between portfolio implementation and the degree to which teachers practice whole language principles. Teachers who took a skills-oriented approach to teaching and learning were less enthusiastic about using portfolios to assess their students; it did not fit their instructional philosophy and they saw it as an add-on to their work. On the other hand, teachers who espoused principles congruent with whole language or math instruction took issue with test-based models of assessment and supported the non-test perspectives and strategies described in this chapter (Cambourne & Turbill, 1990; Ellwein, 1992).

The key to making these alternative assessment strategies work is perceiving assessment and instruction as recursive and the process of learning as dynamic and contextualized. Teachers with other instructional beliefs will find these strategies frustrating, disorganized, and intimidating. Teachers need to understand their own instructional practices, and a sense of their beliefs about learning is a beginning step in implementing these strategies.

Acquiring and Developing Assessment Knowledge

As we stressed earlier in the chapter, teacher training typically does not include much information and practice in models of gathering information about students. While there is strong support for alternative assessment models from a variety of audiences, the methods are still new and underdeveloped. For preservice teachers, we would advocate a move away from the view that assessment is a separate entity, with delivery of information in a single course. All methods classes should have an assessment component spanning both the testing models and more holistic assessment strategies. In that way, instructional and assessment practice is integrated under the umbrella of subject matter content. For many practicing teachers, these methods will be just as new and will require both inservice and consultant services to help them implement assessment as we have described it (Gomez, Graue, & Bloch, 1991). To avoid reinventing the wheel, schools must support teachers so they can work together to develop and share strategies to track their students' work.

Time

The seemingly informal nature of the model we suggest should not lull teachers into thinking it can be implemented easily and quickly. In fact, most teachers who have tried it would probably tell you it can be exhausting, confusing, and overwhelming. It requires a vision of learning and assessment that is broader than required for the traditional testing model. Teachers need to be creative in arranging situations that allow them to learn the things that they need to know about their students. Portfolio use has been described as a labor-intensive process that took untold hours after school to plan activities, review student products, and integrate instruction and assessment ideas (Gomez, Graue, & Bloch, 1991).

Assessment does not lend itself well to large-group instruction and requires intense interaction in small groups. Teachers need to be good observers of events in their classrooms, and that means taking the time to observe. Ms. Benson, the teacher described by Gomez et al. (1991), found it difficult to justify sitting and watching—everything she knew about being a teacher said that she should be teaching, not sitting. Thinking about assessment as part of instruction makes this easier to accept, but still requires a major shift in conception of what teachers do when they are with their students.

Beyond observation, taking time to talk with students about ongoing projects and help them evaluate their own learning requires reallocation of in-class time from classic instructional activity. In addition to rethinking how time is spent in the classroom with students, planning time is pivotal (Gomez et al., 1991). Release time for individuals and groups of teachers, provided consistently, will be needed to plan assessment. In addition, teachers need time to review collections of student work so that they can develop an ongoing picture of student progress. Collaborative evaluation, with teachers working together to understand student growth, provides another rich opportunity in this kind of assessment practice, but one that requires an environment that fosters cooperation among staff members and a commitment to the value of the activity. Space and time for such interaction is not frequently found in today's elementary and middle schools.

Power

One of the problems inherent in old conceptions of testing is that it does not invest much power in local educational settings for negotiation of the form or consequences of testing. For the most part, teachers, parents, and students are passive agents expected to react to the demands of outside authorities. By their very nature, the forms of assessment suggested in this chapter distribute power in different ways than we are accustomed to in schools. They require individuals to take on different roles, to take new kinds of responsibility, and to have different relationships as they negotiate and construct assessment practice.

The most obvious change will occur for teachers, who will have the central role in making these assessments work. Reclaiming the authority and the responsibility for assessment, teachers will need to construct a system of assessment in their classroom, connecting subject matter areas, devising standards, and developing communication strategies for students, parents, administrators, and other audiences. This is a great increase in professional responsibility, requiring more knowledge of subject matter, as well as greater awareness of the ways that culture and language influence learning (Garcia & Pearson, 1991). Building a contextualized view of how learning occurs, teachers can create culturally appropriate assessment activities for all children, rather than rely on tasks developed for White, middle-class children. Probably the most important aspect of this new responsibility will be that a teacher reflects about practice and values the role of the learner as part of instructional activity.

Students will also assume a new role, becoming collaborators with their teachers in building a composite of their learning over time. Given responsibility to develop a case that portrays their development, students can delve into the process of being a student as well as an evaluator of their progress. A new relationship emerges for teachers and students, requiring much more active communication about the student's work and aspirations and the teacher's expectations and standards. This will not occur spontaneously with implementation of portfolio, performance, or authentic assessments.

These relationships and responsibilities must be cultivated over time in each setting, informed by cultural information gathered by teachers. Strategies to include students in decision-making will be as diverse as the students in a classroom and should be responsive to a variety of needs. An interesting question in this kind of assessment involves ownership of both the process and products—who decides what is put into collections such as portfolios and who has the final say in evaluation of these materials? Teachers and students will have new grounds on which to negotiate the assessment process, until now not part of the school scene.

Parents can be drawn into assessment activity in a way that is not possible in the old models. First and foremost, parental knowledge of their children is valued and incorporated in assessment activities in the classroom. A partnership evolves in which home and school information is used to inform the context of schooling. Including parental knowledge of home-related growth provides teachers with contextualized data on the developing student, giving information on transfer of learning.

A caution: All students and parents are not equally able to participate in these activities. Differences in parent participation in schools have been related to both socioeconomic status and race (Graue, 1991; Lareau, 1989). These differences have a tremendous effect on the resources available to families and teachers in the educational process. Just as instructional activities must be developed to be culturally relevant, inclusive assessment activities must take into account the relationship between individuals and the school as an institution. This puts an additional responsibility on teachers to facilitate diverse kinds of participation, respecting the many kinds of information and insights that are offered.

Finally, teachers must find new ways to communicate the progress of their students to audiences outside the classroom. Administrators, who formerly could rely on the authority of standardized test scores to judge the relative effectiveness of teacher practice, will now need to trust a more holistic and ongoing process that relies on many samples of student performance. One advantage is that a principal will find it harder to make sense of students from a look at test forms in an office down the hall—it will become almost mandatory for administrators to visit classrooms regularly. The job will be easiest for teachers if their principal supports such efforts, but will require much work if the promise of this new model of assessment is to be fulfilled.

In this chapter, we have proposed a model for assessment that stretches commonly held ideas about testing practices. We suggest a more dynamic and interactive activity that joins efforts by teachers, parents, and children to get a better understanding of where students are going educationally. We have attempted to expand the purposes, ways, and uses for knowing your students, which redistributes the responsibility for generating tasks, products, and interpretations away from an anonymous authority to participants in the setting. These ideas are presented because we are convinced of the need to reform current testing practices. The old models have excluded teachers, parents, and students from constructing assessments appropriate for their experiences and it is time to change.

Acknowledgment

We are indebted to the many teachers and instructional facilitators from Blue Ridge County, Virginia, schools who taught us about assessment by example. We also would like to acknowledge the support lent by the Commonwealth Center for the Education of Teachers at the University of Virginia.

References

Baker, E. L., & Stites, R. (1991). Trends in testing in the USA. *Politics of Education Association Yearbook, 139-157.*

Brown, A. L., & Palincsar, A. S. (1989). Guided, cooperative learning and individual knowledge acquisition. In L. B. Resnick (Ed.), *Knowing, learning, and instruction: Essays in honor of Robert Glaser* (pp. 393-451). Hillsdale, NJ: Lawrence Erlbaum.

Cambourne, B., & Turbill, J. (1990). Assessment in whole-language classrooms: Theory into practice. *Elementary School Journal, 90,* 337-349.

Clark, C. M. (1988). Asking the right questions about teacher preparation: Contributions of research on teacher thinking. *Educational Researcher, 17*(2), 5-12.

Darling-Hammond, L. (1991). The implications of testing policy for quality and equality. *Phi Delta Kappan, 73*(3), 220-225.

Ellwein, M. C. (1992, April). Watching teachers, watching students. In *More than just measurement: Assessment in the context of instructional practice.* Symposium conducted at the annual meeting of the American Educational Research Association, San Francisco.

Ellwein, M. C., & Glass, G. V. (1989). Ending social promotion in Waterford: Appearance and reality. In L. A. Shepard & M. L. Smith (Eds.), *Flunking grades:* *Research on retention practice and policies* (pp. 151-173). London: Falmer Press.

Erickson, F. (1987). Transformation and school success: The politics and culture of educational achievement. *Anthropology and Education Quarterly, 18,* 335-356.

Garcia, G. E., & Pearson, P. D. (1991). The role of assessment in a diverse society. In E. Hiebert (Ed.), *Literacy for a diverse society: Perspectives, programs, and policies* (pp. 253-278). New York: Teachers College Press.

Glaser, R., Lesgold, A., & Lajoie, S. (1987). Toward a cognitive theory for the measurement of achievement. In J. C. Conoley (Ed.), *The influence of cognitive psychology on testing.* Hillsdale, NJ: Lawrence Erlbaum.

Gnezda, M. T., & Bolig, R. (1988). *A national survey of school testing of pre-kindergarten and kindergarten children.* Washington, DC: National Forum on the Future of Children and Families, National Research Council.

Gomez, M. L., Graue, M. E., & Bloch, M. N. (1991). Reassessing portfolio assessment: Rhetoric and reality. *Language Arts, 68,* 620-628.

Graue, M. E. (1991, April). Construction of community and the meaning of being a parent. In *Connecting to culture, constructing the self—or teaching/ learning in a social/cultural perspective.*

Symposium conducted at the annual meeting of the American Educational Research Association, Chicago.

Gullickson, A. R. (1984). Teacher perspectives of their instructional use of tests. *Journal of Educational Research, 77*, 244-248.

Gullickson, A. R. (1985). Student evaluation techniques and their relationship to grade and curriculum. *Journal of Educational Research, 79*, 96-100.

Gullickson, A. R. (1986). Teacher education and teacher-perceived needs in educational measurement and evaluation. *Journal of Educational Measurement, 23*, 347-354.

Gullickson, A. R., & Ellwein, M. C. (1985). Post-hoc analysis of teacher-made tests: The goodness of fit between prescription and practice. *Educational Measurement: Issues and Practice, 4*(1), 15-18.

Haney, W., & Madaus, G. M. (1989). Searching for alternatives to standardized tests: Whys, whats, and whithers. *Phi Delta Kappan, 70*, 683-687.

Heller, K. A., Holtzman, W. H., & Messick, S. (1982). *Placing children in special education: A strategy for equity.* Washington, DC: National Academy Press.

Johnston, P. (1987). Teachers as evaluation experts. *The Reading Teacher, 40*, 744-748.

Koretz, D. (1988). Arriving in Lake Wobegon: Are standardized tests exaggerating achievement and distorting instruction? *American Educator, 12*(2), 8-15, 46-52.

Lamme, L. L., & Hysmith, C. (1991). One school's adventure into portfolio assessment. *Language Arts, 68*, 629-640.

Lareau, A. (1989). *Home advantage.* London: The Falmer Press.

Linn, R. L. (1986). Educational testing and research needs and policy issues. *American Psychologist, 41*, 1153-1160.

Linn, R. L., Graue, M. E., & Sanders, N. M. (1990). Comparing state and district test results to national norms: The validity that everyone is above average. *Educational Measurement: Issues & Practice, 9*(3), 5-14.

Lissitz, R. W., Schafer, W. D., & Wright, M. V. (1986, April). *Measurement training for school personnel: Recommendations and reality.* Paper presented at the annual meeting of the American Educational Research Association, San Francisco.

McDermott, R. P., & Goldman, S. V. (1983). Teaching in multicultural settings. In L. v. d. Berg-Eldering, F. J. M. de Rijcke & L. V. Zuck (Eds.), *Multicultural education: A challenge for teachers* (pp. 145-163). Dordrecht, Holland: Foris.

McLean, L. (1990). Time to replace the classroom test with authentic measurement. *Alberta Journal of Educational Research, 36*(1), 78-84.

National Commission on Excellence in Education. (1983). *A nation at risk: The imperative for educational reform.* Washington, DC: Author.

Oakes, J. (1985). *Keeping track: How schools structure inequality.* New Haven: Yale University Press.

O'Sullivan, R. G., & Chalnick, M. K. (1991). Measurement-related course work requirements for teacher certification and recertification. *Educational Measurement: Issues and Practice, 10*(1), 17-19, 23.

Resnick, L. B. (Ed.) (1989). *Knowing, learning and instruction: Essays in honor of Robert Glaser.* Hillsdale, NJ: Lawrence Erlbaum Associates.

Rottenberg, C., & Smith, M. L. (1990, April). *Unintended effects of external testing in elementary schools.* Paper presented at the annual meeting of the American Educational Research Association, Boston.

Schafer, W. D., & Lissitz, R. W. (1987). Measurement training for school personnel: Recommendations and reality. *Journal of Teacher Education, 37*, 57-63.

Shepard, L. A. (1989). Why we need better assessments. *Educational Leadership, 46*(7), 4-9.

Shepard, L. A. (1991a). The influence of standardized tests on early childhood curriculum, teachers, and children. In B. Spodek & O. N. Saracho (Eds.), *Yearbook in early childhood education* (pp. 166-189). New York: Teachers College Press.

Shepard, L. A. (1991b). Psychometricians' beliefs about learning. *Educational Researcher, 20*(7), 2-16.

Shepard, L. A., & Kreitzer, A. E. (1987). The Texas teacher test. *Educational Researcher, 16*(6), 22-31.

Sleeter, C. E., & Grant, C. A. (1987). An analysis of multicultural education in the United States. *Harvard Educational Review, 57*, 421-444.

Smith, M. L. (1991). Put to the test: The effects of external testing on teachers. *Educational Researcher, 20*(5), 8-11.

Stiggins, R. J. (1988). Revitalizing classroom assessment: The highest instructional priority. *Phi Delta Kappan, 69*, 363-368.

Stiggins, R. J., & Bridgeford, N. J. (1985). The ecology of classroom assessment. *Journal of Educational Measurement, 22*, 271-286.

Vygotsky, L. S. (1978). *Mind in society.* Cambridge: Harvard University Press.

Wiggins, G. (1989). A true test: Toward more authentic and equitable assessment. *Phi Delta Kappan, 70,* 703–713.

Williams, R. L., Mosby, D., & Hinson, V. (1976). *Critical issues in achievement testing of children from diverse educational backgrounds.* Paper presented at the invitational Conference on Achievement Testing of Disadvantaged and Minority Students for Educational Program Evaluation. Washington, DC: U.S. Office of Education.

Wise, S. L., Lukin, L. E., & Roos, L. L. (1991). Teacher beliefs about training in testing and measurement. *Journal of Teacher Education, 42,* 37–42.

6 Reconstructing Bilingual Education from a Multicultural Perspective

Toni Griego-Jones
University of Arizona

Bilingual education is not a subject or content area, but is an approach to educating students, much as multicultural education is an approach to or way of perceiving education. All subject areas and field experiences discussed in this book are a part of bilingual teaching and can be viewed from a bilingual education perspective as well as from a multicultural social reconstructionist perspective.

The simplest and most common way of defining *bilingual education* is to say that it is education that uses two languages in teaching. The two languages used are usually a child's native language and a second language that the child is learning. To understand bilingual education in today's public schools, then, we must understand what using more than one language for instruction has historically meant in our society and schools.

Contrary to popular notions, the United States has always been a multilingual, multicultural society. From its beginning as a nation, people from many different language groups have made up American society and the use of various languages in schools has often been a source of conflict between linguistic minorities and the linguistic majority. For teachers, the importance of understanding the ongoing struggle over the use of languages other than English in schooling is twofold: First, it helps put current controversies over bilingual education in perspective and second, those who work with children and their families must realize the symbolic power of language in society as well as its instructional function if we are to succeed in educating children. Teachers might want to deal only with instructional and curricular aspects of educating children, but they cannot escape the social and political struggles surrounding use of non-English languages in public schools.

The following section reviews the history of using non-English languages in schooling in the United States. The use of non-English languages was never the result of a pedagogical conviction that children benefit from instruction in languages they understand (Andersson & Boyer, 1978). Instead, such use has been the result of language minority groups' struggles for access to education and their desire to instill pride in cultural heritages in their children. When language minority groups had the political influence to demand instruction in their languages, local schools responded.

❖ Historical Perspective on Non-English Languages in Schooling

Tracing the use of languages other than English in our country, we find that before the arrival of Europeans in the New World, more than 500 Native American languages were spoken in North America. Many of these are still in use today. When Europeans did arrive in the 1500s, it was Spanish speakers who, by colonizing the American Southwest and Puerto Rico, firmly entrenched their language in what is now the United States; Spanish continues to be a dominant language in these areas today. Throughout the 1600s immigrants from almost every northern and western European nation flowed into the Eastern seaboard. At the time of the American Revolution (when English was established as the dominant language of the new country), German as well as Scotch, Irish, Dutch, French, Swedish, Spanish, Portuguese, Danish, and Welsh were widely spoken in the 13 colonies (Andersson & Boyer, 1978; Castellanos, 1985; Crawford, 1989).

When the new country was established with English as the dominant language, the freedom to use other languages in public education became a matter of political conflict. When a language minority group was large enough and politically powerful enough, it was able to insist that its language be used in private or public schooling. In the 1700s and 1800s, Germans were the largest non-English group and consequently, schools using German as the exclusive medium of instruction or in various combinations with English were common until the late 1800s.

At that time, American public schools were locally controlled and therefore responsive to political pressure from ethnic groups attending them. This allowed immigrant groups to incorporate their linguistic and cultural traditions into schools and make the preservation of their cultural identity a legitimate responsibility of public education (Castellanos, 1985). This preservation of cultural identity usually involved instruction in a group's native language in schools, either exclusively or in combination with English.

When the United States acquired what is now its Southwest from Mexico in 1848, Spanish became an important language in our country. American expansion to the West and Southwest was accompanied by immediate confrontation between Spanish-speaking residents of those regions and the English-speaking newcomers. This cultural and linguistic clash still manifests itself today in schools and other public arenas. At various times laws have prohibited the use of Spanish in schools, effectively excluding Spanish speaking students from instructional programs (Carter, 1970; Johnson & Hernandez, 1970; Obledo & Alcala, 1980). In most cases, students were not only denied access to instruction, they were punished in school for speaking Spanish.

Although the sporadic and controversial use of languages other than English in schools has always been a part of our history, the widespread use of bilingual programs in public schools did not occur until the 1960s. Several factors—the development of a bilingual model in Florida by Cuban refugees, rising Hispanic political influence, and the Civil Rights struggle—converged to bring about deliberate development of instructional programs utilizing a non-English language as a medium of instruction in public schools on a national scale.

The influx of Cuban refugees into the United States in the late 1950s and early 1960s brought an educated middle class with experienced teachers to the United States. They helped develop a bilingual program for Cuban and American children at The Coral Way Elementary School in Dade County, Florida. With private funding from the Ford Foundation, the school developed a model of bilingual education that used Spanish to teach Cuban children. And, for the first time, a bilingual program also emphasized the benefit of learning a second language for English speakers.

Academic success of children in the Coral Way experiment provided fuel for Hispanic political advocacy groups who had long demanded bilingual programs. The Florida experiment gave impetus to the political struggle in other parts of the country by showing that a bilingual approach (using two languages) could successfully educate language minority children in an English-speaking society. Hispanic pressure groups began to push for bilingual programs and their increasing political influence helped bring about the passage of the federal Bilingual Education Act of 1968. Federal and state legislation during the 1970s also brought guidelines for programs, funding for teacher training, materials and curriculum development, and various types of monitoring and evaluation.

A third factor, the Civil Rights movement of the 1950s and 1960s, called attention to inequities in schooling of ethnic and language minority students. The Supreme Court decision in *Brown v. Board of Education* (1954), which highlighted inequity in schooling for African American children, also helped point out inequities in schooling for others, including language minority children. Attention began to focus on needs of non-English speaking students and bilingual programs were offered as a way of addressing their instructional needs.

Other court decisions, including the landmark *Lau v. Nichols* (1974), focused exclusively on inequity in education of ethnic and language minority students. Although no specific programs were suggested by the courts to overcome inequities, the use of students' native languages for instruction was promoted by the insistence that children must *understand* instruction for instruction to be equitable. Consent decrees effectively created a presumption in favor of bilingual education (Andersson & Boyer, 1978), and guidelines developed in 1975 by the U.S. Office of Education (commonly called the Lau Remedies) further promoted the use of native languages for instruction in public schools.

Although well intentioned, the casting of bilingual education as a "remedy" for inequities resulted in a mindset that still persists in public schools: that languages other than English are deficiencies and something that should be purged. Students' native languages are often viewed as barriers keeping them from participating in the mainstream culture instead of as valuable communication vehicles for instruction. Unfortunately, something as potentially enriching to education as bilingual programs came to be regarded by educators, the public, funding sources, and even students as remedial or compensatory in nature, as programs aimed at removing language deficiencies in students and getting them ready to learn in "regular" educational settings.

In 1971, 30 states had legislation allowing bilingual instruction while 20 others prohibited it (Ovando & Collier, 1998). By 1983 all 50 of the United States permitted bilingual education, and some even mandated it through state legislation. In 1991, however, a number of state legislatures were caught up in the English-only debate, and some have allowed bilingual education laws to lapse or be repealed. Spanish and English have figured as the most prominent languages in these debates, but other languages, notably German and Chinese, have also been part of the fray.

❖ The Current State of Bilingual Programs in the United States

The most salient characteristic of bilingual programs in the United States today is simply the tremendous variation among them. It is difficult to describe them because of the extreme differences in student composition, program organization, teaching methodologies and approaches, and teacher backgrounds and skills across varying bilingual programs. Probably the only thing they have in common is that they are all aimed at developing proficiency in English. A 1978 U.S. Department of Education study of districts with bilingual programs found that every district's goal was to develop students' English to a level that enabled participation in all English classrooms (Hakuta & Gould, 1987).

Beyond that one general goal of developing English proficiency, the programs differ in their commitment to teaching other subject areas, developing children's native languages, and using children's native languages in instruction. For example, 91 percent of districts in the Department of Education study claimed that their goal was to teach content areas in languages that students understand so that they would not fall behind in school while learning English. Only 15% of the districts listed the maintenance of the students' native language as a goal.

Another variation within bilingual programs is that bilingual teachers often differ from district administrators and policy makers in what they think is important for children. Surveys of bilingual teachers indicate that they, too, want students to learn English but that they place a much greater value on developing students' native languages and the learning of content areas (Ada, 1986; Clark & Milk, 1983; Garcia, 1988; Rodriguez, 1980).

Organizational Models

Bilingual programs are generally sorted according to their main goals and fall under transitional or developmental categories. Most programs are of the transitional type. Their main goal is to bring students to a minimum proficiency in English as quickly as possible with little regard for native language development or even content area learning. The strongest emphasis of transitional bilingual programs is on the acquisition of English and subsequently, of the mainstream American culture. Students' native languages are used for instruction only until they acquire a minimal level of English proficiency, at which time they enter English-only classrooms.

Developmental bilingual programs not only teach children English, they also actively develop students' native languages. Sometimes these programs are called Maintenance programs because they seek to maintain the native language while adding a second one. The goal of these programs is to develop proficiency in both languages to the point of developing fluent bilinguals. Some developmental programs, called Two-Way Bilingual programs, include native English speakers as a part of their program design, and their goal is to develop bilingualism in both English speakers and other language speakers.

Students in Bilingual Classrooms

An estimated 4 million people speak more than 120 major languages in the United States today (Delgado-Gaitan & Trueba, 1991, p. 30), and most large urban systems claim students from at least 70 language groups. Districts try to serve students from non-English homes either through bilingual programs or through English as a Second Language programs. When school districts have large numbers of one language group, bilingual programs are usually implemented; ESL programs are used when districts have smaller numbers of many different language groups.

Because modern bilingual programs were cast as remedies for non-English speaking children, only a few programs enroll English speakers: those with the stated purpose of developing bilingualism in all students (Two Way bilingual programs) and those under desegregation orders. Consequently, most bilingual classrooms are made up exclusively of minority, non-English speaking children. Most students are Spanish speakers, but in a few areas of the country, there are programs for Chinese, Vietnamese, and Hmong speakers.

Even with the expansion of bilingual and ESL programs over the years, however, some non-English students are not in either type of program. Only those students with the *least* proficiency in English are assigned to programs. Placement is exclusively based on measures of students' knowledge of English. Little consideration is given to native language proficiency or subject matter knowledge in placing or grouping students. They are classified strictly according to their level of English proficiency, and those with the lowest scores on English proficiency measures are targeted for bilingual or ESL programs. When students reach a minimal proficiency level in English they are "exited" from bilingual or ESL programs into "regular" classrooms.

Federal and state legislation mandating programs for those least proficient students refer to them as limited English proficient or LEP students. Educators generally adopted that label, but many dislike the limited aspect of the term and use other terms such as English Language Learners (ELL). Most recent national school enrollment information indicates that 2.2 million, or 5.7% of children in public schools, fit the U.S. government's definition of limited English proficient (U.S. Department of Education, 1991, p.10). This count, however, underestimates the numbers of students from non-English speaking homes who could benefit from bilingual programs. There are many children for whom English is a second language who do not receive help in schools. For example, in California, which has the largest numbers of language minority students, one explanation for chronic underachievement of students in some high schools was that many students not identified as LEP, in fact, had difficulty with English because it was their second language (California Department of Education, 1990). The failure to correctly diagnose students' needs has also resulted in an inordinate number of language minority students being placed inappropriately in special education programs for learning disabilities (Baca & Cervantes, 1989; Cummins, 1981; Ortiz & Yates, 1983).

Even when properly identified, however, surveys show that less than a quarter of students for whom bilingual programs were intended are actually in the programs. A 1978 national survey of 1.7 million limited English proficient students aged 5 to 14 indicated that 23% were in bilingual classrooms, 11% were in English classrooms with ESL support, and 58% were in exclusively English-medium classrooms (O'Malley, 1982).

The fact that many, if not most, language minority students are in regular English-only classrooms has implications for "regular" teacher education. So far, teacher preparation has never included information on how to effectively educate students from non-English home backgrounds. Changing demographics and the relatively small numbers of students served in bilingual/ESL programs demand that all teachers, not just bilingual and ESL teachers, need to understand second language acquisition. Indications are that almost half of the nation's teachers (42.2%) have had experience with language minority students, but only 7% of these teachers were in bilingual or ESL classrooms (Wagonner & O'Malley, 1985).

❖ Curriculum and Instruction in Bilingual Classrooms

Bilingual programs are housed in "regular" school buildings, preschool through high school. In large districts with significant numbers of non-English speaking students, bilingual elementary schools often have at least one bilingual classroom at each grade level and secondary schools offer bilingual core content area classes.

Curriculum

The core curriculum in public school bilingual classrooms is the same as that for any other classroom. The only significant curricular difference is the focus on language development (ESL and the appropriate native language) and attention to the cultural heritage of the targeted language minority group. Besides teaching science, math, social studies, art, and music, bilingual teachers must facilitate language learning in everything they do. Given that teachers are concerned with how best to teach non-English speaking students the full range of subjects while developing native and second language skills, what are the most effective ways to create environments which can accomplish all that bilingual classrooms demand?

Instruction

Early bilingual programs in the 1970s reflected practices found in foreign language teaching—drills and memorization of dialogues—and emphasized studying the structures of language. Since then, bilingual teachers have been experimenting with more natural approaches to facilitating language acquisition. Research in second language acquisition has produced sound theoretical bases for using more active, student-oriented approaches such as total physical response, individualized instruction, language experience, and a whole language approach. Many teachers subscribe to a natural approach that creates a nonpressured environment allowing children to learn a second language much as they acquired their first language. Others emphasize a functional approach which centers on English skills necessary for success in academic settings (Ovando & Collier, 1998; Wong-Fillmore & Valadez, 1986).

Because bilingual teachers are part of the larger teaching force, they are involved in the same panoply of strategies and methodologies as other teachers. Any and all approaches current in the teaching of subject areas can be found in bilingual classrooms.

Classroom Management

This is a key issue for teachers juggling two languages of instruction and planning for individual students' abilities and achievement within each language. Programs are experimenting with a variety of management approaches such as alternating days, half days, or weeks for using each language, team teaching using native speakers (teachers) of each language, bilingual teachers working with paraprofessionals, and mainstreaming students for content area subjects and a host of other management plans.

✤ Bilingual Teacher Preparation

Delivering a school's curriculum in two languages requires teachers to have a high level of proficiency in the native language of the students as well as in English. This level of bilingualism is difficult to achieve, and teachers vary considerably in target language and English proficiency. Some are native speakers of the language of the students. Other bilingual teachers are native English speakers who have learned the language of their students as a second language.

Although bilingual teachers are in demand in public schools, higher education has been slow to respond to this demand. Bilingual teacher preparation has not been easily incorporated into teacher education in colleges and universities because of reliance on external funding and the broad, widely encompassing nature of the field. Most teacher preparation programs were initially funded by Title VII of the Bilingual Education Act and are still heavily dependent on federal funding. Programs are usually housed in education departments, most in curriculum and instruction or elementary education (Johnson & Binkley, 1987). But, because bilingual education is inherently an interdisciplinary field, drawing expertise from education, social sciences, and language studies, bilingual teacher preparation programs use faculty and courses from a variety of departments. As in public schools, there is an acute shortage of university faculty for bilingual teacher preparation programs. Scholarly research in second language acquisition, bilingualism, or language minority concerns in general is also woefully underfunded and unappreciated at the university level.

Beyond language proficiency, university preparation for bilingual teaching involves studying first and second language acquisition theory and practice (usually requiring some study of linguistics), cross-cultural studies focusing on the target language group, methods courses, and field experiences in bilingual classrooms. Certification requirements vary nationwide but the endorsement to teach in bilingual classrooms is usually an addition to a teacher's elementary or secondary license. Since 1976, when the first training programs under the Bilingual Education Act began, there has been a dramatic increase in the quality and numbers of professionally prepared teachers, but numbers still fall short of the increasing need (National Forum on Personnel Needs for Districts with Changing Demographics, 1990; Ovando & Collier, 1998; Wagonner & O' Malley, 1985).

Demographic trends in public school populations, the demand for qualified bilingual teachers, and subsequent pressures on teacher preparation programs can only increase. Population growth trends show language minority student populations increasing in all school districts that have traditionally enrolled concentrations of language minority students. Now, language minority students are also enrolling in districts that have never before had significant numbers. Furthermore, there is a greater variety of native languages represented in school populations than ever, and language minority students are increasing even in districts that are experiencing overall decreases in enrollment. All this results in projections calling for as many as 175,000 bilingual teachers in the United States in the next several years, assuming a 20-to-1 student-teacher ratio (National Forum on Personnel Needs for Districts with Changing Demographics, 1990).

The numbers and spread of language minority students also suggest that *all* teachers in public schools will need to know something about second language learning and about the cultural backgrounds of language minority students (Diaz-Soto, 1991; Griego-Jones, 1991; Nieto, 1992). To adequately prepare teachers, bilingual and non-bilingual, colleges and universities must adjust teacher preparation programs to include knowledge and skills involved in teaching language minority students.

✥ Bilingual Education That Is Social Reconstructionist

A multicultural social reconstructionist approach has been defined as one that addresses societal issues that affect students and helps them learn to work collectively for change (Sleeter & Grant, 1988). Social reconstructionist classrooms encourage students to take an active stance on issues and to be in charge of their own lives.

With this definition in mind, reflection on the history and current status of bilingual education in public schools produces questions related to goals and practice in bilingual programs.

- Are the goals and strategies of bilingual education compatible with a social reconstructionist philosophy and approach?
- Is the organization and place of bilingual education in public schooling compatible with a multicultural social reconstructionist approach and philosophy?
- Does the current state of bilingual education reflect a social reconstructionist philosophy?
- Does bilingual teacher training promote this type of approach? If not, what would have to happen in order for bilingual education to reflect social reconstructionist thinking?
- How would the structure and organization of bilingual programs have to change?

Keeping the definition of multicultural social reconstructionist thinking in mind, two aspects of bilingual education will be considered to answer the questions posed. First, we will reflect on bilingual classrooms (the students and curriculum) and second, on bilingual teacher preparation.

Bilingual Classrooms

Students   Perhaps the most important aspect to be viewed from a social reconstructionist perspective is the student composition in bilingual classrooms. There is a tendency to label any classroom that is not White, middle class, and English speaking as multicultural. So, for some people, bilingual classrooms appear to be inherently multicultural settings because they are populated by non-mainstream language minority students.

But, on second glance, we see that most bilingual classrooms are actually very monocultural, containing students from only one language and culture group, usually Hispanic. The practice of assigning only language minority students to bilingual programs seems contrary to multicultural and social reconstructionist thinking.

The isolation of language minority children and lack of attention to interrelationships between minority and majority language groups keep bilingual programs from fulfilling their potential as social reconstructionist programs. They fail to teach language minority children (or the few majority students in them) how to effect social change and intercommunication between groups when curriculum and instruction in bilingual classrooms are so focused on helping minority students move into the mainstream. They prepare language minorities to fit into the English-only classrooms with little thought given to how to change the inequity they will find in the mainstream society they will be entering.

To change this orientation in bilingual classrooms means more than teaching political awareness and strategies for social change. It means a complete reorientation and commitment to social change rather than an absolute acceptance of the social order as it exists. Acceptance of the existing social order is manifest in bilingual classrooms in the preoccupation with "transitioning" students.

The problem with the orientation toward transition is that it not only perpetuates the status quo, it puts the burden of maintaining social order on the language minority child and relieves the rest of society from its responsibility to contribute to social equilibrium. All the attention is focused on how the minority child can fit into the larger society, never considering that what might need to be done is to adjust the mainstream as well.

Curriculum   Bilingual classroom curricula do include study of the target population's history and cultural heritage, but again, the emphasis is on building pride and self-esteem so that language minority students can cope with mainstream society and be "successful." There is nothing multicultural about focusing on transition of one ethnic and linguistic group into the majority society to the exclusion and devaluation of the minority group. It seems contradictory that bilingual programs claim to value language minorities' language and culture and then spend their classroom time pushing students to leave their language and culture and move into another. Instead of framing the classrooms as opportunities to add another language and culture, they are cast as transition "holding tanks" for students until they have acquired a minimal level of English.

Even though most bilingual classrooms may not be achieving their potential from a social reconstructionist perspective, it can be argued that the programs are examples of social reconstructionism at work because they are a response to the inequitable education of a segment of students. However, when bilingual programs are viewed only as vehicles for ridding students of their native languages and cultures, they function as tools of oppression in their role of super-assimilator as much as they are vehicles for empowering language minority students.

Bilingual Teacher Preparation   The second aspect reviewed here, bilingual teacher preparation, also needs adjustment if bilingual education is to become social reconstructionist. Even bilingual educators think small when they allow themselves to be caught in the trap of "remedial" schooling for "limited" students. The orientation toward limited students binds educators' thinking as well as that of the public. They are often caught in a missionary mode of remediating children instead of remediating society. Somewhere a more noble purpose was derailed.

The reorientation of bilingual teachers is key to enabling bilingual education to be social reconstructionist. Teacher education is the most feasible way to alter current practice in bilingual classrooms because it is the most manageable point of departure. Short of massive change in societal attitudes, preparation of knowledgeable, committed teachers is a most effective tool for change in public education (Fullan, 1982; Joyce, 1990; Lieberman, 1988). Thus, bilingual teacher preparation will have to undergo a reorientation in order to bring about a revolution in the classroom.

What little is known about bilingual teacher preparation suggests that the programs do not show how to teach students cross-cultural communication and how to influence social change. Studies that analyzed skill areas and competencies facilitating intercultural communication found that bilingual teacher training programs did not include these kinds of skills (Chu & Levy, 1988; Clark & Milk, 1983). Teacher preparation in general perpetuates the status quo rather than preparing activist change agents; bilingual teacher preparation, by and large, is no different.

In answering the question about whether bilingual education as it exists in public schools today is multicultural and social reconstructionist, the answer would have to be yes and no. Yes, because the very existence of bilingual programs is an example of social reconstruction. However, in examining components of public school bilingual classrooms and bilingual teacher preparation, the answer is no.

Becoming Social Reconstructionist   Many strategies can be suggested for teaching in a multicultural social reconstructionist manner, but bilingual classrooms are in the unique position of offering one megastrategy, that of learning a second language. There is no more effective, potent strategy for facilitating understanding of another culture than learning its language. The capacity to alter human experience by entering the mind and heart of another cultural group through language makes the development of classroom activities incorporating cultural awareness into the curriculum seem like tinkering.

The ability of language to empower individuals and groups, as well as to shut them out, has been at the root of the controversy about bilingual education throughout our history. The empowerment quality of language has tremendous implications for social reconstructionist theory. What better way to empower language minorities than to give knowledge of the dominant society's mode of communication and thought? On the other hand, what better way to enable language *majority*-group students to understand other cultures than to put them in the position of having to articulate their thoughts through another's language? Bilingual classrooms are able to use that most powerful tool of language to transform human experience, and make lessons about oppression and social reconstruction take life for each student (Cziko, Lambert, & Gutter, 1979–80; Lambert & Tucker, 1972; Nieto, 1992; Wong-Fillmore & Valadez, 1986).

Restructured Bilingual Classrooms

Distinguishing characteristics of multicultural and social reconstructionist classrooms would be found in students, curriculum, and teachers. In bilingual classrooms that reflect social reconstructionist philosophy, there would be two language groups represented. Classrooms would not be limited to language minority students but would include English speakers. Although most language minority students are Spanish speakers, any other language group could make up the non-English component. Without this mixture of students it is next to impossible to achieve the goals of multicultural social reconstructionist philosophy. Isolating language minority students only ignores the real conflict over power and oppression and does not come to grips with the powerful role language plays in society's ability to empower and oppress.

The difficulty with accepting the isolation of language minority students is the one-sided expectation of learners. Interaction and social change requires more than commitment and understanding from one group of people. When language minority students meet the outside world, how are they perceived by the majority? What have majority children learned about language minority students that would enable a different type of interaction among them? If majority students have not been in classrooms with language minority students, chances are they have learned little that would change the present society, specifically oppression of other language speakers. Reconstructionist classrooms would not be remedial places to get rid of a language deficiency, but enriching places where all students would learn a second language.

Two-Way Bilingual models fit the student composition requirement and hold promise for teaching in a social reconstructionist manner. They develop students' native languages and cultures as worthy in themselves, not just as vehicles for transition, and they do this for both language groups. Indeed, many suggest that the future for bilingual education lies in the expansion of Two-Way program models (Hakuta, 1986; Ovando & Collier, 1998). This undoubtedly is the preferred model of bilingual educators themselves, but they are not always in charge of their own destiny in schools. Society may be willing to allow experiments, but wholesale bilingual schooling for minority and majority students may be a long way off. Those who have struggled through the evolution of bilingual education know that in fact, advocates started with visions of bilingual benefits for all students, but have had to settle for less (Andersson & Boyer, 1978; Fishman & Keller, 1982).

A solid research base is being developed by anthropologists, sociologists, and educators on the process that language minority children go through in learning a second language and assimilating into a new culture. However, there is little research in the United States on language *majority* children learning another language, particularly a minority language that is less valued by the larger society. Those interested in social reconstructionism should promote research on the effects of learning other languages for English-speaking students. What can majority language students learn about themselves and their relationships to other cultural groups? How does the status of minority languages affect learning those languages, especially if majority speakers are required to learn that language not just as a subject, but as a second language?

The distinction between acquiring a second language and learning a foreign language lies in the amount of exposure a learner has to native speakers of the target language (Ovando & Collier, 1998) and the purpose for learning the new language. Learners of a second language usually need to become proficient and functional in their new language because they are going to have to live and communicate with native speakers of the new language. This is why we talk of language minority students in the United States learning English as a second language, not as a foreign language. Foreign languages are usually learned out of their cultural context and away from native speakers of the language. Second languages become part of a learner's daily repertoire for communication, a ready alternative to the native language.

Learning a second language to the proficiency of a native speaker promotes expectations that the learner's command of the cultural code of a language group will also be proficient. It is this facility in culture as well as language that bilingual classrooms can facilitate by mixing linguistically and culturally different groups. Delgado-Gaitan and Trueba state:

> Language, as the instrument par excellence for social intercourse, is essential in establishing the parameters of membership in social groupings and in opening the lines of communication. Not only through its spoken and written forms, but through kinetic, paralinguistic and other forms of face-to-face communications, language ultimately establishes social relationships and ongoing meaningful exchanges. (1991, p. 25)

Communicative competence, vital to bringing about social change and mutual understanding, would be the expected outcome for the two language groups in multicultural social reconstructionist classrooms. Curriculum in reconstructionist bilingual classrooms would include strong emphasis on development of native language and structured learning of a second language from the first day of elementary school. Increasing exposure and formal instruction in the second language throughout elementary grades would bring students to middle school prepared to attend classes in either language. A sample progression is outlined in Table 6.1.

This model program proposes that the two language groups represented in the classroom would be taught by a team of teachers. The combination of focusing on each language group to develop strong native language and cognitive skills, and then mixing the two language groups to provide opportunities (informal and formal) to learn the second language requires close collaboration between the two teachers.

Each teacher must be a native speaker of one language and have a working proficiency in the other, at least able to understand and communicate with children and parents. The native speaker of each language would instruct students of the same native language in core subjects and would teach his/her native language as a second language to the other group. Team teaching would require joint planning, instruction, and ongoing assessment to ensure learning of subject concepts and language specific to each content area.

Many different management schemes could be used to mix and alternate language groups. Whatever the management scheme, the guiding principle would be to

TABLE 6.1   Sample plan for second language instruction

Level	Native Language	Second Language
Pre-Kindergarten	All content areas taught to group in native language by a native language teacher	Informal, consistent, exposure to second language through contact with each other (e.g., play, games, movies)
Primary 1–3	Subjects (language arts, math, social science, social studies) taught in native language	Continue informal mixing
	Continue teaching language arts in native language	Art, music, p.e. in second language
Upper elementary 4–5	As students gain proficiency in second language, begin to teach math, science, etc., in second, alternating with native language	Continue with above
	Continue native language arts	Introduce formal time for 2nd language and ensure opportunities for using it (contact with other language speakers)
Middle school 6–8	Continue native language arts	Continue format study of second language
	Alternate teaching of all subjects in the native and second language	

facilitate cognitive, linguistic, and social development in the native language *and* the constant, consistent acquisition of a second language through natural contact with other language speakers. As students' proficiency in the second language increases, alternating languages becomes easier. As students develop proficiency in the second language, instruction becomes more like teaching them in their native language. This level of proficiency will usually take at least 7 to 10 years (Collier, 1998).

In some ways it will be more difficult for majority English speakers to acquire a second language. Majority speakers will not have their second language around them outside the classroom like minority language speakers will. An extra effort will have to be made to bring majority language speakers into contact with the minority language community outside the school. This in itself is another opportunity for social reconstructionism.

Experience has also shown that attention will have to be given to upgrading the status of the minority language, because societal attitudes toward it are pervasive and influence students' (majority and minority) attitudes about using and learning it. The relative status of a minority language in both language communities needs to be considered when teaching the second language. Societal uses of, and attitudes toward, language can be part of social studies curriculum as well as language study.

Learning a second language is difficult, serious business and involves personal, permanent behavior change. Sometimes advocates of multicultural education have underestimated the task and given suggestions for just incorporating minority languages into daily classroom routines. Although well intentioned, this almost token attention to the native language of students in the classroom can contribute to the perception of minority languages as lower status.

Curriculum in multicultural social reconstructionist classrooms would use community "funds of knowledge" to address social, academic, and intellectual issues relevant to students (Moll & Gonzalez, 1994). This recognizes strengths of minority as well as majority backgrounds and connects classrooms to the authentic context of society. Development of personal and family histories of all students in the tradition of the Foxfire Project (Wigginton, 1975) would also incorporate childrens' cultural backgrounds. These personal stories would be the starting point for integrating all subjects into a total curriculum that would revolve around the mixture of students in the classroom. Curriculum would reflect the heritages of students and the *current* situations of students, not just information about countries of origin of language minority children. All students would be involved in recording and documenting the developing history of individual class members and the group as a whole in American society.

The role of culture in determining human behavior would be a major part of the curriculum. Usually cross-cultural studies have been limited to the cultural traditions of particular language minority groups and not seen as the study of human behavior. Concepts from anthropology and sociology would be adapted to various age groups and would be taught from elementary through high school. A better understanding of the human condition would begin to shape a socially reconstructed sociopolitical context for public education.

The curriculum would also include study of oppression and inequity in education as well as in social, economic, and political arenas. In analyzing oppression and social inequity, students must deal with those concepts from their own backgrounds and perspectives. A White, English-speaking, middle-class child sees everything, including oppression, through very different eyes than a non-English speaking child of color. How can they understand oppression in the same way? Do they have to understand it in order to change the social order? Don't they both have to proactively work at changing society? It may be necessary to force the *experience* of being in another's culture, not just *learning about* that culture. Learning a second language to fluency can provide that experience.

Learning a second language is offered as a strategy for social reconstructionist class-rooms knowing full well that the majority society has little interest in learning about minority cultures, much less in putting themselves in the uncomfortable, vulnerable position of learning a second language. The obvious question is why would the public want to do that? The shrinking world, economic competition, and multicultural reality of our nation and the world may leave us no choice. Economic necessity alone may force our schools to teach other languages, not as elective subjects, but to a functionally proficient level.

✤ Summary

The historical and current sociopolitical context of the United States determines the organization and place of bilingual education in schools and bilingual teacher preparation programs in higher education. Reflection on the history of bilingual education in our country makes it clear that languages used in schools not only aid or hinder instruction, but also have the ability to provoke or subdue social protest and action. Use of languages other than English has incited public reaction in ways that few other educational strategies have because it is at once an instructional approach *and* an emotional symbol of resistance to oppression for minority groups.

Bilingual education is social reconstructionism at work, but the work is hindered because bilingual classrooms are not acknowledged as places to address oppression and inequity. Instead, they have become places to instruct minority students in the ways of the mainstream and discussions about bilingual education revolve around how best to transition minority students into those ways. The potential of bilingual classrooms to reconstruct society lies in the power of language to promote intercultural communication and inclusion of all groups. Bilingual classrooms are also places to analyze and understand issues about conflict over languages used in schools and society. Curriculum that acknowledges that conflict about language is basically one of status and power in society, not about a method of instruction, would at least clarify issues. Progress is being made as the question of power is more widely recognized and openly acknowledged today than even 10 years ago when one author astutely asked the following:

> Who stands to gain, where "gain" can be operationalized as an indicator of which group benefits in the power struggle. The literature on bilingual education is noticeable for the almost complete absence of such questions. The pious assumption is of course that the children are the ones who stand to gain, with indicators like standardized test scores on school achievement and self-concept. (Paulston, 1980, p. 57)

Hakuta, years later, stated:

> Bilingual education openly acknowledges the legitimacy of non-English languages in a centrally important public institution, and it appears to threaten the status of English. That is what critics are reacting to. Were it not for the symbolic status of bilingual education, one could easily imagine the assimilationists applauding the goals of the current bilingual programs. (Hakuta, 1986, p. 226)

Bilingual classrooms that acknowledge the conflict and strive to resolve it by mutual empowerment of students become social reconstructionist. Neutralizing the conflict by having students learn each other's cultural and linguistic codes even as they jointly develop a new culture could be the result of bilingual classrooms. If everyone has something to gain from bilingual education, perhaps it may be a feasible option for reconstructing public education. If bilingualism were a goal for all students and if American society could accept the worth of *every* language as a communication system, many of the goals of social reconstructionism would be achieved. Bilingual education, conceived as an educational approach for all students instead of as a remedial approach for some students, would be the embodiment of social reconstructionist theory. The role that bilingual education has played in the power struggle to empower language minority students should be expanded to empower all students to live and prosper in a multicultural society.

References

Ada, A. F. (1986). Creative education for bilingual teachers. *Harvard Educational Review, 56*(4), 386–394.

Andersson, T., and Boyer, M. (1978). *Bilingual schooling in the United States* (2nd ed.). Austin, TX: National Educational Laboratory Publishers.

Baca, L. M., and Cervantes, H. T. (1989). *The bilingual special education interface* (2nd ed.). Upper Saddle River, NJ: Merrill/Prentice Hall.

California Department of Education. (1990). *Bilingual education handbook, designing instruction for LEP students.* Sacramento: California Department of Education.

Carter, T. (1970). *Mexican Americans in school: A history of educational neglect.* New York: College Entrance Examination Board.

Castellanos, D. (1985). *The best of two worlds.* Trenton: New Jersey State Department of Education.

Chu, H., and Levy, J. (1988). Multicultural skills for bilingual teachers: Training for competency development. *Journal of the National Association for Bilingual Education, 12*(2), 153–169.

Clark, E. R., and Milk, R. D. (1983). Training bilingual teachers: A look at the Title VII graduate in the field. *Journal of the National Association for Bilingual Education, 8*(1), 41–53.

Collier, V. (1998). *Promoting academic success for ESL students.* Jersey City: NJTESOL-BE in cooperation with the Multicultural Center and Office of Publications and Special Programs at Jersey City State College.

Crawford, J. (1989). *Bilingual education: History, politics, theory and practice.* Trenton, NJ: Crane.

Cummins, J. (1981). Four misconceptions about language proficiency in bilingual education. *Journal of the National Association for Bilingual Education, 5*(3), 31–45.

Cummins, J. (1988). From multicultural to anti-racist education. In T. Skutnabb-Kangas and J. Cummins (Eds.), *Minority education: From shame to struggle* (pp. 127–157). Philadelphia: Multilingual Matters.

Cziko, G. A., Lambert, W. E., and Gutter, R. (1979–80). French immersion programs and students' social attitudes: A multidimensional investigation. *Journal of the National Association for Bilingual Education, 4*(2), 19–33.

Delgado-Gaitan, C., and Trueba, H. (1991). *Crossing cultural borders.* New York: Falmer.

Diaz-Soto, L. (1991). Understanding bilingual/bicultural young children. *Young Children, 46*(2), 30–36.

Fishman, J., and Keller, G. (1982). *Bilingual education for Hispanic students in the United States.* New York: Teachers College Press.

Fullan, M. (1982). *The meaning of educational change.* New York: Teachers College Press.

Garcia, E. (1988). Effective schooling for language minority students. In National Clearinghouse for Bilingual Education (Ed.), *New focus.* Arlington, VA: Editor.

Griego-Jones, T. (1991). Rethinking programs for language minority students. *The Journal of Educational Issues of Language Minority Students, 9,* 61–74.

Hakuta, K. (1986). *Mirror of language.* New York: Basic Books.

Hakuta, K., and Gould, L. J. (1987). Synthesis of research on bilingual education. *Educational Leadership, 44*(6), 38–45.

Johnson, D. M., and Binkley, J. L. (1987). Management and organizational structure in university bilingual education programs: A national survey of Title VII. *Journal of the National Association for Bilingual Education, 11*(2), 95–116.

Johnson, H. S., and Hernandez, W. J. (1970). *Educating the Mexican American.* Valley Forge, PA: Judson Press.

Joyce, B. (Ed.). (1990). *Changing school culture through staff development.* Alexandria, VA: Association for Supervision and Curriculum Development.

Lambert, W. E., and Tucker, G. R. (1972). *Bilingual education of children: The St. Lambert experiment.* Rowley, MA: Newbury House.

Lieberman, A. (Ed.). (1988). *Building a professional culture in schools.* New York: Teachers College Press.

Moll, L., and Gonzalez, N. (1994). Lessons from research with language-minority children. *Journal of Reading Behavior, 26*(4), 439–456.

National Forum on Personnel Needs for Districts with Changing Demographics. (1990). *Staffing the multilingually impacted schools of the 1990s.* Washington, DC: U.S. Department of Education.

Nieto, S. (1992). *Affirming diversity, the sociopolitical context of multicultural education.* New York: Longman.

Obledo, M., and Alcala, C. (1980). Discrimination against the Spanish language in public service: A policy alternative. In D. J. R. Bruckner (Ed.), *Politics and language: Spanish and English in the United States.* University of Chicago: Center for Policy Study.

O' Malley, J. M. (1982). *Children's English and services study: Educational and needs assessment for language minority children with limited English proficiency.* Rosslyn, VA: InterAmerica Research Associates.

Ortiz, A. A., and Yates, J. R. (1983). Incidence of exceptionality among Hispanics: Implications for manpower planning. *Journal of the National Association for Bilingual Education, 7*(3), 41–54.

Ovando, C., and Collier, V. (1998). *Bilingual and ESL classrooms, teaching in multicultural contexts* (2nd ed.). New York: McGraw-Hill.

Paulston, C. B. (1980). *Bilingual education: Theories and issues.* Rowley, MA: Newbury House.

Rodriguez, A. M. (1980, July). Empirically defining competencies for effective bilingual teachers: A preliminary study. *Bilingual Education Paper Series of the National Dissemination and Assessment Center, 3*(12).

Sleeter, C. E., and Grant, C. (1988). *Making choices for multicultural education.* Upper Saddle River, NJ: Merrill/Prentice Hall.

U.S. Department of Education. (1991, June). *The condition of bilingual education in the nation: A report to the congress and the president.* Washington, DC: U.S. Department of Education, Office of the Secretary.

Wagonner, D., and O'Malley, M. (1985). Teachers of limited English proficient children in the United States. *Journal of the National Association for Bilingual Education, 9*(3), 25–42.

Wigginton, E. (Ed.). (1975). *Foxfire 3.* Garden City, NJ: Anchor Press.

Wong-Fillmore, L., and Valadez, C. (1986). Teaching bilingual learners. In M. C. Wittrock (Ed.), *Handbook of research on teaching* (pp. 648–685). Upper Saddle River, NJ: Merrill/Prentice Hall.

7 Multicultural Concerns and Classroom Management

Mary Lou Fuller
University of North Dakota

Without well-planned and well-executed classroom management, the benefits of even the best curriculum will be lost, and teachers will spend a large portion of their days dealing with discipline, organization, and generally "putting out fires." Effective classroom management allows teachers to teach and children to learn in a predictable environment where they can feel secure and can invest their energies in personal growth.

An important factor in quality classroom management is knowing about the students—their physical and emotional development, their learning styles, and the cultural and economic diversity of their homes. Most teachers do a good job with the development and learning-related issues, but are unsure of themselves in the area of diversity, where multicultural education is especially useful.

Multicultural education is an orientation toward the educational process that is sensitive to the diverse backgrounds students bring with them to school (Sleeter & Grant, 1993). Gloria Ladson-Billings (1994) clarifies the teacher's role in multicultural education with the term *culturally relevant pedagogy*. She sees cultural relevancy (understanding students culturally) as a major component of good classroom management.

The purpose of this chapter is to help teachers and preservice teachers consider classroom management from a multicultural perspective. We will examine some general ways to approach learning about children of other cultures and other socioeconomic groups. This process can then be used to gather and interpret information in a range of settings.

This chapter also describes the nature of classroom management and how it is affected by multicultural concerns. It provides a model that is both culturally sensitive and adaptable to your own classroom environment. The model is followed by an exploration of parental involvement, which is important to each child's educational experience generally and classroom management specifically.

From another perspective, good teachers need to develop ways of working with parents whose cultures differ from their own, and some of those strategies are considered in this chapter. The chapter ends with specific suggestions designed to help teachers learn about the cultures of their students. All the issues covered are aimed at helping teachers to develop an understanding of the range of effects a sensitivity to cultural diversity can have on classroom management.

❖ Today's Schools

Schools have changed markedly over the past half century as the number of people from culturally diverse populations has increased in the United States. These changes will continue, and because of some groups' relatively higher birth rates and increased

109

immigration, about 33% of public school children will come from culturally diverse backgrounds by 2010 (Thornton, 1995).

Children of color make up the majority of school children in some states. Currently, 58% of school children in California, for example, are members of minority groups, and by 2020, these groups are expected to exceed the White mainstream population in the schools (Wise & Gollnick, 1996).

Cultural relativity is problematic because more than 87% of public school teachers are White and come from generally middle-class backgrounds (Meeks, 1998) while approximately 31% of public school students are children of color. This demographic disparity is not an aberration; it is a reality in our public schools. Another reality is that while socioeconomic levels are less noticeable than skin color or language, they are equally important. Teachers must consider issues associated with poverty in particular because they permeate the lives of both children and the families from which the children come. Twenty-five percent of the children in this country live in poverty. While this in itself is an appalling number, the figure for young families (family head less than 30 years of age) is even worse—42% live in poverty. In addition, 54% of children of female-headed households live below the poverty line (U.S. Census Bureau, 1993).

Given these realities, what can teachers do to prepare for the diversity of student populations in their classrooms? Clearly, adopting a multicultural (and culturally relevant) perspective that will be useful in managing a classroom is an important answer because students in today's classroom come from ethnic/cultural/racial, familial, and economic milieus that are frequently different from those in which public school teachers were reared.

✛ History of Classroom Management

Attitudes toward the treatment of children have changed dramatically over time. During the Middle Ages, children were routinely beaten in the mistaken belief that they were inhabited by evil spirits that could be exorcised only by corporal punishment—hence the expression "beat the devil out of the child." Caning was a common method of classroom control well into the 20th century, and corporal punishment is still legal in many states.

While most educators take a more enlightened view of child development and how it affects behavior, they often forget other factors such as culture. This issue must be considered in addressing the needs of diverse student populations. As effective educators, we must appreciate and be aware of multicultural concerns in classroom management so that what we do is multicultural and social reconstructionist in nature. Before we can understand any individual child in our classrooms, we need an appreciation for and an understanding of societal equality and cultural pluralism. For schools must "prepare citizens to work actively toward social structural equality; promote cultural pluralism and alternative life styles; [and] promote equal opportunity in the school" (Sleeter & Grant, 1993, p. 211).

✛ Classroom Management, Discipline, and Punishment and the Multicultural Classroom

Classroom Management, Discipline, and Punishment

It is a truism that classroom management is an integral part of all classroom activities. It is also true that while the presence of good management does not guarantee a successful lesson, its absence greatly increases the chances of failure. In short, successful classroom management helps create an environment where learning can take place. Not surprisingly, it is the educator's responsibility to ensure that the environment is both conducive to learning and comfortable for students. Glasser (1986) points out that unless this happens, "teachers and parents needn't bother telling students how valuable school is to them: Unless classroom management works well, students will be dissatisfied; and if they are not satisfied in school, they will get little from the time they spend there" (p. 54).

Discipline is of particular concern to educators and parents. Each year since 1969, the Phi-Delta-Kappa-sponsored Gallup Poll of the public's attitudes toward education asks, "What do you think are the biggest problems with which the public schools in this community must contend?" In most years, the public listed discipline as the No. 1 problem (Gallup & Clark, 1987), and teachers agree (Elam, 1989). The Panel on the Preparation of Beginning Teachers (chaired by Ernest Boyer) identified three major areas of expertise needed by beginning teachers: Knowledge of how to manage a classroom, knowledge of subject matter, and an understanding of their students' [cultural and] sociological background (Jones & Jones, 1997). To be truly effective, a teacher must approach these interrelated areas of expertise from a multicultural perspective. Obviously, classroom management and students' backgrounds overlap.

Of 84 classroom management textbooks published between 1990 and 1997, only two presented multicultural perspectives as an integral part of the textbooks: *Celebrating Diversity: Building Self-Esteem in Today's Multicultural Classrooms* (Siconne, 1994) and *Classroom Behavior Management in a Diverse Society* (Grossman, 1994). Another two books had chapters pertaining to this subject: *Behavior Management* (Zirpoli & Melloy, 1996) and *Classroom Management and Discipline* (Burden, 1995). For the most part, the other 80 books failed even to mention cultural diversity. This is particularly discouraging because a large and growing student population are children of color. Their absence in the literature on classroom management suggests a void in education's consciousness of children of color or the assumption that White mainstream behaviors are the standard by which all classroom behavior should be measured. Both are unacceptable.

What Is Classroom Management?

Educators commonly make the error of looking for "the answer" to classroom management. Preservice teachers and practicing teachers alike enter classroom management courses searching for a formula for creating the perfect classroom. For such a formula to work, however, all ingredients—including students—must be constant and unchanging. And because there are no absolutes when dealing with people, it is impossible for any formula to work with regularity.

But generalizations do exist about people's physical and psychosocial developmental needs. This body of knowledge can be combined with data on socioeconomic and cultural backgrounds to offer educators some basic understandings about the students they teach. These understandings can be interpreted by teachers using their personal philosophies to produce some basic guidelines of good organization, resulting in good classroom management practices.

Educators often err in using the terms *classroom management* and *discipline* as synonyms. Classroom management is much broader in scope than discipline; classroom management includes everything teachers do to increase student involvement and cooperation in the classroom and to establish a healthy, productive working environment for children. Classroom management is "the orchestration of a classroom . . . planning curriculum, organizing procedures and resources, arranging the environment to maximize efficiency, monitoring student progress, [and] anticipating potential problems" (Lemlech, 1991, p. 3).

Discipline and Punishment

Discipline is narrower in perspective. It deals with how children behave in the classroom and the teacher's ability to influence that behavior. Unfortunately, many people think discipline is characterized by autocratic authority using punitive action or rigid control. This view embodies a contradiction, because appropriate theories of discipline are based on tenets of the democratic classroom while those of punishment stand in opposition to that view.

TABLE 7.1.   Discipline vs. Punishment

Aspect	Discipline	Punishment
Student	Is based on logical or natural consequences expressing the reality of the social order (rules which must be learned in order to function adequately).	Is based on the power of an external influence. Is usually painful (e.g. embarrassing, demeaning). Is often arbitrary.
	Responsibility is assumed by the individual. Comes from within.	Is imposed upon student. Responsibility is assumed by the punisher—rather than by the person who committed the act.
	Is ongoing and part of the learning process.	Is finite, and over at the conclusion of punishment.
	Individual has options and input in resolution of problems.	Options for the individual are closed. Individual has no input.
Teacher	An active teaching process involving close, sustained, personal involvement. Emphasizes teaching ways to act that will result in more successful behaviors.	A teaching process which usually reinforces failure identity. Essentially negative and short term.
	Concern for the child as well as the act.	Concern for act. Open or concealed anger.
	Labor intensive and ongoing.	Easy and expedient. Immediate.

Where punishment makes the person with authority the only one with power in the classroom, theories of discipline take a more positive and productive view: discipline should help children move toward self-control. Discipline is a way of helping children assume responsibility for their behavior through introducing the ideas of dignity and respect—for both self and others. Inherent in this approach is the idea that children should behave appropriately—for themselves and their environments. The emphasis on personal responsibility and respect for self and others makes discipline more compatible with a multicultural perspective than does punishment.

The notion of punishment implies, erroneously, that classroom management is a matter of *us* against *them*. In reality, these same views of personal responsibility and respect for self and others allow teachers in multicultural classrooms to be educational leaders who create and maintain an environment in which children can grow as individuals and learn to function as productive members of a group. Discipline is much more complex than the teacher and the students locked in a power struggle (Table 7.1).

✣ A Culturally Appropriate Classroom Management Model

Clearly, an effective classroom management plan is based upon a sound educational philosophy (Figure 7.1). Without a coherent set of beliefs on which to base disciplinary actions, educators' actions become random and unpredictable from the children's perspectives. A well thought out classroom management program

- Starts with a strong set of beliefs.
- Develops disciplinary goals based on these beliefs.
- Considers these goals in light of cultural and socioeconomic factors in the classroom.
- Develops a culturally sensitive plan of action.

For example, the philosophical position that all children have a need to feel a sense of efficacy leads to the goal of providing them with problems to solve to address their needs. If a child's culture suggests that the whole group be involved in problem solving, so be it; however, if the child's culture emphasizes individual activity, then that is the way for that child to address her sense of efficacy.

✣ Philosophy of Multicultural Classroom Management Plan

Basic Beliefs

Philosophy, goals, and multicultural sensitivity are of course more complex than the preceding paragraph implies; it is appropriate to look at these issues in more detail. From a philosophical perspective, multiculturally sensitive classrooms are social reconstructionist in nature[1] and so seek to address inequities related to diversities in race, class, gender, and disability. Considering these factors allows educators a perspective on such crucial educational issues as tracking, learning styles, cooperative learning, resources available to students, pedagogy, meaningful curriculum, student culture, and of course, classroom management. How, one wonders, do classroom demographics play out in each of the educational areas? By doing the kind of inventory implicit in the preceding sentences,

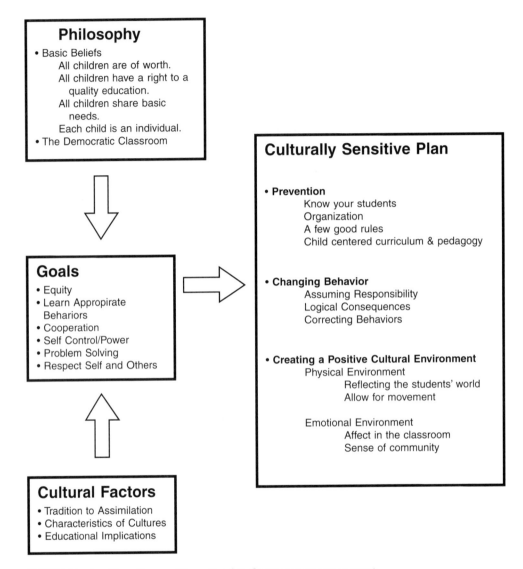

Philosophy
- Basic Beliefs
  All children are of worth.
  All children have a right to a
  quality education.
  All children share basic
  needs.
  Each child is an individual.
- The Democratic Classroom

Goals
- Equity
- Learn Appropirate
  Beharios
- Cooperation
- Self Control/Power
- Problem Solving
- Respect Self and Others

Cultural Factors
- Tradition to Assimilation
- Characteristics of Cultures
- Educational Implications

Culturally Sensitive Plan

- **Prevention**
  Know your students
  Organization
  A few good rules
  Child centered curriculum & pedagogy

- **Changing Behavior**
  Assuming Responsibility
  Logical Consequences
  Correcting Behaviors

- **Creating a Positive Cultural Environment**
  Physical Environment
  Reflecting the students' world
  Allow for movement

  Emotional Environment
  Affect in the classroom
  Sense of community

FIGURE 7.1 **A culturally sensitive plan for classroom management.**

teachers are in a better position to address their responsibilities to work toward equity for all children.

Why would a teacher want to do all this work? Because another tenet of the social reconstructionist philosophy is that all children are of worth and have a right to expect that their teacher will do what is necessary to provide a quality education. And so we now have two ways in which all children are alike (they go through the same physical and psychological developmental stages, and they all are of worth and have a right to a quality education). They differ in that they come from varying cultural and economic backgrounds, and—the point we now wish to focus on—they all differ as individuals. This last point is important because consistent with all children being of worth and deserving of a good education is the idea that each child must be considered individually. Not surprisingly, good classroom management provides an environment in which children can develop as individuals and as part of a group of young and contributing members of society.

A Democratic Classroom

What kind of a classroom allows all this to happen simultaneously? The classroom is child-centered and democratic; indeed, it is difficult to imagine a quality multicultural classroom that does not have a democratic base. The democratic classroom is one characterized by (adapted from Beane and Apple, 1995, pp. 6–7):

- The open discussion of ideas that enables people to simultaneously be as fully informed as possible.
- The opportunity to use critical reflection and analysis to evaluate ideas, problems, and policies.
- Faith in the individual and collective capacity of people to create possibilities for resolving problems.
- Opportunity to participate in the discussions that produce those possibilities and implement those solutions.
- Concern for the welfare of others and "the common good."
- Concern for the dignity and rights of individuals and minorities.
- Understanding that democracy is not so much an "ideal" to be pursued as an "idealized" set of values that we must live by and that must guide our life as a people.
- Organization of social institutions to promote and extend the democratic way of life.

Beane and Apple continue by observing that "Democratic schools, like democracy itself, do not happen by chance. They result from explicit attempts by educators to put in place arrangements and opportunities that will bring democracy to life" (1995, p. 9).

The idea of responsibility is inherent in the democratic (student-centered) classroom: Teachers are responsible for creating an environment in which children are taught how to be responsible members of their society. They must learn to assume age-appropriate responsibility for their own behavior.

Goals of Culturally Sensitive Multicultural Education

Given this philosophical position, we turn now to the goals congruent with it in providing the basis for a multicultural classroom management plan. These goals include:

Equity   Equity must be a goal of any classroom management program because all children are of worth. Please note that *equity* is not synonymous with *equal,* because some children have greater needs than others. The child whose environment lacks the resources and opportunities enjoyed by classmates may have greater needs and consequently require more time, ingenuity, and resources than others. The notion of equity in this situation means addressing the needs of the individual child. It does not mean treating all children exactly alike.

The saying "There is nothing as unequal as equal treatment" summarizes things nicely. The perspective here provides a broader, more holistic view of equity. According to Swadener, Cahill, Arnold, and Marsh (1995) ". . . it can be argued that equity requires social parity, balanced proportions, redistribution of power, access, rights and opportunities" (p. 63). With equity as the goal, distribution of time and other resources over the year may have to be inequitable.

Learning Appropriate Behaviors   The child-centered approach creates a wonderful environment in which children can become socialized to the standards of the classroom specifically, and to larger segments of the community generally. Being able to recognize the appropriate behaviors for a given circumstance gives children a degree of power and control over their lives. In addition, their lives become more predictable and so help them address Maslow's safety (predictability) needs (and other needs, depending on the situation) (Hamachek, 1994).

There may well be several acceptable behaviors for the child to choose among, and this is good. Children in a child-centered classroom are both allowed and encouraged to try different solutions. As educators, we must accept and respect the fact that appropriate behaviors in the child's home environment may differ significantly from those of the school community, and that the behaviors of the home community may suit the child well in that environment. This means both that the child should not hear the non-school options belittled and that the child should have experience choosing among options in school so he'll be better able to make choices in other environments. Children who can select the appropriate behavior in more than one environment have an advantage over those that cannot. From a multicultural perspective, monocultural children do well at making choices only in the culture in which they were socialized; bicultural children are able to make good choices in both cultures with which they're familiar.

Cooperation   *Cooperation* can be understood in several ways, but only two are important here. The first is as a specific learning strategy—*cooperative learning* as described by Johnson, Johnson, and Holubec (1986), where a small group of students works together interdependently on a learning task. The second describes an important characteristic of how a democratic classroom functions.

Children in multicultural classrooms learn to work together, recognizing and appreciating the richness each individual brings to the classroom (implications of group activities will be discussed later in this chapter). Cooperation is an important part of a democratic classroom and is clearly essential when children are learning to work well with others; a child can no more learn to behave appropriately in the absence of opportunities to practice those behaviors than a pianist can learn to play a piano—solo or in concert with other musicians—without drill and rehearsal. The classroom is a wonderful rehearsal hall for just such practice, particularly when it is blessed by ethnic/racial and socioeconomic heterogeneity.

Self-Control/Power   Children learn to assume responsibility for their own behaviors and to make choices that are in their best interest and the best interest of others as they gain some control over their lives. They do this by making decisions in democratic classrooms. This kind of activity has teachers playing roles that are quite different from those in traditional classrooms where they are expected to act as police officers seeing that the rules aren't violated—or at a minimum, providing crowd control. In this classroom the teacher must catch children in misbehavior and punish them; if the children aren't caught, then the misbehavior doesn't count. This is because the teacher, as opposed to the child, is responsible for the child's behavior; the children learn that their role is to rely on others to know if their choices are acceptable.

Problem Solving   An important part of preparing children to assume responsibility for their own behavior is to teach them the skills they need to do so, and problem solving is an important component of such skills. There are a variety of good problem solving programs that can be used in the classroom. However, the problem-solving technique proposed by the Committee for Children (1992) may be the best as it is simple and effective. This plan is also culturally sensitive in that each child can answer the following questions according to her own cultural perspective. Finally, because children vary, adjustments should be made when needed.

- What is the problem?
- What are some solutions?
- For each solution, ask: Is it safe? How might people feel? Is it fair? Will it work?
- Choose a solution and try it.
- Is it working? If not, what can I do now?

Respecting Self and Others   Children must learn to respect themselves before they can value and respect others. The adults in children's lives must model these behaviors. While educators have no control over the adults outside school, they can and must be positive role models by demonstrating that they value and respect themselves and others. A classic study done by Raschke and Raschke (1979) demonstrated that children who feel good about themselves come from families where parents feel good about themselves. This simple and powerful observation has great implications for teachers because in demonstrating respect for themselves and others, they give children permission to like and value themselves. Since respect is culturally defined, how one demonstrates respect is culturally defined; thus teachers are obligated to be knowledgeable about the culture(s) of their students.

High Teacher Expectation for All Children   Teacher expectation is an important factor in how children behave (as well as in their academic achievement) in the classroom. The premise of teacher expectation is that if the teacher expects children to behave well there is an increased chance that they will; the expectation for poor behavior will have like results. Teachers see what they expect to see, and students see what the teacher sees. In other words, teacher expectation becomes students' self-perception. Teacher expectations aren't magic, and wishing does not make things so, but when we have a specific expectation for a child our behaviors become congruent with our expectations. Teacher expectations affect all children but are particularly important with children of color and low-income children, because educators are apt to have lower expectations for these students than for White middle class children.

Teacher expectation is not a new concept but it has only recently received scholarly acceptance. Each of us can remember a teacher who had high expectations for us, inspiring us to work harder, but these experiences are anecdotal in nature and have not been accepted as evidence of this phenomenon. Rosenthal and Jacobson (1968) supported the effects of teacher expectation in their book, *The Pygmalion in the Classroom*. The book was widely hailed as "the answer" to the question of the authenticity of teacher expectation; however, it was also just as widely criticized for faulty research. Perhaps the greatest contribution made by Rosenthal and Jacobson was the profusion of research they inspired in an attempt to prove or disprove their findings. This research has become much more sophisticated and supports Rosenthal and Jacobson's overall findings. Teacher expectation does influence student behavior. Consequently, teachers must have positive expectations for their students and communicate those expectations to them.

✢ Cultural Factors

Ethnic/Racial

Successful classroom management requires cultural sensitivity, because teachers can't address the needs of children whose backgrounds they do not understand or appreciate. What does it mean for teachers to be culturally sensitive? First, teachers must understand their own cultural behaviors, values, and traditions because they view and understand other people's cultural behaviors, values, and traditions against this background. Awareness of our own backgrounds helps us understand our perceptions of students' behaviors and so reduces the likelihood that we will make ethnocentric judgments about students. At a minimum, these judgments hinder communication; at worst, they will cause irreparable harm to the relationships we are establishing with our students.

Cultural sensitivity can help to aovid problems that are simultaneously subtle and profound. Consider, for example, the fact that children in some cultures are brought up to be most considerate of others ("Don't make noise too early in the morning, you will wake the people in the next campsite," and "Play outside with your friends so your brother can study"), while in other cultures, youngsters are taught to be most tolerant of others ("Don't let the radio bother you," and "Learn not to be distracted by other people—the world can't stop because you have to do your homework") (Grossman, 1994, p. 82). If both groups of students are in the same classroom, and the teacher is unaware of their differing expectations, encouraging consideration of others will be confusing to one group of students while encouraging tolerance of others will be confusing to the second group. Understanding the needs and expectations of both groups allows the teacher to tailor her efforts in manners appropriate for all students, and in the process make her job appreciably easier.

While the preceding example highlighted differences across cultures, it is also important to remember that there is dramatic diversity within a culture. This means that a variety of factors must be considered in appreciating people from any given culture. The two most significant for classroom management are degree of assimilation exhibited by a child and socioeconomic groups. We turn first to assimilation.

Tradition and Assimilation

The degree of *assimilation* describes the extent to which a person has internalized the mores and values of a "new" culture—the "new" culture typically being the mainstream culture. A highly assimilated American Indian child, for example, is more comfortable in the mainstream society than in the traditional culture. But even if students appear to be more mainstream than traditional, teachers should be knowledgeable about their traditional culture and its influence on the students' behavior and attitudes. This is especially true if the teacher is to have any contact with parents, since the culture of the students' homes may be more traditional.

Because there is great diversity within cultures, it is impossible to describe each in its entirety; it is similarly impossible to produce a single generalization describing all the people sharing a culture. Overgeneralizing about a culture results in *stereotypes.* Stereotypes are harmful because they deny that variability exists within the stereotyped culture and among its people and thus limit what the observer can see and expect of the people described in such a manner. Stereotyping limits a child's potential.

One way in which stereotyping causes problems for both teachers and students is that a single expectation is applied to all situations. This results in simple explanations for complex cultural phenomena. When teachers use stereotypes, they ignore the complexity of factors that influence children's behavior and thus miss important patterns in their students' actions. This also means that behaviors not fitting the stereotype will seem unpredictable and will often be misunderstood, and this places the teacher at a disadvantage when planning management strategies. Subsequently, in an attempt to understand a behavior, they may turn to their own cultural experiences for an explanation and thus produce ethnocentric explanations for behaviors that would be understood if multicultural perspectives were used. The following paragraphs provide a particularly egregious example. In reading the following paragraphs, think about how you would describe the event if you were the teacher and how your description would differ from that of a Navajo student.

As a beginning teacher, I taught first grade on a Navajo Indian reservation. Children from several classes were lining up in front of their respective classroom doors. There were the usual happy sounds of children giggling, greeting friends, sharing news with teachers, and—suddenly—total silence. One of the teachers had grabbed a student and was vigorously shaking him. As though her behavior was not already inappropriate (both culturally and generally), she yelled, "When I speak to you, you show me the respect of looking me in the eye."

How incredible that must have sounded to the child who was trying to do exactly that—show his respect. He had been taught that being respectful meant not looking directly into the eyes of people in positions of authority. So the teacher's statement was as confusing to him as if she had told a mainstream child, "When I speak to you, you show me the respect I deserve by sticking out your tongue." Later, when the teacher and I talked about what had happened, she blamed the district for not having informed her about the cultural characteristics of her students. She was right, of course; people who prepare teachers and people who employ teachers have a responsibility to inform them about the children they'll be teaching. But when she accepted a teaching position with that reservation school district, she had an overriding responsibility to inform herself about her students. In other words, though everyone except the children had the responsibility to make certain that this teacher was well-informed, it was first and foremost up to the teacher to learn about her students. The general principle here is simple: Educators are responsible for being well-informed about the students who will be in their classrooms; ignoring this responsibility puts them at risk for using stereotypes and making ethnocentric interpretations—which puts their students' school experience in danger.

Educators don't want to risk cultural blunders that might label them as tactless, insensitive, or thoughtless. Avoiding these kinds of problems is a two-step process: First, collecting information about the culture in question, and second, drawing implications from this information which can then be used appropriately in classroom management. The following exercises provide practice in drawing such implications about various cultural groups. These exercises are not in-depth examinations of each of these cultures; rather, they are demonstrations of how one might translate information about students' cultures into culturally sensitive classroom management practices. In considering these cultural descriptions, keep in mind that group membership is not about absolutes, but rather the multiple dimensions of peoples' lives and the roles that race, class, gender, sexual orientation, and language background all play in a person's development. Again, keep in mind that it is the process—and not the cultures presented—that is being examined.

There is diversity within any group; children may appear alike, but they actually vary greatly.

- For example, Carlos Cañas and Lucy Gonzales are both Mexican American. They live in the same neighborhood, attend the same school, and are in the same grade. However, the language of Lucy's home is Spanish while Carlos knows only a few Spanish words. Lucy's family celebrates with joy and enthusiasm many of the holidays of Mexico while Carlos' family celebrates only the holidays of the mainstream society.
- Amy Yazzie and Billy White Bear provide another example. Amy is a Navajo child who was born and lives in Los Angeles while Billy White Bear is a Sioux who lives on a reservation in North Dakota. These two children live culturally different lives as American Indian children. Billy's parents are culturally traditional, while Amy knows very little about her cultural heritage.

Besides cultural diversity, the children also experience environmental diversity: Amy lives in a metropolitan area and Billy lives in one of the most sparsely populated areas in the United States. It may well be that Amy has more in common with Carlos than she does with Billy; Carlos may also find it easier to relate to Amy than to Lucy.

The resources available to a child's family must also be considered. For example, an African American child in an upper-middle-class neighborhood may have more in common with the European American child next door than with another African American child who lives in a federally subsidized housing project.

We have already noted that diversity is as great within a given culture as it is among cultures. This means that to appreciate people from a specific culture, a variety of factors must be considered.

Socioeconomic Grouping

Socioeconomic group is arguably as predictive of behavior as is culture. It reflects financial assets, prestige, and power (Webb & Sherman, 1989) because as a rule, power and prestige are closely tied to financial assets. Further, identifying a person's socioeconomic group usually identifies the person's available economic resources and the options they have (e.g., educational opportunities, health care, etc.). This is of particular importance when considering non-mainstream cultures, because they are apt to be of lower socioeconomic classes and so have fewer economic resources (Bianchi, 1990). In terms of both economic resources and the options they allow, Hispanic/Latino, African

American, and European American children of a given socioeconomic group may well have more in common with one another than with children of their own cultures who are of different socioeconomic groups—as we observed with Carlos and Amy. There are two messages here:

As with culture, lack of knowledge about students' socioeconomic backgrounds is a limitation; it can put teachers in the position of reaching conclusions based on stereotypes, impeding what they want to accomplish in the classroom and unintentionally hurting students.

Second, teachers must be aware of limitations of knowledge and experience with the diversity associated with socioeconomic grouping; they may lack vital information needed to create a learning environment appropriate for students from different socioeconomic groups.

In short, while we must learn all we can about the cultures in our school community, we must also guard against overgeneralizing this information as we strive to understand our students. The following paragraphs present a few examples of how we might take into account who our students are and how we can meet their needs in our classrooms.

✣ Three Cultures as Classroom Management Exercises

The preceding pages beg an important question: How does one go about getting the information needed to be appropriately aware of issues such as ethnicity, socioeconomic status, and culture? The following paragraphs describe four cultures to demonstrate a way of thinking and learning about culture and classroom management. These passages are not definitive nor absolute; they are merely learning activities.

Hispanic/Latino

Background   Hispanic/Latinos are the largest group of people of color in this country; there are now 22.4 million Hispanic/Latinos in the United States (Banks, 1997). Even though there is considerable diversity within the Hispanic/Latino community due to ethnic origin (the community includes Mexicans, Puerto Ricans, Cubans, and others), there is also diversity attributable to socioeconomic group and degree of assimilation. Nevertheless, Hispanics share some broad cultural values and a common language.

Cultural Traits   Family, community, and ethnic group are all central to the life of many Hispanic/Latino students. The family is the most valued of these highly prized institutions, and family inspires great loyalty. Hispanic/Latino parents tend to be affectionate and nurturing, and the extended family plays a more active role in the lives of Hispanic/Latino children than in the European American family (Carrasquillo, 1991). Indeed, grandparents, aunts, uncles, and cousins are particularly important to the Hispanic/Latino concept of family. Age and gender are also usually important factors in determining each individual's status, and sex roles are often more clearly defined than in the larger society (Carrasquillo, 1991; Dodd, Nelson, & Peralez, 1989; Sosa, 1991).

Hispanic/Latino children often develop a strong sense of community. They are generally taught to be cooperative and to have a strong sense of group (Carrasquillo, 1991). This means that Hispanic/Latino children tend to be more warm, concerned about others, and physically affectionate than children in mainstream society (e.g., touching is an important part of interpersonal communication in the culture). A required physical distance between people (also called personal distance) can be much less than in the mainstream society, and handshakes are frequent among acquaintances while hugs are common among family members and close friends (Dodd, Nelson, & Peralez, 1989).

Classroom Management Implications   Because Hispanic/Latino children usually respect adults (age demands respect), the teacher is expected to play a positive role and be an authority figure. Thus, status as an adult and an authority figure means the teacher receives respect.

Competition and individualism are traditions in most U.S. schools; many Hispanic/Latino children feel more comfortable in a cooperative environment. The wise teacher will plan accordingly for Hispanic/Latino children because tensions caused by differences between cultural preference and the tradition of the school can only result in frustration for both the students and the teacher.

Pursuing this idea a bit further, it is to the teacher's advantage to create a sense of community in the classroom by adopting a cooperative attitude toward classroom behaviors. This can be done by pointing out that good behavior reflects on the whole class and, whenever possible, by implementing group problem solving. Glasser's (1986) earlier works and his control theory, as well as Johnson, Johnson, and Holubec's (1986) cooperative learning, would be appropriate resources in largely Hispanic/Latino classrooms. The teacher plays an active nurturing role similar to a parent and the "sense of group" is encouraged and supported.

Nurturance can also be expressed in other ways. Teachers may want to be physically affectionate with their students in age- and gender-appropriate ways. This includes a hand on the arm while talking, a pat on the shoulder while passing, a hug to comfort or affirm, a smile across the classroom. All in all, Hispanic/Latino children will benefit from a warm, friendly classroom.

Because the power of the group is strong, it is often demeaning for the Hispanic/Latino child to be publicly disciplined. Further, the purpose of discipline should always be to change a behavior (as opposed to punishing a child) and it should take place away from the group whenever possible.

American Indians

Background   There are at least 500 recognized Indian tribes and 200 Indian languages in the United States (Gilland, 1992; Swisher, 1991). As with other cultures, there is great diversity among groups and individuals within groups. Some individuals live on reservations, some in rural communities, and some in urban areas (10 percent of school-age American Indian children were born and are reared in cities). Although tribal groups may have unique languages and customs, they also share some basic values.

Cultural Traits   The family is usually an important institution within the culture, and the extended family plays a particularly important role in the life of the American Indian child. In some tribes, aunts play roles similar to mothers, uncles may have some of the responsibilities the dominant culture assigns to fathers, and cousins may be treated like siblings. Occasionally, a grandmother or aunt may actually rear the child (Cleary & Peacock, 1998). American Indian parents also tend to be permissive and accepting of their children.

Emphasis is often placed on the group and the importance of maintaining harmony within the group; the needs of the group are often considered over the needs of the individual. Because of strong feelings of group solidarity, cooperation—not competition—is the desirable mode of operation. American Indian children are often hesitant to show themselves as superior, especially if this would present someone else in a poor light (Cleary & Peacock, 1998).

Furthermore, American Indian children often feel more comfortable participating in class after they have had time to consider their responses or practice their skills. They also are apt to delay answering questions (Sanders, 1987).

Classroom Management Implications   American Indian children tend to be more comfortable in classrooms that are cooperative in nature and that use small group activities as instructional techniques. This may be because the culture enjoyed by American Indian children is generally congruent with a democratic philosophy that emphasizes the whole child and a humanistic perspective. Thus while a child might feel uncomfortable being singled out for praise, this child will feel pride when her group receives recognition. Because the group is so important, it is particularly demeaning to be reprimanded in front of peers (What does this say about the Navajo boy being disciplined on the playground?). In accord with the cooperative preference of this group, the whole class should be involved in identifying desirable class behaviors and then helped to formulate rules to accomplish those goals. The skillful teacher will then refer to those guidelines as "our class rules."

Teachers in traditional classrooms usually allow for a brief response time and assume that students who know will respond immediately. More response time should be allowed for American Indian students, and they should be given many opportunities to practice an activity by themselves before they are expected to show mastery of it.

In planning classrooms, we must have the same basic goal for all students—to create a positive learning environment where children respect themselves and others. The management strategies we use depend on the students' cultural characteristics, and strategies will have to be based on an understanding of our students' cultures. This may well mean addressing the needs of several cultures at the same time.

African American

Background   African Americans represent about 12 percent of the total population (O'Hara, Pollard, Mann, & Kent, 1991) and display great diversity within their numbers. As with other groups, income is the primary reason for those differences.

While there were Black people in this country as early as 1565 helping to establish a colony in St. Augustine, Florida, most share a common history (slavery, civil-rights, discrimination, etc.). Thus African Americans differ from other immigrant groups in that most of their ancestors came to this country as slaves; other immigrant groups came voluntarily because of lack of economic opportunity in their home countries. In contrast, African Americans came involuntarily from countries with well-developed, functioning societies and strong cultures of their own.

Cultural Traits   Geneva Gay reports how slavery created and institutionalized codes of behavior and strategies for maintaining community cohesion; for dealing with oppression, discrimination, and exploitation; for articulating and transmitting values, beliefs, customs, and traditions; and for surviving in a larger society that at worst considered them chattel, and at best treated them as second-class citizens (Gay, 1995). Discrimination and oppression have continued to make these cultural behaviors a necessity for cultural survival. These are also the survival skills that other oppressed groups have employed.

Educational Implications   In writing about African Americans, Irvine observed that the primary goal of culturally relevant teaching is to assist children in developing a relevant Black personality, a personality that allows African American students to choose academic excellence yet still identify with African and African American culture (1990). This assertion is also true for all children of diverse cultural groups, but for the purpose of this discussion we are examining it in the context of the Black student.

Good classroom management allows students to see themselves in their classroom environments. For African American children, their culture, history, achievements, learning styles, and communication styles must be considered and the classroom environment made sensitive to these needs. For example, cooperative learning is not simply a matter of grouping students into heterogeneous groups; effective use of cooperative groups means that in the classroom teachers apply children's preferred style for group formation and interaction. African American children prefer to develop their own leadership structure (this is also true for Hispanic/Latino and Native American children); allowing children to occasionally work in groups of their own making helps them participate more fully in their own schooling (Pang & Barba, 1995).

In considering diverse cultural behaviors, we must be able to translate the needs of our students into our teaching strategies. The teaching style of effective teachers of African American students may vary from teachers of mainstream students; effective teachers of Black children are more likely to give directives to a group of unruly students in a direct and explicit fashion, as opposed to mainstream teachers who are more apt to suggest the behavior they want (Ladson-Billing, 1994).

Children may be punished for behaviors that are culturally appropriate. In dealing with African American children, for example, elevated movement and interaction with peers may be seen as undesirable by a dominant culture teacher when in fact they facilitate learning for many African American students (Delpit, 1995). A wonderful example of this is a description of girls of two cultures playing volleyball in school gymnasiums in St. Paul, Minnesota. The team in one gym consisted of African American girls, and in another Hmong girls. The noise level was very high in the gym with the African American girls—laughing, screams of encouragement, hollering—while in the other gym the only noise that could be heard was the contact of hands with the volleyball. Which of the behaviors was more desirable? Neither? Both? Consider the fact that the girls in each group were enjoying themselves, were comfortable with their behavior, and would have been uncomfortable if expected to behave like the girls in the other gym.

✥ A Culturally Sensitive Plan for Classroom Management

Classroom management must be culturally sensitive to be meaningful. In the absence of sensitivity, both students and teachers will feel confused and frustrated with one another; each will be guided by cultural expectations that the other may not understand.

One problem of establishing a culturally sensitive plan is that the expectations of existing classroom management programs are based on the behaviors of mainstream society. Consequently, in order to be effective we must become culturally knowledgeable about our students, their families, and their communities, and then create a classroom management approach that will be culturally appropriate for our student populations.

Again, we must remind ourselves that no formulas or recipes for classroom management apply to all children or classrooms. After selecting the most culturally appropriate model, we must then continue to customize it to meet the individual and group needs of the children. Using a culturally sensitive plan will provide a better learning environment not only for students of diverse cultures but also for White, mainstream students as it focuses on the needs of children.

This model considers the following: prevention, changing behaviors, and the positive classroom environment.

Prevention

Classroom behaviors deemed appropriate are generally those agreed upon by the dominant culture, and often these are accepted less because they are meaningful to children in classrooms but more because they carry the weight of tradition. For example, we know children learn best when they are actively involved in their learning, and yet in many classrooms "silence is golden" seems to be a whisper from the ghosts of teachers past, a time when children's needs were less well understood. In other words, you must design a management program that meets the needs of the children in classroom.

- **Know Your Students.** The best way to prevent classroom problems is to know your students both collectively and individually. Reflect upon your goals and consider the cultural characteristics present in your classroom. Consider the depth of a child's cultural practices. This information will help you assess how best to attain your goals. Do the students like to work with others? Would they prefer to work independently? Will they respond better to a direct approach than a more suggestive strategy? You will greatly reduce the number of management problems if the students feel comfortable in their classroom and if you recognize and appreciate their cultural practices.
- **Be Organized.** One of the greatest obstacles to good classroom management is disorganization. I was once asked by a school district to work with four first-year teachers who were going to be dismissed if their teaching skills didn't show marked improvement. I met with the teachers and asked them to describe their problem(s) as they understood them. All four placed classroom management at, or near, the top of their lists. When I visited their classrooms I found that all did, in fact, have management problems but that the primary source of the problems for three of these teachers was disorganization. The students' behaviors were the consequence of disorganization and not the cause of the problem.

  If you have to leave the room to get two more sheets of red paper for your art project, or magnets for a science activity, you have lost the lesson and the students. Before you leave school, organize for your next day. Have the Cuisenaire rods on your desk and the map of South America on the wall. Have *everything* ready. You'll find that you and your students will have a much more relaxed and profitable day when you are prepared. Remember that organization doesn't rule out spontaneity.
- **Establish a Few Good Rules.** Democratic classrooms discuss what is acceptable behavior and what isn't. It isn't so much a matter of identifying the "shall nots" as of determining those behaviors that will result in a positive learning environment. After generating a list of desirable behaviors, create a few basic guidelines for behavior. For example, "We will not interfere with anyone's learning—including our own." This

covers a multitude of disruptions (talking too loudly, interrupting a student at work, poking, etc.). And, "We will respect and appreciate ourselves and others" (name calling, physical assault, excluding, etc.). One cannot respect one's self or others without respecting and appreciating one's own culture and the culture of others.

- **Design a Child-centered Curriculum and Pedagogy.** When children are actively involved in their own learning, the frequency of problem behaviors drops dramatically. The challenge is to design a curriculum and develop a pedagogy that meet the needs of students. Understanding a child's cultural characteristics will allow educators to better prepare lessons and present them in a manner that is both culturally sensitive and child centered.

Changing Behaviors

As educators we must employ models of classroom management that are sensitive to the principles of multicultural education. Because multicultural education requires that teachers consider students' cultural and social backgrounds, the relationship of multicultural education and classroom management is obvious.

- **Encourage Students to Assume Responsibility.** Glasser asserts that people must assume responsibility for their own behavior. This is the first step in encouraging students to develop decision-making and citizen-action skills. "The key of the multicultural curriculum [and the key to classroom management] should be to help students develop decision-making and citizen-action skills" (Banks, 1997, p. 25). One of the primary goals of a culturally relevant plan for classroom management is to empower children by giving them some control over their lives.

    William Glasser has been an advocate of strategies that allow children to have control through the act of making good choices. Banks's (1997) description of multicultural goals supports Glasser's views of classroom management: Glasser views students as rational and capable people who can be responsible for their own behavior. Teachers need to help students learn to make choices that will result in appropriate behaviors and reasonable consequences following both good and bad behaviors (Glasser, 1993).

- **Provide Logical Consequences.** Using logical consequences is culturally sensitive as it is concerned with the individual, is never demeaning, and allows children to meet the standards they have helped establish. Logical consequences express the reality of the social order, acknowledge mutual rights, and separate the deed from the doer (Albert, 1989; Dinkmeyer, McKay, & Dinkmeyer, 1997; Dreikurs & Loren, 1993). Although logical consequence follows both desirable and undesirable behaviors, this discussion will concern misbehaviors. For example, a student who pours red paint on the floor would be expected to clean it up (as opposed to the punishment of missing recess, or writing something 500 times). A student who continually disrupts the lunch room gives up the right to eat there (as opposed to the punishment of staying after school, or being deprived of fun activities).

    Logical consequence allows children to correct their mistakes and learn from them without demeaning the child. It also enables teachers to help children recognize the consequences of their actions without becoming angry or frustrated. "Juan, you left the art corner a mess. After our math lesson, please get the pail and rags and clean it."

Logical consequence helps children learn to make good decisions, be productive, interact well with others, and make good use of their educational environments. Through logical consequences, the child comes to realize that self-discipline is "a method of teaching appropriate behaviors and making wise decisions" (Keating, Pickering, Slack, & White, 1990, p. 3).

No child (or adult) likes to be corrected in front of his or her peers, but children of some cultures find it more demeaning than others. Children who are part of cultural groups that prize group (or familial) membership over that of the individual find public retribution particularly humiliating. Most problems can be solved with dignity by addressing them in privacy. "We seem to have a problem. How can we resolve it?" turns a difficult situation into a problem-solving experience.

Creating a Positive Environment

Physical Environment

- **Reflect the Students' World.** The classroom environment must reflect the lives of the students both culturally and geographically. The classroom should be a place where children can see themselves and other members of their community. The students' textbooks should reflect the diversity of the country and their families. Trade books in the classroom need to represent the children in the classroom and also children of other cultures. Pictures and books about people of distinction of all cultures should be available in all classrooms with particular concern for those representing the students in a specific classroom. Another way of making children comfortable in their classroom is to display their work and have them help decorate the room.

    I visited a fifth-grade classroom on the New Mexico-Mexico border. The room displayed pictures of colonial Jamestown and a bulletin board with paper tulips surrounding the calendar bulletin board. When I looked at the calendar, I realized it was May 5th (Cinco De Mayo) and yet there was nothing in the classroom to indicate this holiday. The desert around the community was alive with Mexican golden poppies and other beautiful desert flowers, but they weren't represented in that classroom. One January day I visited a first-grade classroom in southern Texas. Outside, the sun was shining and the children were on the playground without wraps, while in the classroom the walls were decorated with paper snowflakes and snowmen. Their classroom had very little to do with the lives of the students.

- **Allow for Movement.** Finally, a deficit in most classrooms is the limited movement students are allowed. This lack of movement results in a variety of disruptive behaviors. In addition to cultural implications (children of some cultures learn best when they are physically active) there are also major classroom management implications. Classrooms need to be arranged to encourage movement. The class library, science area, computer center, and other centers should be placed in various areas of the room with clear and visible paths leading to them. (Problems can be avoided by teaching children how to use the centers without disturbing others.) Classroom activities should be planned to accommodate activities that allow for movement following sedentary lessons. Children who need more physical movement than others should not only be allowed, but encouraged to move. This will greatly reduce disruptive activities.

Emotional Environment

- **Develop a Comfortable Affect.** The affective environment is perhaps the most important of all. Children feel comfortable in a classroom that reflects the affective nature of their cultures (e.g., some cultures prefer greater personal space than others, some have a more formal relationship with their teachers while some see them as surrogate parents; some are reserved while others are gregarious). While children must be able to see themselves in a classroom, they must also be able to feel emotionally comfortable in that classroom.
- **Establish a Sense of Community.** The classroom should have a sense of unity. It should foster a sense of community where children respect themselves and others. An environment where children learn to work, play, and solve problems together prepares them to work with others and helps children develop a sense of security. The security of knowing they have the support of others and that they belong to a group provides them with an environment in which they can feel safe—a good learning environment. Referring to the class as "our" class helps build a sense of community. And the teacher must be part of the "our." The relationship should be that of a family where pride is taken in each member's accomplishments and where even when there are problems there is the security of knowing one is still a member of the family.

Parental Involvement

The Importance of Involving Parents   Many educators are uncomfortable with and uninformed about the parents of children from diverse student groups. On one hand, teachers recognize that parental involvement is an important part of successful classroom management and that working with parents will be an excellent opportunity to learn about the students. On the other hand, teachers are often afraid that lack of cultural knowledge might result in some great *faux pas* that will offend the parents and embarrass them. The best approach to this problem is to learn as much as possible about the children's families and cultures before meeting with their parents. General information can be collected through reading, and more specific information can be provided by administrators and other teachers at the school.

This information is important as it helps teachers approach and understand their students' families. Remember that teachers and parents already have a common bond: They both care about "their" children, and so they should work as a team to provide the best education possible for those children.

There are some things teachers can do to create a productive educational team. First, they should remember that parents are sending them the best they have—their children. Second, they should convey to parents a genuine appreciation of those children. Third, they should create an environment where parents and teachers must work at understanding the parents' situations including family structure, socioeconomic level, work demands, culture, and so on.

It is also important to understand that lack of information about cultural differences will affect our ability to work productively with parents. Teachers too often assume that parents of color are not as interested in their children's academic performances as European Americans, and this is blatantly untrue; parents of color do want to be involved in their children's educations, but often describe feeling uncomfortable in their children's schools. In addition, they report seldom being invited to participate in their child's school experience (Chavkin, 1989).

The public schools, as institutions, represent the values and behaviors of the White middle class and are designed for children from this community. And they generally work well for these children, as home-school relationships are based on this common cultural tradition. As with any tradition, it works because mainstream parents understand and are comfortable with it.

On the other hand, parents from other cultures may operate under a distinct disadvantage when dealing with the schools; they may not know, understand, or feel comfortable with the traditional home-school relationships that work so well for the dominant community. And because behavior, attitudes, and achievement all contribute to parental involvement, it is to the school's advantage to create constructive relationships with all parents. Learning about the cultures of students and their parents is an important step in establishing a mutually positive working relationship.

The examples that follow are not in-depth representations of different cultural groups; rather, they are examples of situations with a potential for cultural misunderstandings. The purpose of these illustrations is to create an awareness of potential areas of conflict that may impede home-school relations.

American Indians   American Indian parents have a short tenure as invited partners in the educational system. The Bureau of Indian Affairs (BIA) and parochial boarding schools were the primary educational institutions for their children until well into the 20th century. Because the historical goal of these institutions was to "civilize the savage" ("cultural genocide"), parents (as representatives of the "undesirable" culture) were actively discouraged from participating in their children's educational experiences. In addition, the distances from the children's homes to the boarding schools and lack of transportation further complicated home-school relations. Thus, even though most contemporary American Indian children live with their parents and attend schools in their communities, and even though the goals of the schools have changed dramatically, there is no historical tradition of home-school relations. Unfortunately, the old BIA practice of excluding parents from reservation schools is perpetuated by many public schools. Parents are made to believe they have no responsibility for the education of their children—that's the job of the school. This attitude is both counter to promoting parental involvement and tragic.

Another factor complicating the working relationship between American Indian parents and educators is the role of the extended family. As noted earlier, the extended family plays a more meaningful role in the child's life than is the case in much of mainstream society, and the responsibility for rearing an American Indian child is shared by a number of family members. Grandmothers, aunts, and uncles all may have serious responsibilities for and to the child. Parents *and* other relatives may attend school conferences, or the child may live with different family members at different times. The schools often misinterpret this as lack of parental concern or avoidance of parental responsibility when it is neither.

African Americans   Describing cultural patterns of African American students and their parents is difficult. Most studies in the literature are more than a decade old, and the research tends to consider the lower-socioeconomic-level, inner-city children who make up only one part of the African American population. The problem is that these studies do not consider the 45 percent of the population who are middle or upper class or those who are low-income and live in rural areas (Blackwell, 1985). Nevertheless, this literature can be used to examine briefly a continuing problem in African American home-school relations.

Educators often make erroneous assumptions about a particular group of parents, and these faulty assumptions then become the basis for interpreting the parents' behavior. Although published in 1978, Sara Lightfoot's book, *Worlds Apart: Relationships Between Families and Schools,* is still current in its discussion of this problem.

Despite the passionate dreams of Black parents, teachers continue to view them as uncaring, unsympathetic, ignorant of good education for their children and unconcerned about their children's academic success in school. Often they perceive the parents' lack of involvement in ritualistic school events and parent conferences as apathy and disinterest; they rarely interpret it as an inability to negotiate the bureaucratic maze of schools or as a response to a long history of exclusion (p. 166).

Children learn and grow best in schools where the parents and teachers understand one another, share similar visions, and collaborate on guiding children—as in the case in the suburban schools. Lightfoot (1978) also observes that, for a long time, we have understood that the magic of suburban schools is not merely the relative affluence and abundant resources of the citizens (nor their Whiteness), but also the consonance between what the parents want for their children and what teachers believe is educationally sound.

James Comer has successfully achieved this consensus in schools with large African American enrollments (Stocklinski & Miller-Colbert, 1991). In the Comer Model, the parent is a respected, integral part of the program. This model is centered on the idea that if parents, teachers, and staff share control of a school, they will convey a positive attitude to the children, who will then be motivated to learn. The success of these schools demonstrates the power of an educational system in which parents and teachers combine their efforts.

In each of the situations described in the book, the parents' roles in home-school relations were misunderstood. The Indochinese parents' view, for example, came from their experiences with authoritarian schools in their native countries, and the American Indian parents' perceptions are reflected in the U.S. government's historical rejection of them in the educational process. Finally, many African American parents' attitudes emerged from the erroneous assumptions education institutions made about them in the past. In all three cases, parents came to school with attitudes and behaviors that were interpreted according to standards for parents whose culture was that of the school; instead, the school should have tried to understand the parents' expectations, needs, and concerns. To be good teachers, we need to recognize that our students' parents may see their roles in relationship to the school differently than mainstream parents. This means we must work with them to facilitate a positive home-school relationship.

✢ Suggestions for New Teachers

New teachers may well sign a contract with a school district that has a diverse student population whose cultures differ significantly from theirs. Clearly, these teachers must become as well informed as possible about the culture of their students; it is as unprofessional to enter a classroom without knowledge of the students' culture as to agree to teach a subject for which one is unprepared. Being a professional educator doesn't mean new teachers are experts in every aspect of education, but it does mean that they are prepared to teach the students in their classes. They should enter classrooms well informed about their students' cognitive, socio-emotional, developmental, and cultural needs, in addition to being knowledgeable about curriculum and subject matter.

Gathering Information for the Culturally Diverse Classroom

Even though a beginning teacher may feel comfortable with her general knowledge of the children she will teach in terms of their cognitive and socio-emotional development, beginning teachers may know little about them culturally—except that their backgrounds are different from hers, and that she must know more about them if she is to be a good teacher.

New teachers can begin their searches for information by finding answers to the questions that follow, questions designed to help educators collect information about people whose cultural backgrounds differ from their own. The answers to these questions are a starting point; they are the foundation on which to build knowledge of students from different backgrounds as teachers gain experience.

Specific Questions to Ask About a New Culture

1. **What is the group's history?** While you will not become a scholar on the history of a given group, you can become well informed by reading some general books and articles. It is important to be able to recognize names, places, and events that are important to the group in question. It is also important to understand how historical events influenced the ways in which members of this group see things now.
2. **What are the important cultural values of the group?** It is critical to understand the important values of a group. Does the group value family issues over individual concerns? How do members of the group view themselves and others?
3. **Who are outstanding individuals who claim membership in this group?** There will be artists, writers, inventors, historical figures, athletes, and others who are members of the group and who have standing in the local, national, and international communities. Knowing who these people are is helpful to teachers, making it easier to understand who children are talking about and who can act as positive role models. Furthermore, teachers can help the other children in the class appreciate the leaders of different cultural communities through introducing and discussing these cultural personalities.
4. **What are the group's major religions and beliefs?** The answers provide information on values and events in children's lives and are important in explaining to other children what their classmates are doing and how they see things.
5. **What are the current political concerns?** Knowing about these issues means knowing about what is important in the children's home community. Sometimes these concerns will affect the school directly, sometimes they will not; but in all cases, they are issues the children will hear about in the neighborhood and at home.
6. **What are the group's political, religious, and social celebration days?** These are events that are important to the community and, as such, are days children will discuss at school. Good teachers will make use of this information in understanding their students and in planning curriculum.
7. **What are the educational implications of the answers to the preceding questions?** Very often, the answers are important because they affect individual students, and because they have a bearing on the entire class. It is important to know when students will miss school for religious holidays that are not part of the Christian calendar, just as it is important to discuss the political issues facing a specific group with all the students in the class. Because everyone should have an appreciation of

the issues facing students of color, integrating these issues into the curriculum is a good instructional strategy.

Finding the Answers, or, How Does a Teacher Go About Gathering This Information?

Much of the information educators need to begin understanding diverse groups is available in the library. In addition to looking up books and journal articles, using an Educational Resource Information Center (ERIC) computer search can be very helpful. The Current Index to Journals in Education (CIJE) and Resources in Education (RIE) contain useful titles. A good listing of videotapes can be found in *Teaching Strategies in Ethnic Studies* (Banks, 1997); websites about specific cultures are listed in the *Dictionary of Multicultural Education,* edited by Grant and Billing-Ladson (1998).

There is an understanding that comes from being a member of a community that cannot be acquired by commuting. For example, teachers who live on American Indian reservations have a much better understanding of their students and the community than those who commute. But whether you choose to live within the community or to commute, you can attend community activities. If the cultural community publishes an English-language newspaper or magazine, you can subscribe. Technology is also an excellent source of information about various cultural groups.

If the population has a large number of Hispanic/Latinos, agencies providing services to these groups can also provide pertinent information. These people can offer much information that will be useful—both about the groups of people and about ways to work successfully with them.

Visiting community cultural centers and museums can provide valuable information and give you an opportunity to talk with people who work there. They should be knowledgeable about the population and might suggest ways of better understanding the group.

Accept invitations to visit your students' families on special occasions. These might be religious observations or more secular holiday celebrations. In any event, these are opportunities to see people in the community setting, to learn about them, and to enjoy yourself.

Educators should also consider learning the language spoken by the children they teach. This communicates a message to students and their families about how we feel about them. It also allows us to communicate with them in a manner otherwise impossible. Even if we don't become proficient, we will have gained insights into our students' lives as well as demonstrating our respect for them.

In addition to these "do's," there are some "don'ts" teachers need to be aware of. It is not a good idea to ask too many questions initially, because many cultures feel uncomfortable with newcomers who press too hard for information or inclusion in the community. The community will let us know through its behavior when a more active role is appropriate.

✧ Getting Started

For classroom management to be meaningful, it must be culturally sensitive. In the absence of this sensitivity, both the students and the teacher will feel confused and frustrated as they approach one another. The expectations of most classroom management programs are also based on the behaviors of mainstream society, and these are often not applicable to children of diverse cultures. Consequently, we need to become culturally acquainted with our students, their families, and communities, and then determine which classroom management approaches will be most culturally appropriate for our student population.

We will select the model of classroom management that best meets the needs of our students. And we will do so with the understanding that there is no "formula" for classroom management applicable in all classrooms. After selecting the most culturally appropriate model, we need to modify it to meet the needs of our particular classroom. In addition, it is necessary to encourage parental involvement, for we know that parental involvement will enhance classroom management. All of these activities will help us develop classroom management skills resulting in a positive learning environment for our students.

Notes

1. In addition to seeing culture as ever changing, social reconstructionists believe they have a responsibility to promote change that will benefit children (and adults). Inherent in social reconstructionism is action. In other words, educators must actively work for a better environment for students.

References

Albert, L. (1989). *A teacher's guide to cooperative discipline.* Circle Pines, MN: American Guidance Service.

Banks, J. A. (1997). *Teaching strategies for ethnic studies.* Boston: Allyn and Bacon.

Beane, J. A., & Apple, M. W. (Eds.). (1995). *Democratic schools.* Alexandria, VA: Association for Supervision and Curriculum Development.

Bianchi, S. M. (1990). America's children: Mixed prospects. *Population Bulletin, 45*(1), Washington, DC: Population Reference Bureau.

Blackwell, J. A. (1985). *The Black community: Diversity and unity* (2nd ed.). New York: Harper & Row.

Carrasquillo, A. L. (1991). *Hispanic children and youth in the United States.* New York: Garland.

Chavkin, N. F. (1989). Debunking the myths about minority parents. *Horizons, 67*(4), 119-123.

Cleary, L. M., & Peacock, T. D. (1998). *Collected wisdom.* Boston: Allyn and Bacon.

Committee for Children. (1992). *Second step: A violence prevention curriculum, grades 4-5.* Seattle, WA: Committee for Children.

Delpit, L. (1995). *Other people's children.* New York: The New Press.

Dinkmeyer, D., McKay, G. D., & Dinkmeyer, D. (1997). *The parent's handbook: Systematic training for effective parenting.* Circle Pines, MN: American Guidance Service.

Dodd, J. M., Nelson, J. R., & Peralez, E. (1989). Understanding the Hispanic student. *Rural Educator, 10*(2), 8-13.

Dreikurs, R., & Loren, G. (1993). *Discipline: Logical consequences.* Bergenfield, NJ: Plume.

Elam, S. (1989). The second Gallup/Phi Delta Kappa poll of teachers' attitudes towards the public schools. *Phi Delta Kappan, 70*(10), 785-798.

Gallup, A., & Clark, D. (1987). The 19th annual Gallup poll of the public's attitudes towards the public schools. *Phi Delta Kappan, 69*(1), 17-30.

Gay, G. (1995). African-American culture and contributions in American life. In C. Grant (Ed.), *Educating for diversity: An anthology of multicultural voices.* Boston: Allyn & Bacon.

Gilland, H. (1992). *Teaching the Native American.* Dubuque, IA: Kendall-Hunt.

Glasser, W. (1986). *Control theory in the classroom.* La Porte, IN: HarperCollins.

Glasser, W. (1993). *The quality school teacher.* La Porte, IN: HarperCollins.

Grant, C. A. & Billing-Ladson, G. (1998). *Dictionary of multicultural education.* Phoenix: ORYX Press.

Grossman, H. L. (1994). *Classroom behavior management in a diverse society.* Mountain View, CA: Mayfield.

Hamachek, D. E. (1994). *Psychology in teaching, learning, and growth,* 5th ed. Boston: Allyn and Bacon.

Irvine, J. (1990, April). *Black parents' perceptions of their children's desegregated school experience.* Paper presented at the annual meeting of the American Educational Research Association, Boston, MA.

Johnson, D. W., Johnson, R. T., & Holubec, E. J. (1986). *Revised circles of learning: Cooperation in the classroom.* Edina, MN: Interaction Book Company.

Jones, V. F., & Jones, L. S. (1997). *Comprehensive classrooms: Creating communities of support and solving problems.* Boston: Allyn & Bacon.

Keating, B., Pickering, M., Slack, B., & White, J. (1990). *A guide to positive discipline: Helping students make responsible choices.* Boston: Allyn & Bacon.

Ladson-Billing, G. (1994). *The dreamkeepers: Successful teachers of African American children.* San Francisco: Jossey-Bass.

Lightfoot, S. L. (1978). *Worlds apart: Relationships between families and schools.* New York: Basic Books.

Meeks, A. (1998). America's teachers: Much to celebrate. *Educational Leadership, 55*(5), 87–91.

O'Hara, W. P., Pollard, K. M., Mann, T. L., & Kent, M. M., (1991). *African Americans in the 1900s.* Washington, DC: Population Reference Bureau.

Pang, V. A., & Barba, R. H. (1995). The power of culture: Building culturally affirming instruction. In C. Grant (Ed.), *Educating for diversity: An anthology of multicultural voices.* Boston: Allyn & Bacon.

Raschke, H. J., & Raschke, V. J. (1979). Family conflict and children's self-concepts: A comparison of intact and single parent families. *Journal of Marriage and the Family, 41,* 367–374.

Rosenthal, R., & Jacobson, L. (1968). *The Pygmalion in the classroom.* San Francisco: Holt, Rinehart, & Winston.

Sanders, S. (1987). Cultural conflicts: An important factor in academic failures of American Indian students. *Journal of Multicultural Counseling and Development, 15*(2), 81–90.

Sleeter, C. E., & Grant, C. A. (1993). *Making choices for multicultural education: Five approaches to race, class, and gender.* Upper Saddle River, NJ: Merrill/Prentice Hall.

Sosa, A. (1991). *Thorough and fair: Creating routes to success for Mexican American students.* Charleston, WV: ERIC Clearinghouse on Rural Education and Small Schools.

Stocklinski, J., & Miller-Colbert, J. (1991). The Comer process: Moving from "I" to "we." *Principal, 70*(3), 18–19.

Swadener, B. B., Cahill, B., Arnold, M. S., & Marsh, M. M. (1995). Cultural and gender identity in early childhood: Anti-bias, culturally inclusive pedagogy with young learners. In C. Grant (Ed.), *Educating for diversity: An anthology of multicultural voices.* Boston: Allyn & Bacon.

Swisher, (1991). *American Indian/Alaskan Native learning styles: Research and practice.* Charleston, WV: ERIC: Cress. Appalachia Educational Laboratory.

Thornton, M. C. (1995). Population dynamics and ethnic attitudes: The context of American education in the twenty-first century. In C. Grant (Ed.), *Educating for diversity: An anthology of multicultural voices.* Boston: Allyn & Bacon.

U.S. Census Bureau. (1993). Poverty in the United States. In *Current population research series* (pp. 60–185). Washington, DC: U.S. Government Printing Office.

Webb, R. B., & Sherman, R. R. (1989). *Schooling in society* (2nd ed.). Upper Saddle River, NJ: Merrill/Prentice Hall.

Wise, A. E., & Gollnick, D. M. (1996). America in demographic denial. *Quality Teaching, 5*(2), 1–2.

Zirpoli, T. J., & Melloy, K. J. (1996). *Behavior management: Applications for teachers & parents.* Upper Saddle River, NJ: Merrill/Prentice Hall.

The Subject Matters

❖ ❖ ❖

The true aim of everyone who aspires to be a teacher should be not to impart his own opinion, but to kindle minds.

Frederick W. Robertson

You may write me down in history
With your bitter, twisted lies,
You may trod me in the very dirt
But still, like dust, I'll rise.

Maya Angelou

I finish a unit on "racism and Native Americans" for an education class and receive a low grade because my project is called "inappropriate subject material" to be taught to children. I am outraged. My classmates treat my anger and insight with pity; I know they see me as having emotional problems, or, at best, as being politically extreme . . . .

Rosemary Gonzales

Nothing in life is to be feared. It is only to be understood.

Marie Curie

8 Telling and Critiquing Stories of Our Teaching—for Literacy

Mary Louise Gomez
University of Wisconsin-Madison

> The ability of story (prose and poetry) to transform the storyteller
> and the listener into something or someone else is shamanistic
> (Anzaldua, 1988, p. 30).

My 9-year-old daughter Lily[1] has always loved books and stories. In preschool, she never napped. Rather, she gained permission to lie on her cot and "read" a bagful of picture books that I brought from home every day. We have always shared a few books, or a chapter or two, before bedtime. Four years ago, as she struggled to conquer her fears of being in a new school—where noisy "big kids" were in the halls and on the playground—she began to plead for one last story before she slept— "one from the mind"—as she said.

So, each night during that kindergarten year, after we read a few books, and talked about her day, Lily and I composed stories about a hero named Peter, whom we had originally come to know as a character in a favorite book. Now, he romped through our collaborative stories as a citizen of Blueberry Land, Triangle Land, or some other exotic and faraway place. In the pattern of these shared tales, Peter's primary role was to enter a story just when the troublesome children of a kind king or queen required rescuing. Regardless of how careless a story's royal offspring had been in leaving a gate unlocked or wandering too far from their caretakers, Peter was always able to save them. Each day when the monsters were conquered and the kingdom was safe, Peter returned home to his mother. Then our chapter closed, and Lily drifted off to dream.

Anzaldua (1988) says such stories magically link tellers and listeners. They provide solace from the frightening demons that lurk in children's dark bedrooms late at night. Stories also draw us to adventure from which we would otherwise be barred by time, geography, or physical prowess. And they help to "render the horizons of others more accessible" as "we seek to understand landscapes other than our own" (Barone, 1987, pp. 14-15).

Stories make permeable the boundaries of our own and others' life experiences (Smith, 1991) and enable the appraisal of these experiences (Rosen, 1985). Through telling and listening to stories, individuals are able to "put the personal and particular into perspective" (Rich, 1979, p. 43) and to fashion "alternative notions of truth and

---

A draft of this paper was presented at the American Educational Research Association meeting in New Orleans, April 1994.

representation" (Helle, 1991, p. 50). As people, we interpret and secure, challenge and reinterpret our experiences through storytelling.

Narayan (1991) sums the responses of researchers from anthropology, philosophy, psychology, and theology to the question "What happens when we tell stories?" when she writes: "By arranging the flux and welter of experience around a narrative line, we make sense of our pasts, plan for our futures, and comprehend the lives of others" (p. 114). Narayan views stories as opportunities for tellers and listeners to take an alternative perspective on our experiences, to see our lives as composed of stories that can be "observed" and evaluated (p. 125).

Rosenwald and Ochberg (1992) argue that it is the storyteller in particular who has the potential to be transformed through tales:

> The stories people tell about themselves are interesting not only for the events and characters they describe but also for something in the construction of the stories themselves. How individuals recount their histories—what they emphasize and omit, their stance as protagonists or victims, the relationship the story establishes between teller and audience—all shape what individuals can claim of their own lives. Personal stories are not merely a way of telling someone (or oneself) about one's life; they are the means by which identities may be fashioned. It is this formative—and sometimes deformative power of life stories that make them important. (p. 1)

Rosenwald and Ochberg remind us that stories are fashioned by the individual teller within the social and institutional discourses available to her as they acknowledge the possibilities for self-understanding that are inherent in the stories we tell.

I have never spoken directly with Lily, my storytelling partner, about the parallels between her fears of "big kids" who fill school hallways with their large, jostling bodies and who accidentally bump into her when she is least expecting it—and the children of Blueberry and Triangle Land who are stalked by creatures prowling the royal woods. Yet, her requests for our jointly constructed stories began after she had first expressed her fears of the sixth-, seventh- and eighth-graders at her school, and ended later that winter when she became more comfortable with their presence.

Unlike the children in our stories, she had no Peter to rescue her. However, through the telling, I believe Lily came to see that she could conquer her fears and rescue—or transform—herself as we made the strange familiar in our tales. Through telling her stories, Lily gained an alternative perspective on her experiences, one in which she saw herself, like Peter, as someone who could "conquer demons" and return safely home.

Many times since we told the "Peter stories," I have thought about how beneficial the storytelling was for Lily as she became accustomed to a new school, and for me as a mother who wanted to support her in meeting this challenge. Our storytelling was facilitated by the bonds that connect us, as mother and daughter; as people who share a language background, socioeconomic group, gender, and ethnicity; as people who daily work and play together.

As a teacher educator and teacher, I dream of ways I and my colleagues in classrooms around the country might similarly support and sustain children's learning and adults' understandings. Yet, I recognize that it is unrealistic to expect that teachers and students in the United States today share many of the situations that link my daughter and me. Opportunities for teachers to know the feelings and imagine the experiences of the children in our classrooms are inhibited as the student population becomes more diverse and the teacher population remains homogeneous (see Gomez, 1994, for a discussion of how United States teachers' race, socioeconomic group, gender, sexual preferences, and language backgrounds affect their perspectives on diverse student populations' abilities to learn).

As the differences between those teaching and those taught continue to grow, the barriers to understanding one another appear to become greater. The possibilities for teachers forging personal relationships with students and for developing curricula and instructional practices that assist students' learning and meet their needs for academic success become narrowed.

Delpit (1988) contends that teachers can develop personal relationships with students and meet their academic needs only when we become "vulnerable enough to allow our world to turn upside down in order to allow the realities of others to edge themselves into our consciousness" (p. 297). Delpit says we have to develop an insiders' perspective on children's lives if we are to help them learn in school. As teachers, we must see school and its demands from the perspective of children and their families as well as from our own.

In this chapter, I discuss how telling stories of my teaching has allowed me to turn my teaching world upside down and develop new perspectives on my practice. A focus on these stories is teaching for "literacy," an idea that encompasses the teaching of the technical skills of reading, writing, listening, and speaking, but is also more than that. Like Giroux (1993), I see literacy as a means of organizing, inscribing, containing, and contesting meaning.

✧ Telling Teaching Stories: My Own

For the past few years, I have been asking the question (Gomez & Tabachnick, 1992; Abt-Perkins & Gomez, 1993, Gomez & Abt-Perkins, in press): What happens when teachers tell stories about themselves and their work? I have found that in telling teaching stories—narratives in which a teacher and her classroom practices play a central role—individuals can conduct a self-critique of their complex interactions with others in a fresh light. In particular, I am trying to understand how telling teaching stories to their peers (over time and in a supportive setting) can help teachers puzzle through their behaviors toward different students; question accepted schooling practices; unpack the social, economic, and institutional forces against which children and their families struggle; and devise new ways to teach that invite all children to learn.

While I have been a storyteller and writer since childhood, I began in the 1980s to explore formally what Anzaldua (1988) calls the transformative and magical power of personal narrative. Then, through a confluence of teaching and research opportunities, I began considering the potentials of storytelling for teaching. Later in this chapter, I tell about one way I began to consider how telling stories of teaching might affect teachers' thinking and actions.

In 1989, two colleagues, Bob Tabachnick and Ken Zeichner, asked me to write a chapter for their book, which focused on inquiry-oriented teacher education. They asked me to write about a university course I taught that focused on teaching language arts in the elementary school. They were interested in the social justice orientation of the course—how I taught and how students responded to my teaching. They wanted to know what grounded my teaching—why I taught in particular ways, what drove my choices for reading and activities.

I pulled out old paperbacks and recalled reading about teaching and school reform when I was in my 20s—works by Axline (1964), Dennison (1969), Featherstone (1971), Holt (1964, 1967, 1974), Koch (1970), Kohl (1967), Kozol (1967), and Stuart (1970a, 1970b). I also thought about the influence of my father, Manuel Gomez, who explained by his words and actions what he saw as each person's obligation to care for others. I remembered children whom I had taught—in particular, David, who was a first-grader in Black River, Vermont, in the 1970s. I contemplated how I had felt called to teach by the promise it held for changing children's lives. I remembered how I had tried to live out my ideals as a student teacher with David and his friends, and I wrote the following story:

> Twenty years ago in a small Vermont milltown where the looms had long been silent, I was a student teacher. My experiences that year mark my teaching to this day, for it was then that I became David's foster mother. I was drawn to David from the moment I entered his first-grade classroom for my year-long student teaching. David was small and brown; his eyes were large and liquid, sorrowful. He could not identify the letters of the alphabet in September, nor could he do so in May. David's biological mother was a single parent and an alcoholic; she was an absent and sometimes abusive parent. While she was hospitalized during the winter that year, David came to live with me and my husband.
>
> Like many of his peers at Black River School, David and his mother lived in terrible poverty produced by the closing, decades earlier, of the town's factories. Frequently hungry and sleepy, he and his classmates walked from flats adjacent to the railyard to the town's one elementary school. There, Ms. Paterson, their teacher, and I attempted to construct a sanctuary from life as these children knew it. We made cakes for our parties—photographing each step of the preparation and writing group-constructed tales of the work. We made centers for the children's listening, clay modeling, housekeeping, exploration with magnets, and dramatic play. We threw the preprimers and primers for the basal reading series in the closet and gathered books from the town and school libraries for reading. First in the school to put aside textbooks and to teach in ways that we believed were child-centered, we became an admired team.
>
> Late in the springtime, when my student teaching—evaluated as highly successful by all—was nearly completed, David's mother was discharged from the hospital. The state social services department required that we return David to her. Soon afterwards, my husband and I finished graduate school, and we moved away, leaving David in Black River. Neither the social worker assigned to David nor his mother encouraged us to remain in contact with him. So, unhappy about returning him to his flat by the tracks, I buried myself in my new teaching job in the Midwest and did not write or call. I have thought a lot about David in the past years. He would be in his mid-twenties now—about my age when he lived with me (Gomez, 1991).

My reflections about my student teaching in Black River helped me understand how, in attempting to create a sanctuary from their lives outside of school, Ms. Paterson and I failed to build the critical links that bind children's homes to their school classrooms. Missing from our teaching was recognition that all children come to school with knowledge, skills, and experiences upon which we can draw, build, and expand. Our reading and writing program focused on activities and ideas that Ms. Paterson and I chose because we thought the children would enjoy and learn from them. We chose the themes, the books to read, and the forms that the writing would take.

Ms. Paterson and I did not invite the children and their families to make this school their school, because we wanted to replace what they brought to school with what we knew and valued. We failed to value the stories of David and his friends, other than to confirm our own vision of their families' pathology. We did not learn to listen to the children's voices and the voices of their families. Therefore, we could not, in Erasmus's (1989) words, "extend, rather than limit the possibilities these children [brought] to school" (p. 274).

I began to see my intentions as a teacher and the outcomes of those intentions in fresh light. My writing was a telling of my teaching stories, or personal narratives of classroom life. The telling provided me with the time and opportunity to revisit my practices with an imagined sympathetic audience of peers. The telling provided me with multiple perspectives on my work: the perspective of an insider on my teaching as a person who wanted to make children's lives better. It also provided me with the perspective of an outsider, someone who could see that my idea of making children's lives better was to make their lives more like the one I had experienced in a working-class family with middle-class aspirations. I had interpreted a better life as a middle-class life.

In responding to the request to write about why and how I taught a university course, I engaged in self-critique. I interrogated my intentions and what grounded them. I looked closely at how I had enacted those intentions. I analyzed their outcomes for the children. I saw how what I had thought about as classroom teaching grounded in concerns for social justice was actually entrenched in middle-class perspectives on what children should know and learn and do.

❖ Telling Teaching Stories: With Prospective Teachers in an Experimental Program of Teacher Education

During the same period in which I wrote the book chapter, Bob Tabachnick and I were co-directing an experimental multicultural program of teacher education called Teaching for Diversity (1987-92). In the same years, I was developing a graduate course called Teaching Writing to Diverse Learners (now more aptly titled Literacy, Culture, and Schooling). The teacher education (and accompanying research) was aimed at helping prospective teachers prepare for U.S. elementary classrooms where privileged children primarily from White, middle-class backgrounds sit side by side with peers from low-income families, who are often also families of color. Our program was predicated on multicultural and social reconstructionist theories.[2] Our objective was to prepare teachers who were committed to and successful at teaching everyone's children.

Our program spanned the three semesters that the university students were enrolled in course work and field experiences. The students mirrored their peers in the U.S. teaching population: most were White, middle-class, suburban- and rural-born, English-speaking, heterosexual females. Students worked in one of two schools with children from a variety of socioeconomic backgrounds—50 percent of whom in each building were children of color. Most children in these two schools spoke English as a first language; however, there were children from many different language backgrounds enrolled in English as Second Language programs in each building.

Each semester, we led weekly seminars with two teachers from the schools. Over time, we found that our weekly meetings provided opportunities for students in our cohort group to get to know one another well. We also found that the conversations, while guided by readings and assignments, were most exciting and challenging when students talked to one another about their teaching and their understandings of it.

We began to explore how focusing on telling teaching stories in the seminars provided the student teachers with the opportunity to do what I had done for myself in my writing—to critique their classroom practices in relation to their goals for themselves and their students and in relation to the outcomes of their work. We wanted prospective teachers to recognize links between classroom action and children's lives outside of school. We wanted them to see how their perspectives on and interpretations of children's motives and behavior are rooted in their race, socioeconomic group, gender, and sexual preferences just as the children's actions are also rooted in their backgrounds and experiences. We wanted our students to understand how they as teachers and how schools as institutions transformed the multi-faceted, complex dilemmas that families confront into school problems. We wanted prospective teachers to see themselves as a community that had collective responsibility for and investment in the children in their care. Through storytelling, we aimed to question our teaching goals; to consider effective alternatives to our teaching practices so that we continually focused on who the children were and what strengths as well as needs they brought to school; and to reconsider our roles and behaviors as individual teachers. We tried to see ourselves as members of not only a classroom community of children to which we were obligated, but also of a school community and of larger communities outside of school to which we were obligated for social action and justice.

Bobby Jo Johnson's Story

This story illustrates how, through telling teaching stories, prospective teachers were challenged to think about teaching for a literacy that was focused on increasing children's skills of reading and writing and also to consider literacy as a way that people made and challenged meanings. Bobby Jo Johnson, the narrator of this story, is a White woman born in rural Wisconsin and raised on a farm as the youngest of 11 children. She was 25 years old and a candidate for a second bachelor's degree (her first was in economics) as an elementary teacher when she enrolled in our program, Teaching for Diversity.

In a pedagogical autobiography Bobby Jo wrote at the beginning of the program, she said that until she had completed her first university degree she had not thought much about teaching because she thought "money was a critical factor" in her life. However, as she grew older, and was not happy with who she was or what she was doing, she decided she wanted to be a teacher and "make a difference in the lives of [her] students and help as many children as [she] could be lovers of learning." Bobby Jo wanted to be like her favorite teacher, Mrs. Southfield, from second grade. She said,

> I want to be the Mrs. Southfield for every student I have. I want to reach out to the students and help them discover new, exciting interests; to create an environment

where all feel welcome and safe so that they can be comfortable in their learning. But, most of all, I want to be thoughtful and reflective enough to see my weaknesses and mistakes I make in order to correct them. This is what I believe a good teacher does.

At the end of October 1992, during her final field experience as a student teacher, Bobby Jo chose to teach a multiweek unit focused on the presidential election to her fourth-grade students. She did so because the elementary school was located in the politically active eastern corridor of the city and the children in he class talked continually about the election. Many of the girls in the class were especially concerned about the stand that each candidate took on a woman's choice to control childbearing. On their own initiative, several girls were tracking how the candidates represented their views at various campaign stops and with different constituent groups.

As she began planning for the unit, Bobby Jo asked the children to write down questions they had about elections, particularly presidential elections. She used the girls' questions about women's choice as an example of the things the children might wonder about. Once all students had posed their queries, she used them as jumping-off points for the centers that she and a peer, Margaret Smith, who taught another fourth-grade class across the hall, would develop with their cooperating teachers.

Eight centers were developed for the two classes. One featured campaign booths for each candidate where the platforms of Bush, Clinton, and Perot were available for students to read and analyze. Later, the children would stage a mock debate with the data they gathered from the center. At other centers, children could design and construct campaign buttons, banners, and slogans for their favorite candidate/s or about some issue, like children's right to vote. In other centers, children voted in mock election booths, read biographies of each candidate, and analyzed data from various nations regarding who could vote and how voting rights had been determined.

As the days passed, and the actual election drew near, Bobby Jo observed that most of the fourth-graders appeared interested and engaged in the activities. She also observed that the children who had been labeled emotionally disturbed, four of whom were students in her class, seemed to be having fewer self-control problems—fighting, name-calling and general "goofy," off-task behavior—than usual. Bobby Jo said,

> I know we have talked a lot about starting from what kids know and like and do and all that. But, for the first time, I saw how putting everything together . . . in one big unit for over an hour a day made all the difference for kids who usually can't make it all day in our room without some scene and Bob [guidance counselor] or Laurie [the educational assistant] coming on the run. Kids like Marvin and Corry and Danny, who are always popping off at someone or yelling, "I ain't gonna do that [four letter word]!" are hanging in there. Now, maybe they're not reading all of the words in the biographies or the campaign literature, but they are listening to the tapes I made and sitting there and when we talk about the centers, they have something to say. They're not just hanging over their desks with their heads down or trying to make Rollie cry or get angry by snapping a rubber band her way. Marvin was here all day for three days running. Amazing!
>
> What gets me is how during all of this good learning, I hear how we're going to do more testing with Marvin [an African-American boy] so we can label him CD

(cognitively disabled) along with ED (emotionally disturbed). I got so excited today because the learning disabilities staff is trying to tell us that he's done so low on the testing for learning disabilities that . . . I don't want to say it, but that he's mentally retarded. And I'm like . . . there's no way [that is so]. I said that I can prove they are wrong. For one thing, I mean I've watched him listen to a tape and follow along to the reading. I mean I cued him for the first few lines. And when I looked back, he was already on the second column. And, you know, he is able to follow and write the words. This election unit [I taught] really helped me to see how smart he is because all the different learning stations let him use what he knew and what he was interested in knowing. I am going to go to the m-team meeting and argue for Marvin. We need to be better teachers. It's not Marvin—yes, he's certainly got his problems, but we shouldn't label him and say it (not learning) is his fault.

Bobby Jo's descriptions of Marvin as a child who *could* learn and her analyses of who should take responsibility for teaching that would help him build on his interests and the ways he learned best unleashed a torrent of comments from her listening peers. Several other students also gave examples of children of color in their classrooms who were "in a queue" for appointments with various psychologists and learning specialists for testing that would almost certainly result in their being labeled cognitively disabled or emotionally disturbed.

Belinda Davis told about Latanya, an African American child in her kindergarten class, who was struggling with many challenges, including young parents who were jailed. Latanya loved school and was a favored friend of many children in the class. She was small in stature and active—always in motion—and had a sweet disposition. She and some of her siblings were lovingly cared for by their grandmother.

Latanya could not identify any alphabet letters when she came to school in September and did not know how to read or write her name. By December, Latanya could identify many, but not all of the alphabet letters and could write her first name (inconsistently), but not her last. Nonetheless, Belinda saw Latanya as making great progress in both her development of the traditional compartmentalized kindergarten skills of reading and writing and in the ways she talked about and drew about her understandings of the books read to the class, the trips they took around the city, and the classroom activities of measuring, counting, and cooking in which the children took part. Like Bobby Jo's pledge to Marvin, Belinda vowed to keep Latanya from being labeled *disabled.*

"Disabled, yeah," she said, "let's be honest, they want to call her retarded and put her in a special class away from the other kids! I'm going to fight as hard as I can. I'm so disappointed, you know. Even my principal (an African American woman whom Belinda greatly admired) seems to support this testing. I think people just kept talking to her about what's wrong with Latanya and she has started to believe it or wonder about it, too." Belinda felt sad and angry, but also stronger as she realized she was not alone in challenging how low-income children of color in her school were slotted for labeling and "treatment." Knowing that her peers agreed that Latanya and Marvin were smart and could do well in school gave Belinda confidence that she could struggle with Bobby Jo on the children's behalf.

Bobby Jo summed up what she learned from the unit and the story she had told about it to us all a few days after it was completed:

I chose to teach this unit about the election because it was all around them. Lots of kids' parents were campaign workers and the news about the election was everywhere—on their lawns, in their mailboxes, on television, at their dinner tables. What I did not anticipate was how teaching about the election helped me understand how I could stand up and fight for a child's right not to be called disabled. I actually had records of what Marvin could do when he was interested in what he was learning.

Bobby Jo's story helped her understand what had made the difference in literacy learning for Marvin. He could read and write when he was interested, when the tools to support his reading and writing were in place, and when he could contribute to class conversations. Bobby Jo's peers, like Belinda, saw more clearly how they, too, might question ongoing school practices of slotting and labeling learners—especially children of color who were often testing targets—and find ways to act against these for children's benefit. Together, they saw how different meanings and responsibilities for literacy teaching and learning could be assigned that might not result in some children's categorization.

✛ Telling Teaching Stories: In a Graduate Course with Practicing Teachers

The graduate course I was developing at the same time focused on helping practicing teachers develop commitments to reflection and to understanding teaching as a negotiation of meanings. My purpose was to support teachers' reflections on what teaching for literacy meant and on how they might enact a pedagogy that supported their best intentions, despite the societal and institutional constraints on doing so. The syllabus told participants that the course was designed to do the following:

1. Help us understand the perspectives different people have of themselves, of others, and of their experiences with literacy—particularly as these experiences demonstrate the varied ways people are literate and how their literacies conflict with or are not recognized or are not enhanced by schools, schooling, and teachers.
2. Help us develop understandings about ourselves and the personal and professional perspectives that we bring to teaching for and about literacy with different students. Our understandings will develop in part through critical reflections conducted by telling stories about our teaching, our students, and ourselves.
3. Provide opportunities for us to examine, re-examine, and alter the perspectives we bring to schooling different people, and to alter the practices we conduct—in a community of teachers engaged in the same endeavor.
4. Provide opportunities for us to read, discuss, and write about theories of narrative and link them to our understandings of ourselves as teachers and of the roots and outcomes of our literacy teaching.

Through the course, I hoped to heighten teachers' awareness of literacy teaching and learning as activities, on which so much emphasis is placed in schools, teacher education, and in the assessment of individuals. Those activities include reading, discussing, and answering questions about the work of published authors and writing stories, poems, and essays. I also hoped to encourage thinking about ways that people make, negotiate, and contest meanings among others, across time, and in various places.

My intention was that participants acknowledge the sources of their own understandings of what it means to be literate, to examine how they have enacted these understandings, and to envision new practices that open their classrooms to dialogue and debate. In the class, I ask students to read theoretical pieces in which teachers and researchers (e.g., Lisa Delpit, Ann Haas Dyson, Bernardo Ferdman, Paulo Freire, Martin Nystrand, Denny Taylor) lay out their perspectives on teaching for literacy as a potentially dialogic and liberating process, and personal narratives in which poets, essayists, artists, and others from diverse backgrounds (e.g., Michelle Cliff, Mary Crow Dog, Carlos Fuentes, Paula Gunn Allen, David Mura) tell their stories of becoming literate.

The course has four key activities: Students write and share their literacy autobiographies, write weekly journals or reflective essays about the readings, construct projects in which they link their theories about how literacy is encouraged and constrained at home and at school with their practices as classroom teachers or teacher educators, and write and share stories of their teaching with the group.

The readings serve as jumping-off points for the discussions as teachers explore how their personal perspectives on learners and the mandates of schools as institutions often deny the knowledge and skills people bring to classrooms, as we reify particular, school-based proficiencies of reading and writing. Through our discussion of the readings and through the telling of our teaching stories, we explore ways we might enter into relations with children premised on efforts at mutual understanding—respecting, supporting, and sharing their social realities as much as we can as teachers.

Some class members are classroom teachers working on their master's degrees. They most often tell stories of their current work with children and their daily struggles to help children learn to read and write—and to learn *through* reading and writing. Other master's and doctoral students are on leave from or have left public school teaching to pursue college and university careers. Often, they are employed in our university teacher education program supervising the field experiences of prospective teachers. These students generally tell two sorts of stories, those in which they examine their past classroom teaching and those in which they examine their work with prospective teachers.

My goal as the course instructor is to provide an environment where people with diverse backgrounds and experiences can come together to tell teaching stories—to support one another as they challenge their personal perspectives and the institutional perspectives on teaching, learning, and learners, and to critique their own and each other's classroom practices. The following pages contain stories from teachers enrolled in the course. They show how an opportunity to reflect on one's perspectives and practices with an audience of supportive peers can help us reconsider our understandings of teaching.

The stories are from a semester in which 15 graduate students (13 women and 2 men) from diverse backgrounds were enrolled in the course; three were working as classroom teachers at the time. The group ranged in age from 23 to 48. Two of the students were international students for whom English was not a first language. Three of the students from the United States identified themselves as persons of color (one African American woman, one bilingual Latina and one Latino who spoke conversational Spanish as well as his native English); all others identified themselves as White, native English speakers. All but one were either classroom teachers or had been classroom teachers. These cursory descriptions are offered to give readers a glimpse of the varied backgrounds and experiences the students brought to the course and our discussions.

For 15 weeks, we met every Tuesday evening for 2 1/2 hours. While we often told brief stories about ourselves as we explored our understandings of the readings, I also asked that the individuals write personal narratives about their practices three times during the semester. I asked that each person who felt comfortable in doing so read them to the group members, who would comment on the narratives or question the teller. The following stories were told one evening in the 10th week of the semester. They were the second occasion of the semester in which we had told teaching stories. Students were asked to write about their current or past literacy teaching in light of our conversations and the interpretations of the reading we had conducted over the prior weeks.

Lesley Colabucci's Story

One of the first to tell her story was Lesley Colabucci, a master's degree candidate in multicultural education. Lesley, a recent graduate of an eastern university teacher education program, was a teaching assistant in a course on teaching children's literature in which prospective teachers were enrolled. While Lesley usually spoke confidently and easily, she hesitated as she began her story.

> I'm "out there" a bit on this one. I am going to tell you about my teaching last year
> while I was a student teacher in a first-grade class. I have thought about this one child,
> Billy, a lot and I have told stories about him to many people. But now I see differently
> my teaching of him and the responses of children in the class to him. I think while it
> may not sound like it at first, this is a story about literacy, about making and
> challenging meaning and about a discourse that I and the children in my class
> developed when Billy challenged us.

Lesley told us how, in the third week of school, Billy came to her class. He had moved frequently in his life because his parents had separated when he was very young and he had lived alternately with his mother, in a foster home, and with his father. Billy had been sexually abused on many occasions by adults in parental or guardianship roles. He created problems in the class by masturbating openly and frequently; by urinating on other children; by stealing other children's belongings; by eating crayons, pencils, and other supplies; and by licking the carpet, floors, and chalkboard.

Lesley said that for several weeks, she and the other children were upset by Billy's behavior and did all the things people do in school when someone does not follow the rules. Lesley felt compelled to send Billy to the office when he did not comply with her requests to stop stealing other children's belongings or urinating on his peers. Daily, Billy pushed the boundaries of Lesley's patience as well as the patience of her cooperating teacher and the other children. The following lines from Lesley's written story illustrate how, over time, the children and teachers found a way to live with and talk about Billy:

> Then, on the last day of full-time teaching, Billy mooned the class. . . . . I won't even
> begin to get into stories of Billy masturbating in class, of little girls coming up to me to
> complain (My common response was, "Well, [name of child complaining], what do

you think we should do about that?"), of Billy pulling shards of rusted metal out of trash cans, of Billy stealing things from everyone.

And I don't even really know how to get into explaining how we, as a class, coped with everything. But we did. So, on the last day of my teaching that fall, when Billy mooned the class, I knew that we had developed a discourse of our own, a literacy of sorts. Here's how it worked:

We were sitting around singing and playing the drums. I was sitting in the front of the room and students were taking turns coming up in two's to beat the rhythm of the song on the drum. I was pretty much lost in the music and fun of it all, to be honest, so I was shocked when Frederica came up and quietly tapped me on the shoulder.

"Yes, Frederica?"

"Billy just mooned the class."

"Oh."

"I don't think anyone else saw."

"Okay, well thanks for telling me."

"Sure."

At the end of the day, I told the county psychologist, who happened to be around, about the incident, and before Frederica left I made sure she was okay and told her to tell her mom to call me if she was concerned. . . . As I was driving home that day I felt better than I ever had about myself as a teacher. Now I see that my students and I had developed—no, created—our own literacy. We knew what to do now when Billy was having trouble. We didn't have to cringe or cry or scream or get upset or bother him in any way. We simply had to make sure he wasn't hurting himself or anyone else and go on with what we were doing.

This isn't to say that we decided to ignore or marginalize Billy; we worked as hard as we could to include him and to help him cope. The key was we knew how to cope as a class. How to express ourselves about Billy in a way that freed *us* up for learning. I don't know if *Billy* will ever be *free* (Lesley's emphasis).

Lesley later told me that when she realized she had to write a story for our class, she opened her "Billy" file. Previously, she had written poetry about Billy and letters to him that she had never mailed. But, until that night, when she began to plan what she would tell us, she had not thought about the class responses to Billy as a form of "containing" and making new meanings, as being experiences of meaning. "Then I knew," she said, "as I wrote, that we had made new meanings and contested old ones, about Billy, about what it meant to be him and how we could respond differently."

Someone asked Lesley, "What happened, to Billy and everyone, after you left the class?" She continued her story:

One day, later that spring, I came back to visit the children. I walked in on Mrs. Norris [my cooperating teacher] just as tears began streaming down her face. I stood in awe for I don't know how long. Linda was a terrific and experienced teacher. I had attributed my failures with Billy to my amateur-ness so this made no sense to me. Finally, a student spoke out, "Mrs. Norris has allergies." The student and I stared at one another for a minute, knowing allergies had nothing to do with it. I didn't even have to look at Billy to know. Then, I began singing, *If You're All for Freedom*, a Sweet Honey in the Rock version of *If You're Happy and You Know It*, that my students loved. Linda crept quietly out of the room without notice. She returned in time for the last chorus:

If you're all for freedom, clap your hands (clap, clap)
Stomp your feet (stomp, stomp)
Shout hooray ('Hooray!')

Billy had a huge smile on his face as he clapped and stomped and shouted, "Hooray!"

Our university class was quiet for a long time after Lesley concluded. We were thinking about Billy, and Lesley, and what they had both learned that year. Lesley believes that in some ways, Billy found a place for himself in that classroom, a place to learn. She believes that in telling her story to her peers in the class, she acquired new perspectives on her practices. Lesley saw herself again from the viewpoint of an insider to her teaching experience, someone who was angry that Billy was abused and suffered and who was distressed at how Billy's misery manifested itself in classroom behavior that upset everyone, including him.

She also developed an outsider's perspective, one that enabled her to see how over time, she and the children had developed a way of responding to Billy's behavior that made a place for everyone in the classroom to learn academic knowledge and skills, as well as to acquire more personal understandings of suffering and how people live with it. While Lesley still saw many of her individual interactions with Billy and their outcomes as a failure due to her status as an "amateur," she also recognized that she and the children had negotiated new meanings for what they had formerly seen as a child's "bad" behavior.

As listeners, we also developed new understandings of teaching. Another student in the course said to me later:

I cannot get Lesley's story out of my head. I have tried, because it is so tragic and it is hard to keep thinking about it. Every time I think about Billy and how Lesley and the children learned to think about him and what he did, I see how I do the same things. I make a child's actions, especially when they are "bad ones," into something so important that the only way we can all think about Barika or Sam is to think about what they do wrong and how mad they make all of us. Then, that's who Bari and Sam are, who they become for everybody, "bad." But Lesley helped her kids think about Billy in a different way as a person who was hurt. . . . Maybe it's good [she smiled] I can't stop thinking about Billy.

Martha Scheibel's Story

With uncharacteristic hesitation and a flushed face, Martha Scheibel, a White, 42-year-old special education teacher with two decades of experience broke the silence that evening:

Well, I came to understand something new myself when I was thinking about this assignment. I am going to tell you a story about my son, Benjamin. It's also about understanding . . . that comes out of the thinking I did preparing to tell you this story tonight. This is hard for me. It is so close, so . . . personal.

A few weeks ago Daniel [another class member] spoke about how he was concerned that we were addressing the reading of the texts in a superficial way that distanced us from the people and ideas about which we read. I was thinking about what he said and I am going to tell . . . something about my 13-year-old son.

Martha told about two assignments that one of her teenage sons, Benjamin, recently had been given in school. One was to read a mystery book and write a report about how that book exemplified the elements of texts in the mystery genre. As an elementary student, Benjamin had loved reading and being read to. But now he resisted reading at every turn. He grudgingly accepted Martha's maternal efforts to help him complete the assignment and agreed to read a 100-page mystery featuring the relationship between two brothers.

Martha tells how, in struggling with Benjamin, she developed a new understanding of literacy teaching and learning in school and why it so often does not connect with students:

A few weeks ago, Benjamin's language arts teacher presented a unit to his seventh-graders on people with disabilities in observance of National Americans with Disabilities Week. One of the assignments was to write a multifaceted paper about people with disabilities and about what the kids perceived to be their own disabilities.

Benjamin came to me in the kitchen to discuss his writing. We talked and he wrote thoughtfully about how important it is not to group people with disabilities. He wrote persuasively that the person should come before the disability. He didn't understand how he could write about advantages of being disabled, as the teacher had asked, because he thought the advantages were "not worth it." I agreed. "My disability is that I hate to read and that's what you have to do in school."

This lone sentence in my son's writing was the most powerful. The reality I confronted that day will be etched forever in my mind. What could I say? *You can read! Do it more and then you will like it. Oh, come on, Benjamin, at least you can do it! Imagine not being able to read! You just have to put forward a little effort. Change, Benjamin; it's your problem.*

I had heard his complaints before about how hard it was, how boring it was, how long it takes. He and I talked to teachers about his struggles. *Was I truly listening? Was he really saying I hate to read all this meaningless stuff; I'm at a disability, and there's nothing I can do about it? Wouldn't Benjamin change if he could?*

The truth that became a reality for me that day is what Denny Taylor calls the ultimate irony . . . "that when children are given the opportunity to create an authentic foundation for their own existence they do not fail" (1993, p. 26). Taylor says that "we consistently underestimate the enormous potential of children to participate in the construction of their own learning environments." She says we "ignore their abilities" and interests and "blame them" when they "get it wrong."

"So Benjamin," I queried, "when is that mystery book report due?"

"Day after tomorrow."

"So, you've finished the book?"

"Page 30."

"Thirty pages more to read?"

"Nope, seventy."

Silence. . . . I'm thinking. *He doesn't care about filling in the blanks on the book report form. I wonder if he knows what the elements of a mystery are? He doesn't care about getting the assignment handed in on time or maybe at all. So, I stopped. I resisted the ultimatums and the lecture and the consequence giving.*

"Seventy pages. That would be thirty-five a night, unless we just can't put it down!" I said with a grin. "Meet you in your room tonight after dinner."

Benjamin and I read that forsaken mystery together. My boys had broken it to me a few years back that they were too old to be read to. Sadly for me, our nightly reads had ceased. But, somehow Benjamin did not resist this reading. He turned over and around on the single bed next to the one I was stretched out upon as I held the book, straight-armed, above my eyes.

We talked about how the author kept us hanging on. We talked about the characters and the plot and tried to predict who killed Nick's brother. We talked about how hard it would be if Benjamin or his brother died "for real." Together, we filled in the lines of the book report. The warm memories of reading together when my kids were little came back to me. Somehow, I don't think Benjamin hated to read this time.

As I read my own book in bed that night, I heard a quiet knock on my door.

"Thanks for helping me, Mom."

When Martha finished, we asked what she had discovered—about herself, about Benjamin, about schooling? She said she didn't have any simple answers. However, she had learned for certain that the assignments Benjamin was given in school were not encouraging him to read. Rather, they pushed him away from reading as he was asked to dissect the books he read for information his teacher deemed important. Often the reading was accompanied by equally tedious writing assignments that were not connected in any way to the lives and interests of adolescents. She pulled a copy of one of Benjamin's seventh-grade English assignments from her folder:

Look at this! It is titled *Unfinished Stories* and the directions read: "Use the writing checklist below to finish one or more of the stories that follow." Printed on the bottom and back of the handout are two very short stories, one called *Steep and Deep* that opens an adventure at a quarry, and the other called *Race to Taylor's Island* in which some teenagers encourage others to race in a 3-mile swim across dangerous water. In addition to the opening paragraphs of a story, there is a short "cast of characters" for each story and questions to think about as you write. These include the following:

Have I written emphatically by:

1. Using active verbs?
2. Trimming overweight sentences and paragraphs?
3. Using precise and peppy words?
4. Using fresh figures of speech and no cliches?

Have I created good dialogue by:

1. Using idioms, if appropriate for a character?
2. Matching the character's speech and personality?

The more I have thought about Benjamin since he wrote that he hated to read, the more carefully I have read the assignments he gets. I wanted to yell from the rooftops. How can a child know what an "overweight sentence" is when he wrote it and thinks it is good? Why should my kid use peppy words if the story is sad? How could my kid know if an idiom is appropriate for a character or if the character's speech matched his personality when he didn't name or decide on the characters himself? His teacher did, and now all Ben and his friends can do is play a guessing game. How would "Mrs. Olga Beadle, an elderly woman who believes the quarry holds a startling secret" speak? Or, how would "'Scuba' Maynard, a professional underwater diver" talk? Peppily, no doubt!

Martha's words rang in our ears. A few of us wriggled in our chairs as we recalled devising similar assignments for our students. Surely, we chuckled, we hadn't asked anyone to "trim an overweight sentence"; we must have been more "sophisticated" than *that*. Martha's story reminded us how, as teachers, we have been seduced into thinking that by providing students with opportunities to read real novels, to write their own stories with scaffolds like story starters, and to self- and peer-edit, that we are connecting their lives outside school with those they live within its walls. As we listened to Martha, we recognized that Benjamin did not need to change or be fixed; he did not have a disability. We saw how Benjamin's teacher, like many of us, approached literacy teaching as a series of what Reder (1994) calls "a set of decontextualized information processing (e.g., encoding and decoding) skills, which the individual learns and then contextualizes by applying them to a progressively wider range of activities" (p. 40). We understood how teaching this way fails to acknowledge who children are and what they bring to school; teaching this way fails us all.

✥ Telling Teaching Stories: Conclusion

Perhaps Maxine Greene (1982) sums best what Bobby Jo, Lesley, Martha, and I—and our listeners—learned from telling stories of our literacy teaching:

> Teaching for literacy conceives learning as action rather than behavior. The notion of action involves the reflective taking of initiatives: trying out what has been learned by rote, acting on the so-called competencies. This is in contrast to an unreflective, semi-automatic movement through predefined sequences of what is sometimes optimistically called "mastery." A concern for beginnings, for action rather than behavior, is different than an occupation with end points, with predetermined objectives. Indeed, once teachers approach their students as novices, as newcomers to a learning community extending back through time and ahead into a future, they may well open themselves (as well as their students) to all sorts of untapped experiential possibilities. (p. 326)

I believe, like Greene, that teaching that conceives of action taken for fresh starts, just-glimpsed opportunities, and plain hopefulness is what counts in literacy curricula and instruction and in teacher education. This is not a naive view of the possibilities that lie before us; rather, it is a planned and committed endeavor in which concerns for social justice and equity ground the hard work of teachers, children, and families. It is an endeavor aimed at *all* children becoming bi- or tri-dialectal in English as they read, write, listen, and talk—for real purposes—with one another and their teachers, families, and other community members. It is an endeavor that can reap the richest and most fruitful harvest in our country's educational and social life as we offer teachers of all children occasions to tell stories of our learning and rethink our perspectives and our practices.

Acknowledgment

I thank Wayne Otto for his comments on an earlier draft of this manuscript. I am grateful to my students Bobby Jo Johnson, Lesley Colabucci, and Martha Scheibel, and to my daughter Lily Gomez Sasse for allowing me to retell their stories.

Notes

1. The names of all children and teachers in this paper who either tell stories or appear as "characters" in stories are pseudonyms except for the names of my daughter, Lily Gomez Sasse, and graduate student Lesley Colabucci.
2. The experimental teacher education program Teaching for Diversity (1987–92) was grounded in multicultural and social reconstructionist principles that suggest teachers become engaged in (a) self-reflection concerning how cultural identity frames personal development; (b) examination of the activities of classroom life as situated in a larger sociocultural milieu; and (c) collaboration with others for thinking about and conducting social action. For discussion of multicultural and social reconstructionist principles grounding teacher education, see Zeichner & Tabachnick (1991); for a critique and analysis of various approaches to multicultural education, see Sleeter & Grant (1987).

References

Abt-Perkins, D., & Gomez, M. L. (1993). A good way to begin—Examining our personal perspectives. *Language Arts, 70*(3), 193–202.

Anzaldua, G. (1988). The path of the red and black ink. In S. Walker & R. Simonson (Eds.), *The Graywolf annual five: Multicultural literacy* (pp. 13–28). St Paul, MN: Graywolf Press.

Axline, A. (1964). *Dibs: In search of self.* New York: Ballantine.

Barone, T. (1987). Educational platforms, teacher selection, and school reform: Issues emanating from a biographical case study. *Journal of Teacher Education, 38*(2), 12–17.

Delpit, L. (1988). The silenced dialogue: Power and pedagogy in educating other people's children. *Harvard Educational Review, 58,* 280–298.

Dennison, G. (1969). *The lives of children: The story of the First Street School.* New York: Vintage.

Erasmus, C. C. (1989). Ways with stories: Listening to the stories aboriginal peoples tell. *Language Arts, 66,* 267–275.

Featherstone, J. (1971). *Schools where children learn.* New York: Discus.

Giroux, H. (1993). Literacy and the politics of difference. In C. Lankshear & P. McLaren (Eds.), *Critical literacy: Politics, praxis, and the postmodern* (pp. 367–378). Albany: State University of New York Press.

Gomez, M. L. (1991). Teaching a language of opportunity in a language arts methods course: Teaching for David, Albert, and Darlene. In B. R. Tabachnick & K. M. Zeichner (Eds.), *Issues and practices in inquiry-oriented teacher education* (pp. 91–112). London: Falmer.

Gomez, M. L. (1994). Teacher education reform and prospective and novice teachers' perspectives on teaching other people's children. *Teaching and Teacher Education, 10*(6), 1–16.

Gomez, M. L., & Abt-Perkins, D. (in press). Sharing stories of teaching for practice, analysis, and critique. *Education Research and Perspectives.*

Gomez, M. L., & Tabachnick, B. R. (1992). Telling teaching stories. *Teaching Education, 4*(2), 127–138.

Greene, M. (1982). Literacy for what? *Phi Delta Kappan, 63*(5), 326-329.

Helle, A. P. (1991). Reading women's autobiographies: A map of reconstructed knowing. In C. Witherell and N. Noddings (Eds.), *Stories lives tell: Narrative and dialogue in education* (pp. 48-66). New York: Teachers College Press.

Holt, J. (1964). *How children fail.* New York: Dell.

Holt, J. (1967). *How children learn.* New York: Dell.

Holt, J. (1974). *Escape from childhood: The needs and rights of children.* New York: Ballantine.

Koch, K. (1970). *Wishes, lies, and dreams: Teaching children to write poetry.* New York: Vintage.

Kohl, H. R. (1967). *36 children.* New York: New American Library.

Kozol, J. (1967). *Death at an early age.* New York: Bantam.

Narayan, K. (1991). According to their feelings: Teaching and healing with stories. In C. Witherell & N. Noddings (Eds.), *Stories lives tell: Narrative and dialogue in education* (pp. 113-135). New York: Teachers College Press.

Reder, S. (1994). Practice-engagement theory: A sociocultural approach to literacy across languages and cultures. In B. Ferdman, R. M. Weber, & A. Ramirez (Eds.), *Literacy across languages and cultures* (pp. 33-74). Albany: State University of New York Press.

Rich, A. C. (1979). *On lies, secrets, and silence: Selected prose, 1966-1978.* New York. Norton.

Rosen, H. (1985). *Stories and meanings.* Sheffield, UK: National Association for the Teaching of English.

Rosenwald, G. C., & Ochberg, R. L. (1992). Introduction: Life stories, cultural politics, and self-understanding. In G. C. Rosenwald & R. L. Ochberg (Eds.), *Storied lives: The cultural politics of self-understanding* (pp. 1-18). New Haven: Yale University Press.

Sleeter, C., & Grant, C. A. (1987). An analysis of multicultural education in the United States. *Harvard Educational Review, 57*(4), 421-444.

Smith, D. (1991). Hermeneutic inquiry: The hermeneutic imagination and the pedagogic text. In E. G. Short (Ed.), *Forms of curriculum inquiry* (pp. 187-209). Albany, NY: SUNY Press.

Stuart, J. (1970a). *The thread that runs so true.* New York: Charles Scribner's Sons.

Stuart, J. (1970b). *To teach, to love.* Baltimore: Penguin.

Taylor, D. (1993). *From a child's point of view.* New York: Teachers College Press.

Zeichner, K. M., & Tabachnick, B. R. (1991). Reflections on reflective teaching. In B. R. Tabachnick & K. M. Zeichner (Eds.), *Inquiry-oriented practices in teacher education* (pp. 1-21). London: Falmer.

9 Reading Within Multicultural Education: Beyond "Silent" and "Silenced"

Patricia E. Enciso
The Ohio State University

> Come in, come in wherever you've been . . .
> This is the poem in which you're a part.
> This is the home that knows you by heart.
> *From Michael Rosen, "Home"*

The promise of literature, says Bruner (1986), is to enter both the landscape of consciousness and the landscape of action. Beyond these landscapes, literature promises a release from the everyday that allows us to scrutinize our values (Coles, 1989) and imagine ourselves and the world as "otherwise" (Greene, 1994). Furthermore, Sonia Nieto (1996) argues, literacy and literature in schooling should hold the promise of strengthening who we are in the world:

> Rather than attempting to erase culture and language, schools should do everything in their power to *use, affirm* and *maintain* them as a foundation for students' academic success. School policies and practices that stress cultural pride, build on students' native language ability and use, and emphasize the history and experiences of the students' communities would be the result. (p. 292)

This chapter describes practices that have shown promise for attaining the shared goals of reading and multicultural education. The first section focuses on teaching words. Words are the beginning point of oral and written literacy, forming the powerful, lively sounds and images through which we encounter one another and our world. Words, letters, and sounds are quintessentially personal and cultural (Bakhtin, 1981; Vygotsky, 1978); the ways words "work," formally and informally, can be taught, across the grades, with this understanding in mind. The second section describes reading education that reaches beyond word-level instruction. Although this section refers to older elementary and secondary students, even the youngest students who are learning to decode letters and sounds must also discover that stories, poetry, information and ideas that matter to them and their communities can be found in books, in their own writing, and in innumerable electronic and public media. This section also takes up the problem of teaching reading while working to equalize power and status differentials among students as they judge one another's reading competencies and interpretations.

The third section uses Banks's model of knowledge construction (1993) to suggest ways of collecting and presenting literary and media-based texts that will help students recognize and critique multiple representations of "truth."

✜ Teaching Words

> . . . Spanish, even
> Behind the bars
> Of your crib
> When you babbled,
> *Mami, papi, flor, cocos—*
> Nonsense in the middle of the night.
> At school, your friends
> Have to learn Spanish,
> Tripping over *gato,*
> *Y perro,* easy words
> You learned
> When you looked out the back window.
> . . . When you walk home,
> Dragging a stick
> Through the rain puddles,
> Spanish is seeing double.
> The world is twice the size . . .
> (Soto, 1995, p. 7, from "Spanish")

Through his poetry, Gary Soto expresses a love for his home language that we all feel but often do not recognize as an integral part of our very being until that language is challenged, or worse, shamed. He expresses the way our love of language grows in the company of family and friends, at home, in our neighborhoods, and at school. The words we grow up with are part of the fabric of our daily lives and relationships.

Young children expect words to be meaningful in the context of their everyday interactions with people who are working, laughing, making things, and taking care of one another. When children encounter isolated letters, the alphabet, the concept of printed letters relating to sounds, and finally letters and sounds forming words, they are expected to shift their attention from language that was previously learned in the intimate, familiar contexts of human interaction to words represented through abstract, arbitrary, yet conventionalized symbols that express meaning across time and space (Cazden, 1986). This is not an easy shift to grasp, especially if the words students love to say and hear are discounted by the people and books through which they must learn to read and write.

If we expect to achieve reading education that is multicultural and social reconstructivist, we have to begin with daily lessons about language that draw upon the diversity and power of the many languages through which our students have learned to relate to others and the world. Such lessons are not trivial. They indicate to students that, as teachers and teacher educators, we affirm language diversity, we are willing to learn and use the many, dynamic languages of local and more distant communities, and we expect to maintain linguistic diversity in every aspect of our schooling.

Delpit (1995) offers a clear example of teaching that addresses "the politically popular dialect form in this country, that is, Standard English" (p. 53), while also demonstrating respect for linguisitic diversity:

> Amanda Branscombe, a gifted white teacher who has often taught black students whom other teachers have given up on, sometimes has her middle school students listen to rap songs in order to develop a rule base for their creation. The students would teach her their newly constructed "rules for writing rap," and she would in turn use this knowledge as a base to begin a discussion of the rules Shakespeare used to contruct his plays, or the rules poets used to develop their sonnets. (p. 67)

Similarly, Lee (1991), working with African American secondary students who, by all standard measures, were expected to fail English class, scaffolded their understanding of complex literary works by Walker and Hurston through reference to and study of the metaphors, idioms, and ironic turns in their everyday language. Without exception, the students in her study excelled in their reading and interpretation of these and other texts required for study in secondary English programs. Related to Lee and Delpit's work are the findings of Henry (1990) and Ladson-Billings and Henry (1990), who have shown that effective African American teachers draw upon "the rhythms, call and response, and . . . proverbs extant in the expressive vocal communication patterns of the African diaspora" (cited in Foster, 1996, p. 578). Teachers working with African American youth and students of diverse linguistic heritages will certainly build stronger connections between students and reading if they reach toward the language practices cherished and honored by their communities.

The spirit and form of Delpit and Lee's examples can be readily applied to early literacy. Instruction of letters and sounds may be established through the names, places, foods, games, rhymes, and songs children have learned at home and in their communities. These words and songs can be generated and categorized by the children, printed on large pieces of paper or posterboard, and made visible and available throughout the day for children's practice. At the same time, these words and rhymes can become the source for more focused instruction in reading and spelling related to initial sounds (*wh, ch, th*), vowel patterns (/a-e/ /ai/ /ay/), and word endings (*s, ed, ing*). In turn, children can share copies of their community-based rhymes and songs with adults and siblings when they visit the classroom or as they see these rhymes posted in community centers, churches, and grocery stores.

Young children need to learn that writing and reading words gives them a chance to be recognized and understood within their homes and communities. If we can begin with words connected to images and people that students recognize and value, we can help them make the transition from finding pleasure and power in words heard and used in lived contexts to the pleasure and power of words seen and interpreted in abstract forms across texts and contexts.

The Debate That Blinked at Multicultural Education

The so-called "Great Debate" about teaching children the relationship between letters and sounds (the alphabetic code) within "natural" literary contexts versus teaching letters and sounds, separated from "whole" texts and "whole" uses of language is now a foundering if not completely sunken argument. The National Reading Commission report *Preventing Reading Failure in Young Children* (Snow, Burns, & Griffin, 1998) advocates early instruction in the alphabetic code coupled with daily opportunities to hear, read, and write stories and nonfictional texts. Analyses of the report (Allington, 1999; Gee, 1999; Taylor, 1998) point out that the Commission also provides the evidence, although not the ideological backing, for literacy education that emphasizes the strengths in children's home languages and community literacy practices.

Freppon and Dahl (1991) have shown that in early reading instruction situated in "whole language" practices, "children learn the [alphabetic] code through direct involvement with written language, utilize the demonstrations and questioning provided by their teacher, and draw support from the social context of the classroom" (p. 196). Clearly, children need to be taught, not merely immersed in, how letters and sounds work and how print communicates meaningful, entertaining, informational representations—and misrepresentations—of the world.

Confronting the Real Barriers to Early Reading Achievement

Beyond the linguistic balances necessary for teaching early reading, however, educators must also be aware of differential uses of time and emphases given to students during instruction. In terms of multicultural education, the debate about early literacy education should be solidly focused not on letters and sounds learned in context versus "out of context," but on the classroom context itself, where negative interactions and missing interactions between teachers and students lead to limited education for far too many students. Since the early 1970s, numerous ethnographies of classroom literacy have pointed to the urgency of altering the most fundamental, taken-for-granted patterns of exchange between children and teachers, particularly during reading instruction. Allington (1983), Borko and Eisenhart (1989), and Mehan (1979) have clearly documented the limited time spent on actual reading when students are regarded as "low" readers or perceived to lack competence in school reading practices. Rather than receiving reading instruction, students in "low groups" are repeatedly interrupted and given disciplinary instruction. Further, Gilmore (1985), McDermott (1974), and later Bartolomé (1994), Gutierrez and Stone (1997), and Reyes (1992) have noted the significance of seemingly minor but daily misinteractions between teachers and students that quickly lead to teachers' underestimations of students' interests, goals, and abilities, and, in turn, to students' assumptions that teachers are uninformed and uninterested in their education. Eventually, students and teachers actively disengage from learning and teaching.

As teachers strive for a more inclusive, multicultural education for students, it becomes their responsibility to reverse this process of misjudgment and disengagement. Whatever theory of reading education educators subscribe to, they must be alert not only to their attitudes toward students' abilities but also to the daily behaviors and practices that may teach children that they will not become readers. Consider, for example, the following questions:

Are those students who are new to (or struggling with) the alphabet and print encouraged to participate in all literacy experiences or only in the "beginning" lessons that are least likely to demonstrate a wide and involving range of reading experiences? Are expectations and guidelines for participating in literacy-learning activities clearly and positively stated for all children, or are some children more likely to have and enact a tacit knowledge of the guidelines and thus be perceived as good readers? Is the expectation that all children will learn and participate made clear and expressed positively on a daily basis? Are all children initiating ideas and interpretations, or are only a few vocal children doing all the interpretive work? Are a diversity of ideas included and "taken up" by the group, or are only a few predictable ideas considered?

Teachers Questioning What Counts as Literate Behavior

These and other questions direct teachers toward self-examination of their assumptions about what counts as literate behavior and what counts as a meaningful question, answer, or action as students are learning about print. The source for such self-examination begins, as many scholars have argued, with a description and analysis of one's own literacy teaching and learning (Delpit, 1986; Ladson-Billings, 1994; Gomez [this volume]; Hidalgo, 1993) along with a critical understanding of the political and social structures that have sanctioned Protestant, European, upper-class literate practices over others (Luke, 1995). The inquiry of teachers and researchers such as Ballenger (1996), Gallas (1995), and Paley (1997), who have closely examined the literacy journeys of their diverse students, helps us recognize that we all have limited experiences with a diversity of literacy practices, texts, and other linguistic art forms, yet we often act as though a single definition of literate behavior will be a sufficient model for all students. Invariably, our students struggle to teach us otherwise. Indeed, Ballenger's, Gallas's, and Paley's studies have shown that as their own judgments diminished and students' diverse literacy expectations and practices became more visible, the classroom's prevailing models of story telling, word analysis, and writing were reshaped so that more complex ideas could be introduced and explored by all children.

Despite considerable evidence to support the benefits of multiple avenues into literacy learning, it is still a difficult task for many teachers and scholars to re-form the assumptions undergirding their judgments that among students' diverse literacy performances some approaches *should* be *more valued* than others. As further research is undertaken to promote reading education that encompasses the linguistic strengths and traditions of multiple communities, we should heed Delpit's (1986) advice:

> It is the responsibility of dominant group members to attempt to hear the other side of the issue, and after hearing to speak in a modified voice that does not exclude the concerns of their minority colleagues. . . . The key is to understand the variety of meanings available for any human interaction, and not to assume that the voices of the majority speak for all. (pp. 284–285)

❖ Teaching Reading: Beyond "Silent" and "Silenced"

By the time children begin third grade, most will have grasped the significance of letter–sound relationships, learned high-frequency words by sight (e.g., *they, there, said*), and learned to decode unknown words by using a balanced combination of strategies that include letter–sound relationships, the grammar of the sentence (e.g., predict that the next word is a "describing" word), and the meaning of the text overall. If these strategies are not readily used by children, they will become the focus of individual and small-group instruction for the coming weeks and months. However, this instruction should co-exist with reading, writing, and interpreting a wide range of narrative forms (e.g., fiction, nonfiction, poetry, journal and newspaper articles, song lyrics) and everyday print (e.g., grocery ads, menus, weather charts, sports statistics).

Furthermore, students who are able to decode, and those just beginning to master decoding, need to gain fluency in reading; that is, they must be able to retain the meaning of a text as they also figure out words with increasing ease. For many children, across categories of race, gender, and class, this is the point where they decide that "reading is stupid." They become so focused on print decoding and getting through "the tough words" that they lose meaning altogether. Thus, reading deteriorates into a succession of word-by-word decoding that has no point other than to get to the end of the page. Meanwhile, they see other children around them who read page after page without interruption and without distress. Quickly, the class divides into the "cans" and "cannots," based on apparent reading ability but also on the effects of discrimination as described in the previous section—*unless* the teachers' pedagogy is grounded in a profound belief that every child's efforts contribute to the whole class's literacy development.

Questioning Individualism and Hierarchies of Achievement

Such a belief counters the individualistic, hierarchical model of reading achievement that pervades so-called standard practice and separates students on the basis of what appears to be their merit (Gutierrez & Stone, 1997). In an educational context that promotes multicultural, social reconstructivist practices, reading achievement should not be measured by standardized test scores (often grossly inadequate reflections of diverse texts and interpretations) that place responsibility for learning—and failure—on the student. Instead, achievement should be measured by evidence of the limitless potential students have to use and invent a diversity of approaches to understanding words, texts, and one another (Hilliard, 1990). Reading achievement should also be measured by the extent to which students are able to respectfully and deeply consider one another's contributions to learning.

However, these measures of success can be difficult to gauge in reading education, because reading in school and society, as its uses and practices have evolved over the past two centuries in Western cultures (Manguel, 1996), is expected to be silent and bounded: A good reader is a silent, solitary reader. Such a judgment, held by many educators, translates into pedagogies that make it impossible for students to learn about one another's ways of grappling with unfamiliar words; points of view; and narrations of times, places, and events. Fluent readers become increasingly isolated as they silently read an ever wider range of texts and disclose relatively few insights about their reading. Struggling readers, on the other hand, become more public as they are required to participate in tutoring programs or demonstrate their inadequacy as readers during small-group read-aloud sessions. Inevitably, they speak most openly about their lack of interest in or disdain for reading and books (Bloome & Nieto, 1992; Enciso, 1996a).

Reading That Speaks Up

How can shifts in pedagogy and assessment be achieved so that reading education becomes aligned with multicultural education goals? First, teachers must believe and understand that all students bring strengths and interests to the entire classroom community as they learn to read. Second, all students' reading strengths and interests need to be made public through pedagogies that value a shared analysis of reading strategies and viewpoints in the class. In addition, students need to make public a critical analysis of the status and power given particular literacies, viewpoints, and interpretations within the classroom and their communities. For example, a diverse class of fourth and fifth graders, whom I co-taught, held strong and loud debates about the value of rhythm and blues versus rock music and the significance of each for their literacy development. Through a whole-class visit to a museum of African American history (1920–1970), they discovered and discussed the influence of African musical forms on European artists' recordings of what became known as rock. We also considered the race-based inequities in economic gain and public attention given White versus Black performers across the past half-century. Thus, both African American and European American students drew upon their cultural resources and strengths to describe their literacy, but were expected to analyze the differential status they gave and that the American music industry afforded to Europeanist versus Africanist artists.

Third, a wide range of texts, including those produced by the students and their communities, need to be read and enjoyed. However, texts of many kinds must also be critically examined for biases, misrepresentations, and patterns of exclusion that imply or openly describe negative, limited possibilities for students' lives.

❖ Inside a Classroom Where Reading Education Is Multicultural Education

It may be useful to read examples of fourth and fifth grade students analyzing their ways of reading and critically examining the representations in the book they were reading as a class (Enciso, 1998). The following examples, taken from a two-month study of the book *Weasel* (DeFelice, 1990) and related stories of the colonization of Native American lands, illustrate the ways students learned to be engaged, metaphoric, critical readers through public, shared inquiry. The students were heterogeneous across conventional categories of class, race, and ability. Most importantly for reading, they drew upon cultural resources grounded in African American and European American popular and historical images to develop interpretations of texts. Often their differing references required my mediation.

As a co-teacher, I was alert to the ways I might misjudge or undervalue contributions made by students during discussions. I knew that I was not "above" the possibility of diminishing or ignoring students' ideas, particularly due to their immersion in youth and community cultures that were sometimes unfamiliar to me. Indeed, I learned to move away from discussion-based approaches to our analyses and critiques because it was far too easy for me and, primarily, the European American students to revert to practices that allowed a few vocal (male) students to dominate our discussions and transform them into debates over "the facts" of the text. In place of discussion, we often worked through metaphor, using visual representations, dramatic tableau, movement, and music to support a more inclusive pedagogy of reading and interpretation. The use of alternative, artful approaches to analysis and critique of texts and reading meant that students could concentrate on developing compelling metaphors and elaborations on their own and others' ideas, rather than on the inevitable tests of validity that marked earlier debates and discussion.

Seeing Diverse Forms of Engagement in Reading

After reading aloud the opening chapter of *Weasel*, I asked students to find a partner and describe one part of the scene or one character in greater detail. Set in the southern Ohio woodlands during the 1830s, the story begins as two children are summoned by a stranger, Ezra, who asks them to follow him into the woods in search of their father. All of the characters are aware of another man lurking in the woods, Weasel, a notorious hunter and killer of Shawnee Indians who was funded by the federal government to enforce the "removal" of the Shawnee people from the Ohio Valley, but who then became a hunter of townspeople.

As we shared some of our descriptions in the larger group, two girls, both confident speakers and avid readers, offered first an extended description of the family's dogs, which abruptly stopped barking when a strange knock was heard on the cabin door. Their description led us into a larger group exploration of different knocking sounds and what they might convey. One girl also retold the opening scene as if she were there in 1839: "You're out in the woods—and you have a sister and two dogs and there's this knock on the door. And you're like so far out and you think—your Dad must have knocked. But why would your dad knock?" Not surprisingly, these girls readily described their interest in and understanding of the story in quite different but satisfying ways. Unique to their descriptions, however, is the ease with which they "filled in the gaps" (Iser, 1978) of the story and demonstrated their ways of reading once they were given the opportunity.

My goal was to make not only their accomplished reading, but everyone's ways of reading more visible so they could all learn that reading is not a singularly defined performance but rather a multidimensional, imageful experience that requires diverse ways of using one's attention, logic, and concern to create and sustain interest and understanding. Thus, after the girls and other children spoke, I read one more chapter and then asked all of the children to write whatever they were thinking as the second chapter was completed. Their responses reflected a diversity of ways of relating to the story. As I read from students' writing and highlighted each student's strength in their reading, I also made visible and public the range of activities experienced by engaged readers. These are the very experiences that a handful of students learn by chance and continue to exploit as they read more widely, while most students never come close to realizing the potential of deep reading and imagining. As educators, we assume that some children simply read better than others. In my view, some children simply have not been shown how to use multiple resources from their lives and languages to make reading more enjoyable and meaningful. My goal in the lesson described above was to begin to make deep, imaginative reading visible, however that might be expressed among this particular group of children.

Across their writing, the students described their interest in and predictions about the story in a wide range of ways, from their implicit questions of the author's plan to their wondering about how they would react if they were in the characters' predicaments:

- There's more to this story. The whole truth is not being told.
- I'm waiting. I'm not sure what will happen next.

- I think they'll all die. I usually think of the most outrageous thing that could happen.
- It's like *Goosebumps* and other horror stories I've read.
- The author wants you to *think* the man (Ezra) is evil.
- What would I do?
- It reminds me of when I come home from school and no one is home.
- Pa said to his son, "You're the man of the house." What does that mean? That's what I kept thinking about.
- I was feeling scared and excited. I had lots of different feelings.

After summarizing all of the children's ways of reading, I directed them to a poster I had constructed, based on prior research on engaged reading (Enciso, 1990; 1992; 1996a) that could remind them of ways they could create and sustain their interest in reading. Although the chart is not all-inclusive, it was a useful tool that we added to throughout the year and referred to when students needed help describing their reading to one another. The chart lists phrases and related pictorial representations that suggest the following forms of participation or engagement in a story:

- Seeing close up.
- Seeing from a distance.
- Hearing sounds and voices.
- Feeling close to characters.
- Feeling like you have become a character.
- Taking a character's perspective.
- Comparing one perspective with another.
- Feeling like you are there, in the story.
- Wondering what you would do.
- Connecting with other stories.
- Remembering your own experiences.
- Asking "Where am I in this story?"

Across all of these strategies, students needed to draw upon the images, sounds, and relationships that were familiar to them, much as they did when they interpreted almost all of their daily experiences. In this sense, reading was shown to relate to the cultural resources they most valued and understood. But given many of the students' histories with reading, they needed to have these connections between life and reading explicitly described and repeatedly, positively demonstrated. It cannot be taken for granted that all students understand that their particular ways of participating in stories are precisely what they need to use to become readers.

Locating Oneself as a Reader and Member of Interrelated Communities

In my view, the most important question the classroom posters raised was "Where am I in the story?" Educators, researchers, and students often assume that, during reading, everyone is situated close to the same characters or with the same sense of interest in the plot and subplot; for White educators and students, those assumptions are also most likely to be associated with European, Protestant attitudes about what counts as significant in a particular text. Rarely are a diversity of movements or locations made public for serious consideration. Instead, homogeneity is assumed and interpretations or ideas that seem as though they "come from left field" are discounted. With reference to the poem cited at the beginning of this chapter, some students regularly hear the message "Stay out. Stay out. You do not belong," when their ears should be ringing with Rosen's words.

In my work with the fourth and fifth grade students, we used paper cutouts made from colored construction paper to show one another how we believed characters related to one another and how *we* were located in the landscape of the story. Because students were instructed to make or use abstract shapes to represent characters and themselves, these cutouts lent themselves to higher-level, metaphoric interpretations of characters' essence, intentions, and concerns. The location of the reader helped us consider how the same story could be read and interpreted in quite distinctive ways that implicitly supported students' diverse identities and interests.

The students in this example were in small groups, placing five colored construction paper shapes, representing each character, on a full white sheet of paper to depict the relative distance or closeness among characters as they sought and eventually found "Pa" injured in the woods. Notice that as the students moved and described their shapes, they not only developed a sense of the themes and images in the story, but also retold segments of the story and offered conjectures about the characters' points of view. Their talk in this episode was distinctly exploratory compared to the debates about textual details that usually occurred in the class.

Matt called me over to the table where he, Ray, and Sheryl were working. He showed me that their cutouts had formed a shape: "This is like an arrow." I responded, to encourage metaphoric meanings, "What does that mean? Are they going somewhere?" Ray picked up, "Yeah. They might be catching up with Weasel and he might be coming on to them with tracks." I noticed that they had placed the shape for Weasel underneath all the others. "Does that make sense?" I asked. Ray responded, "Yes ma'am. They're [the other characters] up higher than him. He's low because he's bad. He's so mean. They [the other characters] have a better view." I was impressed by the potential of the metaphor he was building related to their moral height or depth. Ray implicitly understood this metaphor, as was evident in his comment that some of the characters could see more clearly than Weasel. I asked him whether Ezra was nice too. Ray responded, "Yeah. They have a better view of being nicer than Weasel."

At this point I encouraged all of the students at the table—about six of them—to stop and listen to Ray's interpretation. It is important to note that until the conversation we were having about *Weasel,* Ray's comments about books, if he offered any, were typically overlooked or discounted. Yet in this conversation he actively shaped and extended an original, insightful interpretation that, I announced, warranted everyone's attention.

He continued, once people were listening, "Weasel's at the bottom because he's dirty. He's cheating and he's kind of like. . . ." Evan interjected, "A dirty lying cheat." Ray continued, "And the other people are on the top because they have more confidence than he does and they're wiser." I concluded, "In a way you're saying they're [the top people] more moral. And he [Weasel] doesn't have any ethics." Later, when I asked him where he was in the story, he pointed to Pa and the children and commented that "they were higher."

An important aspect of this exchange was Evan's support of Ray's interpretation. Evan was an almost obsessive reader who could whip through a book or two per day. He was regarded by the entire class as the *best* reader. Yet, he rarely read with depth or insight; he read for plot. Ray's articulation of the moral underpinnings of the story gave

Ray, a far less fluent and committed reader, the opportunity to "slow down reading" and describe a way of interpreting a text that was new and important for Evan's reading development.

Next, Ray pointed to the arrow shape and said, "The arrow is going somewhere. He's leading them." I wondered if he meant Ezra: "Who's leading them?" Ray said, "Weasel's leading them. It might be a trap." Although Ezra was actually the leader as described in the book, the journey back to Pa was depicted as though a trap might snap at any moment.

Through Ray's extended analysis, I was able to gain a better sense of how he read for moral strengths and limitations and how he might miss key elements of the plot while still constructing the story's themes. Both of these traits in his reading were evident in the coming months and became keys to engaging him and challenging his and other students' reading development.

About half of the students in the class were not yet fluent readers, but that did not prevent us from engaging in sophisticated, challenging explorations of how we read "the word and world" (Freire, 1985). Ultimately, this group of students became readers who learned that decoding is a necessary but not sufficient skill for interpreting texts. They learned to recognize and use multiple, complex aspects of reading that require imagination, participation, and connections across time, place, and texts.

They also learned that their interest in reading could support relationships with the people and communities that matter most to them. For example, Ray, who had claimed little interest in reading earlier in the year and who, as it turned out, knew very few vowel sounds, began to read *The Watsons Go to Birmingham-1963* (Curtis, 1996). With a few brief, ordinary lessons on short and long /i/, /a/, and /e/, he began to tackle his first chapter book. In addition, the book was read to him during the class's "choice reading" time, and later it was read aloud to the whole class. Ray had multiple avenues through which he could gain confidence and fluency as a reader. About halfway through his reading, in early spring, I overheard a conversation in the lunchroom between Ray and his friends, all from other classrooms. They were talking about books they had recently read. Ray described the characters and several episodes in *The Watsons,* as well as a part that was still puzzling to him. In this very public conversation in the lunchroom, Ray was seen as a reader among readers—a friend among friends.

Sociocultural Theory: Understanding Reading That "Makes Noise"

The reading education described here departs from "standard practice" in several ways, while it retains some of the goals associated with upper elementary and secondary reading curricula. Teachers working with students who are able to decode print generally strive for a balance between skills instruction and a range of literary experiences that will support students' reading development. Attention is given primarily to teaching students to find main ideas and themes, to build inferences about characters' attitudes and actions, recall key events, study vocabulary, and apply information available in nonfiction and fiction. In addition, time is often allotted during the day for students to make individual choices for their private reading and for the teacher to read aloud from a chapter, book, or, very occasionally, from poetry collections.

All of these so-called standard dimensions of a reading program are intended to move students toward greater pleasure and insight as readers.

Based primarily on psycholinguistic and constructivist theories of reading, these practices assume a single reader operating with one or more texts, actively, but silently, striving to connect his or her past experiences with print and everyday life to the new words, images, narrative forms, questions, and assignments encountered in the reading program. However, as Willis (1995) points out in her analysis of writing process programs that are founded on pscyholinguistic and constructivist theories, these theories do not adequately account for the sociology and psychology of a fundamentally racist society that tends, in its most benign manifestations, to assume that every student's experiences and strengths will be equally regarded and incorporated into classroom learning environments. Evidence from national and state testing data, surveys of reading materials, and classroom-based research focusing on the social conditions of learning for Latino, African American, and Native American students indicates that the ideas, interests, and needs of these students regarding reading education are not taken seriously by the majority of American educators.

Barrera (1992), for example, points to the simultaneous growth of literature-rich reading programs and the woefully limited inclusion of stories and images reflective of our diverse population's views, contemporary and past ways of life, languages, and histories. In classrooms and schools located on the Texas/Mexico border, she found that those few books that were included in the classroom library to reflect a Southwestern perspective instead reinforced stereotypes through their repetition of tired images of piñatas, tortillas, and burros.

The "official" curriculum of reading, as measured by the content of reading texts alone, silences a diversity of narrative forms and substance that could dramatically increase the possibility that students would see themselves as readers. As Willis (1995) argues, students who do not identify primarily with Eurocentric, Protestant values and everyday cultural practices must constantly translate the meanings of texts and instruction to the meanings and relationships they have learned to value at home and in their communities—and back again to the social milieu of the classroom. Social translation, or "double consciousness" (DuBois, 1968; original 1903), requires students to question the validity of their home cultures before acting on the requests of the school culture, or, vice versa, to initially question or resist school-based requests because of the discrepancy in values or meanings between school and home cultures. To become a reader while doing social translation is, to say the least, socially and cognitively demanding.

Social translation is a complex way of interpreting oneself in the world that most people of color learn early and painfully. I would argue that everyone should learn this way of thinking, particularly White students, who rarely examine their privileges or assumptions in everyday life. However, no student should be expected to learn social translation at the cost of becoming a lifelong reader or a full participant in society.

The pedagogies described in the previous section that highlight diverse approaches to engaging with and interpreting texts are grounded in sociocultural theory that accounts for students' interpretations of themselves as members of a society that is inequitable and discriminatory. Pedagogies that seek multiple ways of opening dialogue about "what we know," "how we know," and "what knowledge matters to whom" create an environment for reading that acknowledges a history of exclusion while it fosters inclusion. Students who are otherwise marginalized as readers—because their culturally based references and behaviors related to reading are not shared by the teacher or because classroom politics favor the most vocal students, who tend to reject a diversity of views—are asked to *lead* others in an inquiry about those references and behaviors, so everyone's understanding about a text and reading might be enlarged and even rearranged.

Many scholars have argued that students should be active informants of and participants in directing their literacy educations. Whether students are using literature or basals as the text for their reading curriculum, they can be encouraged to question representations in the texts, suggest related and alternative readings for comparison, and discuss how reading creates particular classroom politics—and how politics of larger spheres, outside of the classroom, affect classroom reading practices and assessments. Based on their study of children's perceptions of basals, Bloome and Nieto (1992) urged that "children have a role to play in selecting materials and how they will be used—a role that can empower them as readers" (p. 92). Otherwise, children surmise that reading is no more than a place where their ways of being in the world are worthless. It is precisely the opposite message that students need to receive.

❖ Selecting Books That Support Reading for Multicultural Education

Reading for multicultural education means that the texts students read and interpret must be selected in terms of their social and cultural significance, not merely in terms of reading level or availability from previous years. Although multicultural literature is still strikingly limited in numbers compared to the thousands of new books published annually for children and young adults, it is more accessible and more informed than ever before. These books should replace the worn copies of "classics" and basal series that are replete with stereotypes, misleading histories, and Eurocentric accomplishments. New books may be expensive, but they can be found for reduced prices. (Half-Price Books, for example, and other discount stores are able to stock and sell books that either have not been noticed or have been underestimated as significant contributions to so-called mainstream education.)

As teachers seek newer books they will be assisted in their search by several children's literature awards that highlight distinguished contributions to multicultural literature. The Coretta Scott King Award books, for example, are now often displayed each January alongside the Newbery and Caldecott Award winning books. Beyond the benefits of increased accessibility to this literature, the publicity around these books also encourages publishers to seek new African American artists and support those writers and illustrators who have already made outstanding works of literature for children. The Américas Award and Pura Belpré Award recognize distinguished books by and about Latinos and Latinas and also encourage publishers' efforts to promote Latino and Latina artists and writers. In addition, publications such as Violet Harris's (1992) edited volume on multicultural literature and *The Multicolored Mirror: Cultural Substance in Literature for Children and Young Adults* (1991), published by the Cooperative Children's Book Center, offer excellent analyses, annotations, and classifications of literature, making the problem of choosing "best books" both manageable and educative.

Analyzing Multicultural Literature in the Classroom and Community

Many fine contemporary books, classified as "multicultural," can hold demeaning and sometimes wholly inaccurate portraits of diversity. Simply having a "multicultural book" does not excuse teachers or students from close scrutiny and wider reading to gain a sense of a book's strengths as well as its inconsistencies, patterns of inclusion or exclusion, and misrepresentations.

One approach to the analysis of multicultural literature with students is to draw upon the wisdom and insight of parents and community members, who will have varied and enlightening opinions about the ways a book represents a distinct aspect of the children's community. The book may be seriously flawed or, on the other hand, much loved; either way, students, teachers, librarians, and community members will benefit from conversations about the representations of themselves and others in books for children.

A second approach is to collect a range of books on a topic that cut across publication dates, perspectives, contexts, and curricular areas, so that students can compare views and seek patterns in the ways that diversity among people is represented (see, for example, the work of Bigelow, 1995, and Martinez, 1995). The following section describes the use of Banks's model of knowledge types as a guide for selecting and critiquing texts with students.

Knowledge Construction and Critical Reading

Teachers can encourage students' critical reading by creating "text sets" (Short, Harste, & Burke, 1996) or collections of 10 to 20 books that will be read aloud to the whole class and/or closely read by children in small groups. These books are selected because they enable students and teachers to contrast politically dominant views with historically silenced views about people's participation in events and ideas and then consider how they might challenge taken-for-granted assumptions, related to their reading, within their own school and communities. As Shannon and Luke (1991) argue, critical literacy aims to help us understand our own history and culture while also "fostering an activism toward equal participation in all the decisions that affect and control our lives" (p. 518).

Using Banks's (1993) model of five interrelated knowledge types as a guideline, it is possible to create text sets that demonstrate to students that knowledge is not static. Shifts within popular culture, national events, and the emergence of new art forms can alter long-held "facts" and theories. Of course these same assumptions may resurface as political pressures and local or national events return people to their former certainties. Teachers need to be alert to these shifts as much as they are tuned to the range of literature available to students. Students' interpretations will initially refer to their personal and popular cultural experiences—many of which are grounded in misconceptions and false assumptions. By selecting texts that refer to these views, no matter how limited they may be, it is possible to place them in relation to other knowledge types so that students can explore how knowledge is constructed by and for them.

Students can learn, for example, that *mainstream knowledge* about Native Americans presented in children's literature often reproduces old stereotypes about mysterious, noble, historic savages who lost. In contrast, *transformative knowledge,* depicted in books such as *A Boy Becomes a Man at Wounded Knee* (Wood & Wanbli Numpa Afraid of Hawk, 1992), *This Land Is My Land* (Littlechild, 1993), and *The People Shall*

Continue (Ortiz, 1998), encourages students to study contemporary Indian life and politics and to examine the causes and consequences of colonization for both the colonizing and colonized people in this land. *Popular knowledge* about indigenous peoples abounds in magazines, movies, and television shows that reinforce stereotypes and close off questions about the inequitable social relations established between indigenous nations and the U.S. government (Deloria, 1998). Popular images and slogans can be used effectively as the basis from which to ask "Who made this image?"; "What is this image asking you to believe?"; "How is this image made so you will meet their expectations?"; and "How might this image be made differently?" (see Luke, 1995, for further descriptions of critical reading pedagogy). Similarly, *personal/cultural knowledge*—that is, students' mental images, stories from their lives, and connections with other texts they have read—can form a compelling contrast with or parallel to the knowledges they have studied. Finally, students and teachers can examine and make changes in local, *school knowledge*—in essence, the symbolic curriculum—that organizes social relations around texts, with particular texts, and with people represented in texts. All of these knowledge types are important to students' involvement in and analysis of how reading is made *for* them as much as *by* them.

Reading and Rereading Interpretations

When the selection of texts, films, and images is organized to present diverse viewpoints, students can begin to recognize the limitations of a single, decontextualized reading. Yet, students and teachers may not recognize the exclusions that occur *as* they discuss these texts. Again, the invitation to read and discuss multicultural literature is not, in itself, a sufficient pedagogy for mediating diversity in the context of reading education. Britzman, Santiago-Valles, Jimenez-Muñoz, and Lamash (1993) and Ellsworth (1989) argue that when one or even several dimensions of difference and discrimination are deliberately brought to students' attention, other dimensions may be silenced or treated as though they are "given" and unquestionable. In a study of children's response to multicultural literature (Enciso, 1994; 1996b), I documented and analyzed the ways children borrowed from and improvised on popular cultural discourses about race and race relations to interpret *Maniac Magee* (Spinelli, 1991), a story that poses sharp racial divisions. The divide between Black and White as represented in the story seemed to force children to "take sides" with Black and White characters. By embedding popular cultural referents from songs, movies, and cultural heroes in their talk about the story, children implicitly or explicitly aligned themselves with particular characters and one another's racial identities. Children who did not see themselves as Black or White struggled with the story's dichotomous construction of race and with the impossibility of "fitting in" to the discourse about difference that dominated the story and classroom.

Dialogue among students and teachers about diverse histories, identities, and representations must always be *dialogized* (Bakhtin, 1981); that is, multiple voices, images, movement, and stories need to be placed in juxtaposition to one another to create unforeseen opportunities for noticing and negotiating the meanings that matter most to students and their communities. Literature and related texts, treated dialogically with the intention of seeking relationships and absences that had not been considered, can provide a landscape within which students and teachers consider not only how they interpret texts, but also how they interpret one another. Again, teachers need to consider how a text represents diversity and how that representation may be interpreted by students, who will seek alignments with characters and themes while they also seek alignments with one another. Bringing multiple texts into conversations and artful interpretations can diminish the authority of a singular, limited viewpoint, but these texts and interpretations must also be accompanied by continual efforts to read one another's readings.

✥ Conclusion

Reading can be made powerful for every child as the keys to written language are turned by affirming the students' language, the relationships they have with families and peers, and their right to read books that reflect their lives and interests. Furthermore, every student deserves clear guidance from educators, who convey the invitation to be a reader by everything they do. I have tried to show in this chapter that it is possible to draw upon students' language diversity, reading strengths, and relationships, as well as a thoughtfully selected library of books, to create loud, daily solicitations to become readers. I have also outlined ethnographic and teacher-researcher studies that can raise teachers' awareness about how they uphold or dismiss students' effort to be who they are as they also become readers.

One of the ways teachers can reduce the sense among students that some can and some cannot read is to work against pedagogies that promote isolation and silence around students' ways of reading and interpreting texts. In answer to standard practices that create individualized, hierarchical assessments of reading, I have described pedagogies that make reading processes visible and that account for students' varying social locations and cultural resources as they learn to read and interpret texts together.

Finally, I have described guidelines for selecting and sharing multicultural literature with students. And I have considered, briefly, the reponsibility of educators to look beyond the positive step of including multicultural literature in reading programs to the possibility of challenging this literature and the exclusions it might reproduce as one or another so-called difference renders other differences invisible or unspeakable. In the end, reading education must be seen by all students as an unequivocal invitation to participate in shaping their own lives, their classrooms, and their communities.

References

Allington, R. (1983). The reading instruction provided readers of differing reading ability. *Elementary School Journal, 83,* 549-559.

Allington, R. (1999). Critical Issues: Crafting state educational policy: The slippery role of research and researchers. *Journal of Literacy Research, 31*(4), 457-482.

Bakhtin, M. M. (1981). *The dialogic imagination: Four essays.* M. Holquist, Ed.; C. Emerson & M. Holquist trans. Austin: University of Texas Press.

Ballenger, C. (1996). Learning the ABCs in a Haitian preschool: A teacher's story: *Language Arts, 73*(5), 317-323.

Banks, J. (1993). The canon debate, knowledge construction, and multicultural education. *Educational Researcher, 22*(5), 4-14.

Barrera, R. (1992). The cultural gap in literature-based literacy instruction. *Education and Urban Society, 24*(2), 227-243.

Bartolomé, L. (1994). Beyond the methods fetish: Toward a humanizing pedagogy. *Harvard Educational Review, 64*(2), 173-194.

Bigelow, B. (1992). Inside the classroom: Social vision and critical pedagogy. In P. Shannon (Ed.), *Becoming political: Readings and writings in the politics of literacy education* (pp. 72-82). Portsmouth, NH: Heinemann.

Bigelow, B. (1995). Discovering Columbus: Rereading the past. In D. Levine, R. Lowe, B. Peterson, and R. Tenorio (Eds.), *Rethinking schools: An agenda for change* (pp. 61-86). New York: The New Press.

Bloome, D. (1989). Beyond access: An ethnographic study of reading and writing in a seventh grade classroom. In D. Bloome (Ed.), *Classrooms and literacy* (pp. 53-106). Norwood, NJ: Ablex.

Bloome, D., & Nieto, S. (1992). Children's understandings of basal readers. In P. Shannon (Ed.), *Becoming political: Readings and writings in the politics of literacy education* (pp. 83-96). Portsmouth, NH: Heinemann.

Borko, H., & Eisenhart, M. (1989). Reading ability groups as literacy communities. In D. Bloome (Ed.), *Classrooms and literacy* (pp. 107-134). Norwood, NJ: Ablex.

Britzman, D. , Santiago-Valles, K., Jimenez-Muñoz, G., & Lamash, L. (1993). Slips that show and tell: Fashioning multiculture as a problem of representation. In C. McCarthy & W. Crichlow (Eds.), *Race, identity and representation in education* (pp. 188-200). New York: Routledge.

Bruner, J. (1986). *Actual minds, possible worlds.* Cambridge, MA: Harvard University Press.

Cazden, C. (1986). Classroom discourse. In M. C. Wittrock (Ed.), *Handbook of research on teaching* (3rd. ed.). New York: Macmillan.

Coles, G. (1998). *Reading lessons: The debate over literacy.* New York: Hill and Wang.

Coles, R. (1989). *The call of stories: Teaching and the moral imagination.* Boston: Houghton Mifflin.

Cooperative Children's Book Center. (1991). *The multicolored mirror: Cultural substance in literature for children and young adults.* Madison: University of Wisconsin Press.

Curtis, C. P. (1996). *The Watsons Go to Birmingham-1963.* New York: Delacorte.

Davies, B. (1993). *Shards of glass: Children reading and writing beyond gendered identities.* Cresskill, NJ: Hampton Press.

DeFelice, C. (1990). *Weasel.* New York: Avon.

Deloria, P. (1998). *Playing Indian.* New Haven, CT: Yale University Press.

Delpit, L. (1986). Skills and other dilemmas of a progressive Black educator. *Harvard Educational Review, 56*(4), 379-385.

Delpit, L. (1995). *Other people's children: Cultural conflict in the classroom.* New York: The New Press.

DuBois, W. E. B. (1968). The souls of black folks: Essays and sketches. Greenwich, CT: Fawcett. (Original published 1903).

Dyson, A. H. (1993). *Social worlds of children learning to write in an urban primary school.* New York: Teachers College Press.

Edwards, P. (1992). Involving parents in buliding reading instruction for African-American children. *Theory into Practice, 31*(4), 350-359.

Ellsworth, E. (1989). Why doesn't this feel empowering? Working through the repressive myths of critical pedagogy. *Harvard Educational Review, 59*, 297-324.

Enciso, P. (1990). *The nature of engagement in reading: Profiles of three fifth-graders' engagement strategies and stances.* Unpublished doctoral dissertation, The Ohio State University, Columbus.

Enciso, P. (1992). Creating the story world: A case study of a young reader's engagement strategies and stances. In J. Many and C. Cox (Eds.), *Reader stance and literary understanding: Exploring the theories, research, and practice* (pp. 75-102). Norwood, NJ: Ablex.

Enciso, P. (1994). Cultural identity and response to literature: Running lessons from Maniac Magee. *Language Arts, 71*, 524-533.

Enciso, P. (1996a). Why engagement in reading matters to Molly. *Reading and Writing Quarterly, 12*(2), 171-194.

Enciso, P. (1996b). Negotiating the meaing of difference: Talking back to multicultural literature. In T. Rogers & A. Soter (Eds.), *Reading across cultures* (pp. 13-41). New York: Teachers College Press.

Enciso, P. (1998). *Reworking reading positions among African American and European American fourth- and fifth-grade boys and girls.* Paper presented at the annual meeting of the American Educational Research Association, San Diego, CA.

Foster, M. (1996). African American teachers and culturally relevant pedagogy. In J. Banks & C.A. Banks (Eds.), *Handbook of research on multicultural education* (pp. 570-581). New York: Macmillan.

Freire, P. (1985). *The politics of education: Culture, power and liberation.* South Hadley, MA: Bergin & Garvey.

Freppon, P., & Dahl, K. (1991) Learning about phonics in a whole language classroom. *Language Arts, 68*, 190-197.

Gallas, K. (1995). *The languages of learning: How children talk, write, dance, draw, and sing their understanding of the world.* New York: Teachers College Press.

Gee, J. (1999). Critical issues: Reading and the new literacy studies: Reframing the National Academy of Sciences report on reading. *Journal of Literacy Research, 31*(3), 355-374.

Gilmore, P. (1985). "Gimme room": School resistance, attitude, and access to literacy. *Journal of Education, 167,* 111-128.

Greene, M. (1994). Multiculturalism, community, and the arts. In A. H. Dyson & C. Genishi (Eds.), *The need for story: Cultural diversity in classroom and community* (pp. 11-27). Urbana, IL: National Council of Teachers of English.

Gutierrez, K., & Stone, L. (1997). A cultural-historical view of learning and learning disabilities: Participating in a community of learners. *Learning Disabilities Research and Practice, 12*(2), 123-131.

Harris, V. (1992). *Teaching multicultural literature in grades K-8.* Norwood, MA: Christopher-Gordon.

Henry, A. (1990, April). *Black women, Black pedagogies: An African-Canadian context.* Paper presented at the annual meeting of the American Educational Research Association, Boston, MA.

Hidalgo, N. (1993). Multicultural teacher introspection. In T. Perry & J. Fraser (Eds.), *Freedom's plow: Teaching in the multicultural classroom* (pp. 99-108). New York: Routledge.

Hilliard, A. G. (1990). Limitations of current academic achievement measures. In K. Lotomey (Ed.), *Going to school: The African-American experience* (pp. 135-142). Buffalo: State University of New York Press.

Iser, W. (1978). *The act of reading: A theory of aesthetic response.* Baltimore: Johns Hopkins University Press.

Ladson-Billings, G. (1992). Reading between the lines and beyond the pages: A culturally relevant approach to literacy teaching. *Theory into Practice, 31*(4), 312-321.

Ladson-Billings, G. (1994). *The dreamkeepers: Successful teachers of African American children.* San Francisco: Jossey-Bass.

Ladson-Billings, G., & Henry, A. (1990). Blurring the borders: Voices of African liberatory pedagogy in the United States and Canada. *Boston Journal of Education, 172*(2), 72-88.

Lee, C. (1991). Big picture talkers/words walking without masters: The instructional implications of ethnic voices for an expanded literacy. *Journal of Negro Education, 60,* 291-304.

Littlechild, G. (1993). *This land is my land.* San Francisco: Children's Book Press.

Luke, A. (1995). When basic skills and information processing just aren't enough: Rethinking reading in new times. *Teachers College Record, 97*(1), 95-115.

Manguel, A. (1996). *A history of reading.* New York: Viking.

Martínez, E. (1995). Distorting Latino history: The California textbook controversy. In D. Levine, R. Lowe, B. Peterson, & R. Tenorio (Eds.), *Rethinking schools: An agenda for change* (pp. 100-108). New York: The New Press.

McDermott, G. (1974). Achieving school failure: An anthropological approach to illiteracy and social stratification. In G. Spindler (Ed.), *Education and cultural process.* New York: Holt, Rinehart and Winston.

Mehan, H. (1979). *Learning lessons: The social organization of classroom behavior.* Cambridge, MA: Harvard University Press.

Moll, L., & Greenberg, J. B. (1990). Creating zones of possibilities: Combining social contexts for instruction. In L. C. Moll (Ed.), *Vygotsky and education* (pp. 319-348). Cambridge, England: Cambridge University Press.

Nieto, S. (1996). *Affirming diversity: The sociopolitical context of multicultural education* (2nd ed.). White Plains, NY: Longman.

Ortiz, S. (1988). *The people shall continue.* San Francisco: Children's Book Press.

Paley, V. G. (1997). *The girl with the brown crayon: How children use stories to shape their lives.* Cambridge, MA: Harvard University Press.

Reyes, M. de la Luz. (1992). Challenging venerable assumptions: Literacy instruction for linguistically different students. *Harvard Educational Review, 62,* 427-446.

Shannon, P., & Luke, A. (1991) Introduction to critical literacy. *The Reading Teacher, 44*(7), 518-519.

Short, K., & Harste, J., with Burke, C. (1996). *Creating classrooms for authors and inquirers* (2nd ed.). Portsmouth, NH: Heinemann.

Snow, C., Burns, M. S., & Griffin, P. (Eds.), (1998). *Preventing reading difficulties in young children.* Washington, DC: National Academy Press.

Soto, G. (1995). *Canto familiar.* New York: Harcourt Brace.

Spears-Bunton, L. (1990). Welcome to my house: African American and European American students' responses to Virginia Hamilton's House of Dies Drear. *Journal of Negro Education, 59,* 566–576.

Spinelli, J. (1991). *Maniac Magee.* Boston: Little, Brown.

Taylor, D. (1998). *Beginning to read and the spin doctors of science: The political campaign to change America's mind about how children learn to read.* Urbana, IL: National Council of Teachers of English.

Vygotsky, L. S. (1978). *Mind in society: The development of higher psychological processes.* M. Cole, V. John-Steiner, S. Scribner, & E. Souberman (Eds). Cambridge, MA: Harvard University Press.

Willis, A. (1995). Reading the world of school literacy: Contextualizing the experience of a young African American male. *Harvard Educational Review, 65,* 30–49.

Wood, T., with Wanbli Numpa Afraid of Hawk. (1992). *A boy becomes a man at Wounded Knee.* New York: Walker.

10 Mathematizing and the Democracy: The Need for an Education That Is Multicultural and Social Reconstructionist

William F. Tate IV
University of Wisconsin-Madison

What people chose to count and measure reveals not only what was important to them but what they wanted to understand and, often, what they wanted to control. Further, how people counted and measured reveals underlying assumptions ranging from plain old bias—the historian's easy target, when it is detected—to ideas about the structure of society. In some cases, the activity of counting and measuring itself altered the way people thought about what they were quantifying: numeracy could be an agent of change. (Cohen, 1982, p. 206)

How one is categorized is far from a merely academic or even personal matter. Such matters as access to employment, housing or other publicly or privately valued goods, social program design and the disbursement of local, state, and federal funds, or the organization of elections (among many other issues) are directly affected by racial classification. . . . (Omi & Winant, 1986, p. 4)

Scholars who challenge the implicit, unspoken assumption of objectivity in effect claim that knowledge depends on the interaction between the one who sees and what is seen. Reality is not discovered but constructed and invented and this process of invention needs itself to be included within the search for knowledge. (Minow, 1987, p. 175)

The above remarks suggest that the use of mathematics is connected to issues of economic power and social control. Traditionally, mathematics has been described as a discipline unconnected to human affairs. Mathematics is defined as "the science of numbers and operations, interrelations, combinations, generalizations, and abstractions and of space configurations and their structure, measurement, transformations, and generalizations" (Merriam-Webster, 1993, p. 273). Further, mathematical constructs are rigorously exact, precise, and certain. Many in the mathematics community are committed to a belief in the absolute objectivity, neutrality, and exactness of mathematics. However, Ernest (1991) points out that this view of mathematics that promotes itself as value is actually value-laden. He stated:

Abstract is valued over concrete, formal over informal, objective over subjective, justification over discovery, rationality over intuition, reason over emotion, general over particular, theory over practice, the work of the brain over the work of the hand, and so on. These constitute many of the overt values of mathematicians, as well as being shared by much of British and Western scientific culture. (p. 259)

Ernest's remarks provide a backdrop to discuss the following question: Should schools provide students with a mathematics education that prepares them to question the assumptions of objectivity and neutrality that accompany the use of mathematics in our multicultural and democratic society? I contend that curriculum and instruction that present mathematics as objective, value-free, and neutral are problematic. I will argue throughout this chapter that mathematics is embedded in the nexus of society's power relations. Thus, mathematics as a tool to guide social decision making is influenced by the values of those who use it in human affairs.

❖ Understanding Mathematics in Society: Mathematizing

An important way for students to understand mathematics is to know how and why critical issues are mathematized. Putnam, Lampert, and Peterson (1990) described mathematizing as the building of quantitative models to represent non-quantitative relationships. Putnam and colleagues (1990) state that mathematizing assumes:

[A] certain view of the social and physical world, which asserts that the important *elements* [emphasis added] of situations can be represented by numbers and relationships among numbers. In Western society, this view is somewhat of a given, certainly among particular segments of the population who use mathematics to formulate and solve problems and others who *consume* [emphasis added] their work. (p. 98)

How does the mathematizer select the important elements of a situation? Einstein provides some insight into this question:

To the discoverer . . . the constructions of his imagination appear so necessary and so natural that he is apt to treat them not as the creations of his thoughts, but as given realities . . . The stereotypical categories that we use are rarely without some point of tangency with reality (biological, social, medical), but their interpretation is colored by the ideology that motivates us. (Cited in Minow, 1987, pp. 173–174).

The selection of "appropriate" variables/categories to represent a situation is a subjective process (see e.g., Omi & Winant, 1986). Further, choosing the "proper" mathematical technique to model and analyze a situation is a subjective process. The mathematizer can use multiple mathematical techniques to model the same situation. Each technique can provide the mathematizer a different result. This allows mathematizers the freedom to choose a result more consistent with their preordained set of beliefs. In essence, mathematics can serve to "scientifically" reconstruct situations that serve the purposes of the mathematizer (Gould, 1981).

Quantitative methods built on assumptions of objectivity and neutrality can serve to mask the subjective and non-neutral position of the mathematizer (e.g., Rosenberg, 1992).

The philosophical underpinnings associated with mathematics, objectivity, and neutrality are transferred to the value-laden reconstructions of reality made by the mathematizer. This allows the mathematizer to offer solutions to social problems under the guise of being neutral, objective, and fair. I will use a personal experience to illustrate how the mathematizer's ideology influences the reconstruction and interpretation of situations.[1]

College admission requirements that use a combination of test scores and high school class rank are an example of a mathematized method for sorting people into categories (Putnam et al., 1990). When I was an undergraduate, the university administration recommended raising the mandatory ACT score by three points for incoming freshmen. The proposed higher admission requirement was part of a plan to enhance the national status of the campus. Many students favored the proposed change. These students argued that improving the national status of the institution would enhance their opportunities for employment and graduate school admission.

A group of students, including myself, were concerned with how the new policy would affect the number of culturally diverse students admitted to the institution. We formed a committee to analyze the policy. The committee decided that the best way to address the issue would be to determine how the proposed policy would have impacted the admission status of African American freshmen admitted to the university in the prior five fall semesters. African American students were chosen because the university's administration had made public statements about the need to increase the presence of this group on campus. We believed there was a potential conflict between the proposed admission policy and the university's public stance on African American students.

We applied the new admission criteria to the previous five incoming freshmen classes admitted for fall semester. This analysis revealed that a significant percentage of African American students would not have been admitted to the institution. We estimated that 300 out of 1,000 African American students previously admitted would have failed to gain admission.[2] This would have represented a 30% reduction of African American freshmen admitted to the university in the previous five fall semesters.

We presented our results to the university administration. To our surprise, the university's department for institutional research had performed the same mathematical procedure on all fall semester admittees from the past five incoming freshmen classes.[3] The institutional research group's analysis provided the total number of incoming freshmen admitted during the previous five fall semesters who would not have gained admission under the new proposal. They categorized these students into three groups—White, African American, and "other." The institutional research figures confirmed the findings of our student group. That is, 300 out of the 1,000 African American students would not have been admitted under the proposed admission requirements. In addition, the university institutional research group found that 2,000 out of the 10,000 white students and 500 out of the 2,000 students categorized as "other" would not have been admitted under the proposed entrance requirements. The institutional research group argued that only 300 of the 2,800 students not admitted under the proposed entrance requirement would have been African American. Thus, African Americans represented only 10.7% of those students who would not have been admitted using the proposed entrance requirements, as compared to 2,000 out of 2,800, or 71.4% of white students. The university research group argued that the percentage of African American students that would not have been admitted was small in comparison to the percentage of white students.

For both sides involved in the college admission debate, the selection of variables and the analysis performed on these variables were linked to the ideology of each group. Thus, each group responded to several important questions related to using mathematics in the democracy. For example, what methods of mathematical analysis will best support your group's position? What variables should be included within the analysis to strengthen your group's argument? How can you minimize the appearance of variables that may weaken your group's argument? Will percentages or aggregate numbers leave a more striking impression? All of these questions are integral aspects of using mathematics in a multicultural democracy.

Imagine if the university's institutional group had reported their findings without the input of our student group's analysis. For instance, the university institutional group could have reported that 2,800 freshmen admitted to the university over the previous five fall semesters would not have gained admission under the proposed entrance requirements. Further, only 10.7% of those not admitted were African American. In comparison, 71.4% of those not admitted were white students. Would reporting the data in this fashion cause an uproar in the African American student community? Not likely. In fact, it would have probably moved white students to protest against the policy recommendation, especially given that most students are trained to consume numbers. Few students are educated to investigate the ideology that motivates the production of mathematical analysis.

In the end, our student group won the debate. We argued that the new admission policy would have resulted in 300 out of 1,000 African Americans not gaining admission, a 30% reduction, as compared to 2,000 out of 10,000 white students, a 20% reduction. Clearly, the proposed policy would have more negatively impacted African American freshmen enrollment. Although the university institutional report was mathematically accurate, it did not accurately represent the impact of the proposed admission requirements. Instead, it represented the viewpoint of the university policy-makers.

Without the activism and the mathematical input of the student group, an admission policy recommendation would have been enacted that was inconsistent with the university's policy statement on African American student enrollment. Earlier, I asked the question: "Should schools provide students a mathematics education that prepares them to question the assumptions of objectivity and neutrality that accompany the use of mathematics in our multicultural and democratic society ?" I submit that by failing to do so, mathematics teachers will continue to produce a society of mathematical consumers.

The college admissions debate provides a backdrop to begin a discussion of a mathematics education that is designed to prepare students to be producers and critics of mathematics in society, rather than consumers. More specifically, this discussion will look to principles of multiculturalism as a guide for mathematics teaching that prepares students for the challenges of the democracy.

The word *multicultural* may evoke different images both within and across the various learning communities in education. For instance, the concept of multiculturalism has been interpreted differently in the mathematics education community than by scholars who argue for an education that is multicultural and social reconstructionist (EMC). The EMC approach to mathematics education is discussed and developed in this article because it specifically addresses the issue of preparing students to be critical activists within the democracy. Therefore, in order to facilitate communication and understanding between mathematics educators and educators who advocate the EMC approach, the next section of this chapter examines the interrelationship of undergirding philo-sophical tenets of mathematics and multicultural approaches to mathematics education. Included in this discussion are past multicultural recommendations within mathematics education. The final section of this paper is a discussion of two philosophical tenets—centricity and conflict—that undergird a new vision of mathematics education that is multicultural and social reconstructionist.

✣ Multicultural Approaches to Mathematics

Some scholars have argued that the principles underlying the use of mathematics cast this discipline as "elite knowledge" appropriate only for those with privileged status (Cohen, 1987; Kamens & Benevot, 1991). Joseph (1987) posited that the present struc-ture of mathematics education is based on the following historiographic pillars:

1. The inclination not to locate mathematics within a materialistic base and thus to con-nect its advancement with the economic, political, and cultural venues of society.
2. The belief that mathematics should be confined to an elite group who are thought to possess the requisite talent denied a majority of society.
3. The widespread agreement among mathematicians that mathematical discovery can follow only from deductive logic believed to be a product of Greek mathematics; thus, empirical methods are viewed as having little mathematical value.

A great deal of the multicultural movement within mathematics education has been defined by its opposition to the second pillar. That is, mathematics education should be expanded beyond just the elite few (Cuevas, 1984; Ethington, 1990; Johnson, 1984; Research Advisory Committee, 1989; Reyes & Stanic, 1988). More specifically, the multicultural approach in mathematics education has focused on (a) working with cul-turally diverse students to improve affective factors (e.g., self-esteem and attitude); (b) adding more diversity to the mathematics teaching workforce; and (c) introducing multicultural elements into mathematics textbooks (McLeod, 1992; National Research Council, 1989; Valverde, 1984). This body of literature delineates an approach to mathe-matics education principled on all students learning the traditional curriculum in tradi-tional classrooms and being successful in the society as it is currently configured. This scholarship is not completely divorced from Joseph's first and third pillar.

In contrast, educators advocating an EMC approach look to restructure the tradi-tional curriculum by integrating social issues involving inequality based on race, social class, disability, and gender. The primary objective of the curriculum is to prepare stu-dents to be citizens able to reconstruct the democracy based on egalitarian precepts. According to Grant and Sleeter (1989), meeting this objective would involve:

• Promoting and celebrating America's cultural diversity.
• Helping all children achieve academic success.
• Structuring classrooms like a real democracy in order to situate students in realistic opportunities for decision making.
• Developing curricula directly related to the student's lived reality.
• Encouraging social action by involving students in social issues.

Some mathematics educators have made efforts to address one or more of the above themes. However, a paradigmatic tension exists between the philosophy undergirding traditional mathematics and multicultural approaches. According to Kuhn (1970), normal science is based "upon one or more past scientific achievements, achievements that some particular scientific community acknowledges for a time as supplying the foundation for its further practice" (p. 10). The foundation of practice in more traditional approaches to mathematics is derived from Joseph's three pillars. Joseph (1987) provides further insight into the political implications of these foundations of practice:

> Now an important area of concern for anti-racists is the manner in which European scholarship has represented the past and potentialities of non-white societies with respect to their achievement and capabilities in promoting science and technology. The progress of Europe and its cultural dependencies [including the United States] during the last 400 years is perceived by many as inextricably—and even causally—linked with the rapid growth of science and technology. So that in the minds of many, scientific progress becomes a uniquely European phenomenon, to be emulated only following the European path of social and scientific development. (pp. 13–14)

Joseph argued that the void of non-European contributions in the mathematics curriculum is a function of two issues of power. First, for one group to maintain control over another group it becomes important that the knowledge of the dominant group be perceived as most relevant (Apple, 1979; Apple, 1992). If the basis of control is scientific knowledge, as was the case with Europe over its colonies, then Eurocentric mathematical principles must be imposed over those of non-European groups.

The second issue of power concerns the group associated with the development of mathematical knowledge. If mathematics were associated with non-Europeans it would imply that they were capable of creating their own technology-based economies. This implication is counter to the stereotypic mythmaking used to justify the oppressive actions of European domination (e.g., Jefferson, 1954; Crenshaw, 1988). For example, Thomas Jefferson argued that people of African descent were incapable of mathematical reasoning. He used this argument to legitimize the unequal social status of African Americans (i.e., slavery). Jefferson's reasoning was not only morally questionable, he was inaccurate in his position on African Americans and mathematics (Van Sertima, 1988). A body of scholarship has emerged that documents how people of African descent and other cultural backgrounds have contributed to the development of mathematics.

Ethnomathematics

Many scholars view mathematics as an abstract subject devoid of connections with the materialistic base, while for many cultural groups mathematics is directly linked to the structural development of their societies. The study of how various groups and cultures in the world develop and use mathematics is called *ethnomathematics* (Nunes, 1992). D'Ambrosio (1985) defined ethnomathematics as the art of comprehending, describing, coping with, and managing both natural and socially constructed systems—using techniques such as counting, measuring, sorting, ordering, and inferring—developed by well-defined groups like nations, professional classes, children in various age groups, labor groups, and so on. Ethnomathematics provides a lens to view and to comprehend mathematics as a cultural product. Further, ethnomathematics illustrates the validity of the mathematics produced by a wide variety of groups.

For example, Zaslavsky (1991) describes how the Chokwe people of Angola and Zaire use networks to symbolize their beliefs about the beginning of the world. Networks are finite mathematical graphs. In Western society, finite graphs are used to represent telecommunication systems, highways, and other technological applications. For Zaslavsky and others who incorporate ethnomathematics into their classroom instruction, it is very important that all students understand how mathematical representations like networks are connected to the lives of people in various cultures and societies.

Critical Mathematics Literacy

I contend that the elitist bias of mathematics has resulted in a censorship of the ethnomathematics of the American culture. Schools do very little to prepare students for the role of mathematics in American society. Frankenstein (1995) argues that the applications of mathematics taught in schools impart a vision of neutrality and naturalness to specific social configurations that help obscure the class structure of American society. Frankenstein states:

> [M]athematical disempowerment works by presenting mathematics applications that support a particular interpretation and organization of society; and by omitting information that shows the usefulness of statistical data in understanding economic, political, and social issues; and by ignoring data that presents alternative explanations and visions about the structure of society. (pp. 167–168)

In response, Frankenstein has developed a critical mathematical literacy (CML) program. Students learn how and when mathematics is used as a result of studying situations where mathematics is a product. CML provides students an opportunity to analyze data on wealth distribution, the exploitive activity of multinational organizations, and the connection between race, gender, and class exploitation. One theme of the curriculum is "welfare for the rich" or government transfer of monies from the poor to the rich. For example, Frankenstein's students study the mathematics embedded within the Neil Bush Silverado Savings and Loan scandal.

The situational contexts of CML allow the student to construct and reconstruct real, not "realistic," mathematical applications. This process provides students an opportunity to connect mathematics to other knowledge they have about society. Frankenstein suggests this connection catalyzes discussion about the subjective aspects of mathematics. Students begin to see mathematics as context specific. For example, they realize categories are socially negotiated and that reality is obscured by categorizing data in a certain way.

Many educators may question how ethnomathematics and critical mathematics literacy help students understand mathematics. I contend that there are several reasons why these approaches to mathematics education are important.

- Both allow students to gain a sense of how mathematics is developed and used in real settings.
- Both connect mathematics with other subject areas such as history, social studies, economics, anthropology, medicine, and potentially any other domain. The mathematics education reform establishment has argued that this is an important component of numerical literacy (National Council of Teachers of Mathematics, 1989).

- Both challenge the Eurocentric premise that mathematics is a neutral norm devoid of connection to human affairs.
- Ethnomathematics documents the development and creation of mathematics by many cultures and groups.
- Both ethnomathematics and critical mathematical literacy provide teachers of mathematics a literature base to broaden their understanding of how mathematics is used in real contexts.

A mathematics education that is multicultural and social reconstructionist should build on these strengths.

✣ Mathematics and EMC: The Philosophical Underpinnings

The first component of a mathematics education that is multicultural and social reconstructionist is centricity. This component distinguishes the EMC mathematics approach from ethnomathematics and critical mathematics literacy, in that centricity is a paramount consideration.

A mathematics education that is EMC centers the student in the knowledge acquisition process. Students bring culturally relevant knowledge and experiences to classrooms that traditional mathematics pedagogy and other multicultural approaches often fail to acknowledge and build on. The danger of not building on students' experiences and communities is that opportunities to illustrate the subjective aspects of mathematics are lost. Elsewhere I captured this point in a story about a group of African American students from a middle school who responded "strangely" to a question on a school district mathematics test (Tate, 1994). The structure of the test item was similar to the following:

> It costs $1.50 each way to ride the bus between home and work. The weekly pass is $16.00. Which is the better deal, paying the daily fare or buying the weekly pass?

The school district's test designers constructed the problem assuming the students solving the problem correctly would choose the option of "paying the daily fare." The test item design assumes that all people work five days a week and that the worker has only one job. Yet, these assumptions are not congruent with the lived realities of many culturally diverse students (Darity & Meyers, 1989). Therefore, it should not be shocking that a large percentage of the students from this particular middle school chose the "buying the weekly pass" option. When school officials questioned the children about their answers they found many students had personalized the solution process. For example, the students commented on the ability of more than one family member to use a weekly pass. Students also mentioned using the weekly pass on Saturday and Sunday.

Many culturally diverse students live in families where the financial provider(s) have several part-time jobs—on both weekdays and weekends. For these students selecting the weekly pass is economically appropriate, thus mathematically logical. I argue that the correct answer should have been connected to the specific context of the students' lives. Stiff and Harvey (1988) note that students who center their lives and experiences within the process of acquiring mathematical competency risk being penalized for focusing on "tangential matters." As a result many culturally diverse students view mathematics as a subject appropriate only for white males, and they fail to see the usefulness and relevance of the subject (Johnson, 1984).

The failure to provide all students with curriculum and instruction based on their experiences, cultures, and traditions is a major impediment to an empowering education (Asante, 1991; Cummins, 1986; Secada, 1991; Stanic, 1991; Stiff & Harvey, 1988; Woodson, 1933). Molefi Asante (1991) argues that an empowering education would be premised on centricity. He states:

> Centricity refers to a perspective that involves locating students within the context of their own cultural references so that they can relate socially and psychologically to other cultural perspectives. Centricity is a concept that can be applied to any culture. . . . For white students in America this is easy because almost all the experiences discussed in American classrooms are approached from the standpoint of white perspectives and history. (p. 171)

The centric perspective provides a framework for analyzing why many of the Philadelphia middle school children responded incorrectly to the test question. First, the student had to understand that the mode of response should reflect the lived realities of a "mythical" White, middle-class household. Second, the student had to understand the mathematics involved in solving the problem using the White, middle-class perspective as a frame to guide the solution process. This dual level of consciousness must occur if the student is to solve the problem based on the Eurocentric assumptions of the test.

Is the first level of consciousness fair or empowering to students whose experiences are outside the White middle-class realm? Harvey (1984) provides what I consider an appropriate response to this question:

> The advocacy of the values and lifestyles of the dominant white culture is not and cannot be psychologically beneficial to Blacks. The dominant cultural value system, and that of the school admonishes Black students for being what they are while physical and social reality prevents them from being anything else. (p. 446)

To take advantage of the diversity in a single classroom, the mathematics teacher using an EMC approach would allow each student to solve problems using their lived reality. Of course, the mathematical processes used to solve a problem should be consistent with the parameters of the student's life. Similarly, Silver, Smith, and Nelson (1995) argued for the need to enhance the relevancy of school mathematics by building on students' life experience. They offered the following task as a vehicle to explore the complexity of students' thinking and experiences related to the bus problem:

> Yvonne is trying to decide whether she should buy a weekly bus pass. On Monday, Wednesday, and Friday, she rides the bus to and from work. On Tuesday and Thursday, she rides the bus to work, but gets a ride home with her friends. Should Yvonne buy a weekly bus pass? Explain your answer.

Busy Bus Company Fares

One Way $1.00

Weekly Pass $9.00

The structure of this task would allow students to answer the question based on their specific circumstances, yet the context provides more specific parameters to guide the students and assess them across a common condition (i.e., the details of the work schedule). Further, the EMC approach to mathematics education would advocate having students solve the same question from the perspective of different members of the class, school, and/or society. This would be important for two reasons. First, students would have an opportunity to solve the same question using different contextual backgrounds. The various solution processes for each context provide students invaluable insight into the varied nature of problem parameters. More specifically, it would show students that mathematics is embedded in contexts and, as a result, doing mathematics is context dependent. Second, students would have the opportunity to relate and compare their experiences with a variety of groups.

✤ Conflict and Mathematics

The second philosophical principle guiding a mathematics education that is EMC is drawn from conflict theory. Conflict theory provides an explanatory framework for understanding how social systems work. The major premise of this theory is that society distributes its rewards through various social structures and according to the laws that govern these various structures (Appleton, 1983). Social conflicts are a product of groups attempting to secure a favorable position over other groups in the allocation of these rewards (e.g., Allen, 1974; Bell, 1992; Marable, 1983).

One way that educational systems secure a favorable position for various groups is by failing to provide *all students* with instruction that prepares them to expose and reconstruct inequitable conditions. I emphasize "all students" because some students are provided an education principled on a reconstructionist philosophy. For example, Kozol (1991) documented how a White, upper-middle-class group of fourth-graders expanded the concept of "right" after learning about the Bill of Rights and how greed and domination could impact the implementation of the present definition. In the same school, a sixth-grade class learned to question the scientific findings of researchers. One sixth grader wrote the following:

> Gregor Mendel . . . the Austrian monk who founded the science of genetics,
> published papers on his work with peas that some experts say were statistically too
> good to be true. Isaac Newton, who formulated the law of gravitation, relied on
> unseemly mathematical sleight of hand in his calculations . . . Galileo Galilei, founder
> of the modern scientific method, wrote about experiments that were so difficult to
> duplicate that colleagues doubted he had done them. (Kozol, 1991, p. 97)

The students of this school are being provided an education that attempts to demystify the scientific method and begins to prepare them to understand and challenge the use of science in society. Apple (1979) offers two reasons for students to have an education that includes an opportunity to explore the role of conflict in the scientific enterprise. Both reasons apply to mathematics. First, mathematical production is a function of conflict. Knowledge production is conducted by groups or communities of scholars. Like all communities, the mathematics community is governed by both stated rules and a covert value system (Ernest, 1991). Within this community, individuals and groups of mathematicians have a significant history of struggle over what is appropriate knowledge for the discipline. These struggles also include conflicts over data interpretation, credit for discovering ideas, censorship, and many other issues (Eves, 1983). Seemingly, the very nature of mathematical production involves conflict. Yet, school mathematics is presented as a body of static ideas and procedures. Hidden from the student is the role and need for conflict in order to advance mathematical thought.

A mathematics education that fails to prepare students for the conflict involved with mathematical production is problematic for a second reason. The use of mathematics in our democratic/capitalistic society is almost always linked to one group or individual attempting to secure resources over another.

For example, in Major League baseball, fielding averages from .99 to 1 are excellent. Fielding averages under .96 are considered poor. Suppose you are an agent for a professional baseball player. You are responsible for presenting information to an arbitrator on the player's fielding performance as compared to an all-star player.

Do the graphs in Figure 10.1 represent the same information? If you said "yes," you are correct. Which graph should be presented by the player's agent? Which graph should be presented by the team? Which graph is more accurate? Why? If you knew nothing about good or bad fielding averages, what would you have concluded? This example represents how the same information can be "mathematized" and made to appear more consistent with the needs and ideology of the mathematizer.

Ask yourself the following question: "When do you count just for the sake of counting?" My response to this question is "in school." Otherwise, counting and other mathematical activities are performed to move forward or block a particular agenda. Mathematics education should prepare students to recognize that the role of mathematics in the society is to both initiate and resolve conflicts. Further, students should be prepared to initiate and resolve conflicts "centric" to their lives using mathematics.

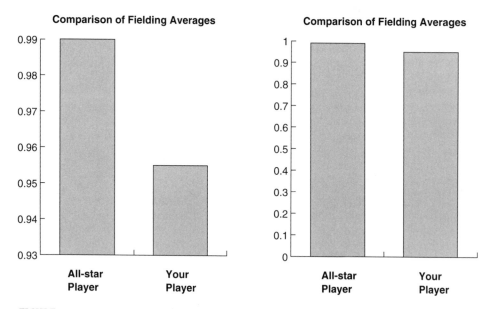

FIGURE 10.1 A comparison of two players' fielding averages.

✥ Final Note

Would you want to be represented by an attorney whose legal education consisted only of memorizing the laws, codes, and regulations of your state? Most likely, you would not. Imagine having this attorney prepare an argument on your behalf in a case involving several different types of institutions in our society—a government entity, a citizen's group, and a large corporation. You would want the attorney to understand the vested interests of each institution and to integrate this background information with the law to formulate a strong case in your behalf. This implies that an attorney must have knowledge of the legal system and of the many different types of institutions that interact within this system. Further, the attorney's reasoning is guided by the context and factors of each case. Merely memorizing the law is inadequate for this profession.

The same issues that apply to an attorney's professional knowledge base apply to the knowledge base of a multicultural and social reconstructionist mathematics teacher. First, mathematics teachers, like attorneys, must work to understand and build on the background, experiences, and culture of their clients/students. Thus, both professions require a centric perspective.

Second, both the lawyer and the EMC mathematics teacher are preparing their clients for the conflicts of the democracy. The EMC approach calls for providing students with a mathematics education which prepares them to make decisions on complex political issues that arise within our democratic society. The EMC approach to mathematics not only requires teachers to have a thorough knowledge of the connections across mathematical topics, but also insists that they know how and why mathematics is used in particular social contexts.

Many students leave school unprepared to use mathematics in real situations in our society. Just as legal education provides the law student an opportunity to apply the law within realistic settings of the profession (e.g., mock trials, internships, and summer clerkships), an EMC mathematics teacher must structure the educational environment so that students have opportunities to construct mathematical understanding within realistic settings where mathematics is a product. The key phrase here is "educational environment." For the EMC mathematics teacher, the world is the educational environment.

Notes

1. Delgado (1990) argues that people of color speak with experiential knowledge that in our society is framed by oppression. This framework gives their stories a common structure warranting the term "voice." A growing body of literature incorporates "voice" to explain the experience of culturally diverse people. These scholars use parables, chronicles, stories, counterstories, poetry, fiction, and revisionist histories to illustrate the irony and contradictions of certain policies in education (Tate, 1994). In this article, I use "voice" scholarship as a vehicle to illustrate the contradictions within the traditional mathematics education paradigm.

2. The data provided in this article are rounded estimates. Please note admission data by race are not mandatory information on most college admission applications. Thus, both the university administration and the student group extrapolated their estimates for the sake of discussion.

3. One member of the student group informed the school administration of our mathematical methods and conclusions.

References

Allen, R. (1974). *Reluctant reformers: The impact of racism on American social reform movements.* Washington, DC: Howard University.

Apple, M. W. (1979). *Ideology and curriculum.* New York: Routledge.

Apple, M. W. (1992). Do the standards go far enough? Power, policy, and practice in mathematics education. *Journal for Research in Mathematics Education, 23,* 421-431.

Appleton, N. (1983). *Cultural pluralism in education: Theoretical foundations.* New York: Longman.

Asante, M. K. (1991). The Afrocentric idea in education. *Journal of Negro Education, 60,* 170-180.

Bell, D. (1992). *Faces at the bottom of the well: The permanence of racism.* New York: Basic Books.

Cohen, P. C. (1982). *A calculating people: The spread of numeracy in early America.* Chicago: University of Chicago Press.

Crenshaw, K. W. (1988) Race, reform, and retrenchment: Transformation and legitimation in anti-discrimination law. *Harvard Law Review, 101,* 1331-1387.

Cuevas, G. (1984). Mathematics learning in English as a second language. *Journal for Research in Mathematics Education, 15,* 134-144.

Cummins, J. (1986). Empowering minority students: A framework for intervention. *Harvard Educational Review, 56,* 18-36.

D'Ambrosio, U. (1985). Ethnomathematics and its place in the history and pedagogy of mathematics. *For the Learning of Mathematics, 5,* 44-48.

Darity, W. A., & Meyers, S. L. (1989). *The problem of family structure, earnings inequality and the marginalization of Black men.* Unpublished manuscript.

Delgado, R. (1990). When a story is just a story: Does voice really matter? *Virginia Law Review, 76,* 95-111.

Ernest, P. (1991). *The philosophy of mathematics education.* Bristol, PA: Falmer.

Ethington, C. A. (1990). Gender differences in mathematics: An international perspective. *Journal for Research in Mathematics Education, 21,* 74-80.

Eves, H. (1983). *An introduction to the history of mathematics* (5th ed.). New York: Saunders.

Frankenstein, M. (1995). Equity in mathematics education: Class in the world outside the class. In E. Fennema, W. G. Secada, & L. Byrd (Eds.), *New directions for equity in mathematics education* (pp. 165-190). New York: Cambridge University Press.

Gould, S. J. (1981). *The mismeasure of man.* New York: W. W. Norton.

Grant, C. A., & Sleeter, C. E. (1989). *Turning on learning: Five approaches for multicultural teaching plans for race, class, gender, and disability.* New York: Merrill.

Harvey, W. B. (1984). The education system and Black mental health. *Journal of Negro Education, 53,* 444-455.

Jefferson, T. (1954). *Notes on the State of Virginia.* New York: W. W. Norton.

Johnson, M. L. (1984). Blacks in mathematics: A status report. *Journal for Research in Mathematics Education, 15,* 145-153.

Joseph, G. C. (1987). Foundations of Eurocentrism in mathematics. *Race and Class, 27,* 13-28.

Kamens, D. H., & Benovot, A. (1991). Elite knowledge for the masses: The origin and spread of mathematics and science education in national curricula. *American Journal of Education, 99,* 137-180.

Kozol, J. (1991). *Savage inequalities: Children in America's schools.* New York: Crown.

Kuhn, T. (1970). *The structure of scientific revolutions.* Chicago: University of Chicago Press.

Marable, M. (1983). *How capitalism underdeveloped Black America.* Boston: South End.

McLeod, D. B. (1992). Research on affect in mathematics education: A reconceptualization. In D. A. Grouws (Ed.), *Handbook of research on mathematics teaching and learning* (pp. 575-596). New York: Macmillan.

Merriam-Webster's Collegiate Dictionary (10th ed.). (1993). Springfield, MA: Merriam-Webster.

Minow, M. (1987). When difference has its home: Group homes for the mentally retarded, equal protection and legal treatment of difference. *Harvard Civil Rights-Civil Liberties Law Review, 22,* 111-190.

National Council of Teachers of Mathematics. (1989). *Curriculum and evaluation standards for school mathematics.* Reston, VA: Author.

National Research Council. (1989). *Everybody counts: A report to the nation on the future of mathematics education.* Washington DC: National Academy Press.

Nunes, T. (1992). Ethnomathematics and everyday cognition. In D. A. Grouws (Ed.), *Handbook of research on mathematics teaching and learning* (pp. 557-574) New York: Macmillan.

Omi, M., & Winant, H. (1986). *Racial formation in the United States.* New York: Routledge.

Piaget, J. (1954). *The construction of reality in the child* (Margaret Cook, Trans.). New York: Basic Books.

Putnam, R. T., Lampert, M., & Peterson, P. L. (1990). Alternative perspectives on knowing mathematics in elementary schools. In C. B. Cazden (Ed.), *Review of research in education* (pp. 57-152). Washington, DC: American Educational Research Association.

Research Advisory Committee. (1989). The mathematics education of underserved and underrepresented groups: A continuing challenge. *Journal for Research in Mathematics Education, 20,* 371-375.

Reyes, L. H., & Stanic, G. M. A. (1988). Race, sex, socioeconomic status, and mathematics. *Journal for Research in Mathematics Education, 19,* 26-43.

Rosenburg, A. (1992). *Economics—Mathematical politics or science of diminishing returns?* Chicago: University of Chicago Press.

Secada, W. G. (1991). Agenda setting, enlightened self interest, and equity in mathematics education. *Peabody Journal of Education, 66,* 22-56.

Silver, E. A., Smith, M. S., & Nelson, B. S. (1995). The QUASAR Project: Equity concerns meet mathematics education reform in middle school. In E. Fennema, W. G. Secada, & L. Byrd (Eds.), *New directions for equity in mathematics education* (pp. 9-56). New York: Cambridge University Press.

Stanic, G. M. A. (1991). Social inequality, cultural discontinuity, and equity in school mathematics. *Peabody Journal of Education, 66,* 57-71.

Stiff, L. V., & Harvey, W. B. (1988). On the education of Black children in mathematics. *Journal of Black Studies, 19,* 190-203.

Tate, W. F. (1994). From inner-city to ivory tower: Does my voice matter in the academy? *Urban Education, 29,* 245-269.

Valverde, L. A. (1984). Underachievement and underrepresentation of Hispanics in mathematics and mathematics-related careers. *Journal for Research in Mathematics Education, 15,* 123-133.

Van Sertima, I. (1988). The lost sciences of Africa: An overview. In I. Van Sertima (Ed.), *Blacks in science: Ancient and modern* (pp. 7-26). New Brunswick, NJ: Transition Books.

Woodson, C. G. (1990). *The mis-education of the Negro.* Trenton, NJ: African World Press. (Original published 1933).

Zaslavsky, C. (1991). Multicultural mathematics education for the middle grades. *Arithmetic Teacher, 38,* 8-13.

11 Learning Science as a Transformative Experience

Jean Lythcott
Martha's Vineyard

James Stewart
University of Wisconsin–Madison

Imagine that when you turn 21 your parents pass on to you an artifact from an ancestor, a long-gone member of the family. Maybe her exact identity has been forgotten by now—someone's great-great-great-aunt, perhaps, or great-great-grandmother. No one knows why the piece was important to the original owner, and so no one is really sure what it is. But the tradition of handing it on to the eldest child has been preserved, and you are the current recipient. You examine it but you can't really connect with it, it has no meaning to you. The threads of connection with its origins are gone, reduced to a tradition of passing it along, intact, and unspoiled. What are you to do with it, except to put it away safely, to pass it along in turn when your time comes?

School science is often like such a tradition—the respectful passing along of decontextualized words and sentences from the past. These words are revered—not to be changed, worked with, nor fitted into the lives of children, but only to be respectfully received from the elders. Listen to the words of science as they exist in the public domain of texts:

> . . . a solid is a state of matter in which a substance has a defined size, shape, and well-defined surfaces that separate it from all other matter (p. 332), and a liquid is a state of matter in which the molecules are free to move from place to place but remain essentially a fixed distance from each other; liquids have a definite volume but they assume the shape of the container in which they rest. (Boeschen, Gerard, & Storin, 1983, p. 330)

These sentences and definitions are terse distillations of meaning, stripped of situational context. They are the decontextualized, abstracted cores of the rich original meaning. This is the language of science that is often taught in schools: sets of words and sentences with their fullest original meanings lost in history.

These pieces of language are our cultural inheritance, passed down to us from the centuries of work, of meaning making, by hundreds of people of different nations, in different contexts, with different materials, asking different questions. The artifacts that are these textbook words and phrases, with their stark, strange, and isolated beauty, have over time become disconnected from the meanings of a cultural past. In science classrooms, the time-honored activity of learning to recite these definitions is like the tradition of passing along an inheritance. And, what is a youngster to do with such strange things that have so little apparent connection with life being actively lived?

How can such artifacts help children make meaning of their world and of themselves in that world? How can receiving these inheritances enable youngsters to transform themselves, to be able to make changes in their own lives and in the lives of others?

Now, to leave this metaphor and to create a different vision, put this book down and collect the following materials:

- One-half cup of cornstarch—any brand from the grocery store will do.
- About four tablespoons of cold water.
- A coffee mug or teacup.
- A sturdy spoon.
- A small container of any kind—but much smaller than the mug. A plastic margarine container works just fine.

Put the cornstarch into the mug, and pour in the cold water. Stir lightly. Adjust the mixture by adding more water or more cornstarch until it is runny when you are not stirring it but dry and somewhat hard when you push it with the spoon. Now scoop the mixture out of the mug with your hand and play with it, in your hands, on the table, in the small container—feel it, drop it, snap it, see what it will do. You might be thinking, "If I just read ahead I can avoid the nuisance of having to do all of this." Maybe so, but you will miss out on something important. By reading ahead you will, in some important respects, only be taking part in the passing-on ritual!

This playing, and feeling, and watching, can spawn conversations that mirror the connections of meaning that grow between the player, the stuff, and the events. Listen to snippets of classroom conversation about this mixture: "It's weird, I mean it's cool stuff—sometimes it's wet, sometimes it's dry"; and "It's like hard and soft, back and forth. When you press it, it becomes hard and solid, then it gets wet and runny again"; another says "It's wet and dry together like it's a liquid but then you pick it up and it turns solid, it's funny." Someone notices something a little different from the others: "It spreads out and it's shiny and loose when it's wet and when it hardens it's not shiny anymore." Now a discussion leader asks: "Tell me how you know when it's being a solid? What is it that lets you know that it is a solid?" and the same question concerning "liquid." The answers come back: "When it's solid you can break it, it just snaps in two, clean, liquids won't do that"; another sees that "When it's a solid the powder, I mean the extra starch, can't penetrate the edges"; someone else says "It has, like edges, that are stiff, not flowing"; and then "You know it's solid when it keeps its own shape, it'll just stand there on its own, you put it in the little jar and for a minute it stands up firm, but then it starts to run down and fills the jar to its shape."

Now the conversation moves to consider the liquidness issue: "It doesn't have a shape when it's liquid, well, not like the solid, but it does when it's stopped spreading out on the table." Another person notices something else: "When it pours out of your hand you know it's liquid. You can pour it and it'll leave part of itself behind, that's a liquid because a solid moves all together in a lump."

What the youngsters knew before they started, from lives lived outside of science class, is crucial to the connections of which meaning is made. Playing with the cornstarch mixture is an experience; it is a context of objects and events out of which children make new meaning for the terms *solid* and *liquid*. When allowed to speak in their own personal language and encouraged to grope for expression of what they think, individuals are free to create meanings for *solid* and *liquid,* to comment and converse about specific bits of the experience that strike a chord of recognition with something they already know.

Listening to the conversation, one can hear the understandings that the students have—the general understanding that things are either solid or liquid and they cannot be both at the same time—and the understanding that for a solid to change into a liquid, and vice versa, is an unexpected event.

Meaning, moreover, is an individual's personal property in this situation. The one who speaks of a solid breaking is not the one who speaks of it having its own shape, nor is it the one who sees that the cornstarch powder cannot penetrate the edges of the solid. The one who saw "pouring" as the liquid leaving behind some of itself is not the one who was struck by it filling the shape of the small container. In this science classroom, the personal contributions of the youngsters are not merely allowed or tolerated, as in some theater of free classroom discourse. Rather, they are the crux of the meanings that the science understandings to come will shadow.

The teacher learns what her students notice, she hears the language they use and begins to negotiate meaning with them: "So, you know that a solid is different from a liquid, you know that solids have fixed edges and so they have a distinct and definite size and shape—the powder cannot penetrate the edges. A solid has surfaces; it takes up a space that nothing else can occupy—we call that its volume."

You have noticed that nothing about a solid moves, it stays still. But a liquid moves by itself—something about the liquid is in motion, pushing the edges of the liquid until it meets the walls of the container and can't go any farther. Somebody noticed that when you hold your hand like this the liquid pours off it, some of it moves and some of it stays behind. The liquid can separate itself; we can think of the liquid being made of tiny pieces that are always moving.

As the meaning is negotiated, the language moves away from the cornstarch mixture. It becomes increasingly detached from and reliant on the particular events and experiences. As the conversation becomes increasingly abstract, the meanings can be connected with a multitude of events not yet experienced, nor even imagined. The science definitions are used, worked with. Each person owns the terse abstractions in a personal way. Rather than inheriting knowledge, the cornstarch players, children and teacher, were the makers of the knowledge they now own. In this way, the science lesson has included children's ideas and experiences as essential to science learning. This is not an easy task for children—making meaning. And it can feel like a discovery to a particular child.

In science class, then, we can provide some experiences and conversation so that youngsters can make the grounded connections that are the stuff of understanding. Returning to the metaphor, these inheritances from the past, these science definitions, will not be strange artifacts to be merely received and put into storage. They have become things with meaning, related and fitted by the youngsters into what they already know. Now they can speak in the language of science, they can use the special words and phrases of science. When they do so, the words and phrases function as language cues to a rich nexus of connections with things and events. The words become included in their lives; students come to speak not about science, but in science.

Our intention has been for you to see the group of children in your imagination. We invited you to join in conversation with us and negotiate meaning about science teaching. This is an impossibility in reality, but perhaps not so in the imagining. What we have been talking about is teachers learning how to teach their children science, starting with materials, events and changes, with something engaging to think and talk about, then listening to their students.

Teachers who have invited children to bring what they know to the table can then negotiate meaning with them from their current understanding. We have been talking about the distinction between a view of science as an artifact to be received and as decontextualized language for which meaning must be created. We have acknowledged that children and teachers use ordinary everyday processes and knowledge of some piece of the world to negotiate and construct new abstracted meaning, in the language of science. It is always the case that youngsters know something that can serve as the foundation for building new ways of explaining and questioning, for noticing new issues, for new language and new meaning.

Our discussion has not concerned the traditional divisions in science education of content versus process; not only do both count, but they are also inseparable. Classifying, for example, is often described as a science process. In playing with and talking about the cornstarch mixture, the youngsters clearly had already classified matter into solid and liquid, but they extended and abstracted that classification through making new decontextualized meaning for the categories in the science class.

The process of classification they used in every day life was also used in science, but to make science meaning, the content and the process were inseparable. Observation is also often mentioned as a science process. The youngsters were certainly observing. They were noticing specific features of the stuff and the changes that occurred. But observing the characteristics that count in science requires one to know what science has said to look for. One child noticed that when the mixture became a liquid it was shiny. That child had observed a characteristic that was indeed interesting and accurate. Whether the observation is useful in science can only be determined from knowing ahead of time what to look for. Only the science meaning for the distinction between solid and liquid tells one whether or not the observation "shiny" is valuable in making science meaning.

This making of meaning is the real basis for the current push for "hands-on" activities in science classes. This is a phrase that makes us laugh a little, for it seems sometimes that there is an idea that knowledge leaks into children's minds through their finger tips! Science meanings do not emerge out of events and experiments. Meaning must be made. No one can see the atoms or molecules of solids and liquids, for example, by observing, touching, and manipulating materials in "hands-on" activities. These particles that scientists have proposed exist must be imagined by each learner. Students get to this imagining by thinking and conversing and struggling for meaning with teachers and with each other about the way things work.

But it is important to understand that although the starting point for learning is real things, "hands-on" activities could be useless as the source of science learning if "minds-off" occurs at the same time, or if children are left to play without the invitation to negotiate science meaning with us. The kind of free, respected discourse in the previous comments of the students does not occur automatically when a fun activity is brought into the classroom. It has to be nurtured by a teacher who knows that children's ideas together with the events and objects at hand are the starting place for learning. In fact, such conversation can be closed down before it has even begun. Suppose the discussion leader, a science specialist, enthusiastically introduced the cornstarch and water task to a group of fifth graders like this:

Today—listen up, class—you will be making a non-Newtonian fluid, spelled n-o-n N-e-w-t-o-n-i-a-n f-l-u-i-d. [writing the letters carefully on the blackboard]. This is a very strange fluid which you will find does not behave according to the regular scientific laws of solid and liquid matter.

The students will probably enjoy playing with the stuff and experiencing its weirdness, regardless of what the leader says. Nevertheless, in this introduction it is clear that the task is not expected to be connected to real life, especially not that of children. Rather it seems to be a science classroom event which has relevance only in the classroom but no connection to life on the outside. Framed in this way, there is no valuing of the voices of the children as a necessary contribution to understanding science, and no notion that the diversity of experience of family, traditions, and culture of a youngster count for anything. Such a teacher has instantly framed school science, not as a connection between, but as a clash of, the cultures of science and children.

✢ Science as Meaning Making

Let us turn our attention to some other events and phenomena. There is a kind of meaning making that should go on in science class, different from the solid-liquid negotiations. It is the struggle to understand in an entirely new way something that already seemed clear. Through open, nonjudgmental conversations with young people, science education researchers have heard the fullness of students' ideas: their way of explaining and describing the world.

For example, children do have ideas about why a thrown ball flies the way it does, how they know that fire is alive, what is going on when iron rusts, where the light goes when the switch is turned off, why the moon looks different on successive nights, and why a child resembles her or his parents. Most of these ideas of children are, not surprisingly, inconsistent with scientific ideas. We know from research studies that youngsters often continue to explain events with similar ascientific ideas both before and after completing a course in college physics, for example, or a sixth-grade science class about atoms. Traditional science teaching does not seem to provide them with new scientific understanding nor to substantively change the ideas that they brought with them to science class.

Traditional science teaching, the inheritance of ritual words, focuses on children getting the artifacts of language, then putting them away somewhere safe and secure. Of course, they easily get lost (buried in the attic); or perhaps they were never put away because the teacher said one thing and the child understood another. The attic is a useful metaphor for the mind, for we know that trying to put something into memory is no guarantee that it can ever be retrieved, nor is it a guarantee that it will still be there in a few days, or that it even made it to the attic. Let us move the conversation to consider the last of these possibilities.

We all, children and adults alike, interpret and translate what is said through our existing knowledge about the way the world is. When people hear the proverbial shout of "Fire!" in the crowded theater, they do not hear a call to set off their muskets! In science class, this interpretation issue can cause misunderstanding. We see and hear with what we know. The meanings that people already have get in the way of making different meanings, especially if they are not invited to struggle to make the distinctions.

Without a negotiation of meaning, without conversation in which children can work with new meanings and their preexisting meanings in a context of real experience, no teacher can ever know what sense children are making of the science language they use.

Often it is this negotiation of meaning that is particularly and precisely necessary in science, when what youngsters know in everyday life is at odds with what science states to be the case. There are many instances of this: In everyday life it suits us to talk of *heat* as stuff that flows out of the opened door on a winter day, or *cold* as stuff that flows out of the refrigerator when it is left open. Because it seems intuitive that a thing doesn't move unless something pushes or pulls it, when we see a baseball moving we say that the pitcher gave it force that is causing it to move; children so often seem to be a blend of the features of their parents that it seems that some mixing of fluid, like blood, makes them who they are. In each instance, however, science disagrees. Under these circumstances, when making a science understanding is contradictory to one's own beliefs, building that new understanding takes a lot more negotiating and struggling to make meaning than in the solid-liquid example.

Here is another activity—collect the following items:

- A hard-boiled egg still in its shell.
- A large empty glass bottle, such as an apple juice bottle, with an opening small enough so that when you set the egg in the opening the egg is just a bit too large to go through (make sure that there are no cracks or other flaws in the bottle).
- A small piece of paper—newspaper is fine.
- A match.

Twist the paper loosely to make a taper about 3 inches long that you can eventually light with the match. Peel the egg. Light the taper and stuff it, flame down, into the glass bottle. Immediately set the peeled egg upright (pointy side down) onto the bottle opening, and watch.

The egg may wobble a little, the flame will go out, the jar will fill with smoke, and the egg will get sucked into the bottle with a distinct squeeze through the neck, an "oomph" sound, and a satisfying thump onto the bottom of the bottle. There is no doubt that you will both see and hear the egg being sucked into the bottle. Even though for science there is no such thing as a "suck" force, scientists and science teachers, who are also regular people, do see and hear the egg being sucked in.

This is the point about "hands-on" alone being insufficient. To make science meaning about this egg-and-bottle experience, we have to interpret it, reinterpret it, and impose new meaning on it. Because they have scientific understanding, science teachers can decide to see this event a different way, to observe not that the egg was sucked in but that it was *blown* into the bottle by outside air. Knowing this, science teachers can ask the youngsters if it is possible to get the egg out again by blowing air into the bottle— the usual answer is "NO!" Demonstrating that, in fact, the unexpected happens and that one can blow the egg out of the bottle begins a conversation driven by the youngsters' need to know.[1]

Even in this demonstration, where the everyday explanation is inconsistent with science, children will tell you words and understandings that are a useful foundation for negotiating new meaning. Your students may say the same or different things from the children we have heard. It is likely, however, that you will hear some of the same things;

for example, mention of a vacuum. You will negotiate the understanding that the burning paper heated up the air in the bottle; that the hot air expanded and pushed up out of the bottle—making the egg wobble a bit—so there was then less air per some standard unit of volume in the bottle than in the outside air; that less air per volume means a lower air pressure when the temperature is the same; that when the flame went out because of lack of oxygen, and the air in the bottle cooled down again, the air outside the bottle moved to get back into the bottle to equalize the pressure. Because the egg was in the way, the air moving back toward the bottle pushed the egg into the neck, sealing it, so that no more air could get in. Eventually the air pushed the egg ahead of it into the bottle. The egg moved because it was pushed by the air that had the greater pressure. It is blown out by exactly the same process, using the same understanding. Blowing a lot of air into the bottle creates greater pressure inside the bottle than outside, and this time the air pressure pushes the egg in the opposite direction.[2]

The conversation that students must have in order to make this meaning for themselves is rich, complicated, and time consuming. They have to make some of this fit with what they already know; they have to acknowledge that the science explanation is a long chain of argument, one piece connecting to and supporting the rest. They have to dissociate the original explanation from the new understanding they are building. They will want to make new experiments, they will want to test their ideas, and they will want to investigate predictions.

These explorations by the children provide times and places for them to converse with the data they get and to check their understanding, their explanations, and the connections. They will each be interested in different issues, and when allowed to set out on their own trail of questioning and answering, they will struggle to make meaning of science and to make science have meaning to them. Clearly, they must be the ones to decide that trail. In trying to answer their own questions it is common sense that what happens will be meaningful to them. Eventually, like the teacher, the youngsters will be able to choose to see the egg either being sucked into the bottle, or being blown in by the air.

The understandings built around science's way of looking at the egg-and-bottle event connect with many other everyday objects and phenomena: vacuum cleaners; the movements of air masses that make weather and climate; pressure, temperature, and volume relationships in balloons and tires; and airplanes taking off. If the teacher continues class negotiations to consider these phenomena, the students will continue to construct ever larger and more secure connections of words and relationships. The conversation of science learning often takes the form of arguing from, about, and with "evidence." At other times, it takes making the familiar unfamiliar through the use of analogy, metaphor, and models. As teachers we must foster connections between what children think and what they see, and between what they see and what they think.

We have said that youngsters come to us with a rich set of understandings about the world they know. We have used a principle of a constructivist perspective about learning to say that what is already known is used to interpret new situations and new information. Because many times ideas that work in ordinary life are different from explanations that scientists make, teaching science is often about learning to see the old things from new perspectives. And we have acknowledged that this is not easy.

❖ Becoming a Teacher of Science

Let us consider the issue of people making themselves teachers. Everyone, having lived in classrooms as students for 12 years or so, has beliefs and understanding about the way teaching is supposed to work. As you read our words, your understanding of them is guided by those understandings about teaching that you already have. You may be understanding as we do; you may be struggling to see science classes in a new way. Whatever is going on, we hope that you are talking, questioning, and struggling to figure out what you think we are saying.

A major assumption guiding this chapter is that some major changes must occur in the way we teach science. The real purpose for rethinking science education is that there is such powerful evidence that what is occurring is not working at all well. Students at every level of education from Ph.D. programs to elementary schools demonstrate a loss of interest and lack of achievement in science. American students who could, through science, gain new understandings about being in charge of their own lives are losing knowledge about science. Equally distressing is the loss to science of U.S. women and students of color with a rich diversity of knowing and questioning. The numbers tell a sad story. There are concerted calls for change in science classrooms and lecture halls, to stem the tide of loss. These calls include the specific issues of women and students of color for several reasons, not the least of which is that they suffer the greatest loss.

But the hard question must be asked: Is it really possible to have hordes of young folk loving and achieving in science in schools and colleges? This question is at the heart of the matter, of course, because for those who believe that girls, children of color, or even most children do not have what it takes to truly understand real science, then there is no point in trying to create change. If one believes as we do, however, that most children can build a "science" way of looking at the world, then one must ask what continues to exclude so many from science at each point in the education process. Let us look at the probable areas of exclusion.

All of the discussion about the necessity for inviting and including children's whole selves into science rests on the assumption that all children can create meaning, can cross the boundary of science by extending themselves into that world. Not everyone agrees with this assumption. The opposite is more common: that real science is accessible only to the few children who are headed in this direction and motivated to do the hard work that is required.

The belief that science is only for the very few is pervasive. Society has conferred on science an extremely high status, the status of high culture. Through science we have gained so much control over aspects of our world that used to bring human misery and travail; many scourges and hardships have been tamed through the interaction of science, technology, and social forces. Science's status is not inappropriate. High culture status involves the specialized activities, rituals and language of a social, cultural and intellectual elite. This high culture defines what a scientist is: in all things, a superbly logical skeptic who accepts conclusions as facts only as they are reasoned from evidence; who thinks and acts in a peculiar way following the "scientific method"; who speaks fluently in a language so specialized that it is difficult to converse with non-scientists—to "come down to their level"; and who probably dresses in a white coat with sharpened pencils in the top pocket.

Within this view of science and scientist, inspiring children in a multi-ethnic classroom to belong to this cultural group is often attempted by displaying pictures of scientists of color or women scientists. The portraits of those who "made it" are hung in texts and on wall posters. Such portraits of the privileged few can be helpful in providing a source of youngsters' imaginings of themselves as adults. When they accompany a high culture view of science, however, they can carry the connotation that crossing the boundaries into that cultural group requires that one's old home self must be discarded, left behind, as unbecoming and unnecessary to science culture status.

It is not enough to post pictures of people, disembodied from their lives, if inspiration is the intent. There must be a different view of science that is inclusive of our origins, our cultural selves. There must be a sense that gaining a scientific cultural self does not require that we discard what we are. Transformative and emancipatory education, a process through which children shape their own lives, can neither entail nor ever suggest the essential loss of self.

There is no doubt that the scientific lens on the world has generated some powerfully reliable and productive knowledge. But we believe it is a serious error to put science on an intellectual pedestal as the best, or the only useful, lens on the affairs of our world. If we can see science not as high culture, but as one of many ways of illuminating our world, then the ways of poets, historians, and artists, for example, can be recognized as equally worthwhile.

This view immediately opens the door of science to everyone who would like to cross the threshold. Such an educative stance allows teachers to ground children's school science experiences in their own beginnings; to let youngsters stretch toward the unknown future of their well-educated selves, with the connections between new learning, family, and tradition providing secure support in that reach. Transformation of self that is a change, not a loss, an evolution out of origins, not a discarding of them, is education in action. By recognizing science as just one of the many valuable ways in which human beings have made sense of the world in which we live, we can take a step toward letting children know that this science world is one in which they can live, work, and grow.

Reconstructing one's view of the nature of science, however, is only one fundamental requirement for transformative science education. There is another boundary that, when erected, excludes many children. This boundary concerns beliefs about the nature of children as learners. Many educators set about their task by identifying in the regular population what is wrong with individual children: This child lacks skills in reading, this one lacks a proper home background, this one lacks basic intelligence. In traditional classrooms the view of children as units of deficiency makes a perfect partner with the view of science as high culture. Students described as deficient in this or lacking in that, who need remediation for some shortcoming, are clearly excluded from membership in high culture science. Such boundaries dictate that those assumed to have deficiencies cannot possibly excel in or even understand this very difficult subject. They are counseled out of science or they exclude themselves. If they do find themselves in science classrooms, all that is left for them is to receive and memorize language, to do busy work and follow scripts for experiments and investigations—at the end of which they are told what they have, or were supposed to have, found.

The inclusion of children, with all of the richness of their lives outside school, into the making of meaning for themselves in science class, springs from the understanding that children are whole, knowing contributors to the process and that science is no elite mystery but one glorious example of human, collective meaning-making.

Questions need to be addressed, however, regarding our sense of children bringing themselves and all they know to active conversation about things and events, and negotiating to make new meaning: How much meaning? What contextualized meanings are appropriate? Lost to nearly everyone except historians of science is the rich set of contexts in which science meaning-makers worked in their times; therefore the original richness out of which the abstracted cores of meaning were distilled is also lost.

It took science hundreds of years to create the most basic definitions of words we use today. These include *matter, mass, force, atom, element, compound, inheritance,* and *evolution.* Scientists in the past were either struggling to resolve the problems that they had set for themselves by sharpening the meanings of their language, or inventing new words and relationships to answer the questions they had asked. A full understanding, then, will surely include the knowledge of those problems, those answers, and those questions.

Gaining contextualized meaning, however, does not require a reinvention of the original contexts from history. Much as we might like to, we cannot usefully imagine that a 4th grader or a brilliant 12th grader is able to reinvent the triumphs of reason and imagination of adult scientists such as Best, Carver, Curie, Dalton, Darwin, or Margulis. They are unlikely to be able to rediscover the foundations of science for themselves. It is futile to attempt to have every child recreate the intellectual pieces of the struggles after meaning that occurred among scientists over hundreds of years—they are, after all, children living in today's, not yesterday's, world. If science is to become part of their lives, though, they do have to create some meaning for themselves, in some real context.

Keeping in mind the twin boundaries of views of high culture science and deficient children, let us explore one way in which those are expressed. Some teachers phrase their curricular tasks in terms of how deeply children can be expected to enter the science world: Chemistry requires math, and children shouldn't study chemistry unless they did well in algebra; what children can do in science depends on their comprehension skills.

Other teachers phrase their curricular tasks in the language of the abstracted cores: I think we should teach photosynthesis; they really should have studied Newton's laws; little kids have to know about atoms and molecules early on, as they are the basis of everything. These teacher phrases make us feel that science teaching and learning are being squeezed into science's world.

Still other teachers do the reverse as they squeeze science into their world of teaching and learning. These teachers phrase their curricular task in the language of events and contexts: These kids are on ice skates almost as soon as they can walk, so we ought to explore collisions and movements like hockey pucks—and force, momentum, and energy; this garbage disposal issue is something they all live with one way or another so let's have them explore decomposition and combustion, and let's see what directions they want to take; perhaps we could get them talking about a litter of kittens to get at how and why they look like their parents. Squeezing science into their own world of teaching and learning allows teachers to be powerful, to demonstrate daring and willingness to take risks. It means that they take ownership; they deny boundaries.

Moreover, it is to invite students to be powerful and to own their work, and to include them in making something work.

Does this happen? Yes! In a New York City middle school, Kahla, an African American student who had not distinguished herself academically, was a part of such a world with such a science teacher. She had told her teacher earlier that she "hated" science, but that he should not take it personally. The teacher, a beginner, was determined to invent an activity that would sponsor meaning-making with his charges. They had completed several days of work on the pieces of a topic that is very intricate, specialized, and complex—protein synthesis.

He framed the task this day as the need to have them tell the whole complicated tale all at once. He brought in a variety of shapes cut from construction paper of different colors and arranged them with tape on the board. The students were first asked to name the pieces with the biological structure that they represented, a piece of a DNA molecule, a ribosome, and so forth. Then he asked them to go up to the board, one at a time, and to move the pieces around—without saying anything. Their task was to recreate the story that biologists have written about how a protein is made—without saying a word, by changing and moving shapes. Everyone was invited to participate to begin the story, to move the next piece along, or to edit the unfolding story by undoing previous moves if that seemed called for. At one point in the story line Kahla stood up, moved a couple of pieces to edit the story, then turned to face her classmates. Putting her hands on her hips, she said: "Well, what I know is that the DNA in the nucleus can't come out of it and go over there, it's the mRNA that does that; then it goes to the ribosome and the tRNA brings its amino acid tails over to it, and they line up to make the protein. Now I may be wrong, but that's what I know!" Whether you understand what she said or not, the point is that it was so clear that she understood. And that is what counts. She owned that story, she knew it with such clarity that she had to have made meaning out of it for herself.

When youngsters are invited to bring themselves into the arena, and when what they have to say is honored and respected, being there has significance: not the significance of being present at a traditional ritual, but the significance of pushing oneself to do something meaningful.

In another classroom, a Latino child was following his teacher's directions to make an event happen. He had a zipper bag with a small container filled with a white solid (ammonium chloride), and some water. He maneuvered the small container so that the solid dropped into the water and dissolved. The bag became very cold. In the milling of students working with this investigation, the boy walked over to the teacher:

Student: "This stuff is crazy cold! Hey, couldn't we use this in air-conditioning?"
Teacher: "It's an interesting idea, what do you have in mind?"
Student: "Well this stuff'll give you your cold that you want . . . you'd have to have a blower to move the air and . . . Hey, how much is this stuff anyway? Is it expensive, like for a lot of it?. . . and you'd blow the room air across this packet like, bigger than this one, it'd be in the bedroom but it could be like [stretching his arms wide] and the warm air will get cool! . . . Hey, how long does it stay cold anyway? D'you think it's still cold enough? . . . then . . . what do you do with it when it's done anyway? Can you start it up again?"
Teacher: "Well what do you want to do to find out?"

The conversation was not about endothermic and exothermic reactions—the intended learning. But can anyone deny the meaningfulness of it? Can you imagine how it would have felt not to be invited to make these connections with his outside school life. His participation in the negotiation of meaning that followed seemed like a most natural transition from his own world across the threshold into the science of energy changes in chemical reactions. In classrooms such as these, children make science meaningful, both in the ways and in the direction toward decontextualized science knowledge that we intend, and also, when invited to take ownership, in the myriad individualistic ways that we cannot predict.

✛ A Classroom of Science Teachers

Throughout this chapter we have talked of science in different ways and at different levels of organization, as decontextualized words and relationships, as explanations for phenomena, and as a way of seeing the world differently. Now we consider another task of scientists: inventing and refining models to explain the world. We do this in the context of people becoming transformative science teachers. To address the education of science teachers is to engage the question of how teachers can create classrooms in which the science taught is related to the particular concerns of their youngsters.

Picture a classroom in which the students are prospective elementary school teachers. They have organized themselves into groups of three or four and each group is examining a half-gallon milk carton-shaped container filled with liquid laundry soap. They have been asked to do what they each consider to be a central activity of scientists; to make observations about the carton, to gather data about it without tearing it apart. So they did: "It's a half gallon container." "It's white, with blue lettering." "The contents slosh around in there." "Let's try pouring some of the detergent out." "It looks like liquid soap. But, hey—it stopped coming out as we poured!" "Try to pour it again." "About the same amount came out—how does that happen?" "Look, it says that there are 48 fluid ounces in here, but it sure looks like the same size as a half-gallon milk carton." "Can we pour the detergent back in?" "What will happen if we hold the container completely upside down?" "Suppose we pour out of the side?" "No, let's pour it out of the side opposite the spout." "Hey, look, there is something across the top about an inch down from the top of the spout."

They continue making observations, with each observation suggesting new things to be done to the container, in turn producing new observations. They are interrupted by their instructor, who comments on the number and quality of their observations but suggests that there is more to science than simply making observations and collecting data. She asks them to imagine what they might see if they could get inside the container, explaining that much of science involves the invention of underlying models or theories of what is not visible to explain what is visible (when was the last time that you saw an electron in the same way that you saw a pizza?).

The prospective teachers, still in groups, are now challenged to invent mechanisms (models) to explain their observations. They are also asked to come up with at least one test of each model: If the world inside the carton is like X, then if you do Y to it, you expect Z to happen. In animated groups they draw, they build three-dimensional objects, they argue, they negotiate, they revise, they collect more observations, they make their own meanings. Then they share representations of their models with the other groups. "Hey, that one is not like ours at all. How does that flap work?" "How would your design allow only a measured amount of detergent to come out?" "What's the right answer?" "When are we going to open up the boxes so that we can see what is really in there?" (they never do open the cartons).

For 2 hours they have been doing things that are similar to what scientists do— they posed problems for themselves, they attempted to solve the problems that they had posed, they tried to persuade other groups that their models worked, and, in many cases, they had to revise their models based on the critiques of their colleagues. They had, for a brief time, been part of a scientific community, sharing with each other, not wanting to give up their own ideas that had been a challenge to create, realizing that their prior experiences (with sugar dispensers that poured a measured amount of sugar; attachments for the tops of liquor bottles that poured measured amounts; valves and floats from experiences with toilet bowl mechanisms) influenced what problems they posed and how they began to think about the mechanism that was at the heart of their explanatory models. They begin to talk about how what they have done is like what those who study atomic structure, or genes, must do.

They begin to wonder if it would be best to open the carton for their own students or even if something like this could be done with elementary school students: "Could fourth graders really do what we have just done?"; "Would they enjoy it?"; "What might they learn from doing it?" Gradually they begin to wonder if it would be possible to teach "real" science, and not just the fun activity of the detergent container, using this model-building approach. The only answer from their instructor is "Well, try it and see what happens."

There are skeptics: "This may be okay for middle or high school kids but it will never work with kindergartners or first graders." But many are willing to see what would happen over the next few weeks that they are teaching in schools.

One young woman, teaching about the human body to first graders, decides to take the challenge, and rethinks how she might do a standard activity which is usually done as a teacher-directed demonstration. Centered on the movements of the upper arm, this demonstration typically involves showing students two pieces of wooden doweling hinged together with screw eyes and with large rubber bands connecting them. The dowels represent the humerus and the combination of radius and ulna, while the rubber bands represent the muscles of the arm that allow it to bend at the elbow.

Rather than passing on this piece of her science education inheritance to her students, she was determined to take a model-building approach. She describes this to her colleagues in the science methods course, painting a vivid picture of her classroom. She had asked her first graders to bend their arms in different ways and to describe what happened; then she asked them to feel the muscles on the front of their upper arms, and on their lower arms as they bent their arms at the elbow. Then they did the same thing with the muscles at the back of the arm (you may want to try this yourself).

The children had made all sorts of observations, including some that she had not made herself or had ever read about in the textbooks that she had consulted in preparing her lesson. She was learning from 6-year-olds; because they were all experiencing on their own, they were not limited to what the textbook writers had determined was important. She was surprised and in some ways worried because the "world" of the arm and elbow seemed so much more complex than she had imagined. On the other hand, the complexity did not seem to bother her first graders.

As they assembled in small groups after making observations, she asked them what materials they thought they would need to make something that worked like an arm. The students came up with many materials, such as flexible soda straws, tape, string, and aluminum foil tubes. She gave them a couple of days to collect the necessary materials and then set them to work building. And they did, for a longer time than first-graders are supposed to be able to attend to anything. They built working models, they revised them when they didn't work like they thought that they should, and they learned a lot about muscles and bones. But they also learned other lessons that they may not have been able to articulate: They were learning that as science learners they could be successful. As this prospective teacher described her experiences to her colleagues, she was having a bigger impact on them than the methods professor—she had been successful, she had created a classroom where children were creating meaning for themselves. It was, in her own words "the highlight of my student teaching."

It is possible to see classrooms in a new way. It is possible to suspend belief in children as units of academic deficiency and in science as something only for the peculiarly bright, to imagine inclusive places without boundaries, where teachers and children learn together, making science meanings and meanings of science together. In these inclusive places it is expected that everyone will have something to contribute to the collaborative tasks of investigating something real, of creating, refining, and eventually decontextualizing reliable and powerful understandings.

Even though a primary emphasis of science education in the elementary school may be on the conceptual and intellectual activities associated with investigations and model building, we need to recognize that there is more to science, and much more to teaching science to elementary school children, than just the conceptual. Rachel Carson, author of *Silent Spring* (1962), the book that helped raise a nation's awareness and conscience about the frailty of the natural environment, wrote another book, *The Sense of Wonder* (1984), that contains rich insights about science teaching from perspectives other than the conceptual/intellectual. We'll end this chapter on science teaching in the elementary school with a quote from *The Sense of Wonder*. The spirit of Carson's thoughts, if we could make them come alive in our own teaching, would contribute to alleviating the "crisis in science education":

> A child's world is fresh and new and beautiful, full of wonder and excitement. It is our misfortune that for most of us that clear-eyed vision, that true instinct for what is beautiful and awe-inspiring, is dimmed and even lost before we reach adulthood. If I had influence with the good fairy who is supposed to preside over the christening of all children I should ask that her gift to each child in the world be a sense of wonder so indestructible that it would last throughout life, as an unfailing antidote against the boredom and disenchantments of later years, the sterile preoccupation with things that are artificial, the alienation from the sources of our strength.
>
> If a child is to keep alive his inborn sense of wonder without any such gift from the fairies, he needs the companionship of at least one adult who can share it, rediscovering with him the joy, excitement and mystery of the world we live in. Parents [and we would add teachers here too] often have a sense of inadequacy when

confronted on the one hand with the eager, sensitive mind of a child and on the other with a world of complex physical nature, inhabited by a life so various and unfamiliar that it seems hopeless to reduce it to order and knowledge. In a mood of self-defeat, they exclaim, "How can I possibly teach my child about nature . . . why, I don't even know one bird from another!"

I sincerely believe that for the child and for the parent [or teacher] seeking to guide him, it is not half so important to *know* as to *feel*. . . . Once the emotions have been aroused . . . a sense of the beautiful, the excitement of the new and the unknown, a feeling of sympathy, pity, admiration or love will emerge . . . then we will search for knowledge about the object of our emotional response. Once found, it has lasting meaning. It is more important to pave the way for the child to want to know than to put him on a diet of facts he is not ready to assimilate. (1984, p. 45)

Science teaching that has the possibility of enabling young and old to transform themselves into owners and makers of their own life's path begins at that spot, paving the way for them to want to know, and supporting them in their efforts to create understanding.

Notes

1. To blow the egg out, first remove the charred paper remains from the bottle, then tip the bottle upside down and shake the egg into position (pointy side out) to come out of the neck. Holding the bottle like that, blow into it as much air as you can with one breath. Remove the bottle from your mouth and the egg will be forced out.

2. Sometimes, people make the argument that the burning paper uses up the oxygen and so reduces the amount of air in the bottle. Since carbon dioxide gas and water vapor are products of combustion (the oxygen is just recombining with other atoms, not being "consumed"), this is not a persuasive argument.

References

Boeschen, J. A., Gerard, J. A., & Storin, D. J. (1983). *Physical science.* San Diego, CA: Coronado.

Carson, R. (1962). *The silent spring.* Boston: Houghton Mifflin.

Carson, R. (1984). *The sense of wonder.* New York: Perennial Library.

Teaching Social Studies for Decision-Making and Citizen Action

James A. Banks

Center for Multicultural Education, University of Washington, Seattle

Social studies, like multicultural education, is a field characterized by competing paradigms and diverse approaches and methods. It also is filled with debates about how social studies teaching in the nation's schools can best help students to develop citizenship skills and abilities (Armento, 1986; Barr, Barth & Shermis, 1977; Shaver, 1977, 1991).

Most social studies educators agree that citizenship, or the development of effective citizens, should be the major goal of social studies teaching. However, educators have conflicting conceptions and ideologies about what constitutes an effective citizen and what kind of curriculum can best develop citizens for a democratic nation-state (Massialas & Allen, 1996). The wide array of social studies scope and sequence schemes and proposed plans for the field reflects the disagreements and tensions within it (Bragaw, 1986).

A number of writers have developed typologies that categorize the diverse approaches and traditions within the social studies. One of the most frequently cited typologies is the one developed by Barr, Barth, and Shermis (1977). They categorize the literature and theories of the social studies into three traditions: (1) social studies taught as citizenship transmission, (2) social studies taught as social science, and (3) social studies taught as reflective inquiry. In the first tradition, citizenship is developed by efforts to instill particular values into students. In the second, it is developed by teaching students the key concepts, theories, and methods of the social science disciplines, including history. In the third tradition, citizenship education focuses on decision-making and solving problems that people face in a democratic society.

This is a useful way to conceptualize developments within social studies education. However, like all typologies, its categories are interrelated. They do not encompass all the approaches and developments in the field, especially those that have emerged within the last three decades. Other approaches include the interdisciplinary conceptual approach developed by Taba, Durkin, Franekel, and McNaughton (1971), and the social issues and decision-making approaches conceptualized by theorists such as Newmann (1975), Engle and Ochoa (1988), and James A. Banks (in Banks & Banks, 1999). Another approach is the critical theory, postmodern approach developed by theorists such as Popkewitz (1977) and Cherryholmes (1982), and based on the work of Habermas (1968). However, the critical theory approach is rarely implemented in social studies lessons and programs in the schools.

✛ Overview

In this chapter, I describe five major periods in the development of social studies education in the United States:

- The traditional or pre-revolutionary period that extends from 1921, when the National Council for the Social Studies was founded, until the publication of *The Process of Education* (Bruner, 1960).
- The era of the social studies revolution of the 1960s and 1970s.
- The public issues and social participation period of the 1970s and 1980s.
- The resurgence of history and the rise of multicultural education during the 1980s and 1990s.
- The quest for standards in the 1990s.

Next, I describe what should be the goals of social studies education in a pluralistic democratic society and a decision-making/social action model designed to attain them. Finally, I discuss a lesson developed and taught with this model.

It is important to keep in mind that when each of the four periods ended, the developments related to it did not end abruptly. Rather, many trends and elements from the previous period continued into the next. However, the characteristics of the new period became the dominant ones.

Also keep in mind that social studies education in the United States can be viewed and conceptualized on at least five different dimensions: (1) research and theory, (2) state and school district policies and curriculum guides, (3) social studies textbooks, (4) inservice development and training programs for social studies teachers, and (5) actual classroom practices.

What happens at one level can differ greatly from what is happening at another. For example, one cannot assume that just because many articles and books were being written about conceptual teaching by experts during the 1960s and 1970s, that most teachers in the classroom were teaching concepts. As a matter of fact, research indicates this was not the case. Even during the height of the social studies revolution of the 1960s and '70s, when conceptual teaching was emphasized by many social studies theorists, most teachers in U.S. classrooms continued to teach in traditional ways, such as emphasizing facts and isolated historical events (Shaver, Davis, & Helburn, 1979).

✛ The Pre-Revolutionary or Traditional Period

Before the 1960s, the social studies was dominated by history and geography. The emphasis was on the development of national patriotism and the memorization of isolated facts about events, places, and people. Yesterday's social studies classrooms were dominated by textbooks, teacher talk, student passivity, recitation, and stories about the historic deeds of the United States and the glorious accomplishments of Western civilization. An important goal of the social studies was to develop patriotic, loyal, and unquestioning citizens. Consequently, little attention was devoted to the nation's problems for fear that its warts might show and undermine the development of such citizens.

Because little attention was devoted to the nation's problems or the problems related to the growth and development of Western civilization, groups that were the society's victims or on the fringes received scant attention in the curriculum and in textbooks. When they were included, they were viewed primarily from the perspectives of upper-class European and European-American males. Consequently, the struggles, victories, hopes, and voices of groups on the margins of society, such as women, people of color, and low-income people, were largely invisible in the pre-1960 social studies curricula, textbooks, and programs (Banks, 1969).

American Indians appeared in traditional social studies textbooks either as groups that were impediments to the spread of European civilization from the east to the west, or as "good" Indians, allies who taught the Europeans how to farm and survive in America. In the first case, American Indians had to be removed so that Western civilization could advance, as the Cherokees were in 1838–39. In the latter case, they were celebrated and venerated, such as Pocahontas and Sacajawea.

African Americans and Latinos appeared in traditional social studies curricula largely in contexts in which they interacted with or became problems for the Europeans in America. Little attention was devoted to African Americans as institutional builders and as shapers of their own fates and destinies. Content about African Americans was limited primarily to slavery and to a discussion of two or three heroes who made contributions to society but did not challenge the prevailing social and political structures. In the 1950s and 1960s, those who appeared in textbooks most frequently were individuals such as Booker T. Washington, George Washington Carver, and Marian Anderson. More radical African Americans such as W. E. B. DuBois, Marcus Garvey, and Ida B. Wells rarely appeared in social studies curricula and textbooks during the 1950s. Most of the content about Mexican Americans in social studies curricula and textbooks of this era dealt with the events that led to the Texas secession from the Mexico union and the United States-Mexican War.

International studies emphasized the study of European nations. Consequently, little was studied about nations in Asia and Africa. Africa was described as the "dark continent." Egypt was conceptualized and viewed as separate and distinct from Africa. Many students studied the great civilizations of Egypt without knowing that Egypt was a nation in Africa. The great kingdoms of sub-Saharan Africa, such as Ghana, Mali, and Songhay, were not mentioned in most history books (Franklin & Moss, 1988). There was little emphasis on active learning strategies, teaching students to question what they read or reviewed, critical thinking, or social action and participation.

✥ The Expanding Communities of Human Beings

During the past eight decades, a rather standardized social studies curriculum has developed within the elementary and secondary schools in the United States. History and geography have dominated social studies during most of this period. In the primary grades, students have studied the communities closest to their experience, such as the family, the school, the neighborhood, and the state. In the middle and upper grades, students studied communities further away from their immediate experience, such as the state; the region; other nations in the Americas; and finally nations in the world, including Europe, Africa, and Asia.

The concept of studying communities close to the child first and branching out later became the dominant curriculum pattern in social studies in the United States. Hanna (1963) helped popularize this pattern, which became known as *The Expanding Communities of Humans* curriculum framework. This curriculum framework has remained tenacious throughout all periods of social studies curriculum reform in the United States and is the most common social studies curriculum framework in the United States today. Superka, Hawke, and Morrissett (1980) found that the topics listed below were the most frequently taught at the grade levels indicated. This sequence is very similar to the Expanding Communities of Humans pattern.

Grade	Topic
Kindergarten	Self, school, community, home
1	Families
2	Neighborhoods
3	Communities
4	State history, geographic regions
5	United States history
6	World cultures, Western hemisphere
7	World geography or history
8	American history
9	Civics or world cultures
10	American history
11	American government

✤ The Social Studies Revolution of the 1960s and 1970s

In September 1959, about 35 scientists, scholars, and educators gathered at the Woods Hole conference center in Cape Cod, Massachusetts, to discuss how science education might be improved in the nation's schools. Based on this 10-day meeting of eminent American scholars and educators, Bruner (1960) wrote a book destined to revolutionize thinking about teaching and learning not only in the sciences but in all subject areas, including the social studies. In this book, *The Process of Education,* Bruner presented his now-famous contention, "Experience over the past decade points to the fact that our schools may be wasting precious years by postponing the teaching of many important subjects on the ground that they are too difficult. . . . The foundations of any subject can be taught to anybody at any age in some form" (p. 12).

Bruner also argued that the fundamentals of every discipline can be reduced to its *structure,* by which he meant its key concepts, key generalizations and principles, key questions that the discipline asks, and its unique modes of inquiry or investigation. Bruner said the structure of each discipline could be identified and that this structure could be taught to all students in some form, regardless of age or stage of development.

By stating that the key ideas of each discipline could be identified and by arguing that these key ideas could be taught to young children, Bruner seriously challenged the leading ideas of developmental psychologists at the time as well as the existing social studies curriculum that had been popularized in the writings of Hanna (1963). *The Expanding Communities of Humans* framework is based strongly on developmental ideas, for example, that children should study the family before they study the larger community.

Based on the idea of the structures of the disciplines and other key ideas set forth by Bruner, social scientists such as historians, geographers, sociologists, anthropologists, and political scientists became heavily involved in the development of social studies curriculum projects during the 1960s and 1970s. Major goals of these projects included helping students to do the following:

- Learn the structures of the social science disciplines.
- Learn the methods that social scientists used to gather data and study society and how to use these methods.
- Learn key concepts and generalizations in each of the social science disciplines.
- Become actively involved in social studies learning.

Bruner was involved in one of these projects, which was designed to teach anthropology to elementary school students. The program was called *Man: A Course of Study.* Bruner described the emphasis in the course:

> The content of the course is man: his nature as a species, the forces that shaped and continue to shape his humanity. Three questions recur throughout: What is human about human beings? How did they get that way? How can they be made more so? (Dow, 1969, p. 4)

To develop a better understanding of what makes people human, the students start by studying salmon, herring gulls, and baboons. The Netsilik Eskimo is studied as an example of a human culture. The course consists of a variety of instructional materials, including films made especially for the project. It deals primarily with the first question raised in the quote from Bruner.

Like any educational movement that tries to change the schools from the outside, the social studies revolution of the 1960s and 1970s had mixed results. It created vigorous discussion, debate, and innovation in the social studies and had a significant influence on social studies curriculum development at the state and school district levels and on textbook writing. It also had a significant influence on the research, teaching, and writing of social studies literature by scholars and university professors.

However, the influence of the *new social studies,* as it was called, on classroom teachers and actual classroom practice was far less than its architects had envisioned. Most of the social studies projects of the 1960s and 1970s were conceptualized by academics and scholars who taught at universities. Few classroom teachers were involved in their creation. Consequently, many teachers had a difficult time understanding and using many of the materials or did not believe they withstood the test of the classroom. Many of the project materials also required extensive inservice training and staff development. Some of the programs, however, such as *Man: A Course of Study* and Senesh's economics program for the elementary grades, *Our Working World*—which was published as a textbook series—became quite popular.

There are probably many complex reasons that schools largely resisted the social studies curriculum reforms of the 1960s. The reformers erred when they assumed that they could create teacher-proof materials and engineer a social studies curriculum revolution from outside the school culture. Teacher development and involvement are essential to the effective implementation of curriculum reforms and projects. This basic principle of curriculum reform was largely ignored by the social scientists who led most of the social studies curriculum projects of the 1960s.

The social scientists who dominated the curriculum reform projects of the 1960s neither understood nor fully appreciated the complex culture of the school. School cultures have their own ethos, symbols, norms, values, and traditions (Bruner, 1996).

Like other cultures and institutions, a school is not easily changed or reformed, especially by outsiders who neither understand nor appreciate its culture and institutional structure (Sarason, 1996). Probably the most important reason that the social studies curriculum reforms of the 1960s failed to become institutionalized on a large scale is the tremendous holding power and tenacity of the culture of the school (Cuban, 1991).

✣ The Public Issues and Social Participation Period of the 1970s and 1980s

Between 1960 and 1980, social movements that pushed for civil rights and social reform were prominent in the United States. These movements included the quests for the rights of groups of color such as African Americans and Latinos, the rights of women, the rights of people with disabilities, and protest over the war in Vietnam. During this period, the United States enacted some of its most enlightened legislation that protected the rights of women, people of color, and people with disabilities, including the Civil Rights Act of 1964, the Bilingual Education Act in 1968 (Title VII of the Elementary and Secondary Education Act), and Public Law 94-142 in 1975, the Education for All Handicapped Children Act.

During the 1970s and 1980s the social reform and civil rights movements influenced the social studies curriculum. Many theorists began to criticize Bruner's structuralist position and argued that it was not sufficient to teach students the key ideas and methods of the social sciences. Bruner's critics argued that the main goal of social studies education should be to develop reflective citizens for a democratic society (Newmann, 1970; Oliver & Shaver, 1966). To become effective citizens, students needed to learn how to apply social science knowledge to the solution of social problems in society, such as racial discrimination, discrimination against women, and the improvement and protection of the environment. The citizenship and public issues curriculum theorists also argued that students need to take social action to improve society and develop a sense of political efficacy (Engle & Ochoa, 1988).

Theorists such as James A. Banks (Banks & Banks, 1999), Metcalf (1971), Newmann (1970), Oliver and Shaver (1966), and Engle and Ochoa (1988) developed theories, materials, and strategies for teaching students to master more than just social science knowledge. Students also would be taught to analyze and clarify their values, identify courses of actions to take, consider alternative actions, and take actions that are consistent with the knowledge and values they have derived and clarified.

Oliver and Shaver (1966) developed a theory of teaching public issues to high school students and published data on the results of their experimental public issues curriculum. Newmann (1970) developed theories and strategies for involving students in social action and civic participation. In its *Curriculum Guidelines for the Social Studies,* the National Council for the Social Studies (1979) stated:

> Extensive involvement by students of all ages in their community is essential. The involvement may take the form of observation or information-seeking, attending meetings, and interviews. It may take the form of political campaigning, community service or improvement, or even responsible demonstration. The school should not only provide channels for such activities, but build them into the design of its K–12 social studies program. (p. 266)

✧ The Resurgence of History and the Rise of Multicultural Education

The 1980s and 1990s were characterized by diverse and conflicting trends in the social studies. One major development was the resurgence of what is called "back to basics," which is a return to an emphasis on history and geography that was dominant during the pre-revolutionary period described earlier. This trend grew out of criticisms by popular writers, who were sometimes joined by historians, who argued that students do not know the basic facts of U.S. history, such as when the Constitution was ratified or when the Civil War occurred.

Hirsch (1987) made this argument in *Cultural Literacy: What Every American Needs to Know*. This book was on the *New York Times* best-seller list for almost 6 months. Its popularity indicated that it articulated important concerns among U.S. citizens about what students were learning in school. Another popular book by Hirsch, Kett, & Trefil (1988), *The Dictionary of Cultural Literacy: What Every American Needs to Know,* also became a best seller. Ravitch and Finn (1987) extended the argument in their book *What Do Our 17-Year-Olds Know?* They describe how students gave many incorrect answers to multiple-choice test items that assessed their recall of factual knowledge in history and literature. Ravitch has argued that the replacement of history teaching with the teaching of the social studies is the main reason that students do not know the basic facts about history and geography.

Writers such as Ravitch, Finn, and Hirsch think the teaching of factual history should be emphasized in the schools. The social studies framework developed and adopted by the state of California, our largest state with more than 30 million people, is history-oriented and incorporates many of Ravitch's ideas (California State Department of Education, 1987). She was one of the major writers of the California curriculum framework.

Another major development in U.S. social studies education during the 1980s and 1990s was inconsistent with the emphasis on factual history. There was a trend toward infusing multicultural content and perspectives into the social studies curriculum. A multicultural social studies curriculum describes concepts, events, and ideas not only from the point of view of mainstream Americans but also from the perspectives of ethnic groups of color such as African Americans and Latinos as well as from the perspectives of women (Banks, 1997a).

Major school districts such as those in Portland, Oregon, and New York City adopted guidelines for infusing multicultural content into all areas of the school curriculum, including the social studies. State departments of education, such as those in Washington and New York state, also developed guidelines in multicultural education. In July 1989, the State Education Department in New York published a social studies curriculum document recommending ways to make the curriculum multicultural: *A Curriculum for Inclusion* (New York State Department of Education, 1989). This report evoked a major national debate in the nation's newspapers and magazines that indicated that Americans are sharply divided on how to describe the balance between national unity and ethnic diversity in the school curriculum. Another document published by the New York State Department of Education (1991), more moderate in tone and language than the earlier document, also evoked considerable controversy and debate in the popular press.

✤ The Quest for Standards During the 1990s

In 1983 an influential commission report stated that the United States was "at risk" because "a rising tide of mediocrity" in the nation's schools "threatens our very future as a Nation and a people" (Gardner, 1983, p. 5). The national concern about the eroding quality of the nation's schools was still alive and debated in 1991 when President Bush initiated America 2000, an ambitious project designed to make U.S. students among the best in the world.

The efforts to establish national standards by many professional associations, including the National Council for the Social Studies, was in part a response to the national movement to increase the academic achievement levels of the nation's students. The movement to establish national standards in the various subject areas taught in the nation's schools has had mixed results. There seems to be general agreement among professional educators that the standards developed by the National Council for Teachers of Mathematics were excellently conceptualized, developed, and implemented and that they have had a positive influence on the teaching of mathematics in the nation's schools.

The standards developed by the National Council for the Social Studies (1994) and the National Center for History in the Schools at the University of California, Los Angeles (1994) have had mixed results. The Standards developed by the National Council for the Social Studies, which contain 10 thematic strands in the social studies, have not evoked much discussion within the profession and have probably had little influence on practice. This is, in part, because the 10 themes identified in the Standards are widely accepted as concepts that should be taught in the social studies by most social scholars and practitioners. They include culture; time, continuity, and change; individual development and identity, and civic ideals and practice.

The standards developed by the National Center for History in the Schools evoked a storm of controversy, culminating in a vote in the United States Senate that rejected them (Nash, Crabtree, & Dunn, 1997). The Senate vote is important not because the history standards were having a significant influence on practice, but because it was an important development in the politics over knowledge production and in the struggle over what is official history, and whose history should be taught in the schools (Banks, 1996). When the first version of the National Standards for United States History was published in 1994, a group of conservatives launched a highly organized and successful attack on them that began with an editorial denouncing them by Lynn Cheney in the *Wall Street Journal.* The conservatives claimed that the standards devoted more time to women and people of color than they did to the founding fathers and other great leaders in American history.

The successful and highly publicized attack on the history standards led to the publication of a second version of them that omitted the teaching examples from the document (National Center for History in the Schools, 1996). The conservatives had focused their attack on the examples that were used to illustrate and amplify the standards rather than the standards themselves. Later, the project published the examples that had been in the original standards document, along with many other examples, in a resource book for teachers (Ankeny, Del Rio, Nash, & Vigilante, n.d.). The development, debate, and fate of the history standards is a painful chapter in the struggle over the control of knowledge and an indication of the extent to which issues of race and diversity are unresolved in the United States as it enters the new century.

❖ Multicultural Education Continues

Multicultural education is a growing development in the nation and will increasingly become integrated into the social studies curriculum in the future. Many of the nation's most prestigious colleges and universities, such as Stanford, the University of California-Berkeley, the University of Wisconsin-Madison, and the University of Minnesota-Twin Cities, require all undergraduate students to take courses in ethnic studies or have integrated ethnic studies readings and knowledge into required courses in the social sciences and humanities.

A major factor stimulating the growth of multicultural education in the United States is the nation's changing demographics (U.S. Bureau of the Census, 1998). The growth rate in the nation's population of color is much greater than the growth rate of the nation's White population. Most (about 85%) of the legal immigrants to the United States today come from nations in Latin America and Asia. Only about 11% of them come from Europe. Today, about one out of every three Americans is a *person of color* (e.g., African American, Latino, Asian, American Indian, etc.). By 2020, if current growth trends continue, students of color will make up about 46% of the nation's school-age youths.

The percentage of students who speak a first language other than English is also growing. In 1990, about 14% of the nation's school-age youth spoke a first language other than English (U.S. Bureau of the Census, 1998). In addition, many students also spoke a version of English different from the version taught in the schools, such as Ebonics or Black English. Because of the nation's changing demographics, more and more Americans are realizing that in order to prepare the nation's students for the America of tomorrow, ethnic content and content about women must permeate the total school curriculum, including the social studies.

The growing awareness among educators that the knowledge, attitudes and skills that constitute multicultural education are needed to keep our society democratic and free is another factor that is contributing to the growth of multicultural education. Multicultural education is an education for freedom in three important senses: (1) it enables students to freely affirm their ethnic, racial, and cultural identities; (2) it provides students with the freedom to function beyond their ethnic and cultural boundaries; and (3) it helps students develop the commitment and skills needed to participate in personal, social, and civic action that will make our nation and world more democratic and free (Banks, 1999).

❖ Goals for Social Studies in a Democratic Pluralistic Society

A major goal of social studies education in a multicultural society should be to help students attain the knowledge, skills, and attitudes needed to participate in the mainstream society. Although social participation is an important goal of social studies in a democratic, pluralistic society, it is not sufficient. Social studies should also help students attain the knowledge, attitudes, and skills needed to help transform and reconstruct society. Problems such as racism, sexism, poverty, and inequality are widespread and permeate many of the nation's institutions, such as the work force, the courts, and the schools. To educate future citizens to merely fit into but not transform society will result in the perpetuation of these problems, including the widening gap between the rich and the poor, racial conflict and tension, and the growing number of people who are victims of poverty and homelessness.

A society that has sharp divisions between the rich and the poor, and between Whites and people of color, is not a stable one. It contains stresses and tensions that can lead to societal upheavals and racial polarization and conflict. Thus, citizenship education for the 21st century must not only help students to become literate and reflective citizens who can participate in the mainstream society, it must also teach them to care about other people in their communities (Kohn, 1991) and to take personal, social, and civic action to create a humane and just society (Banks, 1997b).

Teaching Decision-Making and Social Action

I have developed a model for teaching decision-making and social action in the elementary and high school grades. This section describes the model, and the next section describes a lesson taught by a teacher using it.

This model, summarized in Figure 12.1, assumes that the main goal of the social studies is to help students acquire the knowledge, skills, and values needed to make reflective personal and public decisions so they can take action consistent with American values—such as equality, justice, and human dignity—that will improve and reform society. One essential component of decision making is knowledge.

Knowledge for Reflective Decision-Making

There are many different types of knowledge and ways of validating beliefs and observations. Knowledge that forms the basis of reflective decisions must be scientific knowledge—it must be derived using a process that can be replicated by others, and it must be public as opposed to private. Knowledge used in reflective decisions must also reflect the experiences and perspectives of a wide range of groups within a pluralistic society. Knowledge that only reflects elite groups or ignores the perceptions and experiences of various racial, ethnic, and gender groups cannot result in decisions that reflect the best interests of the commonwealth or civic community.

Figure 12.1 illustrates the major components and process of a social studies curriculum that focuses on reflective decision-making and social action. The unit begins with a decision-problem. The knowledge needed to make the decision is derived with a process of social inquiry. Value inquiry related to the decision-problem leads to clarified values. The knowledge and clarified values are interrelated to make a decision that is implemented by action.

There are various kinds of knowledge and paradigms, as Kuhn (1970) points out in his book *The Structure of Scientific Revolutions.* Some knowledge and paradigms challenge the current social structure and support reform of institutions; other knowledge and paradigms reinforce the prevailing social-class structure and institutional arrangements within society. Kuhn also describes how difficult it is for new knowledge systems or paradigms to challenge or replace existing ones. When this occurs, Kuhn says, a scientific revolution has taken place.

There are many examples of paradigms, theories, and concepts created by elite social scientists that have resulted in decisions and policies detrimental to people of color or different ethnic groups, such as African Americans, Latinos, and American Indians (Banks, 1998). Such paradigms and theories include Phillips's conception of the contented slave (1918), Herrnstein and Murray's (1994) ideas about the intelligence of low-income people and African Americans, and conceptions about culturally deprived

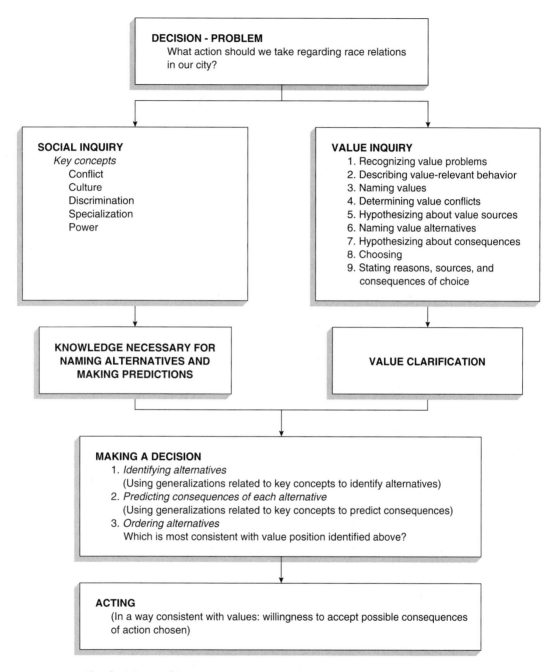

FIGURE 12.1   The decision-making process.

Note. From *Teaching Strategies for the Social Studies: Inquiry, Valuing and Decision-Making* (4th ed.) (p. 457) by J. A. Banks with A. A. Clegg, Jr., 1990, White Plains, NY: Longman. Reprinted by permission.

children that were developed in the 1960s (Riessman, 1962). The cultural deprivation concept has re-emerged in the 1990s in the form of *at-risk* students (Richardson, 1990). The *at-risk* and *culturally deprived* concepts are not identical, but they are similar in several important ways: Both are labels that tend to blame the victim for their situations; both become stigmas for the individuals and groups labeled with the terms.

Value Inquiry and Reflective Decision

To make reflective decisions, students must have clarified and thoughtfully derived values. An important goal of a curriculum focused on decision-making is to help students identify the sources of their values and determine how they conflict, identify value alternatives, and choose freely from them (Banks and Banks, 1999). However, students should be required to justify their moral choices within the context of higher societal values such as human dignity, justice, and equality. If students are not required to do that, value teaching will run the risk of becoming relativistic and ethnically neutral (Banks and Banks, 1999).

After students have mastered interdisciplinary knowledge related to a concept or issue such as racism or sexism, they should participate in value or moral inquiry exercises. The goal of such exercises should be to help students develop a set of consistent, clarified values that can guide purposeful and reflective personal or civic action related to the issue examined. This goal can best be attained by teaching students a method or process for deriving their values within a democratic classroom atmosphere. In this classroom, students must be free to express their value choices, determine how those choices conflict, examine alternative values, consider the consequences of different value choices, and defend their moral choices within the context of human dignity and other American values. Students must be given an opportunity to reflectively derive their own values so they develop a commitment to human dignity, equality, and other democratic values. They must be encouraged to reflect upon their value choices within a democratic atmosphere (Banks and Banks, 1999).

Teachers can use the following value model to help students identify and clarify their values so they can make reflective moral choices. It consists of these steps:

1. Defining and recognizing value problems.
2. Describing value-relevant behavior.
3. Naming values exemplified by the behavior.
4. Determining conflicting values in behavior described.
5. Hypothesizing about the possible consequence of the values analyzed.
6. Naming alternative values to those described by behavior observed.
7. Hypothesizing about the possible consequences of values analyzed.
8. Declaring value preferences; choosing.
9. Stating reasons, sources, and possible consequences of value choice: justifying, hypothesizing, predicting. (Banks and Banks, 1999, p. 444)

Decision-Making and Citizen Action

After students have gathered knowledge, using a scientific process and making sure it represents diverse perspectives and points of view, they should make a decision regarding actions they can take related to the topic, problem, or issue they have studied. In making a decision, they should use the knowledge they have attained to make a list of alternative actions, to predict the possible consequences of each alternative, and to order the alternatives. They should ask, "Which of the alternatives are most consistent with our values?"

The students should take action only after they have thought carefully about the alternatives, weighed and ordered the alternatives, and considered their possible consequences. The actions the students take may be *personal, social,* or *civic.* One possible form of action is inaction. Lewis (1991) has developed a helpful guide to social action activities for students. Primary-grade children who have studied a unit on stereotypes may decide to stop using words and phrases that stereotype American Indians and African Americans. Middle-grade children who have studied a unit on prejudice may decide to read several books on various ethnic and racial groups or to make a friend from another racial, ethnic, or religious group.

Middle school students may decide to do volunteer work for a candidate in a local election who advocates racial equality after they have studied a unit on contemporary race relations. High school students may design, administer, and publish the results of a districtwide survey on racism, as was done by a group of high school students in the Ann Arbor, Michigan, School District (Polakow-Suransky & Ulaby, 1990). In this ambitious project, the students administered the survey to all high school students in the district. Their response rate was 57.4 %, or 2,006 students. Two of the students published an article based on their survey in the *Phi Delta Kappan,* a widely circulated national educational journal. They also presented their findings to the school board and made recommendations. These are among the recommendations:

- Arranging immediate follow-up activities to the survey—including workshops, class discussions, and assemblies—in all high schools.
- Reevaluating the district's policies on tracking, with the goal of discontinuing the practice.
- Requiring students to take a course that would expose them to issues related to racial oppression in the U.S.
- Establishing a task force to evaluate the entire high school curriculum from a multicultural perspective and to draw up guidelines for dealing with the "racial incidents" involving students and school personnel. (Polakow-Suransky & Ulaby, p. 605)

❖ Making Decisions and Taking Action: A Classroom Example

Mr. Carson, a middle school social studies teacher, used the Banks decision-making model to teach a unit on the civil rights movement. Mr. Carson wanted his students to acquire an understanding of the historical development of the civil rights movement and to analyze and clarify their values related to integration and segregation. He also wanted them to conceptualize and perhaps take some actions related to racism and desegregation in their personal life, the school, or the local community. Mr. Carson teaches in a predominantly White suburban school district near a city in the Northwest that has a population of about 500,000. The metropolitan area in which Mr. Carson's school is located has a population of about 1 million.

The Long Shadow of Little Rock

Mr. Carson used the Banks value inquiry model to help his students analyze the value issues revealed in Chapter 8 of *The Long Shadow of Little Rock* by Daisy Bates (1987). In this well-written and moving chapter, Mrs. Bates describes the moral dilemma she faced as head of the National Association for the Advancement of Colored People (NAACP) in Little Rock, Arkansas, when Central High School was desegregated. Nine African American high school students enrolled in Central High School during the 1957-58 school year.

Mrs. Bates was the leading supporter and organizer for the nine students. Her husband, L. C. Bates, was a journalist. They owned a newspaper, *The States Press.* In Chapter 8 of *The Long Shadow of Little Rock,* Mrs. Bates describes how a middle-aged White woman came to her home at 3 p.m. one day and told her to call a press conference and announce that she was withdrawing her support for the nine students and was advising them to withdraw from Central High School and return to the Negro schools. The woman said she represented a group of "Southern Christian women." Mrs. Bates asked the woman what would happen if she didn't do what she told her to do. She looked Mrs. Bates straight in the eye and said, "You'll be destroyed—you, your newspaper, your reputation. . . . Everything."

During a long, anguished night, Mrs. Bates wondered whether she had the right to destroy 16 years of her husband's work—the newspaper. Yet she believed she could not abandon a cause to which she and many other African Americans were deeply committed. By morning, Mrs. Bates had made a difficult and painful decision. She called her visitor and told her no. Later, she told her husband what she had done. He said, "Daisy, you did the right thing." Mrs. Bates' visitor kept her promise. Major stores and businesses withdrew their advertising from *The States Press,* forcing it to close. The Bates family suffered financial and personal turmoil because of the newspaper's closing and because of threats and attempts on Mrs. Bates' life.

Using the Banks value inquiry model, these are some of the questions Mr. Carson asked his students:

Defining and Recognizing Value Problems

1. What value problem did Mrs. Bates face after she was visited by the woman?

Naming Values Exemplified by Behavior Described

2. What did the visitor value or think was important? What did Mrs. Bates value? What did Mr. Bates value?

Hypothesizing About the Source of Value Analyzed

3. How do you think Mrs. Bates's visitor developed the values she had? How do you think Mr. and Mrs. Bates developed the values they showed in this selection?

Declaring Value Preferences: Choosing

4. Try to put yourself in Mrs. Bates's place on October 29, 1959. What decision would you have made?

Stating Reasons, Sources, and Possible Consequences of Value Choices

5. Why should Mrs. Bates have made the decision you stated above? What were the possible consequences of her saying "no" and saying "yes" to her visitor? Give as many reasons as you can about why Mrs. Bates should have made the decision you stated above.

Keep in mind that Mrs. Bates knew that if she said yes to her visitor she would probably have been able to keep her property, but that the nine students probably would have had to return to Black schools and that segregation would have been maintained in Little Rock. On the other hand, by saying no, she risked losing all of her property and her husband's property, including his newspaper. Also, consider the fact that she did not involve him in making her decision.

Decision-Making and Citizen Action

After Mr. Carson's students had derived knowledge about the civil rights movement of the 1950s and 1960s, and clarified their values regarding these issues, he asked them to list all the possible actions they could take to increase desegregation in their personal lives as well as in the life of the school and the community. Mr. Carson was careful to explain to the students that action should be broadly conceptualized. He defined action in a way that might include personal commitment to do something, such as making more friends from different racial and ethnic groups; making a commitment to watch the movie *Roots* and then discussing it with a friend; or reading a play or book to better understand another racial or ethnic group, such as *A Raisin in the Sun* by Lorraine Hansberry or *Beloved* by Toni Morrison. These are some of the possible actions the students listed:

1. Making a personal commitment to stop telling racist jokes.
2. Making a commitment to challenge our own racial and ethnic stereotypes either before or after we verbalize them.
3. Compiling an annotated list of books about ethnic groups that we will ask the librarian to order for our school library.
4. Asking the principal to order sets of photographs that show African Americans and other people of color who have jobs that represent a variety of careers. Asking the principal to encourage teachers to display these photographs on their classroom walls.
5. Observing television programs to determine the extent to which people of color, such as African Americans and Asian Americans, are represented in such jobs as news anchor and program host. Writing to local and national television stations to express our concern if we discover that people of color are not represented in powerful and visible roles in news or other kinds of television programs.
6. Contacting a school in the inner city to determine whether there are joint activities and projects in which we and they might participate.
7. Asking the principal or the board of education in our school district to require our teachers to attend inservice staff development workshops that will help them learn ways to integrate content about ethnic and racial groups into our courses.
8. Sharing some of the facts that we have learned in this unit—such as that by 2050, 47.5% of the population of the United States will be people of color—with our parents and discussing these facts with them.
9. Making a personal commitment to have a friend from another racial, ethnic, or religious group by the end of the year.
10. Making a personal commitment to read at least one book a year that deals with a racial, cultural, or ethnic group other than my own.
11. Do nothing, take no actions.

The Decision-Making Process

After the students had completed the list of possible action (including no actions), Mr. Carson asked them to consider the possible consequences of each of the actions identified, such as:

If I Take No Action   *Then* I will be doing nothing to improve race relations in my personal life, in my school, my community, or my nation. *But* I will not risk trying to do something that could fail. I will also be indicating to others, by my behavior, that I am not concerned about improving race relations in my personal life, my family, school or community.

If I Make a Personal Commitment to Tell No More Racist Jokes   *Then* I will be improving my personal behavior that relates to other racial, ethnic and cultural groups. I will also demonstrate to others that I am concerned about improving race relations in my personal life. *But* I will be doing little directly to improve the behaviors of other people in my family, school and community.

After the students had worked in groups of five to identify and state the possible consequences of various courses of actions, Mr. Carson asked them to select one or two personal group actions they would like to take related to the problems they had studied in the unit. Mr. Carson also asked the students to be prepared to defend or explain the course of action or actions they chose, to tell whether it was feasible for them to carry out the action or actions, and to provide a timeline for its initiation and completion (if possible). These are among the action the students chose:

- Katy and Susan decided to read the play *A Raisin in the Sun* by Lorraine Hansberry to get a better understanding of the experience of African Americans in the United States.
- Clay, Pete, Tessie, Rosie, and Maria decided to prepare an annotated list of books on ethnic cultures and ask the school librarian to order them for the school library. The group planned to ask Mr. Carson to help them find resources to prepare the list of books.
- Roselyn decided to improve her understanding of ethnic cultures by reading these books during the year: *Let the Circle Be Unbroken* by Mildred D. Taylor, *A Jar of Dreams* by Yoshiko Uchida, and *America Is in the Heart* by Carlos Bulosan.
- Aralean, Juan, James, Angela, and Patricia decided to develop a proposal that would require teachers in the district to attend multicultural education workshops. They would develop their plan with Mr. Carson and present it to the principal and then to the Board of Education for possible adoption.

❖ Toward Developing Effective Citizens

Social studies education in the United States is characterized by many conflicting conceptions, paradigms, and ideologies that mirror the tensions, value conflicts, and developments in U.S. society. Although educators hold conflicting conceptions about what should constitute social studies teaching, they agree that the development of effective citizens should be the goal of social studies education.

Barr, Barth, & Shermis (1977) have identified three major traditions within social studies education. The goal of each is to develop effective citizens. The traditions are: (1) social studies taught as citizenship transmission, (2) social studies taught as social science, and (3) social studies taught as reflective inquiry.

Approaches and theories that have developed since within the last several decades are not adequately reflected in the Barr, Barth, and Shermis typology. These approaches include the interdisciplinary conceptual approach, the decision-making and social action approach, and the critical theory paradigm based on the work of Habermas (1968).

In this chapter, I identified and described five major periods in the development of social studies education in the United States, described a model for teaching social studies that focuses on decision-making and social action, and described a social studies lesson on race relations that is organized around the teaching model presented.

Social studies teaching, research, and practice reflect the major social, political, and economic developments in U.S. society. Because social studies deals with the nature of people in society, the social studies curriculum is more likely than other subject areas to mirror the debates, controversies, and tensions within society. The social studies curriculum will continue to reflect the major issues and tensions within American life, as well as mirror the nation's ideals, goals, aspirations, and conflicts. The development of reflective and active citizens who can contribute to and participate in making our nation more democratic and just should be the major goal of social studies education as we enter the 21st century.

Acknowledgment

A section of this chapter is adapted with permission of the publisher from James A. Banks, A curriculum for empowerment, action, and change. In C. E. Sleeter (Ed.) (1991). *Empowerment through multicultural education* (pp. 134–139). Albany: State University of New York Press.

References

Ankeney, K., Del Rio, R., Nash, G. B., and Vigilante, D. (n.d.). *Bring history alive! A sourcebook for teaching United States history.* Los Angeles: National Center for History in the Schools.

Armento, B. J. (1986). Research on teaching social studies. In M. C. Wittrock (Ed.), *Handbook of research on teaching* (pp. 942–951). New York: Macmillan.

Banks, J. A. (1969). A content analysis of the Black American in textbooks. *Social Education, 33,* 954–957, 963.

Banks, J. A. (Ed.). (1996). *Multicultural education, transformative knowledge, and action: Historical and contemporary perspectives.* New York: Teachers College Press.

Banks, J. A. (1997a). *Teaching strategies for ethnic studies* (6th ed.). Boston: Allyn and Bacon.

Banks, J. A. (1997b). *Educating citizens in a multicultural society.* New York: Teachers College Press.

Banks, J. A. (1998). The lives and values of researchers: Implications for educating citizens in a multicultural society. *Educational Researcher, 27*(7), 4–17.

Banks, J. A. (1999). *An introduction to multicultural education* (2nd ed.). Boston: Allyn and Bacon.

Banks, J. A., & Banks, C. A. M., with Clegg, A. A., Jr. (1999). *Teaching strategies for the social studies: Decision-making and citizen action* (5th ed.). New York: Longman.

Barr, R. D., Barth, J. L., & Shermis, S. S. (1977). *Defining the social studies* (Bulletin 51). Washington, DC: National Council for the Social Studies.

Bates, D. (1987). *The long shadow of Little Rock: A memoir.* Fayetteville, AK: The University of Arkansas Press.

Bragaw, D. (Ed.). (1986). Scope and sequence: Alternatives for social studies. *Social Education, 50*(7), 484–534.

Bruner, J. S. (1960). *The process of education.* New York: Vintage Books.

Bruner, J. S. (1996). *The culture of education.* Cambridge, MA: Harvard University Press.

California State Department of Education. (1987). *History-social science framework for California Public Schools, kindergarten through grade twelve.* Sacramento: Author.

Cheney, L. V. The end of history. *The Wall Street Journal,* October 20, 1994, A 26(W), A22(E).

Cherryholmes, C. H. (1982). Discourse and criticism in the social studies classroom. *Theory and Research in Social Education, 9,* 57-73.

Cuban, L. (1991). History of teaching in social studies. In J. P. Shaver, (Ed.), *Handbook of research on social studies teaching and learning* (pp. 197-209). New York: Macmillan.

Dow, P. B. (1969). Man: A Course of Study: An experimental social science course for elementary students. *Man: A Course of Study talks to teachers.* Cambridge, MA: Education Development Center.

Engle, S. H., & Ochoa, A. S. (1988). *Education for democratic citizenship: Decision-Making in the social studies.* New York: Teachers College Press.

Franklin, J. H., and Moss, A. A., Jr. (1988). *From slavery to freedom: A history of Negro Americans* (6th ed.). New York: Knopf.

Gardner, D. P. (1983). *A nation at risk: The imperative of educational reform.* Washington, DC: The National Commission on Excellence in Education.

Habermas, J. (1968). *Knowledge and human interests.* Boston: Beacon Press.

Hanna, P. R. (1963, April). Revising the social studies: What is needed. *Social Education, 27,* 190-196.

Herrnstein, R. J., & Murray, C. (1994). *The bell curve: Intelligence and class structure in American life.* New York: The Free Press.

Hirsch, E. D., Jr. (1987). *Cultural literacy: What every American needs to know.* Boston: Houghton Mifflin.

Hirsch, E. D., Jr., Kett, J. F., & Trefil, J. (1988). *The dictionary of cultural literacy: What every American needs to know.* Boston: Houghton Mifflin.

Kohn, A. (1991). Caring kids: The role of schools. *Phi Delta Kappan, 72,* 496-506.

Kuhn, T. S. (1970). *The structure of scientific revolutions* (2nd ed., enlarged). Chicago: University of Chicago Press.

Lewis, B. A. (1991). *The kid's guide to social action.* P. Espeland (Ed.). Minneapolis: Free Spirit.

Massialas, B. G., & Allen, R. F. (Eds.). (1996). *Crucial issues in teaching social studies K-12.* Belmont, CA: Wadsworth.

Metcalf, L. W. (Ed.). (1971). *Values education: Rationale, strategies, and procedures.* Washington, DC: National Council for the Social Studies.

Nash, G. B., Crabtree, C., & Dunn, R. E. (1997). *History on trial: Culture wars and the teaching of the past.* New York: Knopf.

National Center for History in the Schools. (1994). *National standards for United States history: Exploring the American experience.* Los Angeles: Author.

National Center for History in the Schools. (1996). *National standards for history* (Basic ed.). Los Angeles: Author.

National Council for the Social Studies. (1979, April). Revision of the NCSS Social Studies Curriculum Guidelines, *Social Education, 43,* 261-278.

National Council for the Social Studies. (1994). *Expectations of excellence: Curriculum standards for social studies.* Washington, DC: Author.

Newmann, F. M. (1975). *Education for citizen action: Challenge for secondary curriculum.* Berkeley, CA: McCutchan.

Newmann, F. M., with Oliver, D. W. (1970). *Clarifying public controversy: An approach to teaching social studies.* Boston: Little Brown.

The New York State Department of Education. (1989, July). *A curriculum for inclusion.* Report of the Commissioner's Task Force on Minorities: Equity and Excellence. Albany: State Department of Education.

The New York State Department of Education. (1991, June). *One nation, many peoples: A declaration of cultural interdependence.* Report of the New York State Social Studies Review and Development Committee. Albany: State Department of Education.

Oliver, D. W., & Shaver, J. P. (1966). *Teaching public issues in the high school.* Boston: Houghton Mifflin.

Phillips, U. B. (1918). *American Negro slavery.* New York: D. Appleton.

Polakow-Suransky, S., & Ulaby, N. (1990, April). Students take action to combat racism. *Phi Delta Kappan,* 601-606.

Popkewitz, T. S. (1977). The latent values of the discipline-centered curriculum. *Theory and Research in Social Education, 5,* 41-60.

Ravitch, D., & Finn, C. E., Jr. (1987). *What do our 17-year-olds know? A report on the first national assessment of history and literature.* New York: Harper & Row.

Richardson, V. (1990, Spring). At-risk programs: Evaluation and critical inquiry. In K. A. Sirotnik (Ed.), *Evaluation and social justice: Issues in public education* (pp. 61–75). San Francisco: Jossey-Bass.

Riessman, F. (1962). *The culturally deprived child.* New York: Harper & Row.

Sarason, S. B. (1996). *Revisiting "the culture of the school and the problem of change."* New York: Teachers College Press.

Shaver, J. P. (Ed.). (1977). *Building rationales for citizenship education* (Bulletin 52). Washington, DC: National Council for the Social Studies.

Shaver, J. P. (Ed.). (1991). *Handbook of research on social studies teaching and learning.* New York: Macmillan.

Shaver, J. P., Davis, O. L., Jr., & Helburn, S. W. (1979). The status of social studies education: Impressions from three NSF studies. *Social Education, 43,* 150–153.

Superka, D. P., Hawke, S., & Morrissett, I. (1980). The current and future status of social studies. *Social Education, 44,* 362–369.

Taba, H., Durkin, M. C., Franekel, J. R., & McNaughton, A. H. (1971). *A teacher's handbook for elementary social studies: An inductive approach.* Reading, MA: Addison-Wesley.

United States Bureau of the Census. (1998). *Statistical abstract of the United States* (111th ed.). Washington, DC: U.S. Government Printing Office.

13 The Social Reconstruction of Art Education: Teaching Visual Culture

Kerry Freedman
University of Minnesota

Issues of culture are fundamental to art education. The focus of these issues has changed historically in relation to shifting views of art and culture and changing ideas about the purposes of art in school. Since public school art began in the 19th century, the meaning of culture has ranged from a particular notion of good taste and refinement reflected by fine art to a more general social context in which artistic production and appreciation take place.[1]

This chapter is about representations of culture in art education. Culture, including visual culture, can be represented differently depending on when and where people live, who they are, and how they think. My purpose is to challenge how art is commonly depicted and taught in schools, and to suggest more equitable and enriching ways of teaching and thinking about art.

This chapter has three sections. The first section focuses on the relationship of past and present myths of art education to issues of equity. The second section concerns how cultural knowledge is shaped by art curriculum and instruction. In the third section, recommendations for practice at the elementary and middle-school levels are presented.

✜ Conceptions of Equity: Past and Present

Historically, equity has been dealt with in art education through a focus on two issues: (1) the role of the individual as a self-expressive maker of art and (2) the reflection and reproduction of a "common" culture through common art experiences for all students (Freedman, 1989a). Embedded in art education of the past has been the assumption that focusing on individual self-expression at one level and on promotion of a common culture at another level would override cultural differences and promote equity.

The focus on individualism has resulted in children's cultural commonalities, as well as their differences, being ignored. Except for the similarities among children that have been assumed biophysical and developmental, each child has been viewed as natural, entirely unique, and without attributes of culture.

Late 19th and early 20th century models of artistic ability were borrowed from eugenics to classify children's art abilities based on race, class, and gender (Chalmers, 1992; Freedman, 1989a). More contemporary models of artistic development have represented the characteristics of children's drawings as universal. Only recently have these models been questioned as research has shown that similarities between children's drawings are often copied from common cultural sources (Wilson & Wilson, 1977) and vary between cultures (Brittain, 1990). When children enter school, for example, they have similarities in gendered experience, cultural tradition, and socioeconomic group. Children's artistic production and learning are also bound by the commonalities of schooling. Differences in children's art cannot be entirely individualistic or universal, because they reflect these cultural similarities and differences.

The focus on individualism in school emerged based on 18th-century Enlightenment philosophy and the writings of Rousseau, Pestalozzi, and Froebel. Later, the philosophical notion of individualism in children became mingled with clinical psychology, resulting in a therapeutic purpose for art education by the 1920s. Progressive educators promoted a therapeutic art instruction that was assumed to keep children "natural" and untouched by society and culture (Rugg & Schumaker, 1928). However, the notion of what was natural was culturally based on ideas of self-expression in the fine-art community, the upper-middle-class interests of progressive private schooling, conceptions of childhood in social science, and a political economy of freedom and social mobility.

While the art of a few various cultures began to be included in some art education literature early in the 20th century, and grew particularly in the 1930s and in the 1940s as America began to adopt a more global perspective after World War II, the post-war model for art instruction was that of the fine artist. By the end of World War II, American art educators had become captivated by an ideal of the autonomous fine artist who worked alone in a studio, freely self-expressing and intuitively creating. The ideal was merely symbolic; fine artists are actually part of a professional community that is shaped by cultural norms and values.

Guided by the image of individualistic art, art educators became even more immersed in the practice of therapeutic art education in the hope of confounding the development of authoritarianism in children and nurturing a perceived naturally democratic personality (Freedman, 1989b). This model was tempered somewhat in the 1960s, when art educators began to place a greater emphasis on incorporating formal instruction in other fine-art disciplines, such as art history and criticism (Barkan, 1965), and a multicultural perspective (McFee, 1961), into instruction. Since that time, art education has shifted to include more multidisciplinary art content, but has continued to focus largely on the Western, male-dominated, fine-art community.

The assumption that the dispersal of "common" culture would benefit all has been maintained in art education through the promotion of Western models of aesthetic value and an appreciation of work produced by a male-dominated fine-art community. A purpose of such an education in the United States has been to instill in students a knowledge and appreciation of the symbols of socioeconomic success and the values held by people who have been such successes (Freedman, 1989a; Hamblen, 1990). These values have been seen as cultural capital necessary for social mobility.

This purpose of art education is now viewed as problematic for at least three reasons. First, while teaching common culture has been represented as democratic because it appears to make the elite available to everyone, the notion of elite reflects a power structure not conducive to democratic life. The aesthetic values of a few are instilled in all; they are presented as universal and, in their presentation, become "common." In this way, elite values influence what is valued in non-Western and non-mainstream cultures. It is a strength of education to enable the appropriation of knowledge by those who are excluded to provide avenues for empowerment; however, art education has been reproductive in that it has acculturated students without providing the critical foundation necessary for analyzing underlying assumptions of the aesthetic values taught in school.

Second, visual culture ("common" or otherwise) is continually fragmented and dispersed. When art is not examined from a multicultural perspective, the pluralism that exists in life is not acknowledged and the impossibility of real and stable cultural boundaries is ignored. Modern fine art exemplifies this ongoing transformation because it has been greatly influenced by non-Western sources and is intertwined with traditions of popular art. For example, Picasso was influenced by African masks, Van Gogh by Japanese block prints, and American Indian artist Randy White was influenced by Georgia O'Keeffe and James McNeill Whistler when he painted a picture of O'Keeffe in a pose similar to that of the painting known as "Whistler's Mother."[2] However, these types of cultural conjunctions are rarely presented in school.

Third, the assumption that a common culture can be distributed to students contains a certain irony when juxtaposed with traditions of individualism. It is an illusion to assume that students can adopt a universal model of aesthetics when they are viewing art, yet conceive unique ideas when producing art. Students gain experience in relation to their cultural context and cannot simply put it aside when the demand to view or produce art is made.

✤ Myths of Art Education: The Old and the New

Two decades ago, Eisner (1973–1974) revealed the mythological character of seven beliefs that contributed to the focus on therapeutic self-expression in art education:

1. Children should be left on their own to work with art materials.
2. The purpose of art instruction is to develop children's general "creativity."
3. Artistic process, not product, is important.
4. Children perceive the world more clearly than adults.
5. Children's art should not and cannot be evaluated.
6. Teachers should not talk about art because talk ruins the effect of art.
7. Good art education for young children should provide the widest range of materials and studio activities possible.

Eisner argued that educators should replace these myths with art knowledge and discontinue the practice of determining curriculum based on this mythology.

Consistent with Eisner's aims, educators have shifted toward a greater emphasis on looking at and talking about art in school. However, there has been a continued absence of attention paid to issues concerning the art of multiple ethnic, gender, and socioeconomic groups, as well as other vital cultural issues, such as the ecological implications of art and the visual effects of the mass media. This absence suggests that several new myths of art education need to be examined. The following seven myths reflect current debates concerning multiculturalism in art education.[3]

Myth 1: Art Has Inherent Value   Philosophers since Kant have argued that aesthetic value is inherent within a "masterpiece" and that an educated person will be able to appreciate that value. The irony of this argument is that an education in artistic production and valuing is necessarily socially constructed. It is in relation to time, place, and even social group that art is valued. When the contexts of production and valuing are the same (that is, when the artist and the viewer have the same values), the value may *appear* to be within the work of art; but when the context of valuing is different from the context of production, it is more easily understood that value is largely determined based on issues external to any particular work of art. If this were not the case, European art once considered great, such as Raphael's madonnas, would always be considered great. Though Raphael's paintings were admired in his time, there have been times when they were shunned. Impressionist paintings, once ridiculed, have gained favor.

Even members of the professional art community from the same time and place do not always agree on the value of any particular work of art. The value of a work of art also changes as it moves from one cultural context to another. For example, cere-monial objects used in different cultures and objects traditionally considered decorative that are made by women have only in the last century been viewed as art in European-American culture.

Myth 2: Art Is a Universal Language   While art may take similar forms in sev-eral cultures, the context of production, the intent with which things are made, and the uses to which they are put differ dramatically in different contexts. As is the case with language, technical similarities may exist across the arts of different cultures, but the differences in meaning may be profound and require a specific education to be under-stood. Even the expressive qualities of art that are often considered universal may be cul-turally specific. Recent cross-cultural studies of emotion indicate that there are cultural differences in people's capacities for emotion and the characteristics of their emotional states (Shweder & Levine, 1984). Profound differences such as these influence the pro-duction and appreciation of art.

Myth 3: Art Can Be Studied Effectively Without Studying the Con-text of Production and Appreciation   It may be possible to appreciate, at some superficial level, an artifact from another culture just by looking at it, but one can-not understand it without information about the culture. For example, the pair of beaded earrings meant to be worn during a ritual dance in motion in the sun or before a campfire at night—where they disappear, leaving only light sparkling around the dancer's head—are transformed when placed in a museum case or a photograph. The transformation occurs because the new context shapes what viewers see as art.[4]

Myth 4: There Are Hard and Fast Distinctions Between Fine Art and Other Forms of Visual Production   Although there are dramatic differ-ences between the art forms of different cultures, older, dichotomous categories (such as fine art/non-fine art) may no longer be helpful in understanding these dif-ferences. It is no longer easy to view cultures as totally separate because they inter-act on many levels and through many media. Fine artists borrow imagery from pop-ular culture, men borrow from women, and artists in the United States borrow from other countries. Contemporary visions of art and culture are too complex to be rep-resented dichotomously.

Myth 5: The Interpretation of Art Is the Domain of Experts   Many peo-ple believe that instruction should focus on the opinions of experts in fine art. At least two dilemmas surface resulting from this myth. First, experts in the professional art com-munity do not always agree with each other. For example, women art historians often disagree with men in their interpretations of paintings of and by women. Second, peo-ple knowledgeable about art may not be part of the fine-art community. For example, those who have a deep understanding of an American Indian culture in which art is integrated into everyday life, particularly a member of that culture, can provide infor-mation and aid understanding about art.

Myth 6: All Art Can Be Understood through Certain Analytical (Western) Aesthetic Models   Modern Western models of aesthetics focus on an analysis of objects influenced by Western science and are based on Western conceptions of taste and beauty. However, these models are often treated in curriculum as if they enable objective description; that is, the models give the impression that aesthetics is not socially constructed and culturally located. Currently, most art curricula are based on notions of aesthetics that focus on the reduction of form to elements (such as line, shape, and color) and principles (such as rhythm, balance, and unity) of design or on expressive characteristics considered either unique and personal (different for everyone) or universal (the same for everyone). Subject matter of a work of art and cultural context are usually considered peripheral to these two perspectives. Hence, these models of aesthetics do not include an analysis of the context of production and appreciation (function, underlying assumptions, social effect, etc.) because they do not take into account the multiple cultural influences on art (or on the creation of models themselves).

While these models appear to simply facilitate an analysis of what is contained within a work of art, they actually condition the ways students approach visual culture. The focus on these models in education prepares students to approach art as a series of objects about form and feeling isolated from context. The assumption that any object can be effectively analyzed using such models carries with it the idea that the artifacts of any culture can and should be taught about as if they were Western (male) fine art. This form of acculturation does not promote an understanding of the peculiarities of fine art and aesthetics, nor does it maintain the integrity of other forms of visual culture and alternative ways of understanding.

These Western models of aesthetics also facilitate an education based on a "disinterested" aesthetic experience, which is the form of elation one may feel when encountering a work of art. Such an experience is supposed to defy simultaneous human (personal, social, economic) interests and elevate people to a higher plane of existence. Whether any experience is possible for one isolated from interests is highly debatable, but regardless, this level of experience is merely a perceptual coupling with a work of art, about which the viewer may know nothing. It is only the first simple step toward developing an understanding of visual culture and having the much richer aesthetic experience that comes with depth of knowledge.

Myth 7: Art Education Should Always Start with the Object   It is understandable that the efforts of several decades to move art education away from a focus on the production process, mythological notions of self-expression, and "the child," have resulted in the emergence (actually re-emergence) of this myth.

The professional art community is also currently challenging the notion of individual self-expression and focusing to greater extent on the many communities (professional, cultural) and conditions that make production and appreciation possible.

Information about community and cultural conditions is vital to art knowledge. To start with the object is starting in the middle of the story. This strategy for teaching may convey to children that commodities have privilege over people, purposes, and processes.

Recently, there has been pressure on art educators to overcome these myths and move toward a greater focus on multiculturalism. Several perspectives on the topic have emerged as a result of this pressure. The following sections discuss these approaches and make recommendations for the future.

❖ Teaching Cultural Fragments

Much of the discussion about diversity and reform in art education has focused on change in curriculum. A pervasive view is that teachers should simply supplement published or unpublished curricula that are largely built on models of the disciplines of Western fine art with multicultural content. Stuhr (1991) has equated this activity with the first level of Sleeter and Grant's (1987) multicultural approaches to education.

In part, the pervasive use of this approach to art education is due to the ways government and school district officials have responded to demands for equitable schooling. Their attempts at multiculturalism have often been couched in terms of fair "distribution" or "treatment," suggesting that what is needed is a certain number of lessons about a particular culture or a special (perhaps therapeutic) set of activities where women and men of color are concerned.

In school, the legislation becomes reduced to a requirement that curriculum contains a specified number of artifacts made by people of various cultures. For example, a school district in Minnesota requires that each art lesson taught must include examples of art made by people of at least three different cultures, one of which can be "women." This inclusion may be helpful, but it misses the point of teaching art in a socially sensitive and responsible manner.

The ideal purpose of including these artifacts in curriculum is to promote learning and understanding about disenfranchised groups and inform students about the aesthetic contributions of world cultures. However, art curricula have been published in which non-Western art has been disassociated from its cultural context and analyzed using modernist, Western models of epistemology and aesthetics. The use of these models and quota systems often becomes patronizing and results in inappropriate juxtapositions of culture that misinform students and further disenfranchise the groups curriculum is to support. This occurs, in part, because the *technical* and *formalistic* attributes of artifacts are often focused on in art curriculum, making vitally different cultural artifacts appear to be similar. It also occurs because art is taught with a discourse of extreme individualism, without attention to the ethnocentrism of this idea.

For example, in a second-grade art textbook used by many districts in the United States, a picture of a Navaho woman weaving on a loom is juxtaposed with a close-up photograph of the woven plastic strips of a lawn chair that might be found at a local department store (Chapman, 1987). Rather than addressing the important differences in function, design, and production reflected in these images, the text highlights the relatively less important similarities in the physical structure of "woven" objects. Perhaps a better comparison might be between the Navaho image and a picture of the conceptual work of art titled *Powwow Chair* by American Indian artist Edgar Heap of Birds, which consists of a lawn chair placed on a box of dirt taken from the reservation where the artist resides. According to the artist, this piece was produced to respond to stereotypical questions, such as whether American Indians sit cross-legged during powwows.

In another example, a published curriculum contains a slide of two Northwest Coast Indian totem poles showing one in the background and a part of one in the foreground (Alexander, 1988). The photographer has shown what is important in Western aesthetics: the pole in the background is shown so that the form as a whole can be seen, and in the foreground we see an individual face carved into a pole that has been framed as if it were a portrait (a Western art form). In neither pole are we able to see the interrelationship of figures as one meets another, an important visual and spiritual aspect of the totem in native culture. Curricula are filled with such juxtapositions that reflect a reconstitution of culture as mainstream Western aesthetic theory is drawn upon for interpretation and analysis.

Instruction also has an effect on the way we represent culture in art education. Instruction, as well as curriculum, is often more fundamentally about the structure of schooling and teachers' beliefs than about cultural knowledge and identity. The following vignettes taken from schools illustrate these dynamics in art instruction.

Vignette 1

A third- and fourth-grade class is making papier-maché masks. The teacher is using a published art curriculum that includes reproductions of masks from various countries and cultures. As recommended in the curriculum, she points out some of the physical characteristics of the masks in the pictures and tries to connect the lesson to the life of the students by calling their attention to wearing masks on Halloween. The teacher must make the presentation brief so the students have time to work on their masks. When asked what he has learned about masks as the hour draws to a close, a boy responds, "All people, all over the world, go trick-or-treating."

Vignette 2

A second-grade class has just completed a lesson on the environment. The word "recycle" is still printed on the board and the teacher has placed a recycle bin across the room from the garbage can. The classroom teacher tells the students that the art teacher will arrive soon and that they will be doing a clay project. The art teacher has 45 minutes in each room of two schools, once a week, to set up, teach, and clean up an art lesson. She has more than 600 students and little opportunity to know what they do outside their art period. When she enters the room, the students are spreading newspapers out on their desks in preparation for the lesson. At the end of the lesson, the art teacher tells the students to quickly throw their newspapers in the garbage can because she must get to her next class. Some of the students begin approaching the garbage can, but others appear to be wandering around the room with their paper and not following her directions. To spur them on, the art teacher asks the class, "Now, what are we going to do with our newspapers?" A boy raises his hand and says, "Recycle."

Vignette 3

In a middle-school class, the girls are required to make tissue paper flowers and the boys are assigned intricate pencil drawings of cars. When queried about the two assignments, the teacher responds that after many years of teaching, he has learned that the girls like to make tissue paper flowers and boys prefer to draw cars. He states that it is important to him to teach fairly and that this is the only fair way to teach. "Besides," he adds, "tissue paper is expensive and this solves part of my budget problem."

As Sleeter and Grant (1987) point out, the problem with education is usually assumed to be found in the occurrences that take place in a classroom, rather than being inherent in the structure of schooling. It is also assumed that individual teachers are the agents of change toward multiculturalism. However, these vignettes illustrate that the interests of teaching multicultural art often conflict with other interests of schooling and that the complexity of teaching about diversity and ecology cannot be handled by individual teachers or solely on the level of written curriculum development. Multicultural art education demands a deeper understanding by all concerned with schooling, as well as by the public. The character of instruction and institutional boundaries of schooling, even aspects of schooling that seem neutral such as scheduling, must be reconsidered if such an understanding is to be reached.

The vignettes also give attention to the importance of specificity and the rejection of metanarrative in teaching. Students get mixed messages and fragmentary information which become a misrepresentation when the art of any group is used stereotypically or presented as historically static. It is an important part of the social reconstruction of art education to give clear messages to students about social responsibility. These messages must maintain the integrity of difference, yet attend to equity and global concerns.

It is becoming increasingly difficult to think of cultures as being separate. Consider, for example, the daily interactions of Japanese and American culture. The television show *Dallas* is seen in Japan and *karaoke* takes place in country-western bars in Texas. A Japanese corporation is largely responsible for the restoration of Michelangelo's ceiling of the Sistine Chapel, and a growing number of Western "masterpieces" have been purchased by Japanese businesses (Januszczak, 1990).

There is concern about a negative effect on the national economy from the sale of better-quality Japanese automobiles in the United States. In the name of patriotism, we are pressured to buy lesser-quality American cars. Ironically, Japanese car companies are located in the U.S. and employ American citizens, and vice versa. In school, multicultural education, which should promote understanding and acceptance, has developed a new twist: students now learn about Japanese culture to give the United States a competitive advantage.

While many cultures currently interact, we must struggle to maintain the notion of different artistic traditions in historically separate cultures for the sake of identity. *Identity* is defined, in part, by tradition. It is also important for students to study these historical differences so they can better understand the multidirectional influence that results when cultures touch. Students should understand when and where cultural connections have occurred, because these connections produce cultural change and transform art.

An equitable and reasonable approach to multicultural art education requires a general social reconstruction of the field, wherein all art can be seen as visual culture that is socially constructed and meaningful. This type of art education requires that Western art be anthropologized, made exotic and peculiar, and that the contexts and implications of any art be studied as part of the knowledge necessary to understanding social life.

✣ Recommendations for Practice

Change in art education can promote the transformation of cultural representations in school at large (Lanier, 1969; Neperud, 1988; Stuhr, Petrovich-Mwaniki, & Wasson, 1992). Such a transformation, toward the social reconstruction of art education, could improve schooling in general. If we are to see a social reconstruction of art education, we must be culturally sensitive in our own teaching and ready to oppose institutional structures that push us toward presenting inappropriate understandings of art. Also, preservice and inservice teachers must be made aware of the enriching possibilities of new theoretical contexts for art education and gain a deeper knowledge and appreciation of the importance of teaching visual culture.

It is also imperative that socially reconstructed art curricula be developed. These curricula must reflect an awareness of the power of juxtaposition and include a serious consideration and valuing of all types of art. They must be designed to present a collage that illuminates and demonstrates an awareness of the fragile and fragmentary state of culture and teaching. This requires that the study of art be seen as fundamental to the study of culture and that culture is foundational to art.

Foundations to Understanding: Elementary School Art

To carry out such reconstruction, practical responses to the myths of multicultural art education must begin at the elementary school level. Each of the following guidelines for practice responds to one of the myths discussed above.

Response to Myth 1   We must illustrate to students that while the creation of visual culture is a basic part of human existence and certain psychophysical or perceptual responses to art may be commonly shared, the value of any particular work of art is largely socially constructed. Part of teaching art should be teaching why certain works of art have been valued in the past and why we study them today. Students should also be made aware of the reasons that some art valued today was not valued in the past. Students can begin to learn at an early age about the connections between art and life by studying the art of a few cultures in depth. Only by understanding some works of art in depth can students begin to understand why a particular work of art, and art in general, is valuable.

Response to Myth 2   To develop the understanding that there are many languages of art, children should experience art broadly as well as deeply. They should become acquainted with the art of many cultural groups, and with art by both women and men. They should also become aware that some art and architecture is made in accordance with nature. During elementary school, children begin learning distinctions, categories, and generalizations of many types; it is important that they become aware of the variety of styles, subjects, forms, meanings, and purposes of visual culture. By developing an awareness of these facets of visual culture, students can begin to recognize differences as well as similarities in art. For example, teachers should help students understand that there are different cultural representations of the same subject matter (such as people or animals) and why those differences exist.

Response to Myth 3   Art can be studied effectively only by including the study of production and appreciation contexts. Without cultural context, only a small part of any art form can be understood. Therefore, beginning in the elementary school, children cannot be taught art by activity or product-oriented method alone. Looking at and talking about art is as important as making it. To contextualize art at the elementary-school level, art can be taught in conjunction with other subjects. However, an interdisciplinary approach to art is appropriate only when art concepts are focused on, not merely as support for a science, mathematics, social studies, or English lesson.

Art concepts connect the work of art to its context and include what various art forms look like, how they are similar and different, how and why they were made, and how they were used and viewed. Even young children can think and talk about art concepts that range from the elements and principles of design to concepts emerging from large, philosophical questions that have been debated for centuries, such as, "What is art?" and "How is art different in different places?" Art concepts should be introduced to students in their first year of school and advance in complexity throughout their school years.

Response to Myth 4   The boundaries between art forms are blurred. While classifying and categorizing promotes concept development in students, dichotomies should be used cautiously. Art instruction must be broadened to include many types of visual culture, including visual forms that affect mainstream culture but are not considered fine art, such as the mass media. A fruitful way to distinguish between art forms is to specify how they are meant to be seen or used. For example, some art is meant to be hung on a wall in a gallery or museum, some is meant to be used in a ceremony, and so on. A general connection between the art objects and activities of various cultures may be seen as "making special" (Dissanayake, 1988). Children should be helped to understand that although few cultural universals exist, in many cultures, art is a way of making part of life special and not to be neglected or forgotten. This is an important point to be made not only to students, but to teachers, administrators, and parents, because art is so often ignored in school.

Response to Myth 5   Interpretations of art can come from a variety of sources. Bringing expert knowledge into the classroom is important, but it must be remembered that experts disagree on occasion and that people knowledgeable about art may not be members of the professional fine-art community. Focusing on differences of opinion in the professional community can help students see that there are multiple ways of looking at things and that we need not always look for consensus in the classroom. It is essential to allow students to state their own opinions about art. After all, in a sense, art is about interpretation. However, it is important to help students, at any age, learn to justify their interpretations of art as a way of enriching critical thought. People who are well versed in knowledge about the art of any culture, particularly a member of that culture, should be called on to provide students with information and aid their understanding. A student's own cultural context can also provide important contributions to instruction.

Response to Myth 6   Different notions of aesthetics exist in different cultures and these differences should be included as part of curriculum. Comparing artifacts from different cultures must be done carefully, because what may be similar in appearance may be fundamentally different in purpose and meaning. By pointing out these differences, teachers can help children see that an understanding of art requires a search beyond appearance. This does not mean that every teacher must know all about every culture. Teaching some cultural examples in depth can give students skills in investigation and help them develop a sensitivity to aesthetic differences.

Often, artists and guest speakers from museums and local arts organizations are available to visit classrooms and talk about the art of a particular culture. It is also important to make even young children aware that artists borrow their imagery from many sources and that there are cross-cultural currents in art. These currents are apparent even in television shows and advertisements that children see every day. Consider, for example, the use of art vocabulary and artists' names in the *Teenage Mutant Ninja Turtles* cartoons.

Response to Myth 7   Although the study of visual culture necessarily involves the consideration of objects, it should not necessarily begin with a focus on the physical object per se. Rather, objects should be contextualized so that students can develop an understanding of the conditions (cultural, social, political, economic, environmental) that made the production of the object possible. Teaching visual culture should start with the context of production, but also with the context of appreciation. For example, students should understand why their curriculum includes the study of certain aspects of visual culture and not others, where such visual culture would be found and how it would be used outside a classroom (in a museum, place of worship, ceremony, dwelling), and how visual culture changes by being brought into a classroom (such as through re-production). Contextual information is not peripheral to visual culture, it is integral and therefore fundamental to study. Students cannot understand an art object without having a sense of the people and purposes that are part of it.

These recommendations for the social reconstruction of art at the elementary-school level should be carried over into the middle school with some additional emphases and more complex concepts and activities. The focus of these additions can involve the larger sense of community and culture, including peer culture held by middle-school students, and draw on their capacity for a more sophisticated analysis.

Enriching Apprehension: Critique and Community at the Middle School Level

As students reach adolescence, they become more socially and critically aware. They begin to place a greater emphasis on social rules and mores, and in the process, question as well as accept cultural similarities and differences. This awareness can be enhanced through the development of critique capabilities in art education.

Among the difficulties teachers find with early adolescent critique is that students tend to be concerned with being correct and how they are seen in the eyes of their peers. Students at this age tend to prefer realism in art and are often frustrated when they are unable to produce art that is highly realistic. However, creating a safe environment for writing and talking about adult art can help students understand that multiple representations and interpretations are acceptable and enriching.

Middle-school students can take part in a more sophisticated level of critique and reflection than younger children. They are more aware of social conditions, influenced by local and media culture, and are immersed in the culture of their peers. Culturally sensitive art educators recommend that these students use methods such as interviewing artists in the community to bring local art into the classroom (Chalmers, 1981; Congdon, 1989; Stuhr et al., 1992; Wasson, Stuhr, & Petrovich-Mwaniki, 1990). Students can investigate topics concerning community art, such as where art is located, who makes art, and why art is made.

Students should be encouraged to develop a critical awareness of visual culture they encounter every day, such as film and television. For example, they can use methods from feminist critique to become more aware of gender representations in imagery (Garber, 1990; Hicks, 1990; Many & Cox, 1992), an emerging interest in adolescence. Such investigations could include comparisons of the ways in which men and women have been depicted in fine art and advertising, discussions of intended versus interpreted meanings of imagery, and analyses of art by social groups and about cultural issues. Through these investigations, students can begin to understand the immense power of the visual arts in their capacity to seduce, suggest, and educate.

Lessons concerning the visual arts should include student as well as adult interpretations of art and critical analyses of how art is used in daily life. Teachers can approach these topics, for example, by having students write a dialogue between themselves and a person in a work of art, or select an advertisement that includes a painting or sculpture and explain how and why the advertiser used art to sell something.

Adolescents tend to be particularly interested in the symbolic and metaphorical attributes of art. Instruction in these attributes illustrates to students that art goes beyond the design qualities of the objects. To understand these aspects of art and maintain the integrity of the artist and culture, the context of production should be taken into account. For example, there is a popular art movement in Shaba, the copper-production region of Zaire, that cannot be understood without study of the artists' context (Brett, 1987). These artists create at least three different types of paintings: Things Ancestral, Things Present, and Things Past (Szombati-Fabian & Fabian, 1976). Paintings of *Things Ancestral* refer to early tribal life and customs; they include romanticized images of everyday activities, such as hunting. *Things Present* are representations of contemporary urban industrial life, such as the copper smelting industry. Paintings of *Things Past* involve historical topics from the time following contact of the Shaba people with outsiders; they include images of Arab slave traders and Belgium colonialism. I have seen African art ridiculed and judged as simplistic by middle-school students when the art was analyzed using the formalistic approach prevalent in U.S. schools. However, the same students were intrigued by art from Africa when it was considered in relation to the aesthetic and iconographic context in which it was produced.

Critique of student art can also promote inquiry into issues of art and culture. An important aspect of critique is peer assessment, which provides opportunities for students to address these issues among themselves. Critique can be done in pairs or in a group as large as a class, it can be initiated by students or teacher, and it can be done during or after production. The types of critical analysis used in art education are useful methods for developing reflective general educational practice (Eisner, 1982, 1985; Schon, 1987).

Student interaction during critique disperses control and responsibility in the classroom and promotes student interpretation as part of the construction of knowledge. To participate in small group critiques, which help to get everyone involved and may be particularly helpful when handling sensitive issues, group discussion can focus on specific themes, the quality of art, or lesson objectives. Students can record their discussion, report to the rest of the class, and use student recommendations to improve their work. They can lead small or large group discussions by developing questions to ask one another, such as, Did the work meet the objective? What does the work appear to mean? or What cultural influences are apparent in the work? To help answer these questions, students can use written devices, such as worksheets, or keep journals/sketchbooks as their work develops. These may include information about their research into various aspects of visual culture (artists, styles, methods and techniques, cross-cultural and mass media connections, and so on) that inform their work and illustrate their thinking processes.

When students are producing art, teachers should promote the articulation of art concepts used by students in their work, including the reasons the artist made certain decisions, what appears to be successful about the art and why, and how it can be improved. Through in-class critique, educators can provide students with ways to consider, assess, and act on situations that can help them to make positive changes in their art and in their attitudes about art made by others.

❖ Reconstituting Cultural Knowledge

Cultural knowledge is reconstituted in a classroom. Even when students actually write stories, play music, and make art in school, these are done within the confines of an institution, a classroom, and an assignment. In the reconstitution, we give the knowledge a new meaning. We cannot give it back its original form; however, we can use this new knowledge as a vehicle for the contemplation of life and of what it means to be of a certain gender or culture. We can also use it to understand how culture shapes artistic production and appreciation.

The social reconstruction of education involves a fundamental revaluing of art in curriculum. Art should no longer be thought of as a frill attached to the curriculum to meet the therapeutic activity needs of students imposed by dull, academic school subjects. Beginning in elementary school, art should be at the center of a curriculum on culture because understanding the characteristics of artifacts, ceremonies, costume, and other aspects of visual culture is fundamental to understanding human existence.

Notes

1. People use many different words to represent visual culture. In some cultures, a word similar in meaning to the word *art* does not exist. In mainstream American culture, a range of phrases are used to make distinctions between art forms that serve different purposes and have different socioeconomic locations, such as *fine art, commercial art, folk art,* and *popular art.* Also, some phrases are now viewed as demeaning to nonindustrial cultures, such as *primitive art.* For the purposes of this chapter, I use the phrase *fine art* to denote the work produced by those in the professional community (in advanced industrialized countries) who seek gallery, museum, and other collection recognition. The phrase *Western art* refers to artwork produced as part of the mainstream culture of European and European-American countries. The phrases *art* and *artistic production and appreciation* refer to the visual culture of any group.

2. The title of Whistler's painting is *Arrangement in Grey and Black.*

3. The word *multiculturalism* may be misleading because it suggests to some people that only issues of race and ethnicity are of concern. However, I am using the term in this chapter to signify a general social reconstruction of art education that would effectively respond to a broader notion of culture and include issues of ethnicity, gender, socioeconomics, ecology, mass media influence, etc.

4. The example of the earrings came from a personal communication with Patricia Stuhr.

References

Alexander, K. (1988). *A world of art: Grade six. Learning to look and create: The SPECTRA program.* Palo Alto, CA: Dale Seymour.

Barkan, M. (1965). Curriculum problems in art education. *Seminar on Research and Curriculum Development.* State College, PA: The Pennsylvania State University.

Brett, G. (1987). *Through our own eyes: Popular art and modern history.* London: GMP.

Brittain, W. L. (1990). Children's drawings: A comparison of two cultures. In B. Young (Ed.), *Art, culture, and ethnicity* (pp. 181-192). Reston, VA: National Art Education Association. (Reprinted from *Journal of Multicultural and*

Cross-cultural Research in Art Education, Fall, 1985).

Chalmers, F. G. (1981). Art education as ethnology. *Studies in Art Education, 22*(3), 6–14.

Chalmers, F. G. (1992). The origins of racism in the public school art curriculum. *Studies in Art Education, 33*(3), 134–143.

Chapman, L. H. (1987). *Discover art: Grade 2.* Worcester, MA: Davis.

Clifford, J. (1988). *The predicament of culture: Twentieth century ethnography, literature, and art.* Cambridge: Harvard University Press.

Congdon, K. G. (1989). Multi-cultural approaches to art criticism. *Studies in Art Education, 30*(3), 176–184.

Dissanayake, E. (1988). *What is art for?* Seattle, WA: University of Washington Press.

Eisner, E. W. (1973–1974). Examining some myths in art education. *Studies in Art Education, 15*(3), 7–16.

Eisner, E. W. (1982). *Cognition and curriculum: A basis for deciding what to teach.* New York: Longman.

Eisner, E. W. (1985). *The art of educational evaluation: A personal view.* London: Falmer.

Freedman, K. (1989a). Dilemmas of equity in art education: Ideologies of individualism and cultural capital. In W. G. Secada (Ed.), *Equity in education* (pp. 103–117). London: Falmer.

Freedman, K. (1989b). Art education and changing political agendas: An analysis of curriculum concerns of the 1940s and 1950s. *Studies in Art Education, 29*(1), 17–29.

Garber, E. (1990). Implications of feminist art criticism for art education. *Studies in Art Education, 32*(1), 17–26.

Hamblen, K. A. (1990). Beyond the aesthetic of cash-culture literacy. *Studies in Art Education, 31*(4), 216–225.

Hicks, L. E. (1990). A feminist analysis of empowerment and community in art education. *Studies in Art Education, 32*(1), 36–46.

Januszczak, W. (1990). *Sayonara Michelangelo: The Sistine Chapel restored and repackaged.* Reading, MA: Addison-Wesley.

Lanier, V. (1969). The teaching of art as social revolution. *Phi Delta Kappan, 50*(6), 314–319.

Many, J. & Cox, C. (1992). *Reader stance and literary understanding: Exploring the theories, research, and practice.* Norwood, NJ: Ablex.

McFee, J. K. (1961). *Preparation for art* (2nd ed.). Belmont, CA: Wadsworth.

Neperud, R. W. (1988). Conceptions of art in the service of art and aesthetic education: A critical view. *Arts and Learning Research, 6,* 95–102.

Rugg, H., & Schumaker, A. (1928). *The child-centered school: An appraisal of the new education.* Yonkers-on-Hudson, NY: World Book.

Schon, D. A. (1987). *Educating the reflective practitioner.* San Francisco: Jossey-Bass.

Shweder, R. A., & Levine, R. A. (Eds.). (1984). *Cultural theory: Essays on mind, self, and emotion.* Cambridge, England: Cambridge University Press.

Sleeter, C. E., & Grant, C. (1987). An analysis of multicultural education in the United States. *Harvard Educational Review, 57*(4), 421–444.

Stuhr, P. (1991). Contemporary approaches to multicultural art education in the United States, *INSEA News, 1,* 14–15.

Stuhr, P., Petrovich-Mwaniki, L., & Wasson, R. (1992). Curriculum guidelines for the multicultural classroom. *Art Education, 45*(1), 16–24.

Szombati-Fabian, I., & Fabian, J. (1976). Art, history, and society: Popular painting in Shaba, Zaire. *Studies in the Anthropology of Visual Communication, 3*(1), 1–21.

Wasson, R., Stuhr, P., & Petrovich-Mwaniki, L. (1990). Teaching art in the multicultural classroom: Six position statements. *Studies in Art Education, 31*(4), 234–246.

Wilson, B., & Wilson, M. (1977). An iconoclastic view of the imagery sources of the drawing of young people. *Art Education, 30*(1), 5–11.

Multicultural Approaches to Music Education

Julia Eklund Koza
University of Wisconsin-Madison

When music educators and classroom teachers talk with each other about multiculturalism, they may be speaking different languages. The term "multicultural" may have a different meaning for music teachers than it does for educators who take a multicultural social reconstructionist perspective. Therefore, in order that elementary classroom teachers may better understand their colleagues who are music educators, I begin this chapter with a comparison of definitions of multicultural education. Next, I review the history of multicultural music education as traditionally defined, and describe the current state of multiculturalism within the discipline. In the final section of the chapter, I discuss a new vision of music education that is multicultural and social reconstructionist, with an eye on implications for instruction and curricular content. My goal is to offer an analysis of the successes and shortcomings of music education's past and present multicultural initiatives in an effort to enlighten the discussion of a new and broadened definition.

❖ Defining Multiculturalism

According to Sleeter and Grant (1988), multiculturalism encompasses the "education policies and practices that recognize, accept, and affirm human differences and similarities related to gender, race, handicap, and [social] class" (p. 137). Multiculturalism is, to them, a "different orientation toward the whole education process" (p. 175). A social reconstructionist perspective adds the element of social criticism to multiculturalism; one goal of educators with a social reconstructionist perspective is to help children become citizens who will actively work to promote equality (Sleeter & Grant, 1988). In short, multiculturalism is a perspective that has far-reaching implications for all aspects of schooling, including instruction, curriculum, evaluation, home/school/community relationships, staffing, and extracurricular activities (Sleeter & Grant, 1988).

By contrast, the term traditionally has had a more circumscribed meaning to most music educators. It refers to the teaching of what is sometimes called "ethnic" or "world" music; historically, the multicultural movement within music education has been concerned primarily with curricular content. This is not to say that music educators have been oblivious to issues surrounding social class, gender, and disability. However, in music education these topics are not generally found under the multicultural umbrella. Although some music educators are concerned with specific issues addressed in the multicultural and social reconstructionist realm, there is no concerted movement within the discipline to embrace the dramatic changes in schooling suggested by the latter. In fairness to music educators, many of them are struggling for the survival of their programs. Unfortunately, given the conditions existing in most schools, few of them have time or energy to consider broader issues.

Multicultural music education as traditionally conceived has been surrounded by some ambiguity because the question of what constitutes "ethnic" music has been answered in a variety of ways. As Bessom (1972b) astutely pointed out, *all* music is ethnic; this observation has not informed past definitions, however. Thus, designating specific music as ethnic has also been a process of placing people into the categories of "we" and "they," of articulating which music is "theirs" and not "ours." Definitions of *ethnic* and *multicultural* provide a study in exclusion—whose music typically has been omitted from the canon.

High-art music from Europe and the United States has traditionally constituted "our" music; however, the boundaries between categories have always been blurred and have shifted over time. "Ethnic" has referred to such disparate fare as orally transmitted European songs, African-American rap, ragas from India, and Ojibwa music for wood flute. The placement of some European music, specifically "folk" music, in the multicultural category indicates that socioeconomic group, in addition to ethnicity, has been a factor defining the parameters of ethnic music. Although some music educators are gradually realizing that "they" can be "us," few have discussed or questioned the problematic and limiting nature of current definitions.

✣ Multicultural Music Education, Past and Present

The Beginnings

Multiculturalism is a relatively new movement in music education, generating little interest until the late 1960s. Before that time, only a handful of visionaries saw value in teaching any music from outside the circumscribed borders of a European American canon. For example, from 1914 to 1967, only six articles on the topic of multiculturalism appeared in music education's major trade publication, the *Music Educators Journal.*[1] This small collection of articles is important, however, not only because the authors were progressive, but also because it reflects beliefs, values, and problems that have persisted to some degree to the present and that are ultimately counterproductive to music education that is multicultural and social reconstructionist. Three of these beliefs and problems will be examined in greater depth: (1) a hierarchy that values Western high-art music above all others, (2) divisive distinctions between "our" and "their" music combined with ambiguity concerning what is "ours" and "theirs," and (3) belief in a myth of music as a universal language.

The first problem, a hierarchy that values Western high-art music above all others, fueled the belief that such music was the only worthwhile genre to study. Even the use of the term "high" indicates the privileged status these particular styles traditionally have been given. Using biased standards, and basing their judgments on incomplete and often inaccurate understandings of music of other cultures, many early musicologists and music educators concluded that the music of nearly all of the world's people fell short. High-art music was the benchmark against which all others were measured and invariably deemed inadequate. Music was sorted into "ours" and "theirs"—and ours invariably was better. Well-intended music teachers, whose practices reflected beliefs and values of larger segments of society, concerned themselves with cultivating good taste and exposing children only to music of the "highest quality"; however, the bounds of high quality were narrow.

Belief in the hierarchy was not always openly stated, but its influence is nonetheless evident in early writings about music. For example, the earliest music journal article to address multiculturalism portrayed practices that are grounded in hierarchical thinking. Appearing in 1933, it described an openness to ethnic music in the British schools established on colonized South Sea islands and gave a first-hand account of a music education program in an island school run by a British master (Beck, 1933). After the class had presented a lengthy concert of hymns and American songs in four-part harmony (hallmarks of Western music), one student was allowed to let out a "thrilling old Fijian war-whoop." This final demonstration was considered evidence of British sensitivity, the author concluding that the British "know how to colonize and yet retain the identity of the native" (p. 20).

On the one hand, this article opened the door to consideration of music outside the traditional European American canon, and it emphasized the importance of valuing the culture students bring with them into the classroom. On the other hand, the ratio of indigenous music to European American, and the ordering of selections so that the indigenous music came at the end of the concert (or perhaps *after* it), are telling commentaries on which styles were deemed most worthwhile by the concert's organizers. The well-intended author apparently did not find the school's imposition of large doses of European American music problematic nor did she notice any incompatibility between avowed ideology and actual practice.

This biased hierarchical structure was evident in other articles of the era. For example, a remarkably progressive author advocated studying American Indians of the Southwest United States through an integrated approach reminiscent of John Dewey. Nonetheless, he differentiated between "primitive" people and their music and people of "higher culture"; American Indian music fell into the former category (Otterstein, 1938).

The same article displays another problem often found in early efforts: divisive distinctions between "our" and "their" music combined with ambiguity concerning which musics might be considered ethnic. Teachers were encouraged to introduce children to the people of other lands by singing folk songs from countries such as Holland and Switzerland (Otterstein, 1938). This is a curious suggestion, given the longstanding influence European styles have had on music in United States schools; it indicates that "folk" and "ethnic" may have had socioeconomic group overtones.

In addition to noting where the music of various people of the world was situated on the hierarchical structure, it is important to consider whose music was not mentioned at all. A 1947 article advocating ethnic music as a means of promoting "one world" included a description of a 20-unit audiovisual curriculum, each unit focusing on the music from a specific geographical region (Duffield, 1947). While the tiny countries of Belgium and Switzerland were each allotted one unit, the entire continent of Africa was overlooked.

A third problematic belief is the myth that music is a universal language capable of transcending the barriers of spoken or written word. This myth is but one of many overstated assertions about music's capabilities, some assertions being as old as the ancient Greeks. Many of these claims were drawn on by music educators of the 19th century in their efforts to convince skeptical school boards of the value of music in the curriculum. The legacy of these early music educators is apparent in writings from the first half of the 20th century; the universal language myth was popular then and lingers to some degree now.

Although music is a universal phenomenon, it is bound to social context, and thus, the culture that produces the music also constructs its meaning. Therefore, rather than sending a universally understood message, the music of a particular culture may sound alien and incomprehensible to an uninitiated listener.

A more romanticized notion of the powers of music was present in early discussions of multiculturalism, however. In 1945, shortly after the end of World War II, an article about using music to improve "intercultural relations" included a quotation from President Franklin D. Roosevelt:

> Because music knows no barriers of language; because it recognizes no impediments to free intercommunication; because it speaks a universal tongue music can make us all more vividly aware of the common humanity which is ours and which shall one day unite the nations of the world in one great brotherhood. (Moses, 1945, p. 23)

The article asserted that understanding cultural differences would foster sensitivity to others and that such sensitivity would effect global peace. Other sources echoed similar sentiments. Calling upon "music's universal and unifying message," Duffield (1947) envisioned music as a tool that could bring about a "one world" consciousness (p. 21). Unfortunately, he did not spell out what music's universal and unifying message might be.

Despite the problems just discussed, these older articles are extraordinary. Because their authors opened the door to the possibility of a broader concept of "legitimate knowledge" than had heretofore been envisioned, they courageously challenged "business as usual." However, they probably had little effect on schooling practices, and therefore to call these early efforts a movement is perhaps to overstate their effect.

Modern Multicultural Music Education

The birth of the modern multicultural music education movement came at about the same time as the Tanglewood Symposium in 1967. The symposium was sponsored by the Music Educators National Conference, the most prominent music teachers' organization in the United States. One purpose of the gathering was to suggest ways of improving music education in the face of rapid social change. The Tanglewood recommendation having the most far-reaching implications for multiculturalism declared: "Music of all periods, styles, forms, and cultures belongs in the curriculum. The musical repertory should be expanded to involve music of our time in its rich variety, including currently popular teen-age music and avant-garde music, American folk music, and the music of other cultures" (*Music in American Society,* 1967, p. 2).

Early Problems with the Modern Movement   The mere suggestion of this ambitious goal did not effect a transformation overnight, however. Post-Tanglewood multicultural music education had a slow start and was plagued by problems. One of these problems arose because interest in multiculturalism grew at about the same time that music educators were beginning to apply a conceptual learning approach to music. At that time, music educators usually translated concepts to mean the concepts surrounding the structural or formal elements of the music itself—melody, rhythm, harmony, timbre, texture, and form. Thus, forays into multicultural music often focused on teaching the elements of music through materials drawn from a variety of cultures. Educators spoke of common structural elements that provided a unifying thread for all music and that offered a framework with which to compare musical styles. Concept statements focusing on the structure of the music, such as "Music may move in relation to the underlying steady beat," were illustrated using music drawn from several cultures.[2] The structural concepts remained the same, only the musical examples changed. The common-elements approach was, in effect, an updated version of the universal language myth, except now the assumption was that the elements of music provided the unifying link.

One weakness of the common-elements approach is that it skirts the cultural context of the music being studied. Thus, whether one considers the common-elements approach to be adequate depends on one's definition of understanding music. The unanswered question is whether the technical European American understanding of how music works—derived from the common-elements approach—is sufficient if other understandings, ascribed by the cultures creating the music, are ignored.

For example, an advocate of the common-elements approach might teach a piece of Javanese gamelan music with the intention of helping children understand its formal structure. The goal of the lesson would be to learn that the particular piece exhibits a two-part form and that the gong marks out the structure by sounding on every 16th beat. What I question here is not the accuracy of the information presented but rather the limited focus of the lesson. Concentrating primarily on structure and talking about it in this manner reflect European American ways of understanding music. Familiarity with beliefs that Javanese people hold concerning this music is at least as essential to a student's understanding as is knowledge of structure. Introducing students to the significance of the gong in Javanese culture and to the function of the music in relation to puppet theater and dance produces a different kind of musical understanding.

Using only a European American lens to view musical creations from all world cultures unjustly privileges that way of seeing and thinking. Children may develop a limited idea of what a piece is about unless they explore other aspects of the musical event as well. The common-elements conceptual approach continues to be widely used today. It can be useful as long as teachers keep in mind that it is merely one culturally constructed and, therefore, limited way of thinking about music. It is not the only tool, nor necessarily the best one, that can be brought to bear on new and unfamiliar sounds. Unfortunately, in past practice its own cultural situatedness has often been overlooked by its proponents.

A second post-Tanglewood problem stemmed from the very ambitiousness of the goal established at the symposium: Teach music of all cultures. To learn well the music of one culture is a lifetime endeavor; a thorough knowledge of all cultures is probably beyond the grasp of any human being. However, early proponents were ambitious and idealistic, and the common-elements approach lent itself to introducing musical appetizers from a wide assortment of cultures. A shortcoming of this ambitious goal was the potential for superficiality. Multicultural curricula emerged that amounted to the musical counterparts of "Around the World in 80 Days." For example, a 1972 issue of the *Music Educators Journal* devoted entirely to the subject of multiculturalism covered six continents in a little more than 40 pages (Bessom, 1972a).

The bold music teacher who decided to introduce the music of what was then called a "non-Western culture" often found few suitable materials.[3] Furthermore, what did exist frequently contained overgeneralizations and inaccuracies; the most acute problems tended to occur in introductory materials. For example, complex rhythms were sometimes ironed out, melodies were outfitted with harmonized piano accompaniments when neither harmony nor pianos were part of the culture, and musical instruments were incorrectly identified. Because some of these materials still occupy shelves in elementary classrooms and libraries, a teacher with no experience in the music of another culture should be especially cautious when consulting older sources.

Finally, multicultural music education was (and often remains) a low priority in colleges and universities that trained teachers. Thus, the notion of multicultural music education was handed to unprepared music teachers who had little or no experience with music beyond high-art forms from Europe and the United States. Until recently, few colleges required future music teachers to take a course in ethnic music; even jazz and U.S. popular music are relative newcomers to the college curriculum.

Because many teacher-training institutions placed a low value on the introduction of a wide range of styles, the teachers trained at these institutions, especially those who found employment in relatively homogeneous schools, gave multicultural music education a low priority in their own classrooms. One critic, commenting on the limited curricular fare found in many public schools, noted with acerbity:

> In the Western world the best music has always been made outside the schools and in important ways against the teaching of the schools. And much of the worst has been made in them. Should we not, perhaps, restrict music in the schools to the training of bands, choruses, and orchestras as we have done for the last several decades to the performance of fairly conservative repertoires and leave outside of school music activities something to rebel against? (Seeger, 1972, p. 111)

This remark invites contemplation on whether teaching the exciting music of a multicultural curriculum remains a low priority today—both in colleges and in elementary classrooms. At present few music teachers are prepared to implement a multicultural curriculum, even as it is narrowly conceived within the music profession; the concept of multiculturalism has not filtered into musical training for elementary classroom teachers, either. Therefore, any collaborative attempt at multicultural music education in an elementary school will likely be a new learning experience—not only for the classroom teacher, but for the music specialist as well.

Strengths of the Movement Since Tanglewood   Much good came out of efforts to follow Tanglewood's recommendation. During the past 30 years, a greater emphasis has been placed on recognition of and respect for diversity. Thanks to efforts that began at the time of Tanglewood, the hierarchy that valued high-art music above all others is gradually disappearing. For example, Anderson and Campbell (1989) emphasized that there are "many different but *equally valid* [italics added] forms of musical and artistic expression" (p. 1). Definition of the term "ethnic" has been reexamined as music educators acknowledge the ethnic diversity existing not only outside but also within the United States, and as they recognize the rich cultural heritages children bring with them into the classroom (Anderson, 1991; Campbell, McCullough-Brabson, & Tucker, 1994). Perhaps in recognition of the limitations of the common-elements conceptual approach, some recent resources emphasize the importance to musical understanding of familiarity with cultural context (Anderson & Campbell, 1989; Campbell, 1996a; Campbell et al., 1994; Elliot, 1990).

More and better resources are now available to teachers. Devoting the entire 1972 issue of the *Music Educators Journal* to ethnic music was a bold and unprecedented move; since that time, in addition to a second special issue appearing in 1983, the *Journal* has published a number of individual articles on the topic. These recent articles, along with the ever-growing body of books on related subjects, can be invaluable resources for elementary classroom teachers.

When the first edition of this chapter was written in 1991, the alternate definition of multicultural education I presented was virtually unknown in music education circles. Since that time, a handful of music educators have begun to speak more broadly about multicultural music education, and the work of individuals such as Sleeter and Grant is slowly filtering into the conversation (Campbell, 1996b; Elliot, 1990; Gonzo, 1993; Volk, 1998; Yob, 1995). I see this development as a positive sign; the views of these scholars have yet to become widely accepted and acted upon, however. Thus, multicultural music education today continues to be defined largely as the study of ethnic or world music, the focus of the movement remaining primarily on curricular content. As valuable as the multicultural music education movement has been, the limitations apparent in its roots continue to haunt the discussion.

❖ Music Education That Is Multicultural and Social Reconstructionist

Turning away from the traditional definition of multiculturalism and adopting Sleeter and Grant's broader concept would necessitate changes not only in music content, but in many other facets of music education as well. Let us consider what some of these modifications might be and contemplate how classroom teachers would fit into this new model. I propose changes in four areas: (1) schooling at large, (2) the music education paradigm, (3) instructional practices, and (4) the music curriculum.

Multicultural Music Education and Schooling

Some changes in thinking about schooling at large would facilitate efforts to make music education multicultural and social reconstructionist. If, for example, schooling practices were informed by four assumptions related to music education, significant departures from "business as usual" would occur:

1. Music is worthwhile and deserves as large a share of time and other resources as any subject traditionally considered basic.
2. Any elementary classroom teacher is capable of creating an environment in which children can learn music.
3. The responsibility for helping children learn music rests on classroom teachers as well as on music specialists.
4. Compartmentalizing elementary subject areas, such that music is seen as a discipline apart from social studies, language arts, or physical education, is artificial and often unnecessary.

To elaborate, in current practice music is often considered a frill, a nicety but not a necessity. As mentioned earlier, many music teachers today are struggling to keep their programs alive. While it may be argued that this struggle is a sign of the failure of music education to stay in touch with the needs of children, this explanation is too simplistic. The struggle to give music education legitimacy is at least 150 years old and was present when the subject was introduced into the public schools. The marginalization of music education has been a chronic problem, in part an outgrowth of a pragmatism that saw no use for music. The difficulties music educators historically have faced are reminders that schools sometimes can exclude or marginalize not only individual students but entire domains of knowledge as well. The struggle is a commentary on the values of those who decide what constitutes worthwhile knowledge, and thus the marginalization of music is, in a broad sense, a multicultural issue. Values that marginalize music typically manifest themselves in meager allotments of time and other resources for elementary music education. Overburdened music teachers, some of them traveling from room to room with their supplies on a cart, often work in two, three, or more schools. Some of them see hundreds of children in one day, the average student-to-music-teacher ratio being nearly 500 to 1.[4]

Honoring curricular areas other than the traditional "basics" is an acknowledgment that there are many ways of knowing. Valuing music, as well as the other arts, invites more pluralistic and diverse views about what it means to be intelligent. Valuing music education is a valuing of the affective component of living, of the emotional aspects of life often dismissed as feminine and, therefore, inconsequential. Finally, valuing music and other subjects that may not necessarily lead to gainful employment helps send the message that material wealth is neither the only nor the most important of life's treasures.

Music is often perceived to be such a specialized subject that only an expert, someone with supposedly innate musical talent who has been extensively trained, is qualified to teach it. Given this assumption, elementary classroom teachers may feel ill equipped to offer any form of music education to their students. Aside from a few minutes per week with the music specialist, children may receive no regular music instruction, especially in upper elementary grades and middle schools.

Deferring completely to a music expert is a fairly recent practice in United States education, however. In the early part of the 20th century, music teachers were called supervisors, and their job was to oversee the music education provided by classroom teachers (Coffman, 1987). Unfortunately, as is frequently the case with established schooling practices, the current arrangement, with its total reliance on music specialists, is assumed to be the way things have always been done and, thus, should continue to be done. I am not suggesting that music specialists are unnecessary. Rather, given the inadequate conditions under which many of them work, the quantity and quality of elementary music education might be increased if classroom teachers decided to participate in this portion of schooling.

Even if a classroom teacher is willing to collaborate with a music specialist, scheduling may not permit these individuals to communicate the valuable ideas and information they can offer one another. In many schools, the arrival of the music specialist signals welcomed preparation or release time for overextended classroom teachers. Little opportunity for collaboration between the classroom teacher and the music specialist may cause sharply delineated boundaries to appear between music and the rest of the elementary curriculum.

The four assumptions listed earlier are only indirectly related to multicultural education. However, individual curricular areas do not exist in a vacuum, and the success of elementary music education that is multicultural and social reconstructionist depends on a reconsideration of more basic assumptions about the relationship between music education and elementary education in general. Under the current conditions, many of the changes suggested by multicultural social reconstructionists would be difficult for music specialists to implement without outside assistance. For example, when music instruction occupies only 15 minutes of class time per week and is provided by a music specialist who sees 500 students in a week, it is no small task for that teacher to learn the names of all the students. Achieving the multicultural goal of tailoring instruction to each child and that child's particular interests and needs is probably impossible under such circumstances.

Developing a New Music Education Paradigm

What Is Music Education?   In addition to changes in schooling at large, modifications of the music education paradigm are needed. An analogy may help explain what I mean. I have lived in the Midwest all my life and have never seen a desert. Therefore, my concept of a cactus—my cactus paradigm—has been limited. I envision lanky, leathery green varieties or perhaps squat, spiny barrels. On a recent trip to a cactus display at the Mitchell Conservatory in Milwaukee, I was astonished by a variety called lithops, or Living Stones, which look like the small, smooth, brown pebbles that surround them. A marker at the location of these cacti was the first clue that my cactus paradigm was inadequate. I only saw a few lithops at first, but as my cactus paradigm gradually shifted, I realized that the garden floor was covered with them. As valuable and useful as my original paradigm was, it also limited my vision.

Applying the analogy to music, I maintain that ideas about what constitutes music education, shaped by past experiences, may limit a person's vision of possibilities for the future. Developing a new paradigm may mean putting aside the notion that music education only means participating in large-group singalongs, playing the clarinet in the band, or learning to read standard musical notation. For example, because some music from outside the traditional European American canon does not lend itself easily to large-group performance, multiculturalists may need to carefully reexamine music education's long-standing emphasis on large ensembles and whole-class activities. Furthermore, large-group activities such as band and orchestra involve the purchase of expensive musical instruments, and thus these activities can widen the gap between children who come from wealthy communities and those who do not.

Developing a new paradigm will mean dreaming beyond the boundaries of past personal experience, as well as of what currently constitutes standard practice. Redefining the music education paradigm opens the door to the possibility that classroom teachers, even those with little or no formal musical training, can create environments in which children learn music.

The limitations of a traditional music education paradigm were apparent in a recent incident involving a child, "Katherine," who is deaf and was integrated into an elementary music class.[5] After several weeks of encouraging Katherine to sing, the music specialist learned from the classroom teacher that the rest of the teaching and support staff were trying to train the girl *not* to vocalize. Apparently the child's vocalizations were disruptive; an evaluation team decided the sounds would be a hindrance and an embarrassment to her in social situations. When the conflict of goals was discovered, one person on staff said that she could not understand why a child with little residual hearing was placed in music in the first place and recommended that Katherine be removed from the class.

Indeed, if music education is understood to mean only singing, there may have been scant justification for placing this child in music. However, the incident prompted creative thinking on the part of the music teacher, classroom teacher, and support staff about what music education *might* mean and how a broadened definition might benefit Katherine as well as the rest of the class. It was determined that Katherine needed to work on physical coordination and on overcoming shyness. Instead of taking the child out of music, music education was adapted to the child. Everyone in class learned to sign the songs they sang; Katherine helped teach the class (and the music specialist) how to sign. Dance, taught with a focus on rhythm and accompanied by acoustic instruments, was given more emphasis in the program. Acoustic instruments were chosen over recorded sounds because the former produce strong vibrations that can be felt and can reinforce any residual hearing a child might have.

The changes were not particularly radical, and many other creative possibilities can be imagined. Dancing and signed songs could have been incorporated into a play the children were writing. Class members could provide the background music and sound effects for the play, compose music for the dance, and choreograph it as well. Follow-up activities might include a field trip to see a signed choir or a performance by a troupe of dancers who are deaf. The possibilities are limitless.

However, the simple steps these teachers did take show that even minor modifications in a traditional music education program and small shifts in paradigm can result in an educational setting that is more useful and beneficial to all children. Also, a message was sent: This child is a valued member of the class and her contributions are important; she is entitled not only to be present in the classroom but also to learn, as is *every* child.

Changing the paradigm concerning what constitutes music education will require cooperation from music specialists; without a doubt, some of them will be hesitant to modify the current model. For example, some may contend that Katherine was not receiving a *music* education; instead, music was used as a tool to achieve other curricular ends. These educators are concerned that utilitarianism may compromise the music education profession and further erode its already small plot of turf. A few might argue, "The classroom teacher does not teach music, so why should I be concerned with social studies, or mathematics, or physical education? I have precious little time, and it should be devoted solely to music." However, if one assumes that boundaries between subject areas are artificial and are not always necessary or useful, that classroom teachers *will* teach music, and that music warrants a more prominent place in the curriculum, then these fears have a weaker foundation.

Who Is To Be Educated?   In addition to thinking about what might constitute music education, it is equally important to consider who is to be educated. "Music for every child and every child for music" has been a rallying cry of the profession for decades, but the ideal has rarely been practiced. In general, elementary music specialists have been more conscientious than their secondary counterparts in applying this universal philosophy to their teaching. Even on the elementary level, however, some children slip though the cracks; children with disabilities are the most likely candidates. In some schools, children with disabilities may be excluded from music altogether; if brought into the music class, they may be tacitly excluded by "business as usual" instruction that does not take into consideration their specific needs.

Failure to provide music education for all children becomes an even more serious problem in middle schools and high schools. Recent statistics indicate that only 22% of high school students are enrolled in music (Gerber & Hughes, 1988). Although many factors contribute to this low statistic—among them tight schedules and the elective nature of secondary music courses—the accusation that many middle and high school music programs are elitist and exclusionary cannot be ignored, especially given the strong emphasis these programs frequently place on polished performance of a restricted repertoire of musical styles.

The belief that musical talent is innate and differentially bestowed from one individual to another is a popular but not necessarily accurate assumption that can result in exclusion. This belief often divides children into "haves" and "have nots," effectively prohibiting the "have nots" from ever becoming "haves." In the past, this belief served as justification for giving music instruction to a select few. Today, most music educators advocate music for every child, regardless of perceived ability, but few have considered the possibility that musical talent may be a social and cultural construct; "giftedness" may have far more to do with experience and nurturance than with so-called "natural" gifts.[6] Traditional beliefs about musical talent can lead to tracking, especially on the middle and high school levels. Those perceived to have talent find themselves in a performance organization (band, choir, or orchestra). If every child is required to take a music course, those who are viewed as lacking in talent may be relegated to a general music class.

A few critics may argue that championing music for all children is as insensitive to diversity and individual needs as any other global prescriptive. Perhaps a better way of stating the goal is that every child is entitled to music education tailored to the individual. This is a tall and expensive order, however, and given the current ratio of music teachers to students, it may remain out of the realm of possibility until "business as usual" changes. Taxed music specialists may have considerable difficulty achieving the goal of reaching every child, and this is one area where classroom teachers, who know students well, can offer invaluable insights.

Rethinking Teaching

The concept of education that is multicultural and social reconstructionist invites re-examination of who teaches, as well as how and where learning can take place. Children can learn from people other than teachers and in places other than classrooms. Multicultural education invites a softening of the boundaries between teacher and student, suggesting that we can all learn from each other and can teach each other. Softening the boundaries creates an environment conducive to cooperative teaching and learning. The music specialist and the classroom teacher can learn from each other; students can learn from other students; and teachers can be students themselves, learning much from the children they teach.

Softening the boundaries means that teachers relinquish the hat of the expert, or perhaps, pass the hat around. If one operates under the assumption that everyone has something to contribute—everyone has gifts—then classroom teachers having little or no experience with either traditional or multicultural music education also can make contributions, and they can create an atmosphere conducive to learning music. Nearly everyone has had a vast amount of experience with music—if not with music education. Most people are inundated by music daily, and thus, in some sense, we may all have much more expertise than we realize.

Classroom teachers who feel uncomfortable with their formal knowledge of music, especially of music from cultures unfamiliar to them, may find that inviting others to share in the teaching, including parents, community members, and the students themselves, can be a clever way of introducing students to a diverse array of music while simultaneously circumventing their own lack of expertise. Field trips can be invaluable, and such outings are another way of taking pressure off classroom teachers to be music experts. Although music field trips often have meant visits to the symphony, the fare can be far more varied; outings can help students sample a marvelously diverse mosaic of musics from the United States, the world, and in many cases, from their own neighborhoods.

Rethinking music teaching to make it multicultural and social reconstructionist invites examination of whether instructional emphasis should focus primarily on a child's needs and interests or on more global goals based on perceived needs and interests of children as a group. When a music teacher sees 500 students a week, knowing individual needs, interests, and learning styles becomes nearly impossible. Traditionally, much of public school music education has focused on singing or playing in large performing groups. Only when these activities are no longer perceived as constituting the totality of music education will the student-to-music-teacher ratio fall to a level where individual differences can shape curricular and instructional practices.

When resources have permitted, public elementary music education has also included individual instruction, typically in the form of private lessons on a band or orchestral instrument. Thus, public schools have sometimes made available to a larger segment of the population what historically has been a privilege of the wealthy: private instruction with its potential for adaptation to individual needs and interests. Although one-on-one instruction is not always individualized, greater possibilities for individualization exist when the student-to-teacher ratio is low. Unfortunately, the benefits of private instruction may still go largely to children in wealthy districts that can afford to pay the enormous costs.

Given the status quo, classroom teachers are probably more attuned to a child's needs and interests than is a music specialist; they may be in a good position to implement music curricula and instructional practices that focus on the individual. These practices need not be elaborate. For example, showing respect for the individual can manifest itself in such simple ways as honoring a child's preference not to sing solos by structuring activities so that children can make performance choices with which they feel most comfortable.

In addition to encouraging students to make choices for themselves, multicultural social reconstructionists also suggest that teachers be sensitive to the ways a particular child learns most effectively. Slavish dedication to one way of learning may be a sign of a monocultural bias. The fact that much of the world's population learns and transmits music exclusively "by ear" indicates that aural learning is a valid and effective practice, yet some music teachers consider it a less desirable way of learning than reading notes. Music from many cultures does not easily lend itself to being written down; in fact, "standard Western notation" often proves inadequate. Even music from a fairly mainstream style such as jazz is difficult to notate. Therefore, in some cases not only is written notation inconsistent with the usual manner of transmission, but it can be a hindrance.

Because learning through reading standard notation is privileged by many musicians in power—for example, those who will make decisions about which students will be admitted to the most prestigious music schools and conservatories—it may be argued that children who do not learn this skill will be handicapped. In effect, the ability to read music will separate children into "haves" and "have nots" and will deny "have nots" access to elite and powerful circles. This is a valid and troubling argument, indicating that even well-intended practices, such as acknowledging the equal validity of aural learning, may have negative consequences for individual students. If gatekeepers, i.e., people in positions of power, ever change their perspectives, the shift may come too late for today's students.

The heavy reliance on visual learning notwithstanding, music education at its best, with its emphasis on "hands-on" experience, has been perhaps more sensitive to alternative ways of learning than have other curricular areas. Many students not succeeding in traditional academic courses have found a niche in music. One advantage of a multicultural approach is that teachers may gather invaluable insights by studying how cultures unfamiliar to them transmit musical knowledge; they may, in turn, incorporate these strategies into their teaching.

Rethinking the Curriculum

Content That Is Diverse, Inclusive, and Respectful   Curricular modifications are needed in addition to instructional changes. One of these modifications involves placing greater emphasis on content that is diverse, inclusive, and respectful. Multicultural music education should focus on content representing the diversity of the community, the nation, and the world. This means the inclusion of contributions by people whose music has not been heard in schools in the past, the marvelously interesting music that Seeger, quoted earlier, indicated was being kept out of the schools.

In addition to referring to music created and enjoyed by people of color within and outside the United States, multicultural content can encompass contributions by women, people from many religious backgrounds, and people of various social classes, to name but a few. A multicultural perspective invites consideration of who traditionally has been left out of the collective "we" when people in the past have referred to "our musical heritage." Advocates of multicultural education promote a further consideration of the question of what constitutes good music, while pointing out the narrowness of past definitions that limited the designation to works by dead White, male, European composers.

Multicultural education acknowledges that culture does not merely mean something "out there" and far away but also refers to the varied rich experiences children bring with them to school. Curricular content that is multicultural incorporates, respects, and connects to children's previous musical experiences. A multicultural curriculum begins with a specific child or a particular group of children and expands outward from there. These concepts invite contemplation of whether standardized curricula in music education, which are generally designed to fit all students in all situations, can now or ever be multicultural.

While familiarity with music of *every* culture is probably an unrealistic goal, it is possible to strive toward "polymusicality" for all children.[7] Polymusicality may be defined as the ability to speak and understand more than one musical language—to know the music from more than one culture. Such familiarity does not generally breed contempt; to the contrary, it increases the likelihood that children will enjoy, respect, and celebrate the rich diversity constituting human creative expression.

Recalling the difficulty early educators encountered when attempting to teach the music of all cultures prompts contemplation of whether the appetizer or the four-course meal tactic is more consistent with multicultural goals. In other words, is the breadth provided by a smorgasbord of musical tidbits from a large number of cultures worth the risk of superficiality? Would children be better served if music from a few cultures were discussed in depth and presented in such a way that students learned to remain open to new and unfamiliar experiences? I have no easy answer to these questions; regardless of whether we opt for breadth or depth, however, it is important to focus on instilling values that will foster openness to and respect for unfamiliar music encountered in the future.

Some critics argue that time away from traditional curricular content will be detrimental to the people who most need the empowerment that knowledge of the European American canon can provide. For example, if the elementary music curriculum focuses on learning to play rock drums, or on traditional music of Ghana, or on rap, precious time will be taken away from the study of Bach, Beethoven, and Brahms. The latter knowledge, because it is often more highly valued by people in positions of power in music, can open doors to students who possess it. Socioeconomic class may largely determine which children are exposed to this canon outside of school; thus, an expanded definition of legitimate knowledge may inadvertently disadvantage the children who rely most heavily on schools to provide them with cultural capital. This argument is valid and clearly points out the complexity of the issues at hand. One response might be that balance, rather than abandonment of the traditional canon, is the more prudent route; but this response leaves the question of what constitutes balance unanswered.

Content That Is Contextual and Integrated   Because music is not a universal language and does not speak for itself, multicultural music education must be ever mindful of situating music content within a larger context. Because musical meaning is socially constructed, mediation is often necessary when introducing children to music from cultures unfamiliar to them. Herein lies the beauty of integrating music with curricular areas such as language arts, social studies, foreign languages, physical education, and art. Education that emphasizes the interconnectedness between the arts and other aspects of life will help bring context into focus. Furthermore, in many cultures, music is inseparable from other aspects of life. Boundaries between content areas are somewhat artificial under any circumstances, but they can be especially counterproductive when the goal is multicultural education.

Content That Is Fair   In addition to calling for music curricula that reflect diversity and are contextual, advocates of multicultural education call for curricula that are fair. Equity issues related to music education curricula are legion; the following discussion will focus on just two areas: content that is respectful of religious belief or unbelief, and content that is equitable to both sexes.

Content That Is Respectful of Religious Belief/Unbelief   One "business as usual" music practice related to the issue of respect for religious belief/unbelief is the performance of music in conjunction with Christian sacred holidays. Although public schools in the United States are in theory nonsectarian, their roots lie in Protestantism; nowhere are these roots more obvious than in music education. Some teachers who would not dream of advocating prayer in public schools unflinchingly present wholly sacred Christmas concerts complete with crèches; they lead caroling sessions in classes, hallways, and neighborhoods. The fact that such customs are steeped in tradition lends an aura of legitimacy to them.

Such practices have been under fire for many years, however, and proponents of the traditional approach have presented a varied array of rationales for continuing "business as usual." Some of the most zealous supporters have contended that events such as Christmas concerts are part of an essential ministry to the unchurched. Others present less overtly biased arguments. For example, many assert that sacred music is a central part of "the Western musical heritage"; not to program Christmas music, they argue, is to deny children familiarity with some of the world's greatest art. Others contend that Christmas is as much a secular holiday as a sacred one and, therefore, Christmas carols are not actually sacred songs. Still other arguments are variations on "majority rules" and "when in Rome, do as the Romans."

Siding with proponents who say sacred music has great artistic value apart from its religious significance, courts and local school boards alike have continued to allow the performance of Christmas music in the public schools so long as the intent and effect are secular.[8] In the past, policies concerning the performance of sacred holiday music have given teachers considerable latitude. However, latitude was often interpreted by teachers to mean free license. Teachers used community response to gauge whether their curriculum was appropriate and fair; receiving no complaints meant curricular decisions were wise. Complaints occasionally effected such minor changes as the inclusion of a Hanukkah song or two, but the balance of time and effort remained devoted to Christmas fare. Angered by complaints, some teachers, rather than taking a hard look at whether "business as usual" was a good idea, insisted on continuing to do everything they could get away with. However, as communities have become more culturally diverse, traditional practices have increasingly come under fire, a trend not likely to be reversed in the future.

From a multicultural perspective, a better question than "Is this permitted?" or "Will the community object?" might be "Is the performance of Christian holiday music in conjunction with Christian holidays fair?" Fair curricula assure that no child will feel embarrassed, isolated, or inadequate because of religious belief or unbelief. Put more positively, education that is multicultural affirms who the child is, as the child is.

Excusing children from musical activities that are contrary to their beliefs marks children and can create awkward and unhappy moments for the child who leaves. Such practices suggest that the curriculum is fine and that the problem lies with the child. The message is sent that majority rule means exclusion; this practice devalues minority voices, especially when coupled with large doses of traditional fare.

The heated debate generated by the holiday music question suggests that the issues at stake are much larger than music, the debate evolving out of contrasting visions of society. Opposition to change probably is also fueled by fear. Rather than seeing a more balanced multicultural curriculum as a marvelous opportunity, promising rich rewards in exchange for small concessions, many people, sadly, see only loss.

Few proponents of multicultural education would argue that all Christian sacred music should be removed from the music curriculum; indeed, such music can be an enriching part of a child's education, *as can the music of other religions.* Instead of removal, the usual call is for balance, sensitivity to alternative voices, and thoughtful consideration of the possible consequences of current practices.

If one proceeds on the assumption that sacred music can be taught without proselytizing, and if one opts to keep sacred music in the public school curriculum, then many alternative voices, still silenced by current practice, must be given a fair and respectful hearing. In a nation as diverse as the United States, monocultural public school practices such as caroling, giving Christmas concerts, and confining the study of sacred music almost exclusively to Christian music, are anachronistic, insensitive, and exclusionary. If music associated with every other major world religion is not given a fair share of time, then Christian music belongs in church, not in school.

Equitable Music Content: The Gender Component

Sex equity is another content issue meriting attention from multicultural music educators. Because sexism is so pervasive, it is sometimes difficult to see "business-as-usual" practices as unfair; subtle and overt sexism can slip into curricular content unnoticed.

In the United States, long-standing sex stereotypes exist concerning participation in musical activities. Boys may be reluctant to join in because they have been subtly or explicitly taught that music, specifically singing, is feminine. For example, the stereotype persists that "real men" do not join choir. Despite the feminization of the discipline, however, many musical activities, notably composing and conducting orchestras and bands, have traditionally been reserved for males. Furthermore, except for an occasional vocalist, the performance of rock music and jazz remain male domains. Stereotypes concerning musical instruments also exist. For example, the flute, clarinet, violin, and harp are considered feminine, while drums, trumpets, trombones, tubas, and string basses are deemed masculine (Abeles & Porter, 1978; Griswold & Chroback, 1981). A recent study of the representation of females in music textbook illustrations indicates that textbook content is seriously flawed because it tends to reflect traditional music-related stereotypes (Koza, 1994). Such research raises the question of how teachers might proceed, given the problematic nature of available resources.

First, teachers can examine materials carefully. In addition to including equal numbers of females, and being free from stereotypes that might appear in resources from any curricular area, music materials should portray people of both sexes participating in a wide variety of musical activities and playing a variety of instruments. When analyzing how males and females are represented, it is important to consider not only the written text and illustrations but the musical examples as well. As appealing as it may be to teach favorite songs from one's own childhood, it is nonetheless critical for teachers to first think about whether song texts portray males and females in ways that are considerate, respectful, and fair. For example, "Peter, Peter, Pumpkin Eater" is a traditional favorite in the repertoire of beginning pianists and is based on a familiar nursery rhyme:

> Peter, Peter, Pumpkin Eater,
> Had a wife but couldn't keep her.
> Put her in a pumpkin shell,
> And there he kept her very well.

It is tempting to say, "This is just a cute, silly song; it is absurd to eliminate it from a young pianist's repertoire on the grounds that it is unfair." However, from another perspective ideology is most deeply rooted—and effective—in the seemingly small things. In addition to playing the traditional role of breadwinner, Peter is the active problem solver in the song. All we learn about his wife is that she is kept. Apparently she does not even have a name, and nobody asked her how she felt about being cooped up in a vegetable. Rather than eliminating the song altogether, teachers might invite children to think about Peter's wife and consider her viewpoint on the events. In the spirit of "Fractured Fairy Tales," children could write their own second and third verses in which Peter's beleaguered wife gains a more complex identity and a voice.

If teachers who advocate a multicultural approach that is social reconstructionist use biased materials, they might carefully consider how to incorporate them in ways that are consistent with a goal of being fair and sensitive to all children. A thoughtful question is, "Who might be harmed or served by this representation, especially if it is presented without question or comment?" One alternative to removing materials is to critique them. For example, excerpts from Broadway musicals long have been a popular part of upper elementary and middle school music curricula. However, roles in these musicals have often been sex stereotyped. Teachers can use these musicals as a springboard for critical analysis and class discussion of equity issues. Against-the-grain performances are another effective way of problematizing sexist roles.

Content with a Focus on Social Issues

Finally, it is important to keep in mind that music, because it is a social construct, is intricately related to the society from which it has sprung. Therefore, music is never politically neutral nor value free. This also means that music can be related in many ways to social issues. A music curriculum that is multicultural and social reconstructionist can highlight this relationship in countless ways, four of which are briefly discussed here. Curricular content can focus on such topics as (1) current practices within the field of music and how they are related to larger social problems, (2) social issues and problems of a particular society or culture as reflected in its music, (3) how music is used to sell social and political ideas, and (4) the role music has played in efforts to effect justice and change.

First, students can explore the impact social problems have on the field of music itself. Questions such as "Why are there no women in this book about famous composers?" or "Why haven't more boys signed up to sing in choir this year?" or "Why are there no people of color in this picture of a symphony orchestra?" can lead to exploration of how larger social issues affect the discipline itself. They can provide students with opportunities to think carefully about their own beliefs and values, and they can be starting points for an array of follow-up projects. For example, such questions might lead to a search for music by women composers represented in the Top 40, or to interviews of classmates and parents asking them why boys often do not join choir, or to a letter-writing campaign asking an orchestra association why no persons of color are employed by their organization. Music can be a starting point for efforts to teach children not only how to analyze and critique, but also to debate, coalesce, and take action.

Students can also analyze and critique music with an eye on how it may reflect social issues and problems. For example, an analysis of a rock video or a television commercial can include questions about how women, people of color, or people of various social classes are portrayed in the images and text. Then, in addition to asking questions typical of musical analysis, such as queries on instrumentation or tempo, the issue of how the music itself reinforces the portrayals can be addressed.

Third, students can analyze how music is used to sell not only products—ranging from deodorant to presidential candidates—but ideas as well. For example, propagandists often use music to sell ideas; such sales tactics rely heavily on codes of shared meaning. Children who have watched television in the United States have a vast repertoire of sonic experiences from which they can draw when thinking about what it is in the music itself that prompts particular associations, and when considering how the code of shared meaning is sometimes used to manipulate people.

Finally, students can investigate the role music has played in efforts to effect social and political change. Campaigns that have striven for justice, such as the suffrage, civil rights, and labor movements, have often used music as a way of rallying and sustaining supporters. Sometimes music has come to represent the movement itself. For example, "We Shall Overcome" is one symbol of the efforts of the civil rights movement in the United States. Knowing this music and understanding its significance can help introduce children to people and ideas that have challenged "business as usual."

✣ Keeping the Focus on People

Instructional practices and curricular content are, without question, important for educators to consider. However, from a multicultural and social reconstructionist perspective, the central focus of any educational endeavor should always be people. If in the past music education has sometimes become preoccupied with content and method, and if it has grown isolated from elementary education at large, then multicultural perspectives can offer a new path. The inclusivity suggested by multicultural education can mean welcoming pluralistic content into the curriculum, and more importantly, opening doors to diverse people, ideas, and ways of doing things. Classroom teachers represent one group of people with a wealth of experiences to bring to a new music education paradigm that is both multicultural and social reconstructionist.

Changes in "business as usual" are clearly needed. Sweeping change cannot be effected by music specialists or classroom teachers alone, however, because schools, like classrooms, do not exist in a vacuum. If music education is to survive and if it is to become multicultural and social reconstructionist in the broadest sense, administrators, legislators, taxpayers, and parents must look deep within themselves and reconsider many time-honored beliefs and values. Beliefs and values shape goals, mold policies, and govern priorities; they determine, for example, whether instruments of human destruction or instruments of human expression will receive more resources, whether people or things are given first priority. If equity and justice for all people were placed at the top of the list of goals, both for individual curricular areas and for public education as a whole, then a new perspective would be brought to bear on curriculum and instruction. In the spirit of multicultural education, classroom teachers and music specialists can become politically active and can work together to bring about changes in "business as usual" thinking, not only within, but outside the classroom as well.

Notes

1. In its early days the *Music Educators Journal* was first called the *Music Supervisors' Bulletin* and later, the *Music Supervisors's Journal*. I arrived at the number six by counting the pre-1967 articles cited under the subject heading "Multicultural Education" in Arneson (1987).

2. This conceptual goal was taken from a recent series by Meske, Andress, Pautz, and Willman (1988, p. xxviii).

3. See Anderson & Campbell (1989), p. ix for a discussion of this scarcity.

4. According to information provided by the Music Educators National Conference, in 1983 the student-to-music-specialist ratio was 496.2 to 1. A survey taken in 1987 of 41 states revealed a ratio of 497 to 1.

5. In this particular school, the terms "deaf" and "hard of hearing" are preferred over "hearing impaired"; the latter is perceived to connote deficiency rather than difference.

6. For an unconventional and intriguing view on giftedness, including musical talent, see Bloom (1985).

7. For a contemporary discussion of polymusicality, see Anderson & Campbell (1989, p. 4).

8. For example, Florey v. Sioux Falls School District 49-5 was upheld in the Eighth U. S. Circuit Court of Appeals. The case stemmed from the singing of "Silent Night" in a Christmas concert, and the decision reaffirmed the legality of singing sacred music in public schools.

References

Abeles, H. F., & Porter, S. Y. (1978). The sex-stereotyping of musical instruments. *Journal of Research in Music Education, 26*(2), 65–75.

Anderson, W. M. (1991). Toward a multicultural future. *Music Educators Journal, 77*(9), 29–33.

Anderson, W. M., & Campbell, P. S. (Eds.). (1989). *Multicultural perspectives in music education.* Reston, VA: Music Educators National Conference.

Arneson, A. J. (1987). *The Music Educators Journal: Cumulative index 1914–1987: Including the Music Supervisors' Bulletin and the Music Supervisors' Journal.* Stevens Point, WI: Index House.

Beck, A. L. (1933). Are we making the most of our gifts from other lands? *Music Educators Journal, 19*(5), 20.

Bessom, M. E. (Ed.) (1972a). Music in world cultures. *Music Educators Journal, 59*(2).

Bessom, M. E. (1972b). Overtones. *Music Educators Journal, 59*(2), 5–6.

Bloom, B. S. (Ed.). (1985). *Developing talent in young people.* New York: Ballantine.

Campbell, P. S. (Ed.). (1996a). *Music in cultural context: Eight views on world music education.* Reston, VA: Music Educators National Conference.

Campbell, P. S. (1996b). Music, education, and community in a multicultural society. In M. McCarthy (Ed.), *Cross currents: Setting an agenda for music education in community culture* (pp. 4–33). College Park: University of Maryland Press.

Campbell, P. S., McCullough-Brabson, E., & Tucker, J. C. (1994). *Roots and branches: A legacy of multicultural music for children.* Danbury, CT: World Music Press.

Coffman, D. D. (1987). Vocal music and the classroom teacher, 1885 to 1905. *Journal of research in Music Education, 35*(2), 92–102.

Duffield, P. E. (1947). Global music: An audio-visual approach to the 'one world' concept. *Music Educators Journal, 33*(6), 21, 68–69.

Elliot, D. J. (1990). Music as culture: Toward a multicultural concept of arts education. *Journal of Aesthetic Education 24*(1), 147–166.

Gerber, T., & Hughes, W. O. (Eds.). (1988). *Music in the high school: Current approaches to secondary general music instruction.* Reston, VA: Music Educators National Conference.

Gonzo, C. (1993). Multicultural issues in music education. *Music Educators Journal, 79*(6), 49–52.

Griswold, P. A., & Chroback, D. A. (1981). Sex-role associations of music instruments and occupations by gender and major. *Journal of Research in Music Education, 29*(1), 57–62.

Koza, J. E. (1994). Females in 1988 middle school music textbooks: An analysis of illustrations.

Journal of Research in Music Education, 42(2), 145-171.

Meske, E. B., Andress, B., Pautz, M. P. & Willman, F. (1988). *Holt music* [Teacher's ed., grade 8]. New York: Holt, Rinehart & Winston.

Moses, H. E. (1945). A good-neighbor policy for appreciation classes. *Music Educators Journal, 32*(2), 22-23.

Music in American society: The Tanglewood Symposium. (1967). Washington, DC: Music Educators National Conference.

Otterstein, A. W. (1938). Music in the activity program. *Music Educators Journal, 24*(4), 25, 27.

Religious music in the schools. (1984). *Music Educators Journal, 71*(3), 28-30.

Seeger, C. (1972). World music in American schools: A challenge to be met. *Music Educators Journal, 59*(2), 107-111.

Sleeter, C. E., & Grant, C. A. (1988). *Making choices for multicultural education: Five approaches to race, class, and gender.* Upper Saddle River, NJ: Merrill/Prentice Hall.

Swanson, P. (1991). Who will take up the charge? *The Wisconsin School Musician, 61*(5), 39.

Taylor, R. G. (Ed.). (1983). The multicultural imperative. *Music Educators Journal, 69*(9).

Volk, T. M. (1998). *Music, education, and multiculturalism: Foundations and principles.* New York: Oxford University Press.

Yob, I. M. (1995). Religious music and multicultural education. *Philosophy of Music Education Review 3*(2): 69-82.

15 Curriculum and Instruction in Primary School Physical Education: A Critique and Visionary Perspective for Reform in Teacher Education

Jepkorir Rose Chepyator-Thomson
University of Georgia

Physical education, also called *kinesiology,* is a professional field of study that focuses on knowledge about human movement with its cultural and social connections; motor development with its physiological and psychological connections; methods of teaching; student characteristics; and learning behavior. Physical education pays special attention to physical, cognitive, affective, interpersonal, and emotional development of children as appropriate to their levels and ages of learning. The development of the whole child is the major focus of physical education in elementary and middle school grades and as Nichols (1994) explains, it is "the only area of [school] curriculum that presents motor skills and the study of human movement and provides the opportunity to facilitate their development" (p. 3). Children's development beginning in the early school years through middle school is facilitated through selected curricular and learning experiences developed by specialists in the field of physical education.

As understood by professionals in the field, physical education "is that phase of the general education program that contributes to the total growth and development of each child primarily through movement experiences" (Pangrazi, 1998, p. 4) and represents a part of the education that reflects on the nature and needs of a democratic society, builds on respect for the interests and capacities of all individuals as cultural beings, and is organized into a sequential flow of experiences beginning with early school grades. In concert with democratic principles of education in the United States, the goal of physical education is "the greatest possible development of each individual for responsible democratic citizenship" (Dauer & Pangrazi, 1975, p. 2).

Anchored by cultural, kinesiological, and physiological studies of human movement, physical education has a disciplinary-based knowledge. Teacher education specialists in this area strive to teach children ideas and motor skills inherent in a variety of physical activities, to provide children with experiences to increase levels of health and fitness, to make physical education an enjoyable and satifying experience for children, and to provide opportunities for all children to reap success in movement experiences (Kirchner & Fishburne, 1998). Physical activity allows children to develop their identity formations through sequential curricular experiences in physical education. Physical skills and ways in which they are applied to games and physical activities are grounded in one's culture. As such, a culturally valued physical skill is a movement execution pertaining to a particular culture in society; for example, the jumping activity of the Kalenjin group in Kenya, East Africa, or the lacrosse activity of the American Indians in North America. While the jumping activity of the Kalenjin group is intended to develop strength and rhythmic movements associated with various ceremonies in the culture and is a means to demonstrate manhood among the Maasai, the lacrosse activity of the North American Indians is meant to promote the perpetuation of cultural values and develop physical fitness (Grueninger, 1992).

Although physical education is of greatest importance to children's development in elementary and middle school grades, the development of physical education and its implementation has not been critically examined for its appropriateness for a diverse population of students. Physical education curricula have changed dramatically since the beginning of the 20th century in that more schools are offering more programs with a greater variety of activities; however, there is still a dominant cultural perspective that undergirds the conceptual configurations of physical education and program operations. The dominant perspective has been limited to a specific population, mainly U.S. citizens of European descent.

The literature has not adequately addressed American Indians or African Americans in terms of conceptual frameworks or activity variations. Diversity, as exemplified in the population of the United States, is not focused upon adequately in the literature. Hardly any culturally-based movement skills of North American Indian cultures are taught in physical education programs in elementary and middle school grades. Indeed, traditional culturally-based movement skills have been largely ignored in the primary schools. Scant attention has been paid to the influence of social, cultural, and political factors on the types of physical activities developed for physical education.

In this chapter, I examine the extent to which European cultures influenced the historical development of physical education programs and the differing paradigms that have guided the conduct of physical education in the schools. I offer ways of reforming physical education in teacher education such that varying theoretical perspectives and instructional goals developed by teachers cater to the increasing cultural and social diversity of students populating in public schools.

❖ Historical Development of Physical Education in the United States: The Eurocentric Focus

Cultural Influences

The fabric of United States society has been molded and shaped largely by knowledge derived from European peoples' cultures. This Eurocentric focus has influenced the development of physical education, and in turn, the type of physical activities used in the teaching of physical education in public school systems. In historical terms, German and Swedish immigrants played a major role in the development of physical education before 1900. During this time, German immigrants influenced physical education programs by introducing gymnastic activities which were offered through "Turnverein" gymnastic organizations (Zeigler, 1988). These organizations introduced German gymnastics as a major form of physical education into many United States schools (Van Dalen & Bennett, 1971). Friedrich Jahn, the original developer of the Turnverein organizations, believed that the organizations would develop and maintain physical fitness and discipline among German youth and would help to rehabilitate the spirit and virtues that formed the core of the German culture (Barney, 1975).

The organizations spread knowledge about gymnastic exercises by educating the United States public on the benefits of the German system of exercise (Barney, 1975). The Turners influenced legislation in local and state governments in regard to teaching gymnastics and virtually shaped the United States physical education program in their own image (Barney, 1975). The Turners believed physical training to be an important part of children's growth and development and their moral and mental training (Zeigler, 1988). The preparation of teachers according to the German system was established in 1866 in New York City. By the end of the 19th century, teachers graduating from the German teacher preparatory school taught German gymnastics successfully in the public schools.

The other major European influence on the development of physical education in the United States came from the Swedes. The Swedish form of gymnastics was developed by Per Henrik Ling and his son Hjamar in Sweden; it was introduced into the United States by Dr. Hartwig Nissen (a Norwegian) in 1883 when he came to the United States as a Vice-Consul for Norway and Sweden. The gymnastics form was popularized by a Swedish aristocrat, Baron Nils Posse (Zeigler, 1988). Posse, a graduate of the Royal Central Institute of Gymnastics of Stockholm, and Mary Hemingway, a Boston philanthropist, founded the Boston Normal School of Gymnastics in 1889 with the mission of preparing teachers to teach the Swedish system of gymnastics in public schools and colleges (Zeigler, 1988). The Swedish form of gymnastics was guided by theories of medical and corrective gymnastics (Rice, Hutchinson, & Lee, 1969) and it formed the basis for the development of physical education in many New England states and in other areas of the United States with non-German populations (Zeigler, 1988). The Swedish system was intended to improve the health of school children through light calisthenic exercises (Rice et al., 1969). It focused on the development of flexibility and grace of movement (Zeigler, 1988).

Accompanying the German and the Swedish influence on the development of physical education programs, the Danish people played a role in the development of physical education in this country in the latter half of the 19th century and the first quarter of 20th century. Danish gymnastics were originally designed for Folk Arts Schools in rural areas in Denmark and were believed to develop flexibility and general body conditioning of Danish youth (Zeigler, 1988). The French also had their share of influence, through the Delcarte culture, which brought rhythmic and aesthetic focus into physical education. The movements executed were of a calisthenic type and characterized by repetitive graceful movements (Van Dalen, Mitchell, & Bennett, 1953).

The sports and games of the British have become a part of cultures in many countries that were part of the British Empire, such as Australia, India, and the United States (Rice et al., 1969, p. 95). Although many sports activities such as cricket and archery originated in Britain, many others originated in neighboring European countries. The English and Scots "naturalized" such games as golf and bowling from the Netherlands and Germany, and tennis from France (Rice et al., 1969, p. 95). The British refined these activities and passed them along to the colonies.

The Eurocentric focus in physical education in the United States was discussed and given formality at the Boston Conference of 1899. The conference brought together representatives from several European regions to discuss the direction physical education was to take in the United States (Zeigler, 1988). Dudley Sargent, a dominant figure in the field of physical education at the time, stated that America needed

> . . . the strength giving qualities of the German gymnasium, the active and energetic properties of the English sports, the grace and suppleness acquired from the French calisthenics, and the beautiful poise and mechanical precision of the Swedish free movements, all regulated, systematized, and adapted to our peculiar needs and constitution. (Zeigler, 1988, p. 198).

It is apparent in Dudley Sargent's view that the concept of diversity in physical education was discussed only in terms of European ethnic groups. It can be said that physical education in the United States assumed a Eurocentric focus at its inception not only in terms of content knowledge, but also in terms of structure and philosophy.

Besides the European cultural influences that have been identified, sociopolitical influences on the development of physical education occurred in times of crisis. Physical education was stressed in times of war; the overall physical fitness of citizens was given top priority then and now continues (Zeigler, 1988). In wartime, the major objective of physical education was physical fitness and emphasis was placed on strength, endurance, stamina, coordination, and physical skills that were needed in the military (Van Dalen et al., 1953). During the economic depression period of the 1930s, people's work habits were altered drastically as citizens were put out of work. In that instance, physical education was stressed because it was seen as curing citizens' boredom and inactivity (Zeigler, 1988).

Primary School Physical Education Programs

Beginning with the second half of the 19th century and ending with the first quarter of the 20th century, there were few physical education programs sanctioned in the U.S. (Ragan & Shepard, 1977). The physical education programs that were developed and are still in existence today are of European origin. The Swedish and German gymnastics programs have been considered the first organized physical education in the United States (Nixon, Flanagan, & Frederickson, 1964). During World War II, physical education programs began to stress popular sports and games that have continued to be emphasized in public schools today (Ragan & Shepard, 1977).

Traditionally, school physical education curricula have constituted: (a) sports and games, (b) physical fitness, and (c) movement education. Although the physical education program in elementary school has focused on the introduction of new games and ethnic, folk, and creative dances (Jewett & Bain, 1985), curricular models in place have tended to emphasize activity programs with a movement education focus. According to Locke (1969), movement education has centered on educational dance, basic movement, movement exploration, educational movement gymnastics, and developmental movement (p. 203). Movement education has been a prescription "for the kind of gross motor skills taught to school children and for how such instruction [would be] accomplished" (Locke, 1969, p. 203).

Based on Ennis and Chepyator-Thomson's (1991) analysis of elementary physical education, the dominant curricular approach used has been cognitive or analytical, and the language concepts used have reflected a theory developed by Rudolf Von Laban

(1879-1958), who was born in Hungary, and was a noted dancer and choreographer (Ullmann, 1968).

In terms of middle school, researchers such as Jewett and Bain (1985) have documented the curricula and have pointed out that it has historically stressed survival swimming, sports skills, dance, project adventure, fitness activities, and new games—all expressed under the rubric of lifelong physical activities and health and productive lifestyles which have been perceived to bring about increased productivity in the United States economy. The physical education curricula developed have focused on: (a) the understanding of movement through the refinement of personal skills, (b) creating a depth of social understanding of others outside one's own culture through experiences in movement activities of many cultures, and (c) the invention of new games (Jewett & Bain, 1985, p. 43).

Women have also been excluded in varying programs of physical education. For example, boys have often had more activities available to them. While activities for females have included gymnastics, calisthenics, and dance, activities for males have continued to emphasize team sports (Geadelmann, Bischoff, Hoferek, & McKnight, 1989). Besides unequal activity offerings, boys generally have had superior instruction and facilities. The discrepancy between boys' and girls' curricular and instructional programs has been addressed in recent times through the 1972 Education Act, Title IX, which prohibited discrimination on the basis of sex in federally funded programs.

It is apparent that culture, politics, and social factors have played a major role in the historical development of physical education programs. The Germans, the Swedes, the French, and the British all have had an upper hand role in influencing the type of physical education programs in elementary and middle school grades. In the following section, the different ways in which paradigms function in physical education are discussed in light of politics, culture, and economy.

Differing Paradigms in Physical Education

The concept of paradigm in education has been used in varying ways and it is important to note that "paradigms are not theories" (Gage, 1963, p. 95) but rather ways to contemplate possible formulations of reality. Paradigms impact our thinking, goal setting, problem solving, and values (Gablik, 1991). In this frame of reference, education has allowed people to think in different ways about the subject matter and the outcomes have been several competing perspectives. Researchers and teachers of physical education have conceptualized the subject in different ways: (a) a fitness perspective (Graham, Holt/Hale, & Parker, 1998; Kirchner & Fishburne, 1998); (b) a developmental physical education perspective (Hoffman, Young, & Klesius, 1985; Kirchner & Fishburne, 1998); (c) a movement education perspective (Jewett & Bain, 1985); and (d) a humanistic physical education perspective (Hellison, 1985). Each of these paradigms or perspectives has, at different times in the 20th century, guided thinking about physical education.

Physical Fitness

Physical fitness, defined as the "capacity of the heart, blood vessels, lungs, and muscles to function at optimum effeciency," has been considered an integral part of, and is critical to, a program of quality in physical education (Graham, Holt/Hale, & Parker, 1998). Children's physical fitness has been the major emphasis in the United States elementary school curriculum since the mid-1950s (Graham, Holt/Hale, & Parker, 1998). This emphasis stemmed from public concern about children's health. The number of children who are overweight has increased more than 50% over the past 20 years (Kirchner & Fishburne, 1998). Elementary school children who are physically unfit and are obese are at risk for heart disease, high blood pressure, and high levels of cholestrol. A program of physical education has been to develop the physical fitness of children in order to help improve their health—the child's ability to function adequately in terms of physical, mental, emotional, and social aspects of fitness. This includes the development of strength, endurance, power, flexibility, agility, and speed. From this perspective, achieving optimum physical and mental well-being in children is critical to the nation's social and economic viability.

A fitness-based curriculum that requires specified activity intensities and intervals is composed of health-related and performance-related fitness categories (Hellison & Templin, 1991). Health-related fitness is concerned with muscular strength and endurance, cardiovascular endurance, flexibility, and body composition (Kirchner & Fishburne, 1998). Skill-related fitness, sometimes referred to as motor fitness (Pangrazi, 1998), is concerned with the development of skills necessary for children to engage in sports and other physical activities that require endurance, strength, power, anaerobic capacity, and agility, beyond what is essential to health-related fitness.

The significance of physical fitness for good health and clear thinking—sound body and sound mind—according to Ragan and Shepard (1977), developed in 1926 when United States military draftees were found to be "physically unfit for service" (p. 387). This stirred people in society at large to demand fitness and exercise programs for all United States citizens. Fitness did not become important in schools until the 1950s when one large study indicated that U.S. children were deficient in relation to the fitness levels of European children (Graham, Holt/Hale, & Parker, 1998). Following this publication in 1956, President Eisenhower established the President's Council on Youth Fitness (Ragan & Shepard, 1977) and the school physical education curriculum began to center on fitness.

Today, fitness training for kindergarten and primary school children is the centerpiece of most physical education programs. The fitness programs developed emphasize health-related fitness and are realized through participation in varying aerobic activities such as jogging and rope jumping. Educators who see fitness as a goal of physical education view becoming fit as "an individual matter," and depending on one's level of fitness, a kind of "physical and mental well-being" is ascertained. This way of conceptualizing one's individuality fails to take into account social, political, and economic factors that play a large part in students' lives. The individual focus does not "empower students to make choices based on personal needs and values as well as knowledge" (Hellison & Templin, 1991, p. 16).

Essentially, fitness, important as it is for schooling, is rarely viewed as problematic. Indeed, there are drawbacks in schools' realization of the fitness paradigm in children's schooling.

First, physical fitness is not seen as a social phenomenon implicated in political and economic factors. The segmentation of society into identifiable economically-based neighborhoods such as a suburb, an inner city, or a welfare housing unit, poses problems for students. The socioeconomic status of children is tied to their ability to participate in what are almost always competition-based programs of fitness. Students from higher socioeconomic backgrounds have access to sports clubs where physical activities and individual instruction in sports like tennis, swimming, and golf are available. Furthermore, parents of these students are able to involve their children in after-school physical activities because they have flexible schedules which allow them to take part in recreational activities with their children (Dixon, 1984).

Second, most schools' physical education programs do not adequately meet the physical fitness levels required for children to improve their cardio-respiratory functioning, because physical education requirements vary from state to state. Those in power hold varying perspectives about the subject; consequently, only a limited time is available for the teaching of physical education in elementary and middle schools. For instance, some states have physical education only once a week while others have it twice or three times a week. Based on the Surgeon General's report on physical activity and health, children should engage in endurance type physical activities at a moderate intensity for 30 minutes, preferably every day (U.S. Department of Health and Human Services, 1996). Only in Illinois is physical education offered every day. Thus as currently practiced, school physical education programs generally help students who already have some level of fitness—those students who have access to physical activities in sports clubs or individual instruction as well as those students whose parents have cars to transport them to various community youth programs. Homeless children, children living in inner city housing and others far from recreational areas such as parks, municipal pools, and spaces to play, do not have the same opportunities for after-school or in-school physical fitness programs as upper-class or suburban children. For example, Griffin (1985) discusses the severity of problems in operating a physical education program in one urban inner-city school:

> The lack of outdoor activity space prompted the physical education staff to persuade the principal to schedule physical education once a week for a double period rather than the regular scheduled 45 minute class twice a week. The change gave the classes time to walk across the street and use the athletic fields in the city park. Since this was a *15 minute walk each way,* using the park would have been impossible during the 45 minute class. (p. 158)

In the case Griffin describes, additional problems occurred at the athletic fields: first, the staff discovered that they could not use the fields because of re-seeding operations; second, only small groups of students could be taught in these playing fields as they were not designed for large physical education classes (Griffin, 1985). In out-of-school situations, children in this kind of predicament, like children everywhere, may develop equipment and facilities of their own choosing as a group or as individuals and create new games and play activities or modify games to their particular social and and cultural environments (Chepyator-Thomson, 1990) to make life more livable. African American children's ways of playing basketball attest to this concept of creativity; they have, as explained by Sachs and Abraham (1979), modified basketball play to accommodate their social and cultural milieu by utilizing "moves" to outmaneuver an opponent to the basket (p. 30). For African Americans, basketball has helped the development of self-concept and the achievement of status in the community (Sachs & Abraham, 1979).

To summarize, a fitness paradigm in the public school system requires adequate time, adequate staffing, and the availability of adequate facilities and equipment for the conduct of physical education programs (Ragan & Shepard, 1977). However, far too many schools fail to meet children's needs in ways that would permit an effective enactment of the fitness paradigm. Teachers must be made aware of the social and political factors that influence the development and implementation of fitness activities in the public schools.

Developmentally-Based Physical Education

The developmentally-based program in physical education focuses on children's growth and development. Essentially the program recognizes and fosters an individual child's developmental potential, paying special attention to stages of development and patterns of growth in reference to cognitive, affective, and psychomotor learning (Melograno, 1996). The developmentally-based approach addresses the why, how, and what of human movement and uses a developmental sequence of learning movement concepts and motor skills as appropriate to children's level of ability, interests, and maturity (Kirchner & Fishburne, 1998). A child's psychomotor development, for example, may be reflected in her/his social and emotional development:

> If a child is not capable of coping with his/[her] physical environment with regard to societal expectations, he[/she] becomes less of a person in the eyes of society, thus social and emotional characteristics are affected. If a person lags in social and emotional aspects of total development, there may be lessened tendency to engage in physical endeavours and cooperative play with his/[her] peers. (Auxter, 1973, p. 39)

Developmentally-based physical education uses an activity-based curriculum. While basic games, dance, and gymnastics represent the major groupings of activity at the elementary school level, a variety of lead-up activities in team sports, individual and dual sports units, including fitness and recreational activities, are focused upon mainly in middle school (Kirchner & Fishburne, 1998). The aim of physical education in elementary school is to develop movements skills associated with games, educational gymnastics, and dance (Siedentop, Herkowitz, Rink, 1984), while in middle school, sports-related skills are emphasized; children participate in a wide variety of activities, such as volleyball or soccer, in short 2- to 3-week units (Hellison & Templin, 1991).

Developmentally-based physical education aims at helping children to progress from using simple to advanced patterns of movement. Specifically, activities of classes are arranged so that there is a relationship between each. Also, a sequence that shows how the activities are developmentally structured to enable the children to have optimal participation is provided. The curriculum is organized to reflect the children's developmental stages. In essence, the curriculum takes into account the developmental ability of the children in arranging the essential activities of a class from simple to complex (Auxter, 1973). For example, the gymnasium may be divided into four sections where children throw balls at designated targets using elementary skills in section one, while others practice throwing using more advanced skills in section four. The teacher's plans for developmental experiences help children to acquire qualitative changes in their social, physical, and emotional types of development.

The developmentally-based perspective has one major drawback. There is a tendency for teachers to divide children into groups based on ability for instructional and play purposes within and between classes. Such grouping can result in less skilled children becoming tracked in physical education classes for "less developed" learners. One way to avoid this is to use cooperative learning methods in instruction where, for example, an excellent soccer player would teach a group of children a soccer skill like dribbling. In play situations, a teacher would introduce a "handicap" for outstanding student performers.

Another drawback is that the kind of equipment used could determine placement in the different levels of activity. Familiarity with equipment such as hoops, balls, and pins plays a big role in students' acquisition of content knowledge. The students' exposure to such equipment could be based in part on the socioeconomic standing of the school or the community and also on the parents' economic ability to allow for such exposure in their children's educational development.

Another drawback in developmentally-based physical education programs has been the Eurocentric focus in the types of games played, gymnastic and sports programs developed, and in the dances taught at the elementary and middle school levels. There has not been much deviation from European cultural groups' traditional physical activities in the curriculum and instruction programs used in public school physical education.

Movement Education

Movement education began in England as a counterpoint to structured fitness programs. In the United States, movement education has become the dominant type of curriculum in elementary schools (Nichols, 1994). The goals of movement education are: (a) to teach children about their bodies through physical activities; (b) to teach children to comprehend Laban's movement concepts (Nichols, 1994) which include space and body awareness, qualities and relationship (Kirchner & Fishburne, 1998); (c) to facilitate self-discovery, self-discipline and self-reliance in children so that they can work on their own ideas individually or with others; and (d) to provide opportunities for children to create movements useful in varying environments (Melograno, 1996).

Movement education became the dominant paradigm in elementary schools across the United States especially in the 1960s and 1970s (Nichols, 1994). As a child-centered type of curriculum, movement education emphasizes the technique of individual problem solving and promotes children's abilities to adapt to their own physical and emotional potentials. It encourages a variety of activities and ways of applying the elements of space, force, time, and flow which are essential to this paradigm (Kirchner & Fishburne, 1998). Games, gymanistics, and dance activities are used to bring children's abilities to fruition. The instructional patterns of movement education permit teachers to learn more about each child in a non-competitive and self-expressive manner when children are performing physical activities, to use a conversational tone of voice in addressing the students, and to guide the students individually in educational activities of the class (Kruger & Kruger, 1982). In movement education, teachers provide children with opportunities to learn at their own level of readiness; they enhance children's creativity and independent thinking by teaching in a way that encourages children's "inventiveness, initiative, and imagination" (Ragan & Shepard, 1977, p. 392). Further, movement education is designed to emphasize children's individual responsibility and self-discipline by allowing children to "assume responsibility for their own physical actions," and also to promote the perceptual-motor development of children by helping them to "develop their awareness and control of their bodies" (Ragan & Shepard, 1977, p. 392).

While the goals and instructional plans of movement education appear worthy on the surface, the emphasis on games, gymnastics, and dance brings particular cultural practices and values to the forefront of this paradigm. The games, movement activities, and dances taught by "movement" educators are grounded in Western European cultures. The elements of the movement education paradigm—space, time, flow, and force—are culturally founded on European types of movement; for example, there is a correspondence between children's movements resulting from uses of space, flow, time, and force with movement repertoires expressed in ballet. For the movement education paradigm to reflect African type of movements, as evidenced in *Les Ballet Africains* (a dance group from West Africa which toured the United States in 1991), educators and prospective teachers must be schooled in varying cultural perspectives. *Les Ballet Africains* brings out the rhythms of life in West Africa; life situations are symbolized with strong rhythmic movements characterized by the use of fine motor rather than gross motor muscles.

Humanistic Physical Education

The focus of a humanistic physical education paradigm is on a student's personal liberation and self-actualization (McNeil, 1985), and its major goals are the development of individuals' attitudes and feelings in relation to the subject matter. The program puts an emphasis on children's self-awareness and choice as a basis for personal development and growth (Melograno, 1996). Physical educators of a humanistic orientation believe that "knowledge is personal and subjective and results from a person's interpretation of the world" (McNeil, 1985, p. 5). Thus, students learn the subject matter in the context of their own individual capabilities and perspectives.

Humanistic physical education is a student-centered curriculum that offers children choices of activities and emphasizes process learning in an "atmosphere of understanding, compassion, encouragement, and trust" (Wiles & Bondi, 1984, p. 363). Teachers emphasize students' individuality and ask for student input into how and what they teach. Students' personal excellence in the educational performances of the class are stressed and students' differing learning outcomes are allowed; the teachers acknowledge student individualities.

Hellison's (1985) concepts of irresponsibility, self-control, involvement, self-responsibility, and caring are employed in teachers' instructional plans; these concepts are utilized hierarchically in classroom instruction in physical education as students move from being irresponsible to being self-responsible, followed by caring about others in life situations. With these instructional orientations, children in elementary and middle school are provided with varying movement experiences in which they acquire disciplinary-based and personally-based knowledge; they are taught the subject matter in the context of their individual capabilities and potentials. The movement experiences provided for children are through play, physical fitness, aerobics, and general conditioning activities as well as games, sports, and dance activities.

Humanistic physical education has one major drawback: It leaves out the conditional connections to the school curriculum which include cultural, social, political, and economic factors. School curriculum is not a neutral enterprise but has a correspondence with the society at large. Curriculum is intimately connected to cultural preferences of the dominant culture, the social conditions, the political orientation of the community, and the economic reality existing in the country and/or in the immediate community. For example, physical education for lower elementary school students was eliminated in a city school district in Northwestern New York State, while the suburban area school districts retained their physical education programs.

Since children's interpretation of the world in which they exist is tied to the factors described above, it is paramount that teachers realize the curriculum's shortcomings when constructing the content knowledge and designing the way in which it is going to be implemented. This is essential because it is through the realization of a curriculum that an individual's creation of being is centralized. The experience must be made meaningful to the student. This is considered paramount for physical education programs because in most situations, content development and ways in which it is disseminated have not taken into consideration children's views on either their cultural or social realities.

In summary, several paradigms have guided the philosophical orientation of physical education in elementary and middle schools. The elementary school curriculum is designed to allow children to develop an understanding of fundamental movement concepts and patterns, to perform the movement patterns adequately and efficiently, and to respond cognitively to new circumstances. The aim of the curriculum is to have the children master basic forms of movement and cognition in preparation for their middle school physical education. The middle school physical education curriculum focuses on more advanced and more specific forms of movement and forms of cognition. The children are taught a wide variety of skills in lead-up activities that are specific individual, dual, and team-based activities. The children acquire an appreciation of as many skills and activities as possible and make intelligent choices in activity participation and other related life configurations.

❖ A Visionary Perspective for Curricular Reform in Physical Education

A visionary perspective entails conceptualizing new possibilities for physical education. New physical education curricula should be constructed with societal diversification in mind and with awareness of the changing social, cultural, and political conditions which continually alter the surroundings and goals of schools and their students. Attention must be paid to the multicultural population of learners coming to U.S. schools and to issues of equity and justice as these are realized in school curriculum and pedagogy. Indeed, "The future course of public school education should be defined with respect to the population moving through its institutional system" (Hyland, 1989, p. 132).

Essentially, education with a multicultural perspective requires educational professionals to start developing school programs that aid students' understanding of themselves and others, and that assist students in developing a clear understanding and appreciation of the diverse ethnic and racial groups in the United States. Programs of curriculum and instruction ought to be developed so that they "produce awareness, acceptance, and affirmation of cultural diversity" (Grant & Sleeter, 1989, p. 53). Providing teachers and youngsters with accurate and sufficient knowledge concerning their own and other cultures in educational institutions is crucial for eradicating "myths and stereotypes" about minorities (population-wise) and other racial and ethnic groups in the country (Sachs & Poole, 1989).

Multicultural education "is the recognition and the appreciation of diversity within the teaching content of every discipline and in the context of the whole life of the school" (Department of Education, California, 1977, p. 1). It has been reasoned by Sizemore (1990) and others that " . . . the standard [United States] school curriculum simply does not present the complete facts of history, literature, art, music, drama, science, or other aspects of [United States'] diverse cultures" (p. 82). Sizemore further points out that a curriculum with a pluralistic perspective takes into consideration "all the groups in society and their need for freedom, equality, work, and peace" (Sizemore, 1990, p. 83). Developing curriculum with a multicultural perspective provides "all pupils with a more relevant and appropriate educational experience" (Troyna & Smith, 1983, p. 9). In the following section, the development of paradigm variations in the school physical education curriculum is focused upon with an emphasis on play, games, sports, and movement activities that are multicultural.

The four paradigmatic variations in curriculum discussed earlier have been accepted as viable ways to think about physical education in the United States. Two additional formulations are suggested to help curb problematic situations and discourses influencing our social and cultural milieu. These paradigmatic shifts in thinking are social reconstruction-based and culture-based paradigms, which, like the others, would permeate the curricula and the instructional plans developed by teachers in physical education. In these new conceptions of physical education, social issues and information about cultural groups would be infused into the physical education curriculum and pedagogy.

Physical Education from Social Reconstruction Perspective/Paradigm

A paradigm that requires incorporation into curriculum and instruction in physical education is that of social reconstruction. From this viewpoint, physical education addresses the unequal representation of people's cultural formulations of reality in educational institutions. Representation, as Eisner (1991) terms it, is a "codified" reality (p. 127), and the kind that educational institutions have put in place and legitimized is of an Anglo-centric type. In physical education, a codified reality can be seen in structured movement forms—games, sports (such as basketball), and folk and social dance emphasized in children's classes. The language, codes, and values embedded in physical education curriculum and instruction are of the dominant Anglo-centric culture. Examples include: (a) Competition-based curriculum and instruction in physical education. Essentially, the curriculum and the types of instruction that tend to be used in an activity-based program center on competition. Students are divided into formal teams at the beginning of a unit. The teacher acts as a teacher/coach, overseeing the tournaments. At the end of the unit, a team emerges as the winner of the tournament; (b) Dance-based movement forms. The language and codes used are derived from European dances such as folk and square dance and country-swing (ballroom dance). In part, such curricula continue to permeate United States public schools because students in teacher education are trained in content development and in ways of teaching that follow the social, normative, and economic assumptions of the culture in which they are found (Walters, 1987).

Curriculum and instruction derived from a social reconstruction perspective renders the "collective experiences and interests of a wide range of groups" (Banks, 1991, p. 138) a meaningful status in the United States schools. With a social reconstructionist perspective, physical education students learn to analyze the ways sports have developed and been taught in U.S. schools; they learn how many other cultural groups have been systematically excluded from attention in physical education. Specifically, children learn to play activities and games of other cultural groups in the United States. In addition, they learn the meanings associated with the play activities and games. The social reconstructionist perspective harbors ideals necessary for reforming "society towards a greater equity in race, class, gender, and handicap" (Grant & Sleeter, 1989, p. 54).

Varying movement possibilities and different types of equipment are needed to actualize a social reconstructionist physical education curriculum. The elements of dance, gymnastics, and games across cultures require physical educators to develop curricula and use instructional styles and strategies that meet the needs of all children. This is especially important because the United States' Western-oriented physical education curriculum has alienated children from outside the dominant culture. This alienation has taken several forms: (a) the games and sports children play at home are not part of the school physical education curriculum, (b) the concepts-based physical education curriculum does not use concepts outside the mainstream's cultural frameworks, (c) the teaching methods and strategies such as indirect teaching and an individually-based instructional strategy leave many children out of the teaching and learning situations.

Physical Education from Culture-based Paradigm/Perspective

Culturally-based themes should be included in the development of curriculum in physical education. If play activities and games are perceived to be "integral to our culture" and helping to "enhance the health and vitality of the culture" (Hellison & Templin, 1991, p. 99), then they should be multicultural because U.S. society is composed of many different cultures racially and ethnically. Indeed, the forms of knowledge selected for sharing with children should be culturally based.

Culture is responsible for shaping the way students view themselves and for shaping their relations to various pedagogies and learning (Giroux & Simon, 1988). In this context, it is paramount to pursue the teaching of students from varying perspectives and to consider content development that takes into account the many cultures of the United States. The lack of representation of different ethnic ideals in curriculum and instruction has been noted by Hargreaves (1986), who points out that there is a lack of opportunity for ethnic dance in the schools. Teachers tend to be of an Anglo-centric movement rationality in their teaching of dance. Further, teachers have complained that teaching dance activities to immigrant children from India has been quite difficult because the children tend to be very apprehensive of this type of curriculum; the teachers tend to label them as trouble makers (Hargreaves, 1986).

Given the problematic situations described above, it is paramount that the knowledge selected in the development of the curriculum should reflect the values and life experiences of all students, particularly from the perspectives of race, gender and class. Multicultural knowledge should be taught to students in all schools even though some schools may have a homogeneous student population (Travers & Rebore, 1987). Such knowledge ought to be derived from diverse ethnic sources so that the games played are multicultural (Chepyator-Thomson, 1990). Sources for different cultural information include periodicals, authentic textbooks, and personal communication with people from groups that are not represented in the mainstream United States.

Educators can enhance their knowledge of nonrepresented groups by subscribing to ethnic magazines and journals to acquaint themselves with these groups' social and cultural affiliations. This form of knowledge seeking is important because "curriculum along multicultural lines . . . is seen as crucial . . . in providing all pupils with a more relevant and appropriate educational experience" (Troyna & Smith, 1983, p. 9). Essentially, educators should ascertain that multicultural literature used in curriculum development includes experiences and perspectives from people of color.

Another source of information about students' culture and interests is the students themselves. Drawing on students' own conceptions of how games are organized and played as sources of useful knowledge for curriculum development validates the students' lives and enhances teachers' understanding of their racial, gender, and ethnic backgrounds. The development of a curriculum of this nature can promote pride in children of nondominant groups and respect for their culture in the dominant groups' children. For example, providing all students with relevant education means defining course content such that North American Indian values and customs and their contributions to play forms in the United States are included. Indeed, ". . . American Indians have something different that was bestowed upon [them] by the grace of God, such as [their] songs, tribal dances, arts and crafts, [their] religion, and games and stories" (Wesley, 1961, p. 7). One way of designing a curriculum from a North American Indian perspective is to invite parents to be part of the curricular development team (National Indian Brotherhood, 1984).

Frey and Allen's (1989) study of Alaskan and Indian groups' games has provided a beginning for development of a multicultural curriculum in physical education. The groups' traditional games were identified and were used in the construction of elementary school physical education curriculum in the Anchorage school district. The games were modified for safety and the developmental levels of the children. According to these authors, the games have provided "an enjoyable and efficient way to develop multicultural awareness in students and teachers" (Frey & Allen, 1989, p. 21). The Alaskan and Indian groups value cooperation and self-competition and emphasize "group cohesion, pain tolerance, and respect for environment as important as muscular strength, cardiorespiratory endurance, and speed" (p. 22). The traditional games of the groups reflect these values. The Alaskan and Indian groups' games require "great physical strength, agility, balance, endurance, and concentration" (Frey & Allen, 1989, p. 22). The paradigms of physical fitness, developmentally-based, humanistic physical education could be identified and are valued in such a curriculum.

Although there could be support for the authors' study of the Alaskan and Indian groups' games, there could also be disagreement on the way they have presented the games in relation to the development of the physical education curriculum. First, the idea that "importing traditional, yet unknown, physical activities from different cultures is an exciting way to add creativity and imagination to the physical education curriculum, without having to be creative or imaginative in the traditional sense," is problematic. Frey and Allen's statements seem to rest on the assumption that children do not have to be as creative or imaginative to play and dance these games as when they

FIGURE 15.1   Authentic way of understanding play and games in culture.

Description of the cultural group
Role of the game and play activity in the culture
Contexts in which the game and play activity occur
Description of the game or play activity
Meaning derived from the game or play activity
Comparative perspectives on the game and play activity

might traditionally be asked to be "creative." What should be brought to the forefront is the fact that the traditional dance steps taught in United States elementary school have been derived from European cultures and the children are asked to move "creatively" within this cultural framework. Children from other cultures can also move "creatively" within the Alaskan and Indian groups' cultural frameworks.

Second, Alaskan and Indian games have historically been present within these specific cultures, they were not "unknown," rather they were excluded from United States schools.

Third, Frey and Allen (1989) indicate that Alaskan and Indian groups have "hundreds of games," but only "those activities that have been favorably received by the students and teachers, with teaching hints as appropriate," were presented (p. 22). Although the authors may have thought that the students' and teachers' game preferences were the best way to determine the choice of games to be included in the curriculum, thematic identification of games to be used would have been more adequate as the curriculum developers and teachers would have been forced to identify from Alaskan and Indian groups' perspectives the themes that characterize the games. One helpful way to understand games in culture is to use the information in Figure 15.1.

The paradigm possibilities for reforming the school physical education curriculum have been discussed with a multicultural orientation. Physical education teachers need to develop a multicultural curriculum by researching the literature for play activities and games that are characteristic of diverse groups in U. S. society. This curriculum focus has been perceived to be necessary for a curriculum and its implementation to be inclusive of all students in our educational institutions. In developing a multicultural physical education curriculum, teachers are cautioned that books, texts, or periodical articles on minority groups (population-wise) such as African Americans or North American Indians may either be lacking or inadequate. Therefore, teachers are encouraged to use a variety of sources in developing multicultural games or play activities for teaching physical education in schools.

✢ Implications for Reform in Teacher Education: Curriculum Development and Implementation

Curriculum Development

Physical education curriculum ought to be reformed with multicultural concepts. Trent (1990, p. 360) has argued for the inclusion of "scholarship on race and ethnicity as a core part of the preparation of the nation's teachers" and provides three compelling reasons for this: (a) that the student body is becoming more diverse, (b) that the economic future of the nation depends on meeting the educational needs of this diverse population, and (c) that the teaching force is becoming increasingly more female and more White. For example, Trent mentions a recent national survey that indicates that teachers' competency with Blacks and other people of color is limited due to their "inadequate undergraduate exposure to course content familiarizing them with the experiences of minorities and limited cross-race contact or multicultural experiences in or out of school . . ." (p. 366). In fact, in Delpit's (1995) study, it was indicated that a Native Alaskan teacher said that in teacher education courses, she only learned how to teach White kids [and] learned not one thing about teaching Native kids (p. 197). In general, teachers appear not to comprehend, appreciate, or value differences in students (Rakow & Bermudez, 1993). This trend must be changed, especially in institutions of higher education. Curriculum development must include changes in courses of instruction. For instance, there could be the creation of a "multi-disciplinary course" built around the theme of "understanding ethnic and racial minorities" both in terms of sport activities and cultural practices. The course may encompass issues of gender and class and should reflect the experiences and points of view of people of color as well as the majority perspective in its content. A coordinator and a faculty committee could organize the course. The course could be made up of a series of lectures offered by the best scholars and teachers from the university and elsewhere. The specific aim of this kind of course is to give students a comprehensive knowledge of cultural differences and issues of cultural understanding.

Another way of reforming the curriculum in physical education is to have educators identify play activities and games of their own cultural backgrounds and then conduct a comparative examination of other cultures for similarities and differences (Fig. 15.1). This will assist educators in selecting classroom content that is multicultural; they would be able to conceptualize a curriculum that reflects the diverse clientele in public school systems and teach prospective teachers accordingly.

Having access to diverse ethnic populations is another important concept in reforming the physical education curriculum. Educators in colleges and universities should be exposed to diverse ethnic populations and they should also try to provide prospective teachers with experiences associated with a diverse student body. Further, educators could join multicultural clubs and attend multicultural seminars, concerts, and plays to comprehend other people's forms of culture. For example, attending performances by African American dance groups such as *Les Ballet Africains,* or by American Indian Dance Performers, or by Hispanic American Dance Performers can help teachers view and begin to understand diverse cultures. Knowledge gained from these types of experiences could be used to design relevant curriculum and this would answer the most asked question: "What knowledge is of most worth in curriculum development?" Further, educators could try to "converse with a variety of persons from diverse [cultural] backgrounds to gain appreciation and knowledge of the importance of culture" (Smith, 1991, p. 41).

Teacher Preparation-Pedagogy

Teachers' pedagogical practices are closely related to their individual experiences in education (Guskey, 1986). Indeed, teachers tend to teach students in the same way that they were taught. With this understanding, it is critical to take into consideration that "teachers' ideological beliefs are related, directly or indirectly, to their instructional planning and decision making" (Rich, 1990, p. 82) in physical education classroom or gymnasium settings. The adequacy of instructional plans may be determined in several ways: (a) by examining teachers' values and beliefs, (b) by identifying effective ways to teach students, (c) by finding ways to deal with students positively, and (d) by learning foreign languages.

Teachers' Values and Beliefs   Our sense of self is grounded in our values and beliefs. The values and beliefs that teachers and prospective teachers hold about themselves frame their subject matter knowledge and the practical applications of this knowledge. If we understand the values and beliefs that teachers hold about students and the curriculum, we can discern the extent to which pedagogical knowledge of teachers, as seen in instructional plans, fosters educational knowledge in students. This is critical because the beliefs of teachers and the values that they hold play an important role in their teaching plans (Green, 1986). Thus, teachers need to examine their beliefs and values in relation to curriculum content knowledge presented to children in schools.

Values play an important part in teachers' development of physical activity programs in physical education. Teachers have personal values about physical activity (Hellison & Templin, 1991, p. 44), and these values influence not only teacher-student interactions but also the way the teachers teach. Hellison and Templin (1991) have argued that we want teachers to "get in touch with their motives and values and then examine them to determine whether they hold up under scrutiny and particularly whether they are relevant for [students]" (p. 44). Essentially, teachers and prospective teachers in physical education ought to clarify their beliefs through the develoment of their personal philosophies and to review these periodically as they gain experience and knowledge about the subject matter (Schurr, 1980, p. 31). Teachers also need to take into account that their cultural frames of reference influence the way they teach. It is important to note that children come with their own cultural frames which must be considered in curriculum implementation as they may be in conflict with the teachers' cultural frames.

Given the multicultural orientation vision in physical education, the content of instruction in teacher education ought to acknowledge student experiential differences and the programs should be "the knowledge and experience necessary to enable teachers to envision and implement a model of excellence to which all students are entitled" (Trent, 1990, p. 364). This is a needed critical change in physical education because teacher preparation as currently conducted in some sections of the country does not prepare teachers to teach the diversified student population of the near future, the 21st century.

Apparently, teacher educators have given meager attention to what teacher education curricula and preparation ought to include, and in addition, they have not studied the educational institutions for which teachers are prepared to be full-fledged participants (Beyer & Zeichner, 1982). The literature suggests that radical changes need to be undertaken in not only the institutions of higher education but also in private and public schools in this country for programs in physical education to become truly multicultural.

Such radical changes include developing a multicultural teacher education program in which the focus is on helping "teachers to function effectively with pupils in a culturally diverse society" (Hilliard, 1974, p. 41) and devising different and inclusive strategies for teaching. Multicultural teacher preparation would help prospective teachers improve their teaching of school subjects by cultivating in them appropriate attitudes and cultural experiences that are currently accepted in the society and by helping them to incorporate and structure pedagogical content knowledge to enhance students' learning. As pointed out by Craft (1984), ". . . by learning more about and paying greater respect to minority cultures . . . and by learning more about the varied origins of the majority culture, we are in fact cultivating an intelligent appreciation of diversity" (p. 21). Besides, as Trent (1990) states, "prospective teachers need to understand why the school classroom composition they envisioned is less likely to be available to them now or throughout their careers in teaching" (p. 364).

Effective Teaching   Teachers need to be effective communicators of knowledge in physical education classrooms. In addition, they need to have "detailed knowledge of the perceptions children have of themselves and of the society" (Hannan, 1982, p. 82). Indeed, teachers should be able to comprehend the interests and cultural background of students in order for them to structure desired learning environments. Teaching strategies should include all students. In this context, teacher preparation should focus on unearthing the teachers' incongruencies in teaching physical education and then encouraging them to develop instructional strategies that promote excellence in physical education settings. One instructional strategy is cooperative learning. This strategy, as described by Rich (1990), "remains an instructional strategy seldom used in a systematic manner over the course of a school year or more" (p. 83). Another instructional strategy is what Schoem and Stevenson (1990) term "face-to-face dialogue" (p. 579). Given that face-to-face dialogue involves the teachers' discourse—the outcome of what is spoken interwoven with facial expressions—the extent to which it coincides with students' discourse is important. Teacher educators should pay close attention to this strategy as it provides students with opportunities to "focus on their own communication skills in a setting with different groups and people with different backgrounds and different perspectives" (Schoem & Stevenson, 1990, p. 583).

Teachers need to maintain an environment in which all students see themselves in positive ways in class presentations and activities such as games. This involves structuring activities in creative ways and teaching these to students in ways that enhance their learning, particularly in motor skill development. Essentially, teachers need to promote the academic achievement of all students by responding to their individual needs—regardless of their race, gender, class, or language backgrounds. Teachers need to maintain high and consistent expectations for all students and should diversify their teaching techniques and use cooperative learning techniques when applicable.

Parent-Teacher Relationships: Searching for Effective Discipline Methods   Disciplinary problems are bound to occur in the course of physical education class sessions. In this context, educators may look for effective means of disciplining students by developing a positive working relationship with parents. This is very important because the method of discipline of different groups has often conflicted with that of schools. According to Parmee (1968), for example, Anglo teachers and school officials have not been aware of Apache disciplinary methods, resulting in their use of methods alien to Apache students—shaming the student sometimes in front of his/her classmates and leaving him/her to be laughed at and disapproved by non-Indian peers. In this frame of reference, teachers need to develop, with parents, effective ways of preventing students from deviating from classroom norms and have clear and consistent guidelines for student behavior and interpersonal relationships. Acquiring this kind of information requires a physical education teacher and her/his peers who are regular classroom teachers to visit parents of different cultures and socioeconomic backgrounds in their homes, both to encourage participation as volunteers in physical education classes, and to acquire information about their children and to gather their input about the kind of physical education education program they desire for their children. Teachers ought to acknowledge family differences by carefully considering family situations and by examining the level of involvement possible for parents. An additional way of promoting parent-teacher relationship is to maintain an "open-door" policy regarding parents' visits.

Foreign Language Competency: Searching for Diversity in Communication   All educators ought to be able to speak proficiently in a language other than their own. This perspective has recently been considered in New York State. Beginning in 1993, physical education departments will require new teachers to take a foreign language class to meet graduation requirements. Requiring prospective teachers to have proficiency in a foreign language is important because teachers will then be able to communicate more effectively with students; they will get to know students better as individuals, accept their unique perspectives and their ethnic dialects and mannerisms, and learn verbal and nonverbal communication patterns (Murray, 1991). Further, teachers could model an appreciation for diversity in the words and actions they use in class instructions.

To conclude this section, several ways of augmenting curricular content and implementing curricular goals and objectives in physical education have been discussed. Curricular reform involves: the identification of one's philosophical perspective in terms of values and beliefs; possession of cross-cultural knowledge; conversation with people from diverse backgrounds; and use of students' conceptions of life configurations as classroom content. Restructuring operational plans for curriculum involves the use of effective teaching strategies, conversing in more than one language, and effective disciplinary methods in classroom teaching.

✥ Conclusion

Human movement, with its intimate connections with cultural and social associations, has been the basis for the subject matter taught in physical education. However, the actualizations of this subject matter, as currently exercised in public schools, do not use multicultural games or play activities, discuss issues from varying perspectives, or teach so as to permit the inclusion of diverse groups of learners; hence the provision of visionary perspectives for paradigm curriculum variations, curriculum development and implementation, and for reform in teacher education. Knowledge selection for curriculum development and implementation should use diverse sources and the content emphasis should change accordingly to reflect political, social, and economic changes in society. Further, the knowledge selected for implementation ought to accommodate students from different social and cultural backgrounds.

Teacher education curricula need to be developed with a view toward equipping students with pedagogical knowledge and content-related (subject matter) knowledge to carry out their teaching functions in a multicultural society like the United States. Perhaps the greatest point to be raised in this chapter is that teacher education programs ought to, in some way, ascertain that the graduates produced possess distinctive abilities and outstanding qualities to function multiculturally in the society at large.

Physical education has a special function; it has to contribute to desirable social changes by developing critical perspectives about society in teachers, and by helping them acquire multicultural competences in order to navigate adequately their life configurations in the gymnasium and to respect student diversity fully. For all these desirable accomplishements in physical education, and for us to live together "happily ever after," we must know that "what has been . . . is intimately bound up with what might be: our vision of the future, of diverse possibilities of life and human potential has roots in our experience of the past" (Ngugi wa Thiongo, 1986, p. 39). Physical education should be inclusive of all student backgrounds, particularly in relation to their cultural lives.

References

Auxter, D. (1973). A philosophy of developmental physical education. In R. A. Cobb and P. M. Lepley (Eds.), *Contemporary philosophies of physical education and athletics* (p. 59). Columbus, OH: Charles E. Merrill.

Banks, J. A. (Spring, 1991). Multicultural literacy and curriculum reform. *Educational Horizons, 69*(3), 135-140.

Barney, R. B. (1975). German Turners in America: Their role in nineteenth century expression and physical education legislation. In E. F. Zeigler (Ed.), *A history of physical education and sport in the United States and Canada.* Champaign, IL: Stripes.

Beyer, L., & Zeichner, K. (1982). Teacher training and educational foundations: A plea for discontent. *Journal of Teacher Education, 33*(3), 18-23.

Chepyator-Thomson, J. R. (1990). Traditional games of Keiyo children: A comparison of pre- and post-independent periods in Kenya. *Interchange, 21*(2), 15-25.

Craft, M. (1984). (Ed.). *Education and cultural pluralism.* London: Falmer.

Dauer, V. P., & Pangrazi, R. P. (1975). *Dynamic physical education for elementary school children.* Minneapolis, MN: Burgess.

Delpit, L. (1995). *Cultural conflict in the classroom.* New York: The New Press.

Department of Education, California. (1977). *Bureau of intergroup relations.* Sacramento: Bureau of Publications.

Dixon, M. (September/October, 1984). Participation in physical activity: Option or privilege? *CAHPER Journal, 51*(1), 13-17.

Eisner, E. W. (Spring, 1991). Rethinking literacy. *Educational Horizons, 69*(3), 120-128.

Ennis, C. D., & Chepyator-Thomson, J. R. (1991). Learning characteristics of field-dependent children within an analytical concept-based curriculum. *Journal of Teaching in Physical Education, 10*(2), 170-187.

Frey, R. D., & Allen, M. (1989). Alaskan native games—A cross-cultural addition to the physical education curriculum. *Journal of Physical Education, Recreation and Dance, 60*(9), 21-24.

Gablik, S. (1991). *The re-enchantment of art.* New York: Ballantine.

Gage, N. L. (Ed.), (1963). *Handbook of research on teaching.* Chicago: Rand McNally.

Geadelmann, P. L., Bischoff, J., Hoferek, M., & Mcknight, D. B. (1989). Sex equity in physical education and athletics. In S. M. Klein (Ed.), *Handbook for achieving sex equity through education* (pp. 319-337). Baltimore: Johns Hopkins University Press.

Giroux, H. A., & Simon, R. C. (1988). Schooling, popular culture, and a pedagogy of possibility. *Journal of Education, 170*(1), 9-26.

Graham, G., Holt/Hale, S. A., & Parker, M. (1998). *Children moving.* Mountain View, CA: Mayfield.

Grant, C., & Sleeter, C. E. (1989). Race, class, gender, exceptionality, and educational reform. In J. A. Banks & C. A. Banks (Eds.), *Multicultural education: Issues and perspectives* (pp. 46-65). Boston: Allyn & Bacon.

Green, M. (1986). Philosophy and teaching. In M. C. Wittrock (Ed.), *Handbook of research on teaching* (pp. 479-504). New York: Macmillan.

Griffin, P. S. (1985). Teaching in an urban, multiracial physical education program. *Quest, 37,* 154-165.

Grueninger, R. W. (1992). Physical education. In J. Reyhner (Ed.), *Teaching American Indian students* (pp. 251–264). Norman: University of Oklahoma Press.

Guskey, T. (1986). Staff development and the process of teacher change. *Educational Researcher, 15*(5), 5–12.

Hannan, B. (1982). The multicultural school or schools in search of their culture. In G. Dow (Ed.), *Teacher learning* (pp. 79–110). London, UK: Routledge & Kegan Paul.

Hargreaves, J. (1986). *Sport, power, and culture.* New York: St. Martin's Press.

Hellison, D. R. (1985). *Goals and strategies for teaching physical education.* Champaign, IL: Human Kinetics.

Hellison, D. R., & Templin, T. J. (1991). *A reflective approach to teaching physical education.* Champaign, IL: Human Kinetics.

Hilliard, A. (1974). Restructuring teacher education for multicultural imperatives. In W. Hunter (Ed.), *Multicultural education* (pp. 40–55). Washington, DC: Association of Colleges for Teacher Education.

Hoffman, H. A., Young, J., & Klesius, S. E. (1985). *Meaningful movement for children. A developmental theme approach to physical education.* Dubuque, IA: Kendall/Hunt

Hyland, C. R. (1989). What we know about the fastest growing minority population: Hispanic Americans. *Educational Horizons, 67*(4), 131–135.

Jewett, A. E., & Bain, L. L. (1985). *The curriculum process in physical education.* Dubuque, IA: WM. C. Brown.

Kirchner, G., Cunningham, J., & Warrell, E. (1978). *Introduction to movement education.* Dubuque, IA: WM. C. Brown.

Kirchner, G., & Fishburne, G. J. (1998). *Physical education for elementary school children.* Boston, MA: McGraw-Hill.

Kruger, H., & Kruger, J. M. (1982). *Movement education in physical education.* Dubuque, IA: WM. C. Brown.

Locke, L. F. (1969). Movement education—a description and critique. In R. C. Brown, Jr., & B. J. Cratty (Eds.), *New perspectives of man in action.* Upper Saddle River, NJ: Prentice-Hall.

McNeil, J. D. (1985). *Curriculum: A comprehensive introduction.* Boston, MA: Allyn & Bacon.

Melograno, V. J. (1996). *Designing the physical education curriculum.* Champaign, IL: Human Kinetics.

Murray, M. (1991). Media impact on women in sport and sport leadership. *Journal of Physical Education, Recreation & Dance, 62* (3), 45–47.

National Indian Brotherhood. (1984). Indian control of education. In J. R. Mallea & J. C. Young (Eds.), *Cultural diversity and Canadian education. Issues and innovation* (pp. 131–149). Ottawa, Canada: Carleton Press.

Ngugi wa Thiongo. (1986). *Homecoming.* London: Heinemann.

Nichols, B. (1994). *Moving and learning. The elementary school physical education experience.* St. Louis: Mosby.

Nixon, J. E., Flanagan, L., & Frederickson, F. S. (1964). *An introduction to physical education.* Philadelphia: Saunders.

Pangrazi, R. P. (1996). *Dynamic physical education for elementary school.* Boston: Allyn & Bacon.

Parmee, E. A. (1968). *Formal education and culture change.* Tuscon: The University of Arizona Press.

Ragan, W. B., & Shepard, G. D. (1977). *Modern elementary curriculum.* New York: Holt, Rinehart & Winston.

Rakow, S. J., & Bermudez, A. B. (1993). "Science is ciencia." Meeting the needs of Hispanic American students. *Science Education, 6*(77), 669–683.

Rice, E. A., Hutchinson, J. L., & Lee, M. (1969). *A brief history of physical education.* New York: Ronald Press.

Rich, Y. (1990). Ideological impediments to instructional innovation: The case of cooperative learning. *Teaching & Teacher Education, 6*(1), 81–91.

Sachs, M., & Abraham, A. (1979). Playground basketball: A qualitative field examination. *Journal of Sports Behaviour, 2*(1), 27–36.

Sachs, J. M., & Poole, M. E. (1989). Multicultural education policies in Australia and Britain: Social transformation or status quo? *Education and Society, 71*(1), 9–19.

Schoem, D., & Stevenson, M. (1990). Teaching ethnic identity and intergroup relations: The case of Black-Jewish dialogue. *Teachers College Record, 91*(4), 579–594.

Schurr, E. L. (1980). *Movement experiences for children. A humanistic approach to elementary school physical education.* Upper Saddle River, NJ: Prentice-Hall.

Siedentop, D., Herkowitz, J., & Rink, J. (1984). *Elementary physical education.* Upper Saddle River, NJ: Prentice-Hall.

Sizemore, B. A. (1990). The politics of curriculum, race, and class. *Journal of Negro Education, 59*(1), 77-85.

Smith, Y. R. (1991). Issues and strategies for working with multicultural athletes. *Journal of Physical Education, Recreation & dance, 62*(3), 39-44.

Travers, P., & Rebore, R. (1987). *Foundations of education. Becoming a teacher.* Upper Saddle River, NJ: Prentice-Hall.

Trent, W. (1990). Race and ethnicity in the teacher education curriculum. *Teachers College Record, 91*(3), 361-369.

Troyna, B., & Smith, D. T. (Eds.). (1983). *Racism, school and the labour market.* Leicester, England: AB Printers.

Ullmann, L. (1968). *Modern educational dance.* New York: Praeger.

U.S. Department of Health and Human Services. (1996). *Physical activity and health: A report of the Surgeon General.* Atlanta, GA: U.S. Department of Health and Human Services, Centers for the Disease Control, National Center for Chronic Disease Prevention and Health Promotion.

Van Dalen, D. B., & Bennett, B. C. (1971). *A world history of physical education* (2nd ed.). Upper Saddle River, NJ: Prentice-Hall.

Van Dalen, D. B., Mitchell, E. D., & Bennett, B. C. (1953). *A world history of physical education.* Upper Saddle River, NJ: Prentice-Hall.

Walters, K. S. (1987). Critical thinking in teacher education: Towards a demythologization. *Journal of Teacher Education, 30*(3) 14-19.

Wesley, C. (1961). Indian education. *Journal of Indian Education, 1*(1), 4-7.

Wiles, J., & Bondi, J. C. (1984). *Curriculum development.* Columbus, OH: Charles E. Merrill.

Zeigler, E. F. (1988). *History of physical education and sport.* Champaign, IL: Stipes.

Integrating Diversity and Multiculturalism in Health Education

Veronica M. Acosta-Deprez
California State University, Long Beach

Health is a fundamental concern that transcends all cultures and peoples. It is every human being's desire to feel well and live long. Health affects one's way of looking at the world, the ability to laugh or cry, and the capacity to live and learn. The National Education Association Commission made health the top priority in its list of Seven Cardinal Principles of Education (1976) when they recognized its crucial influence on learning.

Health education is a special field that deals with information that students can integrate and relate to their own lives. Health education involves opportunities and ". . . learning experiences designed to assist individuals, groups, or communities . . . in control of their own health as they define it" (American Public Health Education, 1987). In this respect, it is essential for health educators to find out what views the individuals whom they teach have about health, and to integrate these into their teachings.

Views about health are often influenced by many factors, an important one of which is the culture with which the individual grew up. According to MacDonald (1988), cultural beliefs and practices influence health seeking, health maintenance, and patterns of coping with illness. *Culture* is defined by Wurzel (1988) as the information a group uses to create the meaning necessary for its members to survive as a group. In interacting with their environment, a group establishes rules or guidelines that include preferred ways of perceiving, judging, and organizing ideas, situations, and events. Culture represents these rules or guidelines (Maehr, 1974).

The relationship of culture to health has been widely documented in the health and social science fields. Kelleher and Hillier (1996) offered a range of accounts of how people of diverse ethnic and minority groups view and manage their illness in their book *Researching Cultural Differences in Health.* One of the most widely used theoretical models in health education practice, the Health Belief Model (Greene & Simons-Morton, 1984), postulated that cultural beliefs and practices influence children's perceptions. Four health belief categories are usually examined in terms of the ways in which these influence health behaviors. They are: (1) seriousness of a disease, (2) susceptibility to the disease, (3) benefits and costs, and (4) barriers to taking preventive action. In an earlier study, Stone and Crouch (1979) investigated children's perceptions about health and illness and concluded that children from different cultural and ethnic groups have different orientations to health and illness and, therefore, vary in their perceptions about their vulnerability to health problems. Anglo, Hispanic, and American Indian students were asked to rank the 14 health problems they perceived as "most likely to occur." The answers varied among the three groups. Anglo students ranked upset stomach, headache, and colds at the top of the list, in that order. Hispanic students ranked headache, upset stomach, and colds; while American Indian students ranked sore throat, headache, and colds to be the problems most likely to occur.

It is imperative that health educators integrate cultural elements into their teaching; health education needs to be tailored to the individual's culture. In this chapter, the relationship of culture and health is examined, and a rationale for integrating multicultural concepts into health education is provided. Some challenges in dealing with teaching from a multicultural perspective are described. Additionally, approaches to multicultural health education will be explored, including some perspectives and teaching guidelines.

❖ The Need for Multicultural Health Education

A multicultural approach to health education is necessary for several reasons. First, it enhances instruction and renders it more successful and effective. Second, tailoring information to the culture of students allows them to understand and apply what is being taught to their own lives. Students whose cultural beliefs and practices are consistent with what is taught will more likely adopt health teachers' recommendations. Third, if teachers are aware of students' perceptions regarding their health behaviors and health problems, they are more able to cultivate disease prevention strategies that are consistent with students' beliefs. Fourth, such awareness enables teachers to set up school health services that respond to their students' needs.

Perhaps the most important reason for using a multicultural approach is that health education presents a venue through which the health status of many disadvantaged populations may be improved (Purnell & Paulanka, 1998). Through health education, important information on prevention and treatment that targets at the needs of particular disadvantaged population groups may be disseminated.

One of the three broad goals of Healthy People 2000 (Department of Health and Human Services, 1992) is to reduce disparities in health status among population groups. Obviously, there is great disparity between those who are healthy and those who are not. Often, those who are disadvantaged in one form or another suffer from ill health. Many factors that influence disease or lower health status are traced to physical make up (e.g., genetic predisposition), which is beyond an individual's control. However, risk for disease is unfortunately heightened by factors that are within the individual's and/or society's control. Factors such as low income or poverty, discrimination in relation to race, ethnicity, religion, age or gender, and legislative policies that cater more to advantaged than to disadvantaged populations are examples of the latter. To further illustrate this point, three groups are described here as examples: people with low incomes, certain race or ethnic minority groups, and people with disabilities.

People with Low Income

There is great disparity between the health of the poor and those with higher incomes (Department of Health and Human Services, 1992, p.29). Across the age spectrum, there are twice as many deaths below the poverty level than above it (Amler & Dull, 1987). The risk of death from heart disease is more than 25% higher for low-income people than for the overall population (National Heart, Lung, & Blood Institute, National Cholesterol Education Program, 1990). Poverty has also been associated with infant mortality, and the likelihood of poor pregnancy outcomes such as low birth weight, prematurity, birth defects, and infant death (Institute of Medicine, 1985). Poverty is also linked with high chronic disease incidence, increased vulnerability to risk factors linked to injury and disease such as obesity and high blood pressure, and tobacco use (Feigelman & Gorman, 1989; Office on Smoking and Health, 1987). Significant developmental limitations such as lack of growth and mental retardation have also been linked to poverty (National Health Interview Survey, 1988).

It is important to note that although several studies have suggested a high prevalence of medical- and social-related problems in specific racial or ethnic groups (Furstenberg, 1987; Hopkins, 1987) which are attributed to socioeconomic conditions, "when socioeconomic effects are set aside, disparities experienced by these population groups will still be observed" (Department of Health and Human Services, 1992, p. 32). This means that differences in health status may not be solely linked to poverty, environmental factors, or educational attainment, but to the existence of a combination of factors which place groups in high-risk disease categories.

Racial or Ethnic Groups

Some racial or ethnic groups have suffered disparities in health status compared with the majority population. Many environmental as well as socioeconomic elements push a particular racial and ethnic group to become vulnerable to health problems and disease (Heckler, 1985a, 1985b). African Americans and Hispanics have increased rates of infant mortality. Racial and ethnic groups who live in urban or highly industrialized areas rather than in rural or less-industrialized areas are at high risk for acquiring stress-related ailments. Foods that are high in fat, sugar, and sodium, as well as dietary patterns that characterize certain American diets, may also increase the incidence of malnutrition among racial or ethnic groups living in areas where these diets are prevalent.

Discrimination and inadequate treatment by the current health care system contributes to poor health among a variety of racial and ethnic groups. For example, with the newly enacted Welfare Reform law, many immigrants do not receive the same benefits as non-immigrants from the current health care system, if at all. Other racial and ethnic groups who experience conditions traced to their genetic and physical makeup may not be receiving the care they need. For example, thalassemia and sickle-cell anemia, blood disorders that are more prevalent among people of Mediterranean and African descent, are rare, and health care professionals may not have had the training to deal with these problems. This leads to misdiagnosis or to inadequate or inappropriate provision of treatment.

People with Disabilities

The number of people with chronic disabilities varies from 34 million to 43 million (Department of Health and Human Services, 1992). People with disabilities are represented in all racial, ethnic, age, and gender groups. *Disability* may be defined as a functional limitation which may be in one or more of the following categories: mental/emotional, physical, motor, or sensory. For example, physical disabilities may include an inability to walk resulting from a congenital birth defect, an injury, or leg amputation stemming from an accident. Mental disabilities may include mild to severe degrees of retardation. Emotional disabilities may result from negative environmental and societal conditions such as child abuse, alcohol or drug abuse, and sexual abuse.

People with disabilities are more susceptible to secondary conditions that occur in relation to the main cause of disability. "People with disabilities are at higher risk of future problems that can only increase the limitations they experience" (Department of Health and Human Services, 1992, p.39). Secondary health problems due to lack of adequate rehabilitation, personal assistance, and maintenance therapies, inconsistencies and inequities in existing programs, and lack of insurance are more likely to occur among people with disabilities. Negative family or cultural attitudes may also increase health risks of some people with disabilities

While there is no single solution to the health problems of all students, it is the responsibility of teachers to address as many needs as possible and help all students achieve the highest level of wellness. Teachers can help students think constructively about their health and behaviors and also assist in reconstructing students' environments so that these support and fulfill their needs.

To serve the needs of all Americans, the cultural diversity and richness of this country needs to be acknowledged and incorporated into the present curriculum. "A society as rich in cultural diversity as the United States does students disservice when its educational curriculum is primarily monolithic" (Airhihenbuwa & Pineiro, 1988). A multicultural society in which the desire to "melt" everyone into some stereotypical American image will, at best, serve only a minority elite.

The next section describes prevailing personal as well as professional ethnocentrism among teachers, and potential conflicts that may arise when the teacher's culture clashes with that of the student.

✤ Ethnocentrism and Potential Cultural Conflicts

Teachers often exhibit a degree of personal or professional "ethnocentrism"—a universal pride in one's ethnic or cultural group—which prevents them from presenting unbiased and unprejudiced cultural and ethnic viewpoints. When ethnocentrism is brought into the classroom, cultural conflicts that are detrimental to effective teaching and learning may arise. Additionally, many health topics are morally laden and controversial in nature and cannot be fully explored if teacher bias and prejudice predominate.

Health teachers and health care professionals need to understand that the profession within which they function adheres to one of many cultures of health (Purnell & Paulanka, 1998). This health culture, grounded in the tenets of scientific medicine, attributes the cause of disease to such agents as bacteria, viruses, and chemicals, and uses disease terms such as *pneumonia, influenza,* or *AIDS* to identify the illness. Only those certified by their particular "science-based" profession are sanctioned to intervene and treat diseases and illnesses. Through their teaching and work, health teachers transmit their culture of health to students. Other ways of healing than those that have been "scientifically proven," other types of healers than those who have been certified within the laws of the Western-based medical profession, or other types of health knowledge are not usually recognized or accepted. As such, a sense of cultural ethnocentrism is displayed in the health education profession.

Some students' health cultures are similar to the teacher's. However, many may have different cultures. For example, some health cultures may use terms such as *spirit possession, spells,* and *soul loss* to designate disease cause. They may attribute the cause of disease to another person and not to a pathogen or microorganism. They may sanction spirits, faith healers, or psychic surgeons to intervene in the treatment of disease.

Religious teachings and ethnic beliefs may often conflict with numerous health education tenets.[1] For example, Galli, Greenberg, and Tobin (1987) examined the religious observances of some sects of Orthodox Judaism and found that many of its precepts were incongruent with what is taught in schools, particularly in health education. Topics in the content areas of human sexuality, nutrition, drug education, and death and dying were explored.

Under Jewish Divine Law, as interpreted by some followers of Judaism, it is a man's obligation to "be fruitful and multiply" (Genesis 1:28). It is every man's responsibility to father at least a son and a daughter. Family planning and contraceptive education topics pose contradictions to this law. Several other sex education topics that might conflict with Jewish beliefs include prohibition of male sterilization, vasectomy, induced abortion (except when the mother's life is in danger), artificial insemination (may be done only with the husband's sperm), and homosexuality. In health education, these topics are commonly discussed, dealt with, and provided as viable health options.

Nutrition education is another example where potential conflicts may occur. Various groups within Judaism treat food taboos differently. For example, some interpretations of Jewish law prohibit the ingestion of blood in meats and therefore require that meat be salted and certified kosher. Milk should not be consumed with meat, meat and dairy products should be cooked in separate containers, served in separate plates, and eaten with separate utensils. However, in educating about nutrition, many teachers inform students that certain health practices (i.e., lowering the intake of salt) are good for people. Such teaching pays little or no attention to traditions involving foods, including how they are prepared and served.

Other common health education topics may yield to educational conflict. For example, several topics concerning death and dying, which are commonly discussed and presented as options by health educators, are prohibited by some Jewish beliefs. These topics include euthanasia, suicide, the Living Will, and organ transplants. Teaching about refraining from smoking tobacco may not be seen as advantageous, as some rabbis use tobacco because they believe this is one of God's gifts (Jacobs, 1973).

Some beliefs and values among Hispanic, Indochinese, and Christian Science students may also conflict with health education information. For example, some Hispanics believe in "machismo," which emphasizes the fathering role of males—the more children one fathers, the more "manly" he becomes (Galli, Greenberg, & Tobin 1987; Russell, 1983). A health teacher who discusses contraceptive and family planning education concepts with Hispanic students may find that their teachings contradict the "machismo" belief.

Among some Indochinese, coining disease areas of the skin by scraping the skin to the point of bruising is done as the traditional healing practice of "cao gio." Health educators unfamiliar with this practice may construe the bruises as marks of child abuse and report it to the authorities. This may put health educators in embarrassing and potentially damaging situations.

Many families adhering to the precepts of Christian Science do not believe in the use of medical drugs or treatments such as immunizations, therapeutic procedures, and hospitalization. Yet, these elements and procedures are usually discussed, recommended, and accepted as common practice in health education classrooms.

To implement multicultural health education is to encourage the exploration of alternative ideas of health and illness with students and to provide them with opportunities to explore, critique, and analyze the dominant fundamental assumptions underlying the field of health education. In the following section, a definition of health education that is multicultural and social reconstructionist is provided, and some perceptions and guidelines on how to integrate multicultural concepts into health education are explored.

✤ Health Education That Is Multicultural and Social Reconstructionist

Multicultural health education involves developing and cultivating learning opportunities that are sensitive to the cultural values, attitudes, and beliefs of particular groups. These learning opportunities are designed and developed with the active involvement of the members of the target group, taking into account the group's definition of health, and communicated in ways that are consistent with their level of understanding. Multicultural and social reconstructionist health education extends beyond education to include approaches that teach students to become critical thinkers and cultivate social action skills that enable them to actively participate in and control their own health and destiny (Grant & Sleeter, 1989).

Teachers may think it difficult and even impossible to know everything about a culture, let alone know several cultures. The heterogeneous nature of racial and ethnic groups makes it difficult to compare their health attitudes and behaviors even within their own groups (Pahnos, 1992). Diverse attitudes and behaviors can be found among and within cultures and their individual members. How can teachers fulfill their tremendous teaching tasks and responsibilities, while simultaneously incorporating cultural, ethnic, religious, and social differences, concerns, and issues? The following section provides some perspectives and guidelines to help health teachers integrate multicultural and social reconstructionist principles into their teaching.

Teaching Perspectives and Guidelines

The challenge of incorporating multicultural health education is long overdue. If teachers are to respond to the health problems and needs of various cultural, ethnic, and religious groups, the best programs will promote health through the education of all these groups. In the following paragraphs, perceptions and guidelines are provided for teachers in the following areas: (1) reexamination of their educational philosophies; (2) integration of global and international education; (3) implementation of various teaching approaches, methods, and strategies; (4) recognition of students as our best resource; (5) involvement of parents and other family members in planning health education programs; (6) selection of instructional materials relevant to the target group; and (7) participation in planning and development of health materials and programs.

1. *Reexamining and renewing educational philosophies.*

The success of multicultural health education begins with the reexamination and renewal of teachers' educational philosophies (Pahnos, 1992). Teachers need to reflect on their own teachings; the ideology upon which their profession is based; their biases, prejudices, and ethnocentric conceptions about health; their roles and responsibilities as health educators; and their commitment to helping students achieve higher levels of health and wellness. Because cultural awareness and sensitivity are essential to successful teaching, multicultural health education should not only be added to the curriculum but also integrated into all other areas of teaching (Pahnos, 1992).

Teachers should exhibit a more open view about health as well as about their students and must accept the differences that exist in their culturally diverse classrooms. To do this, teachers may need to develop and practice personal characteristics and qualities that reflect this acceptance. These might include showing respect for students; being tolerant of different views and behaviors; avoiding statements that express bias, prejudice, or judgment; and displaying sincerity, understanding, sensitivity, and compassion for all students. Teachers need to develop positive verbal as well as nonverbal communication skills such as being able to clarify and listen intently to students' views, show interest in students' activities, provide words of encouragement, and accept a wide variety of responses as appropriate.

2. *Teaching multicultural education in the context of global or international education.*

Kalantzis and Cope (1992) offer a perspective about multiculturalism as the key issue of our epoch. They describe the dichotomy between particularism and universalism, multicultural education, and global education. They suggest the propagation of a "new epistemology"—a combination of both: "When we study particular groups, we should use insights gained to try to reframe our understanding of the global" (p. B5). Many health topics are best approached from a transcultural standpoint rather than through a culture-by-culture (ethnicity-by-ethnicity) analysis. For example, we might critically analyze the relationships among poverty, illness, and health, or processes of coping with the AIDS disease as outgrowths of global—not just cultural—change. We might also be able to examine the relationships among politics, illness, and health, or compare health care systems approaches of different countries and relate this to the present global infant morality rate.

Airhihenbuwa and Pineiro (1988) suggested that because health is "a global state with no boundaries," it is important to provide students with "knowledge and appreciation for multiethnicity and the relationship between health and cultural diversity" (p. 241). As such, the authors agree that a K-12 health curriculum should incorporate minority health concepts as well as those related to international health. The authors suggest seven issues that should be covered by such a curriculum: (1) learning about the different ethnic groups in the United States; (2) decision making in minority populations; (3) minority role models; (4) learning from a minority member (contributions of minority health professionals); (5) facing myths and realities regarding ethnic minorities; (6) learning about non-health problems that can affect status, such as unemployment, poverty, poor housing, and racial discrimination; and (7) practicing health by planning activities aimed at improving ethnic minority health status and establishing links among ethnic minorities and other nations or regions around the world.

Health teachers should not become overly enthusiastic about emphasizing differences in cultures and peoples. It is equally important to address the macro-culture—the similarities of health problems and dilemmas in all people. Pahnos (1992) concludes:

Health educators must not be overzealous in their multicultural missions. In stressing the importance of separate cultures and ethnic groups, the unity of being one nation must not be lost. Students need to understand that through individual differences, we gel and collectively contribute to the nation's health practices and advances. Therefore, while we appreciate and respect individual needs and differences, a need remains to reunite and be one regarding important health and environmental concerns. (p. 26)

3. *Using a variety of creative teaching approaches, methods, and strategies.*

Just as students differ in their ways of thinking, so too do they vary in their styles of learning (Kolb, 1984). Because of this diversity of learning styles, teachers should use several teaching approaches, methods, and strategies in teaching about health. Galli, Greenberg, and Tobin (1987) offer some suggestions on how to present health information that is relevant to students' religious and cultural beliefs. These suggestions include the following:

i. Bring a panel of religious leaders to class to explain the tenets of their religions pertaining to health education topics.
ii. Assign projects and papers on various cultural viewpoints towards the topics, emphasizing the value of diversity.
iii. Ask students to rank order such options as physical health, spiritual health, and societal health; ask them to value freedom to choose, moral imperative, and secular law, and to discuss their choices.
iv. Present films in which characters wrestle with conflict between fitting into modern society and maintaining their cultural uniqueness, such as the film *The Chosen*. As an alternative, assign students to read books that portray a similar conflict.
v. Invite to class parents of students who grew up in other countries, and ask them to describe different ways people in their country of birth view health-related topics.
vi. Encourage students to write to the embassies of different countries inquiring about different practices and viewpoints related to health topics studied in class. In particular, have them write to countries with differing major religions.
vii. Have students investigate school practices such as cafeteria meals and food preparation to determine how responsive these practices are to different people. Then students can suggest adjustments in these practices to better accommodate all students. These activities should be feasible and presented in a constructive rather than confrontational manner. (p.179)

King (1982) developed a college course titled Multicultural Health Beliefs that proved to be successful, fun, and enlightening for students. With modification, this course could also be used for other grade levels. The purpose of the course was to increase students' knowledge about Hispanic, American Indian, and African American health beliefs. The course included trips to cultural areas in the southwestern United States, guest lectures on various health topics from members of the three ethnic groups, and writing opinion papers regarding the benefits and problems of experience related to the course.

Trips were made to Juarez, Mexico; to Taos, New Mexico, the home of the Taos Pueblo Indian tribe; to Crownpoint, New Mexico, on the Navajo reservation land; and to San Felipe Pueblo, New Mexico, where a ceremony combining traditional American

Indian and Catholic faith rituals was taking place. Guest lecturers included the director of alcoholism information of the Indian Health Service at Albuquerque, a physician in charge of a diabetes project involving American Indian populations, a student who had recently arrived from Thailand and discussed her culture and specific health beliefs, and a Cuban working to create a biocultural environment within Headstart for Hispanic populations.

The preceding example demonstrates that the success of a multicultural health education initiative depends on the teacher's creativity in using the instructional resources available within and outside the community. Through the activities in the course, students discovered how they were different as well as similar to people of other groups. The promotion of these discoveries among students also depends on the emotional atmosphere that teachers create when they plan endeavors that are relevant and interesting to students. Recognize students as the best teaching resource while using other various resources.

4. Recognizing students as an important instructional resource.

Teachers need relevant multicultural resources to be effective. In attempting to find teaching resources, however, many teachers tend to look outside their immediate surroundings first before realizing the wealth of knowledge their students bring into the classroom. With the abundance of information that students have about health, they may be one of the best resources in teaching many health topics.

According to Poris (1989), diversity in student populations should not be seen as a threat, nor as a problem, but rather as an untapped resource. To capitalize on the wealth of cultures, traditions, and community identifications present among students, health educators can "bring a health topic to life" (Poris, 1989). Poris described some successful activities in the areas of drug education, sexuality education, and other basic health issues, that were implemented in multi-ethnic college classrooms (with some modification, these may be used at other levels). Some of these activities include providing students with opportunities to compare and contrast health-related practices and customs in their home countries with those of the United States; putting together term projects related to drug issues with an application to the student's view of his/her own real world; and having students share, within small group structures, some myths and misinformation about human sexuality that they encountered while they were growing up. Poris concluded that, besides textbooks, there is a wealth of information that students can learn from each other, that student interest and participation are increased if the subject areas relate to the student's ethnic backgrounds, and that capitalizing on students as resources will permit fewer teacher-dominated lessons and greater opportunities for teachers to learn about their students' ethnic and cultural backgrounds, thus broadening their knowledge.

5. Involving parents and other members of the family in the education of their children.

Parents directly and indirectly influence the knowledge, beliefs, values, and behaviors of children. They have the capacity to influence their children in many ways—as "models for appropriate behavior, as gatekeepers for both opportunities and barriers, and as major sources of reinforcement in most of their children's lives" (Perry et al., 1988).

The benefits of parental involvement in their children's education have been widely explored in the area of human sexuality. Fisher (1985, 1988a, 1988b) found that general family communication as well as parent-child discussion about sex seem to be important factors that affect sexuality. It was reported that parent-child communication about sex tends to delay sexual activity and encourages children to become more responsible in their approach to sexuality (Fisher, 1986). A number of studies have also suggested that while discussing sexuality, parents can transmit personal sexual values (e.g. sexual abstinence, the use of condoms and other contraceptives) to their children (Ellias & Gebhard, 1973; Fox & Inazu, 1980a, 1980b; Furstenberg, 1976; Inazu & Fox, 1980; Lewis, 1973; Spanier, 1976). Silverstein and Buck (1986) reported that high degree of parent communication regarding sex education can foster exploration of issues among students.

The extent of the influence that parents and other family members have on their children varies among ethnic groups. In dealing with sensitive health topics, for example, some Hispanics seem more willing to counsel family members about touchy matters and to accept advice, especially from older members, than non-Hispanics (Foulk, Lafferty, & Ryan, 1991). In other cultures, mothers are more likely than fathers to discuss sensitive topics with their children (Fox & Inazu, 1980b). In some cultures, fathers exert more authority.

Health teachers may benefit from understanding the perceptions of family members that are considered to be the most respected and have the greatest influence on children's attitudes and behaviors. It is more likely that these parents will reinforce at home what is learned in school. It is also more likely that these parents will either contradict or support the teaching of various health education content areas in school.

Many health topics are morally laden and controversial. For these topics to be discussed freely in school, parental consent is often necessary. Thus, it may be advantageous for schools to survey parents on the kinds of health education topics they will approve and the age level at which they think these topics may be appropriately taught. In this regard, schools may implement a program that is consistent with views of parents.

Several attitudinal questionnaires are available on various health topics targeted to parents and students. Many of these questionnaires can be used by teachers to assess the views of parents on different kinds of health information. Silverstein and Buck (1986), Fisher (1988a, 1988b), and Acosta (1992) have developed questionnaires on sex and AIDS education topics that can be used by teachers in assessing parental attitudes toward these topics.

6. *Selecting instructional materials relevant to the needs of the target group.*

Many instructional materials portray biased, stereotypical, and prejudiced notions about health, and many schools use these materials, testing students on the information. Sometimes, the information provided conflicts with students' personal beliefs, values, and experiences. The following example describes how information from a health textbook is biased in favor of the U.S. depiction of health.

The U.S. notion of ideal health is influenced, to a large extent, by the media. The ideal healthy female, for example, is portrayed as tall, very thin, and model-like. Such an ideal is beyond the reach of most healthy females. It becomes misleading for many females who do not fit this image to believe that this example is the only model that typifies health.

In one health textbook, a robust, muscular, White male lifting weights in what appears to be an expensive health club is depicted as the ideal healthy man. As with the woman's image, the message conveyed by this picture can be very misleading. It may provide the generalization that a healthy male's body should be similar to that of the one in the picture; or that to be healthy means to subscribe to and rigidly follow the choice of exercises shown in the picture; or, to an even larger extreme, believe that "proper" exercise may only be accomplished in a luxurious gym. While gymnasiums and health clubs are relatively common in the United States, recent immigrants and people living in impoverished areas and in rural localities may not have access to health clubs or even want to join them. For various personal, economic, or social reasons, they are likely to reject the gymnasium or health club milieu.

To implement multicultural health education is to debunk the widespread myths and misconceptions about health that linger within the U.S. cultural health ideal. Teachers must encourage the exploration and reflection of other health "ideals" and encourage discussion of the numerous societal and environmental factors that influence them. In addition, teachers must carefully choose their materials, and steer away from those that exhibit bias and partiality. Sometimes, even excellent books and materials may be biased or misleading in some parts. If these books are used, teachers may need to clarify and discuss these parts, or even present alternatives to the biased information.

7. *Participating in the planning and development of culturally relevant materials.*

An abundance of innovative and creative resource materials exists for health education planning. However, many of these are targeted to the White population and do not meet the needs of other ethnic and racial groups (Orlandi, 1986). Additionally, while a wealth of health education materials have been translated into different languages, much of the information these materials contain is not culturally appropriate for the intended audiences. Nor is the information presented in ways that the targeted groups can best understand and use.

Educational interventions focused on reducing high-risk behaviors often do not include the needs of various high-risk populations and groups (Thomas, Guilliam, & Iwrey, 1989). The increasing number of Blacks, Hispanics, and women who become victims of AIDS, for example, indicates the need for focused educational strategies and resources.

To assure that health education content is relevant to diverse population groups, health educators, especially those that are members of target groups, must participate in the design, development, and planning of these materials and not leave the decisions to non-health educators or non-target group members.

✛ Commitment to Equity: Keeping Abreast of Current Perspectives About Multiculturalism

The effectiveness of health education programs depends on the extent to which teachers can increase students' knowledge about health, enhance favorable attitudes, and promote healthful behaviors. Because students' knowledge, attitudes, and behaviors are associated with their cultural, religious, and ethnic beliefs and practices, the integration of a multicultural and social reconstructionist approach to teaching becomes an essential part of health education.

Multicultural health education programs are more likely to be successful when teachers search for suggestions and guidelines that facilitate personal and professional enhancement. Some of these guidelines include a reexamination and renewal of their educational philosophies; the development and maintenance of traits characteristic of tolerance, openness, and acceptance of all students; the use of a variety of instructional methods, strategies, and approaches that are relevant to their students' needs and interests; the involvement of students as teaching resources and participants in their own learning; and taking part in the careful selection and development of culturally relevant instructional materials.

Although certain guidelines have been suggested in this chapter, the key is for teachers to recognize that what they may be instilling in the minds of students may not be what is always "right" or "good" for all students. Teachers, through health education, have the responsibility of promoting the health of all their students. The success of health education programs depends, to a large extent, on teachers' personal and professional commitment toward Multiculturalism.

Note

1. As an author I realize that by naming particular groups and linking them with specific beliefs and practices, I risk essentializing people. However, in this chapter I hope to clarify how health education practices do sometimes conflict with various cultural groups.

References

Acosta, V. (1992). Parents' perceptions regarding the appropriateness of AIDS education topics for their eighth grade school children. *Journal of Health Education, 22*(1), 45-50.

Airhihenbuwa, C., & Pineiro, O. (1988). Cross-cultural health education: A pedagogical challenge. *Journal of School Health, 58*(6), 240-242.

American Public Health Association. (1987). Technical report: Criteria for the development of health promotion and education programs. *American Journal of Public Health,* Washington, DC. Author.

Amler, R. W., & Dull, H. B. (1987). *Closing the gap: The burden of unnecessary illness.* New York: Oxford University Press.

Becker, M. H. (1974). The health belief models and personal health behavior. *Health Education Monographs, 2* (Winter), 404-419.

Department of Health and Human Services. (1992). *Healthy people 2000 summary report.* Boston: Jones and Bartlett.

Elias, J., & Gebhard, P. (1973). Sexuality and sexual learning in childhood. In A. M. Juhasz (Ed.), *Sexual Development and Behavior.* Homewood, IL: Dorsey Press.

Feigelman, W., & Gorman, B. (1989). Toward explaining the higher incidence of cigarette smoking among Black Americans. *Journal of Psychoactive Drugs, 21*(3), 299-305.

Fisher, T. (1985). An exploratory study of parent-child communications about sex and the sexual attitudes of early middle and late adolescents. *Journal of Genetic Psychology, 147*(4), 543-557.

Fisher, T. (1986). Parent-child communication about sex and young adolescents' sexual knowledge attitudes. *Adolescence, 21*(83), 517-527.

Fisher, T. (1988a). *Parental sexual attitudes, family sexual communications, and adolescent sexual behavior.* Paper presented at the 96th annual convention of the American Psychological Association, Atlanta, GA.

Fisher, T. (1988b). The relationship between parent-child communication about sexuality and college students' sexual behavior and attitudes as a function of parental proximity. *The Journal of Sex Research, 24,* 305-311.

Fischer, T., & Hall, R. (1988). A scale for the comparison of the sexual attitudes of adolescents and their parents. *The Journal of Sex Research, 24,* 90-100.

Foulk, D., Lafferty, J., & Ryan, R. (1991). Developing culturally sensitive materials for AIDS education specifically targeted to migrant farmworkers. *Journal of Health Education, 22*(5), 283–286.

Fox, G. L., & Inazu, J. K. (1980a). Patterns and outcomes of mother-daughter communication about sexuality. *Journal of School Issues, 36,* 7–29.

Fox, G. L., & Inazu, J. K. (1980b). Mother-daughter communication about sex. *Family Relations, 29,* 347–352.

Furstenberg, F., Jr. (1976). *Unplanned parenthood: The social consequences of teenage childbearing.* New York: The Free Press.

Furstenberg, F., Jr. (1987). The AIDS epidemic among Blacks and Hispanics. *Milbank Quarterly, 65,* supp. 2, 460–465.

Galli, N., Greenberg, J., Tobin, F. (1987). Health education and sensitivity to cultural religious, and ethnic beliefs. *Journal of School Health, 57*(5), 177–180.

Grant, C., & Sleeter, C. (1989). Race, class, gender, exceptionality, and educational reform. In J. Banks & C. Banks (Eds.), *Multicultural Education: Issues and Perspectives* (pp. 46–64). Boston: Allyn and Bacon.

Greene, W., & Simons-Morton, B. (1984). *Introduction to health education.* Prospect Heights, IL: Waveland Press.

Heckler, M. (1985a). *Report of the secretary's task force on Black and minority health, volume II: Crosscutting issues in minority health.* Washington, DC: Department of Health and Human Services.

Heckler, M. (1985b). *Report of the secretary's task force on Black and minority health: Executive summary.* Washington, DC: Department of Health and Human Services.

Hopkins, D. R. (1987, November-December). *AIDS in minority populations in the United States. Public Health Reports, 102,* 677.

Inazu, J. K., & Fox, G. L. (1980). Maternal influence on the sexual behavior of teenage daughters. *Journal of Family Issues, 1,* 81–102.

Institute of Medicine. (1985). *Preventing low birth weight.* Washington, DC: National Academy Press.

Jacobs. L. (1973). *What does Judaism say about. . .?* New York: Quadrangle Press.

Kalantzis, M., & Cope, W. (1992, November 4). Multiculturalism may prove to be the key issue in our epoch. *Chronicle of Higher Education,* B3–B5.

Kelleher, D., & Hillier, S. (1996). *Researching cultural differences in health.* London/New York: Routledge.

King, L. (1982, September-October). Multicultural health beliefs in action. *Health Education,* pp. 24–25.

Kolb, D. (1984). *Experiential learning.* Upper Saddle River, NJ: Prentice Hall.

Lewis, R. A. (1973). Parents and peers: Socialization agents in the coital behavior of young adults. *Journal of Sex Research, 9,* 156–170.

MacDonald, J. (1988). Multicultural health education: An emerging reality in Canada. *Hygiene, 7*(2), 12–16.

Maehr, M. L. (1974). *Sociocultural origins of achievement.* Monterey, CA: Brooks/Cole.

National Education Association Commission. (1976). Seven cardinal principles revisited. *Today's Education, 65*(3), 67–72.

National Health Interview Survey. (1988). National Center for Health Statistics, Centers for Disease Control, Public Health Service, U.S. Department of Health and Human Services, Hyattsville, MD.

National Heart, Lung, & Blood Institute, National Cholesterol Education Program. (1990). *Report of the expert panel on population strategies for blood cholesterol reduction.* Washington, DC: U.S. Department of Health and Human Services.

Office on Smoking and Health (1987). Unpublished data from the 1987 National Health Interview Survey.

Orlandi, M. A. (1986). Community-based substance abuse prevention: A multicultural perspective. *Journal of School Health, 56*(9), 394–401.

Pahnos, M. (1992). The continuing challenge of multicultural health education. *Journal of School Health, 62*(1), 24–26.

Perry, C., Luepker, R., Murray, D., Kurth, C., Mullis, R., Crockett, S., & Jacobs, D. (1988). Parent involvement with children's health promotion: The Minnesota home team. *American Journal of Public Health, 78*(9), 1156–1160.

Poris, B. (1989). Student multi-ethnicity: The untapped health education resources. *Health Education, 21*(2), 20–22.

Purnell, L., & Paulanka, B. (1998). Transcultural diversity and health care. In L. Purnell & B. Paulanka (Eds.), *Transcultural health care: A culturally competent approach* (pp. 7–51). Philadelphia: F.A. Davis.

Russell, R. D. (1983). Old ideas still valuable: A review of cultural case studies. *Journal of School Health, 53*(2), 136-139.

Silverstein, C., & Buck, G. (1986). Parental preferences regarding sex education topics for sixth graders. *Adolescence, 21*(84), 971-980.

Spanier, G. B. (1976). Formal and informal sex education as determinants of premarital sexual behavior. *Archives of Sexual Behavior, 5*, 39-67.

Spector, R. (1985). *Cultural diversity in health and illness* (2nd ed.). Norwalk, CT: Appleton-Century-Crofts.

Stone, E., & Crouch, A. (1979, June). Children's perceptions of vulnerability to health problems from a cross-cultural perspective. *Journal of School Health,* 347-350.

Thomas, S., Guilliam, A., & Iwrey, C. (1989). The relationship between knowledge about AIDS and risk behaviors among Black college students. *Journal of American College of Health, 38*(2), 61-66.

Wurzel, J. (1988). (Ed.). *Toward multiculturalism.* Yarmouth, ME: Intercultural Press.

17 Multiculturalism and Educational Theatre

Mark Riherd and Nancy Swortzell
New York University

While most extensively developed in the 20th century, the uses of drama and theatre as methods of teaching and learning have influenced education from the Greeks to the present (Swortzell, 1990). In ancient rituals and later religious ceremonies and secular entertainments, particular civilizations demonstrated again and again the effectiveness of this dynamic and enjoyable method of education. The current century has witnessed worldwide expansion of the field that often calls itself *educational theatre,* a term that includes two separate but interdependent forms: Drama in education (DIE) and theatre in education (TIE). DIE explores a wide spectrum of activities (domestic, social, legal, political, health-oriented, and environmental) as participants are guided by a leader through structured improvisations. By playing different roles, students elicit responses from each other while they spontaneously enact their own. It is a process that allows them to be simultaneously participants and observers of the dramatic action. "Reflection" upon such activity and subsequent decision making are stressed for both the individual and the group. Because DIE emphasizes classroom "improvisation," "role play" and simulation, it is often called *process* drama, whereas TIE involves *product,* a performance in a school auditorium, theatre or classroom by a company or team of actors.

✤ Theatre in Education (TIE)

TIE—distinguished by basic elements of play writing such as conflict, focus, tension, contrast, and symbolism—concentrates on traditional areas of learning and contemporary social issues. TIE programs can include every aspect of the curriculum from the humanities through the sciences. The usual program offers teachers pre- and post-performance activities prepared by the TIE team. The team suggests ways to prepare students for the performance and outlines additional activities to extend the focus of programs after the team has departed.

TIE programs, for the most part, are devised by team members, although a few companies have engaged resident or visiting playwrights to create scripts. The usual devising process entails a period of research and organization of information followed by team improvisations that explore the dramatic context of the topic.

Then members collaborate to focus and refine the materials in rehearsals and early performances. The topical nature often requires frequent changes in text and performance throughout the life of the program. During the final stages of devising, teams begin to structure the workshops that will precede or follow performances.

Before touring programs, members also write drama resource books for teachers that introduce and reinforce themes of the program through suggested dramatic activities. These booklets present ideas for independent student research and also explain basic methods of drama for inexperienced instructors.

Both DIE and TIE are motivated by the conviction that it is the responsibility of the field to bring about positive change in human behavior and social institutions. Through practical involvement followed by individual or group reflection, students often revise their ideas, actions, and perhaps in time, even their institutions. As both participants and spectators, they are placed in the center of the action where they empathize with the characters and issues at hand, reflect upon them, and subsequently make decisions that can permanently alter their attitudes and opinions.

In the early 1960s, Gordon Vallins, the director of Coventry's Belgrade Theatre in England, drafted a working method and structure to serve as a model for other British teams for the next decade. His aim was "to use theatre to tell everyone else about each other's problems" (Redington, 1983, p. 43). Vallins' initial programs used myths, legends, and local history as topics, adapting them so the themes stressed how children could help others. Soon, however, the Coventry team turned to specifically multicultural themes in full-day presentations such as *The Mysterious Wanderers* (prejudice against immigrant "Gypsies"), *How the Rain Came to Hweng Chow* (environment in China), and *The Emergent Africa Game* (political action in Africa). Above all, Vallins implored TIE team members to create programs to overcome superficial thinking and develop a greater understanding of the contemporary world.

The child-centered work in Coventry was not concerned merely with filling minds with information, but took a direct stance against prejudice and injustice (Redington, 1983). One of its strongest multicultural projects, *Rare Earth,* was a TIE program in three parts with participatory workshops (Wyatt & Steed, 1976). In devising the plays, the team members wished to emphasize the difference between attitudes toward the world held by Westerners today and that of less-industrialized peoples.

The first play, sardonically titled *The Only Good Indian is a Dead Indian,* was a poetic dance drama that suggests that in destroying their environment, people destroy themselves. The second play, *Drink the Mercury,* presented in the style of Kabuki theatre, dealt with pollution in Minamatra, Japan. The third play, *The Ramsbottoms,* was a satiric farce that depicted a typical British family of four and focused on international greed for natural resources.

Each play was performed on a separate day, followed by workshops devised and led by members of the class (Wyatt & Steed, 1976). Schools devoted three full days so that material about survival could be experienced firsthand through theatre and drama workshops. Because of the three-day sequence, the program allowed participants time to absorb and develop ideas through the structure of theatre performance and drama workshops. In fact, at the conclusion of the TIE program, many Coventry teachers incorporated drama activities in their classes for several weeks to further explore environmental awareness and protection.

Other important TIE programs, also calling for change in issues of race, gender and disability, are described here, followed by a model incorporating dramatic activities to be employed in the classroom.

Race

The intense desire to combat racial prejudice motivated the Belgrade TIE team in 1976 to devise a controversial program, *Pow Wow,* which depicts the treatment of an American Indian by a White American traveling showman. Mr. Tex tells the audience he holds

Black Elk captive because he is a savage who has killed White men. But later, Black Elk gains the confidence of the children by describing the philosophy of his people and the color of their daily lives. Audience attitudes are tested when they are asked to support one man or the other, and team members select one of two concluding scenes based on the decision of the audience (Redington, 1983).

Raj, written by Paul Swift and performed in 1982 by the Leeds TIE team, is another multicultural program aimed at understanding and overcoming racial prejudice. One actor said he believed ". . . the main connection point was the friendship between characters . . . I think the play raised the possibility that something could be different, something might not have to be. . . . But certainly what it was doing for all is challenging the establishment view" (*Multicultural Images,* 1982, p. 15). Another team member reported that Asian children participated from the moment the program began as if they were saying, "Thank God, this is relevant to me, at last" (*Multicultural Images,* 1982, p. 7).

David Holman combined race, religion and politics as issues in *No Passeran,* produced by the Coventry team in 1977. Without directly presenting a Hitler or Franco, the play concentrated on the prevailing practice of creating scapegoats within European Fascist ideology. Emotionally powerful and socially reconstructionist in attitude, *No Passeran* was approved for inclusion in the local Coventry history curriculum and also has been widely performed in Australia, Canada, and the United States (Holman, 1980).

Racial problems in the Middle East conflict emerged at the heart of the Electric Theatre's 1989 program, *Homeland,* and appeared again in the Greenwich Young People's 1990 program *Circles of Fire.* This script, which examined the characters' responses to living under the apartheid system in South Africa, uses this line of "questioning": What is it that makes one person decide changes are necessary in society while another person is opposed to those changes? Why does one decide to become *actively* involved in trying to effect these changes? How can one bring about these changes? (Circles of Fire, 1990).

In the United States, The Federal Theatre Project (1936 to 1939) also questioned the social status quo through its "learning plays," and in living newspapers and pageants that demanded tolerance and racial understanding (Swortzell, 1986). Much later, in the 1970s, the Creative Arts Team (CAT), the professional educational theatre company of the Gallatin division of New York University, focused on racism in plays about the struggle of Rosa Parks, the career of boxer Joe Louis, and life in South Africa. As a response to an outbreak of racial violence in New York City that culminated in the Howard Beach incident, CAT produced *The Divider,* which has been performed in the United States, Canada, and Scotland.

Gender

Gender study and, in particular, the roles of women in society, has been an ongoing concern of dramatists from Aristophanes' *Lysistrata* to recent works such as *The Heidi Chronicles.* Sexism became a major concern of TIE companies in the 1970s, spearheaded by the Bolton Octagon TIE's *Sweetie Pie.* Advocating women's liberation, the play espoused four goals for women: (1) equal educational opportunity, (2) equal pay, (3) 24-hour nurseries, and (4) free contraception and abortion on demand (*Sweetie Pie,* 1975, p. 15).

Two decades later, some of the attitudes presented in *Sweetie Pie* may seem dated, but certainly the factions supporting and opposing abortion issues still stimulate conflict today. The play paved the way for such other works as *Mates* in 1984 and *No Going Back* in 1990, both devised by the Greenwich Young People's Theatre and both asking young people to make decisions to change attitudes toward stereotypical gender roles and responses.

Disability

Before this century, dramatists often depicted physical and psychological disabilities as studies in deformity and evil. Even Euripides and Shakespeare portrayed people with disabilities for purposes other than sympathetic insight, positive identification, or human compassion. Contemporary practitioners, however, hope to achieve these goals by making audiences aware of how it feels to be physically or emotionally impaired. *Snap Out of It*, a two-part British program devised by the Leeds TIE team, emerged from information provided by the British National Association for Mental Health and from doctors, psychiatrists, and hospital personnel.

Structured to involve audiences in real-life situations, the play created considerable concern for its characters (Chapman & Wilkes, 1975, p. 50). The first half offers a series of satiric sketches that parody a popular television "quiz" format: "by the end of the first part, all material of the 'fun' . . . and the ridicule . . . is entirely replaced by tape-recorded statistics" and the program moves into areas of disturbing commentary (Chapman & Wilkes, 1975, p. 50). This half involves direct participation through which audiences experience the bewilderment, isolation, and confusion of the mentally ill. Powerful emotional feelings raised during the workshop revealed the general ignorance among students about mental illness. The creators described this program as "neither a documentary nor a piece of ordinary 'theatre,' it was an attempt to employ the skills of the actor to augment our understanding of ourselves and our fellow man" (Chapman & Wilkes, 1975, p. 19).

While *Snap Out of It* was directed toward adults, other companies worked on similar themes for a younger audience. The Pit Prop Theatre developed a participation program that presented the problems, frustrations and misunderstandings suffered by a teenager with cerebral palsy. By experiencing the social indignities suffered by the physically impaired, playgoers discovered their own prejudices about the disabled. Similar concerns have generated productions by the GRIPS Theatre in West Berlin, a company that acknowledges its philosophical debt to Bertolt Brecht's *lehrstucke* (learning plays) in its teaching manuals, books, and recordings.

In the United States, *Special Class* (Kral, 1981) calls for a cast of youngsters with and without disabilities drawn from special education classrooms, including youngsters in wheelchairs, and blind, hearing-impaired, and mentally retarded students. As both playwright and director, Kral reflected his belief that "just because an instrument is shaped a little different, doesn't mean it can't play a beautiful tune." Coleman Jennings' script *The Early Life of Louis Braille* effectively dramatizes the struggle of a blind child (Jennings & Jennings, 1990).

Summary of TIE

Almost two decades before educators intensified their focus on multicultural theories and practices, TIE teams were basing their daily work with young people on the same concerns. Without a specific declaration of a multicultural philosophy, and even though no single team combined the issues of race, class, and gender into one play, teams insisted that programs bring their participants an experience related to the "real world" by asking questions about how this world can be changed for the benefit of all. The development of TIE has run parallel to the growth in drama (process) activity both in theory and practice, especially in English-speaking countries.

❖   Drama in Education (DIE)

DIE is generally considered to be made up of informal dramatic activities in schools that are based in role play, improvisation, simulation, and theatre games. They also are aimed at developing the student's imagination, awareness of self and others, aesthetic sense, and life skills. The terms *creative drama, developmental drama,* and *drama-in-education* are basically interchangeable. In an effort to refine definitions, the process has come to mean a group activity of improvisational action guided by a leader who involves participants in role playing and spontaneously enacted situations. Because drama workshops function on the premise that participants possess equal but different talents and contributions, all ideas are listened to, put into action, and considered without respect to race, creed, or gender. Frequently, several solutions to problems are enacted and conclusions or actions left open-ended.

A brief historical survey of the major theorist-practitioners reveals that although drama has been put to various uses in the past 50 years, it is always child-centered in attitude and from the beginning has had its roots in the progressive educational movement.

Harriet Finlay-Johnson was among the first in England to use drama as an effective means of teaching (Finlay-Johnson, 1911). She was followed by Henry Caldwell Cook, whose effect on educational theory eventually came to be praised for his stimulating use of play, role, and ritual, particularly in exploring Greek myths and Shakespeare's plays.

In geography and history classes, students imagined new countries and carried out new systems of government; in science, they visited regional sites and collected and categorized natural elements. Most of Cook's "exercises" stressed that through drama his pupils "be taught to understand as clearly as possible the conditions of this present world in which they live" (Cook, 1917, p. 344).

But it was not until the mid-1960s, after 25 years of studying children at play, that Slade (1969) wrote *Child Drama.* Slade was the first to stress informal drama as an art form in its own right. He believed that in the process of improvising a play, children work out their emotional inhibitions and come to better understand themselves and their world. His major criterion for evaluating participation was the child's degree of involvement, spontaneity, and sincerity. Way, who had worked closely with Slade at the Rea Street Drama Centre in Birmingham, extended Slade's ideas in *Development through Drama* (Way, 1967), which in the 1960s and 1970s became the basis for most drama teaching in English-speaking countries. Way presented a program of systematized observation aimed at developing awareness. His credo rejected the authoritarian stance of traditional education and emphasized "doing drama" to highlight the "uniqueness of the individual" and to foster self-expression.

In the United States, Ward (1957) launched a similar art and educational movement. Moreover, her work spanned both the fields of creative drama and children's theatre. *Playmaking with Children* (Ward, 1957) stresses the values children gain from improvising a "good story." *Theatre for Children* (Ward, 1958) establishes professional guidelines for play writing and production. Ward was one of the first American teachers and directors to call for a scientific evaluation of child audiences.

McCaslin, independent of Ward, also developed an interest in child drama and theatre, which led her to chronicle the history of the movement. McCaslin's international reputation was established by numerous publications, including *Theatre for Children in the United States: A History* (1978), *Children and Drama* (1981), *Theatre for Young Audiences* (1978), and *Creative Drama in the Classroom* (1990), as well as many books for young readers.

Two recent international giants of the drama-in-education world, Dorothy Heathcote and Gavin Bolton, earned their reputations through practical workshops and prolific writing. For the past 25 years, they have revised their methods to train teachers to use drama as education. Heathcote has proposed a total revision of college curricula based on the use of drama as the teaching medium. She begins with the creation of a working climate in which value judgments do not apply, but "where honesty of individual contributions is valued and respect is shown to individual ideas and methods of contribution" (Johnson & O'Neill, 1985, p. 38).

Cultural context areas for her proposed curriculum include subjects such as war, law, health, education, worship, and family. She also explores the sociology of groups, myths, legends, racial tribes, minorities, modes of communication, and anthropological studies (Johnson & O'Neill, 1985). Her drama practices with autistic, blind, and brain-damaged children display a dual focus that allows the less capable child to experience the world and the capable child to comprehend the daily struggle of those less fortunate (Wagner, 1976, pp. 210–217).

For the past two decades, Heathcote and Bolton have worked together in public schools, institutes, and universities in Canada, England, and the United States. Both have shared in the creation of drama guidelines that offer teachers tested methods for conducting workshops (Bolton, 1979, 1984, 1986).

Influenced by Bolton's work, O'Neill (1988) offers teachers tangible methods of using drama in all areas of specialization: Her "structures" adjust to any desired age level or racial or socioeconomic background. One drama lesson, titled "Imagined Worlds," allowed participants to "live through" a role and a situation they would never know, such as life in England immediately after World War II or in a large city of the future plagued by AIDS. Active involvement increases the immediacy of response because by "doing it now," students can offer possible solutions to contemporary problems (O'Neill, 1984).

The assumption that all participants are equal but different in contribution dominates the philosophy of drama-in-education. Drama involves participants in the circumstances of every situation through its use of role play, which allows participants to step directly into another's shoes. In group improvisations, students experience situations of race, religion, gender, and disability; their reflections on actions bring with them new ideas that again may be tested by doing. This insistence upon "doing," "redoing," "rethinking," and "remaking," which is basic for all scientific inquiry, also governs drama as an art form.

An Educational Theatre Model

Of the two forms of educational theatre discussed in this chapter, drama in education is the more accessible and readily employable by elementary and middle school teachers.

Unlike theatre in education, which requires a theatre presentation and workshops implemented by team members, DIE is designed and guided by the classroom teacher alone. The Center Plot, the model curriculum design used in this text, focuses on the subject of prejudice in multicultural education. The program, intended to be carried out in six sessions, incorporates strategies known as "critical thinking through drama," a practice that develops students' decision-making skills. (For more details about this and other drama strategies discussed in the model, see the glossary at the end of this chapter).

The curriculum design for The Center Plot is only an outline or plan and, as such, provides opportunities for teachers to infuse their own ideas as well as those of their students. As long as these themes and events are related to the issue of prejudice, they do not need to be the same as those included in the model. Because the length of sessions and the number of students participating will vary with each classroom, teachers should not be disappointed if they are unable to implement all six workshops or complete each strategy outlined for any one lesson. The model simply offers insights into the varied ways that DIE practices can be incorporated into the curriculum. At every step, the intention is to encourage students through an experiential mode of learning to examine their own attitudes toward people who are different from themselves and, thereby, to better understand multiculturalism. Sessions One through Three are based on a DIE curriculum design devised by the Creative Arts Team at New York University.

The Center Plot

Session One   To begin the session, the teacher assumes the role of the Representative of the Ruler of a mythical country. Using an authoritative demeanor, she welcomes the students to her country and hopes that, because they have been here for several days, they are rested from their long, exhausting journey. The Representative sympathizes about their past oppressed life and suggests that, because conditions will be better here, they should plan a celebration of their new freedom. Stepping out of role, the teacher questions the students about what is happening in the drama, making certain they understand that they are portraying the inhabitants of a new land and that she is also playing a role.

The teacher, once again becoming the Representative, says they should learn more about each other. The students now enact the new Citizens of the land and are asked to state their names and describe the goals they hope to achieve here. The Citizens walk quietly around the classroom, concentrating on their characters and their new lives. When the Representative claps her hands, the Citizens turn to someone nearby and, introducing themselves, describe their hopes. This procedure is repeated several times.

Out of role, the teacher divides the students into small groups and explains that these units represent their new families. They select family names and occupations, which are written on the board, and they decide upon their individual roles within the families.

The Representative says she would like to take a photograph of each family for the Country Records. Each family creates a "tableau" that expresses how the members hope to be remembered by future generations. Each family shares its tableau as the Representative "snaps" the picture.

The families are asked to create an activity to be performed for the Celebration, such as song, dance, poem, or scene, that expresses their feelings about living in a new country. The Celebration begins and the families present their activities.

The Representative reflects that they all seem to be happy, but she recognizes that their lives have not always been so, as they have come to this country to escape prejudices in their homeland. She encourages the Citizens to talk about these prejudices, examples of which are written on the board ("board work"). The Representative asks each family to select one prejudice and, using several examples, to prepare a short improvisation depicting the prejudice that occurred in their former lives.

The Representative asks them which prejudices influenced their decision to leave home. She explains that tomorrow they must begin to build a society based on a constitution with laws appropriate to their new situation. She teaches them the country's pledge of allegiance, which she has written before the class begins.

Follow Up: The students are asked to think of a name for their new location and two to three constitutional laws necessary for everyone's happiness and equality.

Session Two   The teacher asks the students to recall the events in Session One; then they decide on a name for their town (referred to here as New Harmony). The students recite the pledge and assume their roles as Citizens of New Harmony. The teacher, now in role as the Representative, informs the Citizens that they have a difficult but exciting task ahead of them: the building of a new society. She asks them to join their family groups and then produces a large map of New Harmony, divided into plots of land around a center area.

The families are told to select a plot and determine a business to operate there. Each family plans and shares a short improvisation, emphasizing the importance of its business to the community; a member of the group writes the family's name and business on the map. The Citizens are informed that the center plot, as the most convenient and valuable piece of land, should be used for a special purpose, which they will determine later.

The Representative produces a large piece of paper with "CONSTITUTION" written at the top and tells the Citizens they must list the laws that will allow everyone in New Harmony to live together. After a discussion about the rules they consider essential, each family is asked to create one law based on a prejudice inflicted upon them in their old country. The Citizens write their new laws on the constitution sheet, and the Representative reads them aloud. Each family reads the constitution aloud together and, after agreeing to live by these new rules, each family representative signs the constitution.

The Citizens determine the purpose of the center plot of land, being reminded that it is to be used by everyone in the community for something special, such as a public garden, a statue, a shrine, or a public building. The Citizens offer their suggestions and make a decision. The Representative reiterates the importance of the free society they have created. She suggests that each family stand and repeat the pledge in gratitude, a "ritual" that is continued until a high level of excitement is achieved.

Suddenly the Representative becomes distraught and quiets the students, because she has important news: Another group of people has entered New Harmony, and she has heard that they appear to be very different from the Citizens.

Out of role, the teacher questions the students as to what might happen in New Harmony if the information about the Strangers is true. Then, each student creates and repeats to a classmate a negative statement about the Strangers which begins, "I heard that the Strangers . . ." The activity continues with the students taking the information and exchanging it with each other, making certain that each begins, "I heard that the Strangers. . . ."

The teacher explains that some of the students will continue to be the Citizens of New Harmony in the next session, and a few will become the Strangers.

Follow Up: Each student, as a Citizen, writes a letter to the Strangers, describing the importance of the society they have established in New Harmony.

Session Three   The teacher selects a small number of students from each of the family groups who will become the Strangers later in this session. At one end of the room, the teacher forms two groups of students, one a large group and the other a small group. They stand in two lines, facing each other, about 5 feet apart. One person from the larger group stands in front of the smaller group and leads members of the larger group toward the smaller group, expressing a powerful movement and sound. Reacting, the smaller group retreats at the same pace. This activity is repeated several times, with different people from the dominant group continually forcing the subordinate one to retreat. Still in their separate groups, the students discuss the meaning of this activity.

After the smaller group is informed that in this session they will become the Strangers, the two groups are delegated to different areas of the room. The Citizens are told by the teacher to select several members to inform the Strangers about life in New Harmony (the family groups, the plots of land, the pledge, the constitution). Then, the teacher informs the Strangers that their lifestyle is the opposite of the Citizens of New Harmony: (1) They live communally, not in family groups, because they believe that each person is unique; (2) they do not believe in pledges or constitutions but in the right of individuals to live as they choose as long as no one else is harmed; and (3) they are peaceful and have no desire to cause trouble.

To understand their characters, the students portraying the Strangers face each other in pairs; in turn, they practice informing each other about one aspect of their lives and why it is important to them. Simultaneously, the Citizens perform the same task, telling each other about life in New Harmony.

The Representative asks the Strangers to identify a unique skill, such as basket-making, farming, baking, or recording history, that they perform for the society, while the Citizens are encouraged to reflect on the importance of their businesses to the success of New Harmony. Then the Strangers, working individually, "pantomime" the task at which they are expert. The teacher, after determining that the Citizens are prepared to meet the Strangers, asks them to pantomime packing for the journey. "Narration" (by the teacher): "The Citizens set out upon their journey, traveling through the forest and along the river. At midday, they came upon the Strangers at work."

The Citizens, encouraged if necessary by the Representative, challenge the Strangers about not working as a group and explain their constitution and the necessity of living by its laws. They insist that the Strangers sign the constitution as well as learn and recite their pledge. The Strangers explain, politely but firmly, that, based on the principles of their own society, they cannot perform any of these tasks. The Citizens decree that if the Strangers refuse to live by their laws, they must leave New Harmony.

In small groups, the Citizens and the Strangers plan and share improvisations:

The Citizens: A scene depicting their lives if the Strangers remain and refuse to live according to the laws established by the Citizens.

The Strangers: A scene depicting their lives if they remain in New Harmony and are forced to live according to the laws established by the Citizens.

After the scenes have been presented and the students see the opposing views, the Citizens and the Strangers are told to go to different areas of the room and sit.

Narration (to be spoken by the teacher in her own words): "From that day onward, the Citizens of New Harmony and the Strangers lived separate and mistrusting lives with neither group speaking to the other. When anything bad happened to the Citizens of New Harmony, they blamed the Strangers; likewise, when anything bad happened to the Strangers, they blamed the Citizens of New Harmony. And as the days passed into weeks and the weeks into months, and the months, finally, into years, mistrust changed to hatred. One day, the Citizens of New Harmony and the Strangers faced each other and without speaking to or even looking at each other, built a wall around the center plot, separating themselves permanently from each other."

The Strangers are asked to stand and, without speaking, to create a group tableau, entering the picture one at a time, depicting how they feel about the current situation. When all are in place, the teacher asks them to say one sentence to express their feelings. When touched by the teacher, the Strangers deliver their lines. The Strangers sit and the activity is repeated by the Citizens of New Harmony.

Session Four   The teacher asks two students (Student 1 and Student 2) to come to the center of the group and shake hands; the students "freeze," and the class identifies what they see, responding with as many different images as possible.

The teacher tells Student 1 to return to the group, while Student 2 remains in position. Another student (Student 3) joins Student 2 and creates a different image, related to the theme of "People in Conflict." Student 2 leaves and another student joins Student 3 to create yet another image. This activity continues with students depicting people in various conflict situations.

In pairs, the students continue this activity working simultaneously, creating images emphasizing the theme of "People in Prejudice Situations," sharing as many different images as possible in a brief period of time. The students then join in, one at a time, to devise a group tableau titled "Prejudice."

On the board, the teacher writes the word *prejudice* and the students offer their definitions, which are also recorded. Then she leads the students in a discussion of prejudice, referring to their written comments. The students are asked to think of an incident of prejudice they have recently seen or read about. In their groups, they create a tableau, depicting the scene at the height of conflict. They decide on a line of dialogue that they would speak to another character in the tableau. When the characters are touched by the teacher, the dialogue is spoken. Each tableau is shared in the same manner.

Based on their tableaux, the students plan improvisations for which the conflicts remain unresolved. After being presented, one of these scenes is selected for exploration in the next session.

Session Five   The conflict scene from Session Four is replayed. The teacher explains that the students will help resolve the conflict, but that to do so, they will need more information about the characters and the situation; their task is to gather that information.

The characters are "hotseated" by the students who ask questions in rapid succession to gather general information about the characters: "Where were you born?" "How old are you?" "Do you work?" "What are your hobbies?" The characters respond instantaneously, and hotseating continues for the purposes of revealing vital information about the characters and conflict(s) depicted in the scene.

One of the characters is selected to be questioned further. One student from the class stands behind that character and acts as her/his Inner Self ("doubling"). Questioning continues with the character verbalizing what she/he wants people to hear, while the Inner Self speaks what the character is actually thinking.

The teacher leads the class in a discussion about the causes of prejudice and explains that to help resolve the characters' conflicts, they must first discover the origins of the prejudices demonstrated. In small groups, students elect one of the characters and create a "flashback" scene, depicting a situation from the past which contributed to the character's current prejudices. (The characters should not be played by the students who created them). These scenes are shared with the group.

Session Six   Before the original scene is replayed, the students portraying the characters are encouraged to be aware of any new information they may have gained about themselves and how that might affect the way they will play the scene.

The teacher tells the students they are now prepared to help resolve the conflict(s) and asks them what choices the characters have that might help them. After numerous ideas are listed on the board, the students identify one choice they believe would produce positive results and take roles to play that situation. The class assesses the results.

Other positive choices are explored through improvisation with different students taking on the roles and acting out several positive alternatives. Each improvised scene is discussed, emphasizing both positive and negative aspects. After several choices have been enacted, the students decide which would most effectively reduce prejudice. In small groups, the students create an improvisation depicting either a positive or negative result of one of the choices. These scenes are shared and analyzed by the class.

Groups from Session Four are formed again and recreate their original tableaux, depicting characters in a prejudice situation. The students then project what the behavior of these characters would be in 3 years if they lived by the results of their positive choices. They create new tableaux to show this. The students then move slowly and deliberately, improvising dialogue, from the Conflict Tableau to the Resolution Tableau.

Implications of The Center Plot for Multicultural Education

The expected goal of this model is to alter students' prejudicial behavior. However idealistic and unlikely it might be that this goal can be achieved in just six drama sessions, the model nevertheless allows students to learn about another group and experience a change of attitude about them, culminating in a new mode of behavior.

The DIE strategies provided in Sessions One through Three subject students to actual prejudicial behavior as both victims and oppressors. The Citizens establish their new society with laws designed to protect them from discrimination, but their commitment to these laws soon becomes so consuming that they inflict upon others the same oppressions they previously sought to escape. The primary challenge for the teacher in Sessions One and Two is to carefully construct opportunities for the participants to build a belief in the tenets of New Harmony.

As the Representative of the Ruler of an unspecified country, the teacher can be in an authoritative position when necessary. Also, by participating as a central character, the teacher provides students the opportunity to challenge and even contradict that position—a condition they rarely, if ever, enjoy in real life. The teacher in role, on occasion, dictates events in the drama that can be discussed out of role with the students: Was the decision fair? Did it favor some characters more than others? Did the Representative exhibit prejudice toward certain individuals? Could this have been avoided? If not, how could it have been dealt with?

Early in Session One, the teacher in role stresses that the participants previously had lived under oppressive conditions. When she asks them to discover from each other what they hope to gain by living in a new land, she lays the foundation for the conflicts to come that are related to the issue of prejudice.

The formation of family groups allows the students to instigate the development of their own society. The selection of family names and occupations provides students with specific identities and helps them develop a sense of pride. While posing for family portraits reinforces and solidifies familial units, the Celebration is intended to establish a sense of contentment and unity among the Citizens. Only when a sense of family unit has been achieved does the teacher move the drama forward by reminding them that they have not always been content. Under the cautious guidance of the teacher, the Citizens select and depict past prejudices inflicted upon them.

In Session Two, the focus moves from the family to the development of the community and the construction of a new social order. The introduction of the map of New Harmony permits the students to see themselves in relationship to the large community. The students then create their own laws, based on the prejudices they incurred previously. These laws should be carefully constructed by the entire community with the understanding that all, as Citizens of New Harmony, must agree to live by them. The ritual reading and signing of the constitution solidifies and reinforces the seriousness of the situation.

The decision regarding the purpose of the center plot of land is left entirely to the students, with the reminder by the teacher that the space is special and should be used for something special. By empowering the students with this control, the teacher will discover which aspects of society are most important to the students. Then, by announcing that a group of people have arrived, she asks the students to elaborate on those rumors. At this point in the drama, it is vital that the students (1) have a belief in the events of the drama and that the meaning behind this belief is "important" to them, (2) that they have a commitment to their individual family units, and (3) that they are committed to the community as a whole.

In Session Three, prejudice is seen in action. The Strangers live by rules diametrically opposed to those of the Citizens. The Strangers, a small group of people, should not be presented as attempting to change the lives of the Citizens. Instead, they are a peaceful people who want only to live as they have chosen. The conflict arises when the Citizens insist that the Strangers either abide by the laws of New Harmony or leave, demonstrating the infliction of their prejudices upon the Strangers. The workshop concludes with each group suspicious and fearful of the other.

The students in sessions One through Three have experienced or "lived through" situations exploring prejudice. But in Four through Six, they are allowed to critique this issue, stand outside the drama, and analyze their own thoughts, preconceptions, presuppositions, and actions as well as those of the characters being examined. The teacher, in discussions, should refer to the situations experienced by the Citizens of New Harmony and endeavor to see that the following goals are obtained:

1. Participants should consider a variety of choices, as well as predict possible consequences of each and weigh the pros and cons or options before making a decision.
2. Participants should analyze their own attitudes and feelings toward a particular issue, as well as provide new insight into their own preconceptions.
3. Participants should step back and view a situation from another point of view, as well as encourage educated decisions, rather than ones based primarily on self-centeredness.
4. Participants should examine long-range goals that affect others as well as themselves instead of settling for immediate self-centered gratification.
5. Participants should recognize their own potential in producing change in their lives as well as in the lives of others and society.
6. Participants should learn to prioritize choices; to settle, if necessary, and at least temporarily, for a lesser solution to establish a plan for a more satisfactory one.
7. Participants should learn to accept the consequences of their actions.
8. Participants should be able to conceptualize the spiraling nature of decision making; to understand that examination of choices leads to examination of possible consequences which, in turn, leads to decision making. Students should begin to comprehend that decision making is an ongoing process that requires skills for implementation that need constant honing and practice.

Summary of DIE

The theories and practices of drama and theatre in education are catalysts for changing prejudicial attitudes and for ameliorating conflicts by promoting understanding and respect for those who are different from oneself. The model included here illuminates the drama process as it examines sources and conditions of prejudice. Drama workshops offer students the freedom to investigate the world in which they live. They invite and stimulate open, flexible, and imaginative thinking so that avenues of change become apparent to the individual and to the group alike. Through a variety of dramatic activities, students explore specific issues of race, gender, ability, and disability and, rather than hearing a teacher talk about them, they actually "experience" them in performance and reflection.

The scope of multicultural learning presents vast opportunities for the use of drama and theatre techniques in the classroom. For example, the enactment of so simple and traditional a story as *Cinderella* can foster an understanding of such enduring problems as sibling rivalry, oppression, and abuse. Different versions of *Cinderella* as the fairy tale is known in other cultures can offer fascinating comparisons that range from those of ancient Egypt, China, and Russia to American Indians (Swortzell, 1992). The German version of the story even gives us a Cinderella figure who, in fact, is a boy. For older children, this same tale can be explored in its more complex variations as in the story of Cain and Abel and in the tragedy of Shakespeare's *King Lear.*

Timeless global folk and fairy tales are ideal for story dramatization, just as interesting holidays are for the revelations of their similarities and dissimilarities. In performing this age-old material, just as in dramatizing events and issues from current newspapers, different points of view soon become evident and new ideas emerge about the world as it exists today, ideas that are "alive" because they involve, enrich, and empower the students who discover them by "enacting" them.

The model provided in this chapter is not intended to be copied literally but rather to suggest some possibilities available through DIE. The initial challenge confronting the teacher eager to incorporate drama into the curriculum is knowing how to begin. The following suggestions are not meant to be prescriptive, but they do provide a way to begin. As teachers have successful experiences, they will be encouraged to use other dramatic activities and strategies, culminating in the use of DIE for multicultural education as an integral element of the curriculum.

To successfully incorporate drama into their classroom, teachers make a note of the following guidelines:

1. Be thoroughly familiar with the content of the session. It is often beneficial to begin by implementing a single activity requiring no more than 10 or 15 minutes of class time.
2. Establish an attainable learning objective for the students.
3. Consider the dynamics of the students, including their ability to work in small groups and the amount of guidance they will require.
4. Provide enough space and time to work.
5. Realize there may be more movement and noise than usual.
6. Stimulate the students' thinking by compelling them to develop their ideas while remaining focused on the activity.
7. Recognize and acknowledge honest efforts from the students.
8. Encourage the students to develop their assessment skills by guiding their analysis of the drama and by allowing them to offer suggestions for future sessions.
9. Incorporate into the drama other areas of the curriculum, including songs, instrumental music, visual art, puppetry, dance, stories, and poems representative of various cultures.

✢ Glossary

The following strategies have been selected for identification because they are included in The Center Plot model, and are representative of the techniques often used in drama in education workshops, incorporating "critical thinking through drama" techniques.

Board Work   Responses from students during "brainstorming," which are recorded on the chalkboard; they provide concrete evidence of the students' reactions and a visible reference to be used later in the session.

Critical Thinking Through Drama   A methodology incorporating various techniques employed in drama in education and theatre in education as well as other forms of educational theatre, including drama therapy and psychodrama, for the development of students' decision-making skills. The content examines a specific social issue relevant to the participants, such as pregnancy, drugs and alcohol, peer pressure, AIDS, abuse, prejudice, and racism.

A paradigm might begin with the creation of scenes centered on a specific issue of conflict agreed upon by the teacher and the students but intentionally left unresolved. The students then select one situation to explore and resolve, a technique referred to as processing. By employing a series of strategies, including improvisation, role play, hotseating, doubling, flashback, and "flashforward," all interspersed with frequent discussion, the students consider choices open to the characters and examine the possible consequences of these decisions in solving the conflict.

Doubling   A variation of "hotseating" in which a student becomes the "inner self" of the character being questioned. Doubling provides insight into and knowledge about the characters as well as the opportunity to weigh the differences between what characters say and what they think. (See Hotseating.)

Exercise   An activity designed to develop specific skills required for a drama session. While often implemented at the beginning of a workshop as warm-up or preparation, exercises are invaluable throughout the session, especially when the session becomes more complex. Exercises allow students opportunity to step out of the drama and reflect upon what is happening.

Flashback   A scene or "tableau" created by the students depicting a situation from the past, which provides insight into the character's present circumstances, actions, and relationships.

Flashforward   A scene or "tableau" created by the students, most often toward the end of a session, depicting the characters in a situation occurring in the future; this allows the opportunity to consider a realistic or idealistic resolution.

Follow Up   Activities assigned by the teacher and completed by the students before the next workshop which provide continuity between the sessions and allow the teacher to incorporate other areas of the curriculum such as writing, art, music, and map making.

Hotseating   Questioning of characters by the student audience to increase understanding of both motive and circumstance; this technique moves the drama forward and assists in resolving the conflict.

Improvisation   The spontaneous acting out of a situation, which may be (1) unplanned by the participants, (2) planned and often rehearsed in pairs or small groups, or (3) implemented in large groups, guided by the teacher who is frequently in role. Improvisations are unpredictable, belonging to a specific moment of experience and, while not intended for performance before audiences, are shared with other members of the class.

Narration   A narrative description of "what happens next," implemented, usually spontaneously, by the teacher; provides linkage between scenes as well as information important to the participants which has not been provided in the drama.

Pantomime   The nonverbal acting out of an action or situation, in which gesture, facial expression, and movement, rather than speech, are relied upon; silent acting.

Questioning   Interspersed throughout the workshop, this technique encourages the participants to confront the issues of the drama. Though most often implemented by the teacher, questioning by the students, either in or out of role, is invaluable.

Reflection   A time of contemplation initiated through statements or questions, intended to be thought about, not responded to verbally, providing a quiet and private time for the participants to internalize events and to consider the future course of the drama.

Ritual   An activity such as the passing of a sacred object, repeating a pledge, or signing a contract, initiated by the teacher—usually in role—and implemented individually by the participants; this helps build belief in and commitment to the drama.

Role Play   A form of improvisation representing a group of people in a lifelike event such as a party, teachers' conference, or a town meeting; usually, a social situation for which students take on roles and relate to others in the group.

Tableau   Often referred to as a "frozen picture," a "still life," or a "living photograph," this strategy stops the drama at a fixed moment, allowing the participants to reflect upon what is happening and permitting the teacher to comment on the images presented: What do you think is happening here? What is that character thinking? What is the relationship among these people?

Teacher in Role   The taking on of a role by the teacher, permitting participation in the drama with the students, becoming one of them, not isolated or watching. This technique allows the teacher to work from inside the drama, challenging the students, sometimes agreeing with them but often opposing them to move the drama forward.

References

Bolton, G. (1979). *Towards a theory of drama in education.* London: Longman.

Bolton, G. (1984). *Drama as education.* London: Longman.

Bolton, G. (1986). *Selected writings.* London: Longman.

Chapman, R., & Wilkes, B. (Eds.). (1975). *Snap out of it.* London: Methuen Young Drama.

Circles of fire. (1990). Unpublished manuscript. London: Greenwich Theatre-in-Education Company.

Cook, C. (1917). *The play way: An essay in educational method.* London: Heinemann.

Finlay-Johnson, H. (1911). *The dramatic method of teaching.* London: Nisbet.

Holman, D. (1980). *No passeran.* In P. Schweitzer (Ed.), *Theatre-in-education: Four secondary programmes.* London: Methuen Young Drama.

Jennings, C., & Jennings, L. (1990). *The early life of Louis Braille.* Woodstock, IL: Dramatic Publishing Company.

Johnson, L., & O'Neill, C. (Eds.). (1985). *Dorothy Heathcote: Collected writings on education and drama.* London: Hutchinson.

Kral, B. (1981). *Special class.* New Orleans: Anchorage Press.

McCaslin, N. (1971). *Theatre for children in the United States: A history.* Norman, OK: University of Oklahoma Press.

McCaslin, N. (1978). *Theatre for young audiences.* New York: Longman.

McCaslin, N. (1981). (Ed.). *Children and drama* (2nd ed.). New York: Longman.

McCaslin, N. (1990). *Creative drama in the classroom* (5th ed.). New York: Longman.

Multicultural images: Leeds TIE team discuss their programme "Raj" with Geoff Gillham. (1982, September). London: *SCYPT Journal, 10.*

O'Neill, C. (1984, Winter). Imagined world in theatre and drama. *London Drama, 6*(10).

O'Neill, C. (1988). *Drama structures: A practical handbook for teachers.* London: Hutchinson.

Redington, C. (1983). *Can theatre teach?* Oxford: Pergamon Press.

Slade, P. (1969). *Child drama.* London: University of London Press.

Sweetie Pie. (1975). London: Methuen Young Drama.

Swortzell, L. (1986). *Six plays for young people from the Federal Theatre Project.* New York: Greenwood Press.

Swortzell, L. (1990). *International guide to children's theatre and educational theatre: A historical and geographical source book.* New York: Greenwood Press.

Swortzell, L. (1992). *Cinderella: The world's favorite fairy tale.* Charlottesville, VA: New Plays, Inc.

Wagner, B. J. (1976). *Dorothy Heathcote: Drama as a learning medium.* Washington, DC: National Educational Association.

Ward, W. (1957). *Playmaking with children.* New York: Appleton-Century-Crofts.

Ward, W. (1958). *Theatre for children.* Anchorage, KY: Children's Theatre Press.

Way, B. (1967). *Development through drama.* London: Longman.

Wyatt, S., & Steed, M. (Eds.). (1976). *Rare Earth: A programme about pollution.* London: Eyre Metheun, Ltd.

Reading Film and Television in the Classroom: African American Representations in Popular Culture

Ann De Vaney
University of Wisconsin-Madison

> Knowledge, however mundane and utilitarian, plays about in linguistic (and pictorial) images and forms cultural practice (Morrison, 1992, 49).

As the century draws to a close, educators can assess the gains garnered for the classroom by civil rights protestors and subsequent civil rights legislation in the turbulent 1960s and 1970s. During the late 1970s, the 1980s, and even the early 1990s, efforts were made by producers of popular culture to at least include images of some people of color in their media products. Outlets such as Hollywood and broadcast television supported the production, for example, of African American films by directors of color and African American weekly comedy series. In 1991 alone, 19 films by African American writers and directors were produced and distributed by major Hollywood studios. Whatever the economic motives of these producers, this was a moment in time when specific issues of social equity for African Americans, among others, was not only addressed but examined and sometimes creatively explored.

As I write in November of 1998, the political tenor of the nation has changed drastically and my home state, California, has passed a referendum excluding some Chicanos/as from basic rights such as health care and education. Also, the University of California system has banned affirmative action considerations when hiring staff and admitting students, and both California and the state of Washington have banned affirmative action considerations from any aspect of state government. In this time of backlash, fewer African American Hollywood films and situation comedies on broadcast television are included in popular culture rosters.

Cablecast, as opposed to broadcast, television, however, has extended its reach and offers the Black Entertainment Television (BET), a number of African American situation comedies on WB and UPN, as well as reruns of late 1980s and early 1990s African American sit-coms.

Why should this state of affairs in the realm of popular culture concern educators? I contend that Hollywood film and television are teachers, shapers of mores, values, social habits, buying habits, and leisure time. They are powerful educators who compete daily and yearly with the presence of teachers in the classroom. As diversity increases in classrooms and certain textbook publishers and curriculum designers emphasize multiculturalism, what is the effect of that teacher, popular culture, on the learning of students? Is it enough for students to be exposed to stereotypical African American images in rap videos or violent cinema to understand concepts of equity, or do they need as wide a range of Black images as they have of White images on the screen? Certainly, I believe they do. As a teacher I have attempted to help student viewers become critical consumers of media representations of people from any heritage. I am writing this chapter to share the techniques I employ.

In this chapter, I explore ways to help students interrupt the onslaught of stereotypic images from popular culture by providing them with skills that will serve them well now and into the new multicultural century. An ability to understand the messages embodied in representations of people of color, for instance, enables them to distinguish between and among the desires of producers and directors, gives them insight, and consequently power, to weigh the equitability of certain media strategies.

First, I will relate the formation of self-image to mediated images and then explore two methods for reading film and television images. Since this essay is limited, I will concentrate on reading representations of one group, African Americans, but my intention is different from that of many critical media strategies. Space on the screen should and sometimes does become open enough for students of color to see themselves reflected in film or television. Another way of saying this is that the subjectivity of TV programs and film sometimes becomes multiple enough so that diverse subjects in the classroom are able to identity with representations on the screen. The times in which that occurs are teachable moments. With these different strategies I stress the location of complex, credible representations, and simply mention stereotypical images. Borrowing from literary textual analysis I first employ a structural and later a poststructural method. The first concentrates on the manner in which the form or structural features encode the message of the visual text (film or television program); the second focuses on the way in which a visual text positions the viewer or creates its own subjectivity.

✛ Picturing Yourself

Have you considered how you construct your image, develop a picture of yourself? Jacques Lacan (1977) would have us believe that this construction begins at 18 months of age during what he calls a mirror stage, which is the process of differentiating yourself from others and begins when you gain the ability to recognize your reflection in a mirror. Although his period of development includes the society of parents and playmates, it is devoid of other societal images and excludes artifacts and mediated images that also contribute to the formation of a self-image. In a society that prizes individualism, it seems natural to believe that you form an image of yourself and differentiate from others by simply looking into a mirror or the faces of those around you, but the process is not that simple and there is ample evidence to support your dependence on other images.

When I think of the issue of how we form self images, I am reminded of Alicia and her mother, Carol. I was introduced to Alicia when she and her family spent the holidays with me. She was just 5 and by her mother's account somewhat shy and reticent, but after just one day in my house she felt comfortable enough to tell me about her hair. She hated her hair, and I was stunned by that revelation. Whether I like it or not, I know how important hair is to the image of a young girl. I had never encountered a White 5-year-old who hated her hair. Because I was puzzled, my ready reserve of positive responses for children was slow in coming for Alicia, but I told her I admired her corn-rows, and said that my niece always begged her mother to braid her hair in corn-rows. Alicia liked her long hair, but wanted it smooth and shiny, she told me, really smooth and shiny. I thought about this and asked Carol if Alicia had seen Whoopi Goldberg on Sesame Street. "Yes," she replied, but one example, one image is not enough. Then she told me a moving story.

I asked a friend of mine to make an authentic African American doll for Alicia. It was gorgeous, with black hair in corn rows—some tied with colorful ribbons. I put fancy wrappings on the box and placed it under the Christmas tree. On Christmas morning Alicia was casually opening presents until she came to the big box. When she lifted the lid she gasped. It took her breath away. Her face lit up. Perplexed, she asked, "How did I get in there? How did I get in that box?" To this day she treats that doll differently, carefully, and with reverence.

It can only be societal images that prompted Alicia to desire smooth hair. bell hooks recalls similar longings.

> GOOD HAIR—that's the expression. We all know it, begin to hear it when we are small children. . . . Good hair is hair that is not kinky, hair that does not feel like balls of steel wool, hair that does not take hours to comb, hair that does not need tons of grease to untangle, hair that is long. Real good hair is straight hair, hair like white folks hair. (hooks in Gates, 1991, p. 339)

When hooks was young, respectful pictures of African Americans were absent from the majority of mediated images she encountered in books, films, ads, and TV. But the situation was worse for Zora Neale Hurston in the early part of the century when Black media images were most disrespectful.

In her 1937 novel, Hurston tells a poignant story about the way Jane, a 6-year-old, formed an image of herself (*Their Eyes Were Watching God,* 1990).

> So when we looked at de picture and everybody got pointed out there wasn't nobody left except a real dark little girl with long hair standing by Eleanor. Dat's where Ah was s'posed to be, but Ah couldn't recognize dat dark chile as me. So Ah ast, 'where is me? Ah don't see me.'
>   . . . Ah looked at de picture a long time and seen it was mah dress and mah hair so Ah said:
> 'Aw, aw! Ah'm colored! (Hurston, 1990, p. 9)

Janie played with her White playmates in all the rooms of their "big house." Certainly, there must have been a mirror in one of those rooms. Yet, she did not use the mirror to form an image of herself, and most popular representations in her day did not include African Americans; those that did were derogatory. To start forming a picture of herself she used the mirror of a private photo in which she saw her image standing next to those of her White playmates.

I believe people use all available images to create pictures of themselves. From an early age, children see faces on television, in snapshots, on billboards, in magazines, and now in home videos. I have one 9-year-old nephew who has videos of himself from the time he was in utero. What influence, I ask myself, does viewing oneself in a videotaped sonogram and numerous home videos have on self-image? The images children encounter on home videos, however, are only a fraction of the faces in their lives.

All forms of art and popular culture create images by means of representation. Artists and producers use socially constructed signs and symbols to depict children or adults, Black or White, national or international. People use these artistic or popular depictions to construct their own image. Self-image becomes a composite of reflections from real and mediated mirrors. If Black Barbie dolls have long shiny hair and syrup bottles still picture Aunt Jemima, if MTV presents young Black women dressed only as street walkers and Black men continue to be violent partners to White men in cop shows, then African American children will continue to see themselves portrayed in stereotypic ways. A classroom, I believe, can be the place to teach all children to become critical consumers of these images, to reject stereotypes, to identify and ultimately demand credible representations, particularly of people of color. Teachers can acquire and teach those skills necessary to intelligently read photos, ads, films, and television. In fact, most watchers of film and TV have unconsciously adopted those skills; therefore, it becomes the role of the classroom teacher to make that which is tacit, apparent.

❖ Reading Images

Hollywood film, broadcast and narrowcast television are major transmitters of culture today; their practices of production and our manner of reception shape our collective life in a substantial way. Standardized patterns of speech, dress, fashion, family rituals, and other group behaviors are presented in a daily parade of commercial films and television programs. We have evidence that this parade influences our purchasing and voting habits and that it shapes our children's behaviors, beliefs and knowledge. Marshall McLuhan (1964) understood the cultural impact of television when he noted that the TV screen had replaced the hearth. Many immigrants to the U.S. learn not only the English language from television, but also how to dress and behave in their new country. Broadcast, now joined by cablecast, television has been the major influence in the election of every president from John Kennedy to Bill Clinton.

Arguments that these popular media simply reflect culture, i.e., habits, tastes, etc. of the public are reductive, because popular media not only reflect, but shape. In fact, they shape consumption of more items than themselves. To claim that television, for example, only reflects culture actually trivializes the medium and neglects to assign enough influence to it. MTV not only sells music, but clothes and hair styles; in addition to these consumer items it sells mores by modeling certain aspects of male-female interaction. Educators, when citing amazing viewing statistics, such as the fact that children view 3 to 4 hours of television each day, often miss the point of such statistics (Nielson, 1991). Viewing statistics are generally invoked when educators wish to describe reasons for students' failure at school, not to recognize the powerful teacher that is television.

One of the major ways in which television and film teach is through the presentation of human images. It is, after all, primarily a visual medium. I am interested in what faces are presented to children and how these representations help children form self-images and pictures of others. For instance, examples of disrespectful film and TV images of people of color abound, and while it is important to understand the manner in which these images are constructed and the reason for their persistence, it is equally important to seize those scarce complex and credible images of people of color for use in the classroom. Some cognitive theories indicate that if students are presented with "mistakes and errors" before they are given correct examples of the concept being taught, they will first recall the error before recalling the concept itself or the correct application of it; so it is with images. Pictures of Black women dressed as street walkers or Chicanos presented as buffoons have an emotional impact which prompts recall faster than non-stereotypic images, and repetition of these negative representations certainly assists students in their recall. Students should be taught to read both types of images, stereotypic and complex, and understand the messages constructed by them. The two methods I describe here help students read film and television images by questioning the screen, by interrogating the image, by not taking pictures for granted.

✥ Critiquing Film and Television

For centuries, teachers have guided students in methods of critiquing a text; questioning a text to discover author intentions and reader interpretations is a natural classroom activity. Post-modern texts, however, go beyond the written page, and students are bombarded daily with visual texts which transmit much of their contemporary culture. I suggest that the critiquing of those texts is a necessary curricular task and can become a springboard for formation of self-image and understanding, respect and appreciation of diverse people.

Films and television programs are visual texts that can be read in a manner similar to the way one reads newspapers, essays or short stories. A written text consists of words, sentences and paragraphs, while a visual text consists of frames, shots, and scenes or sequences. Just as the study of syntax and grammar of a written text prepares students to read and produce written material, so does the study of syntax and organization of frames, shots, and sequences prepare them to produce and read film and television. Since most people have tacitly acquired many decoding skills, a teacher begins the study of visual texts with an advantage. Studying these skills, it is hoped, will simply uncover them.

Structural Approach

A camera is not a window on the world. People have become so used to commenting on any picture of a child by saying, "Oh. Isn't that a cute baby," that the means for the construction of images become invisible. A baby picture is not reality, but an image mediated by the technology of photography. In this postmodern age images are so ubiquitous they become pleasurable in themselves and it grows easy to mistake an image for reality. Television news, which one wants to believe as true, is also constructed. A televised shot of an urban resistance movement is not a "slice of life." It has been constructed with intent by a director and camera-person and transformed by the technology of the video camera. It probably represents the most sensational aspect of the resistance and needs to be read by mentally juxtaposing less fiery or less violent scenes.

A structural method of critiquing an image relies on the notion that the form or structure of a communication is as important in delivering a message as is the content. The structures of a TV program, for instance—frame, shot, transitions and scene—fabricate the message that a viewer receives. Questions such as these help students uncover messages hidden in the form. What do you imagine lies outside the frame? What is the angle of the shot? What kind of lighting is used in the scene? What is the distance of the camera from the focal point? What types of edits are used and how are they paced? What is the sequence of scene or segment presentation?

Frame   The smallest structural unit in film and television is a frame, that which can be differentiated and identified when one holds film stock to the light, or—for purposes of this chapter—that which one can capture by pressing the pause button on a video cassette recorder. What is included in a frame is read not only by its content, but by what has been excluded. If viewers see a single televised shot of Michael Jordan advertising athletic shoes on a basketball court, they interpret his movement as if set within a stadium, although they may not have actually seen the stadium. In other words, they create the geography of the frame by imagining the space outside of it. This reading of visual information within the frame by mental reference to what viewers suppose lies outside the frame is a learned skill that viewers acquire as children. Students can be made aware of their ability to construct the geography of a frame if one asks them to question the frame. What lies inside and outside that electronic border? The need for such exercises, though, may not be readily apparent.

Many teens today are such facile TV viewers that they may claim not to be influenced by the medium and maintain that they know when a message is authentic or fabricated, but the point here is that all the messages are fabricated and most TV watchers do not realize that fact. For example, during the 1989 Loma-Prieta earthquake that hit the San Francisco Bay area with great force, TV viewers across the country were aghast at scenes of burning buildings. It appeared that San Francisco was in flames when, in fact, television cameras were consistently trained on a small area of the Marina where houses were on fire. A viewer would have to tell herself that what lies outside the frame is probably not in flames.

The opposite scenario was played out on TV after the 1994 Northridge earthquake in Southern California. There, news teams consistently showed the same footage. One large apartment house in Sherman Oaks had collapsed, and that was displayed frequently, as were scenes of laborers and their families camping in Red Cross tents in local parks. The newspapers indicated that damage was widespread in wealthy sections of Los Angeles, such as parts of Santa Monica, the foothills of Thousand Oaks, Brentwood, and sections of West Los Angeles. The discrepancy between newspaper reporting (without pictures) and TV coverage was telling. I believe an effort was made by the producers of news, who themselves lived in those neighborhoods, to exclude pictures of upper middle and upper class neighborhoods for fear of raids. In this case, a viewer might think of the damage as contained, less widespread than it was. In both earthquakes viewers would have to ask what lies outside the frame. But viewers want to believe that the camera is a window on the world, even when they know better.

Angle, Lighting, Distance   Other structural features besides the frame are used in the production and interpretation of a shot on television. The angle of the camera, lighting, and distance of the camera from the focal point are used by directors to construct the shot and by viewers to read the shot. A medium shot allows students to compare and contrast people or objects within its frame. The camera may move from close-up for detail, to medium shot for comparison and contrast, to long shot for establishment of locale or to give an overview. It also moves from low angle, where viewers feel less powerful than the person depicted, to a level angle where they are "on the level" with the person's image, to a high angle where they may feel more powerful than the person depicted. Lighting in the shot can move through a range of low-key, suggesting a quiet, somber or fearful mood, to high key, suggesting a cheerful or celebratory mood. Without thinking, spectators use these structural clues to read film and television images.

An interior shot of Hilton Lucas's kitchen may communicate its meaning by being constructed with high key (bright) lighting for a cheerful and busy mood. Hilton may be standing in the doorway and the camera shoots him from a low angle which forces viewers to look up to him; the shot actually encourages people to admire him; conversely, a high angle shot would make viewers look down upon him. He may be sitting on the sofa in his studio living room after having made a fool of himself, and the director selects a high angle shot to reduce his stature for the moment. If the camera then zooms out from a tight shot of Hilton Lucas on the sofa to a medium-long shot of the living room, viewers are able to smirk at Hilton at close range and then see who else may be in the room smirking. Here the camera is detailing the geography of the visual space to help viewers makes sense of the intended messages.

Motion   Within a shot the camera can move in a limited number of ways, and directors use each of these to layer different meanings on the shot. A camera can only zoom in or out, tilt up or down, and pan, left or right. If a director moves the whole camera, she can only dolly or truck the camera in a smooth path moving along with the moving object in the shot. Traditionally, these structural features were used in a seamless, hidden manner and were designed not to be noticed. In other words, a director did not want to call attention to them; viewers were not encouraged to notice them, but were led to believe they were watching a "slice of life." Matched cuts within shots were consistently used in 1950s film and television so that viewers understood where they were in the geography of visual space.

Current films and television programs often call attention to themselves by using jump cuts and dizzying motion. Directors accent those structural units used by viewers to read TV. This is apparent on MTV and in the numerous films and programs imitating MTV. Innovative use of within-shot motion techniques and between-shot edits allows viewers to take notice of the screen itself; it calls attention to the clever use of production styles. After generations of attempting to imitate reality, many film television formats are calling attention to themselves, and it is within these formats that one can learn the nature of the medium itself. It is as if a director were saying to viewers, "Look at what I can create," instead of saying, "I don't want you to know that camera is here."

Shots   Frames are static, but when a camera moves from frame to frame, it is called a shot; a shot is a series of frames. Shots are juxtaposed in film and television just as sentences are juxtaposed in a paragraph. The mixing and matching of shots can deliver as many different messages as the mixing and matching of sentences in a paragraph. There are a limited number of edits or transitions from shot to shot in film and television; these are cuts, wipes, dissolves, and superimpositions. Often the last two are combined and, as I indicated, a director can use seamless editing by matching the geography of one shot to that of another and attempt to keep the camera invisible, or she can use jump cuts to jar spectators and toss them around in the geography of the visual space, thereby calling attention to the ingenuity of the people behind the camera. MTV and imitators make frequent use of jump cuts, as did Serge Eisenstein in early Russian films such as *Ivan the Terrible* and *Potempkin.* (Eisenstein used jump cuts to establish the practice of cinematic montage, which can be powerful and encourage mental metaphors in spectators).

Shot Transitions Traditionally, a shot transition or edit which suggests no passage of time or place is a match cut. A wipe is like the curtain coming down or going up on the stage and suggests the close or opening of a scene plus a passage of time and possibly a change of place. When a TV image dissolves to black it also signals a passage of time, but if a dissolve and superimposition are used together it is usually for aesthetic or decorative purposes and may enhance the mood. The speed of edits, transitions from one shot to the next, can set the tone for the scene or sequence just as tempo can set the mood in music. Staccato editing, as in the shower scene from *Psycho,* can build tension and be frightening. Long uninterrupted shots can call attention to the dialogue or other aspect of the scene that the director believes is important, or they can be used to suggest a sense of boredom.

Film and Television as Visual Text

Like rhythm in music and syntax in language, these structural features pace the presentation of film and TV images and provide program continuity. Without thinking, students tacitly use these features to read the screen; this process is similar to the linguistic process of reading a printed text. Television and film are visual texts which viewers read daily. If spectators read MTV in a traditional fashion, expecting the physical cues of matched cuts and seamless editing, they will be tossed around in the geography of the space by all the jump cuts. Since younger viewers have accrued thousands of TV viewing hours, they may be challenged by jump cuts; they may enjoy making sense of the geography of the visual space, and may employ visual metaphors without thinking. (While some designers of visual literacy curricula tout this ability as cognitive sophistication, it is actually lower-order thinking).

Codes In film and TV texts, messages are visually encoded and a code in these media is a syntax pattern which can best be illustrated by reference to a written code. Syntax refers to the organization or arrangement of a communication—whether a sentence or a visual scene. When an arrangement is consistently repeated in the production of a communication, a code develops (DeVaney, 1991). "Have a nice day" has become a code in the United States for a well-wishing goodbye. "Don't have a cow, man" is a code borrowed from television for telling someone to take it easy. "Who's been sitting in my chair?" is a familiar code for the child listening to *The Three Bears.* Codes develop only through repetition, and readers of printed or visual texts tacitly understand the meaning of codes often before they can verbalize that meaning. In movie theaters it was Alfred Hitchcock who taught spectators to be afraid by offering a visual syntax pattern or code that he and other film directors frequently repeated. Current film or TV watchers are frightened by this code when a hand-held camera presents a villain's point of view (POV) shot while the camera stalks a victim in the woods or down the dark corridor of a house.

This syntax pattern grew from daily production practices that were repeated often in murder mysteries or horror formats; they included hand-held cameras for tentative humanlike movement, POV subjective shots, medium shots of dark corridors or somber paths in the woods. Another visual syntax pattern or code that Hitchcock taught us is the use of fast-paced transitions as in the shower scene in *Psycho.* That fast-paced editing along with jump cuts of body parts and specific music has become a code for murder in a horror film.

Codes of Realism   Even when Bernard Shaw presents the news on CNN, codes of realism are employed to make viewers believe in him and the news. But they are not watching Mr. Shaw read the news; they are watching a televised representation of him. This image is one remove from reality, and it is important to note that camera and structural codes are used to imitate reality. Using television news codes, a director usually shoots Mr. Shaw on the level, so viewers see him "eye to eye" and he gains their trust. Current codes of realism employed in the construction of TV news include shooting the newscaster on the level, employing a moderately high key lighting pattern for an upbeat effect, allowing viewers to see the geography of the news studio in a medium shot, and allowing viewers to see the cameras and camera operators. These were not the codes of realism in the 1970s, nor will they be the codes of realism in the next decade. It is difficult but necessary to remember that the camera always lies; it presents a fiction. It may record an authentic event, but that event is reshaped by the technology of film or television and presented as a story to viewers.

In this section I have drawn upon a method of literary analysis to explain the basic structural units of film and television. By questioning the screen, its frame, shot, motion, lighting, editing, and scene building, students can uncover the manner in which these forms fabricate media messages. By identifying syntax patterns or codes, viewers can relate the program they are watching to other visual texts.

Students will be enabled viewers if they understand that everything they watch in film and television is a text that has been constructed with intent by a director, encoded in socially constructed signs and symbols, and interpreted by them as members of a community that has access to those signs and symbols. These popular media, therefore, can be explained in a discursive fashion. To heighten student's understanding, teachers can encourage their students to experiment with video cameras, so they may experience the construction of a visual text as they do the construction of an essay. This capacity, however, is only the first step in the process of recognizing complex and credible representations of any people; such recognition includes the development of additional skills.

❖ African Americans on Television

As filmgoers witness the diminution today of Hollywood films from African American directors, TV watchers are confronted with another cultural dilemma. While the number of African American situation comedies on the major broadcast networks, (ABC, NBC, and CBS) has been reduced to two on CBS (in this 1998–99 season), certain cablecast networks (Fox, WB, and UPN) are catering to a specific niche, the African American audience (Gay, 1998). At first glance this situation may appear hopeful for educators seeking to capture complex images of people of color for the classroom, but more shifts than the transition of African American programs from broadcast to cablecast networks may have occurred between the early and the late 1990s. Commenting on the efforts of WB and UPN to present African American programs, critics and artists have taken the networks to task. Writing in the *Boston Phoenix,* television critic Jason Gay (1998) notes that while these networks are committed to attracting African American viewers, they are less committed to giving them something worthwhile to watch. Even "Rapper Chuck D dismissed UPN as the 'United Plantation of Negroes' " (Gay, 1998). Certain chapters of the

NAACP have cited these networks for their "horrible" representations of Black life, and Spike Lee said "I would rather see Amos 'n' Andy . . . At least they were straight-up about Uncle Tommin" (Gay, 1998). But critical opinion is mixed and some artists (Marlon Wayans) and political groups (national NAACP) think that what WB and UPN offer audiences is helpful for the African American image. Nonetheless, the suitability of these programs for educators seeking to capture the complex representation of African Americans is problematic, and the issues are further complicated by niche viewership.

In the early 1990s broadcast television and Fox included more situation comedies and dramatic series with African American casts in prime time than ever before, and producers were aiming their programs at a crossover audience (DeVaney, 1992). On ABC, NBC, CBS, and cablecast, Fox programs such as "The Cosby Show," "Family Matters," "In Living Color," "A Different World," "True Colors," "I'll Fly Away," "Homefront," "Fresh Prince of Bel Air," and "Roc" attracted White audiences as well as people of color. Since these programs often addressed issues of African Americans living and thriving in a White society, they were rich sources for appropriating complex and credible images of African Americans. Today, with the proliferation of cable channels and the backlash to multicultural education, few if any producers are reaching a crossover audience. For example, in the 1998–99 season the five most popular programs that have African American casts ("Between Brothers," 1, Fox; "Living Single," 2, Fox; "Hope Street," 3, Fox; "Steve Harvey Show," 4, WB; and "The Wayans Brothers," 5, WB), had a low viewership in White households. The top five White programs ("ER," 1, NBC; "Seinfeld," 2, NBC; "Veronica's Closet," 3, NBC; "Friends," 4, NBC; and "Touched by an Angel," 5, CBS) had a much lower viewership in Black than in White households. Producers, in seeking niche audiences, have segregated viewership.

While this segregated situation and the quality of some television programs presents problems for educators, they are not insurmountable. In fact, broadcast and cablecast television in general has a much better record than does Hollywood for producing African American programs or films. And television has taken more risks in representing complex African Americans than has Hollywood. The presence, however, of video stores that stock both films and older television programs can be a rich source for those educators and students seeking to capture video clips of multiple representations of African Americans.

❖ Old and New Television Programs

Since images of people of color tend to remain stereotyped, teachers will have to search between and among films or television programs for clips to include in the curriculum. In the old "Family Matters," Urkel, for example, is more of a caricature than a character—his antics are similar to a modern Step 'n' Fetchit. And although his role is extended to include the antics of a smart nerd in the new "Family Matters," he is still a pitiful caricature. In his new incarnation he has graduated from a Step 'n' Fetchit symbol to a grotesquely satirized intelligent student. In this program and in the current (1998–99) "Steve Harvey Show" (WB), any and all students who study, who may be smart and who communicate that interest are made objects of derision. (In fact, "The Steve Harvey Show," ranked number 4 this season with African American households, not only derides intelligent students, but allowed male students in one episode to move physically close to their female principal, signaling her with verbal sexual innuendoes. [Episode airing 11/5/98, in the Madison, Wisconsin market]. Unlike other popular Black sit-coms, e.g., "For Your Love" [WB] or "Jamie Foxx" [WB], in which women are generally treated with respect, "The Steve Harvey Show" continues in this episode and elsewhere to reproduce old male and female sexual stereotypes, thereby closing down multiple subject positions for its male and female cast members.)

Moments can and do occur, however, in both formulaic and creative African American programs which open the door on a nonunified Black subject. In November 1998, episodes of "The Cosby Show," CBS; "For Your Love," WB; and "Jamie Foxx," WB, viewers were treated to Hilton's comic disappointment in the selection by his daughter of a male airline attendant to be her fiancee, the consternation of Jamie Foxx when he discovers that his mother is engaged to a man his age, and the patience of a husband in the face of his psychiatrist wife's overburdened schedule. In these examples I find a variety of role representations (occupations and social strata) and locate diverse problems confronting these varied characters. At first glance these roles and responses may appear mundane and suggest "business as usual," but that is the manner in which White programs are constructed. Efforts are made in White comedies to include a wide range of everyday occurrences. This complexity, this nonunified subjectivity has been missing from many African American TV programs. For these reasons, they may be captured for classroom use.

Other television moments may provide an understanding of racial dilemmas. "The Wayans Brothers," for example, is a fairly formulaic situation comedy which sometimes takes small risks and in doing so opens the window on cultural Black problems. In one episode, Braxton exhibits agency by confronting his internal confusion about dating a White women. He is reluctant to be seen in public with her and struggles with the interracial concept. Such moments are ruptures in the visual narrative, and their existence can validate some Black viewers' feelings while challenging White audience belief in the unity of African American values.

Another aspect of some current African American sit-coms ("The Wayans Brothers," WB; and "Jamie Foxx," WB) is their habit of featuring a musical group within an episode, often including their members in the plot. As the credits for the program are rolling at the end of an episode, one band member, usually a singer, is responding to interview questions. The singer is presented on 3/4 of the screen and is usually delivering a message about her/his music that is encouraging to female or male teens. This musical feature is not part of White sit-coms and is a measure of respect for selected pop stars.

❖ Agency

There is another way that educators and students can identify complex and credible images of African Americans on television. Some responsible representations are self-evident, such as the image of Whoopi Goldberg on Sesame Street talking about what it feels like to have black skin and curly black hair. Or, one might look for ruptures in narratives as cited above, but literary analysis offers additional methods. In novels characters are said to be human if they incorporate *agency,* that is, if they are instrumental in forwarding the plot. If characters act rather than just react to situations, and/or if the author allows a character to grow or change in some way, he or she has agency. If the reader feels the power of a character because she has acted, not only reacted, that character can be credible.

In simulating reality, producers of narratives most often display the agency of a character by allowing her/him to face odds from a protagonist or protagonist force. The central character's humanity is shown by the manner in which she faces and overcomes or does not overcome those odds. In such a display the audience may be able to see some growth in the character. Two of the central characters, Paul D. and Denver in *Beloved* (the movie) are credible because they face and overcome personal odds within the movie. Likewise, the troubled Sethe is credible, because at first she overcomes incredible odds and then life overtakes her. Yet, the viewer sees her thinking and struggling in a most humane way to make sense of her life. These three characters have agency in this film production.

In a 1991 episode of "A Different World," the women in a dorm of a Black college create a comic pageant of stereotypic images of Black women and yet exhibit agency. These modern college women assume the roles of mammies, maids, and street walkers. Mimicking the stereotypes, the young women illustrate the destructiveness of these images, but continue to probe the representations for any unique qualities. An argument arises between those who wish to totally deny the stereotypes and those who wish to embrace them as part of their heritage, but retain only their strong characteristics. Those who embrace these stereotypes carry the day. The message of the program is that, although media have exaggerated the representation of these Black women, the ingenuity and persistence of the original models gave courage to the Black college women. Their situation in comparison to the situation of a mammy was completely different, yet they were able to appreciate the strength and ingenuity of these slaves and embrace them as forebears of the Black women's cultural heritage. (This position is one with which I disagree. As a television analyst, I think the use of stereotypic images does more harm than good. I can respect this position, however, as an authentic one.)

The level of sophistication of Black images in this episode is rarely found on television. The sophisticated female scenario that appeared in "A Different World" would have been impossible to portray with African American men. Black male stereotypes were created to portray these men as socially impotent, because of the threat of their perceived physical prowess.

In this section I have drawn upon structural methods to examine contemporary film and television representations of African American images; use of these techniques will enhance a student's visual literacy. Assessing a character's agency will also help students identify complex representations of people of color. Structural methods stress the visual text, film or television, as the site of meaning, while post-structural methods locate meaning construction in viewers as they interact with visual texts. Both approaches offer different but pragmatic skills. Now I will consider a post-structural approach to reading film and television.

✥ Reading and Viewing

Since television and film are both communication media, they are subject to rules governing the sending and receiving of messages. Like any communication medium, they have their own language and grammar, but that grammar is negotiated and renegotiated in daily production practices, just as meaning is slowly renegotiated in the use of any language. As I described above, when the signs and symbols of film and television are patterned in daily use, codes (syntax patterns) accrue. From a post-structural stance, meaning is created when viewers interact with or read, among other things, media codes which are familiar to them. Codes are usually format-specific, such as those particular patterns and conventions which grew up around the production of television talk shows, news broadcasts, sports programs, Hollywood dramatic narratives, comedies, horror films, etc. Viewers become familiar with format codes and with the way messages are created within a format; consequently, they have expectations for understanding and interpreting talk shows, news broadcasts, sports programs, comedies, or horror films.

❖ Reading Positions

Post-structuralists propose reading theories, and viewers, like readers, interpret messages constructed in the visual text of television or film. If they accept the dominant message, they are reading "with the program"; if they read "against the grain," they may reinterpret messages in light of codes which have been established in some community of readers such as a subculture. High school students, for instance, read the films of John Hughes in the 1980s differently than did adults, because Middle American adolescents were privy to and helped establish the codes of teenage communication in their everyday lives (De Vaney, 1987). Other reading positions, therefore, that depend upon the cultural construction of the subject may be occupied. Viewers are offered an invitation by the film or television program (Ellsworth, 1988) to accept or "buy" the dominant message offered in each format; they may accept or reject that invitation and occupy another reading position, another subject position.

Some key concepts of post-structural or reader theories which inform this approach to media interpretation are text, reader, reading, subjectivity, and discourse. Since most reader theories are post-modern these key concepts are usually not defined, but described and contested. Although they are appropriately contested in post-modern discourse, agreement, however ephemeral, upon the trajectory of these categories in specific curricular tasks allows analysis to take place.

As a viewer I espouse a social construction of knowledge and believe that communities of viewers, as described by early Fish (1980), participate in constructing meaning while viewing film or television. Reading, therefore, occurs in the process of creating meaning while viewing TV or film. The program forms a communication that has been encoded by socially constructed signs and symbols that remain dormant until they are received by the viewer/s. Viewers, therefore, not the medium, create meaning.

Although text is a shifting category in post-structural discourses, I will continue to refer to film and television as texts. I would like to distinguish, however, between my understanding of a physically bound text, such as a book or a TV program, and a text "writ large" with blurred boundaries, such as a discourse. A discourse can be identified as an informal system of thought; it contains certain knowledge, concepts, definitions, values, attitudes, etc., while excluding others. In post-structural analysis, one can relate physically bound texts, such as films, to larger texts or discourses. Large and small texts are constructed by authors and contain socially encoded messages that may be variously interpreted by readers. Readers or viewers, however, must have access to the community which has encoded the message.

❖ Viewing Positions and Subjectivity

Within a discourse or informal system of thought an idea of a human person is constructed. Depending on the discourse, that person ideally incorporates those beliefs, values, attitudes, and knowledge that are part and parcel of the discourse; that person is ideal for the specific discourse. Sometimes referred to as the *subject* of a discourse, that concept of what a person should be and do gets incorporated tacitly or overtly in all discursive formations. A subject is a paradoxical concept, intended to be double edged. It emerges in discourse or in visual texts drawn from certain discourses as producers and directors communicate their ideas, desires, values, assumptions, knowledge, etc. They can be aware of what they are doing or the values of a discourse may speak through them. In other words, they create and control their own visual images, but meanings about those images may have already been socially established, since certain interpretations belong to larger social discourses. Producers and directors are members of communities which incorporate these discourses; therefore, they are subjected to the values and assumptions of discourses. In fact, the rhetoric of a community to which directors belong may be so naturalized as to be transparent, and often they do not recognize the constructed nature of a shot, for instance; the discourse, therefore, speaks through them. They are subjected to or enslaved by the discourse; that subjects can be rulers and slaves of meaning in discursive space is the paradoxical nature of subjectivity.

A shortcut to ascertaining subjectivity in a communication was established by Ellsworth (1987) when she posed the question, Just whom does that text think its readers are? Forms of address and other cues within the text can reveal the manner in which the communication thinks of and constructs a human. Reader theorists Jauss (1982), Iser (1978) and Fish (1980) all agree that the text holds clues to ascertain the subject.

Some post-structural questions for classroom students are: Just what types of invitations are offered to viewers of contemporary film and television or of a specific film or program? What are the subject positions students are being asked to occupy when it comes to reading, viewing, and interpreting African American images and representations in specific films and programs? Can and do students occupy different viewing positions when confronted with stereotypical images in specific film and television programs? A post-structural approach need not vitiate the structural, but may build on it. In considering the film *Beloved,* from Toni Morrison's book of the same title, I asked myself how the movie positioned its viewers.

✛ *Beloved,* the Movie

One might ask, when viewing *Beloved,* who is being addressed by this film? Cues within the filmic text itself help situate the audience and hence identify the subjectivity/ies of the film. Like rules for language production, filmic codes are format specific and the dramatic narrative format of *Beloved* dictates certain production practices. As I indicated above, these codes (syntax patterns) come about simply in the practice of shooting films on a daily basis (they do, however, change just as language syntax changes). A dramatic narrative filmic tradition dictates that the actors on screen look only at one another and not at the audience. This code arose when cinema was attempting to imitate the legitimate stage. Directors thought it would help viewers to read the screen if they thought a drama was taking place before them. In live dramas, characters usually address and look at one another, not at the audience. If a character looks at the audience, it is usually in an "aside." The concept behind such exclusion of the audience is a willing suspension of disbelief. A dramatic narrative, whether on stage or film, calls for a suspension of disbelief; therefore, by allowing the narrative to take place in front of but excluding the viewers, spectators may be better able to envision an encompassed scene, to go along with the fiction. Another aspect of this refusal to gaze at the audience is a respect for the dramatic narrative strategy of identification. As an encompassed drama is taking place before filmgoers' eyes, they are able to identify with one or two of the characters and involve themselves in the plot. Identity provides the pleasure and power of narrative. It is a comfortable position and one which gives viewers the freedom to identify or not, as they are moved. The integrity of a dramatic narrative is broken when a player addresses the audience.

Repeatedly in *Beloved* the director, Demme, makes the decision to break the dramatic narrative format, and that decision is crucial in deciding just whom he is addressing. In the scenes where Sethe or Paul D. recall life on the ironically named Sweet Home plantation, Demme breaks the format. As Sethe or Paul D. recall specific horrific events, they begin by talking and looking at one another. (In these scenes they are on screen together.) As the scene progresses the camera technique and actor gaze shifts, and after that shift occurs Sethe or Paul D. are then shot as a "talking head" in a shoulder-up shot; each looks directly at the audience. Sethe tells the filmgoer just what her experiences were at Sweet Home and the telling is interspersed with horrible flashbacks. Paul D. is given the same directorial treatment in his scenes of recollection. To understand why the director included the viewers, addressing them directly, one needs to identify where these camera techniques are traditionally used. "Talking heads," shoulder-up shots with a participant addressing the audience, is used in documentary films. Nichols (1988) believes that this form of direct address—participant on screen as opposed to participant or narrator voice-over—is the most credible and powerful form of address for a documentary. (A documentary exists, contrary to popular belief, for rhetorical purposes. In other words, it exists to convince an audience of a director's point of view about a specific theme.) Sethe bears witness to atrocities, looks directly at viewers, and talks to them. Like documentaries that also dramatize scenes to provide evidence of the director's thesis (usually presented in the audio track), dramatic flashbacks are interspersed with Sethe's or Paul D.'s recollections.

The stark shift in format from dramatic narrative to documentary takes place at some of the film's most crucial and important moments. (These moments are important because they establish the credibility of the central characters, especially Sethe. Among other things, the audience, in order to understand Sethe's action against her own child, must believe she suffered atrocities almost beyond human endurance.) Within these shifts, it is as if the director is saying "I must interrupt your willing suspension of disbelief as you watch and listen to this story; I must disrupt your ability to identify with Sethe, Paul D., or both characters. Now, I will position you not as a voyeur of this story in which you receive narrative pleasure, but as a receiver of news, facts, as a viewer of a documentary that gives witness to history. You will get firsthand accounts of atrocities. Be careful; you are not these people, not Sethe nor Paul D. Don't let my little narrative fool you. This happened to them and you are the receiver of this information." Demme shifts viewer positions here from one of narrative identification to one of outsider witnessing historical atrocities. This position of witness extends beyond the movie itself, beyond the willing suspension of disbelief. It creates a powerful and disturbing, but extended subjectivity in a discourse about unequal treatment of African Americans.

In other dramatic, and to my way of thinking, very moving, scenes Baby Suggs, Sethe's mother-in-law, preaches. She has become the preacher for the post-Civil War Black community outside of Cincinnati. The woods form her church with a tree stump as her pulpit, and she gathers her African American neighbors in circles around her. In one scene she asks the children to step forward in a circle and start laughing; then she asks the men to step forward and start dancing. In another scene when speaking to her neighbors, she asks them to love their hands, to love their skin and their hearts, because she notes that those people—and she points beyond the circles formed around her (the viewer cannot actually see "those people")—do not love your hands, skin, nor hearts. Her Black neighbors always form circles around her in the geography of the visual space in these scenes. Demme goes as far as to use some documentary camera techniques here, swinging the camera around the circles of neighbors, around her body and some-times around her head, but no one ever gazes at the filmgoer. Since the predominant number of shots are the backs of heads of Baby Suggs and members of the crowd, the filmgoer is further excluded. In fact, all the camera techniques and actor gazes deliber-ately position the audience as outsiders, as the people beyond those closed circles of ex-slaves. This camera work further suggests that the filmgoers are those residing beyond the circles, those who hate the hands and skin of these Black bodies.

✤ Multicultural Curriculum

Since film and television are teachers who compete daily with classroom teachers, an educator can design a curriculum which makes space for that competing teacher. Teachers can appropriate for the classroom examples of non-stereotypic African Amer-icans in popular culture artifacts. In this chapter, I have presented two methods of analysis for visual texts. These methods should enable students to assess the complex-ity and credibility of representations. Students enjoy gaining the ability to read and in-terpret visual representations in structural and post-structural ways.

References

Bove, P. (1992). *Mastering discourse.* Durham, NC: Duke University Press.

DeVaney, A. (1987). The world of John Hughes. *Framework, 1*(1), 16-26.

DeVaney, A. (1991) A grammar of educational television. In D. Hlynka & J. C. Belland (Eds.). *Paradigms regained: The uses of illuminative, semiotic and postmodern criticism as modes of inquiry in educational technology* (pp. 241-280). New York: Educational Technology Publications.

Ellsworth, E. (1988). Media interpretation as a social and political act. *Journal of Visual Literacy, 8,* 27-38.

Fish, S. (1980). *Is there a text in this class?* Cambridge, MA: Harvard University Press.

Gay, J. (Feb. 26–March 5, 1998). Prime time apartheid: How television has divided the races. *The Online Boston Phoenix.* http//www.bostonphoenix.com 80/alt 1/arts.html

hooks, b. (1991). Black is a woman's color. In Henry Louis Gates, Jr. (Ed.). *Bearing witness—selections from African American autobiography in the twentieth century* (p. 339). New York: Pantheon Books.

Hurston, Z. N. (1990). *Their eyes were watching god.* New York: Harper Perennial.

Iser, W. (1978). The act of reading. Baltimore: The Johns Hopkins University Press.

Jauss, H. R. (1982). *Towards an aesthetic of reception.* (T. Bahti, Trans). Minneapolis, MN: University of Minnesota Press.

Lacan, J. (1977). *Ecrits: A selection.* Alan Sheridan (Trans.). New York: Norton.

McLuhan, M. (1964). *Understanding media: The extensions of man.* New York: McGraw-Hill.

Morrison, T. (1992). *Playing in the dark.* Cambridge, MA: Harvard University Press.

Nichols, B. (1988). The work of culture in the age of cybernetic systems, *Screen, 29*(1), 22-46.

Nielson Media Research. (1991).

The Classroom and the Community

❖   ❖   ❖

No person is your friend who demands your silence, or denies your right to grow.

Alice Walker

What happens to a dream deferred? Does it dry up like a raisin in the sun?

Langston Hughes

A community is democratic only when the humblest and weakest person can enjoy the highest civil, economic, and social rights that the biggest and most powerful possess.

A. Philip Randolph

A society committed to the search for truth must give protection to, and set a high value upon, the independent and original mind, however angular, however rasping, however socially unpleasant it may be; for it is upon such minds in large measure, that the effective search for truth depends.

Carl P. Haskin
(New York Times, *December 9, 1963*)

Here everybody is now from the same village even if they come from different parts of China.

Amy Tan
The Joy Luck Club (New York: Ballantine, 1989), 300.

Field Experiences: Planting Seeds and Pulling Weeds

Marilynne Boyle-Baise
Indiana University

Christine E. Sleeter
California State University-Monterey Bay

What does it mean to experience racism? Do different racial groups experience racism the same way? What does it mean to hold a job and still live in poverty? Does housing discrimination really happen today? Do students of color resist school learning that devalues their identities? Can a family consisting of a grandmother, two children, their cousin, and their neighbor be functional?

These are examples of questions that require exploration if one is to offer children an education that is multicultural and social reconstructionist. Such an education demands substantial restructuring of classroom instruction and of schooling in ways that build on strengths and aspirations of oppressed groups. This restructuring should also help all students learn and think multiculturally and examine and challenge various forms of oppression.

How do we approach such questions for ourselves, particularly with reference to groups we do not belong to? In university course work, teacher education students may encounter information about areas such as racism, classism, sexism, learning and communication styles, and cultural world views. Often this information is presented as something to memorize for a test—only to forget it later; it is not connected to any life experiences.

Duckworth (1991) tells a story from the radio show "A Hitchhiker's Guide to the Galaxy":

> In one episode, a computer is built expressly for the purpose of answering the question, "What is the meaning of life, the universe, and everything?" When it is ready, they ask if it can answer that question. It says, yes, it can, but that it will take . . . seven million years. They say, "Well, OK, go to it." Seven million years later, whoever is around goes to learn the answer. The computer says that it does have the answer, but that it might be a little disappointing. "No, no," they say, "go ahead, what is it?" "Forty-two," the computer says. (p. 7)

Without an experiential basis in which to locate cognitive information about diversity and inequality, terms such as *institutional discrimination, oppositional identity*, or *fictive kinship system* have about as much meaning as "forty-two".

In the teacher education program, field experiences can provide preservice teachers with some experiential basis for theory presented in their course work. Learning in the field is vital to developing understandings of education that is multicultural. However, field experiences as they are normally structured are not useful for this purpose.

Here we critique field experiences as most preservice teachers experience them, cite examples of some that are structured differently, and provide suggestions for learning from the field. We also suggest applications of this discussion of teacher education to teaching in the elementary and middle school classroom.

✥ The Importance of Perspective

Teachers make decisions based on what seems important and reasonable to them, as-sumptions which are rooted in their perspectives. Teacher perspective is defined as the following:

> A construct that captures the ideas, behaviors, and context of particular teaching acts; [it is] anchored in the world of actual situations and [has] reference to particular behaviors. Therefore, a teacher perspective is a theory of action that has developed as a result of the individual's experiences and is applied in particular situations. (Ross, 1988, p. 102)

Teachers' perspectives are rooted partially in their prior experience in school. When preservice teachers enter classrooms, they enter familiar places, even if the stu-dents are unfamiliar. Familiarity with what constitutes teaching and schooling influ-ences what they attend to and encourages them to accept and try to replicate what they see teachers doing (Britzman, 1986; Feiman-Nemser & Buchmann, 1985).

Teachers' perspectives are also rooted in their general life experiences, which provide a basis for generalizations, decisions about what is important, and styles of re-lating to others. Perspective acts as a filter through which preservice teachers interpret course work and other experiences, as well as shaping how they approach teaching. (Lauderdale & Deaton, 1993; Sleeter, 1993). Most preservice teachers take their own perspectives for granted, as natural, as the "way things are" (Armaline & Hoover, 1989). A student may not realize that his or her perspective is only one way of perceiving re-ality and that it may include inaccuracies, such as what children's home lives are like, how students learn, and what their community regards as worth learning.

How does teacher perspective relate directly to diversity and inequality? We will illustrate with a comparison of two groups of teachers or preservice students. McDi-armid (1990) studied a group of White, middle-class, female preservice students. Within their perspectives, good teaching was defined as covering textbook materials while keeping the classroom operating in an orderly manner. Children, especially those of color or who were poor, needed to master basic skills (as opposed to higher order thinking skills). They believed that children who performed poorly were responsible for their own failure because their home environments were inadequate or they lacked the proper attitude or ability for learning.

Similarly, Ginsburg and Newman (1985) found that 12 of 14 preservice students in an urban university believed social inequality was due either to lack of effort and cul-tural deprivation within a free and open social system, or to individual attitudes and prejudice; only two viewed it as a result of unfair institutional structures.

In contrast, research on effective teachers for students of color illustrated a dif-ferent perspective. Ladson-Billings (1995) studied eight effective teachers of African

American students. She found that one of the most important factors they had in common was their culture of reference, or the cultural group on which they drew most heavily in constructing their perspectives about teaching. Seven of the eight (both African American and White) considered African American people when constituting their main culture of reference; they conscientiously turned to African American adults as their primary source of information about education of African American students.

As a result, their teaching was highly congruent with experiences and styles of their students, and built on the African American community's valuing for education. They perceived students' home and cultural background as a resource for learning rather than a cause for failure. In an ethnographic study of secondary schools, Metz (1990) found that White teachers experienced great difficulty contacting many of the African American parents, but the African American teachers, who had a good conceptual map of the African American community and therefore knew how to locate the parents, did not experience this difficulty. Lack of familiarity with the African American community led the White teachers to assume their difficulties were rooted in parents' lack of concern for education.

In other words, teachers who have a strong familiarity with a racial minority group regarded students' home and neighborhood as a strong departure point for further learning; teachers without this familiarity regarded it as a hindrance to learning. One does not need to be a member of another cultural group to develop a perspective about education that genuinely includes other groups. For example, Gillette (1996) found that some White student teachers, placed in a school serving African American youth from low-income families, were able to rethink status quo and deficiency views of schools and students. The "rethinkers" were willing to reconsider stereotypes based on information that contradicted their previous perspectives and define their teaching success by the degree of academic and personal growth students experienced. However, without working at it, one's perspective about teaching is not necessarily inclusive of any cultural groups other than one's own.

To teach within a framework of education that is multicultural and social reconstructionist requires an understanding of how institutions—including schools—perpetuate inequality, and the ability to visualize alternative institutional arrangements. As Cochran-Smith (1995) argues, this kind of teaching requires teachers to grapple with some of the "toughest questions there are about how to work effectively in the local context with learners who are like them and not like them" (p. 520). One way to begin to build this understanding is to examine one's own perspectives and compare them with those of other preservice teachers to determine the ideas and beliefs that guide teaching actions.

Some of the questions that need to be raised include the following: (1) What group(s) serves as the main culture of reference for teaching? (2) What is known about the aspirations, cultural patterns, and strengths of oppressed groups? (3) In what ways should teaching relate to students' life experiences? (4) To what extent are the notions of educational equality and equity integrated into beliefs and actions? We propose that teacher education programs help preservice teachers reconsider and perhaps reconstruct their perspectives to support greater equality and multiculturalism. One way to examine and challenge the "web of beliefs" (McDiarmid, 1990) of preservice teachers is to carefully construct field experiences that provide a foundation on which alternative perspectives can be built.

❖ Field Experiences in Teacher Education

Although some educators are skeptical of their value, most teachers and preservice teachers regard field experiences as the most important part of the teacher education program, and as a potentially powerful vehicle for connecting theories and generalizations with the "real world" of the school. Field experiences have been a part of teacher education longer than any other component, and are the most widely accepted component of teacher education. A century ago, formal teacher education consisted of practicing in the classroom, with supervision and feedback. Gradually, course work was added to precede student teaching. The longer and more complex this course work became, the more programs began to accompany at least some of the course work with early field experiences (Cruickshank & Armaline, 1986). While most states increased the number of hours required in the field, there was little alteration in the design of field experiences (Zeichner, 1981–1982). But "more" is not necessarily "better." Early field experiences do help preservice teachers move through the stages of anxiety and concern about self, and toward a focus on student learning by the time they student teach (McDermott, Gormley, Rothenberg, & Hammer, 1995).

However, time spent in the classroom can also encourage new teachers to copy what they see, which for children from marginalized groups is not necessarily beneficial (Zeichner, 1981–1982). Preservice teachers use field experiences mainly as a transition from the university to assumption of a teacher's role. Applegate and Lasley (1985), Evans (1986), and Killian and McIntyre (1988) found preservice teachers used field experiences to determine whether teaching was really for them, discern what good teachers did by watching them, acquire techniques to use later, practice using skills, and find out how teachers handled problems.

In addition, a considerable amount of research has found that what preservice teachers do in field experiences usually encourages imitation. Goodman (1985) studied field experience students, and summarized what generally happened in the field (see also Joyce, 1988; Tabachnick, Popkewitz, & Zeichner, 1980; Zeichner, 1980):

> Students had little control over either what or how content would be taught. Only a few students used techniques to encourage pupil problem-solving, self-directed learning and research, and thoughtful interpretation and expression of content. The vast majority were observed doing routine, mechanical types of teaching activities involving little creativity. However, the quantity of field experience meant that each [student teacher] said that by the end of their final practicum, they were "ready to teach." What most students meant was that they had become technically proficient: they had learned how to manage and organize the given curriculum and classroom schedule, and they had learned enough discipline techniques to feel secure in facing a classroom of twenty to thirty children. (p. 36)

In general, most preservice students perceive themselves as having learned how to teach once they have learned to take over management of routines in a cooperating teacher's classroom smoothly (Feiman-Nemser & Buchmann, 1985).

To challenge this preoccupation with copying patterns of behavior, some teacher educators encourage preservice teachers to think reflectively about teaching when they are in classrooms (Beyer, 1984; Grant & Zeichner, 1984; Zeichner, 1981–1982; Zeichner

& Liston, 1987). Reflective teaching is rooted in the work of Dewey (1938), who was concerned about educating students (and teachers) in a way that would help them continue to learn. To Dewey, experimentation and reflection were essential to learning and further learning; on the other hand, imitation hindered further growth and learning.

To encourage reflective teaching, Dewey described three attitudes that were prerequisites to reflective behavior:

1. Teachers need to be open-minded or willing to consider alternative possibilities or inaccuracies in accepted ways of thinking.
2. Teachers need to take responsibility for the consequences of their actions. For example, responsible teachers regard their choice of what and how to teach as important decisions about what is considered worth knowing or doing.
3. Reflective teachers need to pursue the attitudes defined above with wholeheartedness; this means open-mindedness and responsibility are integrated within normal, daily approaches to teaching and learning. (Grant & Zeichner, 1984)

Further, Dewey warned that placing teaching candidates in classrooms before they have developed the habits of reflection will result in candidates adopting the methods and recommendations of their supervising teacher (Denton, 1986).

Those who argue that field experiences should promote reflectivity disagree about exactly what this means, and consequently address it differently (Gore, 1987). The approach exemplified by Cruickshank (1985) is concerned about helping preservice teachers learn to apply pedagogical and psychological theories to facilitate the achievement of predetermined teaching goals (such as having students learn a particular concept in the given curriculum). The assumption of this approach to reflection is that schools are structured as they should be, but that to maximize effectiveness, teachers should base as many decisions as they can on scientifically validated theories. Cruickshank developed a laboratory-type process in which preservice teachers teach a carefully controlled lesson and then analyze what happened, focusing mainly on the methods used and their effect.

A different approach to reflective teaching, exemplified by Zeichner (1981–1982), is more concerned about having preservice teachers examine links between schooling and broader political and ethical issues. Zeichner encouraged preservice teachers to examine curriculum and instruction for emphasis on particular content and certain habits of learning, consider who benefited from these curricular and instructional designs, and think about the extent to which the nature of teaching is just and fair for all students. The assumption behind his approach to reflection is that schools are not necessarily structured and run fairly for all students, and that bringing about changes that are just requires educators to question rather than take what they see for granted.

Service learning, although not a new concept, has rapidly become a pedagogical approach that many educators are using to help preservice teachers learn to reflect about and act upon social issues. The Alliance for Service-Learning in Education Reform (1993) defines service learning as:

> a method by which young people learn and develop through active participation in thoughtfully-organized service experiences: that meet actual community needs, that are coordinated in collaboration with the school and community, that are integrated into each young person's academic curriculum, that provide structured time for a

young person to think, talk, and write about what he/she did and saw during the actual service activity, that provide young people with opportunities to use newly acquired academic skills and knowledge in real life situations in their own communities, that enhance what is taught in the school by extending student learning beyond the classroom, and that help to foster the development of a sense of caring for others. (p. 1)

Service learning is increasingly being developed as a way of helping preservice teachers reflect on social issues in the context of community participation (Wade, 1997). At the same time, it is important to recognize that engaging in service in the community does not necessarily help young people understand structural roots of op-pression. Rather, service can reinforce well-meaning but implicitly condescending atti-tudes about helping (Kahne & Westheimer, 1996). This often occurs when power dif-ferences between the server and those served are not questioned, diverse meanings of "common good" are not examined, or causes of social problems are not investigated (Varlotta, 1997).

We support Dewey's ideas about reflectivity and the importance of practicing re-flective behavior in preservice experiences, and are attracted to potentials of service learning. For purposes of learning to teach from a position of multiculturalism and so-cial reconstructionism, field experiences need to be structured from the orientation to the reflection described by Zeichner rather than the one described by Cruickshank. Our discussion in the remainder of this chapter sketches alternative field experiences that actually plant seeds of awareness about social issues, and that pull the weeds of imitation.

❖ Reconstructing Teaching Through Work in the Field

To construct an education that is multicultural and social reconstructionist, one must (1) understand how oppression is institutionalized through various institutions in-cluding schools, and how people respond to it; (2) have a rich working knowledge of cultural groups other than one's own—which may entail getting past a period of ini-tial culture shock in which negative stereotypes may be reinforced; (3) believe strongly in the desire and ability of members of oppressed groups to achieve, and rec-ognize steps they are taking to do that; and (4) be able to translate this knowledge and belief into actions in schools that may look quite different from what one has ex-perienced.

In reviewing the literature on field experiences in teacher education, we found only a small proportion that discussed how they could be structured to accomplish these goals. However, we also found some useful models. We will organize our descrip-tion of these models into four broad categories: (1) placement in classrooms with cul-turally diverse student populations; (2) ethnography in communities, schools, and class-rooms; (3) action research in classrooms; and (4) immersion in culturally diverse communities.

Teacher education students may wonder how such information will be helpful to them, because their field experiences usually are already structured. We suggest that preservice teachers apply as much of the following as possible in their field experi-ences, and that they supplement these as much as possible with experiences outside their programs, even if they do not receive university credit for them. In our experience, suggestions such as those discussed here have benefited many students.

Field Experiences in Classrooms with Culturally Diverse Students

Teacher educators often recommend that preservice teachers have field experiences in culturally diverse schools to prepare them for the likelihood that they may teach in such schools. The assumption is that contact with children from other racial backgrounds will help develop positive attitudes, a sense of comfort, and perhaps some knowledge. A small amount of research assessed this assumption, and reported that such field experiences did indeed promote positive attitudes, although the improved attitudes may not last very long (Gipe, Duffy, & Richards, 1989; Hennington, 1981).

However, we do not support the unqualified benefits of such an experience. Interactions within classrooms are limited and, often, do not provide the experience needed to counteract negative attitudes toward culturally diverse students, their families, and their communities. Preservice teachers may end up reinforcing, rather than examining, their biases and stereotypes (Zeichner & Melnick, 1996). For example, if one sees a few students who fit an ethnic stereotype, and one lacks the benefit of community counsel and context, prior beliefs can be confirmed.

Further, most teachers and administrators are White, middle-class professionals, and unless they have broadened their primary culture of reference, their schools and classrooms reflect almost exclusively the norms and expectations of mainstream society (Tellez et al., 1995). For example, raising one's hand before speaking is a common norm for acceptable student behavior. African American children in the classroom sometimes do not adhere to this rule and are reprimanded. On the surface they may appear boisterous and disobedient. However, African American children may be expected to speak up in their home environments where lively discussions are normal. African American children can learn a different rule for classroom behavior, but many respond negatively to constant reprimands for a rule that may not have been explained and differs from the pattern at home.

Having said this, we encourage preservice teachers to locate as many field experiences as possible in schools with diverse cultural populations. Look for classrooms in which the teacher has an excellent knowledge of the strengths and interests of the students' communities, and excellent teaching skills. Such teachers have developed an understanding of the cultural group of the majority of the students, and probably are very comfortable with students. They are also highly successful with the students they teach. Teachers usually share with preservice teachers their own perspective about their students; the most helpful perspective will be one that accurately highlights students' strengths. For example, spending time in a classroom populated by language minority students, and being taught by a skilled bilingual teacher, provides an opportunity to learn what effective classroom instruction should look like.

There is evidence that working with effective teachers can help novice teachers learn to "teach against the grain." Goodman and Fish (1997) studied the impact of a teacher education program on 15 students. The program was designed around a progressive teaching philosophy. Preservice teachers who worked in classrooms in which the teacher was open to and supportive of progressive teaching—even if the teacher was not skilled in using progressive teaching approaches him or herself—learned not only how to teach in a child-centered and socially-critical way themselves, but also how to negotiate freedom to be different within the constraints of the school.

Thus, it appears that field experiences in classrooms with culturally diverse students and excellent teachers make a significant difference. These experiences should be combined with additional activities we describe later.

Ethnography in Communities, Schools, and Classrooms

Ethnography is not a familiar type of inquiry to many teacher educators or preservice teachers. Ethnographic research is a part of anthropology. Ethnographers try to understand complex settings through the eyes of the observer and the participants, and assume that to understand a social setting one needs to connect the observed behavior with rationales for that behavior. They collect as many kinds of information as feasible, including observations, interviews, maps, artifacts, and photographs. In addition, the ethnographer seeks to report the "truth" of a setting by including many "voices" or perspectives in the telling of the story.

Ethnographic techniques of careful observation and interviewing, and practice in discovering patterns one had not previously paid attention to, are useful for teachers. Such investigation can help teachers understand communities, schools, and classrooms, especially in culturally diverse settings, where actions and meanings are complex and people view them differently. Preservice teachers can learn to use processes of ethnographic research to examine the familiar world of schools and classrooms as students might see and experience them. In addition, preservice teachers can use ethnographic research to discover strengths and perspectives of a sociocultural group that is different from their own. Examples of both focuses for ethnographic investigations follow.

In our experience, most preservice teachers are largely unable to delineate dimensions of classroom life or consider what classrooms would look like from a multicultural perspective. We use this as a starting point for ethnography. For one project, one of us introduced six components of the classroom that preservice teachers were to observe and describe:

1. Aesthetic/visual environment
2. Instructional materials
3. Content of lessons
4. Social organization of the class
5. Student-student interaction
6. Student-teacher interaction

Questions to consider were developed about how the classroom functioned for students from different race, class, or gender groups. For example, in regard to the aesthetic/visual environment, preservice teachers drew pictures of bulletin boards, mobiles, other decorations, and learning centers. To encourage reflection from a multicultural perspective, they were asked: What kinds of people seem welcome here? Does the room reflect the children's and teachers' work and interests? Are there stereotypes, or are groups of people omitted? Class time was used to help preservice teachers analyze their findings. We discussed the relationship between the site population and their observations, and considered how race, class, and gender relationships in the community at large (local, state, and national) influenced what they saw in classrooms.

For this project, preservice teachers learned to use ethnographic methods to investigate the curriculum taught in schools. They collected artifacts that represented the curriculum, including textbooks, assignments, bulletin board displays, posters, and projects. These artifacts were categorized in terms of what information, skills, or attitudes were deemed "important to know" and what were relegated to the status of "nice to know" (Boyle-Baise, 1996).

The preservice teachers also asked questions such as the following to analyze the curriculum: What information, skills, and attitudes were emphasized? To what extent was the information correct, nonstereotypic, and unbiased? To what extent was it weighted toward European American male accomplishments? And what messages were sent about race, social class, and gender through "need to know" and "nice to know" distinctions?

Gottleib and Cornbleth (1988) and Teitelbaum and Britzman (1991) used ethnographic inquiry to examine the context of the school rather than the classroom. Preservice teachers were encouraged to investigate such areas as discipline procedures, racial integration, and teacher work. They were urged to speak to teachers, students, and administrators about each area. Investigations could include collection of discipline codes, neighborhood walks, school-grounds surveys, and interviews with varied members of the school population. Data collected from such assignments can be analyzed in terms of equitable treatment of students across race, class, and gender.

Using discipline procedures as an example, the following questions could be raised: What is considered appropriate behavior? For which cultural group(s) are these expectations similar to behavioral norms in students' homes? Who is suspended most often, for what offenses? Are suspensions proportionate to the population of particular groups in the school?

Ethnographic investigations can be complex or simple, depending on available time and what one wants to accomplish. For example, some preservice teachers view playgrounds in inner cities as chaotic; with help in observing systematically, in a short period of time they can learn to identify organized behavior and purpose in children's activity. Speakers of "Standard English" often view other English dialects as haphazard and full of errors. With guidance, they can learn to identify grammatic and phonemic patterns they had not noticed earlier.

Ethnographic investigations can also be carried out in the community, in the context of service learning pedagogy. For example, preservice teachers can identify community agencies that serve a particular sociocultural group (such as community centers, ethnic clubs, homeless shelters), and volunteer their time, in connection with coursework focusing on issues of culture and community. While there, they can begin to understand why people come to the center; or they can become sensitized to the deprivations many people experience. It can also provide them with an insider's view of a self-help agency that is run by a sociocultural group the student may not have perceived as having self-help organizations.

As another example, preservice teachers can compare the prices of gasoline and groceries in the inner city and the suburbs. They could then investigate the type of transportation available to an inner-city resident who might want to shop in a suburban store. Preservice teachers who have done this kind of investigation have been surprised to realize that the inner-city resident pays more for some items than does the suburbanite, and may need to take a long bus ride—transferring two or three times—to reach the better prices and better merchandise. The notion of institutional discrimination begins to take on substance during such investigations.

Preservice teachers will need help learning to interview and listen to what they hear, and to observe as carefully as possible. Much of the value of ethnography to a teacher is learning to tune in carefully to the perspectives and experiences of others, and to recognize and suspend one's own assumptions. Usually preservice teachers will need help interpreting their findings; the instructor should plan an active role in processing their investigations.

This is especially important when ethnography is used to learn about institutional inequality or perspectives of oppressed people. For example, Teitelbaum and Britzman (1991) reported that they cautioned their preservice teachers about developing generalizations from the limited data of one ethnographic study, but at the same time helped them relate their findings to social norms: "We probably play our most active role in class discussions in helping to clarify for preservice teachers the relationship between the experiences they observed within the school and the social structures that exist 'outside' " (p. 181).

Action Research Activities in the Classroom

Action research is an investigation of one's own teaching practice. For example, preservice teachers may investigate how they initiate lessons, or the types of questions they use to guide discussion, or the extent of their consistency in carrying out managerial procedures.

The task of self-inquiry takes place through a cycle of reflection, which includes the following dimensions: plan, act, observe, and replan. Preservice teachers plan to study an area of their teaching, act or teach in accordance with their plan, observe or have a colleague observe their teaching, and replan or reflect about the area of study based on data collected (Gore, 1991; Noffke & Brennan, 1991; Zeichner & Liston, 1987).

Many teacher educators use action research to challenge the tendency of preservice teachers to imitate the teacher. They argue that the process accomplishes several purposes: First, what is taken for granted about practice is treated as problematic—opening the door for discussion. Second, preservice teachers have the opportunity to take charge of their own practice and learn how to modify it if necessary (Ferguson, 1989; Hollingsworth, 1988; Noffke & Brennan, 1991; Zeichner, 1983).

Action research can promote a multicultural perspective if preservice teachers study dimensions of race, class, and gender in their teaching, although action research was not usually focused in this way in the research literature we examined. This focus could easily be built into the proposal stage, during which teachers consider what aspects of their teaching they want to study and why this has educational significance.

For example, preservice teachers might investigate the attention they pay to individual children. Questions for the planning stage of action research could include: What is the purpose and pattern I use for giving students attention? Who gets the most and least positive and negative attention and why? Are my actions biased in relation to race, class, or gender? The lesson could then be tape-recorded or videotaped, then analyzed for patterns in distribution of attention to students.

As another example, a preservice student could study the use of cooperative learning to promote positive cross-group interaction. During planning and analysis the following areas could be investigated: How should children be grouped and what tasks should be assigned to accomplish positive interaction among children who may differ by race, gender, social class, or learning abilities?

Action research is limited for several reasons. First, preservice teachers usually have time to complete only one cycle of inquiry or research one question (Noffke & Brennan, 1991). These studies just begin to shed light on teaching practice and the process of studying one's own teaching. We think of it as planting seeds for further growth. This limitation can be eased somewhat by sharing inquiries in seminars. This provides a repertoire of teaching experiences and projects that speak to equity in some way.

Second, this research—like ethnography—is a case study, and in generalizing from one particular context to teaching in general, one must be cautious at the very least. For example, what can we determine about the use of multicultural literature after reading a few stories to children? What does the teaching of poetry through rap rhythms at one site tell us about teaching at other sites? These caveats do not argue for the limitation of action research itself, but rather for careful consideration of the results of the research. It is necessary to guard against reproducing practice just because it worked for one or two preservice teachers; this is the definition of experience that we challenge.

Immersion Experiences

The activities just discussed can help preservice teachers think critically about teaching, but are limited primarily to schools and classrooms. Ultimately, the best way to reconstruct one's own perspective about a wide range of topics is to spend extended time living with the people in a culturally different community.

Several things usually happen if one stays long enough. First, stereotypes about the group as a whole begin to evaporate as one gets to know individuals who differ widely from each other, many of whom contradict whatever stereotypes one came with. Second, one can see firsthand how people construct their daily living in functional and meaningful ways. At first their ways may seem different, but the longer one spends with a particular group, the more sensible their ways of doing things become.

One also gains a sense of the richness of another group's experiences, finding things that are delightful, or heartwarming, or valuable that one had not anticipated. For example, many non-Indians are immediately struck by a different conception of time on a reservation. Clock-time is often disregarded, and non-Indians are uncertain when to arrive at places or when they can expect events to happen. One's first reaction may be critical. ("They don't respect me," "They are lazy," or "No wonder nothing ever gets done around here!") But after giving one's own sense of time a chance to readjust (this may take a while), one realizes the value in structuring activities around natural rather than artificial rhythms; inner feelings become more important than the face of the clock, and one begins to pay attention to feelings one normally tunes out.

A third important feature of immersion experiences is the opportunity to listen to adults talk about circumstances they face, and how they view things. For example, in African American households it is not uncommon for dinner-table conversations to revolve around some aspect of racism that someone in the family or neighborhood has experienced (in White households, this rarely happens). If one listens nondefensively, one can learn very different perspectives about common areas of life (such as renting an apartment) that are experienced quite differently in other sociocultural groups.

Some teacher education programs have structured quite extensive immersion experiences. Campbell (1986) described a 14-year-old program that placed 250 teachers in rural areas. Preservice teachers lived with rural families for 8 weeks and taught in rural schools as well. The tenure and size of this program attested to positive results, and program leaders said their best advertising came from students urging others to participate in the experience.

Several programs placed preservice teachers in either remote or urban areas where people of color constituted the majority of the population and, more often than not, poverty was pervasive (Batteson & Sixsmith, 1995; Clark, 1987; Liebert, 1988; Noordhoff & Kleinfeld, 1991). Teachers stayed in the placement for as little as 2 weeks or for their entire preservice experience.

Common to these field experiences was course work about the history, culture, communication patterns, lifestyles, and political issues important to the context in which students were placed. In several programs, course work on how to collect field data was included (Noordhoff & Kleinfeld, 1991); or field projects were required and student teachers completed case studies about the community (Liebert, 1988; Noordhoff & Kleinfeld, 1991).

The results of immersion experiences reported in the literature are positive across the board. Each program enrolled more preservice teachers each year, who indicated that they were learning to understand and respect the lifeways of people different from themselves. Several reports were based on many years of collecting information from preservice teachers' journals and evaluations (Campbell, 1986; Clark, 1987). In addition, they developed units of study that showed deep understanding of culture and ways to integrate cultural information into subject matter and teaching strategies (Liebert, 1988; Noordhoff & Kleinfeld, 1991).

One of us was certified to teach in an 8-month immersion experience, and considers it one of the most powerful experiences of her life. The main difference between such an experience and the other kinds of field experiences we have described is that one is forced to rethink many taken-for-granted ideas when confronted with a different cultural group's daily experiences. One cannot simply go home after a few hours in a site and interpret what one has seen based on familiar and comfortable ideas. One's ideas and prior beliefs are challenged and confronted, sometimes in painful ways. For White, middle-class preprofessionals, such an immersion experience may provide the first time the concept of racism or institutionalized poverty actually sinks in, and the first time strengths and perspectives of adult members of an oppressed group are truly recognized.

The drawbacks of this type of experience relate to time, organization, and personality. As Mahan reported (Clark, 1987), time in the field, often in remote areas, is required. In addition, organizing the field experiences and procuring placements take tremendous dedication from teacher educators. Also, all preservice teachers must take a long look at their ability to be flexible enough to live and work in a culture different from their own.

Community-based service learning experiences have goals similar to extended immersion experiences. Usually in service learning experiences, preservice teachers do not actually live in the community, but rather spend several hours a week there engaged in service. While actually living in a community is a powerful way to learn, well-structured community-based service learning experiences can also stimulate a good deal of learning.

Levesque and Prosser (1996) described a community-based service learning experience in which preservice teachers worked with homeless children in a literacy project. The teachers got to know the parents and community context in the process. Some of them began to construct culturally-relevant pedagogy, as described by Ladson-Billings (1995). Interviews with teachers also revealed the degree to which the experience helped them to grapple with moral issues by grounding such issues in real experiences.

We have engaged preservice teachers in community-based service learning experiences for several years, and find them very beneficial. In a study of 65 preservice teachers, one of us found that 20 hours of service with culturally diverse and poor children and adults with disabilities assisted preservice teachers in questioning stereotypes, becoming comfortable among diverse people, understanding the workings of poverty, and realizing the shortcomings of normal schooling (Boyle-Baise, 1998).

As another example, one of us has organized a 50-hour field experience in community centers (Sleeter, 1996). This is a powerful learning experience for many preservice teachers. One White preservice teacher, for instance, began to reconstruct her perspective about African Americans during the experience. She was initially frustrated by her inability to understand the young people's dialect, and assumed it was bad grammar. In her university course she was taught some grammatical rules of Black English, and encouraged to listen for patterns. She returned to the community center and discovered that what she had perceived to be random errors were now patterns she could discern. Excited, she went to the library and sought books about Black English for a paper for another course. A profound transformation in her perspective was taking shape. Before the field experience she had not given much thought to African American culture, assuming it to be impoverished and only moderately interesting. In her field experience, combined with university course work, she discovered that it was not impoverished at all; the language (and other aspects of culture she would later discover) was highly patterned, interesting, and could be understood if one took the time.

Relatively short field experiences rarely result in a major transformation of perspective. But even if a field experience does not completely change one's perspective, if it is well constructed, it can plant seeds that will grow.

✤ Field Experiences in the Classroom

Most preservice teachers are excited and yet overwhelmed by the thought of teaching differently than they have been taught. It is difficult for them to perceive alternatives, because this requires consideration of teaching approaches that are unfamiliar, and redefinition of the essence of teaching. We find that our preservice teachers seem relieved to realize that they can learn along with students, through designing and completing field-experience-type learning activities. Several examples of field experiences that preservice teachers can accomplish with students follow.

The following example comes from Schniedewind and Davidson's (1998) resource guide of learning activities to promote race, class, gender, and age equity. "Who's Who In Our School?" and the extension activity "And How Do They Feel About It?" involves the examination of the division of labor at school as a way to understand the roles that racism and sexism play in work. Students identify the race, gender, and number of school personnel including teachers, custodians, secretaries, cafeteria workers, and administrators. They analyze the data by figuring the percentages of men, women, and people of color in each category and calculating these in terms of the total staff. The teacher guides a discussion of the findings and asks, for example, "In what areas did you find racial or sexual balance?" An extension of this inquiry involves interviewing staff about job opportunities, choices, and feelings about work.

Other field-experience-type activities that preservice teachers can develop for classroom use include collecting oral histories, taking neighborhood walks, and performing community service. Oral histories are the "his-stories" and "her-stories" of people who are real to students: mothers, fathers, neighbors, friends, and acquaintances. Histories can be collected by young children and young adults, but the number of questions asked and the depth of the answers vary.

We tried "recipe histories" successfully with our preservice teachers (and they did the same with their students). Students asked a relative to describe a favorite family recipe, remember who first made it and why (e.g., in one family, a flourless cake was first developed because of rationing in World War II, and in another, oxtail soup called for inexpensive meat). The preservice teachers asked how the recipe became a family tradition (e.g., in several cases the recipe was passed down for generations and made only on certain occasions). We constructed this project around several research questions: What stories will be related to these recipes? Will the stories have anything to do with race, class, or gender? This project engendered discussion of socioeconomic issues and the nature of history, and planted seeds for further research.

Taking a walk through the school neighborhood is another activity in which sights and sounds relevant to children can be noted. Teachers as researchers pay attention to such sights as types of homes, businesses, religious centers, and community agencies; geometric shapes in building designs, kinds of plant life and rocks; and sounds of music and language. The information collected can be used to answer questions such as: What is our neighborhood like? How does our neighborhood reflect the people who live here? What are some of the most positive things we saw in our neighborhood? What things do we think could be improved? In addition, the data provide a reference point for lesson planning relevant to the children.

Offering community service is another activity, which is becoming popular in schools across the country. Services may range from reading to preschool children to participating in a community self-help project. The essential component for these experiences is positive interaction with people active as "helpers" in the community. Examples of projects include taking part in a neighborhood cleanup effort, volunteering in a community agency, and "adopting" an elderly resident of a retirement home. (An excellent collection of service learning ideas is found in Wade, 1997).

Yet another activity is based upon inter-school exchange. While preservice teachers probably would not be able to arrange this experience, we offer these examples to encourage consideration of the needs of children in monocultural schools. For these teachers, action must be taken beyond school walls to provide multicultural experiences. A mini-magnet could be developed around a theme that draws "sister classes" together to study for a while. Preservice teachers could visit "sister schools" for a day-in-the-life type of exchange. Intramurals could become intermurals as sister schools exchange sports events in which all children may participate. Rather than schools creating theatrical events on a school-by-school basis, a joint project could be planned.

These are just a few suggestions for extending the learning environment beyond the classroom walls. Experiences such as these can provide a rich reference of real, relevant information to use to raise questions related to the construction of our social world.

✥ Planting Some Seeds

Providing an education that is multicultural and social reconstructionist requires a firm knowledge about how oppression works and what oppressed groups are doing to cope with and resist their oppression. One cannot just study these issues abstractly, because then they will not mean much more than the computer's answer of "forty-two."

One must ground one's awareness of oppression and diversity in experience. Field experiences can provide the opportunity to plant seeds of awareness that may continue to grow and develop. Field experiences that are well constructed can also pull the weeds of ignorance and misconception that all of us have about groups of which we are not members.

We hope that this chapter planted some seeds of ideas and possibilities for change, and pulled some weeds of traditional thinking about the nature of the learning environment. Teachers who take them to heart and cultivate them in practice are on the way to becoming "outstanding in the field."

References

Alliance for Service-Learning in Education Reform. (1993). *Standards of quality for school-based service learning.* Chester, VT: Author.

Applegate, J. H., & Lasley, T. J. (1985). Students' expectations for early field experiences. *Texas Tech Journal of Education, 12*(1), 27–36.

Armaline, W. D., & Hoover, R. L. (1989). Field experience as a vehicle for transformation: Ideology, education, and reflective practice. *Journal of Teacher Education, 40*(2), 42–48.

Batteson, C. & Sixsmith, C. (1995). Reflections on an experiential, inner-city placement for preservice teachers. *Journal of Education for Teaching, 21*(2), 229–233.

Beyer, L. (1984). Field experience, ideology, and the development of critical reflectivity. *Journal of Teacher Education, 35*(3), 36–41.

Boyle-Baise, M. (1996). Multicultural social studies: Ideology and practice. *The Social Studies 87*(2): 81–87.

Boyle-Baise, M. (1998). *Community service learning for multicultural teacher education: An exploratory study with pre-service teachers.* Manuscript submitted for publication.

Britzman, D. P. (1986). Cultural myths in the making of a teacher: Biography and social structure in teacher education. *Harvard Educational Review, 56*(4), 442–456.

Campbell, M. (1986). Preparing rural elementary teachers. *Research in Rural Education, 3*(3), 107–110.

Clark, H. (1987, July 9). Coming to understand others: J. Mahan's cultural immersion projects. *The Christian Science Monitor,* p. 27.

Cochran-Smith, M. (1995). Color blindness and basket making are not the answers: Confronting dilemmas of race, culture, and language diversity in teacher education. *American Educational Research Journal 32*(3), 493–522.

Cruickshank, D. R. (1985). *Models for the preparation of America's teachers.* Bloomington, IN: Phi Delta Kappa Educational Foundation.

Cruickshank, D. R., & Armaline, W. D. (1986). Field experiences in teacher education: Considerations and recommendations. *Journal of Teacher Education, 37*(3), 34–40.

Denton, J. (1986). Do early experiences in teacher education provide a meaningful context for acquiring pedagogical knowledge? *Teacher Education and Practice, 3*(1), 41–46.

Dewey, J. (1938). *Experience and education.* New York: Collier Books.

Duckworth, E. (1991). Twenty-four, forty-two, and I love you: Keeping it complex. *Harvard Educational Review, 61*(1), 1–24.

Evans, H. L. (1986). How do early field experiences influence the student teacher? *Journal of Education for Teaching, 12*(2), 35–46.

Feiman-Nemser, S., & Buchmann, M. (1985). Pitfalls of experience in teacher preparation. *Teachers College Record, 87*(1), 53–56.

Ferguson, P. (1989). A reflective approach to the methods practicum. *Journal of Teacher Education, 40*(2), 36–41.

Gillette, M. (1996). Resistance and rethinking: White student teachers in predominantly African American schools. In F. Rios (Ed.), *Teacher thinking in cultural contexts* (pp. 104–128). New York: SUNY Press.

Ginsburg, M. B., & Newman, K. K. (1985, March/April). Social inequalities, schooling, and teacher education. *Journal of Teacher Education,* 49–54.

Gipe, J. P., Duffy, C. A., & Richards, J. C. (1989). A comparison of two types of early field experiences. *Reading Improvement, 26*(3), 254–265.

Goodman, J. (1985). Field-based experience: A study of social control and student teachers' response to institutional constraints. *Journal of Education for Teaching, 11*(1), 26–49.

Goodman, J., & Fish, D. R. (1997). Against-the-grain teacher education: A study of coursework, field experience, and perspectives. *Journal of Teacher Education 48*(2), 96–107.

Gore, J. M. (1987). Reflecting on reflective teaching. *Journal of Teacher Education, 38*(2), 33–39.

Gore, J. M. (1991). Practicing what we preach: Action research and the supervision of student teachers. In B. R. Tabachnick & K. Zeichner (Eds.), *Issues and practices in inquiry-oriented teacher education* (pp. 186–202). London: Falmer Press.

Gottlieb, E., & Cornbleth, C. (1988). Toward reflective social studies teaching. *Teaching Education, 2*(1), 60–63.

Grant, C. A., & Zeichner, K. M. (1984). On becoming a reflective teacher. In C. A. Grant (Ed.), *Preparing for reflective teaching* (pp. 1–19). Boston: Allyn and Bacon.

Hennington, M. (1981). Effect of intensive multicultural, non-sexist instruction on secondary student teachers. *Educational Research Quarterly, 6,* 65–75.

Hollingsworth, S. (1988). Making field-based programs work: A three-level approach to reading education. *Journal of Teacher Education, 33*(4), 28–36.

Joyce, B. R. (1988). Training research and preservice teacher education: A reconsideration. *Journal of Teacher Education, 39*(5), 32–43.

Kahne, J., & Westheimer, J. (1996). In service of what? The politics of service learning. *Phi Delta Kappan, 77*(9), 592–599.

Killian, J. E., & McIntyre, D. J. (1988). Grade level as a factor in participation during early field experiences. *Journal of Teacher Education, 39*(2), 36–41.

Ladson-Billings, G. (1995). Toward a theory of ulturally relevant pedagogy. *American Educational Research Journal, 32*(3), 465–491.

Lauderdale, W. B., & Deaton, W. L. (1993). Future teachers react to past racism. *Educational Forum, 57*(3), 266–276.

Levesque, J., & Prosser, T. (1996). Service learning connections. *Journal of Teacher Education, 47*(5), 325–334.

Liebert, D. (1988). Enhancing field experience through multicultural placements. *Teaching Education, 2*(2), 68–72.

McDermott, P., Gormley, K., Rothenberg, J., & Hammer, J. (1995). The influence of classroom practical experiences on student teachers' thoughts about teaching. *Journal of Teacher Education, 46*(3), 184–191.

McDiarmid, G. W. (1990). Challenging prospective teachers' beliefs during early field experience: A quixotic undertaking? *Journal of Teacher Education, 41*(3), 12–20.

Metz, M. H. (1990). How social class differences shape teachers' work. In M. W. McLaughlin, J. E. Talbert, & N. Bascia (Eds.), *The Contexts of Teaching in Secondary Schools* (pp. 40–110). New York: Teachers College Press.

Noffke, D. E., & Brennan, M. (1991). Student teachers use action research: Issues and examples. In B. R.

Tabachnick & K. Zeichner (Eds.), *Issues and practices in inquiry-oriented teacher education* (pp. 186-202). London: Falmer Press.

Noordhoff, K., & Kleinfeld, J. (1991, April). *Preparing teachers for multicultural classroom: A case study in rural Alaska.* Paper presented at the annual meeting of American Educational Research Association, Chicago, IL.

Ross, E. W. (1988). Becoming a teacher: Development of preservice teacher perspectives. *Action in Teacher Education, 10*(2), 101-109.

Schniedewind, N., & Davidson, E. (1988). *Open minds to equality: A sourcebok of learning activities to affirm diversity and promote equity* (2nd ed.). Boston: Allyn and Bacon.

Sleeter, C. E. (1993). White teachers construct race. In C. McCarthy & W. Crichlow (Eds.), *Race, identity, and representation in education* (pp. 157-171). New York: Routledge.

Sleeter, C. E. (1996). *Multicultural education as social activism.* New York: SUNY Press.

Tabachnick, B. R., Popkewitz, T., & Zeichner, K. (1980). Teacher education and the professional perspectives of student teachers. *Interchange, 10,* 12-29.

Teitelbaum, K., & Britzman, D. P. (1991). Reading and doing ethnography: Teacher education and reflective practice. In B. R. Tabachnick & K. Zeichner (Eds.), *Issues and practices in inquiry-oriented teacher education* (pp. 186-202). London: Falmer Press.

Tellez, K., Hlebowitsh, P. S., Cohen, M., & Norwood, P. (1995). Social service field experiences and teacher education. In J. M. Larkin & C. E. Sleeter (Eds.), *Developing multicultural teacher education curricular* (pp. 65-78). Albany, NY: SUNY Press.

Varlotta, L. (1997). Confronting consensus: Investigating the philosophies that have informed service learning's communities. *Educational Theory, 47*(4): 453-476.

Wade, R. C. (Ed.). (1997). *Community service-learning.* Albany, NY: SUNY Press.

Zeichner, K. (1980). Myths and realities: Field-based experiences in preservice teacher education. *Journal of Teacher Education, 31,* 45-55.

Zeichner, K. (1981-1982). Reflective teaching and field-based experience in teacher education. *Interchange, 12*(4), 1-22.

Zeichner, K. (1983). Alternative paradigms of teacher education. *Journal of Teacher Education, 24*(3), 3-9.

Zeichner, K., & Liston, D. (1987). Teaching student teachers to reflect. *Harvard Educational Review, 57*(1), 23-48.

Zeichner, K., & Melnick, S. (1996). The role of community field experiences in preparing teachers for cultural diversity. In K. Zeichner, S. Melnick & M. I. Gomez (Eds.). *Currents of reform in preservice teacher education* (pp. 157-171). New York: Routledge.

20 It's Got to Be in the Plan: Reflective Teaching and Multicultural Education in the Student Teaching Semester

Maureen D. Gillette
William Paterson University

Reflective teaching has been referred to as the "new zeitgeist," or fad, in North American teacher education (Tabachnick & Zeichner, 1991, p. 1). Numerous definitions of reflective teaching can be found in the education literature. The purpose of this chapter is not to detail these definitions, but to argue for a specific one that represents a multicultural, social reconstructionist approach to examining teaching. It is important for prospective teachers to learn to develop habits of inquiry and critical reflection as they refine their teaching practice during early field experiences and in the student teaching semester.

This chapter begins with a brief discussion of reflective teaching as it relates to multicultural education. Reflective teaching and multicultural education will then be examined through two vignettes, each of which describes the experiences of a prospective teacher during the student teaching semester. The manner in which each prospective teacher thought about and acted on his or her practice will be analyzed within the context of the classroom and society today.

✤ The Reflective Teacher in a Social Reconstructionist Framework

In the previous chapter, Boyle-Baise and Sleeter noted that the roots of reflective teaching could be found in the work of Dewey (1938). Dewey defined a *reflective* teacher as one who engages in reflective action, rather than one who acts in what he called a routine manner. Routine practice is guided by unexamined tradition or imitation. Reflective action is behavior "which involves the active, persistent, and careful consideration of any belief or practice in light of the grounds that support it and the further consequences to which it leads" (Grant & Zeichner, 1984, p. 4).

Dewey (1933) described three characteristics of a reflective teacher: open-minded, responsible, and wholehearted. Each of these can be considered in light of concerns about issues of race, class, gender, language difference, differing physical and mental abilities, and sexual orientation as they manifest themselves in the classroom.

Open-mindedness is "an active desire to listen to more sides than one, to give full attention to alternate possibilities, and to recognize the possibility of error even in the beliefs that are dearest to us" (Dewey, 1933, p. 4). From a multicultural point of view, this would include such things as a willingness to see variances in students' abilities, lifestyles, and ways of problem solving as differences to be explored rather than deficiencies to be remediated or rejected without consideration.

Responsibility "involves the careful consideration of the consequences to which an action leads" (Dewey, 1933, p. 4). It is rare to find anything in teaching that is inherently neutral. Almost every decision a teacher makes and every course of action a teacher chooses have possible positive and negative consequences for students and teachers. Educators must consider the implications of their choices and actions. For example, researchers (American Association of University Women, 1991; Sadker & Sadker, 1994) have documented that females fail to receive the same attention from their teachers that male students do, that their lessons often come from gender-biased textbooks, and that they are not encouraged to pursue careers in mathematics as are their male counterparts.

Teachers do not deliberately set out to ignore or neglect the females in their classrooms; however, part of being a responsible teacher is to systematically examine classroom policies, procedures, routines, and materials to ensure gender equity in the classroom.

Finally, *wholeheartedness* is the effort teachers put forth in becoming and remaining open-minded and responsible. Prospective teachers must take an active role in their own education by demonstrating the willingness and commitment to continually investigate and improve their teaching. This does not mean student teachers should automatically condemn or negatively criticize current classroom practices. It does mean they must approach any classroom situation with a questioning mind, turning what appear to be "normal" (or traditional) classroom practices on end and taking nothing for granted. It requires asking "why" and thinking through alternatives.

A student teacher may decide an existing practice is best; however, this decision should be reached through careful consideration of what the teacher wants to accomplish, what alternatives exist, and what the consequences of these alternatives are for the teacher and the students, now and in the future. In other words, in choosing to use a certain strategy, implement a particular curriculum, administer a certain punishment, etc., a conscious, deliberate, and informed choice has been made. The teacher does not continue a practice just because "that's the way it has always been done."

Tabachnick and Zeichner (1991) note that it would be difficult to find teachers who would say they were not reflective. Therefore, it becomes important to examine how the word *reflection* is used in practice. Often prospective teachers believe they are being reflective. They leave their field placement each day with school events weighing heavily on their minds. They spend many hours thinking about the children, their lesson plans, their interactions with the cooperating teacher, as well as myriad other factors related to teaching.

Most prospective teachers have a sincere desire to work hard at improving their teaching practice but, despite all of their thinking, some continue to implement similar management procedures and lesson plans, and have the same types of interactions with the children. They do this even if they do not consider these practices important, relevant, or effective in achieving their teaching goals (e.g., student achievement, a caring classroom environment).

Other student teachers examine their practice in a way that makes a substantial difference in their teaching and their understanding of the students. They gather data about, plan for, and implement practices they believe will help them make the educational process rewarding, personally and academically, for themselves and their students. What might make this difference?

Dewey's (1933) notion of reflective teaching is underpinned by an emphasis on self-examination that is often absent in many teacher's conceptions of reflection. It is much easier to look outside one's own practice for the cause of students' academic or social problems. It is common to hear educators placing the blame for school failure on the students (e.g., lack of motivation, laziness, learning disabilities, language differences), on family situations (e.g., single-parent homes, teen-age parents, "latch-key" children), or on larger societal problems (e.g., homelessness, drugs, violence).

While these are certainly all factors that affect a child's success in school, it is equally important for teachers to focus on their own practices in the classroom. It is possible to identify areas where they can systematically examine these practices and make changes that will maximize learning for all children by assessing the factors over which the teacher has control. These factors include designing curricula to meet the needs of a particular group of students and selecting an instructional method based on students' preferred learning styles. These assessments are more constructive than focusing on factors over which teachers have little or no control, such as the fact that a student lives in a homeless shelter.

Reflective, social reconstructionist teachers seek to understand how their actions have consequences for students both inside and outside of the classroom. They understand that schools and society play a reciprocal role in structuring inequalities and recognize the need to incorporate a concern for issues of oppression based on race, ethnicity, social class, language, physical and mental ability differences, and sexual orientation. A reflective, social reconstructionist teacher understands the importance of connecting the school and the community. This approach will be briefly compared with issues that come to the fore in other versions of reflective teaching. Then, two student teaching vignettes will illustrate some of the differences among these various approaches.

Tabachnick and Zeichner (1991) identified four varieties of reflective teaching practice that are based on Zeichner and Liston's (1990) analysis of teacher education reform traditions. The first has *academic* focus. This version "stresses reflection upon subject matter and the representation and translation of subject matter knowledge to promote student understanding" (p. 3). The second variety, a *social efficiency* model, "emphasizes the thoughtful application of particular teaching strategies that have been suggested by research on teaching" (p. 3). The third version takes a *developmental* approach, "prioritizing teaching that is sensitive to students' interest, thinking, and patterns of developmental growth" (p. 3). The fourth version, the *social reconstructionist* approach, "stresses reflection about the social and political context of schooling and the assessment of classroom actions for their ability to contribute toward greater equity, social justice, and humane conditions in schooling and society" (p. 3).

While each version of reflective teaching emerged from a particular historical tradition related to the purposes of schooling and teacher education, these are not mutually exclusive. Proponents of each acknowledge the importance of attending to issues raised in other models; however, Tabachnick and Zeichner (1991) point out that the differences among the traditions of reflection are defined in terms of "the emphasis and priority that is given to particular factors within traditions" (p. 4).

It is the degree of emphasis on a certain way of viewing reflective teaching that makes the difference. For example, those who advocate a social reconstructionist view certainly acknowledge the importance of subject matter, student understanding, research-based teaching techniques, and an emphasis on the students' interests, thinking, and development. Teachers who practice a multicultural, social reconstructionist version of reflective teaching view the substance of other versions through the lens of the larger society. Such teachers realize that without solid subject matter taught using appropriate and effective instructional techniques, as well as curricula based on the needs, interests, talents, and learning styles of the children, students will not attain the knowledge base and skills necessary to become active, participating members of society. Knowledge, skills, and personal development are not seen as individual ends but as essential components of a wider educational endeavor that helps students become active participants in improving our democratic society. A concern for issues of equity, justice, and human rights in both the teaching and the learning process serves as the backdrop for examining teaching and schooling. Tabachnick and Zeichner (1991, pp. 8–9) listed three characteristics of multicultural, social reconstructionist reflective teaching:

1. In a social reconstructionist conception of reflective teaching, the teacher's attention is focused both inwardly at their own practice . . . and outwardly at the social conditions in which these practices are situated. . . . (Kemmis, 1985).

2. A social reconstructionist conception of reflective teaching has a democratic and emancipatory impulse and the focus of the teacher's deliberations is upon substantive issues that raise instances of inequality and injustice within schooling and society for close scrutiny. Recognizing the fundamentally political character of schooling, the teacher's reflections center upon such issues as the gendered nature of schooling and of teachers' work, the relationships between race and socioeconomic group on one hand, and access to school knowledge and school achievement on the other, and the influence of external interests on the process of curriculum production. . . .

3. A social reconstructionist conception of reflective teaching includes a commitment to reflection as a communal activity. . . . It is felt that the empowerment of individuals is inadequate, and that the potential for institutional and social change is great, if teachers see their individual situations as linked to those of their colleagues. (Freedman, Jackson, & Boles, 1986).

The process of becoming a multicultural, social reconstructionist reflective teacher and sustaining this vision is not easy. It requires time, effort, and commitment. Most importantly, it requires a willingness to critically examine one's practice in light of the characteristics mentioned thus far. The following two vignettes relate the stories of two student teachers struggling with becoming reflective.

Vignette 1   "It's Not in the Lesson Plan, It's in You"

Carol,[1] a 27-year-old White female, was student teaching in an urban elementary school. She was placed in a second-grade classroom of 22 students, 9 girls and 13 boys. Five students were African American (2 girls, 3 boys), 1 was biracial (a girl), 1 was an American Indian (a girl), 1 was a Latino (a boy), and 14 were White (5 females and 9 males). The class was also socioeconomically diverse, consisting of the sons and daughters of physicians, lawyers, and local politicians as well as a number of students whose parents were unemployed or were receiving state or federal assistance.

Academically, the group was heterogeneous. Several students' reading, writing, and calculation skills were well beyond those expected of a second-grader. A large portion of the class was considered to be achieving at grade level, in that they were beginning to read, write, and calculate with ease. There was also a small group of students who had trouble identifying letter sounds and numbers and who regularly experienced difficulty completing assigned tasks.

Carol's cooperating teacher attempted to foster a humanistic environment in the classroom; however, she used a form of "assertive discipline" (Canter, 1976; 1992) that involved extrinsic rewards and public accountability (i.e., names placed on the chalkboard followed by check marks to indicate rule infractions). Although Carol was given permission to adapt classroom practices to her personal style of teaching, she attempted to maintain consistency by using her cooperating teacher's system of discipline.

As she began to assume more of the teaching duties in the classroom, she became uncomfortable with the "assertive" approach. Carol addressed her uneasy feeling with her student teaching supervisor and cooperating teacher during the seventh week of the 16-week semester. The following conversation occurred after a small group reading lesson that was observed by the supervisor:

Supervisor (toward the end of the conference): The children were reading most of the time with the exception of Tom. . . . he didn't seem to be having his best day ever, did he?

Carol: No.

Cooperating Teacher: He hasn't had a best day all week.

Supervisor: What's happening with the checks? Tell me what happens with those.

Carol: Well, we have an elaborate money system. We give them five dollars a day and then for every check they lose a dollar. And Hope is . . .

Cooperating Teacher: . . . on her way to her last check, and they get a time out in the office if they lose all five dollars.

Carol: Yes, they get a time out in the office. I really notice that I'm so different, so inconsistent. Like some days I'll just barely give one or two checks and today I said to myself, "I'm just giving them checks, I'm sick of talking."

Supervisor: How do you react to that if you think you're being inconsistent? How do you feel about that?

Carol: Well, I guess I'd rather be consistent. But, if I'm inconsistent for all the kids on the same day it's not as bad. What I've really been noticing is sometimes I'll let the better kids by. I'll give them a look or something, whereas a kid who already has two or three checks, I'll give them another check. I really hate that about myself.

Supervisor: When you say "better" kids, do you mean better academically or behaviorally?

Carol: Better behaved, but a lot of times those are the better students academically.

Supervisor: Is that a certain group of children? I mean, when you say that do you have names in mind?

Carol: Yeah, I think it's those girls, Kitty and Diane and the two Lauras. And I really want to change that but I don't know why I don't.

Supervisor: . . . All the names you mentioned were female.

Carol: It just happens that those four girls are smart and pretty well-behaved, but not always. They kind of get off with each other. But that group of the other four girls I give checks to regularly.

Supervisor: Which group?

Carol: It's more kind of a halo effect, you know.

Supervisor: Can you think about that from a multicultural point of view? Are you comfortable talking about that, the other group?

Carol: Yeah, it's Sherry, Val, Felicia, and Hope. I guess what bothers me is that two of those girls are Black and one is American Indian and that three out of four are from lower socioeconomic backgrounds and it happens that the other four girls are all White and upper middle class.

Supervisor: And that leaves Sheila.

Carol: Sheila is kind of in the middle academically. Behavior-wise she's great, though. The only way she gets checks is for being late.

At this point, the conversation moved away from the topic of Carol's inconsistent discipline and the check mark system, and focused on Sheila. As the conference drew to a close, though, Carol returned to her confusion over her own practice:

Carol: . . . I hate to say it but those four girls, academically and behavior-wise they're real low. Their being Black or American Indian or whatever is a contributing factor but it's not the reason. I don't think I look at them and say, "You're Black so you're going to be at the bottom" but they work together. I was bringing that up in seminar and Professor Stevens said, "You know, you have stereotypes right away." I was really confused about that. It made me think twice about it, yet I have a hard time.

Carol gave a lot of thought to her inconsistent disciplinary techniques over the course of the semester. Although she lost sleep on a couple of occasions and more than once shed some tears over this dilemma, she continued to experience difficulties, especially with the group of four girls. At the end of the semester, her concerns about fair and appropriate disciplinary techniques remained unresolved. In response to, "Tell me about your student teaching semester," Carol stated the following:

Carol: Okay, well, a couple of things were really hard for me. . . . The discipline was really hard. That was one of the hardest things this year. I got better at it. I got better at when to let things go and when to really get on something and feel more comfortable. . . . And the kids, I think they got more mature toward the end of the year which helped me. . . .

Interviewer: . . . You've talked a lot about discipline. One time I observed a conference with you and your supervisor and you were not satisfied with the check system of discipline because you saw that the non-White kids were getting checks every day. You weren't happy with your consistency. How did you ever resolve that?

Carol: I don't think I addressed it so much. I think what I did start doing was taking the kids' side more, asking them "What's wrong? What do you want to change?" I was dealing with them on an individual level and we didn't actually use the check system as much. I think maybe at the end of the year they were maturing. I don't think we had as many discipline problems. So I guess it just kind of resolved itself. . . . I have learned that school is people, these kids, and they have their own way. You can have the best ideas in the world but they might not work out the way you planned, so you have to change. I think that's why multicultural education has to be a part of you rather than something in your lesson plan.

Carol as a Reflective Teacher

Was Carol a reflective teacher? She certainly spent many hours thinking about her discipline dilemma, but none of Carol's deliberations were systematic, nor did they result in any changes in her practice. She began by implementing a disciplinary policy from a "social efficiency" approach. This caused her uncomfortable feelings when she inconsistently doled out check marks.

Indeed, Carol recognized that her actions impinged unfairly on the females of color and certain males yet she took no action to document, confirm, or negate her suspicions. She did not attempt to analyze her practices in any way. Carol then moved into a developmental approach where she reported that she tried, toward the end of the semester, to consider the students' perspectives when dealing with discipline problems.

From a multicultural point of view, Carol was not a reflective teacher. It is important to examine her dilemma and her actions on two levels, the micro (or classroom) level and the macro level, projecting the consequences of her action (or inaction) into the lives of the children outside of school and to their futures.

Carol neglected to examine the consequences of her decision to use assertive discipline procedures, despite her feelings of uneasiness. At the level of the classroom, the results of her actions can be viewed from several perspectives: the students whose names were consistently placed on the board, the students whose names were not consistently placed on the board, and the effect of her actions on the social relationships among the two groups of females and in relation to several males whose names were consistently placed on the board in the classroom.

Carol was implementing a practice that occurs in many classrooms across the United States. Children's names are placed on the board for a variety of reasons such as inappropriate behavior or missing assignments. Often a pattern develops, as in Carol's class, where the same children's names are placed on the board day after day. What consequences might this have? The children whose names are repeatedly placed on the board for behavioral reasons rarely improve their demeanor over the course of the year. Instead, they often live up to a teacher's expectations.

They begin to see themselves as "bad" or less able than their classmates because they never seem to behave according to teacher expectations or manage to complete their assignments in the allotted time. Their classmates, too, begin to ascribe these negative characteristics to their peers. At the same time, they view themselves as "good" or superior because they have successfully internalized the teacher's rules or are able to complete assigned tasks in the requisite amount of time. As Carol noted about her own practice, once this pattern is established, a teacher often continues to focus on those children who have established a reputation as "bad" or "incapable" while overlooking undesirable behaviors in those children who have established themselves as "good."

This cycle can have detrimental effects on the social relationships in the classroom. In Carol's room, the females had already segregated themselves by race and social class. The non-White females, whose names regularly appeared on the board, worked and played together. Carol correctly noted that these four girls, who came from families whose income was at the low end of the socioeconomic scale, were below grade level academically. The four White girls, whose inappropriate behaviors Carol admittedly overlooked on a regular basis, came from families in upper-level income brackets and were academically at or above grade level.

It is possible to consider the effects of these patterns on the children's lives as they progress through school and face the reality of racism, sexism, and classism outside of the classroom. Evidence indicates that once a child is labeled as behaviorally or academically different from what is considered to be normal for a grade level, this label follows a child throughout school (Goodlad, 1981, Oakes, 1985, 1994). Compounding this problem is evidence related to the relationship between a teacher's expectation and a student's academic progress. Decades ago, it was documented that children in classrooms tend to behave and perform academically according to the teacher's expectations (Rosenthal & Jacobson, 1968).

Given the situation in Carol's classroom, it is likely that the female students of color and the males whose names continuously appeared on the board will carry negative labels about themselves in their heads as they move through the grades. These labels may manifest themselves year after year if a teacher does not stop to examine what is behind the label or what factors are affecting a student's behavior and academic performance.

For the students in Carol's class, it is a grim projection. Currently, females of color are more likely to drop out of high school and college and be unemployed between the ages of 20 and 35 than White females and males. Those females of color who do not hold full-time jobs often occupy minimum-wage positions and earn lower weekly salaries than their male or White female counterparts (U.S. Bureau of the Census, 1991; U.S. Department of Education, 1996). It is essential that all students, but especially female students of color, are provided with positive educational experiences and early academic success if the cycle of undereducation and underemployment is to be broken.

In addition, the social relations in Carol's classroom are being cemented by academic grouping that places children of like backgrounds together for much of the school day. When a teacher groups students according to ability, often students of color are placed in the "low" group, as was the case with the girls in Carol's classroom. In a situation such as this, the children are rarely afforded the chance to work with other classmates. Opportunities to learn about and appreciate the talents and abilities, the uniqueness and similarities among class members are lost. When the peer group is limited by ability grouping or tracking, students miss the opportunity to debate issues with others who may have different opinions, or to listen to and consider multiple perspectives. In short, the degree to which students are able to become open-minded, critical thinkers is in jeopardy.

Could Carol have considered these consequences on her own, or with the assistance of her cooperating teacher and supervisor? Could she have changed her teaching patterns in response to these types of considerations? The answer is yes, if Carol had been willing to take a few risks.

The first risk would have been for her to move beyond her feelings of uneasiness and admit that, as the teacher, she played a key role in determining the behavior patterns which manifested themselves in the classroom. Carol never understood this. Rather, she concluded at the end of the semester that the behavior problems in her classroom had diminished because the students had matured. While this may have been a factor, placing the onus on the students provided Carol with an excuse for not looking further into her own actions and the effect they have on the students.

The second risk Carol needed to take was to assume the role of teacher-researcher. Once she identified the discipline dilemma, Carol could have initiated a data-gathering process to help her examine the effect of the check mark system in her classroom. For example, audiotaping or videotaping herself would have provided Carol with access to her lessons as an "outsider." She could have examined the situations in which she issued check marks. Carol also might have used a personal journal or enlisted the aid of her supervisor to assess the extent to which other factors, such as the thoroughness of her planning, affected her frustration level with the students during the lesson.

Carol sensed that the girls in her class had gathered into two social groups, one consisting of upper-middle-class Whites and the other of lower-class females of color. She could have gathered data to confirm or deny this suspicion. If she confirmed it, she could have taken action to prevent this type of segregation in the classroom. For example, she could have administered a sociogram to assess the friendship patterns in her class, adding to this other data from informal observations conducted in social settings such as the lunchroom and the playground. She then could have arranged numerous cooperatively grouped learning activities where she selected the group members and arranged the learning task in a way that fostered a recognition and appreciation in all the girls for the talents and abilities of their classmates.

Carol was letting herself off the hook when she said a teacher could not plan to be a multicultural teacher, that it had to come from inside one's self. To some extent, she was correct. The characteristics of open-mindedness, responsibility, and whole-heartedness suggest that a teacher must have an awareness and an understanding of multicultural issues to address them in the classroom. But it is equally important for a teacher to *plan* for curricular and instructional practices that incorporate multicultural concerns. The second vignette provides an example of a prospective teacher who used some of the techniques noted here and planned for effective multicultural teaching in the student-teaching semester.

Vignette 2   "You Gotta Get Them Where They Are"

Tom, a 32-year-old White male, was student teaching in Mrs. Kelly's sixth-grade classroom in an urban middle school. His class was more racially, ethnically, linguistically, and socioeconomically diverse than Carol's because several elementary schools with diverse populations fed into the middle school. This brought in children who lived in one of several nearby homeless shelters as well as children who were recent immigrants from Southeast Asia.

Mrs. Kelly gave Tom freedom to design his curricular and instructional plans so that he could develop a personal teaching style. While she was concerned that he cover the material traditionally taught in the sixth grade, she was flexible and did not require him to use the textbooks and worksheets that were commonplace in her teaching.

Tom's college supervisor required that he conduct an investigation of some aspect of his teaching. Tom spent several weeks getting to know his students and their abilities. This was a challenge for him because his cooperating teacher was paired with another teacher across the hall. As a result, he taught several groups of students daily.

Tom was most concerned with a specific class that contained 16 students who had been designated "at risk"[2] for failure by the school district. He taught this group for two periods a day, once for math and once for social studies. Because the district was experimenting with mainstreaming, a resource room teacher (a specialist in learning disabilities) was assigned to assist the students while Tom taught. After much thought, Tom decided to focus on this particular class and to examine his own teaching practices as they related to student learning styles.

Tom spent about 2 weeks researching the topic of learning styles before deciding to limit his investigation to auditory, visual, and kinesthetic learning. He began his self-study by collecting data related to the students' preferred learning styles. First, he distributed a questionnaire that asked the students questions such as, "I work best (check one), alone, with one other person, in a small group" and "I like the teacher to give (check one) specific directions for homework assignments, general directions, options for homework."

Next, he began a series of individual interviews to discover how students solved problems posed in math class. At the same time, he collected observational data on different occasions with the help of his supervisor and the resource room teacher. For example, he noted the names of children who asked to have directions repeated, who talked while they worked, who seemed to need quiet, and who used manipulatives to solve math problems. Tom also tape-recorded his lessons and later listened to himself and his students. He gleaned information about the students as well as his teaching, such as the amount of "wait time" he was giving during social studies discussion periods.

The initial data-gathering period lasted about 3 weeks. After Tom sifted through his notes and categorized the students' surveys, he discussed his data with the resource room teacher to receive her input. He made some interesting discoveries. The survey data revealed that the majority of the students preferred learning kinesthetically, that is, in a "hands-on" manner and with the help of manipulative materials. The students also preferred to work in pairs or small groups rather than alone.

Tom's observational data revealed that many of the students exhibited underdeveloped listening skills, yet the primary mode of instruction in this middle school classroom was lecture. Tom discovered that most of the students benefited greatly from concise, written instructions. A small group of students had limited reading ability and required continued reliance on direct visual cues in conjunction with oral instructions and information. This information changed the way Tom structured the learning environment for these students. Following the data-gathering period, he had the following conversation with his college supervisor:

Supervisor: So, tell me how your teaching is going so far.

Tom: The data that I collected so far has been really interesting. I found out that these particular students, all labeled "at risk," really are able to articulate how they learn best. What I realized was that almost all of them prefer to see *and* hear information and that many of them do better when they have some type of manipulatives, even in social studies.

It occurred to me that all we ever do around here is lecture to them. According to what the kids said, and my observations, that is the least effective way to get information across. Almost all of them said they like to work in pairs or small groups. Only one preferred to work alone. Almost everything we do here is done in large group lessons and there is a lot of competition—some of the kids put pressure on themselves but a lot of it comes from messages we (the teachers) send out. We're always talking about grades, the expectations that will be placed upon them in high school—succeeding, you know. I'm not really sure they understand the importance of school success later on.

Supervisor: Have you thought about how you'll use all of this data you've collected?

Tom: Well, I'm really concerned about this particular group. They are already losing interest in school and I can see that some have quit trying. They've dropped out without leaving school. I think I can change the way I teach so that my lessons still teach them the stuff they need to know, yet make it interesting and fun. I'm planning on beginning some cooperative grouping activities in math and social studies. I guess I'm really going to concentrate on math first because I see that as something they'll need immediate success in so they will not be afraid to take the courses they need should they choose to go to college.

Supervisor: What will your first steps be?

Tom: Starting next week, I'm planning on having every lesson I teach use the three modalities—not only am I going to lecture to them, I'm going to provide visual aids and manipulatives. I really have to work on setting the environment so that manipulatives are seen as desirable. Some of them think they are too old to use things to help them solve math problems. I also am going to try a group process for solving problems and sharing strategies. I really need to work on the cooperative aspect rather than the competitive.

Supervisor: Anything else?

Tom: Oh yeah (laughing). Let me read you some of the problems I made up to begin reviewing fractions next week. (Tom reads aloud)

1. Angelo got $12 in tips for doing chores for the senior citizens in his neighborhood. He spent 1/3 of the money getting a fade at the barber and the rest on a compact disc. How much was the fade and how much was the disc?

2. Linda, Shatiqua, and Ricki agreed to split the cost of a pizza and some soda after the basketball game. Pizza Hut had a 12-slice pizza for $12. A large Pepsi was 75 cents. Across the street at Pizza Village, there was a 9-slice pizza and pitcher of Coke for $12.50. Which was the better deal? Why? And how much did each girl pay?

I used each kid's name in a problem based on what I've learned about them and what they like to do outside of school. I figure that once they get the idea, I'll have them begin to generate some problems of their own and we'll share them in groups. I guess it could get pretty wild if they like them as well as I think they will but, hey, who says math can't be fun!

Anyway, I've got a weeklong plan where I'm balancing my lecturing about math strategies with multiple methods, like using the overhead projector, with the students working in small groups to find solutions cooperatively and share strategies. I've tried to structure the instruction and the problems according to their interests and their preferred learning styles. Wish me luck. Will you be back next week to see how this is going?

Tom began to change his instructional techniques, using cooperative strategies in mathematics to increase the students' understanding and mastery of fractions. The students reacted so enthusiastically to Tom's problems that it was difficult for him to keep up with them. The session in which students shared strategies sometimes took a whole class period, but Tom's observational notes and the students' math scores indicated that they were increasing their ability to think critically about a problem. They did not shy away from story problems and their assignments indicated they were able to apply their reasoning to problems in the textbook, a task which the cooperating teacher considered necessary to demonstrate understanding.

Tom also applied what he was learning to his social studies and science instruction. In science, he was preparing the students for a weeklong outdoor education experience. It was necessary for the students to learn many difficult concepts before the special week. They also needed to learn how to get along and appreciate the talents of their peers because the sixth grade would be spending the entire week at a campground together, an unfamiliar experience for these children of urban backgrounds.

Social studies proved especially rewarding for Tom. His experiment in math gave him the courage to develop a video magazine project in a format fashioned after *Newsweek* magazine. Students were divided into cooperative groups and assigned a general area from the magazine to research (e.g., International Affairs, National Affairs, Business, The Arts, Lifestyle). Tom prepared research packets and guided the students through the process of selecting a topic, gathering and organizing data, and making a presentation. The students developed a project that resembled a classic mix of CNN and MTV. Tom videotaped each segment and the students critiqued themselves based on criteria the teacher and the students designed together in advance.

Tom wrote the following in his journal at the end of his student teaching experience:

> With the information I gained, I had a much clearer understanding as to how I should approach providing instruction. . . . I was able to assess individual learning styles and know if there was a correlation between a student's performance on a given task and the mode of instruction. The strength of the correlation was striking to me. The improvement shown by the students when provided with manipulatives and multiple source information was dramatic when compared with their performance when given isolated written or verbal instructions. Lots of varying explanations can probably be made, taking into account my collected data and the rather crude parameters of this investigation; however, one thing is clear. . . . Students showed remarkable improvement in their ability to solve mathematical problems of a similar nature and degree of difficulty when the instruction and the learning environment was sympathetic to their desired learning style.
>
> Cooperative learning is and will be a major instructional method in my classroom. Grouping of students is traditionally random or done so as to ensure appropriate (teacher desired) classroom behavior. Recognizing the value of learning style information, grouping in and of itself can become a learning enhancer for the teacher. Students can be grouped by the teacher to provide a variance of styles (in addition to abilities), allowing students to be exposed to alternative learning strategies with a successful common goal and a positive atmosphere. I was able to implement this in my math class and the results were very encouraging. I had an ongoing project where I placed students in groups of four. Within each group, I selected individuals who demonstrated varying learning style preferences while being aware to also mix students to read technical information, extract and record necessary data, synthesize/evaluate the material and, finally, present the results. . . .
>
> In the end, the students had worked through relatively complex problems based on data from an ecological phenology study I had prepared. It fit nicely into their

science unit on mammals. Most of the questions posed to the groups were at a difficulty level beyond the individual. The group process was not only beneficial but necessary!

Tom as a Reflective Teacher

Was Tom a reflective teacher from a multicultural, social reconstructionist perspective? He may not have demonstrated all the traits listed earlier in the chapter, but as a beginning professional, he was well on his way. Tom clearly saw himself as a key to the students' academic and social success. He understood the connections between the students' success in the sixth grade and their future life opportunities. He wanted academic success for his students, the first step toward getting rid of the stigma caused by others who labeled them "at risk."

Tom accepted this responsibility by setting out to change *his* practice and *his* way of thinking about teaching to have a positive effect in the classroom. Rather than interpret the data he gathered in a way that would require the students to immediately adapt to modes of learning typically found in school (i.e., lecture), Tom concluded that it was *he* who needed to adapt his teaching style to the students. He made informed choices and sound decisions based on information he gathered about the talents, interests, and academic needs of the pupils. Tom refused to be guided solely by tradition and unexamined practice. He believed that the learning environment could and should be designed to address academic needs, to incorporate sound teaching practices, and to capitalize on students' interests.

He set out to help this group acquire the knowledge, critical thinking strategies, socialization skills, and positive attitudes necessary to be successful students. Tom used his personal knowledge of their experiences inside and outside of school to make learning relevant and fun. In these ways, he saw himself as contributing toward a more equitable and just school experience for this particular group.

Tom also attempted to involve his colleagues. He enlisted the resource teacher and his college supervisor to assist his data gathering. He consulted with school colleagues about his data and sought their advice about designing learning experiences. Tom also took charge of the supervision process, directing his supervisor to provide feedback on areas of his teaching that were of importance to him.

Tom focused his attention on his own practice, acknowledging the fact that the category "at risk" is a socially constructed label that means different things to different people. He did not let the students' diversity or an "at risk" label stand in the way of helping them to achieve success. Rather, he looked upon diversity as a positive attribute, one that he could use to build a foundation for learning. He attempted to create what Ladson-Billings (1992; 1994) has characterized as a learning community, a place where teachers and students work collaboratively and an interdependence is fostered.

Tom recognized the importance of education in shaping one's life chances and he knew that his group of racially, ethnically, and linguistically diverse students would need a solid set of academic and social skills to succeed in a school environment and a world that, in many ways, puts them at a disadvantage. Are there other things that Tom could have done in his efforts to be a reflective, social reconstructionist teacher? Of course! There is always more a teacher can do. As the students' positive attitudes and success in mathematics increased, Tom needed to move them beyond a traditional role as "consumers" of mathematical knowledge to one in which they become producers of such knowledge (Tate, 1994). In this model, the teacher "situates students in realistic problem contexts found in our multicultural society and has them analyze and solve these problems" (p. 13).

This approach requires more than addressing pizza and haircuts as topics for mathematical problem solving. Tom could have used current databases, such as demographic and employment statistics, in his teaching. For example, the students might have learned graphing skills by translating gender-based employment data (usually provided in tables) to bar, circle, and line graphs (Schniedewind & Davidson, 1998). In this way, students develop and hone important mathematical skills while learning about salary inequities and the extent to which the presentation of statistics can alter the reader's perceptions about the data. It is the teacher's role to develop and facilitate these mathematical activities and to lead discussions about their results in ways that help students make connections between mathematics and their lives. Further, the teacher must follow up such lessons by assisting the pupils in finding opportunities to use their new skills and knowledge to directly challenge existing inequities in their school, in the community, or in the larger society.

Tom did not directly address community involvement or social action. He could have done more to foster in the students a sense of themselves as politically active participants inside and outside the classroom. He did not access the community in his attempts to connect the curriculum to the lives of the students. Yet, achievements in the student teaching semester are often limited by factors such as time, degree of autonomy, and the hard work of learning to teach. Tom built a foundation to continue his growth as a reflective, social reconstructionist teacher.

Tom concluded his teaching journal with some ideas about how he, as a teacher, could share the type of information he gleaned in his data collection with parents so they could better become partners in the educational experiences of their children. For Tom, all of this was part of "getting them where they are" so he could help take them where they wanted to go in life.

✥ Conclusion

Grant and Zeichner (1984) have argued that becoming a reflective teacher is "both possible and desirable" (p. 17). They further suggested that this process is a necessary condition if those laboring in schools wish to contribute to revitalization and renewal of the educational system; however, they noted that prospective as well as practicing teachers have a choice: to give direction to their own professional development or to allow others to direct it for them. Given the current crises in education, a teacher has no choice. Becoming a multicultural, social reconstructionist, reflective teacher is an inherent part of becoming an effective educator. Smyth (1989) quotes Jean Rudduck stating that "not to examine one's practice is irresponsible; to regard teaching as an experiment and to monitor one's performance is a responsible professional act" (p. 6). Without a multicultural, social reconstructionist type of reflectivity, teachers run the risk of indefinitely perpetuating those current school practices that turn students off to school and limit the range of possibilities in their lives.

Practicing a multicultural, social reconstructionist version of reflective teaching is essential if teachers are to play an active part in assisting all students in becoming participating citizens. Without an explicit, systematic examination of classroom practices, it becomes very difficult for a teacher to meaningfully connect his or her work in the classroom with its effect outside of school.

This is not to say that becoming a reflective teacher is easy. It requires a willingness and commitment to the time, effort, and risk taking required to alter our actions in the classroom, especially those tied to "time-honored traditions." In Chapter 19, Boyle-Baise and Sleeter discuss several ways teachers can begin to engage in activities that encourage open-mindedness toward multicultural issues, responsibility to act on them in the classroom, and wholeheartedness in this effort. Becoming a reflective teacher includes all the things mentioned by these authors, but includes a specific focus on the place "where the action is"—the classroom.

Several advocates of a social reconstructionist model of reflective teaching (Carr & Kemmis, 1983; Smyth, 1989; Zeichner, 1996) encourage teachers to begin by examining their personal biographies and their professional histories. By doing so, they can uncover the roots of taken-for-granted beliefs about the way things are "supposed to be" in teaching. This opens the door for teachers to begin "sketching out the contours of actual situations and posing problems about concrete situations" in the classroom (p. 5). Beginning teachers can focus on those things, under their own control, "which perplex, confuse, or frustrate them" (p. 5) by engaging in four forms of action with respect to their own teaching. These are described in terms of four questions that represent cyclical stages of action. Smyth (1989) uses the following as guides:

1. Describe . . . what do I do?
2. Inform . . . what does this mean?
3. Confront . . . how did I come to be like this?
4. Reconstruct . . . how might I do things differently? (p. 5)

Other questions can be added to this list to address the interplay of school and society:

5. If I do not do things differently, what will the effect be for the students, now and in the future?
6. Will this effect be different for different students?
7. How can I connect my efforts to those of others and to larger societal issues related to equity, justice, and human rights?

Embarking on the process of becoming a reflective, social reconstructionist teacher helps student teachers take control of their learning process by considering ways of reconstructing teaching that do not depend solely on "the way it has always been done" or on the methods of the cooperating teacher. Student teaching can provide an environment for the type of collegial, communal reflection described earlier as one of the three characteristics of multicultural, social reconstructionist reflective teaching.

The student teacher, the cooperating teacher, and the student-teaching supervisor can collaborate to create the type of classroom environment where multicultural, social reconstructionist reflective practice is the norm. Some may argue that this type of cooperative effort is not possible in the student teaching semester. It is true that classroom teachers, college or university programs and personnel, and student teachers themselves often set up roadblocks (e.g., policies, evaluation procedures, unwillingness to take risks) in the journey toward reflectivity; however, it does not have to be this way.

A growing body of evidence indicates that a relationship that supports reflectivity can be established among the student teacher, the cooperating teacher and the college supervisor (Gore, 1991; Noffke & Brennan, 1991; Wood, 1991; Zeichner & Hoeft, 1996). Most importantly, student teachers can, either alone or in concert with their cooperating teacher and supervisor, begin to develop habits of reflection that will ultimately make their teaching responsive to our increasingly diverse student population— a task that will benefit all of us. For unlike Carol's comment that teaching with a concern for multicultural issues cannot be "planned for," Tom's story clearly indicates that being reflective must be a part of each teacher's plan!

Notes

1. The vignettes are developed from the actual work of student teachers; however, pseudonyms are used throughout the chapter.

2. For a discussion of the problematic nature of the term *at-risk,* see Boyle-Baise and Grant (1992), Nieto (1992), or Swadener (1991).

References

American Association of University Women. (1991). *Shortchanging girls, shortchanging America.* Washington, DC: Author.

Boyle-Baise, L., & Grant, C. (1992). Multicultural teacher education: A proposal for change. In H. C. Waxman, J. Walker de Felix, J. E. Anderson, & H. Prentice Baptiste (Eds.), *Students at risk in at risk schools: Improving environments for learning* (pp. 174-193). Newbury Park, CA: Corum Press.

Canter, L. (1976). *Assertive discipline: A take charge approach for today's educator.* Santa Monica, CA: Lee Canter & Associates.

Canter, L. (1992). *Lee Canter's assertive discipline: Positive behavior managment for today's classroom.* Los Angeles, CA: Canter & Associates.

Carr, W., & Kemmis, S. (1983). *Becoming critical: Knowing through action research.* Victoria, Australia: Deakin University Press.

Dewey, J. (1933). *How we think.* Chicago: Henry Regnery.

Dewey, J. (1938). *Experience and education.* New York: Collier Books.

Freedman, S., Jackson, J., & Boles, K. (1986). *The effect of teaching on teachers.* Grand Forks, ND: North Dakota Study Group on Evaluation.

Goodlad, J. (1981). *A place called school.* New York: McGraw Hill.

Gore, J. (1991). Practicing what we preach: Action research and the supervision of student teachers. In K. M. Zeichner & B. R. Tabachnick (Eds.), *Issues and practices in inquiry-oriented teacher education* (pp. 253-272). London: The Falmer Press.

Grant, C. A., & Zeichner, K. M. (1984). On becoming a reflective teacher. In Grant, C. A. (Ed.), *Preparing for reflective teaching* (pp. 1-18). Boston: Allyn and Bacon.

Kemmis, S. (1985). Action research and the politics of reflection. In D. Boud, R. Keogh, & D. Walker (Eds.), *Reflection: Turning experience into learning* (pp. 139-164). London: Croom Helm.

Ladson-Billings, G. (1992). *Liberatory consequences of literacy: A case of culturally relevant instruction for African American students.* Paper presented at the annual meeting of the American Educational Research Association, San Francisco, CA.

Ladson-Billings, G. (1994). *The dreamkeepers: Successful teachers for African-American children.* San Franciso, CA: Jossey Bass.

Lawson, M. (1992, February 12). School's glass ceiling imperils girls, study says. *Education Week, 1,* 17.

Nieto, S. (1992). *Affirming diversity.* White Plains, NY: Longman.

Noffke, S. E., & Brennan, M. (1991). Student teachers use action research: Issues and examples. In B. R. Tabachnick & K. M. Zeichner (Eds.), *Issues and practices in inquiry-oriented teacher education* (pp. 186-201). London: The Falmer Press.

Oakes, J. (1985). *Keeping track: How schools structure inequality.* New Haven, CT: Yale University Press.

Oakes, J. (1994). Tracking, inequality, and the rhetoric of reform: Why schools don't change. In J. Kretovics & E. J. Nussel (Eds.), *Transforming urban education.* Boston, MA: Allyn & Bacon.

Rosenthal, R., & Jacobson, L. (1968). *Pygmalion in the classroom: Teacher expectation and pupils' intellectual development.* New York: Holt Rinehart & Winston.

Rudduck, J. (1984). *Teaching as an art: Teacher research and research-based teacher education.* Second Annual Lawrence Stenhouse Memorial Lecture, University of East Anglia.

Sadker, D., & Sadker, M. (1994). *Failing at fairness: How America's schools cheat girls.* New York, NY: Maxwell Macmillan International.

Schniedewind, N., & Davidson, E. (1998). *Open minds to equality: A sourcebook of learning activities to affirm diversity and promote equity.* Boston, MA: Allyn & Bacon.

Smyth, J. (1989). Developing and sustaining critical reflection in teacher education. *Journal of Teacher Education, 40*(2), 2-9.

Swadener, E. B. (1991). Children and families "at risk": Etiology, critique, and alternative paradigms. *Educational Foundations, 4,* 17-35.

Tabachnick, B. R., & Zeichner, K. M. (1991). Reflections on reflective teaching. In K. M. Zeichner & B. R. Tabachnick (Eds.), *Issues and practices in inquiry-oriented teacher education* (pp. 1-21). London: The Falmer Press.

Tate, W. (1994). Diversity, reform, and the professional knowledge of mathematics teachers: The need for multicultural clarity. In D. B. Aichele (Ed.), *Professional development for teachers of mathematics.* Reston, VA: National Council of Teachers of Mathematics.

U.S. Bureau of the Census. (1991). *Statistical abstracts of the United States: 1991* (11th ed.). Washington, DC: U.S. Department of Commerce.

U.S. Department of Education. (1996). *The condition of education, 1996.* Washington, DC: Office of Education Research and Improvement.

Wood, P. O. (1991). The cooperation teacher's role in nurturing reflective teaching. In B. R. Tabachnick & K. M. Zeichner (Eds.), *Issues and practices in inquiry-oriented teacher education* (pp. 202-210). London: The Falmer Press.

Zeichner, K. M. (1996). Teachers as reflective practitioners and the democratization of school reform. In K. M. Zeichner, S. Melnick, & M. L. Gomez (Eds.), *Currents of reform in preservice teacher education.* New York: Teachers College Press.

Zeichner, K. M., & Hoeft, K. (1996). Teacher socialization for cultural diversity. In J. Sikula (Ed.), *Handbook of research on teacher education.* New York: Simon & Schuster Macmillan.

Zeichner, K. M., & Liston, D. (1990). *Traditions of reform in reflective teaching in U.S. teacher education* (Issue Paper 90-1). East Lansing, MI: National Center for Research on Teacher Education.

Index

Note: Page numbers followed by *f, n,* and *t* indicate figures, notes, and tables, respectively.